MW00998191

Christian Apologetics

A Comprehensive Case for Biblical Faith

Douglas Groothuis

IVP Academic

An imprint of InterVarsity Press
Downers Grove, Illinois

Apollos
Nottingham, England

InterVarsity Press, USA
P.O. Box 1400
Downers Grove, IL 60515-1426, USA
World Wide Web: www.ivpress.com
Email: email@ivpress.com

APOLLOS (an imprint of Inter-Varsity Press, England)
Norton Street
Nottingham NG7 3HR, England
Website: www.ivpbooks.com
Email: ivp@ivpbooks.com

InterVarsity Press®, USA, is the book-publishing division of InterVarsity Christian Fellowship/USA® <www.intervarsity .org> and a member movement of the International Fellowship of Evangelical Students.

Inter-Varsity Press, England, is closely linked with the Universities and Colleges Christian Fellowship, a student movement connecting Christian Unions throughout Great Britain, and a member movement of the International Fellowship of Evangelical Students. Website: www.uccf.org.uk

All Scripture quotations, unless otherwise indicated, are taken from the THE HOLY BIBLE, NEW INTERNATIONAL VERSION®, NIV® *Copyright © 1973, 1978, 1984, 2011 by Biblica, Inc.™ Used by permission. All rights reserved worldwide.*

Chapter 6 appeared in similar form in Reclaiming the Center *(Wheaton, Ill.: Crossway, 2004).*

Chapter 7 was originally published as "Why Truth Matters Most: An Apologetic for Truth-Seeking in Postmodern Times" in Journal of the Evangelical Theological Society 47, no. 3 (2004). *Used by permission.*

Chapter 18 originally appeared in Journal of the Evangelical Theological Society 41, no. 2 (1998). *Used by permission.*

Chapter 19 by Craig Blomberg is copyright © 2008 by Christ on Campus Initiative (CCI). Used by permission.

Some material from chapter 20 originally appeared in Jesus in an Age of Controversy *(Eugene, Ore.: Harvest House, 1996).*

While all stories in this book are true, some names and identifying information in this book have been changed to protect the privacy of the individuals involved.

Design: Cindy Kiple
Images: Solar system: ©Baris Simsek/iStockphoto
Sunburst: ©Christian Miller/iStockphoto
Iron cross on textured background: ©cstar55/iStockphoto
Page of Bible text: ©Kevin Russ/iStockphoto
Sculpture of Aristotle: ©Snezana Negovanovic/iStockphoto
Old Pakistan flag: ©Zeffss1/iStockphoto
Fingerprint: ©Tolga TEZCAN/iStockphoto

USA ISBN 978-0-8308-3935-3
UK ISBN 978-1-84474-539-5

Printed in the United States of America ∞

Library of Congress Cataloging-in-Publication Data

Groothuis, Douglas R., 1957-
  Christian apologetics: a comprehensive case for biblical faith/
Douglas Groothuis
    p.cm.
  Includes bibliographical references (p.) and indexes.
  ISBN 978-0-8308-3935-3 (casebound: alk. paper)
  1. Apologetics. 2. God (Christianity) I. Title.
  BT1103.G76 2011
  239—dc22

2011013645

British Library Cataloguing in Publication Data

A catalogue record for this book is available from the British Library.

P 20 19 18 17 16 15 14 13 12 11 10 9 8 7
Y 30 29 28 27 26 25 24 23 22 21 20 19 18 17 16 15 14

To Rebecca Merrill Groothuis,
astute and intrepid editor,
dedicated follower of Jesus Christ,
beloved wife.

Contents

Acknowledgments

CHRISTIAN APOLOGETICS COMES OUT OF my Christian life and all who have contributed to it. Since this book is as close to a magnum opus as I will ever have, I should thank as many people as possible who, in one way or another, contributed to its existence. However, I will attempt to be mercifully brief.

A number of people were instrumental in my intellectual development as a Christian philosopher. Karsten Museaus taught an undergraduate course on worldviews ("The Twilight of Western Thought: A Christian Response") through the Sociology Department at the University of Oregon in the late 1970s that significantly shaped my thinking. I later taught this course for nearly five years. Our faculty sponsor, Dr. Benton Johnson, professor of sociology at the University of Oregon, was most gracious and helpful in preserving this rather offbeat class from being censored by secular attacks. During that time (1979-1984) I worked for The McKenzie Study Center, a Christian think tank focused on the University of Oregon. My thanks go to the Center's director, Wes Hurd, for giving a young, idiosyncratic, aspiring thinker a lot of room to develop his skills in campus ministry and in writing. Of great encouragement during this formative time was also Richard Beswick, a campus minister with whom I would later work at the University of Oregon. My gratitude also goes to two of my best friends, Stuart Smith and Pat Knapp, who have given me so much encouragement and insight on my Christian pilgrimage. My mother, Lillian Groothuis Dunn (1930-2010), was a lifelong encourager and supporter. I owe to her more than a few words could possibly say, and I miss her.

Professor Keith Yandell was my advisor at the University of Wisconsin-

Madison, where I received my M.A. degree in philosophy in 1986. From Keith I learned the rigors and virtues of analytic philosophy and what it could mean for Christian philosophers. My doctoral advisor at the University of Oregon was Robert Herbert (d. 2006), who further sharpened my thinking by being a devout critic whose seldom-heard praise could keep me going for weeks.

Editor Andrew Le Peau, of InterVarsity Press, exercised great patience and accommodation when this book doubled in size and became a textbook. He never rushed me, but provided encouragement for me to write the kind of book I had to write. My thanks also go to Sarah Geis, who provided much help in adjusting footnotes, compiling the bibliography, finding parallel biblical texts and doing other literary chores that freed me up to finish the main manuscript. The Denver Seminary library staff provided me with needed interlibrary loan material in short order. I am also grateful to the leadership of Denver Seminary for granting me sabbatical time that helped greatly in writing this work.

David Werther and Paul Copan carefully and critically evaluated the entire text and made it far better than it otherwise would have been. I also received important help from Jonathan Wells regarding my critique of Darwinism, from Timothy McGrew on the resurrection of Christ, from Harold Netland on religious pluralism, from Michael Sudduth on natural theology, and from Ed Komoszewski and Robert Bowman on the claims and credentials of Jesus. Of course, any errors that remain should be credited to me, not them. The chapters contributed by my colleagues Craig Blomberg and Richard Hess make this volume far better than it would be otherwise, and for this I am grateful.

I have been greatly inspired and encouraged by two pioneering Christian thinkers who preceded me at Denver Seminary: Dr. Gordon Lewis and Dr. Vernon Grounds (1914-2010). Both received doctorates when few evangelicals even considered such an undertaking, and both have made tremendous contributions to the kingdom of God through their philosophical skills. I am also grateful to my many students who over the years have both learned from me and taught me. Many others, too numerous to mention, also provided important insights and references for *Christian Apologetics*.

My greatest debt of thanks goes to my wife, Rebecca Merrill Groothuis, whose editorial contributions touch every page of this large volume (and every page of all of my books). Rebecca is an editor (and writer) extraordinaire, who continually makes me a better writer and thinker. She improved the quality of this book in a multitude of ways. Moreover, as this project dragged on and on, she encouraged me to finish the race and worked very hard to finish the editing of this huge volume of material, despite her own considerable obstacles toward achieving that end.

PART ONE

Apologetic Preliminaries

1

Introduction

Hope, Despair and Knowing Reality

IS THERE HOPE FOR THE UNIVERSE? THERE certainly is hope *in* the universe, given the presence of hopers—we who think and speak in the future tense, who invest ourselves in that distinctively human tense through anticipation, imagination, rumination and speculation (both informed and reckless).[1] But is there any hope *for* the universe and its intrepid hopers? One is hard-pressed to find a larger, more significant question than this imperious query concerning the cosmos. For all our cynicism, we are—at the end of the day—inescapably creatures of hope. We look forward; we yearn for something more, something better—anything to give meaning, value and substance to our short lives. Even when our hopes for family, friends, country and ourselves are satisfied—by a happy reunion, an election that goes our way, a job promotion, a negative biopsy—larger hopes (and fears) still loom.

Yet we strive after the future. Even when we reflect back on our lives, our species and our planet, we wonder: *What does it mean? What will endure? Is history progressing toward a goal or merely staggering along? What of the present instant, the ongoing now of my unfolding—or unraveling—life?* From here and now we look back and we strain ahead. But what is possible for me to hope, to know and to do? As we explore the tenses of life, we often fear that our hopes are empty, hollow, mere specters without a home, that in the end it is hopelessness that will rule the day and our destiny. For the possibility of despair is always close at the elbow of hope, acting as a

---

[1]George Steiner has reflected on the significance of the human use of the future tense, "the grammar of hope," in *Real Presences* (Chicago: University of Chicago Press, 1991), p. 56.

debating partner if not a heckler. Can one agree with the biblical philosopher that "love is as strong as death" (Song of Solomon 8:6)? Or will death
have the last laugh on us all?

How we answer these questions—or if we attempt to answer them at
all—will shape who we are and who we become. We are all citizens of the
universe—anxious travelers, much of the time, passing through our days
and nights in uncertainty and confusion concerning what matters most. In
one sense, we are alone. No one else will live our life or die our death. Each
self is unique, responsible and indissoluble. Yet our fate is bound up with
our world and our fellow travelers, each of whom has a particular way of
coping with—or avoiding—these insistent immensities. We are alone—
together.

What if these perennial human questions, yearnings and wrestlings
with destiny are merely human, all-too-human? What if hope cannot extend beyond human endeavor itself and is never answered by anything
beyond it? What if the millennia of human cries echo only into the empty
sky and no further? That possibility must be faced if the quest itself is to
have any meaning. In the end, hope without truth is pointless. Illusions
and delusions, no matter how comforting or grandiose, are the enemies of
those who strive for integrity in their knowing and being. Statements such
as "I like to think of the universe as having a purpose" or "The thought of
an afterlife gives me peace" reflect mere wishes. These notions do not address the truth or falsity of there being purpose in the world or of our
postmortem survival, because there is no genuine claim to *knowledge:* a
warranted awareness of reality as it is. A hearty, sturdy and insatiable appetite for reality—whatever it might be—is the only engine for testing and
discerning truth. Truth is what matters most, particularly truth concerning our human condition in the world—its origin, its nature, its purpose (if
any) and its destiny. Knowing the truth and living according to its requirements should be the hope and aspiration of the reflective person. Only our
knowledge of truth—our awareness of reality, no matter how sketchy or
partial—can help resolve the inner bickering between the claims of hope
and the fears of despair.

The very concept of objective truth is under fire today. Some esteem it
as nothing better than a philosophical hangover from less realistic days, a
chimera impossible to attain yet still alluring for too many. (We return to

these denials and deniers in chap. 6.) Truth may also be shunned in a more pedestrian manner. Instead of being philosophically pummeled, the concept of truth may simply be shunted aside with a shrug and a smirk—as antique and extraneous to "real life," which then is defined as little more than what lies within one's short-term memory and what enflames one's immediate expectations.[2] Yet humans are privileged with the ability to transcend their immediate experiences and ponder other matters. Such is the stuff of philosophy, literature, religion and late-night discussions in college dormitories (at least one hopes these still occur).

Perhaps instead of our seeking a reason for hope or asking for life's meaning or meanings, the situation is reversed. Perhaps *we* are on the witness stand before the jury of life. This is just how the late psychiatrist Victor Frankl put it in his classic work *Man's Search for Meaning:*

> Ultimately, man should not ask what the meaning of his life is, but rather must recognize that it is *he* who is asked. In a word, each man is questioned by life; and he can only answer to life by *answering for* his own life; to life he can only respond by being responsible.[3]

"The gas chambers of Auschwitz, Treblinka, and Maidanek," Frankl observes, "were ultimately prepared not in some ministry or other in Berlin, but rather at the desks and in the lecture halls of nihilistic scientists and philosophers."[4] As a prisoner of Hitler's death camps, Frankl noted that those captives with a sense of meaning that reached beyond their immediate experiences maintained hope and dignity, even in their Nazi hell. Those without benefit of this conviction tended to atrophy and die in the pressure cooker of evil, even if they were spared the gas chambers.

Nevertheless, one may live or die for a lie; one may hope in something that gives meaning, direction and even courage for life and be on the wrong side of the truth. Zeal does not insure knowledge; in fact, zeal may serve as a beguiling surrogate for knowledge. It may even blind us to what matters most—and destroy others as a result. After months of meticulous

---

[2]C. S. Lewis writes of the temptations to avoid deeper matters through a fixation on "real life"—or the immediate stream of experience—in the first letter of his classic fictional work *The Screwtape Letters* (1942; reprint, San Francisco: HarperSanFrancisco, 2001), particularly pp. 2-4.

[3]Victor Frankl, *Man's Search for Meaning: An Introduction to Logotherapy* (New York: Pocket Books, 1959), p. 172.

[4]Victor Frankl, *The Doctor and the Soul* (1955; reprint, New York: Vintage Books, 1986), pp. xxviii.

preparation, nineteen young zealots boarded four American passenger flights on September 11, 2001, to carry out a mission that was centered on and animated by a particular interpretation of reality. They were no nihilists—barren of meaning—seeking to destroy for no reason, as some early commentators intoned. They endeavored to accomplish the will of God (Allah) itself—at the expense of their earthly lives, but in the hope of a paradise of very earthly delights. Their lives they gave, and over three thousand lives they took, and the civilizations of the globe will never be the same as a consequence.

This apocalypse of terror not only shook New York, the Pentagon, an open field in Pennsylvania and world opinion. It rattled the worlds of not a few cultural relativists. Even the *New York Times*, that apotheosis of secularity, editorialized that these horrific events put the lie to postmodernist relativism and called out for "a transcendent moral standard."[5] This kind of language breaks out of and moves beyond mere personal preference and political analysis. It invokes essential issues of how the world is and how it ought to be. It is outrage in search of a worldview, an upsurge of conscience making universal claims. In a similar vein David Brooks wrote in the *Atlantic Monthly* that a "recovering secularist" like himself needs to realize that "he has been too easy on religion." By wrongly assuming that religion was playing a diminishing role in human affairs, many secularists have taken a patronizing approach to it, not bothering to evaluate its claims against reality. To do that would be impolite and stir up too much trouble. "Is Wahhabism [a movement within Islam adhered to by Osama bin Laden and his assassins] a vicious sect that perverts Islam? Don't talk about it." But in light of recent events, Brooks changed his mind and his method. "In a world in which religion plays an even larger role, this approach is no longer acceptable. One has to try to separate right from wrong."[6] Tragedies may indeed help clear the mind of some conceptual rubble.

Years before the events of September 11, 2001, political scientist Samuel Huntington spoke of a "clash of civilizations" that lay ahead. This thesis was in stunning contrast to a much-celebrated and debated book on

---

[5]Edward Rothstein, "Attacks on U.S. Challenge Postmodern True Believers," *New York Times*, September, 22, 2001, p. A17.
[6]David Brooks, "Kicking the Secularist Habit," *The Atlantic Monthly*, March 2003, p. 28.

world civilizations by Francis Fukuyama published in 1992 that heralded "the end of history." Reworking some themes from Hegel's philosophy of history, Fukuyama claimed that the liberal democracies of the West set the standard for world emulation. In that sense history had reached its end or telos. Other nations would soon follow the lead of these enlightened Western nations. Global conflicts over which form of government was ideal would diminish since that issue was really settled with the failure of Communism and the ascent of liberal democracy worldwide. Fukuyama wondered if this democratizing and stabilizing process might eventually lead to a kind of boredom, but he did not foresee the events that now enshroud us.[7]

But Huntington saw another, less felicitous world. The struggles between civilizations, he claimed, would not primarily be fueled by nationality, politics, ideologies or economics, but by different "cultures" and their perspectives on reality.

> Peoples and nations are attempting to answer the most basic questions humans can face: Who are we? And they are answering that question in the traditional way human beings have answered it, by reference to *the things that mean most to them*.[8]

What means the most to them is, in the final analysis, their worldview: that complex of concepts that explains and gives meaning to reality from where they stand—given their diverse ancestries, histories, institutions and religions.[9] The slogan "One person's terrorist is another's freedom fighter" may be correct on a descriptive or sociological level, but it rings hollow philosophically, since it avoids the vexing questions of hope, meaning, truth, morality and rationality. As Brooks and others have noted, religion is not withering away under the conditions of modernity, nor can it be adequately accounted for on the basis of social and political factors. It has its own intrinsic power in world affairs and in the minds of mortals.[10]

But these observations, while important, cannot settle the question of which religion (if any) is true and worth following. Nor can the resurgence

---

[7]Francis Fukuyama, *The End of History and the Last Man* (New York: Avon Books, 1992).

[8]Samuel Huntington, *A Clash of Civilizations* (New York: Simon & Schuster, 1996), p. 21, emphasis added.

[9]Ibid.

[10]See Peter L. Berger, ed., *The Desecularization of the World* (Grand Rapids: Eerdmans, 1999).

of religion in the world—particularly Islam and Christianity in the third world[11]—count intellectually against a secular worldview that leaves no room for God in its understanding of reality. Truth is not determined by counting noses. To begin to answer these questions regarding ultimate reality, we must dig deeper than charting or anticipating social change. We need to think hard, ponder and assess the options in light of the sharpest reasoning and the best available evidence.

I am convinced that a solid and compelling case can be made that what matters most for everyone in this life and beyond is one's orientation to Jesus of Nazareth, the incarnation of God. Hope here finds its goal—in the truth that satisfies and liberates. Finding one's way to this discovery may take many routes. This book carves out a path of intellectual investigation and argument. It is a work of apologetics, the ancient and ongoing discipline of defending and advocating Christian theism. This book is applicable to both unbelievers and those believers who seek a stronger reason for their hope. To this end we will explore the core claims of Christianity in light of the counterclaims of its major rivals in the contemporary world. I do not pretend to be neutral on this score; I am a professing Christian who believes the Christian worldview to be true, rationally compelling, existentially engaging and socially, globally, and perennially pertinent. However, the book will appeal to rational and factual considerations that any thinking and concerned person should be able to appreciate.

Before outlining the contours of my approach in more detail, a few words about my own journey may be apropos, since one's biography invariably shapes one's thinking—although a book is better judged by the merits of its arguments than by the credentials of its author. After my conversion to Christianity in 1976 at age nineteen, I was counseled by some (although not in so many words) to give up the life of the mind—which I had just begun to explore in my first year of college—in favor of a faith rooted in experience. I attempted this for a few tormenting months. I failed, but I did not give up on being a Christian. There was another and better way. The inquiring mind needs satisfying answers, not merely experiences. As Aristotle put it in the opening sentence of his *Metaphysics*, "Man by nature desires to know"—and this is no less true of the Christian than of anyone

---

[11]See Philip Jenkins, *The Next Christendom* (New York: Oxford University Press, 2002).

else. Moreover, a Christian anthropology affirms that humans were made to know their Maker and to love God with all their minds (Matthew 22:37-39). This is often a demanding task, but also a rewarding one. Since my failed experiment in unreflective faith, I have pursued the life of the mind as a calling from Christ.

Accordingly, I earned graduate degrees in philosophy and worked for twelve years in campus ministry at two secular universities. I have written extensively on diverse topics for many different kinds of publications (academic and popular), and have been a full-time professor of philosophy since 1993. I make it a point to speak and write in forums where the truth of Christianity is not taken for granted. I do this in order to challenge the audience with its revolutionary claims as well as to test my own mettle in intellectually demanding situations. So, while this book makes no claims to be "the final word" on the subject, it does flow from a life consistently and continually occupied with the themes it addresses. The book does not presuppose the truth of Christianity, nor does it want to beg any philosophical questions. My approach is that of Francis Schaeffer, who said, "I try to approach every problem as though I were not a Christian and see what the answer would be."[12]

Christian Apologetics begins by laying out the biblical case for apologetics and the apologetic method necessary for defending the faith. That faith (i.e., the Christian worldview) is then explained and defended against various false charges. This initial ground clearing is followed by a defense of the concept of objective truth and the need to seek truth passionately, especially given the high stakes of the Christian message (heaven or hell). The next several chapters address the case for God from natural theology—ontological, cosmological, design, moral and religious-experience arguments for God. To these arguments for theism are added arguments for why the uniqueness of humanity—our greatness, misery, consciousness and rationality—is best explained by Christian theism. The next several chapters defend the historical reliability of the Bible, particularly the New Testament. With that foundation, we take up the identity of Jesus Christ, his claims, credentials, incarnation and resurrection. In arguing for these

---

[12]Francis Schaeffer, "How I Have Come to Write My Books," in *Introduction to Francis Schaeffer* (Downers Grove, Ill.: InterVarsity Press, 1974), p. 35. This is a study guide with no author listed.

things we will also be considering alternative views and how they fare intellectually. Having made this overall case for Christianity, we then take up three significant challenges to it: the challenge of religious pluralism (Christianity cannot be the only way, given so many religions), the resurgence of Islam and its claims to be the one true religion, and the problem of evil (God cannot be all-good and all-powerful, given the evils of the world). The final chapter exhorts those confident of Christian truth to lead lives that radiate those convictions before the watching, waiting and weeping world. Two appendices attend to significant questions that have not been fully explored earlier in the book. The first appendix defends the biblical doctrine of hell as rooted in the wise and sobering teachings of Jesus himself, and the second appendix (by Richard Hess) tackles some vexing questions related to the reliability and morality of the Hebrew Bible.

2

The Biblical Basis for Apologetics

Is the Christian worldview true and rational? Is it worth believing and living out? Within these questions resides the discipline of Christian apologetics. It offers answers based on rational arguments, yet these arguments can never be divorced from the apologist's personal character. Therefore, apologetics is necessarily both theoretical and personal, both intellectual and relational. Along with the method of the apologetic argument comes the manner of the apologist himself. Both are equally vital, as we will see.

The task in this chapter is to tighten up our understanding of apologetics by explaining its basis in Scripture. After these basics are battened down and the course charted, we can launch out into intellectual adventures argument by argument in the chapters that follow.

THE MEANING OF APOLOGETICS AND ITS BIBLICAL BASIS

The word *apologetics* is often used today in a derogatory way to mean a biased and belligerent advocacy of an indefensible position. Yet the idea of presenting a credible "apology" for a legitimate position or viewpoint has a long and rich history. For example, the American founders presented an apology (or apologetic) for what would become the American form of government in *The Federalist Papers*. These learned and eloquent apologists explained and rationally defended a political perspective in the face of objections. An apologist, then, is a defender and an advocate for a particular position. There are apologists aplenty for all manner of religion and irreligion. The position is not reserved for Christians or other religionists. Richard Dawkins, for example, is a tireless apologist for atheistic Darwinism and, as such, an equally tireless opponent of all religion, but particularly of Christianity.[1] While apologists may resort to propaganda or even coercion in order to win approval for their positions, they need not do so. Of course, the Christian, following Christ's example, must never do so.

Christian apologetics is the rational defense of the Christian worldview as objectively true, rationally compelling and existentially or subjectively engaging. The word *apologetics* comes from the Greek word *apologia*, which can be translated as "defense" or "vindication." In the days of the New Testament "an apologia was a formal courtroom defense of something (2 Timothy 4:16)."[2] The word, in either the noun form *apologia* or the verb form *apologeomai*, appears eight times in the New Testament (Acts 22:1; 25:16; 1 Corinthians 9:3; 2 Corinthians 7:11; Philippians 1:7, 16; 2 Timothy 4:16; 1 Peter 3:15). The term is used specifically for a rational defense of the gospel in three texts: Philippians 1:7, 16, and most famously in 1 Peter 3:15-16.[3]

> But in your hearts revere Christ as Lord. Always be prepared to give an answer *[apologia]* to everyone who asks you to give the reason for the hope that you have. But do this with gentleness and respect, keeping a clear conscience, so that those who speak maliciously against your good behavior in Christ may be ashamed of their slander.

Peter writes to strengthen Christians who are suffering for their faith. The reason they can endure and even find hope in suffering is Jesus himself. But simply saying "Jesus" when someone asks why you have hope in times of suffering is to fail to give a full apologetic. Although this passage does not directly address the whole scope of apologetics, it does encourage believers to articulate the reason for their Christian confidence. In light of this, we should also explain why we believe in Jesus in the first place; that is, why Jesus is our sufficient comfort and inspiration for difficult conditions.[4]

---

[1]We will return to Dawkins's attacks on Christianity in chap. 13.
[2]L. G. Whitlock Jr., "Apologetics," in *Evangelical Dictionary of Theology*, ed. Walter Elwell (Grand Rapids: Baker, 1984), p. 68.
[3]See Kenneth Boa and Robert Bowman, *Faith Has Its Reasons: An Integrative Approach to Defending Christianity*, 2nd ed. (Colorado Springs: NavPress, 2005), p. 2.
[4]James Sire says concerning this passage that "it is important to see that the core notion of apologetics—the defense of the Christian faith—is not the focus of this passage" (*A Little Primer for Humble Apologetics* [Downers Grove, Ill.: InterVarsity Press, 2006], p. 16). His point is well taken, but the apologetic enterprise is a valid extension of the basic point Peter makes.

Apologetics defends the defining Christian truth claims against various challenges from unbelievers (see chap. 5). This definition of apologetics invokes both rational legitimacy (objective truth) and emotional appeal (subjective attractiveness). As such, it harks back to Pascal's programmatic comment on his own never-finished apologetic project.[5]

> Men despise religion. They hate it and are afraid it may be true. The cure for this is first to show that religion is not contrary to reason, but worthy of reverence and respect. Next make it attractive, make good men wish it were true, and then show that it is. Worthy of reverence because it really understands human nature. Attractive because it promises true good.[6]

Many people are, at least initially, wary or even resentful of Christianity—its demand for faith, humility, submission to divine authority, willingness to sacrifice for the Christian cause, repentance (meaning the end of indifference and hedonism) and so on. They fear that if it is true, they are on the hook, and if they submit to its terms, their lives will get worse. But if it is true and they fail to submit, God will get them in the end.[7] The antidote to this conundrum is to defend Christianity's core claims rationally in order to show that Christianity is indeed objectively true. But more than this, apologetics needs to demonstrate that Christian truth is winsome because it explains who we are and how we can flourish as creatures in this life and beyond, if we are reconciled to our Creator.

But apologetics is offered not only in response to the doubts and denials of non-Christians.[8] It also fortifies believers in their faith, whether they are wrestling with doubts and questions or simply seeking a deeper grounding for their biblical beliefs. When John the Baptist was in prison and wondering whether Jesus was truly the Messiah, as John had previously proclaimed, Jesus provided evidence of his identity as the Messiah. Jesus did not rebuke John's questions but answered him by listing his unique

---

[5]For an explanation of Pascal's apologetic efforts, see Douglas Groothuis, "The Character and Plan of the *Pensées*," in *On Pascal* (Belmont, Calif.: Wadsworth, 2003).

[6]Blaise Pascal, *Pensées* 12/187, ed. and trans. Alban Krailsheimer (New York: Penguin, 1966), p. 34. The first number (12) refers to the Lafuma enumeration used in the Penguin edition; the second number (187) refers to the older Brunschvicg system, used, for example, in the Great Books edition. This convention will be used throughout this book.

[7]This prudential concern is appropriate and will be discussed in chap. 8.

[8]For an excellent treatment of the problem of Christian doubt, see Os Guinness, *God in the Dark* (Wheaton, Ill.: Crossway, 2006).

credentials as the Messiah who supernaturally fulfilled prophecies from the Hebrew Scriptures (Matthew 11:1-11). One reason Christianity has failed to exert much influence on the major intellectual institutions of America is that too many Christians hold their beliefs in an uninformed and precarious fashion. Instead of pursuing answers to the toughest questions an unbelieving world can marshal, they attempt to preserve certainty through ignorance and isolation, relying on platitudes rather than arguments.

Near the end of his noteworthy apologetics book *The God Who Is There*, Francis Schaeffer chides and challenges his Christian readers:

> When we understand our calling, it is not only true, but beautiful—and it should be exciting. It is hard to understand how an orthodox, evangelical, Bible-believing Christian can fail to be excited. The answers in the realm of the intellect should make us overwhelmingly excited. But more than this, we are returned to a personal relationship with the God who is there. If we are unexcited Christians, we should go back and see what is wrong.[9]

Enthusiasm at the prospect of knowing and advocating Christian truth does not exclude rational rigor. The apologist, in fact, cannot substitute bare emotional fervor for intellectual acumen and hard study. Rather, they should work hand in hand.

APOLOGETICS' RELATIONSHIP TO THEOLOGY AND PHILOSOPHY

Apologetics is an aspect of the philosophy of religion (broadly understood), which is the rational investigation of religious truth claims. Certainly, one may engage in the philosophy of religion as a critic of Christianity (such as William Rowe or Michael Martin) or as an advocate of the Buddhist or Islamic worldviews. However, the Christian apologist employs the tools of the philosophy of religion in service of the Christian worldview.[10]

---

[9]Francis A. Schaeffer, *The God Who Is There*, 30th anniv. ed. (Downers Grove, Ill.: InterVarsity Press, 1998), p. 190.

[10]In the past few decades Christian philosophers have been mounting an impressive case for Christian truth at the highest levels of philosophy. However, noted apologist John Warwick Montgomery makes the claim that apologetics is not philosophy. He seems to be saying that there is more to defending Christianity than giving abstract logical arguments. There is no disputing that, but every kind of apologetic defense requires rigorous philosophical reasoning, whether it concerns cosmology or historiography or psychology. Montgomery also affirms that

Apologetics is linked to theology, philosophy and evangelism, but it is not reducible to any one of these disciplines. The conceptual content of apologetics depends on theology, the goal of which is to systematically and coherently articulate the truth claims of the Bible according to various topics, such as the doctrine of God, salvation and Christ. The apologist who has a strong commitment to the truth of Scripture endeavors to defend what Scripture teaches, and nothing less. Therefore, the discipline of apologetics requires skill in reading the Bible aright, since one would not want to defend something not warranted by Scripture, which is the ultimate authority when properly interpreted by the principles of logic and hermeneutics.[11] Defending a straw man is just as fallacious as attacking one.

While apologetics in one sense may be considered a branch of theology, it also walks arm in arm with philosophy. The definition of philosophy is not easy to stuff into a nutshell, but I suggest that philosophy, whatever else it might be, is the investigation of significant truth claims through rational analysis.[12] In that light, the necessary and sufficient conditions for being a philosopher (whether good or bad, major or minor, employed or unemployed) are a strong and lived-out inclination to pursue truth about philosophical matters through the rigorous use of human reasoning and to do so with some intellectual facility.

A Christian-qua-apologist, then, must be a good philosopher (even if not a professional philosopher). This is nonnegotiable and indispensable. As a logical and persuasive discipline, the connection of apologetics to philosophy is vital. Those who do not yet believe the Bible typically are not interested in expositions of biblical doctrine per se. Of more pertinence to the unbeliever is whether the arguments under consideration are rationally compelling.

"life is bigger than logic" and insinuates that philosophy can close down inquiry by insisting on logical consistency. This must be disputed. As I will argue in chapter three, logical consistency is a necessary, negative test for truth in all realms, given the law of noncontradiction. See John Warwick Montgomery, "Apologetics in the 21st Century," in *Reasons for Faith: Making a Case for Christian Faith*, ed. Norman L. Geisler and Chad V. Meister (Wheaton, Ill.: Crossway, 2007), pp. 43-44.

[11]On hermeneutics, see Craig L. Blomberg, William Klein and Robert Hubbard Jr., *Introduction to Biblical Interpretation*, rev. ed. (Nashville: Thomas Nelson, 2004).

[12]For a detailed Christian reflection on the meaning of philosophy, see J. P. Moreland and William Lane Craig, "Argument and Logic," in *Philosophical Foundations for a Christian Worldview* (Downers Grove, Ill.: InterVarsity Press, 2003).

APOLOGETICS AND EVANGELISM

The defense of Christianity as objectively true, rationally compelling and subjectively engaging also plays a leading role in evangelism. Many leading evangelists, such as Billy Graham, make almost no use of apologetics; but Graham does not disparage apologetics. On the other hand, I once spoke with a gifted evangelist who could not fathom why apologist Ravi Zacharias spent so much time explaining and critiquing postmodernism during his lectures to college audiences before inviting people to convert to Christ. From this man's perspective, "all this philosophy" was a waste of time that would have been better spent explaining the gospel and giving the "invitation." I believe this evangelist's complaint was grounded in a misunderstanding. Apologetics can be used to remove or diminish intellectual obstacles that hinder people from embracing Christ as Lord; thus it serves as pre-evangelism. In some cases—especially in academic settings where unbelief has become second nature for so many—"all this philosophy" *is* required for evangelism to become even a possibility. J. Gresham Machen (1881-1937), the great biblical scholar and apologist, understood this well in the early twentieth century.

> God usually exerts power [for conversion] in connection with certain prior conditions of the human mind, and it should be ours to create, so far as we can, with the help of God, those favourable conditions for the reception of the gospel. False ideas are the greatest obstacles to the reception of the gospel. We may preach with all the fervour of a reformer and yet succeed only in winning a straggler here and there, if we permit the whole collective thought of the nation or of the world to be controlled by ideas which, by the resistless force of logic, prevent Christianity from being regarded as anything more than a harmless delusion.[13]

In a time when people are worried about "religion being shoved down their throat," it is important to draw a distinction between apologetics in service of evangelism and proselytizing. *Proselytizing* and *evangelizing* can be used synonymously in some contexts, but *proselytizing* is usually used pejoratively to mean the exercise of untoward or unethical influence on a person. However, Christian persuasion (involving both apologetics and

---

[13]J. Gresham Machen, "Christianity and Culture," in *Christianity, Education, and the State*, ed. John W. Robbins (Jefferson, Md.: Trinity Foundation, 1987), p. 51.

evangelism), if it is true to Scripture and the Holy Spirit, eschews any undue pressure, personal threats, power plays, coercion or deception. The goal of conversion does not justify *every* means of convincing, but only those means that flow from Scripture itself. Christlike apologetics labors to communicate the truth in love and with wisdom (Ephesians 4:15). In truly Christian persuasion, one simply seeks to make known the Christian message so that others may hear it, believe it and live it out. The results are left to God's sovereignty and the judgment of those who hear. The apostle Paul sets the standard in his letter to the Thessalonians:

> For the appeal we make does not spring from error or impure motives, nor are we trying to trick you. On the contrary, we speak as those approved by God to be entrusted with the gospel. We are not trying to please people but God, who tests our hearts. You know we never used flattery, nor did we put on a mask to cover up greed—God is our witness. (1 Thessalonians 2:3-5; see also Galatians 1:10).

THE BIBLICAL JUSTIFICATION FOR APOLOGETICS

Before exploring the rudiments of apologetic method in chapter three, a strong biblical support for apologetics needs to be established, since it seems many Christians deem apologetics unnecessary at best and harmful at worst. Some claim that the ways of God are incorrigibly mysterious and beyond figuring out, thus leaving no place for rational argumentation for Christian truth. "You cannot argue anyone into the kingdom," it is often said. Yes, an infinitely wise God has myriad ways of getting our attention and revealing his saving truth. But the biblical evidence, as we will see, indicates that arguments in favor of Christianity are one way by which God reaches those in need of God's provision. The claim that no one is argued into Christianity is simply false. Although reasoning with unbelievers can prove frustrating, this may be more the fault of poor arguments, poor presentations or poor character than of the fruitlessness of apologetics per se. William Lane Craig and J. P. Moreland, two leading Christian apologists and philosophers, claim that arguments have been pivotal tools in their evangelistic strategies, particularly on college campuses.[14] They go

---

[14]Moreland and Craig, *Philosophical Foundations*, p. 4. My own less extensive, but not insignificant, experience in speaking to university groups since 1979 confirms their judgment.

further: "To speak frankly, we do not know how one could minister effectively in a public way on our university campuses without training in philosophy."[15] Moreover, noteworthy intellectuals such as John Warwick Montgomery and C. S. Lewis trace their conversions to key transformations in their thinking wrought through rational arguments.[16]

Rob Bell, a popular young pastor and writer, claims that Christianity is so mysterious it cannot be argued for. Because its many paradoxes cannot be resolved, it must be celebrated, as one celebrates a loved one, instead of rationally defended.[17] While there are mysterious elements to the Christian worldview, the prospect of celebrating unresolved paradoxes is hardly attractive or compelling.

The foundation of apologetics is the very character of God. There is but one God, whose nature and revelation must be affirmed and declared by the faithful in the face of multiple counterfeits (Exodus 20:1-3). We discover the importance of reasoning regarding religious claims throughout the Old Testament. As Moreland points out:

> Regularly, the prophets appealed to evidence to justify belief in the biblical God or in the divine authority of their inspired message: fulfilled prophecy [Isaiah 40–45], the historical fact of miracles [Elijah and prophets of Baal], the inadequacy of finite pagan deities to be the a cause of such a large, well-ordered universe compared to the God of the Bible [Jeremiah 10:1-16], and so forth. They did not say, "God said it, that settles it, you should believe it!" They gave a rational defense for their claims.[18]

This is highlighted by the words of God through Isaiah, the prophet,

---

[15]Ibid., p. 5.

[16]See C. S. Lewis, *Surprised by Joy: The Shape of My Early Life* (New York: Harcourt, Brace & World, 1955). For an excellent account of the intellectual aspects of Lewis's conversion, see David C. Downing, *The Most Reluctant Convert: C. S. Lewis's Journey to Faith* (Downers Grove, Ill.: InterVarsity Press, 2002). Many of the accounts of the pilgrimages of leading Christian philosophers involve strong apologetic elements as well. See Kelly James Clark, ed., *Philosophers Who Believe* (Downers Grove, Ill.: InterVarsity Press, 1993); and Thomas Morris, ed., *God and the Philosophers* (New York: Oxford University Press, 1995). See also the entry by Keith Yandell, "Christianity and a Conceptual Orientation," in *Professors Who Believe*, ed. Paul M. Anderson (Downers Grove, Ill.: InterVarsity Press, 1998).

[17]Rob Bell, *Velvet Elvis* (Grand Rapids: Zondervan, 2006), pp. 34-35. This short and insubstantial book seems to dismiss apologetics as irrelevant.

[18]J. P. Moreland, *Love Your God with All Your Mind* (Colorado Springs: NavPress, 1997), p. 132. I have added biblical references, which should be taken merely as a partial representation of the many biblical citations available.

"'Come now, and let us reason together,' says the LORD" (Isaiah 1:18 KJV). We can add that Israel was given rational tests for the prophets. If they denied the religion that had been given to Israel, they were false prophets, even if their predictions came to pass (Deuteronomy 13:1-5). If their predictions did not come to pass, they were deemed false prophets (Deuteronomy 18:20). The creation account of Genesis 1 may have been written as a polemic or apologetic against the mythical cosmologies of other Near Eastern cultures. Genesis's emphasis on one Creator who is separate from his nondivine creation radically contradicted the polytheism of surrounding cultures.[19] While the ruler of the universe is certainly in a position to issue threats and make pronouncements when needed, he also deigns to reason with his creatures who are made in his image and who, therefore, share (in a finite and fallible way) the ability to reason.

JESUS AS APOLOGETIC EXEMPLAR

Because Jesus, echoing the Hebrew Scriptures, affirmed that we should love God with all of our being, including our minds (Matthew 22:37-39), believers should defend God's truth when it is assailed. Jesus himself did just this throughout his ministry. He was an apologist and a philosopher, although these categories are rarely applied to him today.[20]

Consider just one example of Jesus' ability to escape neatly from between the horns of a dilemma when challenged intellectually.[21] The Sadducees attempt to spring a trap on Jesus by questioning him about the afterlife. They, unlike the Pharisees, did not believe in life after death, or in angels or spirits (although they were theists), and they granted special authority only to the first five books of the Hebrew Bible. So the Sadducees remind Jesus of Moses' command "that if a man dies without having children, his brother must marry the widow and raise up offspring for him" (Matthew 22:24). Then they propose a scenario in which the same woman is married to and then widowed by seven brothers, none of whom sire any children by her. Then the woman dies. "Now then, at the resurrection,

---

[19]See Gerhart Hasel, "The Polemical Nature of the Genesis Account," *Evangelical Quarterly* 46 (1974): 81-102.

[20]See Douglas Groothuis, "Jesus as Thinker and Apologist," *Christian Research Journal* 25, no. 2 (2002): 28-31; 47-52.

[21]Another example of Jesus escaping the horns of a dilemma is found in Matthew 22:15-22. See Groothuis, *On Jesus*, pp. 26-27.

whose wife will she be of the seven, since all of them were married to her?"
they ask pointedly (Matthew 22:28).

Their argument is brilliant. The Sadducees know that Jesus reveres
the law of Moses, as they do. They also know that Jesus, unlike themselves, teaches that there will be a resurrection of the dead. They think
that these two beliefs are logically at odds with each other; they cannot
both be true. The woman cannot be married to all seven at the resurrection (Mosaic law did not allow for polyandry), nor is there any reason
why she should be married to any one out of the seven (thus honoring
monogamy). Therefore, they figure, Jesus must either come against
Moses or deny the afterlife if he is to remain free from contradiction.
They are presenting this as a logical dilemma: either A (Moses' authority) or B (the afterlife).

Philosopher Michael Martin and others have asserted that Jesus praised
uncritical faith and threatened more than he argued.[22] If these charges
were correct, one might expect Jesus (1) to dodge the question with a pious
and unrelated utterance, (2) to threaten hell for those who dare question
his authority, or (3) simply to assert two logically incompatible propositions with no hesitation or shame. Instead, Jesus forthrightly says that the
Sadducees are in error because they have failed to know the Scripture or
the power of God.

> At the resurrection people will neither marry nor be given in marriage; they
> will be like the angels in heaven. But about the resurrection of the dead—
> have you not read what God said to you, "I am the God of Abraham, the
> God of Isaac, and the God of Jacob"? He is not the God of the dead but of
> the living. (Matthew 22:30-32)

Jesus' response has an astuteness that may not be obvious. First, he
challenges their assumption that belief in the resurrection means that we
are committed to believing that all of our premortem institutions will be
retained in the postmortem, resurrected world. None of the Hebrew Scriptures teach this, nor did Jesus believe it. Thus, the dilemma dissolves. Jesus
states a third option that exposes this false dilemma as such: there is no
married state at the resurrection.

---

[22]Michael Martin, *The Case Against Christianity* (Philadelphia: Temple University Press, 1993),
    p. 167.

Second, as part of his response to their logical trap, Jesus compares the resurrected state of men and women to that of the angels, thus challenging the Sadducees' disbelief in angels. (Although the Sadducees did not believe in angels, they knew that their fellow Jews who did believe in angels thought that angels did not marry or procreate.)

Third, Jesus cites a text from the Sadducees' own esteemed Scriptures (Exodus 3:6), where God declares to Moses from the burning bush that he is the God of Abraham, Isaac and Jacob. Jesus could have cited a variety of texts from writings outside the first five books of the Bible in support of the resurrection, such as the prophets (Daniel 12:2) or Job (Job 19:25-27), but instead he deftly argues from their own trusted sources, which he also endorsed (Matthew 5:17-20; John 10:31).

Fourth, Jesus capitalizes on the verb tense of the verse he quotes. God *is* (present tense) the God of Abraham, Isaac and Jacob, all of whom had already died at the time God uttered this to Moses. God did not cease to be their God at their earthly demise. God did not say, "I was their God" (past tense). God is the God of the living, which includes even the "dead" patriarchs. "When the crowds heard this, they were astonished at his teaching," for Jesus had "silenced the Sadducees" (Matthew 22:33-34).

OTHER BIBLICAL TESTIMONY

Many other examples of Jesus' intellectual acumen and apologetic savvy may be mustered, but the point is that Jesus unapologetically engaged in apologetics with his sharpest critics. If he is the model for Christians, we should do so as well. Jesus' apostles and other writers of the New Testament certainly recognized this. Peter admonishes the followers of Jesus to be ready with an answer (apologetic) concerning their hope in the gospel and to present this in a gentle and respectful spirit (1 Peter 3:15-17). Likewise, Paul speaks of coming against arguments that deny the knowledge of God (2 Corinthians 10:3-5;[23] see also Colossians 2:8-9). Jude joins the chorus by writing: "Dear friends, although I was very eager to write to you about the salvation we share, I felt compelled to write and urge you to contend for the faith that the Lord has once for all entrusted to God's holy people" (Jude 3).

---

[23]The context here is church discipline, but the idea has a universal application, which includes apologetics. See Sire, *Little Primer*, pp. 21-22.

Luke, the author of the Gospel of Luke and the Acts of the Apostles, recognized the need for *certainty* on behalf of the original recipient of his Gospel.

> Many have undertaken to draw up an account of the things that have been fulfilled among us, just as they were handed down to us by those who from the first were eyewitnesses and servants of the word. With this in mind, since I myself have carefully investigated everything from the beginning, I too decided to write an orderly account for you, most excellent Theophilus, *so that you may know the certainty of the things you have been taught.* (Luke 1:1-4, emphasis added)[24]

Not only do the writers of the New Testament commend apologetics, they engage in it as well—just as their Master did. The sermons of Peter and Paul recorded in Acts all have a strong apologetic backbone. For the Jews, these apostles develop an apologetic of Jesus as the fulfillment of ancient Jewish prophecy concerning the Messiah.[25] For the Gentiles, the emphasis rests more on the evidence of God's workings through nature and history in general.[26] One sermon of Paul's deserves a bit more commentary, since it exudes apologetics aptitude.

PAUL IN ATHENS: APOLOGIST EXTRAORDINAIRE

Paul came to Athens after fleeing persecution by the Thessalonians in Berea (Acts 17:13-15). His witness at Athens is the most detailed account in Acts of a Christian teacher challenging non-Jewish thinkers.

Athens in Paul's day was not at the height of its intellectual, cultural or military influence, but it *was* still a cultural powerhouse. It was much like a major college town today. Yet Paul was "greatly distressed" because the city was full of idols (Acts 17:16). But instead of unleashing a thundering condemnation on the Athenians, Paul began to reason with the Jews in the synagogue and with the God-fearing Greeks day by day, as was his custom.

There was "a group of Epicurean and Stoic philosophers" in Athens who "began to debate" with Paul (Acts 17:18). Although they wrongly

---

[24]Craig Blomberg discusses the reliability of the New Testament in chap. 19 of this volume.
[25]This argument, sometimes neglected in apologetics, will be discussed in chap. 20.
[26]See F. F. Bruce, *The Defense of the Gospel in the New Testament* (Grand Rapids: Eerdmans, 1977).

accused him of being a "babbler" (or intellectual plagiarist) who advocated "foreign gods," they nevertheless invited him to speak to the Areopagus (Acts 17:18-19). This was a prestigious group of thinkers who deemed themselves the custodians of new ideas.

From creation to Creator. Paul found common ground by noting that they were "very religious," given their many "objects of worship" (Acts 17:22-23). Paul knew this was *idolatry*, but he used a neutral description in order to build a bridge instead of erecting a wall. We too should be distressed by the emblems of unbelief in our midst, yet we should try to discern and capitalize on points of contact with these other worldviews.

Paul then reports that he had found an altar to "an unknown God" (Acts 17:23). But what they took to be unknown, Paul now declares to them. His declaration (Acts 17:24-31) is a masterpiece of Christian persuasion, the beauty of which cannot be captured in a short space.[27] Knowing the perspective of the philosophers he was facing, Paul begins not with the message of Jesus but the biblical doctrine of creation—a belief alien to both Stoics and Epicureans (and to all Greek thought).

Paul affirms that a personal and transcendent God created the entire universe, which depends on him for its continued existence. "He himself gives everyone life and breath and everything else" (Acts 17:24-25; see also Hebrews 1:3). This sets up a sharp antithesis between Christianity and both philosophical camps. The Stoics believed in an impersonal "world soul"—something like today's New Age spiritual principle or "the Force" in the *Star Wars* movies—while the Epicureans believed in several deities who had no interest in humanity.

This Creator, Paul declares, is also closely involved with humanity. He created all people from one man and established the conditions in which they live. He did this so that people "would seek him and perhaps reach out for him and find him, though he is not far from any one of us" (Acts 17:27).

Against the Athenian philosophies, Paul presents a God who is personal, transcendent, immanent and relational. He conveys all this before uttering a word about Christ. Paul should be our apologetic model here as well. Unless we establish a biblical view of God, people will likely

---

[27]See D. A. Carson, "Athens Revisited," in *Telling the Truth*, ed. D. A. Carson (Grand Rapids: Zondervan, 2000).

place Jesus in the wrong worldview, taking him to be merely a guru or swami or prophet rather than Lord, God and Savior (Philippians 3:20; Colossians 2:9).

Finding common ground. Having established the antithesis between "the Lord of heaven and earth" (Acts 17:24) and the false gods of the Athenians, Paul again makes a point of contact with their worldview by citing Greek poets: "'For in him we live and move and have our being.' As some of your own poets have said, 'We are his offspring'" (Acts 17:28).

Although their fundamental worldview was off base, the Greeks had some sense of the divine as well as their dependence on it. They were partially right, although largely wrong. Given God's general revelation in creation and conscience (Romans 1–2), Christian witnesses should always try to find the scattered elements of truth embedded within darkened worldviews.

Paul continues by arguing that since we are God's offspring, we should not think that the divine being is like any humanly crafted image. As Adam Clarke writes:

> If we are the offspring of God, He cannot be like those images of gold, silver, and stone which are formed by the art and device of man, for the parent must resemble his offspring. Seeing therefore that we are living and intelligent beings, He from whom we have derived our being must be living and intelligent. It is necessary also that the object of religious worship should be much more excellent than the worshipper; but man is . . . more excellent than an image made of gold, silver, or stone. And yet it would be impious to worship a man; how much more so to worship these images as gods![28]

The logic of Paul's argument is compelling. Furthermore, he makes his case on the basis of the Athenians' own beliefs about God and humanity. Paul displays an astute apologetic prowess.

Defending the faith. Paul lastly says that in the past God overlooked ignorance about himself, but now "he commands all people everywhere to repent" because he has "set a day when he will judge the world with justice by the man he has appointed." God has proven this to be true by raising Jesus from the dead (Acts 17:30-31). Acts only gives us a summary of Paul's

---

[28]Adam Clarke, *Commentary on the Holy Bible: One-Volume Edition,* abridged by Ralph Earle (Grand Rapids: Baker, 1967), p. 1006.

speech; he would have spoken far longer than the written text permits. So, we can be sure that Paul explained the full meaning of Jesus' life, death and resurrection (see 1 Corinthians 15:1-8).

Paul is not content to give a philosophical lecture comparing the biblical and Greek worldviews. He calls his audience to respond individually and existentially to Jesus Christ. Likewise, apologists today should be alert to when they should invite people to repent and accept the crucified and resurrected Jesus Christ as Lord.

The author (Luke) concludes this remarkable narrative by describing the various reactions: some sneered at Paul, others wanted to hear more, and some became "followers of Paul" (Acts 17:32-34). To win this response from a group of worldly philosophers is a noteworthy achievement.

With Paul as our model, we should be disturbed at the unbelief in our midst. Therefore, we should winsomely, lovingly and courageously enter the marketplace of ideas as apologists who defend the Christian world-view. We do this by establishing common ground with our audience, distinguishing the Christian worldview from alien philosophies and calling unbelievers to respond rightly to the truth of Jesus Christ.

Establishing a strong justification for the imperative of apologetics is not sufficient for the endeavor, however. The bad man with a good argument is only half clothed. One may have a sword (arguments) but lack a shield (godly character), and thus become vulnerable and ineffective. Therefore, it is wise to consider briefly the spirituality and character of the apologist before looking at the details of apologetic method.

THE SPIRITUALITY OF THE CHRISTIAN APOLOGIST

Humility is the cardinal virtue of the apologist (and of every Christian). Humility does not require abjuring religious certainty in favor of intellectual timidity. On the contrary, in a verse with multiple applications to apologetics, Paul declares that "the Spirit God gave us does not make us timid, but gives us power, love and self-discipline" (2 Timothy 1:7). Humility recognizes the source of all good things—intellectual and otherwise—as rooted in God's grace. As such, they are gifts deserving of thanks. It is difficult to be dependent on God and thankful to God while being arrogant. As Andrew Murray points out, human humility is grounded in our very existence as creatures. We are beholden to our Creator for everything and should keep that in the forefront of our minds.[29] Humility lives only in love. We love God only because he loved us first; we love others and want them to live as lovers of Christ, only because God loves them and has commissioned us to love them as well. So, the virtues of love— patience, kindness, endurance, truthfulness and so on—should animate all apologetics (1 Corinthians 13).

Humility, for the Christian, also stems from our status as forgiven violators of God's goodness. As such, "You are not your own; you were bought at a price"—the price of Christ's shed blood and broken body on the cross (1 Corinthians 6:19-20). If we grow in apologetic ability—or any other area of competence in ministry—without growing in the grace of humility, an ugly arrogance results, which threatens to blunt or even undermine the force of the best apologetics. The apostle Paul, one of the stellar minds of antiquity, knew this well: "But we have this treasure in jars of clay to show that this all-surpassing power is from God and not from us" (2 Corinthians 4:7). There is no room for boasting in oneself, as Paul points out: "May I never boast except in the cross of our Lord Jesus Christ, through which the world has been crucified to me, and I to the world" (Galatians 6:14). Because of our fallen propensity to rest in proper beliefs while letting our spiritual maturity lag behind the truth of what we believe, Paul exhorted Timothy to watch both his life and his doctrine closely (1 Timothy 4:16). Apologists must do likewise.

PRAYER AND APOLOGETICS

Humility embraces prayer and lives within its embrace, whether for apologetics or any other enterprise. Paul requested prayer for his outreach to unbelievers (Colossians 4:2-4). The praying and fasting of Paul's sending church (Acts 13:1-3) were behind his dramatic encounter with a sorcerer who sought to dissuade Paul and his companions from explaining the gospel to the sorcerer's superior, Sergius Paulus, an intelligent man who sought out Paul's teaching (Acts 13:1-12). Paul prevailed in sidelining the sorcerer and converting Paulus through the power of the Holy Spirit and in accord with the prayer and fasting of his sending church.

---

[29]See Andrew Murray, *Humility* (Minneapolis: Bethany House, 2001); Douglas Groothuis, "Humility: The Heart of Righteousness," in *Christianity That Counts* (Grand Rapids: Baker, 1994).

Prayer enters deeply into every aspect of apologetics. The apologist must pray for wisdom in preparation for apologetic engagement, for the right words and spirit in an apologetic opportunity, and for the audience to receive the truth and respond positively and wisely (see John 16:13 and Ephesians 6:18). Francis Schaeffer affirmed that a solid apologetic is not in competition with prayer for the moving of the Holy Spirit. "When I am talking to an individual, or sitting on a platform talking to 5000 people and answering questions, very often, more often than most people know, I am praying for them."[30]

One needs to find courage and zeal for apologetics through prayer (and perhaps fasting). It is easy to become complacent and unfeeling about outreach in a pluralistic culture where we are greeted with the signs of unbelief every day. We are told that life is about possessions, self-esteem, appearance and fame—and we almost believe it. We are told that all religions are good and that we should pick the one that works best for us—and we almost believe it.[31] The antidote is biblical realism. The gospel is infinitely precious because it is the only way out of sin, death and hell—and the only way into forgiveness, a new creation in Christ and eternal life.

THE GOAL OF APOLOGETICS: CHRISTIAN CONVERSION AND INTELLECTUAL CONFIDENCE

Biblically understood, conversion is a radical turn away from sin, selfishness and Satan, and a turn toward God and his kingdom. This incorporates the whole person, not merely the intellect. However, there is no reason to follow and obey the God of the Bible unless Christianity is true and worth obeying. If it were false, it would not matter how attractive it might be. If it were true but unimportant, why should anyone even care?[32] Therefore, conversion is necessarily intellectual and involves cognitive assent to propositions taken to be objectively true. For this to occur, we must understand what the gospel requires of a person and on what basis it requires it. This understanding is classically known as *notitia*. One cannot be a Christian without knowing

---

[30]Francis A. Schaeffer, *The God Who Is There*, 30th anniv. ed. (Downers Grove, Ill.: InterVarsity Press, 1998), pp. 205-6.

[31]Sadly, many self-described "evangelicals" and "born again" Christians do believe that God offers salvation through other religions. This is taken up in chap. 23.

[32]I agree with Alvin Plantinga's comment that Christianity is "the maximally important truth" (*Warranted Christian Belief* [New York: Oxford University Press, 2000], p. 499).

what Christianity actually is. Here the Christian worldview and doctrine are primary. Any candidate for conversion should believe that (1) God exists as a holy being before whom all humans are held morally accountable for their transgressions (sins); (2) the malady of sin is so deep and pervasive that any rectification of the problem must come from outside of our wounded and rebellious beings; (3) God, the loving and just author of salvation, sent his only Son, Jesus Christ, to live the perfect life we cannot live and to make atonement for our sin in order to provide the way of reconciliation between us and God; (4) the reality of this work was vindicated by Christ's unflinching obedience to the Father, his death on the cross and his death-defeating, life-affirming resurrection from the dead. The path of forgiveness and restoration is open to all, but only by faith alone and only through the finished work of Jesus Christ alone.[33]

Only if we believe in the truth of the Christian message will we be able to trust the object of that message: God as revealed in and through Jesus Christ. This component of faith is *fiducia,* or trust; it is closely related to belief, but involves more than bare assent. It includes entrusting oneself in an existential act to Christ and his cause. While Scripture speaks of the need to "believe" in God, it also speaks of those who "received" him (John 1:12). A person believes that certain biblical propositions are objectively true; then the person subjectively appropriates these truths as his or her own. In so doing, the person gives allegiance to the object of these truths: Christ himself. Trust in this case may be likened to marriage. A lover believes many favorable things about his or her beloved before marriage, but only becomes married after sincerely affirming, "I do," and giving oneself to that partner.

Faith in Christ, biblically understood, guides and inspires a new way of knowing, being and doing. It has effects that James summarizes as "good works" (James 2:14-26; see also Ephesians 2:9). These works—which include inward renovation, both intellectual and moral, as well as outward behavior—are not the basis or warrant for one's favorable standing with God. That status comes by grace alone and is received by faith alone in Christ alone (Ephesians 2:8-9; Titus 3:5). However, where faith takes root, fruit takes hold and grows (Matthew 7:15-23). This understanding is

---

[33]See Francis A. Schaeffer, *The Finished Work of Christ* (Wheaton, Ill.: Crossway, 1998). More will be said on the nature of the gospel message in chap. 20.

vital for apologetics because of the pandemic problem of false conversions and nominal Christianity. Given biblical criteria, far more Americans claim to be Christians than are truly glory bound. Apologetics aims at conversion, not generic spirituality or religious externalism. Conversion requires repentance, as Jesus and John the Baptist and all the Hebrew prophets made so clear (Matthew 4:17). While a call to repentance might be thought more the job of evangelism, it factors into apologetics for two reasons. First, apologetics labors to present the Christian worldview. One aspect of that worldview is that people are disordered in their passions, self-centered, guilty before a holy God and in need of radical forgiveness and transformation. Repentant faith is the way into new life in Christ.[34] Second, apologetics should show that repentance makes sense because Christianity is true, rational and, in Pascal's sense, "attractive"—it promises our "true good." This true good is the restoration of the person through the achievements of Jesus Christ.

Apologetics also equips questioning or doubting Christians to find the intellectual confidence to be a wise witnesses to the truth of the gospel. As Christians master apologetic arguments, their knowledge of the truth and rationality of their beliefs increases, thus giving them a stronger platform for explaining and defending "the good news of God's grace" (Acts 20:24). The Christian's goal should be to gain "all the treasures of wisdom and knowledge" concerning the Christian worldview (Colossians 2:3).

DIALOGICAL AND CONTEXTUAL APOLOGETICS

The articulation of a sound philosophical method of apologetics is the burden of chapter three. However, I conclude this chapter by relating some very practical issues of apologetics pertaining to dialogue, discernment and context.[35]

The forums for apologetic presentation are legion, and we should use our sanctified imaginations to figure out new ways to present ancient truths. However, some forums are, in a sense, static. One publishes an argument, either in a book, an article, a letter to the editor, a tract, a post-

---

[34]On the necessity of repentance for conversion, see John MacArthur, *The Gospel According to Jesus* (Grand Rapids: Zondervan, 1988).

[35]See also David Clark's excellent treatment in *Dialogical Apologetics* (Grand Rapids: Baker, 1994); and Greg Kokl, *Tactics: A Game Plan for Discussing Your Christian Convictions* (Grand Rapids: Zondervan, 2009).

ing to a webpage or blog, or through some other written form—and that's that.[36] These statements may elicit a response, which in turn can be responded to by the apologist, but the dialogical aspect is usually minimal. Other forums are more dialogical because they involve direct discussion. These include face-to-face meetings, lectures with a question-answer session, debates, letters, e-mails, phone calls and so on. Although dialogue can devolve into a pointless exchange of mere opinion with little intellectual challenge, it need not do so. The spirit of persuasive dialogue was alive in the teaching and preaching of Paul throughout the book of Acts. Paul rationally engaged Jew and Gentile, common person, royalty, and philosopher—all for the cause of Christ. This, in fact, is true for all the outreach in Acts. As Ajith Fernando says, "All the messages recorded in Acts had a strong apologetic content."[37]

We can seek similar dialogues with unbelievers of all sorts. These dialogues necessarily involve all of the virtues requisite to apologetics discussed previously. Especially important is the humility that involves the willingness to listen and temper our responses to the intellectual and spiritual condition of the one who is engaged. This requires certain relational skills as well as worldview discernment. Love for the lost also carries a cost for the apologist, as Schaeffer noted:

> This kind of [apologetic] communication is not cheap. To understand and speak to sincere but utterly confused twentieth-century people is costly. It is tiring; it will open you to temptations and pressures. Genuine love, in the last analysis, means a willingness to be entirely exposed to the person to whom we are talking.[38]

In defending and commending the faith, Christians need to detect exactly what their dialogue partners believe about reality. While the technical discussion of worldviews falls into set categories—theism, deism, pantheism, naturalism, polytheism—people's beliefs are not always that well categorized. Through hundreds of interviews over a period of twenty

---

[36]While many Christian tracts are reactionary, simplistic or otherwise offensive, the medium itself is worthwhile. I have written tracts and distributed them over the years. For a discussion of the use of tracts, see Douglas Groothuis, "Event Specific Evangelism," in *Confronting the New Age* (Downers Grove, Ill.: InterVarsity Press, 1988).

[37]Ajith Fernando, *Acts*, The NIV Application Commentary (Grand Rapids: Zondervan, 1998), p. 30.

[38]Schaeffer, *God Who Is There*, p. 149.

years, my students in Christian apologetics at Denver Seminary have found that people often hold a smorgasbord of beliefs that do not easily fit into any unified worldview. There may be a dash of Christianity (left over from Sunday school), heaps of New Age spirituality (for personal enrichment), a dose of naturalism (about scientific matters) and, of course, substantial seasoning by relativism (which is everywhere). The savvy apologist must shift through this welter of conflicting beliefs through intent listening, as well as caring but challenging responses. The apologist should reveal that he or she is trying to understand what the unbeliever's beliefs are, how these beliefs relate to each other and how they are connected to the external world and the individual's life.

Once a person's worldview has been identified, the apologist should work on establishing common ground with the unbeliever in order to move closer to the Christian perspective. If the unbeliever is an atheist, we must start from scratch and argue for theism. However, the atheist may (inconsistently) believe in objective moral truth. If so, there is significant common ground. If the unbeliever is a theist, but not a Christian theist, then the emphasis will be on things unique to Christian theism, particularly the incarnation.

But besides worldview detection and looking for points of common ground, we need relational wisdom as to when and how to present arguments for Christian truth. Apologetic "dumping" or "blasting" with little concern for the state of the soul of the unbeliever may relieve pent up tension and display the apologist's knowledge, but it does little to bring anyone closer to eternal salvation. Some people are quite ready to get an earful of Christian truth; others are so closed that one must retreat and restrategize for another occasion.[39] We need discernment into the human heart for wise apologetics, as Pascal highlighted:

> We think playing upon man is like playing upon an ordinary organ. It is indeed an organ, but strange, shifting and changeable. Those who know only to play an ordinary organ would never be in tune on this one. You have to know where the keys are.[40]

Another crucial matter for apologetic encounters is context or situation. Since our culture places little value on genuine intellectual dialogue and

---

[39]See Jesus' discussion of "pearls before swine" in Matthew 7:6.
[40]Pascal, *Pensées* 55/111, p. 44.

discourse (which takes time, effort and discipline), we must deliberately seek out contexts in which these ideals may be lived out. Although we may find ourselves in apologetic discussions "on the fly" in less than ideal situations (God often engineers such divine appointments), the best intellectual environment is usually one in which there is silence and time to reflect and discuss the things that matter most. This ambience should be as free as possible from distracting stimuli—particularly television, the great destroyer of truth and rationality—and the hurried and harried atmosphere of contemporary culture.[41] Silence, however, is a rich atmosphere for rationally engaging truth, and should be cultivated.[42]

The virtues of hospitality and conviviality loom large on the apologetic horizon. Opening up one's home for discussions with unbelievers is ideal. Sadly, however, it is infrequent, given the breakdown of community and the tendency to "cocoon" inside one's home, spending more time in front of the home entertainment center than with other humans in conversation about what matters most. Much of the success of Francis and Edith Schaeffer's ministry in reaching unbelievers came as a result of inviting unbelievers to live with them at their L'Abri ministry in the Swiss Alps.[43] Of course, few of us have chalets in the Alps, but the principle of closely associating with and loving unbelievers holds true nevertheless.

THE SUM OF THE MATTER: DEFEND THE TRUTH

Here is the sum of the matter. We must earnestly endeavor to know the truth of the biblical worldview and to make it known with integrity to as many people as possible with the best arguments available. To know God in Christ means that we desire to make Christian truth available to others in the most compelling form possible. To be created in God's rational, moral and relational image means that our entire being should be aimed at the glorification of God in Christian witness. A significant part of that witness is Christian apologetics.

---

[41]See Douglas Groothuis, "Television: Agent of Truth Decay," in *Truth Decay* (Downers Grove, Ill.: IVP Books, 2000); and Neil Postman, *Amusing Ourselves to Death*, 20th anniv. ed. (New York: Penguin, 2005).
[42]On the importance of silence, see the Kierkegaard quote on p. 154.
[43]For the remarkable story of the Schaeffers, see Edith Schaeffer, *L'Abri*, 2nd ed. (Wheaton, Ill.: Crossway, 1992); and Edith Schaeffer, *The Tapestry: The Life and Times of Francis and Edith Schaeffer* (Waco, Tex.: Word, 1981).

3

Apologetic Method

Evaluating Worldviews

MUCH INK HAS BEEN SPILLED OVER apologetic methodology. Various schools have contended that their way is superior to others. Some apologists have spent as much or more time attempting to refute their fellow apologists' methods than they have in attempting to bring apologetics to the people who need it most: unbelievers and doubting followers of Jesus. Evangelist Dwight L. Moody was once criticized by another Christian for his approach to evangelism. Moody's response was that he liked the way he did evangelism better than the way his critics didn't do evangelism. This lesson applies to apologetic method as well.

Apologetics means philosophical engagement, and philosophy trades on logic. Therefore, a brief discussion of basic logical principles is imperative. Some Christians have disparaged the use of logic in either defining or defending Christian faith on the basis that logic is "merely human" and that we cannot limit God in this way. Worse yet, they have claimed that whatever benefit there may be in logic, it has been defaced by the Fall such that the human mind cannot grasp God through reasoning. On this understanding, faith means believing something without or against evidence and logic. Faith may even be taken as inversely related to evidence and logic. The less evidence and logic, the more need for faith; the more evidence, the less need for faith. Therefore, the highest and most commendable faith has the slimmest foundation in evidence and logic. This position is known as fideism or "faith-ism." I will return to fideism in more depth later in the chapter, but first we need to establish the indispensability of basic logic for apologetics.

LAWS OF LOGIC: NOT JUST GOOD IDEAS, BUT THE LAW

The logic of truth begins with the logic of *the law (or principle) of noncontradiction*. First codified (but not invented) by Aristotle, this law states, "Nothing can both be and not be at the same time in the same respect."[1] Nothing can possess incompatible properties; that is, nothing can be what it is not. For example, Jesus cannot be both sinless and sinful. If there is exactly one God, there cannot be many gods. This logical principle is not the unique possession of Christianity; it is a truth of all creation. God ordained us to think in this way because the world operates this way. Despite what some theologians have claimed, Christian faith does not require that we somehow transcend this law (or any law) of logic. God is consistent and cannot lie. God cannot deny himself or assert what is false, nor can he make something both true and false in the same way at the same time. This is no limit on God; it is a virtue.

Those who claim that this basic principle of thought is false must assert this principle in order to deny it. In so doing, they make a mockery out of all thought, language, communication and the very notion of truth. Consider the statement "The law of noncontradiction is false." For this statement itself to be true, it must contradict its opposite: that is, that the law of noncontradiction is true. But in so doing, it must affirm the duality of truth and falsity—which is the very thing that the law of noncontradiction itself affirms. Some think that modern physics has done away with the principle of noncontradiction because light behaves like both a wave and a particle. But this is false. The discovery of quantum electrodynamics (QED) near the turn of the last century showed that

> light is essentially made up of particles but that all elementary particles are capable of "wave-like" behavior. By showing in a logically consistent manner how light was capable of behaving like a wave on some occasions and a particle on others, this breakthrough produced one self-consistent paradigm that satisfactorily resolved the confounding puzzle of "wave-particle duality."[2]

---

[1]Aristotle *Metaphysics* 1005 b19-20.

[2]Scott R. Burson and Jerry L. Walls, *C. S. Lewis and Francis Schaeffer: Lessons for a New Century from the Most Influential Apologists of Our Time* (Downers Grove, Ill.: InterVarsity Press, 1998), pp. 86-87. The authors cite as their source Richard P. Feyman, *QED: The Strange Theory of Light and Matter* (Princeton, N.J.: Princeton University Press, 1985), p. 37. For more on how modern physics does not refute the law of noncontradiction, see R. C. Sproul, *Not a Chance: The*

Some may argue that since there are situations that involve self-contradictory elements, the law of noncontradiction is not universally true. Someone may be conflicted as to whether to study philosophy or to play video games, for example. So, that person wants to perform both A and non-A. But contradictory elements in *tension* with each other in our minds do not constitute logical contradictions "in which one and the same thing both is and is-not at the same time and in the same respect."[3]

The law of noncontradiction combined with the specificity of Christian truth claims and the high stakes involved in choosing whether to believe in Christ means that truth for the Christian is confrontational. While the postmodern world beholds the great welter of lifestyles, trends and façades, and can only utter "whatever" with a smirk, a slouch and a yawn, the followers of "*the* Way" (Acts 9:2) cannot be so nonchalant and easily pacified.

The law (or principle) of excluded middle trades on the same essential insight as the law of noncontradiction by stating that any factual statement and its denial cannot both be true. Either Jehovah is Lord or he is not Lord. Either Buddha was enlightened or he was not. There is no middle option. Jesus assumes this principle when he warns that "no one can serve two masters. Either you will hate the one and love the other, or you will be devoted to the one and despise the other. You cannot serve both God and money" (Matthew 6:24). Some may protest that not everything is black or white; some things are gray; so the principle does not hold universally. It is true that everything is not black or white; but the law of excluded middle does not reduce everything to binary relationships. Rather, it affirms that no statement and its denial can both be true: a statement cannot be both gray or not gray.[4]

The law (or principle) of bivalence states that any unambiguous declarative statement is either true or false—not neither true nor false and not both true and false. (Statements with intended double meanings or meaningless or ambiguous statements do not fall under this principle because they fail to assert any one thing.) The statement "Muhammad is the seal

Myth of Chance in Modern Science and Cosmology (Grand Rapids: Baker, 1994).
[3]Ed L. Miller and Jon Jensen, *Questions That Matter*, 5th ed. (Boston: McGraw-Hill, 2004), p. 33.
[4]Miller and Jensen, *Questions That Matter*, p. 33.

of the prophets" is either true or false. The statement "Jesus was God in the flesh" is either true or false. Moreover, both of these statements cannot be true because of the law (or principle) of noncontradiction. Muhammad cannot be the last and greatest of the prophets ("the seal of the prophets") if he was fundamentally mistaken about Jesus' identity. However, both of these statements could be false if there is no God, since there would be no God-inspired prophets and no divine incarnation.

Some have disputed the law of bivalence by claiming that sentences may have many meanings, depending on the interpretation. Thus, a sentence cannot be either true or false if it has many meanings, each of which has its own truth value. But this objection misses the point, since the law does not address questions of *interpretation* (hermeneutics) but the *truth value* of a statement *once its meaning is determined*. When the meaning is fixed, the truth value is strictly binary—true or false.

One final principle rounds out the logic menu. *The law (or principle) of identity* simply states that something is what it is: A = A. A thing is itself and nothing other than itself. If we say, "You're not yourself today!" we don't violate the principle of identity. We mean, rather, that you are acting out of character, acting strangely or unexpectedly, given what we know about you. The person is still identical to him- or herself even if he or she is acting strangely. Nor does this law deny the fact that things change over time. What it denies is that something cannot be what it isn't at any given time.[5] I cannot be fifty-one years old and fifty-two years old at the same time.

Some multiculturalists have claimed that basic logical principles are Western or male and thus not universally valid. To assert their universality is to engage in a kind of intellectual imperialism or cognitive colonialism. Whether one uses these logical principles is a matter of convention or even taste. To insist on their universality is wrong and narrow-minded. However, the last statement, in order to be meaningful at all, must assume the principle of noncontradiction as necessarily true. Furthermore, the foundational principles of logic are not the property of any one ethnic or reli-

---

[5]While this law is deceptively simple, we will later find it a powerful weapon against a materialist account of mind. Hint: if mental and material properties are not identical, they cannot be the same thing. Thus, mind-body identity theory is false. See J. P. Moreland, *Scaling the Secular City* (Grand Rapids: Baker, 1987), pp. 83-84.

gious group. Paul Griffiths, a noted scholar of Buddhism as well as a Christian philosopher, puts the lie to the idea that there is a special "Buddhist logic" distinct from Western logic. Reflecting on his experience in reading the first-millennium Indian Buddhist writers, he says:

> I immediately felt a great sense of familiarity, of recognition. Here was a philosophical tradition I could recognize, feel at home with, understand. Here was a tradition for which virtually all of the philosophical questions which had troubled me and my tradition—questions about knowledge, truth, personal identity, language, and reference—were burning issues. Here, I felt, was a tradition which also placed great stress upon the probative significance of valid arguments with true premises.[6]

These observations fit the biblical claim that all humans are made in the divine image and so think in essentially similar ways, despite significant cultural differences.[7] This fact should give us confidence to develop a fundamental apologetic method that trades on logic and develops arguments rationally.

WORLDVIEW HYPOTHESIS EVALUATION

The best method of apologetic reasoning is hypothesis evaluation and verification. The Christian worldview is taken as a large-scale hypothesis (or metanarrative) that attempts to explain what matters most. Some might balk at regarding Christian faith as a hypothesis, since it is a living relationship with God to which one is absolutely committed. To some, Christianity as a hypothesis sounds too tentative, clinical and academic. I offer two responses. First, when we are commending the Christian worldview, we cannot transfer our own attitude toward that worldview to those who do not share it. To unbelievers, Christianity is not yet believed to be true. It is merely a possibility (at best). Second, a worldview—Christian or otherwise—should be put forth as a hypothesis because it presents itself as a candidate for the most important truths (as do all religions and worldviews). A worldview hypothesis is a broad-ranging theory of everything, in

---

[6]Paul Griffiths, "Philosophizing Across Cultures: Or, How to Argue with a Buddhist," *Criterion* 26, no. 1 (1987): 11. For an application of the thesis that arguments can be made across religious traditions, see Paul Griffiths, *An Apologetic for Apologetics* (Maryknoll, N.Y.: Orbis, 1991).

[7]See Francis A. Schaeffer, *Escape from Reason* (1968; reprint, Downers Grove, Ill.: InterVarsity Press, 2007), pp. 46-47.

that it tries to account for the nature and meaning of the universe and its inhabitants. While worldviews can be dissected intellectually, they also reflect and address the orientation of one's innermost being—that is, the heart. Thus, while the commendation of the Christian worldview is necessarily an intellectual enterprise, it should also take stock of the biases, prejudices, loves and hates that lie at the root of the human being.[8]

How does one present an argument for the Christian worldview as the best hypothesis? The answer: carefully, slowly and piece by piece. First, the hypothesis needs to be formulated clearly. For apologetics, this means paying close attention to the components and implications of the Christian worldview, with an eye for detecting false stereotypes and caricatures.[9] Second, identify the worldviews that are potential rivals to Christianity. These will be the worldviews that are plausible—or "live hypotheses," to use William James's term.[10] A plausible worldview is one that holds interest and appeal for a significant number of people at a particular time and place. So, Islam is plausible in Iran, while secular humanism is plausible in the United States. *Plausibility* should not be confused with *credibility*, which deals with whether or not any claim is true and rational.[11] The credibility of a worldview is determined by whether or not arguments marshaled in its favor are compelling and logically coherent. A worldview that is plausible is not necessarily credible.

The major worldviews that have vied for acceptance throughout history are monotheism, deism, dualism, polytheism, pantheism and naturalism. Today in the West, monotheism (particularly Christianity and Islam), naturalism and pantheism are the most plausible worldview contenders, although some argue for dualism (in the form of gnosticism) and polytheism (of a Mormon variety). Of course, each worldview has various versions with differing aspects. For example, both Islam and

---

[8]See James Sire, *Naming the Elephant: Worldview as a Concept* (Downers Grove, Ill.: InterVarsity Press, 2004). For a review of some of the weakness of this book, see Jonah Schupbach, *Denver Journal* <www.denverseminary.edu/article/naming-the-elephant-worldview-as-a-concept>. Blaise Pascal was a master of addressing the whole person in his apologetic. See Pascal's *Pensées*, ed. and trans. Alban Krailsheimer (New York: Penguin, 1966).
[9]Some of these will be discussed in chap. 5.
[10]William James, *The Will to Believe and Other Essays on Popular Philosophy* (New York: Dover, 1956), pp. 2-3.
[11]I owe this basic distinction to a lecture by Os Guinness. For a discussion of the plausibility of religion in relation to Western secularization, see Peter Berger, *A Rumor of Angels* (Garden City, N.Y.: Anchor Books, 1970).

Christianity are monotheistic, but Christianity affirms, while Islam denies, that God is a Trinity and that Jesus Christ is God incarnate. The third and final step in presenting an apologetic argument for the Christian worldview is to apply the same criteria or tests of truth to each of the contending worldviews.

Some argue that the criteria for truth are worldview dependent. That is, each worldview defines for itself what will count as a test for truth. Therefore, these criteria cannot be used to assess competing worldviews. Missionary and apologist Lesslie Newbigin, for example, claims that criteria for truth are worldview dependent. I have critiqued his view in some detail elsewhere, but suffice to say that if each worldview sets up its own test for truth, then apologetics becomes impossible.[12] For example, a Christian might say that the Trinity is an utter mystery and cannot be logically explained, yet insist that if a defining doctrine of another worldview is "an utter mystery logically," then that worldview must be rejected. But this will not do. If we allow opaque mysteries in our own worldview, we have to allow them everywhere. Or if we demand logical consistency in other worldviews, we must demand it of our own. That is, the criteria for rational evaluation must be objective. There must not be any special pleading.

Without objective criteria, each worldview would be hermetically sealed off from other worldviews, since each would have its own truth claims and its own ways of verifying them. But if Christians desire to demonstrate the truth and rationality of Christianity to those who hold other worldviews, they must apply objective criteria to the contending worldviews. If none are given, there is no apologetic, but only preaching.[13]

Before discussing the eight criteria for worldview evaluation, the difference between constructive and negative apologetics needs clarification. Constructive apologetics (usually called positive apologetics) builds a case

---

[12]For more on Newbigin, see Douglas Groothuis, *Truth Decay: Defending Christianity Against the Challenges of Postmodernism* (Downers Grove, Ill.: InterVarsity Press, 2000), pp. 153-59.

[13]Christians do have and use rational criteria that are dependent on their worldview, but these are not pertinent to apologetics. For example, John says that we must test the spirits to determine whether they are from God. The test (or criterion) is christological (see 1 John 4:1-6). But this test depends on the idea that Christianity is true. As such, any spirit that denies that "Jesus has come in the flesh" is not of God and is of the antichrist. However, it makes no apologetic sense to say to a Muslim, "1 John 4 says your teaching is antichrist. Therefore, it is false." This statement is true, but it carries no apologetic weight, since the Muslim will deny the truth of 1 John in favor of the teachings of the Qur'an.

for Christian theism by arguing that Christianity best fits the appropriate criteria for worldview assessment. The central point of this book is constructive apologetics. Most chapters will construct a case for Christian theism. Here the apologist is on the offensive. On the other hand, the term *negative apologetics* can be used in two ways. First, when another worldview claims to be rationally superior to Christianity (such as naturalism or pantheism), it is appropriate to evaluate that worldview against appropriate criteria in order to show its logical deficiencies in relation to Christianity. We will argue in this way as well. This is an offensive approach because it brings non-Christian worldviews into question. Second, if a genuine objection is brought against Christianity—for example, that it is nothing but wish fulfillment, lacking objective reality—that challenge should be rebutted. The obstacle or roadblock to faith should be removed through argument. This is a defensive strategy. Later chapters will defend Christian theism against religious pluralism (which challenges Christianity's uniqueness and supremacy) and the problem of evil (which challenges the coherence of a worldview that affirms the coexistence of evil and God's goodness and power).[14]

The following criteria should be applied to all types of apologetic engagement. I take these criteria to be immediately obvious, since they are employed in any area of life where hypotheses are advanced and tested. For each criterion I will first give a general explanation of the criterion and then follow with a more formal statement.

CRITERIA FOR WORLDVIEW EVALUATION

The first test of any worldview is that *it explains what it ought to explain*. A *world*view has a broad reference range; it attempts to map the rudiments of reality comprehensively. If it gives us no explanation for important aspects of life—matters pertaining to meaning, morality and mortality—something is amiss, since these questions are perennial and pertinent. Although there are limits to the kinds of explanations that finite mortals can give, it is not appropriate to invoke "mystery" or "paradox" too often when defending a worldview. Otherwise you cannot defend it at all.

---

[14]For more on how various apologists have understood the constructive and negative task of apologetics, see Kenneth Boa and Robert Bowman, *Faith Has Its Reasons*, 2nd ed. (Colorado Springs: NavPress, 2005).

Criterion 1. If a worldview asserts an essential proposition X, and X is utterly mysterious or unintelligible and sheds no light on anything (it is a bare assertion), then the assertion of X is a rational strike against that worldview.

To telegraph this point, in following chapters I will argue that at key points both naturalism and pantheism fall into this error because they cannot explain key features of the universe and human persons. But Christians may tumble into this pit as well when they play the "mystery card" promiscuously. Some Christians, when called on the logic of the Trinity (How can three be one?) and the incarnation (How can an infinite God become a finite human?), simply affirm these doctrines as paradoxes or mysteries.[15] If this is all that can be said, then two defining features of Christian monotheism have no explanatory value and are concepts that seem contradictory. This does not bode well for apologetics, theology or anything else constructive for the Christian cause.[16]

The second criterion is *internal logical consistency*. The essential or constitutive elements of any worldview must accord with one another without contradiction. By "essential or constitutive element," I mean a conceptual plank in a worldview that is necessary for the worldview itself. For example, the ideas of karma and reincarnation are essential and constitutive elements of Hinduism (in all its various schools). Internal consistency of all the essential elements of a worldview is a *necessary* test for every worldview, but it is not sufficient to establish any worldview as true and rational. A worldview might be internally consistent but fail to accurately describe objective reality. Internal *in*consistency, however, is a *sufficient* indicator that a worldview is false.

Criterion 2a. If a worldview affirms X, Y and Z as essential elements of that worldview, and none of these individual elements contradicts another essential element, the worldview *may* be true because it is not logically inconsistent.

Criterion 2b. If a worldview affirms X, Y and Z as essential elements, and any of these elements contradict another essential element (say X contradicts Y), or is self-contradictory, this worldview is necessarily false because it is logically inconsistent.

---

[15]The Trinity will be discussed in chap. 4, and the incarnation in chap. 21.
[16]This is not to say that the concept of mystery has *no* place in a Christian worldview. We will return to this in chaps. 18 (concerning original sin) and 25 (concerning the problem of evil).

Not all inconsistencies within a worldview are fatal to a worldview. For example, a critic may charge that Christianity is false because some Christians baptize infants and some baptize only those who profess faith in Christ. But baptism, while part of Christian discipleship and indispensable in some form, is not at the core of the Christian worldview, and a specific form of baptism is not essential to the Christian worldview. It is true that both those who baptize infants and those who do not hold opposing beliefs, both of which cannot be correct. But whoever holds the incorrect view of baptism has not invalidated the Christian worldview in so doing. People hold worldviews, and people make honest mistakes. Worldviews should always be evaluated in their best representative forms, not withstanding the idiosyncrasies of their adherents.

The third criterion by which worldviews should be evaluated is *coherence*. This test is related to consistency, but moves beyond it to speak of the essential propositions of a worldview being tightly interrelated and conceptually linked. A collection of noncontradictory ideas is not sufficient to form a coherent worldview. Consider these statements:

1. Willie Mays was the best defensive center fielder in the history of baseball.

2. John Coltrane was the best tenor saxophonist in the history of jazz.

3. Alaska is the largest state in the union.

These statements are all consistent logically.[17] However, this triad of isolated facts is hardly a *coherent* worldview.[18] Now consider quickly Christian claims about God, humans and salvation. God is a personal being who created humans in his image. The metaphysics of God and humans are closely related on this account. Humans fell into sin against God, but God provided atonement through his own actions in Christ. Again, the being and the behavior of God are interrelated with the human condition. And so on. Like consistency, coherence is a necessary, but not a sufficient, condition for the truth of a worldview. To take an obvious example, the mythical world of Tolkien's *Lord of the Rings* is very coherent, but utterly imaginary.[19]

---

[17]Statement 3 is unarguably true (Texans to the contrary), while 1 and 2 are arguably true.

[18]I owe this insight to philosopher Keith Yandell, a professor at the University of Wisconsin, who used another example to illustrate the idea.

[19]Its being imaginary does not rule out that this mythic world is significantly influenced by

> *Criterion 3.* If a worldview's essential propositions are coherent (meaningfully interconnected conceptually), it is more likely to be true than if its essential propositions are not related in this way.

The fourth criterion is *factual adequacy.* This concerns the historical and empirical dimensions of life. A worldview may be internally consistent yet inconsistent with respect to the reality it attempts to describe. For example, Buddhism, Hinduism and some forms of naturalism claim that the universe is eternal; it did not come into being out of nothing, as is affirmed by Judaism, Christianity and Islam. If there is strong scientific and philosophical evidence that the universe did come into being out of nothing, then any worldview denying this is factually inadequate on this essential point. Worldviews often disagree over historical—as well as cosmic—facts. For example, Islam denies that Jesus Christ affirmed his own deity and instead teaches that this is a later distortion of the church. The New Testament affirms that Jesus did claim deity, and Christianity confesses the deity of Christ at the very center of its worldview. Both claims, of course, cannot be true. The resolution of the conflict must come by arguments over historical facts and their proper interpretation.

> *Criterion 4.* The greater the extent to which a worldview's essential factual claims can be established in various empirical, scientific and historical ways, the greater is the likelihood that this worldview is true.

Existential viability is the fifth criterion. This is a kind of factual adequacy, but focuses on the inner reality of human beings.[20] Simply because a person claims that a certain worldview "works for me" does not mean this worldview is existentially viable. To claim that a worldview is existentially viable means that it can be affirmed without philosophical hypocrisy. *Philosophical hypocrisy* is not *moral hypocrisy.* The latter involves failing to live to up to a *livable* standard and then failing to admit this failure to self and others.[21] This manner of hypocrisy testifies to the

---

Tolkien's Christian beliefs, as was also the case with the fiction of C. S. Lewis. On how fiction can nevertheless communicate truth, see Michael Jubien, "Is There Truth in Fiction?" in *Contemporary Metaphysics* (New York: Blackwell, 1999).

[20]This criterion of *worldview assessment* needs to be distinguished carefully from the *pragmatic definition of truth,* which will be addressed in chap. 6.

[21]The classic denunciation of hypocrisy is found in Jesus' preaching against the scribes and

56

bad character of the person, but it does not necessarily bring the world-view of that person into question. Philosophical hypocrisy requires a person to engage in perpetual doublethink in order to live according to his or her worldview. Consider any worldview—such as Christian Science or most forms of New Age spirituality—that affirms that there is no objective evil in the world. Apparent evil is merely "in the mind"; it is only a lower form of consciousness. The adherent of such an evil-denying worldview must always redefine and dismiss evil as unreal or illusory. Rape or murder cannot be condemned as truly evil. But who can consistently live on that basis? On another score, if a worldview affirms that (1) life has no purpose, (2) death is the end of the person, and (3) one should live joyfully and hopefully, this worldview may also be existentially unlivable (as well as internally inconsistent).[22]

Criterion 5a. For a worldview to be a likely candidate for truth, its essential propositions must be existentially viable.

Criterion 5b. If a worldview leads habitually to philosophical hypocrisy, it is rationally disqualified, since this indicates that it does not correspond to reality.

Related to livability, but put more positively, is the sixth criterion, *intellectual and cultural fecundity.* If a worldview is (1) truly explanatory, (2) internally consistent, (3) coherent, (4) factually adequate and (5) existentially viable, then it should inspire cultural and intellectual discovery, creativity and productivity. If a worldview fits reality, it should motivate its followers to embrace and master that reality with confidence and energy. J. P. Moreland captures this idea in his reflections on the nature of truth and its power: "This is why truth is so powerful. It allows us to cooperate with reality, whether spiritual or physical, and tap into its power."[23]

This is not to say that fundamentally false worldviews will not generate impressive cultural effects. Nazism produced its own warped and powerful culture—for a time. Moreover, this test is not a sufficient test for a world-

---

Pharisees in Matthew 23.

[22]More on the inconsistency of these three naturalistic beliefs will be discussed in chap. 15, which argues that naturalism entails nihilism, which is unlivable.

[23]J. P. Moreland, *Love Your God with All Your Mind* (Colorado Springs: NavPress, 1997), p. 81.

view, but a necessary one. It must be factored into the other tests to be used appropriately. So, we cannot simply say that Islam has produced a great civilization and continues to appeal to people globally, therefore, it must be true.[24] If Islam fails any of the previous five tests (such as factual adequacy with respect to the identity of Jesus), its cultural success—such as it is—cannot count decisively in its favor.

> *Criterion 6.* If a worldview is true, it should lead to *intellectual and cultural fecundity.* The greater the beneficial fecundity, the greater evidence that the worldview is true.

Seventh, *radical ad hoc readjustment* is an important negative criterion for testing worldviews. When a worldview is faced with potentially defeating counterevidence, an adherent may readjust its core claims to accommodate the evidence against it. Various theories and worldviews can legitimately refine their beliefs over time, but radical ad hoc readjustment reveals a deep problem at the heart of the worldview in the dock. Two examples should explain this:

(1) A deep philosophical problem for the doctrine of karma (held by Hinduism and Buddhism) is that karma operates automatically and impersonally. It must do its work of comprehensive cosmic ordering without a conscious agent who records acts of good and bad karma, and metes out karmic rewards and punishments. Since an impersonal and automatic process cannot explain karmic outcomes, the theosophist Annie Besant invented the doctrine of "the lords of karma," thus positing conscious spiritual agents to accomplish the work. Yet this idea is absolutely alien to both Hinduism and Buddhism; it is an ad hoc readjustment that brings the entire karmic system into serious question.[25]

(2) Another type of radical ad hoc adjustment to a worldview occurs when sound Christian doctrine is altered unnecessarily. Consider, for example, openness theology.[26] Those who advocate this understanding of

---

[24]Moreover, Islam's previous cultural achievements are often overstated for ideological purposes. See Robert Spencer, *Religion of Peace: Why Christianity Is and Islam Isn't* (Washington, D.C.: Regnery, 2007); and Alvin Schmidt, *The Great Divide: The Failure of Islam and the Triumph of the West* (Boston: Regina Orthodox Press, 2004).

[25]See Paul Edwards, *Reincarnation: A Critical Examination* (Amherst, N.Y.: Prometheus, 1996), pp. 40-41.

[26]This has been advocated in recent years by William Hasker, Gregory Boyd, Clark Pinnock, John Sanders and others.

the Bible claim that we cannot solve the problem of evil without reconsidering the nature of God.[27] Therefore, they assert that if God has a strong providential control of history, evil must be attributed to his agency. To avoid this they allege that God leaves much of the future open; thus it is unknowable to him. I address the problem of evil in chapter twenty-five, but the point here is that such a sweeping readjustment to the doctrine of God—one that is supported by neither the Bible nor the creeds and confessions of church history—is a not strong candidate for truth because it distorts the original understanding of God that is intrinsic to Christian theism.[28]

Thus a radical ad hoc readjustment may indicate that the original worldview is salvageable only through an illegitimate move (as with karma), or it may reveal that the original worldview itself has been sold short in favor of a foolish alternative.[29]

> *Criterion 7.* If a worldview substantially alters its essential claims in light of counterevidence, it loses rational justification.

Eighth, all things being equal, *simpler explanations are preferable to unnecessarily complex ones.*

How this criterion plays out depends on what is being explained. For example, a materialist may claim that any materialist explanation is better than a theistic one, since materialism is simpler than theism, which includes both God and the material world. But this is simple to the point of being simplistic. For materialism to win the day, it must make a better case than theism for whatever it attempts to explain, given its intrinsic resources and limitations as a worldview. For example, it cannot appeal to immaterial states of any kind, nor can it ground human reason in any kind of design plan for humans and the larger universe. As we will discover in later chapters, these

---

[27]They also offer other philosophical reasons for their position, but I take the problem of evil to be the leading impetus for their views.

[28]As I argue in chap. 25, the problem of evil is best understood in terms of God's sovereignty. There is no need for openness theology. However, openness thinkers have tried to make their case from biblical exegesis. See John Sanders, *The God Who Risks*, 2nd ed. (Downers Grove, Ill.: InterVarsity Press, 2007). For a critique of open theism, see John Piper et al., *Beyond the Bounds: Open Theism and the Undermining of Biblical Christianity* (Wheaton, Ill.: Crossway, 2003).

[29]I believe this is also the case for those who advocate theistic evolution. Ridding the world of the evidence of design (as does Darwinism) is not compatible with Christian theism. It is a radical ad hoc readjustment. This will be addressed in some detail in chap. 13.

are serious and (in fact) lethal weaknesses that overwhelm the brute assertion of simplicity.

Criterion 8. Worldviews should not appeal to extraneous entities or be
more complex than is required to explain what they propose to establish.[30]

How each of these eight criteria plays out may involve subsidiary
considerations of more sophistication. For example, factual adequacy in
the area of historical claims involves the application of historiographical
tests regarding documents. Where scientific claims are made (regarding
the origin of the universe, life and humanity), considerations of simplicity, elegance and other epistemic values come into play. Nevertheless,
these eight criteria are essential in charting the course of our worldview
evaluation.

By applying each of these eight tests to Christianity and its rivals, a
cumulative case argument is formed. Several lines of evidence converge
on the hypothesis that Christian theism is the best-attested worldview.
This might be likened to a courtroom situation in which several diverse
witnesses concur in their testimony regarding the guilt or innocence of a
defendant. Each witness in isolation gives only part of the story, but
when multiple witnesses, all speaking from different areas of knowledge,
agree on their judgment, the overall case is strengthened considerably—
if their testimony outweighs any competing claims and if each of the
lines of argument formed by the cumulative case agrees with all other
lines of evidence.

Therefore, chapter by chapter we will argue that the testimony of the
cosmos, human experience and history all point to Christian theism as the
most probable explanation for the facts. However, competing worldview
explanations (if you will, opposing witnesses) will be consulted along the
way, since our goal is to argue that Christianity presents a better explanation, or a better hypothesis, than its rivals. Of course, more time will be
spent on the positive case for Christianity than on the negative case against
other worldviews. Indeed, giving a strong positive case for a Christian
worldview will automatically eliminate other views. For example, a strong
case for a transcendent lawgiver will rule out naturalism and Eastern reli-

---

[30]For a development of this claim, see Richard Swinburne, "How We Explain Things," in *Is
There a God?* (New York: Oxford University Press, 1996).

gions, neither of which can abide such a conclusion.

This cumulative-case model differs from that of the brilliant apologist Edward John Carnell in that Carnell and followers typically fail to employ arguments for the existence of God.[31] Instead of arguing for a general monotheism and then arguing for Christian particulars, they argue for the whole of Christian theism at every stage of the argument. Part of this strategy may be based on the historical fact that Carnell developed his method in the late 1940s, when theistic arguments—outside of the Thomist tradition—were all but dead in philosophical circles. That situation has radically changed in the past few decades, thanks to the work of philosophers we will be consulting in the pages that follow.

Unlike Carnell and his followers, my approach is to verify the Christian worldview by arguing for its essential elements one by one. For example, I will argue that good cosmological arguments establish the existence of a singular, personal and all-powerful being who created the universe out of nothing. These arguments also refute every worldview that denies creation ex nihilo (such as Hinduism, Buddhism, Taoism and naturalism). Cosmological arguments do not speak directly to the existence of the Trinity or to the incarnation; neither do they speak against them. In fact, these specifically Christian doctrines become more credible after the existence of an omnipotent and personal Creator is rationally grounded. Then we may argue for the Trinity and the incarnation on the basis of their logical coherence, the well-established testimony of Scripture, their existential significance and so on.

OTHER APOLOGETIC SYSTEMS

Before moving on to address constructive and beneficial apologetic arguments, we must assess briefly the strengths and weaknesses of other apologetic methods: fideism, presuppositionalism, Reformed epistemology and evidentialism. A more involved discussion of natural theology awaits in chapter nine.

Fideism. Fideism is an attempt to protect Christian faith against the assaults of reason by means of intellectual insulation and isolation. Some,

---

[31]See Edward John Carnell, *An Introduction to Christian Apologetics* (Grand Rapids: Eerdmans, 1948). An especially noteworthy Carnellian is my esteemed colleague Gordon R. Lewis. See his *Testing Christianity's Truth Claims* (Chicago: Moody Press, 1976).

who believe apologetics does not comport with the nature of Christian faith, see fideism as an antidote to apologetics. There are various stripes of fideism, some more defensible than others, but they all share the strategy of making belief a self-certifying and self-enclosed reality that needs no intellectual fortification from the classical arsenal of apologetics—natural theology, evidence for biblical reliability and arguments against other worldviews.[32] Not all who reject the efficacy of arguments for God's existence are fideists, since they may substitute another apologetic in its place, but all fideists reject natural theology.[33] Some claim faith is a divine gift, which removes it from the efforts of reasoning and discourse. Many claim that the effects of sin on the mind (the noetic effects of sin) are so great that they significantly retard the ability to reason to the truth of the gospel.

I have already argued for the indispensability of logical principles for rational discourse of any kind. To exempt the Christian worldview from logic is special pleading and wins no respect from unbelievers. Nor does it help Christians who are struggling with their faith. But some fideists may grant that while logical principles are useful in understanding the nature of Christianity, we can build no bridge from unbelief to belief through their employment, given the terrible effects of sin on the mind.

While Scripture warns us that every aspect of humanity is corrupted by sin and that reason alone is not sufficient to receive the things of God, it also speaks of God's general revelation in nature (Romans 1–2). The Bible also evidences apologetics in action repeatedly (see chap. 2). Thus, there is no a priori reason to forbid apologetics. Certainly, the effects of the Fall make apologetics more difficult, but they need not render it impossible.

Last, while biblical Christians agree that salvation is a gift of grace re-

---

[32]See C. Stephen Evans, *Faith Above Reason: A Kierkegaardian Account* (Grand Rapids: Eerdmans, 1998). Evans gives a very sympathetic account of Kierkegaard's philosophy of religion and attempts to vindicate him from the charge of irrationalism. While considered a fideist, Kierkegaard presents an insightful kind of psychological apologetic in many of his works, particularly *The Sickness Unto Death*—a work that helped me become a Christian in 1976. One textbook sees fideism as a type of apologetic method and includes Pascal along with Kierkegaard and others as proponents. See Kenneth D. Boa and Robert M. Bowman, *Faith Has Its Reasons*, 2nd ed. (Waynesboro, Ga.: Paternoster, 2005), pt. 5. For reasons made clear in my book *On Pascal* (Belmont, Calif.: Wadsworth, 2003), I deny that Pascal was a fideist, but much depends on the exact definition of that term.

[33]I discuss the role and power of natural theology for Christian apologetics in chaps. 9-16.

ceived by faith, this need not banish the vigorous use of the mind in weighing the case for faith, since we are not justified by the use of our intellect but by the objective work of Jesus Christ in history. If we come to faith partially through recognizing good apologetic arguments, as did C. S. Lewis, we should give thanks that we could use our mind this well and that the arguments were at hand for inspection and reception. There is nothing in the apologetic enterprise that conflicts with salvation as a gift of God's grace.

Presuppositionalism. Presuppositionalism is a school of apologetics influenced by Reformed Christianity that rejects the tools of classical apologetics.[34] But it does so without resorting to irrational fideism. Its leading proponents in the last century were Cornelius Van Til, Gordon Clark and Carl F. H. Henry.[35] Presuppositionalism claims that the Christian should presuppose the entire Christian worldview and reason from this conviction with unbelievers. It thus limits positive apologetics to showing the logical coherence of Christian doctrine and relies on negative apologetics to refute non-Christian perspectives. It claims that unless a person presupposes Christianity, he or she cannot make any sense of the world morally, logically or scientifically, since Christianity alone supplies the required conditions for these areas of life to be intelligible. We cannot find sufficient common ground with unbelievers to build successful arguments for Christianity based on reason and evidence. Presuppositionalists critique the arguments of classical apologetics as both logically defective and theologically improper. The latter charge (made by Van Til) follows from the claim that an appeal to shared principles of evidence and logic is an appeal to autonomous and God-rejecting reason, which, of course, will resist recognizing the one true God. Van Til, unlike Clark and Henry, even claimed that we cannot

---

[34]This by no means implies that all or most apologists who hold to Reformed theology ascribe to this method, although Cornelius Van Til and his followers claim presuppositionalism is the method most consistent with Calvinism. Deeply Reformed thinkers such as John Gerstner and R. C. Sproul vigorously disagree (see John Gerstner, R. C. Sproul and Art Lindsley, *Classical Apologetics* [Grand Rapids: Zondervan, 1984]). Moreover, the old Princeton school of apologetics (Charles Hodge and B. B. Warfield) employed a classical approach fruitfully.

[35]See Cornelius Van Til, *The Defense of the Faith*, 4th ed. (1955; reprint, Phillipsburg, N.J.: P & R Publishing, 2008); Gordon Clark, *Reason, Religion, and Revelation* (Philadelphia: Presbyterian & Reformed, 1961); and Carl F. H. Henry, *God, Revelation, and Authority*, 6 vols. (Waco, Tex.: Word, 1976-1982). Volume one speaks most directly to apologetic method and epistemology.

impose human logic on God, who transcends it.

While I learned much from Van Til, and particularly from Clark and Henry, I cannot embrace their apologetic systems. Without giving a full-fledged critique of presuppositionalism, I will note just a few points.[36] First, if Van Til's statement about logic were taken seriously, it would doom any apologetic or theology. If human logic does not apply to God, we are left with nothing to affirm theologically and nothing to defend apologetically. Clark, however, insisted that the law of noncontradiction was a necessary and negative test for truth.[37] Second, there is nothing impious in using arguments with unbelievers that employ their God-given reasoning abilities. *Good* reasoning is not "autonomous" or "apostate," but rather a God-given way to discover truth. Because of the noetic effects of sin, apologetics is more difficult, but it is not futile. Moreover, the presuppositionalists use logic extensively in their tearing down of non-Christian worldviews (negative apologetics). Why, then, they forbid its use to build up a positive case for Christianity is unclear.[38] Clark, Van Til and Henry essentially repeated charges made by David Hume and others against the theistic arguments, all of which have been successfully rebutted—as will be argued later in this book.[39]

Van Til and his followers (such as Greg Bahnsen and John Frame) sometimes appeal to a "transcendental argument" that claims that unless we presuppose a Christian worldview, we have no reason to trust our rational faculties, since they would otherwise rest ultimately on chance.[40] The

---

[36]For excellent critiques of Clark and Van Til, see Lewis, "The Rationalism of Gordon Clark," and "The Biblical Authoritarianism of Cornelius Van Til," in *Testing Christianity's Truth Claims*.

[37]See Ronald Nash's treatment of "The Law of Noncontradiction" in *Life's Ultimate Questions* (Grand Rapids: Zondervan, 1999).

[38]I owe this astute insight to a comment made by John Montgomery to me in 1980 at an apologetics conference in Eugene, Oregon.

[39]Clark did give one positive argument for God's existence based on the existence of truth. See his *A Christian View of Men and Things* (Grand Rapids: Baker, 1981), pp. 318-23. In this, he relied on Augustine. For a book-length, multiauthor challenge to Hume's attack on natural theology, see James Sennett and Douglas Groothuis, eds., *In Defense of Natural Theology* (Downers Grove, Ill.: InterVarsity Press, 2005).

[40]Van Tillians engage in heated arguments over which of these two, Bahnsen or Frame, is the true disciple of Van Til, but I will not take up these arguments, since I do not endorse the basic method. For a contemporary application and interpretation of Van Til's method, see the entries by John Frame in Steven Cowan, *Five Views of Apologetics* (Grand Rapids: Zondervan, 2000); John Frame, *Cornelius Van Til: An Analysis of His Thought* (Phillipsburg, N.J.: Presbyterian & Reformed, 1995); and John Frame, *Apologetics for the Glory of God* (Phillipsburg, N.J.: P & R Publishing, 1994). For another take on interpreting and applying Van Til, see Greg L.

structure of this argument is good and does not beg any questions, but the argument need not carry the entire weight of an apologetic.[41]

Reformed epistemology. In the last three decades or so, sophisticated Christian philosophers such as Alvin Plantinga, Nicholas Wolterstorff and William Alston have developed an epistemological approach to Christianity known as Reformed epistemology, which has apologetic implications.[42] The rigor and complexity of their arguments does not lend itself to any simple summary or critique.[43] The following assessment will focus on some broad themes from Plantinga, largely from his major work *Warranted Christian Belief.* Reformed epistemologists argue that secular thought has placed an undue burden on Christian apologetics. It demands that Christians offer proof for their beliefs on pain of being irrational. Plantinga has extensively argued that this demand is based on a self-refuting epistemology known as classical or narrow foundationalism.

Roughly put, classical foundationalism holds that a belief only becomes knowledge if that belief is true *and* if either (1) the belief is self-evident or necessarily true or evident to the senses, or (2) the belief can be supported in some way by what is self-evident, necessarily true or evident to the senses. Beliefs of type (1) serve as the *foundation* (hence, *foundationalism*) for all other beliefs of type (2) and not the converse.

Both Christians and critics of Christianity worked within this paradigmatic epistemology for centuries, but Plantinga rejects it for two reasons. First, many beliefs do not fit within the strictures of classical foundationalism; nevertheless, we take them to be true and reasonable. For instance,

---

Bahnsen, *Van Til's Apologetic Readings and Analysis* (Phillipsburg, N.J.: Presbyterian & Reformed, 1998), and *Presuppositional Apologetics: Stated and Defined*, ed. Joel McDurmon (Powder Springs, Ga.: American Vision, 2008). See William Lane Craig's assessment of Frame and other presuppositionalists in *Five Views of Apologetics*, pp. 232-235.

[41]This kind of negative apologetic against naturalism fares far better in the hands of philosophers such as Alvin Plantinga and C. S. Lewis, as we will see in chapter seventeen.

[42]The treatment on Reformed epistemology draws heavily on my review/essay on Alvin Plantinga's *Warranted Christian Belief,* which was published in the *Journal of the Evangelical Theological Society* 45, no. 1 (March 2002): 178-82. A fairly early statement of Plantinga's, Wolterstorff's and Alston's views, with contributions from all these authors, is Alvin Plantinga and Nicholas Wolterstorff, eds., *Faith and Rationality* (Notre Dame, Ind.: University of Notre Dame Press, 1983).

[43]For a sympathetic overview of this project, see Kelly James Clark, *Reason and Belief in God* (Grand Rapids: Eerdmans, 1990); and Ronald Nash, "The Evidential Challenge to Religious Belief" and "Foundationalism and the Rationality of Religious Belief," in *Faith and Reason* (Grand Rapids: Zondervan, 1988).

memory beliefs (such as what we had for breakfast) are not self-evidently true, necessary truths or evident to the senses; neither are they based on beliefs outside of memory itself. Yet we take memory to be generally reliable. Such "properly basic beliefs," as Plantinga calls them, are not held on the basis of other beliefs and are not necessarily true (as is the statement, "All bachelors are unmarried men"). Second, classical foundationalism suffers from self-referential failure. It cannot fulfill its own requirements for knowledge. The tenets of this epistemology are not themselves self-evident, necessarily true, evident to the senses or based on such items of knowledge. Therefore, classical foundationalism is faulty and should not be employed for testing knowledge, including religious knowledge.[44]

Plantinga's key philosophical move in light of the failure of classical foundationalism is to argue that belief in God and the entire Christian worldview is one kind of belief that may be properly basic. If it is, we need not argue for God's existence on the basis of things we already know through different forms of arguments (reasoning from premise to conclusion). Rather, we come to believe in God "in the basic way." This belief may be occasioned by looking at the beauty of nature or feeling divine displeasure over something we have done, but the belief in God is not evidentially based on these events. These events are "nonpropositional" experiences that serve as episodes for coming to belief in God.

Plantinga says that a Christian belief

> can have warrant, and warrant sufficient for knowledge, even if I don't know of and cannot make a good historical case for the reliability of the biblical writers or for what they teach. . . . On this model, the warrant for Christian belief doesn't require that I or anyone else have this kind of historical information.[45]

Thus Plantinga often invokes the special status of Christian belief as properly basic in order to deflect criticisms. If we don't have to play the evidence game, so to speak, we need not be threatened by certain anti-Christian arguments. Plantinga further argues that if Christian belief re-

---

[44]I am not sure that Plantinga's critique is fatal to all forms of strong foundationalism. Timothy McGrew defends a carefully nuanced (and non-Cartesian) foundationalism in "A Defense of Classical Foundationalism," in Louis Pojman, *The Theory of Knowledge: Classical and Contemporary Readings*, 2nd ed. (Belmont, Calif.: Wadsworth, 1998).

[45]Alvin Plantinga, *Warranted Christian Belief* (New York: Oxford University Press, 2000), p. 259.

quires outside evidence for God's existence and the specifics of Christian orthodoxy, we are at an epistemological disadvantage. The classical method of arguing for theism and then giving Christian evidences (as exemplified by Richard Swinburne) fails to offer a sufficient case; in other words, warrant cannot be established in this way. However, if we believe "in the basic way," then warrant for Christian belief very likely obtains. Given Christian belief as properly basic, Plantinga rejects the model that presents the Christian worldview as a hypothesis to be verified or falsified by appeals to evidence and argument (namely, the apologetic model commended in this chapter). Rather, Christian belief is more like memory beliefs:

> Everyone . . . accepts memory beliefs. We all remember such things as what we had for breakfast, and we never or almost never propose such beliefs as good explanations of present experience and phenomena. And the same holds for theism and Christian belief.[46]

So, for Plantinga, Christianity can be taken as a properly basic belief in the same category as memory beliefs; and, like memory beliefs, it does not have to serve as an explanation for anything, thus exempting Christianity from being the best explanation for phenomena.

Taking Christian belief "in the basic way," however, does not exempt one from having to address certain potential "defeaters"—that is, claims or arguments that would render Christian belief unwarranted or worse.[47] Neither does believing "in the basic way" necessarily make one a fideist, since Christian belief is taken to be rational (as a properly basic belief).

Despite his emphasis on the "proper basicality" of Christian belief, Plantinga does not eschew all positive arguments for God's existence. His "evolutionary argument against naturalism" claims that unless theism is true, we have no reason to trust our cognitive abilities, since they would rest merely on impersonal and chance forces with no designing wisdom to

---

[46]Ibid., p. 330.

[47]Plantinga deals with five potential defeaters in *Warranted Christian Belief:* (1) the claims of Freud and Marx that religious belief is merely a projection, (2) the arguments of liberal scriptural scholarship that deny biblical truth, (3) the challenge from postmodernism (mainly in the person of Richard Rorty) that the traditional correspondence view of truth itself (required for Christian truth claims) be rejected, (4) the accusation that religious pluralism undercuts the unique and final truth of Christianity, and (5) the objections of recent formulations of the problem of evil.

insure their proper functioning.[48] He also claims that all naturalistic accounts of warrant for knowledge fail (both conceptual and perceptual), thus leaving a theistic account as more plausible.[49] Nevertheless, positive arguments are not required for warranted belief in God or for Christian theism.

Plantinga is right to affirm that God may inspire someone to believe in the Christian God apart from formal evidence or arguments. This happens all the time. Further, Plantinga's work seems to show that the unbeliever cannot refute the Christian's belief simply on the basis that the Christian cannot support it through the traditional means of apologetics. If a believer can fend off relevant defeaters and articulate how he or she believes God led him or her to belief, the Christian may be warranted in that belief. Moreover, even a young child could believe in Christianity and be rationally justified in so doing, given the inspiration of the Holy Spirit.[50] Nevertheless, his approach to apologetics is limited in several ways.

First, Plantinga relies on a specific theistic version of an epistemology known as externalism. His earlier work *Warrant and Proper Function* developed the idea that one's beliefs receive warrant on the basis of their functioning properly in an environment divinely designed to be conducive to cognitive success. Plantinga argues that the Christian worldview provides the metaphysic required for this epistemology. As long as there are no in-principle reasons not to believe in Christianity—that is, as long as belief in Christianity is not shown to be intrinsically irrational—one may believe the Christian faith rationally.[51] This is because Christian belief comes through "instigation of the Holy Spirit." So, according to Plantinga, the believer can have warrant for his or her belief without having evidence for that belief. While this may be so, one wonders how a believer, who holds belief in God "in the basic way," would deal with intellectual doubts about the truthfulness of those beliefs. Yes, the person may be able to "defeat defeaters" of some kinds. But what if he or she questions God's

---

[48]More on this in chap. 17.

[49]See Alvin Plantinga, *Warrant: The Contemporary Debate* (New York: Oxford University Press, 1993); and Alvin Plantinga, *Warrant and Proper Function* (New York: Oxford University Press, 1993).

[50]I owe this insight to David Werther.

[51]On this subject, Plantinga marshals impressive arguments against the antibiblical arguments of those who attempt to discredit Christianity on this basis. See his *Warranted Christian Belief,* chaps. 1, 2, 5.

very existence or the reliability of the Scriptures? According to Plantinga, traditional strategies for defending these beliefs do not offer enough rational justification to make them convincing. In fact, he denies that Christianity is a hypothesis to be verified by appeals to different kinds of evidence.[52] Rather, one comes to believe in the inspiration of Scripture simply because the Bible is "self-authenticating" to those who believe through the Spirit.[53] But in the case of the doubting Christian, "basic belief" would seem insufficient.

Second, given Plantinga's system, philosophy is unable to pronounce on the *truth* of Christianity; it can only render it *rational* to believe. If the Christian God exists, then one can be warranted in this belief, but the existence of the Christian God cannot be rationally established through arguments that appeal to nonbasic knowledge—despite the strength of some of Plantinga's arguments for generic theism. At the end of his 499-page magnum opus Plantinga says:

> But *is* it [Christianity] true? This is the really important question. And here we pass beyond the competence of philosophy, whose main competence, in this area, is to clear away certain objections, impedances, and obstacles to Christian belief. Speaking for myself and of course not in the name of philosophy, I can say only that it does, indeed, seem to me to be true, and to be the maximally important truth.[54]

Yet it seems that one should hope more of apologetics, as did Augustine, Anselm, Aquinas and other apologists—both ancient and modern.[55]

Plantinga may be right, but since I (along with other Christian philosophers) take the cumulative evidential case for Christian theism to be much stronger, this book will aim for the truth and cogency of the Christian worldview, not just for its rational acceptability. In so doing, I will appeal to what is called internalism in epistemology. That is, in many cases, we can and should have access to reasons and evidence for our deepest beliefs. This is especially the case concerning our worldview, our deepest and most significant intellectual commitments. The reader must make his or her

---

[52]Ibid., p. 329.
[53]Ibid., pp. 259-60.
[54]Ibid., p. 499.
[55]For more on Plantinga in relation to apologetics, see Keith A. Mascord, *Alvin Plantinga and Christian Apologetics* (Eugene, Ore.: Wipf & Stock, 2006).

own judgment as to the success of this endeavor.[56]

Evidentialism. Evidentialism is a method in apologetics that argues that the most significant historical events in Christianity—particularly the resurrection of Jesus—are matters that can be established through proper historical argumentation, even apart from any prior arguments for the existence of God. Classical apologists argue first for the existence of a monotheistic God and then argue for the particulars of Christianity—the reliability of the Bible and the claims and credentials of Jesus. This is a two-step strategy which trades on the idea that if monotheism is first established, the probability of God working in history—through miracles, special revelation, and the incarnation and resurrection—increases dramatically. In this sense it is easier intellectually to move from theism to Christianity than to move from a nontheistic worldview directly to Christianity through the evidence for Christian particulars. Evidentialism either minimizes or dispenses with arguments for God's existence from nature and instead opts for a one-step argument for Christianity. Two leading and prolific contemporary evidentialists are John Warwick Montgomery and Gary Habermas.[57] N. T Wright's multivolume effort defending the reliability of the New Testament and the resurrection of Jesus seems to fit into this category as well.[58]

Evidentialists are sometimes criticized for not sufficiently factoring in the role worldview plays in the assessment of evidence. Our preunderstandings shape how we interpret evidence. Or, as the saying goes, "What my net doesn't catch ain't fish." A diehard naturalist will likely reject all evidence for the resurrection of Jesus—or any other miracle—since this supernatural event is deemed impossible. However, if a very powerful evi-

---

[56]For a good exposition of internalism, see Douglas R. Geivett, "Is God a Story? Postmodernity and the Talk of Theology," in *Christianity and the Postmodern Turn: Six Views*, ed. Myron B. Penner (Grand Rapids: Brazos Press, 2005); and J. P. Moreland and William Lane Craig, "The Structure of Justification," in *Philosophical Foundations for a Christian Worldview* (Downers Grove, Ill.: InterVarsity Press, 2003).

[57]See John Warwick Montgomery, *Faith Based on Fact* (Nashville: Thomas Nelson, 1978). His overall apologetic method is summarized and systematized, but without full documentation (strangely), in *Tractatus Logicus Theologicus* (Bonn: Culture and Science, 2002); Gary Habermas, *The Historical Jesus* (Joplin, Mo.: College Press, 1996); and his contributions to *Five Views of Apologetics* among many other books.

[58]N. T. Wright, *The New Testament and the People of God* (Minneapolis: Fortress, 1992); *Jesus and the Victory of God* (Minneapolis: Fortress, 1997); and *The Resurrection of The Son of God* (Minneapolis: Fortress, 2003).

dential case is marshaled for the resurrection, a person may convert from
naturalism directly to Christianity in a one-step process. If so, so much the
better for the evidentialist and the new convert. However, if an apologist
argues according to several lines of evidence for the existence of a personal
and supernatural God before arguing for the resurrection of Jesus, miraculous events will be considered more probable. The evidence for miracles
will not have to be as strong as when one starts from a nontheistic worldview. To use an example from Swinburne, if a person knows in general
that stars sometimes explode, then one can make a more convincing case
for a particular star having exploded.[59]

Another potential problem for the evidentialist is that an unbeliever
may be convinced that a particular supernatural event occurred but not
place that event into a coherent worldview. For example, Jewish New Testament scholar Pinchas Lapide argues for the literal resurrection of Jesus
but believes that Jesus is the Savior only of Gentiles, not of Jews, who
continue to have their own separate covenant.[60] It seems that Lapide is
unwarranted in believing in both the resurrection and a limited role for
Jesus, but this underscores that more apologetic reasoning is required than
simply establishing isolated facts, however crucial they may be.[61]

In later chapters we will find much evidence for the veracity of events
described in the New Testament. Here the work of evidentialists is very
helpful (far more helpful than presuppositionalists, who largely ignore this
area). But their insights should be placed into a larger, cumulative case approach to apologetics.

THE LIMITS OF APOLOGETICS

Although various apologetic systems have proved useful, even the best
apologetic method must squarely face its limits. While a thorough and
wide-ranging apologetic is sorely needed today, apologetics is bounded by
at least three realities.

First, the Bible is a long, ancient and sometimes perplexing book for
contemporary people. Defending what the Bible teaches is no simple task,

[59]Richard Swinburne, *Is There a God?* (New York: Oxford University Press, 1996), p. 118.
[60]Pinchas Lapide, *The Resurrection of Jesus* (Minneapolis: Fortress, 1985).
[61]For example, why would Lapide believe in the resurrection accounts on the historicity of the
resurrection but fail to believe Jesus' statements that he is the Lord of both Jew and Gentile?

and certainly does not admit of a formula. Even the stellar apologist must face his or her intellectual limits and never bluff knowing more than he or she knows. However, to admit this difficulty is not to revel in mysteries, paradoxes or (worse yet) absurdities. Rather, we should realize that all of our intellectual endeavors—especially those dealing with the broadest and deepest questions of life's meaning—will be dogged to some degree by misunderstanding, ignorance and intellectual disappointment. To hold that the Christian worldview is the best rational explanation for the things that matter most does not imply that we have a lock on all the best arguments or have attained all the truths we need.

Second, apologetics is limited not only by the difficulty of the subject itself, but by the weaknesses of the subjects who practice it—us. We commend and defend Christianity through our speech, our writing and our demeanor. And we are sinners. We are the medium for this matchless message, but we are flawed. The best argument carried forth by a bad character will not likely have the desired effect. We may know strong apologetic arguments but lack courage to present them, or, conversely, we may confidently offer arguments that we think are strong, but are not. We may study too much and pray too little, or the opposite. And so it goes. Yet we may be thankful that "God can make a straight line with a crooked stick," as the medieval saying goes.[62] If we fall short as apologists, this does not mean that Christianity is untrue or irrational, or that all our efforts are vain. Our job is to faithfully give the best arguments possible from the purest heart possible.

Third, apologetics must be understood within the framework of God's secret councils, as Calvinists like to put it.[63] God often does not tell us how or why he brings some things about. As William Cowper's hymn puts it, "God moves in a mysterious way, his wonders to perform." God may use any means at his disposal, and all means are at his disposal. As the majestic Westminster Confession of Faith puts it, "God, in his ordinary providence, maketh use of means, yet is free to work without, above, and against them, at his pleasure" (5.3). The apologist might be likened to a physician trying to cure an ailment. He can only use the tools of his trade,

---

[62]See also Francis Schaeffer, "The Weakness of God's Servants," in *No Little People, No Little Places* (Downers Grove, Ill.: InterVarsity Press, 1974).
[63]They typically appeal to Deuteronomy 29:29; see also Romans 11:33-36.

but he realizes that some people spontaneously recover without treatment, and some do not respond well to treatment that should help them. Nevertheless, he does not despair of his task.

SUMMARY: A CUMULATIVE AND WINSOME APPROACH

While much more could be written on apologetic method—and entire books are dedicated to just that—we will now begin to apply the model sketched out here by advancing numerous and concurring arguments for the truth of the Christian worldview.[64] I will neither presuppose Christianity is true apart from the need for positive evidence (fideism, presuppositionalism or Reformed epistemology) or suppose that by amassing legions of historical facts we can convince someone of Christian truth (evidentialism). Rather, I will offer a variety of arguments that verify or confirm the Christian worldview as superior to its rivals, thus showing that Christianity alone makes the most sense of the things that matter most. This chapter has stated worldview criteria rather technically, but the chapters that follow need not cite them verbatim to make the needed points. Simply put, if a worldview fails to explain what it promises to explain, fails to make sense on its own terms (internal consistency), fails to describe what is there (objective and inner reality), fails to give intelligible meaning to life, or fails to be intellectually and culturally productive, it is disqualified from consideration. I will argue that Christianity passes these tests better than any of its competitors.

---

[64]See Boa and Bowman, *Faith Has Its Reasons;* Cowan, *Five Views of Apologetics;* Gordon Lewis, *Testing Christianity's Truth Claims* (Chicago: Moody Press, 1976); and Bernard Ramm, *Varieties of Christian Apologetics*, 2nd ed. (Grand Rapids: Baker, 1962).

4

The Christian Worldview

THE TERM *CHRISTIANITY* HAS SUCH BROAD application and such a range of meanings that we need to offer some definition and delimitation of its meaning if we are to have any hope of defending Christianity rationally. The understanding I offer is, I hope, deeply biblical without being narrowly sectarian, since the task of apologetics is not to fortify only one Christian tradition but to defend the core tenets of Christianity broadly understood.

RELIGION AND WORLDVIEW

Christianity, understood as a religion, can be addressed in a number of dimensions. Philosopher of religion Ninian Smart suggested that all religions can be understood in six dimensions: sacred narrative,[1] doctrine, ritual, social and institutional expression, experience, and ethics.[2] Without trying to settle what the necessary and sufficient conditions of a religion must be,[3] this sixfold analysis describes well the various aspects of the world's religions. Defending the truth and reasonableness of Christianity involves all of these dimensions in one way or another. For a work of apologetics, however, the main concern will rest on doctrine, not the history or institutions of Christianity.

The best way to fathom the doctrinal dimension of Christianity is to

---

[1]Smart uses the term *myth* as a synonym of sacred narrative, but he does not mean this necessarily in the sense of "false story," but as a story that has symbolic and cosmic value. However, the "sacred narratives" of some world religions (especially in Hinduism and Buddhism) make no necessary claim on being factual history.

[2]See Ninian Smart, *Worldviews*, 3rd ed. (New York: Prentice-Hall, 1999), chaps. 3-8.

[3]On this vexed question, see Winfried Corduan, *Neighboring Faiths* (Downers Grove, Ill.: InterVarsity Press, 1998), pp. 20-21.

consider it as a worldview.[4] The term *worldview* is sometimes used to mean one's view of the world situation—matters of war and peace, immigration, foreign aid and so on. How we view these issues is part of our larger worldview but is not what I mean by worldview. Nor is a worldview simply the entirety of a person's beliefs—items such as an individual's age, favorite saxophonist and knowledge of baseball statistics. A worldview is forged out of beliefs that have the most consequence for a comprehensive vision of reality. It is an overall conception of reality that touches on the key areas that philosophy and religion have always addressed. Through a worldview, one orients oneself intellectually to the universe. As William Halverson notes, a worldview is "a comprehensive view of reality in terms of which one attempts to understand and 'place' everything that comes before one's consciousness."[5] It is an interrelated cluster of central assumptions or presuppositions about reality. These basic conceptions about life may be held in a well-articulated fashion (say by a philosopher or theologian) or in a largely unconscious manner by someone who is not even familiar with the term.[6] A worldview will typically include narrative elements as well; that is, our most important beliefs are often shaped by the sense of an unfolding story of the cosmos and human history, and not just by a set of abstract statements. This is certainly true for Christianity, whose sacred book (the Bible) is deeply rooted in many historical accounts of God's working with human beings, individually and collectively.[7]

Moreover, worldviews may be held at various levels of certainty and commitment. There are very convinced and committed atheists as well as Christians with considerable and nagging doubts that hinder their expression of faith. Worldviews may also be believed with various degrees of integrity and consistency. For an assignment in my apologetics course, my students ask a non-Christian these questions: (1) What is the ultimate reality or what is most real? (2) What is the nature of humanity? Who are

---

[4]For an in-depth treatment, see David Naugle, *Worldview: The History of a Concept* (Grand Rapids: Eerdmans, 2002).

[5]William H. Halverson, *A Concise Introduction to Philosophy*, 3rd ed. (New York: Random House, 1976), p. 452.

[6]Although I have not directly quoted him, I am indebted to James W. Sire's understanding of worldview. See "A Universe Charged with the Grandeur of God: Christian Theism," in James W. Sire, *The Universe Next Door: A Basic Worldview Catalog*, 5th ed. (Downers Grove, Ill.: InterVarsity Press, 2009).

[7]See Naugle, *Worldview*, pp. 297-303.

we? What is our nature? (3) How can spiritual liberation be attained? That is, what is the answer to the human problem? (4) Who is Jesus Christ? (5) Why do you believe 1-4? In the course of the interviews, it becomes plain to many of the students that their interviewee holds incompatible beliefs in a rather haphazard configuration. Some of the worldviews on display were a strange mix of Christianity, deism, naturalism and New Age thought. However, a person of intellectual rectitude will strive to believe truths that fit coherently in an overall pattern, free from spin and equivocation.

Our worldview shapes who we are and what we do. We are driven by our deepest beliefs and interpret the world according to them, often almost automatically. While worldviews necessarily involve truth claims about reality, these beliefs are often held in a pre-reflective and unexamined manner, often for emotional as well as intellectual reasons. Given the diversions, distractions and amusements of postmodernity, many people fail to bring their worldviews into critical focus. While it is a uniquely human capacity to call one's beliefs into question, a torrent of social forces encourages us to be unconsciously swept along with the surging culture that we might obediently consume its products, endorse its ideology and generally do its bidding.

THE CHRISTIAN WORLDVIEW AS TRUTH-CLAIMING

Like every other worldview, a Christian worldview, at its deepest level, is a system of truth claims or assertions about reality. This must be underscored because some have wanted to erase Christianity's claim on truth while retaining some other form of "Christianity." This is akin to the smile of Lewis Carroll's Cheshire Cat when the cat has disappeared. Nevertheless, some contemporary writers influenced by Ludwig Wittgenstein—particularly Don Cupitt and D. Z. Phillips—have claimed that Christianity can exist apart from any objective truth claims because the essence of religion is not a description or explanation of reality, but a way or form of life that is meaningful. For example, belief in "the last judgment" is not the expectation that we will literally stand before God one day to give an account for all we have done. It is rather an approach to life where responsibility is at the forefront of our thinking. It is a statement of value, not of fact. This approach is known as religious nonrealism. Some "postliberal" theologians seem to move in this direction as well, since they exchange any

objective claims of biblical revelation for merely living within the param-
eters of the biblical narratives. Instead of viewing biblical revelation as
propositional (or truth-affirming), they see it as expressive of the thoughts
and feelings of the biblical writers. Sadly, even some members of the
emerging church are flirting with, if not embracing, this idea.[8]

The best antidote to any form of Christian nonrealism is some sustained reading of the Bible itself, as well as a healthy dose of the great
thinkers and activists who have sworn allegiance to it. Martyrs have not
gone to the death for a "way of life" divorced from truth claims. Apologists such as Augustine, Aquinas and Pascal have not defended the
meaningfulness of living within the Christian narrative apart from its
objective and eternal truth. No, the truth of the Christian narrative is
precisely what makes the Christian life meaningful and worthwhile.
Nonrealists to the contrary, statements of theological value that have
meaning are also assertions about reality. Christians strive to live a good
and faithful life because they know their deeds will eventually come
under the final scrutiny of God.[9] Fact and value meet and kiss each
other. The only sufficient reason for wanting to blend one's own narrative with the narrative of the Bible is that what the Bible describes about
creation, fall and redemption is true and worth believing and obeying. If
it is not, then to live within this story line is literally to live a lie—and to
advocate that others live this lie as well.

What really lies behind nonrealistic forms of religion is a capitulation
to non-Christian worldviews. The reasoning is that if Christianity cannot
succeed in the world of ideas—if it cannot compete, say, with the materialistic worldview—then its only recourse is to abandon all truth claims and
emphasize tradition, ritual, symbolism, experience and community. There
are two compelling reasons to reject such a move. First, as this book will
argue, Christianity has *not* lost out in the world of ideas. Therefore, there
is no reason to exempt it from the demands of reality. Second, if Christianity cannot intellectually compete with other worldviews, the only sane
and logical alternative is to abandon it completely. Christianity claims

---

[8]See D. A. Carson, *Becoming Conversant with the Emerging Church* (Grand Rapids: Zondervan,
2005); and R. Scott Smith, *Truth and a New Kind of Christian* (Wheaton, Ill.: Crossway,
2005).
[9]This does not mean that we are justified before God according to our merits, but that our life
comes under divine review, even if we are justified by the grace of God in Christ.

to be true. If it is not, it has lied and must be left behind. As Paul said, if Christ has not been raised from the dead, Christians are the most deceived and miserable urchins on the planet (1 Corinthians 15:17-19).[10]

When one speaks of "the Christian worldview," this does not mean that Christians can or should agree on everything, but that they must agree that their view aims at biblical truth. Christians throughout history and today differ in their understanding of what their convictions should be. However, a biblical worldview tries to capture the essential ideas of Christianity, its fundamental doctrines, and how they hang together in explaining God, the universe and humans. Some, to the contrary, think of Christianity as more of a set of behaviors and feelings and symbols, as opposed to a bona fide worldview. Dorothy Sayers lamented during the dark days of World War II that "we have rather lost sight of the idea that Christianity is supposed to be an interpretation of the universe."[11] Even Nietzsche, that colossal anti-Christian, knew this. When speaking of the English tendency to reject belief in God but to keep Christian ethics, Nietzsche proclaimed: "Christianity is a system, a whole view of things thought out together. By breaking one main concept out of it, the faith in God, one breaks the whole: Nothing necessarily remains in one's hands."[12]

While the vast majority of Americans believe in a God, few have well-articulated worldviews. This is revealed in poll after poll showing that high percentages of Americans both (1) believe in God and (2) are moral relativists. This means that God, the ultimate reality in any theistic worldview, has nothing to say about the conduct of one's life. This mass of worldview underachievers includes professing evangelical Christians. A 2003 Barna poll (often the harbinger of grim news, it seems) reported that only 12 percent of evangelicals knew what a worldview is or could provide

---

[10]For a careful and devastating critique of nonrealism in religion, see J. L. Mackie, *The Miracle of Theism* (New York: Oxford University Press, 1981), pp. 217-29. Mackie was an atheist but understood nonrealism as radically out of step with the claims of theism. For a critique of more recent nonrealist accounts of Christianity, see Kai-Man Kwan, "A Critical Appraisal of Non-Realist Philosophy of Religion: An Asian Perspective," *Philosophia Christi*, series 2, vol. 3, no. 1 (2001): 225-35; and Peter Bryne, *God and Realism* (Burlington, Vt.: Ashgate, 2003).

[11]Dorothy L. Sayers, *The Letters of Dorothy L. Sayers: 1937-1943, From Novelist to Playwright*, vol. 2, *The Letters of Dorothy L. Sayers*, ed. Barbara Reynolds (New York: St. Martin's Press, 1998), p. 158; quoted in Naugle, *Worldview*, p. 4.

[12]Friedrich Nietzsche, *The Twilight of the Idols*, in *The Portable Nietzsche*, ed. and trans. Walter Kaufmann (New York: Viking Press, 1975), pp. 515-16. We will return to Nietzsche's point about morality in chap. 15.

a proper definition for one. A scant 4 percent said they should know any-thing about the concept.[13] Added to this are repeated polls indicating massive biblical illiteracy, which may at least partially account for the dearth of evangelical influence in the world of ideas. Many Christians live in an intellectual ghost town and possess ghost minds.[14] They may know something of a rich (but lost) intellectual heritage and be able to point to a few intellectuals "on our side" (like C. S. Lewis), but they have not attuned themselves to the cultivation of their inner map of reality.

Putting forth the lineaments of a Christian worldview is necessary in order to stipulate just what the rest of this book will advance as true and reasonable. We cannot defend something of which we are ignorant. As William Wilberforce observed, people admit that "vigorous resolution, strenuous diligence, and steady perseverance" are required for learning, wealth and military excellence, yet we "expect to be Christians without labor, study or inquiry!"[15]

> This is more preposterous because Christianity, a revelation from God and not an invention of man, shows us new relations with their correspondent duties. It contains also doctrines, motives and precepts peculiar to itself. We cannot reasonably expect to become proficient accidentally.[16]

The very articulation of the Christian worldview may have a weighty apologetic effect, even apart from its philosophical defense. There are at least two salient reasons for this. First, by clearly explaining what Christi-anity affirms and what it does not affirm, we may remove obstacles to belief generated by false stereotypes. Second, when the Christian vision is

---

[13]"A Biblical Worldview Has a Radical Effect on a Person's Life," *Barna Group*, December 1, 2003 <www.barna.org/barna-update/article/5-barna-update/131-a-biblical-worldview-has-a-radical-effect-on-a-persons-life>. More recent Barna studies indicate little change in these results: "Barna Survey Examines Changes in Worldview Among Christians Over the Past 13 Years," March 6, 2009 <www.barna.org/barna-update/article/21-transformation/252-barna-survey-examines-changes-in-worldview-among-christians-over-the-past-13-years?q=worldview>.

[14]On the concept of a ghost mind, see Os Guinness, *Fit Bodies, Fat Minds* (Grand Rapids: Baker, 1994), sec. 1.

[15]William Wilberforce, *Real Christianity*, ed. James Houston (1829; reprint, Minneapolis: Bethany House, 1997), p. 4.

[16]Ibid. Similarly, Francis Schaeffer remarked, "Every day of our lives we should be studying the Scriptures to make sure that what we are presenting really is the Christian position, and that we are presenting it as well as possible in our day" (Francis A. Schaeffer, *The God Who Is There*, 30th anniv. ed. [Downers Grove, Ill.: InterVarsity Press, 1998], p. 158).

presented in its wholeness and significance as a view of all of existence, which has engaged some of the greatest minds of history, this may constructively influence those in search of a broad and deep worldview. The same effect may be produced when a vitally functioning Christian mind (rooted in a Christian worldview) is brought to bear on any number of pertinent social, political, moral and aesthetic issues.[17] Harry Blamires notes that the Christian mind is "a mind trained, informed, equipped to handle the data of secular controversy within a framework of reference which is constructed of Christian presuppositions."[18]

SOURCE OF ULTIMATE AUTHORITY: THE SCRIPTURES

A Christian worldview begins with the basis of authority for knowing reality: the sixty-six books of the Bible.[19] All worldviews have some basis for authority, some source of knowledge that is normative.[20] For the Christian, this is the Bible—properly interpreted and applied. A Christian worldview takes the Bible to be God's written revelation to humanity.[21] Although written by numerous authors over a long period of time and in different places, God, a personal and moral agent, guided the writers to communicate what God intended to make known to the original audience and subsequent readers for their own good and for God's honor and glory. A Christian's beliefs ought, then, to comport with what is taught in the whole council of the Scriptures. One's worldview, however, will include more than the content of the Hebrew Scriptures and New Testament, since a worldview integrates all

---

[17]This was the vision of the great Dutch theologian, educator and statesman Abraham Kuyper (1837-1920), who stressed much the necessity of possessing a thoroughly Christian worldview sufficient to challenge the attacks of unbelief. For a summary of Kuyper's thinking on worldview, see Naugle, *Worldview*, pp. 16-25. Kuyper's own system is laid out in his 1898 *Lectures on Calvinism* (Grand Rapids: Eerdmans, 1931). Despite my respect for Kuyper's vision and his many stellar achievements, I must part company with his apologetic method, which lies at the root of the presuppositionalism of Cornelius Van Til and his followers.

[18]Harry Blamires, *The Christian Mind: How Should a Christian Think?* (1963; reprint, Ann Arbor, Mich.: Servant Books, 1978), p. 43.

[19]Roman Catholics include books not canonized by Protestants, referred to as the Apocrypha. On the nature of the Catholic deuterocanon and why Protestants do not accept it, see Neil R. Lightfoot, *How We Got the Bible*, 3rd ed. (New York: MJF Books, 2003), pp. 163-70.

[20]The biblical worldview can be laid out according to various schemes and orders. For instance, compare the conceptual schemes of James Sire, "A World of Difference: Introduction," in *Universe Next Door*; and Ronald Nash, "What Is a Worldview?" in *Faith and Reason* (Grand Rapids: Zondervan, 1988).

[21]See the discussion of biblical inspiration and authority at the end of chap. 20.

of life into a meaningful intellectual model. The Bible itself encourages this kind of integration, since it claims that God is the ultimate source of all truth, whether that truth is recorded in Scripture or not.[22] Moreover, as we will discover, claims of the Bible's authority—its truthfulness in all it asserts—need not be made in an intellectual vacuum. The reliability and wisdom of Scripture can be tested in various ways.[23]

EPISTEMOLOGY: HOW WE KNOW WHAT WE KNOW

It is in human beings that heaven and earth meet in thought. Made in God's image, we are personal beings who can detect God's fingerprints in creation and his voice in conscience and through Scripture. We were designed to know God, ourselves, others and God's creation. As James Sire puts it, "Human beings can know both the world around them and God himself because God has built into them the capacity to do so and because he takes an active role in communicating with them."[24]

Scripture affirms that human beings, though east of Eden, are not banished to utter darkness concerning themselves, their world or God. God has made knowledge of these realms possible, though not all will attain a true and rational understanding of these things. The Gospels indicate that Jesus had a well-formed epistemology. He believed that objective truth is knowable (realism), that factual evidence is crucial in supporting truth claims, that noncontradiction is a necessary test for truth, that the truth Jesus reveals has experiential effects, that the imagination is a key organ for receiving truth (his use of parables and figures of speech) and that one's ability to know truth is closely tied to one's moral rectitude.[25] All of these principles will be brought to bear in the course of this book.[26]

IN A NUTSHELL: CREATION, FALL AND REDEMPTION

Taking the Bible as the ultimate authority for Christian thought, we can

---

[22]On this, see J. P. Moreland, *Love Your God with All Your Mind* (Colorado Springs: NavPress, 1997), pp. 53-57.

[23]See chap. 19 and appendix 2.

[24]Sire, *Universe Next Door*, p. 36. For a development of this theme, see Ronald Nash, *The World of God and the Mind of Man* (Phillipsburg, N.J.: P & R Publishing, 1992).

[25]See Douglas Groothuis, "Jesus' Epistemology," in *On Jesus* (Belmont, Calif.: Wadsworth, 2003).

[26]However, the role of the imagination in knowing will not be discussed to the degree that Jesus' other epistemic principles will be addressed.

organize a Christian worldview into three broad categories: creation, fall and redemption.[27] After sketching out this triad, a more detailed approach will be considered.

Creation. Biblically understood, the universe is the handiwork of a tri-une, supernatural, personal and moral being who created it out of nothing. Unlike unitarian monotheism (Judaism, Islam and unitarianism), Scripture teaches and the Christian creeds affirm that the divine being is one God who exists eternally in three coequal persons: Father, Son and Holy Spirit. So, the universe has not always existed; neither did it pop into existence without cause or reason. The origin of the universe is supernatural, not natural, based on the unique creative action of the Trinity. Further, the universe is not itself divine (pantheism) but contingent on God for its creation, conservation and culmination. What God created was good, since it came from a Perfect Being. Humans are "very good" since they bear the divine image and are ordained to glorify God by cultivating the creation through godly relationships.

Fall. Despite its divine origin and good nature, the universe is fallen. The first humans disobeyed God's clear command and thus turned against God, themselves and creation (Genesis 3). This disruption adversely affected the entire universe such that it groans in awaiting its final redemption (Romans 8:18-26). Women and men are now incapable of serving God properly given their own resources, and nothing in this fallen world can redeem them. We are prone to selfishness, obsession, addiction, idolatry and false religion of all kinds. We worship the creation rather than the Creator. As such, we are under God's righteous condemnation and without hope in ourselves.

Redemption. Yet God has not left his erring creation to rot in its ruinous ways. Immediately after the Fall, God clothed our first parents and made an oblique promise that a liberator would come and undo what the serpent had initiated (Genesis 3:15). God continued to pursue humans east of Eden by graciously selecting a particular people for his redemptive

---

[27]The creation-fall-redemption triad is a major theme in the philosophy of Herman Dooyeweerd and his followers, who often refer to it as the Christian "ground motive." For a contemporary application of this theme to contemporary issues, see Nancy Pearcey, *Total Truth* (Wheaton, Ill.: Crossway, 2004). Dooyeweerd's magnum opus is the four-volume work *A New Critique of Theoretical Thought*, trans. David H. Freeman and William S. Young (Phillipsburg, N.J.: Presbyterian & Reformed, 1969).

purposes, inspiring prophets, giving visions and intervening in history—all with a view toward the revelation of the divine Messiah. In the fullness of time God sent the Son, who did not hold on to his equality with the Father but came into the world to culminate God's plan of redemption. He accomplished this by living a perfect life through the Holy Spirit, by dying a horrendous death to atone for human sin and set us right with God, and by rising from the dead to defeat all the powers of death and darkness, sin and Satan.

This explanatory triad of creation, fall and redemption outlines the biblical drama of God, humanity and the cosmos. But the outline needs to be expanded considerably in order to adequately explain the Christian view of reality. We start, appropriately enough, with the ultimate or supreme reality: God.

ULTIMATE REALITY: GOD

The opening chapter of Genesis declares that "in the beginning God created the heavens and the earth" (Genesis 1:1). This tells us that God is the Creator of the universe and that he transcends the universe as such. God is not some subtle aspect of nature, nor does God emerge over time through natural processes. The creation is not an emanation of the being of God. Rather, God is metaphysically distinct from creation eternally and inexorably. God, the Creator, is personal. The act of creation was not an automatic effect of an impersonal being or system but flowed from the will of an intelligent and active Creator. God initiated and was pleased with the creation (Genesis 1) and even delighted in his handiwork (see Proverbs 8). These are the marks of personality, not impersonality; the marks of an agent, not a mechanism. Christian theism is a thoroughly and radically personal worldview. God personally created the world to be populated by people, as the prophet Isaiah revealed:

> For this is what the LORD says—
> he who created the heavens,
>   he is God;
> he who fashioned and made the earth,
>   he founded it;
> he did not create it to be empty,
>   but formed it to be inhabited. (Isaiah 45:18)

Christian metaphysics allows for no property, power or principle deeper than that of the divine person himself. Scripture portrays God as hearing (Exodus 6:5), creating (Genesis 1:1), knowing all things (Psalm 147:5; John 3:20) seeing (Psalm 94:9) and having volition (1 John 2:17). Thus, God is a self-conscious and reflective being, "an omnipotent, omniscient, and omnipresent Personality, who manifests every dimension of personality."[28]

While God is essentially invisible and immaterial, he is no less personal or relational for that. The doctrine of the Trinity highlights God's personality by emphasizing that God is intrinsically relational. The one God exists eternally in three coequal persons (Deuteronomy 6:4; Matthew 28:18). Chesterton's quip is not glib: "It was not God for God to be alone."[29] God did not need to spring humans into existence in order to experience communication and have a relationship, bad Christian teaching to the contrary. He was not lonely before creation. Rather, in creating personal beings for loving relationships, God was expressing something vital about his own nature.

God is one with respect to deity (or Godhead). This is often referred to as "one substance." But God is three with respect to persons who are coequal and coeternal: the Father, Son and Holy Spirit. So, the best way to understand the Trinity is that God is three-in-one. The Athanasian Creed captures the heart of the idea:

> Now this is the true Christian faith: We worship one God in three persons and three persons in one God, without mixing the persons or dividing the divine being. For each person—the Father, the Son, and the Holy Spirit—is distinct, but the deity of Father, Son, and Holy Spirit is one, equal in glory and coeternal in majesty. What the Father is, so is the Son, and so is the Holy Spirit.[30]

While some have regarded the idea of a triune God as a contradiction (three equals one), it is not presented as such in Scripture or by the church's best thinkers throughout the ages. Proving that the Trinity is contradictory is a difficult task. To refute such a claim, the apologist needs only to

---

[28]Walter Martin, *Kingdom of the Cults* (Minneapolis: Bethany House, 1974), p. 284.
[29]G. K. Chesterton, *Orthodoxy* (1908; reprint, New York: Image Books, 1959), p. 135.
[30]This is only part of the creedal statement on the Trinity. The author was not Athanasius, but he may have contributed to the formulation.

provide one or more plausible strategies that are biblically faithful and noncontradictory.[31]

The Trinity is not a logical puzzle or an embarrassment to the Christian or the Christian worldview. For in the Trinity we find the philosophical basis for love at the highest order possible and the key to explaining the human propensity toward and need for loving relationships. Love at its richest level requires a lover, loving and a beloved.[32] The doctrine of the Trinity affirms that each member of the Trinity has been in an eternally loving relationship with each other member of the Trinity. As Schaeffer said:

> The universe had a personal beginning—a personal beginning on the high order of the Trinity. That is, before "in the beginning" the personal was already there. Love and thought and communication existed prior to the creation of the heavens and the earth.[33]

So, from the biblical worldview, there is nothing deeper than personal love. That is the foundation for the universe. This theological and cosmic personalism contrasts sharply with both naturalism and pantheism, both of which assert that the loveless impersonal (either mindless nature or an impersonal god) is the ultimate reality, thus rendering love either a cosmic accident (naturalism) or an illusion (pantheism).

Importantly, without the doctrine of the Trinity, the incarnation, which is the lynchpin of Christianity, makes no sense. Jesus Christ, the second person of the Godhead, took on a human nature for our redemption and for the restoration of the cosmos (Colossians 1–2).

God, as a metaphysically distinct and personal being, is free to interact with his creatures in any number of ways. The Author is involved in his story. The universe is neither divine nor divorced from the divine. God may intervene in history through miraculous actions, in ways im-

---

[31]For an excellent summary of some recent philosophical approaches by evangelical Christians, see Thomas Senor, "The Incarnation and the Trinity," in *Reason for the Hope Within*, ed. Michael J. Murray (Grand Rapids: Eerdmans, 1999); J. P. Moreland and William Lane Craig, *Philosophical Foundations for a Christian Worldview* (Downers Grove, Ill.: InterVarsity Press, 2003), chap. 29. For a detailed theological treatment, see Millard Erickson, *God in Three Persons: A Contemporary Interpretation of the Trinity* (Grand Rapids: Baker, 1995).

[32]See Richard Swinburne, *The Christian God* (New York: Oxford University Press, 1994), p. 177.

[33]Francis A. Schaeffer, *Genesis in Time and Space* (Downers Grove, Ill.: InterVarsity Press, 1972), p. 21.

possible if the world were left to its natural laws and operations. This involves, for example, the supernatural inspiration of the prophets and the written revelation of the Bible, as well as the miracles of Jesus' healings and exorcisms.

The universe is thus an open and rational system of cause and effect.[34] The universe is not a self-enclosed machine, but neither is it chaotic. Rather, it is an orderly and meaningful environment in which divine, human and angelic agents, each in their own way, find their proper sphere of operation. But just who are humans in this scheme of things?

HUMAN BEINGS: QUESTION MARKS IN SEARCH OF AN ANSWER

Humans are the loudest and oddest question marks in the cosmos. They endlessly interrogate themselves about the universe and their place in it—and whether there is anything beyond it. The great Jewish philosopher Abraham Heschel wrote: "The Bible is not man's theology, but God's anthropology."[35] This insight is deeply biblical, since the psalmist asked God about humans when he wrote of their stature in relation to the world:

> When I look at your heavens, the work of your fingers,
> the moon and stars that you have established;
> what are human beings that you are mindful of them,
> Mortals that you care for them? (Psalm 8:3-4 NRSV)

The response is that God has made mortals "a little lower than the angels" and has "crowned them with glory and honor" (Psalm 8:5). As such, they are "rulers over the works of your hands" by exercising their prowess over the rest of the creation (Psalm 8:7-8). This, along with the earlier verses of the psalm, causes the writer to exclaim:

> LORD, our Lord,
> how majestic is your name in all the earth! (Psalm 8:9)

---

[34]See Francis A. Schaeffer, *He Is There and He Is Not Silent*, 30th anniv. ed. (Wheaton, Ill.: Tyndale House, 2001), p. 38; Francis Schaeffer, *The Church Before the Watching World: A Practical Ecclesiology* (Downers Grove, Ill.: InterVarsity Press, 1971), p. 13; For the idea of an open universe, including miracles, see chap. 22 of this book.

[35]Abraham Heschel, *God in Search of Man: A Philosophy of Judaism* (New York: Farrar, Straus & Giroux, 1976), p. 412.

The majesty of God himself is somehow mirrored in these beings, for God is ever mindful and watchful.

The psalmist's words echo the account given in Genesis that men and women were created by divine design for the purpose of knowing God, filling the earth with humans, and governing and cultivating God's good earth (Genesis 1–2). A Christian worldview esteems humans as having been made in the image and likeness of God (Genesis 1:26; 9:6) and refuses to reduce them to the unintended byproducts of time, matter and natural laws. As bearers of the divine image, humans have a created nature and telos (or purpose) under God and within all of creation. This human nature fits the rest of the world and was intended to do so by God's omniscient design. So humans are not, in Bertrand Russell's memorable phrase, the result of an "accidental collocation of atoms."[36] On the other hand, humans are not divine—not even when they were in their original and pristine state. With God, they share the attributes of personality—agency, intelligence, creativity, rationality, emotion and relationality—but in a form forever finite, limited and contingent. Humans are more like God than anything else in the universe, yet they are only a small part of the universe, and they fall far short of the divine majesty discussed in Psalm 8. Thus, from a Christian perspective, we perennially face the dual temptation either to demote ourselves below what we truly are (despair) or to promote ourselves above our true status (hubris). All in all, humans are *unique among the living.*

Genesis reports that God breathed his Spirit upon mere dust to create living beings (Genesis 2:7). While humans are integrated beings, they are not reducible to an assemblage of merely material parts, as is a computer or an automobile. Humans are embodied and highly developed souls; that is, they possess an immaterial substance, which interacts with their physical dimensions.[37] This was the overt teaching of Jesus, revisionists to the contrary.[38] The Christian vision of humanity exalts neither the immaterial at the expense of the material (as in idealism, pantheism, gnosticism) nor the

---

[36]Bertrand Russell, "A Free Man's Worship," in *Why I Am Not a Christian*, ed. Paul Edwards (New York: Simon & Schuster, 1957), p. 107.

[37]That is, while they are on earth. The Bible affirms that people continue to exist as souls or spirits after the demise of their physical bodies (2 Corinthians 5:1-10). However, their final state will be as a resurrected body-soul (1 Corinthians 15).

[38]See Douglas Groothuis, *On Jesus* (Belmont, Calif.: Wadsworth, 2003), pp. 40-42.

material at the expense of the immaterial (as in physicalism). The earth may be our material domicile, but it is our sister, not our mother.[39] This aspect of biblical anthropology has profound implications for our understanding of human personhood, life after death, spirituality and much more.[40]

Although God has crowned humans as royalty, they have been ousted from their peaceful occupancy of the throne—and are ever questing to be reinstated. Such is the psychological energy for utopias, self-deception and insanity. The doctrine of the fall of humanity is more fully developed in the New Testament, but it is summarized keenly in the book of Ecclesiastes: "This only have I found. God created mankind upright, but they have gone in search of many schemes" (Ecclesiastes 7:29). The apostle Paul declares that through "one man," sin entered the world, thus disrupting everything— yet not without remedy, since through "another man," Jesus Christ, salvation has been secured for those who rightly respond (Romans 5:12-20; 8:19-23).[41] As a result of the first couple's rebellion against God's commandment, they were held responsible for their rebellion and were subjected to divine punishment by being banished from the garden and put out into a now hostile, dangerous and deadly world.

Humans were once naturally in concord with themselves, others, nature and God. Yet through moral transgression against God, humans were banished from such harmonious arrangements and suffered a constitutional corruption that has been passed down to every human being (save Jesus Christ, who is sinless). This has historically been called the doctrine of "original sin." Now all humanity experiences the same alienation and disharmony chronicled in Genesis 3 and made plain in the rest of the Bible's account of the human condition—one of both war and peace, heroism and cowardice, love and lust, commitment and betrayal, love and hate, faith and unbelief.[42]

---

[39]Chesterton, *Orthodoxy*, p. 119.

[40]See J. P. Moreland and Scott R. Rae, *Body and Soul* (Downers Grove, Ill.: InterVarsity Press, 2000). I will develop the mind-body issue further in chap. 17.

[41]Paul writes of the symmetry between the "one man" who brought sin and the "one man" (Jesus Christ) who brought redemption. However, Paul knows that both the woman and the man were responsible for sin entering the world when they succumbed to the temptations of the serpent (Genesis 3). He speaks of Eve's sin in the Fall in 2 Corinthians 11:3 and 1 Timothy 2:13-15. The latter passage has often been misinterpreted to mean that greater blame is placed on the woman.

[42]On original sin, see Bernard Ramm, *Offense to Reason: The Theology of Sin* (San Francisco: Harper & Row, 1985); Harry Lee Poe, *See No Evil: The Existence of Sin in an Age of Relativism*

Questions as to the historicity of the Genesis account and its relationship to evolutionary theories must wait until chapter twelve.[43] However, many biblical texts outside of Genesis, including statements by Jesus himself, appeal to the historicity of the first humans as our first parents (Matthew 19:4-5; Romans 5).

The point to recognize and ponder is that humans are estranged from their original earthly home. We were designed to thrive here, but we are out of step in our own backyard. Given our mixed state, we strain upward to the stars but are pulled down to the earth—and below. We are the only part of the universe that can consciously return praise to God—and curse our Maker. But Christianity cries out that humans east of Eden are not banished from hope and healing. We are still under a watchful and caring heaven. Since our origin is noble, our end may be glorious. But redemption must originate from beyond the royal ruins of the self. It must issue from God above. What, then, is this salvation that God has offered us?

SALVATION: FROM GOD, FOR US

From Genesis to Revelation, the Bible records God in pursuit of his human creatures. After creation and the Fall, the triune Creator made provision for human sinfulness and held humans accountable for their rebellion through his judgments at Babel and in the flood. He later called Abraham to follow his guidance and establish a great people of God's own choosing. God delivered this people from the bondage of Egypt and put them in the Promised Land. He made his covenant with them to be a people set apart, and he revealed his will, summarized in the Decalogue.

Despite their forgetfulness and hardness of heart, God sent prophets again and again to declare neglected truths and to bring God's people back to their Creator and Redeemer. The prophets further spoke of a coming Messiah who would both rescue Israel and bring salvation to the uttermost parts of the earth. And this Messiah came, not merely as another prophet, but as God incarnate.[44] Jesus of Nazareth accredited himself through signs and wonders, his matchless teaching, his impeccable character, his death

---

(Grand Rapids: Kregel, 2004). We will also take up this issue in chap. 18.

[43]Some Christians have retained the doctrine of the Fall as somehow compatible with Darwinism; others (myself included) reject this harmonization in light of the biblical texts and because of evidential and logical problems intrinsic to Darwinism.

[44]The logical coherence of Christ as both divine and human will be taken up in chap. 21.

on a bloody Roman cross, and finally through his rising from the dead in a glorified body. The resurrected Christ imbued his followers with a new way of life that must be taken to the nations, so that they may know that God has acted decisively in Jesus Christ to reconcile God and humanity and to create a new community of faith, hope and love that awaits his final coming at the end of the age.

This brief and inadequate account of God's doings in the world demonstrates the fact that God is a God of action who participates in history. History, then, has a purpose: it is the theater of a divine drama of judgment and restoration. It is linear (as opposed to being cyclical or unreal) and is providentially guided by God, but in a manner that does not undermine the creaturely agency of human beings, who either submit to or rebel against God and his ways.[45] As a character in C. S. Lewis's novel *The Great Divorce* puts it, "There are only two kinds of people in the end: those who say to God, 'Thy will be done,' and those to whom God says, in the end, 'Thy will be done.'"[46]

SOURCE OF MORALITY

Ethics, according to the Christian conception, is anchored in the reality of a personal and moral God who is free to interact with his creation in order to impart moral knowledge. God has implanted in his image-bearers a conscience that acts as a moral monitor (Romans 2:14-15), unless it has been willfully sullied by sin. God's character is eternally good; thus his commands are holy and just. Further, God's directives—known through conscience and Scripture—are in accord with the contours of the universe and the nature of human persons. God's moral principles are not artificially or arbitrarily imposed on a morally neutral creation, nor are they essential moral principles up for revision. Since God is both good and just, Christian ethics equally emphasizes love and justice. Our first duty is to love God with all our being, then to love others as ourselves. In a broken world, Christians are summoned to work for peace, justice and reconciliation—not in their own strength, but by the grace and empowerment of God. Jesus is their supreme example, since he not only provided spiritual

---

[45]The relationship of providence and human agency will be discussed in more depth in chap. 25.

[46]C. S. Lewis, *The Great Divorce* (1946; reprint, New York: Macmillan, 1976), p. 72.

salvation through atonement and forgiveness, but healed the sick, fed the hungry, loved and taught the outcasts, and spoke truth to corrupted power. Throughout Scripture God expresses deep concern for the powerless—the last, the least and the lost—those who have been marginalized and oppressed by the uncaring and prideful. James even defines true religion on the basis of the Christian's response to these people and situations: "Religion that God our Father accepts as pure and faultless is this: to look after orphans and widows in their distress and to keep oneself from being polluted by the world" (James 1:27). Following the Creator, Lawgiver, Savior and Judge entails not only worship on the vertical level but moral action on the horizontal level under God's watch. As the prophet Micah declared,

> He has shown you, O mortal, what is good.
>   And what does the LORD require of you?
> To act justly and to love mercy
>   and to walk humbly with your God. (Micah 6:8)

HISTORY AND THE AFTERLIFE

It is appropriate to center on Jesus' teaching on the biblical worldview of history and the afterlife since the kingdom of God is focused on Christ, and through him the afterlife is made known most manifestly. Jesus speaks of God as both the Creator of the world and the sovereign of history. He often refers to divinely orchestrated events in the history of the Jewish people as illustrating moral and spiritual truths. He heralds the coming of a new chapter in the kingdom of God as demonstrated in his own teaching, preaching and ministry.

For Jesus the kingdom of God indicates God's intervention in history to accomplish both redemption and judgment. The kingdom refers to God's authority and dominion, rather than a set location or one group of people. It has both present and future dimensions. In the person and actions of Jesus the kingdom breaks forth in new power, but much more is yet to come.

First, Jesus connects the coming of the kingdom in a new and unprecedented way to his own identity and mission. As F. F. Bruce puts it:

> In Origen's great word, Jesus was the *autobasileia*, the kingdom in person;
> for the principles of the kingdom of God could not have been more com-

pletely embodied than in him who said to his Father, "not my will, but thine be done," and accepted the cross in that spirit.[47]

Jesus claims that his authority over the spiritual realm serves as evidence that the kingdom of God has come (Matthew 12:28).

Jesus says to his disciples that "the knowledge of the secrets of the kingdom of heaven has been given to you" (Matthew 13:11). "Blessed are your eyes because they see, and your ears because they hear. For truly I tell you, many prophets and righteous people longed to see what you see but did not see it, and to hear what you hear but did not hear it" (Matthew 13:16-17).

Second, the kingdom of God is not limited to the Jewish nation but is offered broadly, even to Gentiles (Luke 13:29-30). In fact, many Jews would fail to recognize the coming of the kingdom in Jesus and so would forfeit its benefits (Luke 14:15-24). This claim of God's universal purposes beyond the Jews scandalized many in Jesus' audiences.

Third, Jesus views the kingdom of God and the flow of history as intimately related to his own ongoing and perpetual authority. After his resurrection, Jesus announces to his disciples that he possesses all possible authority and that they are to disciple the nations, baptizing converts in the name of the Trinity and teaching them what Jesus taught them (Matthew 28:18-20). Jesus also tells his disciples that they will receive power through the Holy Spirit to be his witnesses "in Jerusalem, and in all Judea and Samaria, and to the ends of the earth" (Acts 1:8).

Jesus also speaks of a postmortem existence either with God in blessing or outside of God's blessing in a state of regret, loss and forfeiture. Jesus announces to the criminal crucified next to him that he would be with Jesus in paradise that very day (Luke 23:43). In the parable of Lazarus and the rich man, Jesus contrasts the beggar Lazarus, who "died and the angels carried him to Abraham's side," with the oppressive rich man who died and found himself in "Hades, where he was in torment" (Luke 16:19-23). Jesus also warns of a day when he will eternally separate the "sheep" from the "goats" on the basis of how people lived in response to him and to their neighbors (Matthew 25:31-46). Jesus implicitly builds on certain passages in the Hebrew Scriptures to this effect (Daniel 12:2), but he makes himself the key agent of eternal judgment.

---

[47]F. F. Bruce, *New Testament History* (Garden City, N.Y.: Doubleday, 1972), p. 173.

Jesus teaches that one passes from death into a disembodied intermediate state—either into God's presence or away from it—and that at some future time this will be followed by Jesus' own return to earth in final judgment. After this the permanent resurrection of the body will occur (John 5:28-29). Jesus claims to have the authority to render final judgment at that time (Matthew 7:21-23).

A VERY SMALL NUTSHELL: THE TOUCHSTONE PROPOSITION

William Halverson claims that at the core of every worldview lies a "touchstone proposition," which is the "fundamental truth about reality and serves as a criterion to determine which other propositions may or may not count as candidates for belief." [48] If any proposition is deemed to be inconsistent with the touchstone proposition it must be rejected. [49] At the risk of oversimplifying matters, I suggest that the touchstone proposition for Christian theism is something like this:

> The universe (originally good, now fallen and awaiting its divine judgment and restoration) was created by and is sustained by the Triune God, who has revealed himself in nature, humanity, conscience, Scripture and supremely through the Incarnation, that God may be glorified in all things. [50]

CHRISTIAN EXISTENCE: LIVING IN THE TRUTH

Christianity means far more than holding a worldview or supporting it rationally through apologetics, although these are necessary for Christian witness. The Christian worldview, because of its objective and compelling truth, inspires a distinctively Christian way of living. When an apologist defends the truth, rationality and pertinence of Christianity, he or she is also advocating a Christ-centered, Spirit-led, Bible-honoring way of being.

The Christian worldview summons people to follow Christ, to recognize and obey the truth that sets them free. "To the Jews who had believed him, Jesus said, 'If you hold to my teaching, you are really my disciples.

---

[48]William Halverson, *A Concise Introduction to Philosophy*, 3rd ed. (New York: Random House, 1976), p. 384.
[49]Ibid.
[50]I have expanded on the "touchstone proposition" given by Ronald Nash, *Faith and Reason* (Grand Rapids: Zondervan, 1988), p. 47.

Then you will know the truth, and the truth will set you free'" (John 8:31-32). This new life bestows freedom from false masters: the world, the flesh and the devil. It is a new life offering freedom from meaninglessness, since all should be done for the eternal glory of God (Ecclesiastes 12:13-14; 1 Corinthians 10:31; Colossians 3:17) as we seek the kingdom of God to be made manifest in our midst (Matthew 6:33). The Christian life gives freedom from self-deception, since, in Christ, we can face our greatest sins, repent of them and know that because of Christ's finished work on the cross we are forgiven and empowered for kingdom service (1 John 1:8-10). The Christian is offered freedom from the tyranny of self, since we are commanded to deny ourselves, take up our cross and follow Jesus Christ by loving our neighbors and even our enemies (Matthew 5:43-48; Luke 9:23-24) through the power of the Holy Spirit. The Christian life manifests freedom from self-dependence since we must live in moment-by-moment dependence on God for all that we do (John 15). The Christian is given a new life that frees us from the fear of death or nonbeing. Since Christ has been raised immortal from the dead, Christians have a strong hope (based on knowledge) that they too will conquer death in the end (Hebrews 2:14-16).

This new free life is a life of spiritual adventure, not because it is glamorous or thrill-seeking, but because each Christian is a unique person with a distinctive role to play in God's eternal kingdom. Each Christian has been given gifts of treasure, time and talents, and has a calling on his or her life to manifest truth and love whenever and wherever possible, no matter what the cost.[51] Last, and most important, new life in Christ sets us free to love God and rejoice in the very being of the triune God. In light of this enjoyment of the divine, no sacrifice is too great and no human achievement can ever compare with it. And this joy is not without effect, for "the joy of the LORD is your strength" (Nehemiah 8:10; see also Psalm 90:14-15).[52]

An accurate understanding of the richness and distinctiveness of the

---

[51]On the doctrine of calling see Os Guinness, *The Call* (Nashville: Thomas Nelson, 1998); John Piper, *Don't Waste Your Life* (Wheaton, Ill.: Crossway, 2003).

[52]For a profound elaboration on the theme of the enjoyment of God as our highest good and greatest strength, see John Piper, *God Is the Gospel* (Wheaton, Ill.: Crossway, 2005). For help when Christian joy is distant, see John Piper, *When I Don't Desire God* (Wheaton, Ill.: Crossway, 2004).

Christian worldview is necessary for any apologetic that honors the God at the center of that worldview. Christianity is both a coherent system of ideas and the true story of the universe, its Maker, and our place within the divine drama. Nevertheless, the good news of the Christian message is often put in a bad light through caricature and distortion. To this problem we now turn.

Distortions of the Christian Worldview— Or the God I Don't Believe In

WE LIVE IN A MEANINGFUL WORLD UNDER the providence of a good and powerful God who has given us the opportunity to side with his cause, which is assured to triumph in the end because of the matchless achievement of Jesus Christ. Despite our pain and suffering, our destiny is to live forever in a restored universe with all those who share in God's goodness.

This outline of the Christian worldview, set forth in chapter four, may seem appealing to many, even those who are not Christians. Some may even wish it were true but are taken aback by repeated accusations that Christianity is without excuse because of one or more of its intrinsic defects: anti-intellectualism, an antiscience stance, racism, sexism, homophobia, imperialism, ecological disregard and a boring conception of the afterlife.[1] These epithets are hurled often and loudly against Christianity. The effect is that Christianity is sometimes taken to be so implausible that it is not deemed worthy of further investigation.[2] In this chapter, I will give a brief response to each of these objections to the Christian worldview.

ANTI-INTELLECTUALISM: CHRISTIANITY AS INTELLECTUAL SUICIDE

Some refuse to give Christianity the time of day because they deem it anti-intellectual—a religion that values ignorance and credulity far above criti-

---

[1]Other objections to the Christian worldview will be considered later in the book, including the very significant objection that Christianity cannot be true because it has such a narrow view of salvation. This will be treated in chap. 23.

[2]Plausibility should not be equated with credibility. This distinction was discussed in chap. 3.

cal intelligence. In his satirical book *The Devil's Dictionary* (1911), Ambrose Bierce defined faith as "Belief without evidence in what is told by one who speaks without knowledge, of things without parallel." In a book on how to leave one's religion behind, Marlene Winell writes of a young man named Sandy who was in her "religious recovery support group," who lost his faith in college through an encounter with an anti-intellectual pastor. The young man was experiencing doubts as a result of what he was exposed to in college. Instead of addressing these questions head-on, the pastor kept changing the subject. One day, when pressed by the young man, the pastor replied, "Sandy, it's about time we call this what it is—sin." The young man left the church and Christianity, being unwilling to follow "a religion that made thinking a sin."[3]

No one should be willing to follow a religion that decapitates critical thinking. Anti-intellectualism has quite a grip in many aspects of American culture, not only in the Christian church.[4] The reasons for the irrational faith shown in some aspects of American Christianity are numerous and will not concern us here except to say that none of the reasons flow from the Bible itself or from the best and truest elements of the Christian tradition.[5] While some have pitted faith against reason, the Bible does not endorse blind leaps of faith in the dark but rather speaks of the *knowledge of God* gained through various rational means. Instead of a *leap* of faith, it commends a well-informed and volitional *step* of faith.[6]

Jesus said the greatest commandment is to love God with all of one's being, including the mind (Matthew 22:37). Jesus' own ministry led him into intellectual debates with the best thinkers of his day, none of whom bested him in argument. We find Jesus using various argumentative strategies, such as reductio ad absurdum, a fortiori, modus ponens and appeals

---

[3]Marlene Winell, *Leaving the Fold: A Guide for Former Fundamentalists and Others Leaving Their Religion* (Oakland, Calif.: New Harbinger, 1993), p. 80.
[4]Richard Hoffstadter, *Anti-Intellectualism in American Life* (New York: Vintage, 1963).
[5]On the problem of anti-intellectualism in American Christianity, see Os Guinness, *Fit Bodies, Fat Minds* (Grand Rapids: Baker, 1994); Mark Noll, *The Scandal of the Evangelical Mind* (Grand Rapids: Eerdmans, 1994); Charles Malik, *The Two Tasks* (Wheaton, Ill.: Billy Graham Center, 2000); J. P. Moreland, *Love Your God with All Your Mind* (Colorado Springs: NavPress, 1997); and John Piper, *Think: The Life of the Mind and the Love of God* (Wheaton, Ill.: Crossway, 2010).
[6]For more on the beliefs and posture required for salvation, see Francis A. Schaeffer, *The God Who Is There*, 30th anniv. ed. (Downers Grove, Ill.: InterVarsity Press, 1998), pp. 163-67; and chaps. 2, 20 and 23 of this book.

to evidence.[7] He further reasoned from a well-developed theistic world-view.[8] The apostle Paul reasoned with the philosophers on Mars Hill (Acts 17:16-31), and the apostle Peter challenged his readers to "give an answer" for their hope in Christ (1 Peter 3:15-16).

When Paul refers to the wisdom of God as foolish to unbelievers in 1 Corinthians 1–2, he is not derogating the intellect per se. He is rather stressing that God's initiation through divine revelation is required for a saving knowledge of Christ, and that human pride and arrogance deem it unreasonable to submit humbly to this necessity. God's revelation is not unreasonable, yet the unaided human mind could not produce it on its own. Similarly Paul warns his readers not to be taken captive by "hollow and deceptive philosophy," which is merely human and divorced from God's revelation (Colossians 2:8). This is not a condemnation of all philosophy, only false philosophy.[9] Paul himself reasons carefully throughout his many intellectual encounters in the book of Acts and in his many New Testament letters. We do not lose our intelligence by being filled with the Holy Spirit.[10]

Not long ago Christian apologists faced an uphill battle against well-entrenched philosophies of unbelief. Natural theology was deemed long dead, having been slain by the swords of Hume and Kant. Arguments for God's existence were at best philosophical museum pieces revealing the errors of unenlightened intellectuals. Higher critics had reduced the Gospels to ragtag collections of scattered facts, idiosyncratic theologizing and existentially gripping myths. Philosophers and apologists were doing well to argue for the *intelligibility* of religious language (considered nonsense by logical positivists), let alone its rationality or truth. Evangelical apologetics—when pursued at all—was typically practiced outside the academy and often lacked intellectual power (although this could not be said of twentieth-century evangelical stalwarts such as J. Gresham Machen, Gor-

---

[7]For more on this, see Douglas Groothuis, "Jesus' Use of Argument," in *On Jesus* (Belmont, Calif.: Wadsworth, 2003); and James W. Sire, "Jesus the Reasoner," in *Habits of the Mind* (Downers Grove, Ill.: InterVarsity Press, 2000).

[8]See Groothuis, *On Jesus*, chaps. 4-7.

[9]For more on these passages, see Moreland, *Love Your God*, pp. 58-59, and Piper, *Think*, chaps. 10-11.

[10]More on the nature of Christian believing and the relation of faith and reason will be discussed in chap. 7.

don Clark, Bernard Ramm, Edward John Carnell or Carl Henry).[11]

But seismic shocks in the philosophy of religion have realigned the intellectual world of unbelief in the past three decades, opening up fissures and toppling edifices. Atheist philosopher Quentin Smith wrote in the skeptical philosophical journal *Philo* that the philosophy departments of the academy have been "desecularized" since the late 1960s, largely due to the pathbreaking work of Alvin Plantinga's writings. Given the renaissance in Christian philosophy during the past few decades, atheistic philosophers can no longer assume that their naturalism is justified. Smith even allows that "the justification of most contemporary naturalist views is defeated by contemporary theist arguments."[12] As of 2008, *Philosophia Christi*, the journal of the Evangelical Philosophical Society, had the largest subscription base of any philosophy of religion journal and features a roster of stellar contributors. In two important books, *Philosophers Who Believe* and *God and the Philosophers*, many leading philosophers wrote of how their Christian beliefs inform their philosophical pursuits.[13]

We find then that Christianity should encourage a robust life of the mind and that many philosophers today are owning and defending Christianity philosophically. There is therefore no reason to refuse to consider Christianity on the (false) basis that it demands intellectual suicide.

THE SUPPOSED WARFARE BETWEEN CHRISTIANITY AND SCIENCE

Many object to Christianity on the basis that it is hostile to scientific progress. Much has been made of the alleged "warfare between science and religion," as if the forces of retrenchment and obscurantism (religion) were always hurling their ideological ordnance against the forces of reason, experimentation and enlightenment (science).[14] This caricature has been kept alive by Richard Dawkins in his bestselling book *The God Delusion* (2006). On this account, Christianity is reactionary and antiscience. But

---

[11]For essays on these important thinkers see Walter A. Elwell, *Handbook of Evangelical Theologians* (Grand Rapids: Baker, 1993). Many of the theologians were also philosophers.

[12]Quentin Smith, "The Meta-Philosophy of Naturalism," *Philo* 4, no. 2 (2001) <www.philoonline.org/library/smith42.htm>.

[13]Kelly James Clark, ed., *Philosophers Who Believe* (Downers Grove, Ill.: InterVarsity Press, 1994); Thomas Morris, ed., *God and the Philosophers* (New York: Oxford University Press, 1995).

[14]Andrew D. White, *The Warfare of Science and Religion* (1895; reprint, New York: George Braziller, 1955).

on the other hand, if Christianity has in fact contributed significantly to scientific betterment, then this would be of positive apologetic value.[15]

The relationship between Christianity and science is extensive and multifaceted. We will look at two apologetic responses to this matter. The first response is historical: how has Christianity related to scientific discovery? The second is philosophical and theological: how does the Christian worldview address the nature of the universe and matters of scientific discovery?

The historical record is not one of unmitigated hostility of the church against science, resulting in science always claiming victory over benighted theological assertions. On the contrary, the Christian understanding of nature often inspired scientific research. As part of a long and fascinating research project concerning the relationship of Christian monotheism to Western history, sociologist Rodney Stark claims that the medieval Christian worldview provided a wellspring of intellectual resources for the development of science, technology and commerce. He argues that the later achievements of the scientific revolution were not the results of "an eruption of secular thinking" but were "the culmination of many centuries of systematic progress by medieval Scholastics, sustained by that uniquely Christian twelfth-century invention, the university."[16] This development was rooted in the Christian belief that nature is rationally knowable and should be investigated and used for the common good and the glory of God.

Science only reached its glories in the Christian West during the scientific revolution in the seventeenth and eighteenth centuries, when new discoveries were made in physics, astronomy, mathematics and other sciences. This was due in part to the rejection of some of the inherited Roman Catholic ideas of nature held by the church on the basis of its adoption of Aristotelian philosophy. For example, Francis Bacon and Blaise Pascal (both Christians) rejected certain a priori accounts of nature that were strongly influenced by Aristotelianism and opted instead for a more experimental/empirical approach. Bacon developed an inductive approach to science (although he engaged in a few experiments) and Pascal performed

---

[15]See the apologetic criterion concerning human betterment in chap. 3, "Apologetic Method."

[16]Rodney Stark, *The Victory of Reason: How Christianity Led to Freedom, Capitalism, and Western Success* (New York: Random House, 2005), p. 12.

significant experiments concerning the vacuum, the behavior of fluids and so on.[17] Other seminal scientific figures such as Isaac Newton, Johannes Kepler and Galileo held to a theistic worldview that encouraged the study and development of creation.[18] They did not view the Bible as inhibiting science but as being compatible with the best investigations of nature.

Despite this record of harmony between religious commitment and scientific aspiration, there has been discord as well—although not to the degree that is usually assumed. Two examples of this discord were Galileo's conflict with the Roman Catholic authorities and the infamous Huxley-Wilberforce debate over Darwinism. These icons of church-science warfare need to be knocked off the secularists' trophy shelf.

Galileo, as noted, was a confessing Christian who discerned no discord between the Bible and natural science. He famously stated that the Scriptures tell us how to go to heaven, but not how the heavens go. By this, he meant that Scripture should not be pressed beyond what it was intended to communicate. He was not denying the truth of the Bible, but rather its misinterpretation. Galileo built on the Copernican heliocentric theory and confirmed it through telescopic observation. The church objected to Galileo's theory more on the basis of its commitment to Aristotelian principles concerning nature than on a conflict between the Bible and new scientific findings. Further, Galileo was rather intemperate in his opinions and thereby left himself open to censure. He was placed under house arrest but was not tortured or imprisoned in any cruel manner. Galileo's mistreatment was certainly indefensible, but the whole sorry episode fails to represent any incorrigible conflict between the Bible and scientific progress.[19]

We will discuss Darwinism in detail in later chapters. However, one event is often invoked to demonstrate the futility of criticizing the es-

---

[17]For a brief account of Pascal's philosophy of science see Douglas Groothuis, "Scientist and Philosopher of Science," in *On Pascal* (Belmont, Calif.: Wadsworth, 2003). Bacon and Pascal were key players in the scientific revolution, but they held different understandings of nature. Bacon was far more optimistic about human progress through science than was Pascal. See Douglas Groothuis, "Bacon and Pascal on Mastery Over Nature," *Research in Philosophy and Technology* 14 (1994): 191-203.

[18]Not all these thinkers held to an orthodox Christian view. Newton may have been an Arian. Nevertheless, they were religious people who held a theistic worldview and who did not deem science as antithetical to religious convictions.

[19]See Rodney Stark, *For the Glory of God: How Monotheism Led to Reformations, Science, Witch-Hunts, and the End of Slavery* (Princeton, N.J.: Princeton University Press, 2003), pp. 163-66.

sentials of Darwinism: the debate between Thomas Huxley (known as "Darwin's bulldog") and Samuel Wilberforce, an Anglican bishop. Occurring shortly after the publication of Darwin's *Origin of Species*, the debate came to be characterized as a rout for Huxley, who exposed the benighted clergyman as a buffoon through an especially apt one-liner. But the reality was quite different. The event caused very little controversy at the time and was not written up in local papers until some time later. There was no consensus that Huxley was the victor. Wilberforce, who is usually dubbed as opposing Darwin for theological reasons alone, in fact marshaled a *scientific* critique of his theory based on a previously written fifty-page article. Far from forever banishing rational criticism of Darwinism, this debate revealed two capable intellects sparring over a very significant topic.[20]

Having briefly looked at historical matters, we need to consider in more detail the intellectual reasons why the Christian worldview encouraged science in the Middle Ages and especially in the scientific revolution. The rise of science in the West is unique in world history. As Stark says,

> Real science arose only once: in Europe. China, Islam, India, and ancient Greece and Rome each had a highly developed alchemy. But only in Europe did alchemy develop into chemistry. By the same token, many societies developed elaborate systems of astrology, but only in Europe did astrology lead to astronomy. Why?[21]

The answer lies in the Christian West's view of God, creation and humanity. Unlike cultures elsewhere, "Christians developed science because they *believed* it *could* be done, and *should* be done."[22] Philosopher and mathematician Alfred North Whitehead noted in *Science and the Modern World* that the medievalists insisted on "the rationality of God, conceived as with the personal energy of Jehovah and with the rationality of a Greek philosopher. Every detail was supervised and ordered: the search into nature could only result in the vindication of the faith in rationality."[23]

The deities of other religions (outside of monotheism) were irrational

---

[20]See J. R. Lucas, "Wilberforce and Huxley: A Legendary Encounter," *Historical Journal* 22, no. 2 (1979): 313-30.
[21]Stark, *Victory of Reason*, p. 14.
[22]Ibid.
[23]Alfred North Whitehead, *Science in the Modern World* (New York: Macmillan, 1925), p. 18.

and impersonal, and could not serve as the foundation for belief in an orderly and knowable creation. Lacking any doctrine of creation, these other
cultures could only posit a universe that is, according to Stark, "a supreme
mystery, inconsistent, unpredictable, and arbitrary. For those holding these
religious premises, the path to wisdom is through meditation into mystical
insights and there is no occasion to celebrate reason."[24] But Christianity,
on the contrary, "depicted God as a rational, responsive, dependable, and
omnipotent being and the universe as his personal creation, thus having a
rational, lawful, stable structure, awaiting human comprehension."[25]

Although Islam affirms a doctrine of creation, its views of God and
humanity are far different from that of Christianity. The God of Islam is
an unknowable commander and humans are Allah's slaves, not made in
his image. Creation is controlled moment by moment by God's arbitrary
will such that laws and processes cannot be discerned. Basic scientific
theories are not discoverable, since they depend on natural regularities.[26]
According to eminent historian and philosopher of science Stanley Jaki,
Islamic thinkers—having assimilated Aristotle nearly wholesale—did not
have a conception of God that was "adequately rational to inspire an effective distaste for various types of pantheistic, cyclic, animistic, and magical
world pictures which freely made their way into the *Rasa'l* [an early Islamic encyclopedia of knowledge]."[27] While Christian thinkers believed in
miracles, they deemed them as rare and as not interfering with the basic
patterns of the natural order established by God himself.[28]

Kenneth Samples has aptly summarized ten ways in which Christian
belief creates a hospitable environment for scientific inquiry.[29]

1. The physical universe is an objective reality, which is ontologically distinct from the Creator (Genesis 1:1; John 1:1).

2. The laws of nature exhibit order, pattern and regularity, since they are
   established by an orderly God (Psalm 19:1-4).

---

[24]Stark, *Victory of Reason*, p. 15.
[25]Stark, *Glory of God*, p. 147.
[26]Ibid., pp. 154-55.
[27]Stanley Jaki, *The Savior of Science* (Grand Rapids: Eerdmans, 2000), p. 207, quoted in Stark, *Glory of God*, pp. 155-56.
[28]I will explain more of the biblical understanding and defense of miracles in chap. 22.
[29]Kenneth Samples, *Without a Doubt* (Grand Rapids: Baker, 2004), pp. 192-94. I have modified his ten points somewhat, but within the spirit of what he wrote.

3. The laws of nature are uniform throughout the physical universe, since God created and providentially sustains them.

4. The physical universe is intelligible because God created us to know himself, ourselves and the rest of creation (Genesis 1–2; Proverbs 8).

5. The world is good, valuable and worthy of careful study because it was created for a purpose by a perfectly good God (Genesis 1). Humans, as the unique image bearers of God, were created to discern, discover and develop the goodness of creation for the glory of God and human betterment through work. The creation mandate (Genesis 1:26-28) includes scientific activity.[30]

6. Because the world is not divine and therefore not a proper object of worship, it can be an object of rational study and empirical observation.

7. Human beings possess the ability to discover the universe's intelligibility, since we are made in God's image and have been placed on earth to develop its intrinsic possibilities.

8. Because God did not reveal everything about nature, empirical investigation is necessary to discern the patterns God laid down in creation.

9. God encourages, even propels, science through his imperative to humans to take dominion over nature (Genesis 1:28).

10. The intellectual virtues essential to carrying out the scientific enterprise (studiousness, honesty, integrity, humility and courage) are part of God's moral law (Exodus 20:1-17).[31]

While Christianity and science have had their scuffles, there is nothing inherent in the Christian worldview that is inimical to science rightly understood. We will take up the relationship of Christianity and science (particularly Darwinism) in more detail in chapters thirteen and fourteen.

RACISM AND SLAVERY

Sadly, people have used the Bible to promote racism in various forms.

---

[30]On the significance and depth of the creation mandate see Francis Nigel Lee, "The Roots of Culture," in *The Central Significance of Culture* (Phillipsburg, N.J.: Presbyterian & Reformed, 1976).

[31]On the presuppositions of science, see also J. P. Moreland, *Scaling the Secular City* (Grand Rapids: Baker, 1987), pp. 198-201.

Especially noteworthy for Americans is the fact that Southern Christians before the Civil War sought to justify from Scripture the perpetual institution of slavery. However, the broad themes of Scripture do not endorse slavery. All humans are equally made in God's image and likeness (Genesis 1:26), and all have equally fallen into sin (Romans 3). Even God's election of Israel was not because of their superior race or ethnicity, but solely because of God's unconditional grace (Genesis 12:1-3). Israel was divinely elected to be a light to the Gentiles. Through its lineage came the Messiah, who calls all people to himself (Matthew 11:28-30; 28:18-20). In the end, people from "every nation, tribe, people and language" will rejoice before God's throne in celebration of their redemption (Revelation 7:9).

But if Christianity is nothing but a white man's religion, it is remarkable that it is growing most prolifically in nonwhite parts of the world, particularly in the Southern Hemisphere, as Philip Jenkins has documented.[32] Yet in much of Europe and the United States, Christianity as a movement is arguably stagnant, dying out or decadent.

Over the centuries, many who have been invested in slavery have cited Genesis 9:20-27 to ground their view that the darker-skinned races were inferior and under an enduring curse, "the curse of Ham." When Noah awoke from a drunken stupor to find that Ham had asked his brothers Shem and Japheth to cover Noah's nakedness with a garment, Noah cursed Canaan (Ham's son), not Ham himself. The Canaanites later became the enemies of Israel and the recipients of God's judgment. However, there is no specific racial component involved, since all the parties were Semites. Just how and when the races became differently pigmented is not addressed in the Bible, probably because skin color makes no difference whatsoever to God.

The Bible's references to slavery are not meant to enshrine it as a God-ordained, normative institution. Slavery, as practiced under Old Testament law, was not based on the race of the enslaved peoples but on ancient laws regarding the spoils of war. In fact, the slavery in the cultures of biblical times bore little relation to the race-based slavery practiced, for example, in the United States before the Civil War.[33] Old Testament laws

[32]Philip Jenkins, *The Next Christendom* (New York: Oxford University Press, 2002).
[33]See Robert Hutchinson, "You Were Called to Freedom," *The Politically Incorrect Guide to the Bible* (Washington, D.C.: Regnery, 2007).

regulating the extent and form of slavery had the effect of humanizing the existing institution to some degree.[34] More importantly, the Hebrew theocracy was not meant to be a perpetual institution.[35] The best was yet to come in the messianic age.

Slavery in Greco-Roman times was not as harsh and cruel as American slavery, although it certainly was no model for any society.[36] References to slaves submitting to their masters in the New Testament are not endorsements of the institution but temporary injunctions given certain social realities. This is evident when Paul refers to slave traders as evil (1 Timothy 1:10) and when he bids slaves to seek freedom lawfully when they can (1 Corinthians 7:21). The book of Philemon did much to revolutionize the Christian view of slavery. Paul writes to Philemon that since Onesimus, his slave, is his brother in Christ, he should be treated well, "no longer as a slave, but better than a slave, as a dear brother. He is very dear to me but even dearer to you, both as a fellow man and as a brother in the Lord" (Philemon 16).[37]

A specific indictment of slavery cannot be found in the Gospels—or in any other literature of the world at that time. But an omission of condemnation is not the same as an endorsement of an institution's perpetual and crosscultural legitimacy. The Gospels do not portray Jesus primarily as a social reformer who directly challenged all illegitimate authority. His mission was more focused than that. However, his instruction that his followers not lord it over others but rather prize servanthood sets in motion an ethic ultimately incompatible with slavery (Mark 9:35).

While misguided Christians used texts out of context as pretexts for slavery,[38] Christians with a deeper sense of the Bible's meaning of liberation opposed slavery and eventually prevailed in both the British Empire (largely through the efforts of William Wilberforce) and in the United States.[39]

---

[34]On the nature of slavery in the Bible see Walter J. Kaiser, *Toward an Old Testament Ethics* (Grand Rapids: Baker, 1983), pp. 288-90; and Christopher J. H. Wright, *An Eye for an Eye: The Place of Old Testament Ethics Today* (Downers Grove, Ill.: InterVarsity Press, 1983), pp. 178-82.

[35]Consider the Old Testament references to the new covenant in Jeremiah 31 and Ezekiel 37.

[36]See Hutchinson, *Politically Incorrect Guide*, pp. 165-72.

[37]Some have argued that this book does not address the problem of slavery, but this has been the minority position. For a full discussion, see Joseph Fitzmyer, *The Letter to Philemon*, Anchor Bible Commentary (New Haven, Conn.: Yale University Press, 2000).

[38]See J. Oliver Buswell III, *Slavery, Segregation, and Scripture* (Grand Rapids: Eerdmans, 1964).

[39]On Christianity's role in abolishing slavery, see Stark, *Glory of God*, pp. 291-366.

IS CHRISTIANITY SEXIST?

Some believe that Christianity is a male-dominated religion that reduces women to an inferior status. How can we trust a sexist book (the Bible) as a revelation from God? Many women have felt the anguish of being treated as second-class citizens in a man's world. They have been stereotyped and marginalized by men who fail to see their real abilities and understand their real desires.

Christians should be sensitive to these concerns, since God calls us to respect everyone equally on the basis of the truth that we are all created in the image of God (Genesis 1:26). We are to love our neighbor as ourselves (Matthew 19:19) and recognize our unity and equality in Christ (Galatians 3:26-29). Yet sadly, many women and men see the Bible itself as justifying the mistreatment of half the human race.

Many non-Christian feminists claim that the God of the Bible is male. If God is male, then men are more like God than are women. This belief devalues women who, because of their gender, will never have the privileged status of men. Some feminists also complain that since the incarnation of God occurred in the form of a man, Jesus, this God cannot properly relate to women's experience. Because of these problems with Christianity, they say, women must turn to a feminine understanding of the divine, the goddess.

But those who are drawn to the goddess must come to terms with the real Jesus, not a sexist caricature. First, the God of the Bible is not male in any sense, because God is not a sexual being. Jesus taught that God is Spirit (John 4:24) and not one who brings things into existence through procreation. God is not to be represented as either a male or a female (Exodus 20:4; Deuteronomy 4:16). Scripture refers to God as "he" and Jesus called God his Father not to emphasize masculinity against femininity but to highlight that God is a personal and powerful being. Unlike the idea of the goddess, the biblical God is a knowing, willing, holy and loving personal agent who reveals himself in the Bible and through taking on a human nature in Jesus Christ.

Throughout human cultures, men have had more authority than women. The Bible uses the terms and concepts that would best communicate God's power and prestige, and his role as our protector and provider. Nevertheless, the Bible uses feminine imagery when it speaks of God as giving birth to Israel (Deuteronomy 32:18) and to the Christian (James 1:18). Jesus said he longed to gather rebellious Israel to himself as a mother hen gathers her chicks (Matthew 23:37-39). These kinds of metaphors reveal that although God is not a sexual being, he possesses all the qualities that we appreciate in both men and women, for God is the giver of every good and perfect gift (James 1:17).

Moreover, Jesus did not set up a male-dominated religious system in which women would be permanently subjugated. He surprised his followers by teaching theology to women in private and in public (Luke 10:38-42; John 4:7-27; 11:21-27) at a time when women were excluded from such affairs. Although he esteemed the family, Jesus stipulated that a woman's principal purpose in life is not reducible to motherhood and domestic work, but is found in knowing and following God's will (Luke 10:38-42; 11:27-28). Jesus also appeared to Mary after his resurrection and appointed her as a witness to this world-changing event—in a time when the witness of a woman was not respected (Matthew 28:5-10; John 20:17-18). His model of leadership was based on mutual service and sacrifice, not hierarchical authority structures:

> Jesus called them together and said, "You know that the rulers of the Gentiles lord it over them, and their high officials exercise authority over them. Not so with you. Instead, whoever wants to become great among you must be your servant, and whoever wants to be first must be your slave—just as the Son of Man did not come to be served, but to serve, and to give his life as a ransom for many. (Matthew 20:25-28)

In addition, in the early church, women served as prophets (Acts 2:17-18; 21:9) and teachers (Acts 18:24-26). Paul clearly articulated the spiritual and ontological equality of male and female believers when he said, "In Christ Jesus you are all children of God through faith, for all of you who were baptized into Christ have clothed yourselves with Christ. There is neither Jew nor Gentile, neither slave nor free, nor is there male and female, for you are all one in Christ Jesus" (Galatians 3:26-28).

Third, the incarnation of God in Jesus does not imply that God is male or that God excludes or devalues women. For God the Son to take on human nature, he would have to be either a male or a female. He could not be both simultaneously. Moreover, the divine nature of the Son is not gendered, since sexuality is a human, not a divine attribute. The most important fact about Jesus' *humanity* was not his maleness but his moral perfection and his identification with the entire human race. Jesus understands us all from the inside out: "For we do not have a high priest who is unable to empathize with our weaknesses, but we have one who has been tempted in every way, just as we are—yet he did not sin" (Hebrews 4:15). Although Jesus lived in perfect harmony with the Father and the Holy Spirit, when he joined the human family he personally experienced what it was like to suffer and feel pain, even as we do (Hebrews 5:7-9).

Those who gravitate toward the goddess because of the problems they perceive with the God of the Bible should realize that Jesus Christ died for the sins of the world, including the sins that men commit against women. Jesus neither endorses nor excuses any sin, but calls everyone to repent of sin and accept him as his or her Savior, Master and Friend (John 15:15). An impersonal principle, power or presence romantically called the goddess can be no one's friend, let alone their Savior.

While goddess religion is speculatively reconstructed from the dark recesses of prehistory, the drama of Jesus is enshrined in datable, space-time, human history. God has a human face, the visage of Jesus. His story has spoken to countless millions of women and men worldwide for the last two thousand years—and continues to speak to us today. Jesus, in fact, scandalized the religious establishment (and even his own disciples) through his respect for women demonstrated in many circumstances.[40] Even though the Bible was written in and to patriarchal cultures, it lauds several women leaders in various capacities, such as judge, prophetess and teacher.[41] The promise of the kingdom involves both men and women filled with the Spirit and serving Christ (Acts 2:17-18; see also Joel 2:28-32).

ARE CHRISTIANS AFRAID OF HOMOSEXUALITY?

Christianity is often accused of being homophobic. The term is usually used imprecisely as more of a thoughtless invective than conveying any

---

[40]On this see Douglas Groothuis, "Jesus' View of Women," in *On Jesus* (Belmont, Calif.: Wadsworth, 2003).

[41]Female leaders, teachers and prophets in the Bible include Miriam (Exodus 15:20; Micah 6:4), Deborah (Judges 4–5), Huldah (2 Kings 22:14-20; 2 Chronicles 34:11-33), Noahdiah (Nehemiah 6:14), the wife of Isaiah (Isaiah 8:3), Anna (Luke 2:36), Philip's daughters (Acts 21:8-9), Priscilla (Acts 18:24-26; Romans 16:3-5; 1 Corinthians 16:19), Junia (Romans 16:7), and Phoebe (Romans 16:1-2).

clear meaning. However, the idea is that Christianity is regressive and bigoted to its core and so is not a serious candidate for one's allegiance.

In order to ascertain whether this is a distortion of the Christian worldview, two issues need to be considered. First, we need to consider just what the Scripture states concerning homosexuality. Second, if homosexual practice cannot be condoned by Scripture, what does the Bible advocate Christians do in light of the reality of homosexuals in their midst?

Despite some revisionist attempts to justify homosexual relationships from the Bible, the biblical paradigm is heterosexual monogamy, which is rooted deeply in the foundational Genesis narrative concerning men, women, marriage and children. In Genesis 1–2, God created man and woman to cultivate and develop creation, to be one flesh in marriage and to procreate (Genesis 1:26-28; 2:23-25). Jesus further ratifies this when he is asked a question about divorce. "'Haven't you read,' he replied, 'that at the beginning the Creator "made them male and female," and said, "For this reason a man will leave his father and mother and be united to his wife, and the two will become one flesh"?'" (Matthew 19:4-5).

The one-flesh relation of the man and the woman is the very meaning of marriage in the Bible and the original pattern for human satisfaction under God. Homosexuality, on the other hand, stems from the fall of humanity into sin. Paul brings this home when he describes what happens when people fail to honor God for who God is. Part of the result of this fallen pattern is homosexual behavior.

> God gave them over in the sinful desires of their hearts to sexual impurity for the degrading of their bodies with one another. They exchanged the truth about God for a lie, and worshiped and served created things rather than the Creator—who is forever praised. Amen.
>
> Because of this, God gave them over to shameful lusts. Even their women exchanged natural sexual relations for unnatural ones. In the same way the men also abandoned natural relations with women and were inflamed with lust for one another. Men committed shameful acts with other men, and received in themselves the due penalty for their error. (Romans 1:24-27)

These sexual behaviors are against creation and so are shameful, unnatural and injurious. Therefore, whether or not a homosexual orientation is a matter of choice, it cannot be condoned as naturally good or fitting.

Further, Paul writes of those who were so inclined but who have repented and are washed clean of their sin through the Lord:

> Neither the sexually immoral nor idolaters nor adulterers nor men who have sex with men nor thieves nor the greedy nor drunkards nor slanderers nor swindlers will inherit the kingdom of God. And that is what some of you *were*. But you were washed, you were sanctified, you were justified in the name of the Lord Jesus Christ and by the Spirit of our God. (1 Corinthians 6:9-11, emphasis added)

Whether one takes the biblical teaching on homosexuality to be normative depends on whether one reckons the Bible to be divinely inspired.[42]

Even though homosexuality cannot be approved by Christians, this does not mean Christians should hate or be alarmed by homosexuals. Jesus said to love our neighbor; and the homosexual is our neighbor. Jesus also called people to look at the log in their own eye before considering the plank in another's (Matthew 7:1-5). So, there is no room for censoriousness or condescension. But Christian love includes a call to repent (Acts 17:30). Several Christian ministries seek to help homosexuals who want to become Christians and to turn from their homosexual ways. However, conversion does not guarantee that homosexual urges will immediately or completely vanish. But the Christian labors to obey God's commands in the power of the Holy Spirit, no matter how difficult that might be.

However unpopular the biblical understanding of homosexuality may be, if the Christian worldview is well supported, then the biblical perspective provides the believer with a rational and balanced view of the matter. Moreover, it gives real hope for forgiveness and constructive change for homosexuals.

COERCION AND IMPERIALISM

Christians in many parts of the world, such as Sri Lanka, are often accused of siding with Western imperialism rather than having solidarity with their own people. This is one result of nations in the Two-Thirds World having been colonized by Western powers. Although I cannot give the

---

[42]Or one might have independent, extrabiblical reasons for taking homosexuality to be aberrant. See Scott Rae, *Moral Choices*, 3rd ed. (Grand Rapids: Zondervan, 2010), pp. 284-85; and Robert George, "Nature, Morality, and Homosexuality," in *In Defense of Natural Law* (New York: Oxford University Press, 1999).

history of imperialism, there are biblical principles that militate against it and differentiate it from genuine Christian witness (apologetics and evangelism).

Christianity was born and developed in a largely hostile environment in the ancient Mediterranean world. Nevertheless, it expanded as it reached out to both Jews and Gentiles through its teaching, preaching, miracles and acts of service. Since neither Jesus nor the apostles ever sanctioned coercion as a method for mission, neither did the early church. While the state is given "the power of the sword" (Romans 13:1-7), the church is not. Its weapons are spiritual and have greater power (2 Corinthians 10:3-5; Ephesians 6:12). After Christianity was legalized in the Roman Empire by Constantine, and especially after Christianity became the state church, the situation became more complex. We know from history that the church has sometimes used the coercive power of the state to threaten or force conversions (or ostensibly Christian behavior where true faith was lacking). Yet we cannot find any basis for this strategy in the Bible itself.

In light of the postmodernist criticism that "totalizing metanarratives" (worldviews claiming objective and universal truth) are intrinsically unjust, we should note that Jesus commissioned his followers to persuade and influence people through teaching and actions that are empowered by the Holy Spirit (Matthew 28:18-20; Luke 24:46-49; Acts 1:8). He never authorized imperialism, exploitation, coercion, threats or any other means of illicit power over others. Instead, he tells us to love our neighbors and even our enemies (Matthew 5:43-48). The book of Acts shows the early Christians winning conversions through persuasion, not coercion or manipulation. We find Christians, such as Stephen (the first Christian martyr), being persecuted and killed for their faith. This did not lead the Christians to an armed revolt but to fervent prayer, fasting and acts of faith in the face of opposition. Sadly, some later Christians who held the reins of political power did enforce Christian conformity through the sword. We would be hard pressed, though, to find any warrant for this in the teachings of Jesus or the apostles.

Some may hearken back to the territorial imperatives given by God to ancient Israel in which the Israelites were to take land from their neighbors and in some cases to exterminate them.[43] Suffice to say that these injunctions were meant only for a particular people at a particular time and for a particular purpose. There is no warrant to regard the holy wars of the Hebrew Bible as general principles for Christian endeavors. Further, the purpose of these wars was not the conversion of the inhabitants of the land but their military defeat.[44] Therefore, there is no parallel to Christian witness today, which has nothing to do with conquering lands by force.

While the Christian crusades are often invoked as evidence against the goodness and truth of Christianity, this is simply not true. Much could be said about the distorted views of the crusades (especially their extent and purposes), but suffice it to say that they were a relatively short-lived and largely defensive action instigated by Roman Catholic popes to reclaim the Holy Land for Christendom from Islam.[45] Since this book defends a Protestant understanding of Christianity and so rejects the office of the pope as unbiblical, these papal pronouncements on the crusades lie outside of anything I wish to defend as true or rational. Claims made by popes that the soldiers dying in a crusade would be guaranteed heaven are entirely unbiblical and, in fact, resemble Islamic claims more than anything found in Holy Scripture. The call for a holy (military) crusade made by the church is always out of sync with the Bible itself.[46]

DOES CHRISTIANITY NEGLECT ECOLOGY?

Christianity is often characterized as displaying little concern for the non-human realm of nature and focusing instead on only the salvation of souls

---

[43]See appendix 2 by Richard Hess.

[44]On the moral question of the conquest of Canaan, see also C. S. Cowles, Eugene H. Merrill, Daniel L. Gard and Tremper Longman III, *Show Them No Mercy: Four Views on God and Canaanite Genocide* (Grand Rapids: Zondervan, 2003); Paul Copan, "Is Yaweh a Moral Monster?" *Philosophia Christi* 10, no. 1 (2008): 7-37; Paul Copan, *Is God a Moral Monster? Making Sense of the Old Testament God* (Grand Rapids: Baker, 2011); Bob Siegel, "Why Did God Command the Israelites to Wipe Out the Other Nations?" in *I'd Like to Believe in Jesus But . . .* (Wheaton, Ill.: Campus Ambassadors Press, 1999).

[45]See Robert Spencer, *The Politically Incorrect Guide to Islam and the Crusades* (Washington, D.C.: Regnery, 2005), part two; and Thomas Madden, "The Real History of the Crusades," *Crisis Magazine,* March 2002 <www.crisismagazine.com/2011/the-real-history-of-the-crusades>; Dinesh D'Souza, "Rethinking the Inquisition," in *What's So Great About Christianity* (Washington, D.C.: Regnery, 2007), esp. pp. 204-6.

[46]This should be distinguished from the just war tradition, which stipulates conditions under which the state (not the church) can engage in warfare morally. See Darrell Cole, *When God Says War Is Right* (Colorado Springs: WaterBrook, 2002).

and their eternal state in heaven above. Humans are deemed free to exploit the earth as its masters. The earth will be destroyed at the end of the ages anyway. Given this caricature of Christianity, many green activists and environmentalists have rejected a Christian view of nature and have gleaned heavily from non-Christian religions, which they take to be more respectful of nature. "Love Your Mother," reads a bumper sticker with a depiction of planet Earth on it. Earth Day (started in 1970) is close to a sacred holiday for many groups. Yet pagan religions have done a fine job of polluting and disrespecting nature, as René Dubos pointed out in his refutation of Lynn White's influential essay claiming that Christianity was responsible for "the ecological crisis."[47]

The Christian worldview neither deifies nature nor denigrates its worth. According to the Bible, creation is not divine and should never be worshiped. Yet it is neither intrinsically evil nor illusory, so it should be treated with respect. The universe was created as good by God and given to humans that they might develop and cultivate it through their God-given ingenuity. Women and men's "dominion" over creation—critics to the contrary—was never intended to mean lawless exploitation at the expense of creation (see Genesis 1–2; Psalm 8). However, the Fall set creation against itself such that harmony between humans, animals and the rest of nature is difficult to attain (Genesis 3). But now the entire creation has been dignified by God's decision to take on a human nature and live on earth for the sake of cosmic redemption. In the end the balance will be restored and nature in all its nooks and crannies will be reinstated with untrammeled goodness and grace (Romans 8:18-26; Revelation 21–22).

Nevertheless, the Bible's ecological concern does not require vegetarianism, nor does it put animals on an equal or higher moral level than human beings, who alone are made in God's image and likeness. Jesus spoke of humans as being "much more valuable" than "the birds of the air" (Matthew 6:26). Under the old covenant, God ordained animal sacrifice to portray the need for blood atonement for sin. The Passover meal, prefiguring Christ's death for sin, features the consumption of lamb (Exodus

---

[47]René Dubos, *The Wooing of the Earth* (New York: Charles Scribner's, 1980), pp. 70-78. See also Francis Schaeffer and Udo Middleman, *Pollution and the Death of Man* (1970; reprint, Wheaton, Ill.: Crossway, 1992). Middleman provides the introduction to the new edition but did not write the main text.

12:21). Jesus himself ate this meal at the Last Supper (Matthew 26:17) and ate fish after the resurrection (Luke 24:40-43). Yet the Bible does not regard animals as without value or as mere fodder for human exploitation. The old covenant law speaks of the need for letting the land rest and for the proper treatment of animals.[48]

Although Christians of good conscience will find themselves in disagreement as to which policies are in the best interest for God's green earth, all Christians should work for what Francis Schaeffer called "substantial healing" for the earth, even before the second coming.[49]

Although some writers have emphasized the imminence of events signaling the end of the world, Jesus proclaimed that no one knows the precise timing of his return from heaven (Mark 13:32; see also Acts 1:11). Until that time, his followers should bring as much *shalom* (justice and peace) to earth as possible. They should put their talents to good use while they have time (Luke 19:11-28). This includes tending the garden God bequeathed to earthlings for safe keeping. In fact, in recent years, many evangelical Christians have become more interested in these matters.

THE CHRISTIAN AFTERLIFE IS UNAPPEALING

Although it is seldom mentioned in Christian apologetics texts, some have dismissed Christianity as unappealing partially because they take its view of the afterlife to be monotonous and boring. This often stems from half-remembered Sunday school lessons, bad religious art or popular presentations of people playing harps on clouds for no apparent reason—forever. The root of this problem is a false concept of heaven, which is often perpetrated by the church itself. Biblically understood, the afterlife has two stages: (1) life after death and (2) life after life after death.[50] For the believer in Christ, physical death means that the soul separates from the body and enters into the presence of God. The Bible does not reveal much about this stage, except to that one is "with the Lord" but nevertheless "unclothed," lacking a

---

[48]See Rousas John Rushdoony, *Institutes of Biblical Law* (Nutley, N.J.: Craig Press, 1973), p. 245.
[49]See Schaeffer and Middleman, *Pollution and the Death of Man;* and Alister McGrath, *The Reenchantment of Nature: The Denial of Religion and the Ecological Crisis* (New York: Doubleday, 2002). McGrath argues that secularism fails to honor nature by taking away its status as God's good creation.
[50]See the interview by David Neff with N. T. Wright, "You Can't Keep a Justified Man Down: An Interview with N. T. Wright," *Christianity Today On Line Exclusive*, April 1, 2003 <www.christianitytoday.com/ct/2003/aprilweb-only/4-14-42.0.html>.

physical body (2 Corinthians 5:1-10). That is, this disembodied and intermediate state—between mortal life and the resurrection of the body—is incomplete. We were created to be a physical and spiritual unity, but death (due to sin) has shattered this unity. At death the Christian is freed from the chains of earthly, sin-affected existence but has not yet put on the resurrected body promised to those redeemed through Christ. There are some descriptions of redeemed spirits praising God in the book of Revelation, a highly symbolic book, where harps are mentioned (Revelation 14:2; 15:2). Even so, the activity of praising and worshiping an infinitely majestic God cannot possibly be boring or pointless. We may praise and honor finite beings to some extent, but even standing ovations for virtuoso musicians (rightly) end at some point. However, the worship of an infinite and Perfect Being has no termination, since finite beings will always be in God's debt and will always have more of God's endless life to joyfully experience through worship throughout all eternity. That is what paradise is—to be with the incomparable and matchless Jesus Christ (Luke 23:43).

The final state of creation is "the new heavens and new earth" (Revelation 21–22). Humans were created to cultivate and develop the world and glorify God thereby (Genesis 1–2). Jesus Christ came to redeem not only humans but the entire creation (Romans 8:18-26). So, in the world to come, redeemed women and men will take their place on earth to continue the task of cultivation and development.[51] Moreover, although it is not commonly taught in American evangelicalism, there is a strong biblical case (emphasized by the Calvinistic tradition) that humanity's cultural achievements will be purified and brought into this resurrected world. "The wealth of the nations" shall be brought into the eternal kingdom, thus giving its citizens ample occasion for enjoyment and appreciation.[52] Beyond these historical monuments to God's cultural grace are the manifold cultural creations that will flourish in a restored universe which is free of the Fall and filled with the manifest presence of God as the waters cover the sea (Isaiah 11:9, Revelation 21–22).

So, if one takes the Bible seriously, the afterlife cannot be viewed as

---

[51]See Michael Wittmer, *Heaven Is a Place on Earth: Why Everything You Do Matters to God* (Grand Rapids: Zondervan, 2004).
[52]See Richard Mouw, *When the Kings Come Marching In: Isaiah and the New Jerusalem*, rev. ed. (Grand Rapids: Eerdmans, 2004).

insipid or uninspiring. As Irenaeus wrote, "The glory of God is man fully alive"—and the redeemed will be fully alive in their glorified state.[53]

FROM DISTORTIONS TO REALITY

Due to their popularity and the passion with which they are promoted, distorted accounts of Christianity keep many from pondering the genuine Christian message. But popularity and passion do not guarantee truth. This chapter has argued that Christianity can counter the caricatures raised against it. It is neither anti-intellectual nor antiscience, but rather embraces the life of the mind in order to understand reality rationally and empirically. The Christian worldview affirms that all humans are made in God's image, however fallen they are. As such, it does not discriminate on the basis of race or gender, but offers life and hope to all through the gospel. While it deems homosexual conduct as antithetical to the purposes of creation, it does not encourage homophobia but rather love and restoration. Christianity should commend itself on the basis of persuasion, not coercion. Whenever the Christian cause is promoted by the sword, it becomes unfaithful to its highest authority, the Bible. The biblical doctrine of creation, far from demeaning the importance of nature, means that the earth should be revered as God's handiwork. God so highly esteems it (and us) that the afterlife for the redeemed will be lived out amid the endless joys of a restored physical universe.

---

[53]Irenaeus *Against Heresies* 4.20.7. On how the symbolism of heaven relates to objective realities, see C. S. Lewis, "Hope," in *Mere Christianity* (1952; reprint, San Francisco: HarperSanFrancisco, 2001), bk. 3, chap. 10. For more on why heaven could not be tedious, see Jerry L. Walls, "Heaven and Hell," in *The Routledge Companion to Philosophy of Religion*, ed. Chad Meister and Paul Copan (New York: Routledge, 2007), pp. 593-94. On the related objection that the afterlife does not give meaning to this life, see J. P. Moreland, *Scaling the Secular City* (Grand Rapids: Baker, 1987), p. 130.

6

Truth Defined and Defended

"What is truth?" said jesting Pilate; and would not stay for an answer.

FRANCIS BACON[1]

IF APOLOGETICS FINDS ITS MEANING and mission in defending the truth of Christianity rationally, it must take pause when the historic Christian view of truth itself is brought into question or rejected outright.[2] In 1968, Francis Schaeffer wrote that the problem with communicating Christianity to a new generation was centered on a new view of truth that detached it from objective and knowable reality.[3] Schaeffer was prophetic, and the dangers he discerned then are epidemic now. Truth, especially spiritual truth, is now widely taken to be a matter of perspective, a mere social or personal construction. Truth no longer concerns the nature of things, nor is it subject to intellectual analysis.

Yet Scripture repeatedly affirms that faith must be factual, that believing means connecting with reality. Consider Paul's statements to the Corinthians who were disputing the resurrection of the dead.

> If Christ has not been raised, our preaching is useless and so is your faith.
> More than that, we are then found to be false witnesses about God, for we

---

[1]Francis Bacon, "On Truth," in *Bacon: A Selection of His Works*, ed. Sidney Warfaft (Indianapolis: Bobbs-Merrill, 1965), p. 47.

[2]This chapter appeared in a similar form as "Truth Defined and Defended" in *Reclaiming the Center,* ed. Millard J. Erickson, Paul Kjoss Helseth and Justin Taylor (Wheaton, Ill.: Crossway, 2004).

[3]Francis A. Schaeffer, *The God Who Is There*, 30th anniv. ed. (Downers Grove, Ill.: InterVarsity Press, 1998), p. 25. Schaeffer referred to the biblical and classical view of truth as "true truth."

have testified about God that he raised Christ from the dead. But he did
not raise him if in fact the dead are not raised. For if the dead are not raised,
then Christ has not been raised either. And if Christ has not been raised,
your faith is futile; you are still in your sins. Then those also who have
fallen asleep in Christ are lost. If only for this life we have hope in Christ,
we are of all people most to be pitied. (1 Corinthians 15:14-19)

Paul's argument presupposes a truth claim concerning the resurrection of
Jesus in space-time history. Paul stakes everything on the objective truth
of Jesus' resurrection. His strength in believing in it, or his community's
comfort in affirming it, is irrelevant if it is not objectively true.

Nevertheless, many Christians are abandoning any objective and rationally knowable concept of truth concerning Christianity itself. They claim
that this concept of truth limits Christian witness and ties it to an outmoded modernist account of truth that has failed to deliver.

TRUTH AND EVANGELICALS

In his popular book *A New Kind of Christian*, which became the first of a
trilogy, Brian McLaren defends postmodernism as the only way forward
for an irrelevant and hopelessly modernistic evangelicalism. McLaren
weaves a story in which Dan, a disillusioned Christian considering leaving
the pastorate, is strengthened in his faith through his lively interaction
with Neo, the winning and winsome protagonist of postmodernism.[4] In
one significant exchange, Neo tells Dan that

> the old notions of truth and knowledge are being, hmm, I was going to say
> "deconstructed," but we don't need to get into all that vocabulary. The old
> notions are being questioned. New understandings of truth and knowledge
> that might improve on them haven't been fully developed yet. So, Dan, I'm
> not saying in any way that truth isn't important. But I am saying that truth
> means more than factual accuracy. It means being in sync with God.[5]

While Neo claims that truth is "more than factual accuracy," the rest of
the book proceeds to question whether truth concerns factual accuracy at
all. Neo describes modernity—the bogeyman—as "an age aspiring to absolute *objectivity*, which, we believed, would yield absolute certainty and

---

[4]Postmodern thinkers Stanley Grenz, Leonard Sweet and Nancey Murphy are all favorably
mentioned in the footnotes.
[5]Brian McLaren, *A New Kind of Christian* (San Francisco: Jossey-Bass, 2001), p. 61.

knowledge" at the expense of poetry, narrative, religion and the arts. It was also "a *critical* age." If you believe in "absolute, objective truth, and you know this with absolute certainty, then of course you must debunk anyone who sees differently from you."[6] Neo believes that evangelicals have taken on the worldview of modernity (despite its criticisms of religion) in that they emphasize objective, absolute and knowable truth and the need to refute those who disagree with it. This modernistic hangover, according to Neo, must be soundly rejected.

The postmodernist "deconstruction" of objective truth and rationality, on which Neo does not directly elaborate, amounts to this: truth does not lodge in statements that correspond to reality. That modernist notion needs to be deconstructed or reduced to its "true" elements. Truth is a matter of perspective only; it is something that individuals and communities construct, primarily through language.

If this postmodernist view is accepted, objective truth is ruled out in principle. Truth dissolves into communities, ethnic groups, genders and other contingent factors. No one "metanarrative" (or worldview) can rightly claim to be a true and rational account of reality. That would be arrogant and impossible.

Since McLaren has already diluted the notion of truth, he must now redefine the nature of Scripture to fit these conceptions. The older liberals held to a classic correspondence view of truth and claimed that many biblical statements—particularly those truth claims related to history and science—failed to correspond with reality.[7] On the other hand, Christians who are attracted to postmodernism change the very concept of truth itself and then apply their new concept of truth to the Scriptures. The Bible is thus relieved of the pressure to exhaustively conform to an objective and given reality outside of its own words and outside the perspectives of its readers. The Bible is now "true" in the sense that it is found meaningful by the believing community, that it gives us great narratives and that it inspires us spiritually. Perfect agreement with fact is no longer an issue. Realizing this, for McLaren and those he represents, means becoming "a new kind of Christian."

---

[6]Ibid., p. 17.
[7]For a classic critique of the older theological liberalism, see J. Gresham Machen, *Christianity and Liberalism* (Grand Rapids: Eerdmans, 1923).

In his survey of "the younger evangelicals," Robert Webber addresses their views of apologetics. Those whom Webber consults appear suspicious of Christian truth viewed as objective, propositional and defensible through compelling rational defense.[8] Webber cites three key propositions from Carl F. H. Henry's magnum opus, the six-volume *God, Revelation, and Authority* and summarily announces that younger evangelicals—the cutting edge of the movement, to his mind—simply do not have that focus. These are the statements he cites:

(1) God's revelation is rational communication conveyed in intelligible ideas and meaningful words, that is, conceptual verbal form.

(2) The Bible is the reservoir and conduit of divine truth.

(3) The Holy Spirit superintends the communication of divine revelation, first, by inspiring the prophetic apostolic writings, and, second, by illuminating and interpreting the scripturally given Word of God.[9]

Webber concurs with their rejection of a heavily propositional understanding of Christian truth. The old view of truth must go.

Some think truth is already on the way out and are lamenting its demise. The American pollster George Barna has reported that only 9 percent of "born again Christians" possess a biblical worldview. He defines such a worldview in the following way:

A biblical worldview was defined as believing that absolute moral truths exist; that such truth is defined by the Bible; and firm belief in six specific religious views. Those views were that Jesus Christ lived a sinless life; God is the all-powerful and all-knowing Creator of the universe and He still rules it today; salvation is a gift from God and cannot be earned; Satan is real; a Christian has a responsibility to share their faith in Christ with other people; and the Bible is accurate in all of its teachings.[10]

---

[8]I wonder about the adequacy of Webber's sample. I know of many younger evangelicals who hold to a strong objective view of truth and the necessity of rational apologetics. This is true of most all of the philosophy of religion graduate students at Denver Seminary that I have known since 1993.

[9]Robert Webber, *The Younger Evangelicals* (Grand Rapids: Baker, 2002), p. 97. For Henry's entire treatment of these propositions, see Carl F. H. Henry, *God, Revelation, and Authority* (Waco, Tex.: Word, 1976-1983), vols. 2-4.

[10]"A Biblical Worldview Has a Radical Effect on a Person's Life," *Barna Group*, December 1, 2003 <www.barna.org/barna-update/article/5-barna-update/131-a-biblical-worldview-has-a-radical-effect-on-a-persons-life>.

Barna further reports that "among the most prevalent alternative world-views was postmodernism, which seemed to be the dominant perspective among the two youngest generations (i.e., Busters and Mosaics)."[11]

On a more academic note, in their volume *Beyond Foundationalism: Shaping Theology in a Postmodern Context*, Stanley Grenz and John Franke appropriate ideas from the descriptive sociology of Peter Berger and Thomas Luckmann to explain Grenz's and Franke's concept of truth. From within the discipline of the sociology of knowledge, Berger and Luckmann write of the "social construction of reality" through language. Berger and Luckmann do not make philosophical claims about the nature of truth, but describe how beliefs are formed and how they function in various social contexts. Strictly speaking, the sociology of knowledge is not about *knowledge* in the philosophical sense (i.e., justified true belief), but merely about how beliefs gain plausibility in various cultural settings.[12]

Nevertheless, Grenz and Franke take this notion of constructing reality through language and adopt it for theological purposes. While they grant that there is a "givenness to the universe apart from the human linguistic-constructive task" (even postmodernist maven Richard Rorty grants this), they do not consider language as rightly or wrongly relating to an objective reality. Rather, they make the rather remarkable statement, "The simple fact is, we do not inhabit the 'world-in-itself'; instead we live in a linguistic world of our own making."[13] (If this were so, there would be precisely no "simple facts.") Furthermore, they claim that there is no "objectivity," understood as "a static reality existing outside of, and cotemporally with, our socially and linguistically constructed reality; it is not the objectivity of what some might call 'the world as it is.'"[14] Instead, "objectivity" concerns only what God will eventually bring about in the future, eschatologically.[15] Grenz and Franke, therefore, deny that language can truthfully con-

---

[11]Ibid.

[12]See Peter Berger, "The Perspective of Sociology: Relativizing the Relativizers," in *A Rumor of Angels: Modern Society and the Rediscovery of the Supernatural* (Garden City, N.Y.: Anchor Books, 1970).

[13]Stanley Grenz and John Franke, *Beyond Foundationalism* (Grand Rapids: Eerdmans, 2000), p. 53.

[14]Ibid.

[15]This claim is illogical. If language cannot *now* represent the objective world, why think that language can represent a *future* world? If language is socially constructed in essence, it remains

nect with an extralinguistic reality outside of itself—the objective world as it now is. This is a significant and momentous departure from the correspondence view of truth and any kind of theological realism (the claim that theological statements in harmony with Scripture reflect an objective reality).

This chapter defends a concept of truth that is challenged by those who journey down the postmodern road away from objective truth. It is a vision of truth both ancient and logically compelling. Nevertheless, many evangelicals are brushing it aside with little critical engagement. At worst, some evangelicals seem to abandon—or at least marginalize—this venerable view of truth simply because many postmodern people are questioning or abandoning it.

THE TRUTH QUESTION

The question of truth has at least two core components. First, what is the nature of truth itself? What does it mean for something—a belief or statement—to be true as opposed to false or nonsensical? These sorts of questions address the metaphysics or "being" of truth. Truth claims can be made about pedestrian facts (Is it raining today?) or about ancient and consequential worldviews (Which of the many religions is true, if any of them?). Second, since contradictory truth claims greet us on every hand, truth claims need to be rationally tested. This invokes the field of epistemology, or the study of how we know what we know. While this chapter will not address epistemology directly, it is imperative to note that no epistemology works independently of a theory of truth.[16] Therefore, a rational theory of truth is required for a rational and truth-seeking epistemology, whether it is applied to philosophy, theology or any other discipline.

Meaning and truth. Before assessing the four leading theories of truth,

---

a construct in reference to future claims as much as it does to present claims. Moreover, the authors want us to believe that their statements about eschatological reality are true *right now*. If so, these words must be more than mere social constructions. If so, it also follows that we do not—as they claim—inhabit a "linguistic world of our own making," but that we have some cognitive claim on the "world-in-itself." So, their perspective seems self-contradictory: they presuppose a view of truth that they explicitly deny. Their perspective echoes themes from Jürgen Moltmann and Wolfhart Pannenberg. For a critique of Pannenberg's and Moltmann's eschatology and overall worldview, see Carl F. H. Henry, "Shall We Surrender the Supernatural?" in *God, Revelation, and Authority*, 6 vols. (Waco, Tex.: Word, 1976-1983), vol. 6.

[16]The epistemology of worldview testing is given in chap. 3, "Apologetic Method."

a word is in order on the matter of meaning. For a statement to either be true or false—however we understand the concepts of truth and falsity—it must be meaningful; that is, it must put forth an understandable truth claim. It must stake out a share of reality conceptually and be intelligible. For example, the statement "Green ideas sleep furiously" is neither true nor false, because it doesn't advance any statement about anything. The statement may be grammatical, but it is, nonetheless, meaningless. The statement "God is three-in-one" (made by Christians) is meaningful. The statement "God is not three-in-one" (made by Muslims) is meaningful.[17] The statement "There is no God" (made by atheists) is meaningful. The statement "There are many gods" is meaningful.[18] Of course, these statements cannot all be true. At most only one of these statements can be true.[19]

Of course, one must correctly interpret the meaning of any given statement if that statement's truth claim is to be discerned and assessed. The refutation of a misinterpreted statement leaves the truth or falsity of that statement untouched. This holds true for entire worldviews as well. Many have misinterpreted the meaning of certain aspects of Christianity and so have attributed to it claims of wrongdoing for which it is not guilty. By failing to discern the meaning of Christianity's claims, some have thus rejected it unfairly.[20] In fact, any worldview that is caricatured and then criticized on that basis has not been fairly interrogated.

The correspondence theory of truth. Although it can become quite technical in some of its details, the correspondence view of truth—often referred to as realism—is commonsensical and employed at least implicitly by anyone who affirms something about reality.[21] Aristotle got to the heart of the matter centuries ago:

> To say of what is that it is not, or of what is not that it is, is false, while to

---

[17]Some have taken the doctrine to be contradictory, but few have claimed it was meaningless.

[18]See Douglas Groothuis, "Meaning," in *Encyclopedia of Empiricism*, ed. Don Garrett and Edward Barbanell (Westport, Conn.: Greenwood Press, 1997), pp. 244-46.

[19]These statements do not cover all the logical possibilities with respect to metaphysics.

[20]See Philip J. Sampson, *Six Modern Myths About Christianity and Western Civilization* (Downers Grove, Ill.: InterVarsity Press, 2000), and chap. 5 of this book.

[21]Not all who hold to some version of realism are happy to endorse what is called the correspondence view of truth, but these differences are fairly technical and do not affect the material that follows. See Alvin Goldman, *Knowledge in a Social World* (New York: Oxford University Press, 1999), p. 60.

say of what is that it is, and of what is not that it is not, is true; so that he who says of anything that it is, or that it is not, will say either what is true or what is false.[22]

A belief or statement is true only if it matches with, reflects or corresponds to the reality it refers to. For a statement to be true it must be factual. Facts determine the truth or falsity of a belief or a statement. It is the nature and meaning of truth to be fact dependent. In other words, for a statement to be true, there must be a *truth-maker* that determines its truth. A statement is never true simply because someone thinks it or utters it. We may be entitled to our own opinions, but we are not entitled to our own facts. Believing a statement is one thing; that statement being true is another. In this sense truth is an achievement. Not all truth candidates are elected by reality. Some are defeated. Not all statements hit their targets. Some are off the mark. For epistemologist Alvin Goldman, the relationship of beliefs to truth is like betting on a horse race. Whether we bet, or on what horse we bet, is up to us. Who wins the race is not up to us. "Once you form a belief . . . its 'success' or 'failure' is not up to you; that is up to the world, which in general is independent of you."[23] In other words, "only the world [i.e., reality itself] confers truth and falsity."[24] A true statement, then, is a "descriptive success," which means that it is faithful to reality.[25] Another way of explaining this is that truth claims are intentional. This means that they are *about* something or *pertain* to something. They are *directed* at a state of affairs, and, if they are true, they capture that state of affairs conceptually. "God exists" is a statement about God's being there as opposed to being absent. God, then, is the intentional object of the intentional statement "God exists." If a statement fails to find its intentional object, it is false. An example is

---

[22]Aristotle *Metaphysics* 4.7.

[23]Goldman, *Knowledge in a Social World*, p. 20. In some limited cases, however, one can make a belief or statement true by something one does or says. For instance, if I say, "I am speaking now," my saying this makes the statement true. Similarly, some utterances make their contents true, as when a minister says, "I now pronounce you husband and wife." (Technically, this is called a "performative utterance.") Or predictions can help make statements come true, as when someone says to a tennis player that she will win the match, and this, in fact, helps give her the courage to win the match (see ibid., p. 21). But in the cases of the truth of worldviews concerning matters of God, humanity, salvation and eternity, these kinds of conditions do not obtain.

[24]Ibid., p. 21.

[25]Ibid., p. 60.

"Albert Gore won the 2000 U.S. presidential election."[26]

Matters become trickier when we speak of the truth or falsity of statements made in the future tense; that is, when we make predictions about things that do not yet exist. This is not abstruse metaphysics with no purchase on the present. We want and need to know if certain promises are true, particularly those relating to cosmic history and personal immortality. In these cases we can't claim that the statement "Jesus will come again" is true on the basis that it *now* corresponds to a present or past objective event, since the event of the second coming is future. This differs from the statement "Jesus lived in ancient Palestine," since that is a past event of objective history. Yet in the case of the second coming, the claim is meaningful: it stipulates intelligible states of affairs, and it is certainly true that either Jesus will come back or he will not. Only one of these antithetical realities will happen. So, the statement is not exempted from the condition of being either true or false.[27] The particular truth value of the statement "Jesus will come again" is still based on its correspondence to God's perfect knowledge and infallible plan for the world. Moreover, according to the Christian worldview, the predictive statement will, at some unknown time in the future, correspond to the actual event of the second coming by being fulfilled in history.

The truth of moral and logical principles does not correspond to reality in the same way as do statements about observable empirical facts. The law (or principle) of noncontradiction is true not because it corresponds to any one slice of reality but because it corresponds to all of reality. The fact that nothing can be itself and not itself in the same way and in the same respect (A is not non-A) is a universal condition or requirement of existence. It is true at all times and at all places, and must be so. It is a necessary truth; it cannot be false. Further, the truth of the law of noncontradiction corresponds to the workings of God's mind. God is a God of truth and not of falsehood. God does not contradict himself and cannot deny himself. He

---

[26]On statements as intentional in relation to intentional objects, see J. P. Moreland and William Lane Craig, *Philosophical Foundations for a Christian Worldview* (Downers Grove, Ill.: InterVarsity Press, 2003), pp. 136-37.

[27]Some philosophers debate whether or not a statement about contingent truths concerning the future are true or false before the events they predict occur, but I will not take that up here. For a view that all statements are always true or false (with a fatalistic implication), see Richard Taylor, *Metaphysics*, 4th ed. (New York: Prentice Hall, 1990), pp. 63-67.

knows all things truly and knows that neither his being nor his creation can contain logical contradictions.

Moral statements are also true because they match reality. The statement "Adultery is wrong" is true because the statement corresponds to the objective, universal and absolute moral law revealed by God, which is in accordance with his eternally stable character and the character of his creation.[28] It therefore applies to all of reality—to all marriages. We don't verify the wrongfulness of murder in the same way we verify an individual fact of history; nonetheless, meaningful statements about morality are true or false, depending on whether they match the moral law. Another way that the truth of moral statements obtains is that they correspond not only to the moral *law* but to objective states of *value*. That is, acts of adultery have the objective moral property of wrongness (because they violate the moral law) whenever they occur. On the other hand, acts and attitudes of love in marriage—and in other divinely sanctioned relationships—have the moral value of being good (because they obey the moral law) whenever they occur.[29]

Truth, then, is an exclusive property that is not shared with all assertions. But what exactly possesses this property of truthfulness? What is the *truth-bearer*? A truth-bearer must be a unit of conceptual meaning. To grasp this, we need to distinguish sentences from propositions. A sentence may be written, spoken or thought in the mind (without an external linguistic indicator). Declarative sentences, unlike questions or commands, stake claims on reality by stipulating that such and such is the case. A proposition is what a declarative sentence asserts; that is, what it means. Different sentences in the same language may have the same propositional content, such as "Jesus is the Lord" and "the Lord is Jesus." If a sentence is translated faithfully from one language to another—say, from New Testament Greek to an English translation—both sentences mean the same thing; that is, they assert the same proposition. Language cannot get on without propositions, since so much of language involves targeting facts with words.

---

[28]The relation of God and goodness is taken up in chap. 15.

[29]See Moreland and Craig, *Philosophical Foundations*, pp. 137-38. This paragraph assumes moral objectivism and God's character as the source of the objective moral law—claims that will be defended in chap. 15.

The biblical view of truth. The Bible does not set forth a technical view of truth, but it does implicitly and consistently advance the correspondence view in both Testaments. If the Bible had presented its own unique, idiosyncratic view of the basic nature of truth—one not generally shared by other worldviews—this would insulate and isolate the Bible from any assessment of its truth claims by outsiders, thus making apologetics impossible. Further, if Scripture had offered only a particular Christian account of the basic meaning of truth, Christianity would be "true" by definition, but only in a trivial sense.[30] Any other worldview could also claim its own view of truth and be so exempt from criticism.

The Hebrew and Greek words for truth are rich in meaning but have at their core the idea of conformity to fact.[31] Scripture also emphasizes that God is true to his truth, meaning that he is faithful and will not lie (Hebrews 6:18). God is a God of truth, whose word is truth (John 17:17). The Holy Spirit is "the Spirit of truth" (John 14:17; 15:26; 16:13) and so will teach us true things. Jesus, the Son of God, is "full of grace and truth" (John 1:14), and declared himself to be "the way and the truth and the life" and that no one could come to the Father apart from him (John 14:6). The prophets (Jeremiah 8:8), Jesus (Matthew 24:24) and the apostles (1 John 4:1-6) warn of those who pervert the truth of God through errors and lies. Hence, all of Scripture puts God's revealed objective truth at the solid center of spiritual and ethical life and faithfulness. God's truth must be learned (Acts 17:11), meditated upon (Psalm 119) and defended (1 Peter 3:15-17; Jude 3). Error must be addressed in love (2 Corinthians 10:3-5; 2 Timothy 2:24-26), whether it is theological or moral, and whether it concerns the false beliefs of unbelievers or the false beliefs of errant Christians.[32]

Versions of the correspondence view of truth have been held by the majority of ancient philosophers (Plato, Aristotle), medieval philosophers (Augustine, Anselm, Aquinas), modern philosophers (Descartes, Locke, Hume, Leibniz, Russell) and contemporary philosophers (John

---

[30]Ibid., p. 131. There is a specific Christian understanding of truth broadly understood, but this includes the commonsensical or classic view of truth as correspondence to reality.

[31]See Douglas Groothuis, *Truth Decay: Defending Christianity from the Challenges of Postmodernism* (Downers Grove, Ill.: InterVarsity Press, 2000), pp. 60-64.

[32]For much more on the biblical view of truth, see Groothuis, "The Biblical View of Truth," in *Truth Decay.*

Searle, William Alston, Alvin Goldman and Thomas Nagel). Nevertheless, two other theories of truth deserve some attention: postmodernist
and coherence.

Does truth exist? Postmodernist challenges. Is all this protracted musing
on the nature of truth just pretentious philosophizing that is out of touch
with contemporary realities? Is the imperious and singular truth something we should shed in favor of opening up the field to many truths?[33]

The case against the correspondence view of truth as it has been explained previously is an ancient one. The ancient philosopher Protagoras
claimed that "man is the measure of all things" instead of being measured
by them. Socrates, of course, didn't take this lying down. Instead, as related in Plato's *Theaeteus*, he quickly dismantled the claim by asking Protagoras a series of philosophically embarrassing questions. Protagoras was
a teacher, but who has anything to learn from an authority if we determine
truth and falsity by mere opinion? Moreover, does not Protagoras disagree
with those who deny his proposition? But how can he? "Man is the measure of all things" means that each man is his own measure and there is no
measurement apart from each person's measuring.[34] Despite this ancient
refutation of Protagoras, the spirit of his thinking has been reincarnated
(with a few twists) in a host of postmodernist philosophers, historians and
sociologists of recent decades.

In a nutshell postmodernism holds that truth is not determined by its
connection to objective reality but by various social constructions devised
for different purposes. Put another way, various cultures have their own
"language games," which describe reality very differently. However, we
cannot adjudicate which language game or which linguistic "map" correlates more correctly with reality, since we cannot get beyond our own cultural conditioning. But instead of affirming skepticism (there is an objective reality, but we have no access to it), postmodernists typically affirm
that there is no knowable objective reality apart from our languages and
concepts. To say we know the objective truth about ultimate issues is to set
up a "metanarrative" that is intrinsically oppressive and exploitative (Jean-

---

[33]I have addressed the case against the classical view of truth in "The Truth About Truth," in
Truth Decay.

[34]For a very clear treatment of this issue, see Ronald Nash, *Life's Ultimate Questions* (Grand
Rapids: Zondervan, 1999), pp. 231-32.

François Lyotard). Various "interpretive communities" (Stanley Fish) determine their own truth. Texts, whether religious or otherwise, do not have any fixed, objective meaning; therefore they are neither true nor false in themselves (Jacques Derrida). Truth is what our colleagues will let us get away with (Richard Rorty) or what the power structures deem to be so (Michel Foucault). Finally, there is no "God's-eye view" of anything; therefore, there is no objective truth.

Postmodernist claims come in various forms and should be evaluated individually, but, since they all reject the correspondence view of truth, they are all subject to several general criticisms.[35] First, metanarratives are not oppressive by virtue of being comprehensive truth claims (or worldviews). At some level, everyone has a worldview or a take on how the world is and how it works. These views may or may not be oppressive toward those who do not hold the worldview. That is a question of the intellectual content (or truth claims) of the worldview in question. The Marxist worldview historically has been very oppressive and unliberating, despite propaganda to the contrary. The Wahhabi version of Islam, the ideology of Osama bin Laden and his destructive followers, fueled the atrocities of September 11, 2001, and similar horrors globally. The Christian worldview, while frequently distorted, is not intrinsically oppressive given its ethic of incarnation, love and justice.

Second, postmodernist pronouncements on rejecting objective truth tend to contradict themselves in that they claim to be applicable to reality itself, not merely to their own language game or constructed map. Yet this is just what postmodernists themselves claim cannot be done. For example, the claim that all metanarratives are oppressive is itself a metanarrative or large-scale explanation of reality. Therefore, these kinds of claims are self-refuting and false. Moreover, while deconstructionists of various stripes claim that texts have no fixed and objective meaning, they still object when others "misinterpret" their own writings. But this presupposes a *proper* interpretation—based on the author's intended meaning—which becomes the objective standard by which to judge interpretations. If so, the central postmodernist claim about the endless plasticity of texts cannot be true.[36]

---

[35]For detailed analysis of Derrida, Foucault, Fish and Rorty, see Millard Erickson, *Truth or Consequences* (Downers Grove, Ill.: InterVarsity Press, 2001).
[36]See Millard Erickson, *Postmodernizing the Faith: Evangelical Responses to the Challenge of Post-*

Third, right-thinking people judge certain acts—such as racism, female genital mutilation, rape, child abuse, the murderous terrorist attacks on America on September 11, 2001—as objectively evil, as atrocities, and not as merely relative social constructions. If such assessments are correct, then the postmodern view cannot be sustained logically, since in the postmodernist account there are no objective moral facts but only endlessly differing interpretations. As some have unwisely said, "One person's terrorist is another person's freedom fighter." This may be so on a descriptive level—there are differing opinions on the moral status of the perpetrators of violence—but it makes no *objective judgment* about the moral status of the persons involved.

Fourth, by emphasizing the irresolvable diversity of truth claims, postmodernism provides no reliable criteria to *test* these claims against reality. Instead, it succumbs to a kind of intellectual indifference. Truth is what you (or your culture) make it, nothing more. This stance thwarts the fundamental concern for truth discussed so far in this book. Although postmodernists have no objective criteria by which to evaluate truth claims, they nevertheless make objective moral judgments—in spite of themselves. After the *New York Times* editorialized against postmodernism in the wake of the terrorist apocalypse of September 11, 2001,[37] Stanley Fish claimed in an op-ed piece later in the same newspaper that his postmodern view did, in fact, allow him to make moral judgments against such acts. However, he admitted that he had no objective criteria by which to level such judgments and that none were available.[38] If so, his judgments are nothing more than subjective assertions of value that are posited within an objective value vacuum.[39]

Although no major religion adheres to the postmodern view of truth, this frame of mind has affected how many people view religious expression. In nations with religious freedom (especially the United States), the default position for many citizens is that religion is a matter of choice, taste

---

offmodernism (Grand Rapids: Baker, 1998), p. 156.

[37]Edward Rothstein, "Attacks on U.S. Challenge Postmodern True Believers," *New York Times*, September 22, 2001, p. A17.

[38]Stanley Fish, "Condemnation Without Absolutes," *New York Times*, October 15, 2001 <www.nytimes.com/2001/10/15/opinion/15FISH.html>.

[39]Alvin Plantinga develops the absurdity of this kind of postmodern relativism (against Richard Rorty in particular) in "The Twin Pillars of Christian Scholarship," in *Seeking Understanding: The Stobb Lectures, 1986-1998* (Grand Rapids: Eerdmans, 1998), pp. 129-34.

and preference. Dialoging about one religion being true or another false is beside the point. All are "true" in the postmodern sense because they give meaning and direction to people's lives. However, when it comes to certain Muslim beliefs on the duty to die in a jihad against the Western "infidels," postmodernist "tolerance" may begin to crack open. A total relativism concerning religious belief is difficult to sustain.

The postmodernist view also bears on the increasing tendency of some contemporary people to create their own religions (or "spirituality") by mixing and matching elements of several religions, however incompatible these may be. If spiritual truth is a matter of social or individual construction, then one need not be constrained by logical consistency or by adherence to a received tradition (say Buddhist, Jewish, Christian or Islamic). There is an element of pragmatism here as well. If it "works" for someone to combine elements of Hinduism (the practice of yoga) and Christianity (church attendance, the golden rule and prayer), one need not worry about intellectual consistency or spiritual fidelity to an ancient tradition or revealed authority.[40] But this smorgasbord approach lacks intellectual integrity because it makes religious belief something to use instead of something to discover and live by.

Postmodernity often erodes religious confidence. What results is a free-floating spirituality largely devoid of certainty or sustained convictions. The sheer number of religious options combined with the intellectual superficiality of much contemporary religious expression encourages a less committed and less thought out kind of religious believing. This is seen in the shift from "religion" to "spirituality." Religion is deemed too structured, authoritative, exclusive and rigid. Spirituality, on the other hand, is more customized, subjective, inclusive and open to pragmatic experimentation. Sociologist Robert Wuthnow speaks of Americans moving from an orientation of "dwelling" within an established religious worldview and set of practices to a spirituality of "seeking," wherein they "negotiate among competing glimpses of the sacred, seeking partial knowledge and practical wisdom."[41] This tentativeness is

---

[40]On the worldview and dangers of yoga, see Douglas Groothuis, *Confronting the New Age* (Downers Grove, Ill.: InterVarsity Press, 1988), pp. 76-83; and Brad Scott, "Yoga: Exercise or Religion?" *Watchman Expositor* 18, no. 2 (2001) <www.watchman.org/na/yogareligion.htm>.

[41]Robert Wuthnow, *After Heaven: Spirituality in America Since the 1950s* (Berkeley: University of California Press, 1998), p. 3.

reflected in our language about spiritual concerns. When someone holds strong convictions on religious matters he or she will speak of them (or of the most important ones) in terms of "knowledge," "certainty" and other cognitively strong notions. This is what sociologist Peter Berger calls "firm objectivations," which are "capable of supporting world views and ideas with a firm status of objective reality within the consciousness of their adherents."[42] Yet when a social consensus that makes religious beliefs plausible breaks down, religious language also loses its intellectual strength. Instead of the "knowledge of God," we speak of "beliefs," "opinions" or "feelings" instead. Rather than speaking of faith as a way of confident knowing, we speak of the "leap of faith," along with "religious preference."[43] These kinds of tentative references reveal what Berger calls "the deobjectivation of the religious tradition."[44] Deobjectivation indicates a common tendency exhibited by those suffering under the pressures of postmodern pluralism.

Coherence theories inadequate. Coherence theories of truth argue that what makes a statement or belief true is its coherence or consistency with other beliefs. If my "web of belief" is large and internally consistent—that is, if none of my beliefs contradict each other—my beliefs are true. A belief is false if it fails to cohere with the rest of my beliefs. In other words, truth is defined simply as logical coherence.

The main problem with this view is that a set of beliefs held by fallible human beings may be coherent but false. Suppose all the evidence in a murder case indicates that the defendant is guilty, but the evidence has been rigged against an innocent person. Then the evidence is false precisely because it fails to hook up with reality. Further, it is possible for two worldviews each to be internally consistent logically and still contradict each other regarding core truth claims. Even if Islam and Christianity were both internally consistent, they could not both be true in essential beliefs, since Christianity is trinitarian and incarnational, and Islam is not. Moreover, two contrasting but internally consistent scientific theories may describe and explain the same phenomena in very different ways. Both

---

[42]Peter Berger, *Facing Up to Modernity: Excursions in Society, Politics, and Religion* (New York: Basic Books, 1977), p. 174.
[43]Ibid.
[44]Ibid.

geocentrism and heliocentrism may be formulated in logically consistent forms. Yet both cannot be true.

Worse yet, on the coherence theory, one may hold to the correspondence view of truth coherently. Therefore, the correspondence theory—a view that contradicts the coherence theory—would then be true. This indicates that something is badly amiss with the coherence account of truth.

Coherence or logical consistency cannot be what makes a truth claim true, although logical coherence is a necessary and negative test for truth. That is, if a worldview contains core beliefs that contradict each other, that worldview must be false. The logical test of coherence, however, concerns epistemology (theory of knowledge), not the nature of truth per se.[45]

Pragmatism: Not a useful theory of truth. Pragmatic theories of truth have been advanced (in somewhat different forms) by American philosophers such as Charles Peirce, William James and John Dewey. Richard Rorty, although considered a postmodernist by many, is an heir to the pragmatist legacy as well and has influenced at least one evangelical writer significantly.[46] To simplify a bit, the general pragmatic understanding of truth is that a belief is true only if it produces desirable or beneficial effects in the long run.[47] Something is true because it works in various ways found to be favorable. This theory of truth dispenses with considerations beyond some kind of utility. According to William James, a belief's "cash value in experiential terms" is all that counts.[48] The pragmatic *definition* of truth should not be confused with the means by which a claim may be verified or falsified by experience or evidence. The ways that truth is discovered or verified concern *epistemology*. The pragmatic view of truth, however, is a *metaphysical* claim. It maintains that truth *is* what works, not that actual living demonstrates some things to be true and some things to be false (an epistemological claim).

---

[45]For more critical analysis of the coherence view of truth, see Moreland and Craig, *Philosophical Foundations*, pp. 142-44.

[46]See Philip Kenneson, "There Is No Such Thing as Objective Truth and It's a Good Thing, Too," in *Christian Apologetics in the Postmodern World*, ed. Timothy Phillips and Dennis Okholm (Downers Grove, Ill.: InterVarsity Press, 1995), pp. 155-70.

[47]This section of the chapter cannot do justice to the different views of truth given by Peirce, James and Dewey. For a detailed treatment see Gertrude Ezorsky, "Pragmatic Theories of Truth," in *The Encyclopedia of Philosophy*, ed. Paul Edwards (New York: Macmillan, 1967), 6:427-30.

[48]William James, *The Moral Philosophy of William James*, ed. John K. Roth (New York: Thomas Crowell, 1969), p. 295.

Defining truth in terms of positive outcomes is untenable for several reasons. Bertrand Russell, among others, provides some helpful reflections on the central claims of the pragmatic view of truth, particularly that of William James. These criticisms are apropos for the navigator of the contemporary postmodern intellectual landscape as well, since when a person drops the correspondence view of truth, pragmatic considerations loom large in the selection and maintenance of belief.

According to Russell, James requires that a belief is deemed true when its effects are good, that is, when it "works." If this idea is to be useful (which is only fitting given the pragmatist's view of truth), we must know two things before we can know whether a belief is true: (1) what is good and (2) what the effects of this or that belief must be. For "it is only after we have decided that the effects of a belief are good that we have a right to call it 'true.'"[49] But this is deeply problematic. We must measure beliefs by usefulness, yet in many cases we just don't know ahead of time what the usefulness of a belief will be. Russell gives the example of believing that Columbus came to the New World in 1492. According to pragmatism, we cannot just look this up in a book. We have to determine what effects this belief will have on us. But how can we know this ahead of time?[50]

Added to this is the problem of knowing after the fact how beneficial our beliefs have been. Beliefs have consequences, no doubt, but determining just what the causal connections are between beliefs and effects and whether they are beneficial may be difficult in many cases. Russell gives an example: "It is far easier, it seems to me, to settle the plain question of fact: Have Popes always been infallible? than to settle the question whether the effects of thinking them infallible are on the whole good."[51]

Moreover, what does it mean for an idea to "work"? Arthur Lovejoy pointed out that James seems to confuse two senses of what this means. One view is that a theory is verified if it makes true predictions about events. There is nothing objectionable about that. Those who predicted that George W. Bush would win the 2000 presidential election were proved right when he was so elected. In that sense, their prediction worked

---

[49]Bertrand Russell, *A History of Western Philosophy* (New York: Touchstone, 1967), p. 817.
[50]Ibid., p. 817.
[51]Bertrand Russell, *Philosophical Essays* (London: Longmans, Green, 1910), p. 135.

by being factually verified (which, of course, presupposes the correspondence view of truth). But "working" could also mean simply that the effects of believing that Bush would be elected are deemed valuable to the individual. Certainly, optimism lifts the soul, but optimistic thoughts are either true or false (in light of the facts), irrespective of how happy or fulfilled they may make someone feel.[52]

Russell disputes James's contention that the meaning of truth is simply its ability to produce desirable states of affairs. This ignores the common meaning of truth. Consider the difference between two statements: (1) Other people exist. (2) It is useful to believe that other people exist. If James's view of truth were correct, (1) and (2) would have the same meaning; they would be synonymous. That is, they would express the same proposition, since James *defines truth as usefulness*. But they clearly do not. Therefore, the meaning of truth cannot be a belief's usefulness, even though some beliefs are more useful or fruitful than others.[53]

Furthermore, a belief may "work" and not be true. A woman may believe she lost a large sum of money due to being disorganized. Taken aback, she reforms her life, gets organized and becomes a successful businesswoman. Later, however, she discovers that the money she thought she lost was in fact stolen by a roommate. Her belief that she lost the money was false, however fruitful the consequence of that false belief may have been.[54]

What makes a belief true, according to the correspondence theory, is that it matches reality. So, what makes it true that Columbus came to the New World in 1492? It is true because this event occurred in the fifteenth century. This historical fact is what makes my belief true; it is the truthmaker. The effects of this belief are irrelevant to its truth value. But James claims that "on pragmatic principles, if the hypothesis of God works satisfactorily in the widest sense of the word, it is 'true.'"[55] In fact, James thought that various and conflicting religious beliefs could "work" and thus be "true" on the pragmatic theory.[56]

---

[52]Arthur Lovejoy, "The Thirteen Pragmatisms, II," *Journal of Philosophy* 5 (1908): 29-39, cited in Ezorsky, "Pragmatic Theories of Truth," p. 428.

[53]Russell, *Philosophical Essays*, p. 135.

[54]The inspiration for this example comes from Winfried Corduan, *No Doubt About It* (Nashville: Broadman & Holman, 1997), pp. 60-61.

[55]James, *The Moral Philosophy of William James*, p. 339.

[56]William James, *Essays on Pragmatism* (New York: Havner, 1955), pp. 159-76.

Those postmodern evangelicals who abandon the correspondence view of truth often appeal to the meaningfulness of Christian community—its language, symbols, rites, traditions and fellowship—instead of any apologetic method that might verify the objective truth of Christianity over against rival worldviews.[57] These postmodernist evangelicals would have very little to say that would be persuasive to a member of another religious group (say, a Mormon) who finds their group meaningful and "true" in a pragmatic sense. Russell's comments on this pragmatic conception of religion are on target:

> This simply omits as unimportant the question whether God really is in His heaven; if He is a useful hypothesis, that is enough. God the Architect of the Cosmos is forgotten; all that is remembered is belief in God, and its effects upon the creatures inhabiting our petty planet. No wonder the Pope condemned the pragmatic defense of religion.[58]

G. K. Chesterton compactly dispensed with pragmatism as a theory of truth by discerning an ironic contradiction within it. He observed that the pragmatists are correct in affirming that humans should attend to those truths that bear on their lives: "There is an authoritative need to believe the things that are necessary to the human mind. But I say that one of those necessities precisely is a belief in objective truth." While the pragmatist tells us to disregard anything absolute, the concept of absolute truth is most necessary to thought. Thus, the pragmatist, who professes to have a humanly oriented and highly relevant philosophy, "makes nonsense of the human sense of actual fact."[59]

In light of these objections, it should be evident that the pragmatic theory does not describe the nature of truth, nor can it slake the soul's deepest thirst for reality. However, if a belief is true to reality, it should produce effects in keeping with its promises. A true worldview should be livable; it should not commit us to perpetual intellectual and moral frustration. If it does, something is amiss. But this is one of several *tests* for truth (in the area of epistemology). Pragmatic results do not *determine* the

---

[57]This perspective is evident in the later work of the late Stanley Grenz. For a critique of some of his statements to this effect, see Groothuis, *Truth Decay*, pp. 116-17.

[58]Russell, *A History of Western Philosophy*, p. 818. For Russell's positive views of truth, see "Truth and Falsehood," *The Problems of Philosophy* (1912; reprint, New York: Barnes & Noble, 2004).

[59]G. K. Chesterton, *Orthodoxy* (1908; reprint, New York: Image, 1959), pp. 36-37. For a similar judgment, see, Martin Buber, *The Eclipse of God* (New York: Harper & Row, 1952), p. 70.

truth of a belief. Therefore, the pragmatic theory of truth is false and should be rejected—by evangelicals and anyone else serious about matters of truth and falsity.

Cosmic impiety. Any concept of truth that deems truth to be somehow dependent on our culture or our minds or wills makes truth into something that we (either collectively or individually) create and control. This is the case for all views of truth that abandon correspondence as the essence and meaning of truth. This disregard for reality encourages what Russell called "cosmic impiety."

> The concept of "truth" as something dependent upon facts largely outside human control has been one of the ways in which philosophy hitherto has inculcated the necessary element of humility. When this check is removed, a further step is taken on the road towards a certain kind of madness—the intoxication with power.[60]

Russell is on to something deep and rich—a truth about truth and untruth. When people untether themselves from any responsibility to get reality right, to be true to the truth come what may, they forfeit the humility of being beholden to a reality outside of themselves—a reality that may prove then right or wrong, but which they do not command. People must rather obey—or disobey. Whether an atheist or a theist or anything else, cosmic piety means submission to the truth of the cosmos—and whatever may be beyond it as well.

CORRESPONDENCE: VINDICATED AND ESSENTIAL

Examined against the standard of the correspondence theory of truth, the postmodern, coherence and pragmatic theories of truth clearly fall short.[61] A culture may construct beliefs that grant it meaning and significance—for example, the idea that if one perishes in an Islamic jihad, one goes directly to paradise—yet those beliefs may be false in light of the facts. A set of beliefs may be internally coherent and not match reality. A set of beliefs

---

[60]Russell, *History of Western Philosophy*, p. 828.
[61]This chapter does not cover all the theories of truth, but does, I think, address those most likely to be addressed in apologetic endeavors. Another view of truth being discussed in philosophical circles is called minimalism or the deflationary account of truth. See Daniel Stoljar, "The Deflationary View of Truth," *The Stanford Encyclopedia of Philosophy* <http://plato.stanford.edu/entries/truth-deflationary>.

may produce some good outcomes (at least in this life) and fail to connect with reality in important ways. We are, then, left with the reality of the truth—truth that is intransigent and resistant to any coercion. Christians, of all people, must strongly affirm the notion that truth is what corresponds to reality—and must do so unswervingly, whatever the postmodern (or other) winds of doctrine may be blowing in our faces.

Why Truth Matters Most

Searching for Truth in Postmodern Times

THE WORD *TRUTH* IS A STAPLE IN EVERY LANGUAGE.[1] We cannot imagine a human language lacking the concept of truth. Such a language would never inform anyone of anything; it would lack any intellectual access to reality. No language *qua* language could be so constrained (although some political and celebrity "discourse" comes close). The idea of truth is part of the intellectual oxygen we breathe. Whenever we state an opinion, defend or critique an argument, ask a question, or investigate one kind of assertion or another, we presuppose the concept of truth—even if we don't directly state the word, even if we deny that truth is real or knowable.

The notion of truth haunts us, ferreting out our shabby thinking, our lame excuses, our willful ignorance and our unfair attacks on the views of others, both the living and the dead. Conversely, when our own ideas are misrepresented or our personal character falsely maligned, we object by appealing to something firm that should settle the issue—namely, the truth. Truth seems to stand over us like a silent referee, arms folded confidently, ears open, eyes staring intently and authoritatively into everything and missing nothing. Even when an important truth seems out of reach on vital matters, we yearn for it as we yearn for a long-lost friend or the parent we never knew. Yet when the truth unmasks and convicts us, and we refuse to return its gaze, we seek to banish it in favor of our own self-serving and protective version of reality.

This chapter develops a general apologetic for the significance and

---

[1]An earlier version of this chapter was originally published as "Why Truth Matters Most: An Apologetic for Truth-Seeking in Postmodern Times," in *Journal of the Evangelical Theological Society* 47, no. 3 (2004): 441-54.

value of both objective truth and truth seeking.[2] Many works of Christian apologetics assume that unbelievers want to know the truth but are unaware of good arguments to that end. While good arguments for Christian truth claims are indispensable, they are not sufficient. Many unbelievers never seriously consider these arguments simply because they are unconcerned with truth.

Reflecting on Jeremiah 17:1-5, Eugene Peterson notes that "the presumption here is that the kinds of lives we lead, who we are, not just what we do, are huge factors influencing our access to truth, any truth, but especially the Truth that is God." In other words, "The understanding of the knower must be *adequate* to the thing being known."[3] Many in the postmodern world have given up on the existence of objective truth entirely and so find no need to pursue it. There is, therefore, an apologetic need and duty both to defend the concept of a knowable and objective truth philosophically (which was done in chap. 6) and to commend the virtues requisite to attaining it.

In the pursuit of an honest reckoning with truth for apologetic purposes, we will discuss (1) the relationship of truth, self-deception and personal virtue, (2) the will to disbelieve, (3) how humility relates to the quest for truth, (4) the vice of intellectual apathy, (5) the truth-avoiding temptations of diversions, and (6) the truth-attracting possibilities of silence.

TRUTH, SELF-DECEPTION AND VIRTUE

We all have some intuition of the meaning of truth, even if we cannot articulate it very well philosophically. Truth is something we may know or fail to know, but it is not something we should try to manipulate according to our own desires, fears, whims or hatreds. Winston Churchill quipped that "men occasionally stumble over the truth, but most of them pick themselves up and hurry off as if nothing had happened." This barb underscores the value of truth to life. Brushing away truth in the rush and tumble of life is somehow wrong—and we know it. If so, there must be another way of life that seeks, honors and is willing to submit to truth,

---

[2]For more on the postmodern view of truth, see Douglas Groothuis, *Truth Decay: Defending Christianity Against the Challenges of Postmodernism* (Downers Grove, Ill.: InterVarsity Press, 2000), and the treatment of this in chap. 6 of this book.
[3]Eugene Peterson, *Subversive Spirituality* (Grand Rapids: Eerdmans, 1997), p. 81.

especially concerning matters of supreme consequence.

This orientation requires a kind of courage—one of the classical virtues—since the truth may not be what we would prefer. It is revealing that so many people today express approval by saying, "I'm comfortable with that," and disapproval by saying, "I'm not comfortable with that." Comfort is important when it comes to furniture and headphones, but it is irrelevant when it comes to truth.

Conversely, the pursuit of truth requires that we must shun sloth—one of the classical vices—since truth may be tucked under the surface of things and not be easily ascertainable. Moreover, studiousness should be cultivated instead of mere curiosity. Curiosity may be no more than lust for what we need not know (or should not know), and it may driven by ulterior motives such as vanity, pride or restlessness. Curiosity is not intrinsically good, because it can lead to gossip, violations of privacy (snooping) and wasted time and effort—as represented by the content of any issue of *People* magazine. In other words, curiosity can be a vice, despite the fact that it is a principal passion (or lust) of contemporary Western culture. Studiousness, on the other hand, earnestly inquires after what ought to be known in ways fitting the subject matter. Studiousness sniffs out its own areas of ignorance and pursues knowledge prudently, patiently and humbly—not resting until what needs to be known has been pursued to its end. Thus, we labor to avoid both gullibility (holding too many false beliefs) and extreme skepticism (missing out on too many true beliefs).[4]

While Jesus frequently engaged in intellectual arguments, he was acutely sensitive to the moral status of those with whom he was communicating, realizing that the state of a person's soul affected his or her ability to know certain things.[5] The Gospel of John reports Jesus saying to some unbelieving religious leaders, "I have come in my Father's name, and you do not accept me; but if someone else comes in his own name, you will accept him. How can you believe [in me] since you accept glory from one another?" (John 5:43-44). Jesus claimed that an unhealthy concern for approval or status could impede proper judgment—in this case, a sober

---

[4]On this see the classic essay "The Will to Believe," in William James, *The Will to Believe* (New York: Dover, 1956).

[5]On this see Douglas Groothuis, "Jesus' Use of Argument," in *On Jesus* (Belmont, Calif.: Wadsworth, 2003).

assessment of his own identity and the proper response to it. After discussing the love that God manifested in "his one and only Son" in order to provide eternal life to those who trust in him, Jesus went on to reflect on those who will not avail themselves of this gift and why. His language is stark and gripping.

> This is the verdict: Light has come into the world, but people loved darkness instead of light because their deeds were evil. Everyone who does evil hates the light, and will not come into the light for fear that their deeds will be exposed. But whoever lives by the truth comes into the light, so that it may be seen plainly that what they have done has been done in the sight of God. (John 3:19-21)

We must be ruthless with ourselves in the process of pursuing truth, given the manifold temptations to self-deception and denial. The well-respected physicist Richard Feynman highlighted this imperative in his 1974 commencement speech at the California Institute of Technology. After discussing scientific integrity, Feynman said, "The first principle is that you must not fool yourself—and you are the easiest person to fool. So you have to be very careful about that. After you've not fooled yourself, it's easy not to fool other scientists."[6] After offering a parable concerning the danger of seeking worldly benefit instead of loving God, Kierkegaard warns of "failing to invest your life upon that which lasts: to love God in truth, come what may, with the consequence that in this life you will suffer under the hands of men. Therefore, do not deceive yourself! Of all deceivers fear most yourself!"[7]

THE WILL TO DISBELIEVE

But not all exercise this healthy fear of self-deception. The great essayist and novelist Aldous Huxley (1894-1963) gives us a window into the machinations of the human soul in this candid revelation about the philosophy of his youth.

> I took it for granted that there was no meaning. This was partly due to the

---

[6]Richard Feynman, *Surely You're Joking, Mr. Feynman: Adventures of a Curious Character* (New York: Bantam, 1989), p. 313.
[7]Søren Kierkegaard, "An Eternity in Which to Repent," in *Provocations: Spiritual Writings of Kierkegaard*, ed. Charles Moore (Farmington, Penn.: Plough, 1999), p. 47. See also Jeremiah 17:9.

fact that I shared the common belief that the scientific picture of an abstraction from reality was a true picture of reality as a whole; partly also to other non-intellectual reasons. I had motives for not wanting the world to have a meaning; consequently, I assumed that it had none, and was able without any difficulty to find satisfying reasons for this assumption.

Most ignorance is vincible ignorance. We don't know because we don't want to know. It is our will that decides how and upon what subjects we shall use our intelligence. Those who detect no meaning in the world generally do so because, for one reason or another, it suits their books that the world should be meaningless.[8]

Huxley coveted freedom from the received political, economic and sexual norms of his day, all of which were substantially influenced by Christianity. "There was one admirably simple method of confuting these people and at the same time justifying ourselves in our political and erotic revolt; we could deny that the world had any meaning whatsoever."[9]

In another noteworthy confession, contemporary philosopher Thomas Nagel admits that theism repulses him at a level deeper than its "objectionable moral doctrines, social policies, and political influence" or its "acceptance of empirical falsehoods."[10]

I am talking about something much deeper—namely the fear of religion itself. I speak from experience, being strongly subject to this fear myself: I want atheism to be true and am made uneasy by the fact that some of the most intelligent and well-informed people I know are religious believers. It isn't just that I don't believe in God and, naturally, hope that I'm right in my belief. It's that I hope there is no God! I don't want there to be a God; I don't want the universe to be like that.[11]

Nagel's candid pronouncements are not made in an intellectual void; he attempts to explain the existence of eternal moral and intellectual truths

---

[8]Aldous Huxley, *Ends and Means*, 3rd ed. (New York: Harper & Brothers, 1937), p. 312.
[9]Ibid.
[10]Nagel does not specify what he has in mind with these references. Concerning "empirical falsehoods," does he think that the Bible is committed to a flat earth or to geocentrism? If so, he is mistaken since references to "the four corners of the earth" or to "sunrise and sunset" can be viewed as phenomenological or perspectival language and not to physical specifics of cosmology. We still use these figures of speech today with full knowledge that the world is round and that the sun revolves around it.
[11]Thomas Nagel, *The Last Word* (New York: Oxford University Press, 1997), p. 130.

(against relativism) without recourse to theism.[12] Nevertheless, Nagel's visceral disclosure resembles the apostle Paul's description of those who, in opposition to the divine knowledge of which they have access, suppress the truth of God's existence, fail to give God thanks and thus become darkened in their understanding (see Romans 1:18-21).

Another great philosopher, equally hostile to the Christian worldview, also rejected the idea of an omniscient deity who peered into the human situation—apparently on the basis of the *argumentum ad horrendum* ("too horrible to be true"). Friedrich Nietzsche's (1844-1900) critique of Christianity is multifaceted, but his rejection of a personal God appears as much instinctive or dispositional as philosophical. Consider this statement from *Thus Spoke Zarathustra,* where the "ugliest man" speaks of God:

> But he had to die: he saw with eyes that saw everything; he saw man's depths and ultimate grounds, all his concealed disgrace and ugliness. His pity knew no shame: he crawled into my dirtiest nooks. This most curious, overobtrusive one had to die. He always saw me: on such a witness I wanted to have my revenge or not live myself. The god who saw everything, even man—this god had to die! Man cannot bear it that such a witness should live.[13]

This passionate statement is hardly a rational argument against God's existence; it is, rather, revulsion at the thought of a holy and all-knowing deity gazing into human uncleanness. It defies as much as it denies.

Nietzsche's observations emphasize the importance of honesty before reality, whether it is the face of God, a faceless and indifferent universe, or something else. On other occasions Nietzsche wrote equally passionately about the demands of truth.

> Truth has had to be fought for every step of the way, almost everything dear to our hearts, on which our lives and our trust in life depend, has had to be sacrificed to it. Greatness of soul is needed for it, the service of truth is the hardest service. For what does it mean to be honest in intellectual things? That one is stern toward one's heart, that one despises "fine feelings," that one makes every Yes and No a question of conscience![14]

---

[12]I find these arguments wanting (see Douglas Groothuis, "Thomas Nagel's 'Last Word' on the Metaphysics of Rationality and Morality," *Philosophia Christi*, series 2, 1, no. 1 [1999]: 115-22).

[13]Friedrich Nietzsche, *Thus Spoke Zarathustra*, in *The Portable Nietzsche*, ed. Walter Kaufmann (New York: Viking Press, 1975), p. 379. The book's hero, Zarathustra (a kind of atheistic antiprophet), speaking in Nietzsche's voice, approves of the speech.

[14]Nietzsche, *The AntiChrist*, section 50, in *The Portable Nietzsche*, ed. Walter Kaufmann (New

It is questionable that Nietzsche was able to reconcile his overall philosophy with a true respect for objective truth, yet the moral advice of this quote is worth pondering.[15]

An honest pilgrim on the path to truth will not recoil from truths that seem distasteful (or *argumentum ad horrendum*), since what is the case may or may not be pleasing to us.[16] Truth should be sought for its own sake, but also in tight relation to the intellectual flourishing of the individual. That is, there should be a conviction that it is best for us to follow truth wherever it leads, whatever the effect may be—and that this is the imperative for anyone with a modicum of intellectual rectitude. In a famous and poetic essay, "A Free Man's Worship," Bertrand Russell (1872-1970) articulated a worldview that was anything but cheerful. In one passionate half-page sentence he wrote that in this universe humanity appears as the result of blind causes "which had no prevision of the end they were achieving," and that all of a person's heroism, intensity of thought and feeling were futile to "preserve an individual beyond the grave." Indeed, "the whole temple of human achievement must inevitably be buried beneath the debris of a universe in ruins."[17] We should salute Russell's courage to face up to the implications of what he took to be true, whether or not we agree with his perspective. Indeed, his essay gives no *arguments* to support the conclusion of a godless world, but rather draws out the consequences of such a view.[18]

In a note related to his unfinished apologetic treatise, Blaise Pascal (1623-1662) laid down his goal for the work:

> I should, therefore, like to arouse in man the desire to find truth, to be ready, free from passion, to follow it wherever he may find it, realizing how far his knowledge is clouded by passions. I should like him to hate his concupiscence [lustful desire] which automatically makes his decisions for him,

York: Viking Press, 1975), p. 632.

[15]For a brief critique of Nietzsche's perspectivalism, see Groothuis, *Truth Decay* pp. 107-8; 198-202. In *Truth and Truthfulness* (New York: Princeton University Press, 2002), pp. 12-19, Bernard Williams claims that Nietzsche was not a perspectivist, but he glosses over several Nietzschean texts that seem to refute his theory.

[16]See Peter Geach, *Truth and Hope* (Notre Dame, Ind.: University of Notre Dame Press, 2001), p. 6.

[17]Bertrand Russell, *Why I Am Not a Christian and Other Essays on Religion and Related Subjects*, ed. Paul Edwards (New York: Simon & Schuster, 1957), p. 107.

[18]We will address this worldview in chap. 15.

so that it should not blind him when he makes his choice, nor hinder him once he has chosen.[19]

Pascal spoke further of the gravity of truth and the possibility of forfeiting it. "Truth is so obscured nowadays, and lies so well established, that unless we love the truth we shall never recognize it."[20] Moreover, once having recognized it, truth must have its way with us. "Weaklings are those who know the truth, but maintain it only as far as it is in their interest to do so, and apart from that forsake it."[21] As T. S. Eliot observed, "Humankind cannot bear very much reality."[22] It takes courage and fortitude to interpret existence aright.

TRUTH AND HUMILITY

When the quest for truth is successful, the virtuous person is humbled, not puffed up with pride. We do not create the truth; we can only discover it. Those who discover "the great things of the Gospel" (Jonathan Edwards) find a truth that is both humbling and ennobling. The saving truth of Jesus Christ is a gift of God's grace. As sinners, we can only receive it in humility. Yet Jesus declared that the gospel is a truth that sets us free (John 8:31-32). This Christ-wrought freedom for the Christian should not lead to timidity or uncertainty, but boldness to make known the only truth that will ever set anyone free (2 Timothy 1:7).

However, intellectual tentativeness about objective truth—held under the guise of "humility"—is sometimes advocated by evangelical writers. While rightly warning of the dangers of arrogance and triumphalism in apologetics, John Stackhouse affirms an attitude quite foreign to the great apologists of Christian history by claiming that Christianity cannot be known to be true "beyond a reasonable doubt."[23] Yet if this were the case there would be epistemic warrant for the Christian to doubt his or her faith on an ongoing basis—and without any resolution. One would not only be *reasonable* in so doing but would be unreasonable not to do so. While doubts can be an aid to a deeper faith, if they are properly

---

[19]Blaise Pascal, *Pensées* 119/423, ed. and trans. Alban Krailsheimer (New York: Penguin, 1966), p. 60.

[20]Ibid., 739/864, p. 256.

[21]Ibid., 740/583, p. 256.

[22]T. S. Eliot, *Murder in the Cathedral* (New York: Harcourt, Brace & World, 1963), p. 69.

[23]John Stackhouse, *Humble Apologetics* (New York: Oxford University Press, 2002), p. 111.

handled, a mandate to doubt would lead to a diminished Christian life.

He further claims that naturalism and Buddhism can be believed rationally.[24] If this were so, it is hard to see how a Christian could engage in fruitful apologetics with a Buddhist or a naturalist, since their view must be no less rational than the Christian's. Further, Buddhism and naturalism deny the existence of a personal Creator God in the biblical sense. If Buddhism and naturalism are rational, how does this square with Paul's affirmation that creation has given ample evidence of God's existence to all humans, but humans as sinners have suppressed this knowledge foolishly (Romans 1:18-21)?

After quoting 1 John 1:1-3, Stackhouse remarks that "John did not pretend to have cataloged the religious and philosophical options of the ancient world and to have judged Christianity somehow superior to others."[25] Although John did not offer a worldview catalog or a detailed argument for the superiority of Christianity over all other worldviews, John did, nevertheless, emphatically affirm on the basis of firsthand evidence the uniqueness and supremacy of Jesus Christ. This can be found in many passages in 1 John, such as 1 John 2:28; 4:13; 5:9-12, 14-15; and in the Gospel of John 1:1-3, 14, 18; 14:1-6. Moreover, John refutes the incipient Gnosticism (or proto-Gnosticism) of the day with his emphasis on Jesus' having "come in the flesh" (1 John 4:2; John 1:14). The suggestion that John's personal experience of Christ rendered his perspective less than certain is not warranted by this text or by any of John's writings. John exudes certitude in his letter and wants his readers to share in it.

But Stackhouse goes further, claiming that "postmodernity concurs" with 1 John 1:1-3 and that "no human being knows anything for certain."[26] This supposed humility is ill-advised for at least five reasons. First, the apostle John would never agree with the statement "No human being knows anything for certain," since he set forth hard evidence of Christ—not just as his own story or preference but in order to proclaim to others that Jesus Christ is God incarnate. Second, most postmodernists are not skeptics but nonrealists. Knowledge for them is not difficult but easy: just assent to the language game in which we find ourselves—unless we deem

---

[24]Ibid., p. 150.
[25]Ibid., p. 166.
[26]Ibid.; see also p. 232.

it a totalizing metanarrative—and stop worrying about objective truth. Third, Stackhouse asserts that he *knows* that no human being knows anything for certain. If Stackhouse is *certain* of this proposition, then it is not clear how he could know the proposition to be true. In fact, it is self-refuting. Fourth, there are plenty of counterexamples of propositions we know for certain—statements everyone agrees with (or should), such as (1) torturing the innocent merely for pleasure is always wrong, (2) the law of noncontradiction is universally true, (3) murder is wrong, (4) there are physical objects. Fifth, Scripture repeatedly promises that confident *knowledge of God* is possible for humans rightly related to their Maker (see Romans 8:15-16). Being "humble" in apologetics should not commit us to an epistemological quagmire. We may have justified certainty apart from absolute proof.[27]

Any intellectual quest is sabotaged by quarantining certainty at the outset. It is like injuring a horse before a race on the general principle that a strong, swift and healthy steed is too proud to compete fairly or honestly. We should assess the strength of a given conclusion on the basis of the arguments given to support that conclusion, not by stipulating some "humble" ideal that forswears certitude in principle and in perpetuity. After the dust of a good argument settles, we may err by either understating or overstating the force of our conclusions. If we understate, we are not being humble but timid. If we overstate, we may be too proud to admit the limits and weakness of the argument. The ideal is neither timidity nor grandiosity. Honest and rational truth seeking should set the agenda.

In 1908, the prolific Christian apologist, novelist and essayist G. K. Chesterton faced a similar worry about the use of humility to forestall argument. "Humility," he wrote, "was largely meant as a restraint upon the arrogance and infinity of the appetites of man."[28] For anyone to enjoy the grandeur and largeness of the world, "he must be always making himself small." But Chesterton worried that humility had moved from "the organ of ambition" to "the organ of conviction, where it was never meant to be. A man was meant to be doubtful about himself, but undoubting about the truth; this has been exactly reversed." Instead of true humility, one may

---

[27]Ibid., p. 166.
[28]G. K. Chesterton, *Orthodoxy* (1908; reprint, New York: Image Books, 1959), p. 31.

assert oneself, but doubt "what he ought not doubt—the Divine Reason."[29] Chesterton frets that "the new humility" might give up on finding truth through reason entirely.[30] Indeed, misplaced humility continues to bedevil discourse a hundred years after Chesterton's musings.[31] Certainty is no vice, as long as it is grounded in clear and cogent arguments, is held with grace, and is willing to entertain counterarguments sincerely.

While the postmodernist dismissals of objective truth end up ringing hollow and intellectually unsatisfying, the postmodernist suspicion of received metanarratives (or worldviews) has some point. Some of the grand narratives that inspired so many for so long in the twentieth century have been brought into question, particularly Freudianism and Marxism, both of which are intrinsically atheistic. Even the edifice of Darwinism is being challenged scientifically and philosophically. While we cannot reduce the concept of truth to power relationships and nothing more, the way in which cultures view truth and falsity is partially determined by who controls the discourse—or who "owns the microphone."[32] Views may be marginalized not because they are intrinsically illogical or lacking in evidence, but because they are threatening or subversive or simply out of style.

It is likewise true that even within a rationally supported worldview, some aspects of that system of belief may be reified or absolutized beyond reason. Even if we argue convincingly that Christianity is a rationally warranted worldview, it is still the case that some Christians have made improper judgments as to what their worldview entails. For example, some Christians supported slavery and female subjection as perpetual and God-ordained institutions when, in fact, they do not appear as such in Scripture itself. The postmodernist "hermeneutic of suspicion" calls us to reevaluate such claims to see if they may be based more on the vested interests of the powerful than on truth itself.[33] But this hermeneutic of suspicion itself must presuppose that the true can be separated from the false according to

---

[29]Ibid.

[30]Ibid., p. 32.

[31]The entire chapter from which these reflections are drawn, "The Suicide of Thought," is still amazingly pertinent to the contemporary intellectual situation. See ibid., pp. 30-45.

[32]See Phillip Johnson's reflections on this in relation to how the creation-evolution controversy is often handled in *Defeating Darwinism by Opening Minds* (Downers Grove, Ill.: InterVarsity Press, 1997), pp. 32-34.

[33]On the use and abuse of this method, see Merold Westphal, *Suspicion and Faith* (Grand Rapids: Eerdmans, 1993).

wise judgment. So, if we look back at the interpretation of Scripture held
by the Southern slave owners and traders, we discern that their reading
was adversely affected by their investment in the institution of slavery.
That is, both their hermeneutic and their racist views were wrong, false
and out of alignment with reality. The hermeneutic of suspicion cannot
properly function without the concept of objective truth.

APATHY AND TOLERANCE: ENEMIES OF TRUTH

Denizens of the twenty-first century may also be taken hostage to another
enemy of truth: intellectual apathy. Writing in the *Atlantic Monthly*, Jonathan Rauch coined the term *apatheism* to describe a relaxed attitude toward religion and irreligion that he takes to be laudable.[34] He is not alone.
Apatheism rests on a benign indifference, refusing to become passionate
about one's own beliefs or the beliefs of others. A person may have religious preferences, but they are not the engines of energetic commitment,
nor do they fuel controversy. This person is neither called nor driven by
these beliefs, but just has them. In apatheism, beliefs simply do not mean
that much, nor should they. Rauch defends this attitude by claiming that
apatheism is not a "lazy recumbency, like my collapse into a soft chair after
a long day." Rather, "it is the product of a determined cultural effort to
discipline the religious mindset, and often of an equally determined personal effort to master the spiritual passions. It is not a lapse. It is an
achievement."[35] He takes apatheism to be the antidote to both religious
extremism—so evident in the world of Islamic militancy—and the tyran-
nical secularism of the Chinese government.

Rauch's advocacy of apathy as the tonic to incivility is a clear case of a
virtue that has run amuck. That virtue is tolerance, which, as understood
by the American founders, is a kind of patience that refuses to hate or
disrespect those with whom we disagree, even when disagreement concerns the things that matter most. The ideal of tolerance, in the Western
classical liberal sense, is compatible with strong convictions on religious
matters and with raging controversies. In fact, John Locke, one of the
leading proponents of early modern tolerance, was himself a professing
Christian who engaged in apologetics. Rauch's notion of tolerance would

---

[34]Jonathan Rauch, "Let It Be," *The Atlantic Monthly*, May 2003, p. 34.
[35]Ibid.

exclude in principle the discovery of and adherence to any truths not found comfortable by people who place tranquility above *truth*. Moreover, his recommended attitude is antithetical to the teaching of all religions and sound philosophy: that we should care about our convictions and put them into practice consistently. Contemporary forms of tolerance tend to fall into the abyss warned of by novelist and apologist Dorothy Sayers when she wrote of the sixth deadly sin, *acedia* (or sloth).

> In the world it calls itself Tolerance; but in hell it is called Despair. It is the accomplice of the other sins and their worst punishment. It is the sin which believes nothing, cares for nothing, seeks to know nothing, interferes with nothing, enjoys nothing, loves nothing, hates nothing, finds purpose in nothing, lives for nothing, and only remains alive because there is nothing it would die for.[36]

Nevertheless, apatheism seems to be, if not epidemic, at least a widespread toxin in the United States. Rauch finds it in his "Christian friends who organize their lives around an intense and personal relation with God but who betray no sign of caring that I am an unrepentantly atheistic Jewish homosexual."[37] For the serious Christian, however, an attitude of apathy over the eternal destiny of another human being is not an option. Jesus warned the church of Laodicea that he was nauseated by their lukewarm (or apathetic) attitude (Revelation 3:14-16). For decades polls have consistently indicated that while belief in God is very high in America, and most people identify themselves as Christians, there is a dearth of knowledge of the Bible. Further, high percentages of "believers" are relativists whose behavior differs little from professed unbelievers. It seems an inescapable conclusion that many of those who identify with an ancient and worldwide religion claiming to possess and dispense a body of life-changing knowledge seem to have little genuine interest in matters of truth and the difference it makes. This is certainly not the case for vast regions of Islam, which takes its authoritative claim to reality seriously and seeks to make it known globally, however much that might threaten many in the West.[38]

---

[36]Dorothy Sayers, *Christian Letters to a Post-Christian World* (Grand Rapids: Eerdmans, 1969), p. 152.

[37]Rauch, "Let It Be," p. 34.

[38]See Irving Hexham, "Evangelical Illusions: Postmodern Christianity and the Growth of

Intellectual sloth is age-old. Both Socrates and Jesus combated it through their probing questions, dialogues and debates. But cognitive apathy is strengthened in the contemporary world by several defining features of postmodernity. This apathy is not only justified in the name of tolerance, as indicated by Rauch, but also encouraged by the endless diversion supplied by a culture of entertainment.

DIVERSION: TRUTH ON HOLD

In the middle of the seventeenth century in France, Blaise Pascal went to great lengths to expose those diversions that kept people from seeking truth in matters of ultimate significance. His words still ring true. In his day diversion consisted of hunting, games, gambling and other amusements. The repertoire of diversion was minute compared with what is available in our fully wired and overstimulated postmodern world of cell phones, radios, laptops, video games, omnipresent television (in cars, restaurants, airports, etc.), extreme sports and much else. Nevertheless, the human psychology of diversion remains unchanged. Diversion consoles us—in trivial ways—in the face of our miseries or perplexities; yet, paradoxically, it becomes the worst of our miseries because it hinders us from ruminating on and understanding our true condition. Thus, Pascal warns, it "leads us imperceptibly to destruction." Why? If not for diversion, we would "be bored, and boredom would drive us to seek some more solid means of escape, but diversion passes our time and brings us imperceptibly to our death."[39] Through the course of protracted stupefaction, we learn to become oblivious to our eventual oblivion. In so doing, we choke off the possibility of seeking real freedom.

Diversion serves to distract humans from a plight too terrible to encounter directly—namely, our mortality, finitude and failures. There is an ineluctable tension between our aspirations and the reality of our lives.

> Despite [his] afflictions man wants to be happy, only wants to be happy, and cannot help wanting to be happy. But how shall he go about it? The best thing would be to make himself immortal, but as he cannot do that, he has decided to stop thinking about it.[40]

Muslim Communities in Europe and North America," in *No Other Gods Before Me?* ed. John Stackhouse (Grand Rapids: Baker, 2001), pp. 137-60.
[39]Pascal, *Pensées* 414/171, p. 148.
[40]Ibid., 70/165, p. 45.

Pascal unmasks diversion as an attempt to escape reality, and an indication of something out of kilter in the human condition. An obsession with entertainment is more than silly or frivolous. It is, for Pascal, revelatory of a moral and spiritual malaise.

Diversions would not be blameworthy if they were recognized as such: trivial or otherwise distracting activities performed in order to temporarily avoid the harsh and unhappy realities of human life. However, self-deception comes into play. In the end, "we run heedlessly into the abyss after putting something in front of us to stop us seeing it."[41] According to Pascal, this condition illustrates the corruption of human nature. Humans are strangely not at home in their universe. "If our condition were truly happy we should feel no need to divert ourselves from thinking about it."[42] Woody Allen highlights this in a scene from the movie *Manhattan*. A man speaks into a tape recorder about the idea for a story about "people in Manhattan who are constantly creating these real unnecessary neurotic problems for themselves because it keeps them from dealing with more unsolvable, terrifying problems about the universe."[43]

The compulsive search for diversion is often an attempt to escape the wretchedness of life. We have great difficulty being quiet in our rooms, when the television or computer screen offers a riot of possible stimulation. As Pascal said, "Our nature consists in movement; absolute rest is death."[44] The postmodern person seeks diversion and overstimulation—a desperate bid to elude mortality by keeping higher realities out of sight.

SILENCE AND TRUTH

Diversions and the omnipresent noise and clutter of contemporary culture erect barriers to the serious and disciplined pursuit of truth. Although I do not believe it is included in any apology for the Christian worldview (it is scarcely mentioned anywhere at all), one of the key elements in considering Christian truth claims is not an argument at all, but a condition in which arguments may be understood and appreciated. That condition is silence. No one has stated it better than Kierkegaard, who wrote before the

---

[41]Ibid., 166/183, p. 82.
[42]Ibid., 641/129, p. 238.
[43]*Manhattan*, directed by Woody Allen, cited in Tom Morris, *Making Sense of It All: Pascal and the Meaning of Life* (Grand Rapids: Eerdmans, 1992), p. 32.
[44]Pascal, *Pensées* 641/129, p. 238.

onset of electrification and its manifold mind-numbing media.

> In observing the present state of affairs and of life in general, from a Chris-
> tian point of view one would have to say: It is a disease. And if I were a
> physician and someone asked me, "What do you think should be done?" I
> would answer, "Create silence, bring about silence." God's Word cannot be
> heard, and if in order to be heard in the hullabaloo it must be shouted deaf-
> eningly with noisy means, then it is not God's Word; create silence!
>
> And we humans, we clever fellows, seem to have become sleepless in
> order to invent every new means to increase noise, to spread noise and in-
> significance with the greatest possible ease and on the greatest possible
> scale. Yes, everything has been turned upside down. The means of com-
> munication have been perfected, but what is publicized with such hot haste
> is rubbish. Oh, create silence![45]

In the silence of rational reflection, truth may disclose itself to the receptive soul.[46]

---

[45]Kierkegaard, in *Provocations*, p. 372. For an absorbing treatment of the meaning of silence, see
   Max Picard, *The World of Silence*, trans. Stanley Goodman (Chicago: Henry Regnery, 1952).
[46]On the dangers of diversion in our technological society see Douglas Groothuis, *The Soul in
   Cyberspace* (Grand Rapids: Baker, 1997).

Faith, Risk and Rationality

The Prudential Incentives to Christian Faith

*I should be much more afraid of being mistaken and then finding out that
Christianity is true than of being mistaken in believing it to be true.*

BLAISE PASCAL[1]

APOLOGETICS THAT DEFENDS THE CHRISTIAN worldview as ob-
jectively true, rational and pertinent is essential to Christian witness today.
So I have argued thus far. Moreover, Christianity makes a stupendous
promise on the basis of its truth: one can enter a new and richer mode of
being—both in this life and the next—by embracing Jesus Christ on his
terms. In chapter seven, I commended the earnest pursuit of truth as an
intellectually virtuous endeavor; for no matter how strong the case for
Christianity may be, if it is not investigated, its verities can be neither accepted nor appreciated. As John Montgomery surmised, if the average
person put as much time into investigating Christianity as he or she put
into a college course on the humanities, most of these people would come
to faith.[2] Yet how many today would even consider such an independent
study? And why should they, especially in light of the many spiritual alternatives available from anthroposophy to Zen?

---

[1]Blaise Pascal, *Pensées*, ed. and trans. Alban Krailsheimer (New York: Penguin, 1966), 387/241,
   p. 143.
[2]John Warwick Montgomery, "Contemporary Apologetics," taped lecture, Trinity Theological
   Seminary, Newberg, Ind., 1976.

THE PLACE OF PRUDENCE IN APOLOGETICS

This chapter will address prudential considerations with respect to Christian belief. *Prudence*, as I use the term here, concerns personal benefit and detriment in matters of belief in general and concerning Christianity in particular. Life today provides us with a panoply of possible beliefs about a plethora of topics, and many face this welter of worldviews with a stupefied indifference. Those so anaesthetized will, of course, show no interest at all in pursuing Christian truth claims. The best arguments concerning the greatest issues, if left unheeded, do no good. So, a vital part of apologetics must address how to stimulate interest in Christian topics among the unconverted. In a world awash with spiritual options, playing the prudence card is not unwarranted—if and only if it is done tactfully and respectfully and in a way that comports with our sense of prudence in other areas of life.

We all must develop some considered beliefs about our professions in order to flourish within them. Beliefs about our health are taken quite seriously as well. An ambiguous physical symptom that could indicate a serious medical threat needs to be investigated. But what about belief pursuits that are more elective? What beliefs are necessities and what beliefs are luxuries? What should we even consider worthy of belief or unbelief? The previous chapter argued that the virtuous person pursues truth and follows it wherever it may lead. It also claimed that knowledge of Christian truth claims is possible and desirable. But this response, while required for intellectual rectitude, gives but part of the answer. We should believe what is true and well supported by evidence. But what truth claims should claim our attention in the first place? In other words, where should we direct our investigations on matters of truth and falsity?

PASCAL ON PRUDENCE IN RELIGIOUS BELIEF[3]

It should be no surprise that Christians contend that non-Christians should investigate the claims and credentials of Christianity. Christians often encourage this on the basis of their own experiences. Christ changed their lives for the better, and he can do the same for others who come to him on his

---

[3]Some of the following material is adapted from Douglas Groothuis, "Wagering a Life on God," from *On Pascal* (Belmont, Calif.: Wadsworth, 2003).

terms. This approach is fitting, so long as it does not devolve into pragmatism. Nevertheless, it is only part of the incentive that may be needed for an unbeliever. While keeping a firm backbone of objective truth, Christian apologetics should also commend Christianity on a prudential basis. Here we can invoke some insights from Blaise Pascal's famous and much-debated wager argument. My concern here is not to defend Pascal against his critics, but rather to apply the heart of his argument to the apologetic situation today (along with some help from William James).[4]

Unlike many philosophical debates, the wager captures the imagination and triggers strong passions on both sides. I once heard a philosophy graduate admit that he was not a Christian because of the way the wager argument was presented to him. One of my own Christian students had such an aversion to this argument that he refused to attend my lecture on it. But before tackling objections to the wager, a clearer understanding of the role of prudence in belief formation needs to be developed.

We first should note that Pascal is not advising us to treat God as merely a means to the end of escaping hell and inheriting eternal life. However, the prudential aspects should play a strong role in stimulating a person's interest in Christianity's truth claims. Pascal believes that by emphasizing these prudential concerns the apologist may elicit the religious interest of an otherwise unconcerned unbeliever. However, Pascal wants the unbeliever to reach true faith.

> True conversion consists in self-annihilation before the universal being whom we have so often vexed and who is perfectly entitled to destroy us at any moment. . . . It consists in knowing that there is an irreconcilable opposition between God and us, and that without a mediator there can be no [salvation].[5]

Let us move on to Pascal's prudential considerations proper.

Succinctly put, if Christianity is true and one becomes a Christian, there is much to gain and little of *ultimate* importance to lose. Pascal says, if one is a Christian and Christianity is true, there is "an infinity of an infinitely happy life to be won."[6] He is speaking of the eternal state of the believer, who dwells with God in a restored creation with all the redeemed

---

[4]See ibid.
[5]Pascal, *Pensées* 378/470, pp. 137-38.
[6]Pascal, *Pensées* 418/233, p. 151.

(see Revelation 21:1–22:6). We may add to this the benefit of knowing the truth in this life and receiving the divine blessings of a restored relationship with God and the privilege of seeking and serving a kingdom that cannot be shaken (Matthew 16:18; Hebrews 12:28). When someone receives these temporal and eternal benefits, he or she also escapes the pains of hell, although Pascal does not mention hell overtly in his famous argument. Moreover, if Christianity is true and a person becomes a Christian, he or she also becomes an instrument of truth and goodness in the world in a way not otherwise possible. This introduces an altruistic element to the equation.[7] Of course, a true follower of Christ will repent of and thus lose some worldly enjoyments (Romans 12:1-2; 1 John 2:15-17); he or she also inherits a tension with the world system that can result in religious persecution by family, friends, strangers or the state. But even in this, those so afflicted are "blessed," because "great is [their] reward in heaven" (Matthew 5:11-12; see also 1 Peter 4:12-19). Yet Jesus does challenge his potential disciples to "count the cost" of following him. His way is not a casual endeavor or a hobby for one's spare time:

> Then he said to them all: "Whoever wants to be my disciple must deny themselves and take up their cross daily and follow me. For whoever wants to save their life will lose it, but whoever loses their life for me will save it. What good is it for you to gain the whole world, and yet lose or forfeit their very self?" (Luke 9:23-25)

In the same passage that Jesus speaks of the cost of following him, he also warns of the greater cost—an eternal one—of not following him. Jesus was not afraid to marshal the resources of prudence, although he did not limit his argumentation to such warnings.[8]

On the other hand, if Christianity is true and one fails to become a Christian, there is much to lose and little of final importance to gain. Even Antony Flew, writing (at that time) as an atheist, realized this: "If there is a chance at all that we are in danger of unending misery, then knowledge which might show us how this is to be avoided must become overwhelmingly important."[9] How, then, might the apologist engender a concern for knowledge in this area?

---

[7]Peter Kreeft, *Christianity for Modern Pagans* (San Francisco: Ignatius Press, 1993), p. 297.
[8]See Douglas Groothuis, *On Jesus* (Belmont, Calif.: Wadsworth, 2003), esp. chaps. 1, 3.
[9]Antony Flew, *God and Philosophy* (Amherst, N.Y.: Prometheus, 2005), p. 34.

PRUDENTIAL CONSIDERATIONS AND ACTIVITIES

If we take a basic inventory of our beliefs (what constitutes our noetic structure), we realize that some beliefs are more important than others; that is, some beliefs have more existential impact on ourselves and on the world around us than other beliefs.[10] For example, discerning whether someone would make a worthy mate is no small matter. Marriage is a serious endeavor carrying with it very high stakes, since an individual is choosing his or her most intimate friend and life partner. On the other hand, beliefs about the relative greatness of sports figures, while interesting, hardly carry the same consequences. So, it is rational to spend more effort investigating one's potential marriage than debating who the greatest hitter in the history of baseball might be.[11]

But many want to remain uncommitted and apathetic about Christian claims. To this, Pascal argues that we *must* wager for or against Christianity. Uncommitted agnosticism is not an option: "There is no choice, you are already committed. Which will you choose then?"[12] With regard to the truth or error of two mutually exclusive propositions A and B, we can (1) believe A (and so disbelieve B), (2) believe B (and so disbelieve A) or (3) suspend judgment about A and B. Although we could remain uncommitted concerning Christianity, the option becomes "forced," to use William James's term, when a prudential element is added.[13] We cannot avoid the issue by remaining skeptical because "although we do avoid error in that way *if religion be untrue*, we lose the good, *if it be true*, just as certainly as if we positively chose to disbelieve."[14]

In other words, not to believe in Christianity, either as a committed unbeliever or as an agnostic, means to forfeit the *benefits* promised only to the believer (eternal life), should Christianity be true. Deciding not to choose has the same result as not believing in God. In this sense, "you are already committed." In the final analysis, to be apathetic is to be antithetical to Christ. As he said, "Whoever is not with me is against me, and whoever does not gather with me scatters" (Matthew 12:30).

---

[10]On noetic structure, see Ronald Nash, *Faith and Reason* (Grand Rapids: Zondervan, 1988), pp. 21-24.

[11]The answer is Ted Williams.

[12]Pascal, *Pensées* 418/233, p. 150.

[13]See William Rowe, *Philosophy of Religion* (Belmont, Calif.: Wadsworth, 1978), pp. 178-80.

[14]William James, *The Will to Believe* (New York: Dover Publications, 1956), p. 26.

Our lease on earthly life is of limited duration, and we don't know when it will be up. Therefore, the decision should weigh heavily on us. In William James's words, such a decision is "momentous" and not "trivial" because the stakes are high, the opportunity is unique and the choice is irreversible.[15] What lends urgency to the situation, as Pascal mentions elsewhere, is that if one dies "without worshipping the true principle" (that is, the true God), that person is forever lost.[16]

Pascal denounces indifference toward religion as violating the principles of reasonable self-interest. Here he narrates the speech of a skeptic who expresses his utter lostness in the cosmos:

> Just as I do not know whence I come, so I do not know whither I am going. All I know is that when I leave this world I shall fall forever into nothingness or into the hands of a wrathful God, but I do not know which of these two states is to be my eternal lot. Such is my state, full of weakness and uncertainty. And my conclusion from all this is that I must pass my days without a thought of seeking what is to happen to me. Perhaps I might find some enlightenment in my doubts, but I do not want to take the trouble.

At this point, Pascal issues four red-hot questions.

> Who would wish to have as a friend a man who argued like that? Who would choose him from among others as a confidant in his affairs? Who would resort to him in adversity? To what use in life could he possibly be turned?[17]

These questions are not mere ad hominem attacks; they form a cogent argument. If it is a good thing to be a trustworthy friend, and if such a friend would never be as nonchalant as the skeptic, then it is not a good thing to be a negligent, skeptical person. This kind of skeptic has failed to discharge a basic human duty to investigate matters of extreme moment. In confronting this intellectual indolence, Pascal is as much an existential therapist as a philosopher. He realizes that he must treat such worldly complacency with psychological explosives by stimulating the imagination, as in this memorable parable.

---

[15]Ibid., pp. 3-4. We should amend James by noting that a person may put off a religious decision or change religious beliefs before death. However, in biblical language, we may so "harden our heart" that such a deathbed conversion becomes a psychological impossibility.

[16]Pascal, *Pensées* 158/236, p. 82.

[17]Pascal, *Pensées* 427/194, p. 158.

> A man in a dungeon, not knowing whether sentence has been passed on to
> him, with only an hour left to find out, and that hour enough, once he
> knows it has been passed, to have it revoked. It would be unnatural for him
> to spend that hour not finding out whether sentence has been passed by
> playing piquet.[18]

Pascal challenges us to face our mortality. But unlike Martin Heidegger,
who in his *Being and Time* (1927) saw humanity's "being unto death" as a
call to live authentically for a *finite* period of time, Pascal wants to spark a
hope for transcendence, for an *infinite* life conferred by God's grace in
Christ.

If Christianity is true, the prudential benefits for believing (eternal life)
far exceed those offered by believing in atheism or any other worldview
(finite pleasures). The prudential detriments of not believing if Christianity is true (loss of eternal life; gaining of hell) also far outweigh the detriments of not believing atheism or another other worldview if the non-
Christian view is true (loss of some finite pleasures).[19] Pascal is right to
affirm that eternal bliss outweighs any finite good, and eternal loss is far
worse than mere extinction.[20]

PRUDENTIAL CONCERNS AND OTHER RELIGIONS

Only one other religion is as prudentially charged as Christianity: Islam.
It too claims that being a Muslim is the only way (or at least the surest) to
eternal felicity. So, given prudential concerns, why should someone investigate Christianity over Islam? First, prudential matters do not determine
beliefs; they merely prime the pump for investigation and consideration.
One must consider the *credibility* of any religious claim in addition to its
prudential promises. Chapter twenty-four will assess the essential claims
of Islam and find them intellectually wanting. This fact in itself would
cancel out Islam's numerous threats of hell for those who do not submit to
Allah. Second, Islam makes no *promise* of eternal life to any of its followers. Unless one dies in a jihad, no Muslim is given certainty as to whether

---

[18]Pascal, *Pensées* 163/200, p. 82.

[19]Unless Islam is true, since Islam, like Christianity, threatens hell and promises heaven. This is
discussed later.

[20]Pascal does not overtly mention hell in the wager, but it seems implied; he endorses the doctrine of eternal punishment in *Pensées* 152/213, p. 79, which emphasizes the fragility of life
situated between heaven and hell.

he or she will enter paradise. One can only hope that one's good deeds outweigh one's bad deeds or that Allah will somehow show mercy.

Christianity could not be more dissimilar on this score. Christ and the apostles *promise* eternal life (beginning in the here and now) to the true believer on the basis of God's love and grace (Romans 8:16), which is received by faith alone (Ephesians 2:8-9). Jesus promised this: "I am the resurrection and the life. The one who believes in me will live, even though they die; and whoever lives by believing in me will never die" (John 11:25-26). So, if Christianity is true, the believer can find assurance of salvation; if Islam is true, a Muslim can only work for salvation and hope he or she ends up in paradise. Of the two options, Christianity is, then, much more attractive. Of course, truth claims are not decisively settled by which ones are the most attractive, but Christianity, if true, would offer far more to the believer than would Islam if it were true. Thus, the seeker is prudentially justified in investigating Christianity first.

Contemporary Judaism holds a variety of beliefs on the afterlife.[21] The more orthodox schools of Judaism affirm the existence of eternal states of reward or punishment. However, conservative Jews believe that non-Jews can be acceptable to God through obeying basic moral commands; they do not have to be Jewish to be acceptable to God. Jews may believe that Gentiles are missing the richness of religious life by not engaging in Judaism, but the Gentiles' nonparticipation in Judaism per se has no eternally deleterious consequences. So, the prudential incentive to consider Judaism is far less than that offered by Christianity and Islam.[22]

To illustrate this prudential principle, consider a more pedestrian scenario. In considering two insurance companies, one reads that company A's benefits far exceed company B's benefits. But at this point the interested person knows nothing else about company A and B. If so, all things being equal, it is more rational to pursue the facts about company A rather than company B. This is, of course, a prima facie consideration; it could be that company A makes false promises and company B delivers on its less impressive benefits.

---

[21]For an overview of Judaism, see Winfried Corduan, *Neighboring Faiths* (Downers Grove, Ill.: InterVarsity Press, 1998), pp. 45-76.

[22]I will not offer a critique of Judaism in itself. In defending of Christianity, I claim that the Hebrew Bible (or Old Testament) is divinely inspired in chap. 20. However, the arguments for Jesus as the Messiah entail that Christianity is the fulfillment of Judaism.

Other religions lacking the doctrines of heaven and hell may also offer prudential incentives, but they are less charged prudentially than Christianity and Islam. Both Hinduism and Buddhism teach the doctrine of reincarnation, wherein the postmortem state is not seen as necessarily eternal. Any number of lifetimes may be needed to neutralize bad karma and attain ultimate enlightenment, after which one escapes samsara (the wheel of rebirth) and need not reincarnate. According to Hinduism and Buddhism, if one wagers incorrectly—say on Islam or Christianity—in this life, a religious adjustment is available in another incarnation. But Christianity (Hebrews 9:27) and Islam offer no such second (or millionth) chance.[23] The stakes are higher and the time allotted to wager is far shorter—one life. Therefore, even if someone finds the apologetic case for Hinduism or Buddhism attractive, given the prudential considerations of Christianity and Islam, that person should attempt to rule out these high-risk monotheistic faiths before pursuing Hinduism or Buddhism—unless, of course, the person deems Hinduism or Buddhism so intellectually superior that he or she can find no rational interest in Christianity or Islam at all.

Even if other spiritual possibilities were *conceivable*, this would not, in itself, undermine the prudential and evidential warrant of a Pascalian experiment. If we become convinced through apologetics that we have sufficient reason, both epistemic and prudential, to believe in Christianity, then further experiments would not be in order in light of Christianity's claims to religious sufficiency and uniqueness. Yet this does not mean that we could not choose to cease believing in Christianity. But as long as a person believes, no other quests are appropriate, because religious faith—more than the initial spiritual experiment—makes a total demand on a person.[24]

EMOTION, REASON AND RELIGIOUS BELIEF

Despite all the prudential reasons to seek Christian faith, and even though we may see the benefits in believing, belief often remains difficult to attain because of emotional dispositions, fears or loves that keep us from seri-

---

[23]Some have argued for a postmortem opportunity for salvation, but the biblical evidence for this is quite weak. See appendix 1.

[24]See Douglas Groothuis, "Obstinacy in Religious Belief," *Sophia* 32, no. 2 (1993): 25-35.

ously considering this alternative. Pascal realized this and famously urged the one considering Christian faith for prudential reasons to act in religious ways in the hope that faith might emerge. Pascal is often accused of advocating religious brainwashing in this regard. But he is not here suggesting that a person simply become habituated to the proposition "God exists," such that he or she comes to believe it. This protocol would give no rational justification for the belief. Habituation is not argumentation. If the genesis of any belief is reducible to habituation alone (sans epistemic considerations), then that belief is not epistemically justified. However, there is a more charitable and philosophically promising understanding of Pascal's advice.

An unbeliever's passions may inhibit belief when prudential reason would otherwise impel him or her to believe. Thus an individual should consider attempting to neutralize these inhibiting passions such that belief becomes possible. This is not brainwashing but a kind of testing. Pascal says elsewhere in a dialogue:

> "I should have given up a life of pleasure," they say, "if I had faith." But I tell you: "You would soon have faith if you gave up a life of pleasure. Now it is up to you to begin. If I could give you faith, I would. But I cannot, nor can I test the truth of what you say, but you can easily give up your pleasure and *test* whether I am telling the truth."[25]

As an Augustinian, Pascal believed that people are essentially motivated by either lust or charity—in other words, by our fallen nature or by grace. If we are dominated by lust, religious truth is unavailable. If we are willing to suspend or at least attenuate foul passions, charity may break through and faith may ensue. For example, Jesus says to some unbelieving religious leaders, "How can you believe [in me] when you seek approval from others?" (John 5:44). He contends that prideful regard for status could keep a person from seeing the truth.

Along these lines, consider the case of a prideful actor named Charles who, now past his prime, refuses to recognize the brilliance of a younger actor, Rodney, who is superbly executing the roles Charles once excelled in performing. But because of his age, Charles can no longer play the parts that once made him famous and which are now catapulting Rodney into

---

[25]Pascal, *Pensées* 816/240, p. 273, emphasis added.

fresh celebrity. The elder's pride and jealousy blinds him to the talents of his younger "rival." But Charles is counseled by a wise friend—who is interested in reconciling him to Rodney—to watch Rodney's best acting performances on video three times within one week. In so doing, the friend hopes that Charles's obtuseness will be overcome. Charles reluctantly agrees and later confesses Rodney's greatness, along with admitting the blindness of his former pride. Now he has eyes to see.[26]

Pascal's recommendation of religious practices does not advise brainwashing but rather a vulnerability to persuasion through various religious practices that may serve to temper the passions and thus open one to certain claims not otherwise convincing and to experiences not otherwise possible. Pascal elsewhere speaks of habituation or "custom" as helping to ground certain beliefs in a rational manner.[27]

IS IT TRUE FAITH?

Critics argue that wagering faith little resembles true religious faith for at least two reasons. First, we cannot be said to have faith if there is any tentativeness involved. The idea of testing a commitment with a spiritual experiment is inherently irreligious because religion demands absolute faith and commitment. Second, wagering faith is rejected because it is cultivated only to save one's own skin and get a heavenly payoff; it is merely mercenary. To this, I give two responses.

First, Pascal's Christian tradition offers incentives for those not yet fully convinced to seek fuller assurance. Jesus advises that if his hearers ask, seek and knock they will receive an answer (Matthew 7:7-8). When Jesus is confronted by a man who pleads, "I do believe, help me overcome my unbelief," he does not rebuke the man but responds to his imperfect faith and grants him his desire (Mark 9:14-29). Jesus also comments that faith as small as a mustard seed is sufficient for great things (Matthew 17:20).

Second, a person who wagers on God need not be a religious mercenary who commits all intellectual and moral integrity to the flames for the off chance of infinite reward. One need not transgress any intellec-

---

[26]For more on this, see Douglas Groothuis, "Wagering Belief: Examining Two Objections to Pascal's Wager," *Religious Studies* 30 (1994): 479-86.
[27]Pascal, *Pensées* 821/252, p. 274.

tual or ethical standard by wagering on God. Self-interest, a normal human regard, need not be selfish (see Ephesians 5:29). Jesus invoked self-interest, along with a comparison of finite and infinite goods, when he asked, "What good will it be for someone to gain the whole world, yet forfeit their soul? Or what can anyone give in exchange for their soul?" (Matthew 16:26).

Following the advice of the wager can be seen as a first step in the process of possible belief development.[28] Because beliefs cannot just be taken up at will, a process is undertaken which may result in full-fledged belief, if certain conditions obtain. Pascal himself is aware of the difference between true conversion and prudential exploration. The wager appeals to self-interest but precludes brute selfishness, if for no other reason than that the one wagering must begin to inhibit his or her worldly passions for the sake of religious participation.

To act as if one believes means to engage in activities thought to build or strengthen faith. This could include involvement with religious services, the reading of Scripture and devotional materials, prayer and meditation, and association with believers on matters of spiritual concern. This kind of active participation need not be a case of uncritical engagement but rather of sympathetic involvement. Ninian Smart has rightly observed that philosophers have tended to treat religious questions as merely metaphysical assertions in abstraction. Yet some sympathetic imagination and even participation is required to understand a religious claim in the holistic milieu in which it functions, even if this falls short of total commitment.[29] Pascal emphasizes both the cognitive and physical sides of spirituality:

> We must combine outward and inward to obtain anything from God; in other words, we must go down on our knees, pray with our lips, etc. . . . If we expect help from this outward part we are superstitious, if we refuse to combine it with the inward part we are being arrogant.[30]

The conclusion is that someone may act "as if" he or she were a believer, but only if hypocrisy and self-deception are ruled out. Pascal certainly does not want to encourage self-deception: "Men often take their imagination

---

[28]See Nicholas Rescher, *Pascal's Wager: A Study of Practical Reasoning in Philosophical Theology* (Notre Dame, Ind.: University of Notre Dame Press, 1985), pp. 117-33.
[29]Ninian Smart, *The Philosophy of Religion* (New York: Random House, 1970), p. 25.
[30]Pascal, *Pensées* 944/250, p. 324.

for their heart, and often believe they are converted as soon as they start thinking of becoming converted."[31]

PRUDENCE, TRUTH AND APOLOGETICS

The case for Christianity stands or falls on the arguments presented on its behalf and the arguments presented against pertinent worldview rivals. But these arguments will have no effect unless people seriously investigate them. A prudential consideration of the Christian truth claim can, when offered wisely, invoke a healthy self-interest that encourages unbelievers to inquire into Christianity. Further, since we are not merely disembodied intellects—but beings of emotion and will, as well—the investigation of Christianity should also include exposure to its public expression, its forms and practices. This could be called a "devotional experiment." As Pascal observed, these activities (along with rational reflection) may help one truly discern the state of one's own soul before God and the glories of the Christian revelation itself.[32]

[31]Pascal, *Pensées* 975/275, p. 347.

[32]For more on the evidential value of a spiritual or devotional experiment, see Caroline F. Davis, *The Evidential Force of Religious Experience* (New York: Oxford University Press, 1989). Davies, however, extends the religious experiment idea to justifying religions other than Christianity. See also chap. 16 of this book.

PART TWO

The Case for Christian Theism

9

In Defense of Theistic Arguments

NATURAL THEOLOGY CONSISTS OF theistic arguments (sometimes called theistic proofs). They are rational arguments for the existence of a monotheistic God that do not appeal to sacred scriptures for their cogency. These arguments claim that there are sufficient reasons to believe that monotheism is objectively true. Monotheism affirms that there is only one God and that this God is a personal and Perfect Being of unlimited power, knowledge and goodness who created the universe out of nothing. This being is worthy of adoration and worship, is distinct from the world but continuously involved in it, and is capable of generating miracles. The concept of God must be logically coherent for any argument or combination of arguments to establish the existence of such a being, since there are no good arguments for incoherent entities (such as square circles).[1]

Such theistic arguments have a long and complicated history, involving not only Christianity but other monotheistic religions as well. This chapter will explain the major types of theistic proofs, consider how they contribute to Christian apologetics and defend them against two types of criticisms.

ARGUMENT FORMS

The term *proof* can mean an argument in which the premises deductively entail a conclusion such that the conclusion is secured beyond any doubt. That is, if the premises are known to be true, then the conclusion must be

---

[1]I have given a preliminary argument in chap. 4 that the concept of God, including the Trinity, is coherent. This question also arises in chap. 10 (concerning the ontological argument) and in chap. 21 (concerning the incarnation). We will return to the coherence of believing in such a God and in the existence of evil in chap. 25.

true. So, a theistic proof in this sense would establish the existence of God in the same way that theorems are deductively derived from axioms in geometry. Some theistic arguments have such a deductive form. However, the phrase *theistic proof* can mean any argument—even if inductive or abductive—for God's existence.[2] Theistic proofs are a product of *natural theology*, which is distinguished from *revealed theology* (what can be derived by proper exegesis and theologizing from sacred texts). For example, the plan of salvation through Jesus Christ is known only through God's acts in history and subsequently through the written biblical revelation; it is not known through rational reflection on the creation alone.

Theistic proofs thus form part of Christian apologetics, but not the whole of it. Their aim is to establish rationally the existence—and certain core attributes—of God. They do not fully fill out all of the attributes of the Christian God, nor all the Christian worldview. It is deism, not Christian theism, that claims that our knowledge of God is exhausted by what can be known about God through nature and unaided reason.

TYPES OF THEISTIC ARGUMENTS

Theistic proofs are grouped into two main categories. Each category is a family of arguments, since there are various versions of the ontological argument, the cosmological argument, the design argument, the moral argument and the argument from religious experience. All of these arguments have been updated and made more analytically rigorous in recent decades. In fact, they are flourishing in the philosophical literature thanks to the works of virtuoso philosophers such as Richard Swinburne, J. P. Moreland and William Lane Craig. First, there are a posteriori or empirical arguments. These arguments—cosmological, design, moral and religious experience— depend on some evidence in the world as a basis from which to infer God's existence. A second category of theistic argument is a priori. These arguments rely on what is rationally known apart from the empirical world. So, ontological arguments trade on the philosophical implications of the idea of God in itself, and not on states of affairs in the world. These arguments claim that, combined with certain logical principles, the very idea of God as a greatest possible being rationally demands that God exists.

---

[2]I use an abductive form of argument in chap. 18 when arguing that Christian theism gives the best explanation of the greatness and misery of the human condition.

While the effectiveness of each kind of theistic proof must be evaluated individually, the savvy apologist can combine several types of arguments to form a cumulative-case argument for theism that is stronger than the force of any argument taken by itself. One may use a cosmological argument to establish the existence of God as Creator, a teleological argument for God as Designer, a moral argument for God as the source of the moral law and so on. Each argument is like a witness in a trial; each testifies in its own way for the truth of theism. Similarly, the best scientific theories (such as the big bang) are corroborated by several discrete lines of converging evidence, as I argue in chapter eleven. The larger case for Christian theism includes even more lines of converging evidence, such as the resurrection of Christ.

The Bible affirms that God has revealed certain knowable truths about himself in creation. This is classically called general revelation and is rooted most prominently in Romans 1:19-20, where Paul discusses the culpability of the human race before God:

> What may be known about God is plain to them, because God has made it plain to them. For since the creation of the world God's invisible qualities—his eternal power and divine nature—have been clearly seen, being understood from what has been made, so that people are without excuse.

John Stott notes that this "is one of the principal New Testament passages on the topic of 'general revelation,'" which is distinguished from special revelation in four ways. First, this revelation is "general" because it is made known to everyone everywhere, as opposed to special revelation received by those who knew Christ or who read the biblical authors. Second, it is "natural" because it is disclosed through the natural order of creation as opposed to the supernatural work of Christ or the inspiration of Scripture. Third, it is "continuous" because it has gone out "since the creation of the world" without abatement, as opposed to the final and finished work of Christ and the Scripture. Finally, it is "'creational,' revealing God's glory through creation, as opposed to 'salvific,' revealing God's grace in Christ."[3]

While general revelation is necessary for natural theology, it is not

---

[3]John Stott, *The Message of Romans: God's Good News for the World*, The Bible Speaks Today (Downers Grove, Ill.: InterVarsity Press, 1994), p. 73.

sufficient. Nor are these two terms synonymous. General revelation means that God has revealed himself in nature and conscience. Natural theology engages in logic in order to derive rational arguments for God's existence. However, some think that although God has revealed his existence through nature and conscience, general revelation is not sufficient to support philosophical arguments defending God's existence. That is, God may have revealed himself in a way not susceptible to argumentation. If so, this general revelation would be more a matter of intuition than intellection. However, given the reality of general revelation, the long history of natural theology and the revival of natural theology today (in sophisticated analytical forms), the burden of proof is on those who would deny its biblical permissibility or its logical possibility. Nevertheless, several arguments have been advanced against natural theology, all of which I find unconvincing.

NINE OBJECTIONS TO NATURAL THEOLOGY

The objections can be divided into two categories: in-principle objections, which claim there is something intrinsically wrong (in a spiritual or theological sense) with theistic arguments, and practical or in-practice objections, which claim theistic arguments simply don't live up to our expectations, however much we wish they did. First we turn to the in-principle arguments. Despite the seeming advances of theistic arguments for the cause of Christian apologetics, various Christian thinkers, including some apologists, have rejected them or minimized their value.

1. Biblical omission argument. Pascal argued that since Scripture fails to offer examples of natural theology, we should shun such endeavors as well.[4] The Bible does claim that nature speaks of its Creator and that it is the fool who says there is no God (Psalm 14:1; 53:1), but we are hard pressed to find a developed philosophical argument in Scripture for God's existence.[5] Since Pascal labored to be faithful to Scripture, he took

---

[4]Blaise Pascal, *Pensées* 463/243, ed. and trans. Alban Krailsheimer (New York: Penguin, 1966), p. 179.
[5]Some suggest that the germ—if not the full fruit—of natural theology can be found in biblical passages such as Romans 1:18-32 and Acts 17:16-34, which appeal to nature as evidence for God's existence. Biblical commentator Adam Clarke identifies this argument from Paul in Acts 17:29, which argues for God given the audience's assumptions:

1. If we are the offspring of God, He cannot be like those images of gold, silver, and stone which are formed by the art and device of man, for the parent must resemble his offspring.

this philosophical omission as normative and exemplary. If Pascal was right, the considerable work done by philosophers recently to defend theistic arguments must be theologically illegitimate, whatever its philosophical value may be.

But Pascal's observation only shows that no biblical writer deemed natural theology pertinent to *his situation*. This is not surprising, since atheism was not a significant issue in the ancient world of the Hebrews and their neighbors, and natural theology is usually aimed more at atheism than at other worldviews.[6] People who rejected the biblical deity were much more likely to be polytheists or pantheists, or to have another monotheistic or henotheistic god. The biblical writers use a different argumentative strategy in combating these worldviews. For example, Isaiah refuted the ersatz gods of his day by claiming that they cannot infallibly predict the future, as does the God of Israel (Isaiah 40–45). The omission of natural theology may also indicate that from a biblical perspective, one may be justified in believing in God apart from any formal philosophical arguments for God's existence.[7] But this does not, in itself, disqualify natural theology for apologetic purposes.

In the end Pascal's case against natural theology seems to be a fallacious argument from silence. Since there is no explicit prohibition of theistic arguments in the Bible, and since the emphasis on general revelation is so rich, the absence of any developed natural theology does not seem to imply that it is forbidden or pointless in all circumstances.[8]

2. Biblical authority argument. A related argument claims that since the Bible is the ultimate authority on God, its claim that God exists needs

---

2. Seeing, therefore, that we are living and intelligent beings, He from whom we have derived that being must be living and intelligent.

3. It is necessary also that the object of religious worship should be much more excellent than the worshipper; but man is, by innumerable degrees more excellent than an image made of gold, silver, or stone. And yet it would be impious to worship a man; how much more so to worship these images as gods.

4. Comment: "Every man in the Areopagus must have felt the power of this conclusion; and, taking it for granted that they had felt it; he proceeds" (Adam Clarke, *Commentary on the Holy Bible* [Grand Rapids: Baker, 1967], p. 1006; I have added the enumeration).

[6]Successful natural theology does, however, help defeat pantheism and polytheism, as will be shown later in this book.

[7]See the comments in chap. 3 on Plantinga's claims that belief in the Christian God may be properly basic.

[8]For a further development of this argument, see Douglas Groothuis, "Pascal's Biblical Omission Argument Against Natural Theology," *Asbury Theological Journal* 52, no. 2 (1997): 17-26.

no external support. For some thinkers, the biblical pronouncement on the existence of God—and all else—is "self-attesting" or "self-authenticating." The need for external rational support would undermine its superlative authority. This view was held by Cornelius Van Til and Herman Bavinck, who said, "Scripture . . . does not make God the conclusion of a syllogism, leaving it to us whether we think the argument holds or not. But it speaks with authority."[9]

Nonetheless, whatever speaks with authority must be viewed by others as having authority if it is to be recognized as authoritative. For example, a text on physics may be the definitive statement on the subject and thus have the highest scientific authority. This authority would not be damaged by those who refuse to view it as authoritative out of ignorance, perversity or disagreement. Neither would its authority be diminished if someone were to defend its credentials. Even if its authority needed to be corroborated, it would still have the highest authority as a physics text. Certifying its credentials as an authority does not undermine its authority but rather establishes it. Similarly, although the intrinsic authority of Scripture is not dependent on the arguments of natural theology, God's existence may be demonstrated or rendered more rational through such arguments. If so, the Bible would gain authority in the eyes of those who had previously dismissed as irrational the existence of God and any God-inspired book.

3. The noetic effects of sin argument. Another in-principle argument is that human reason is too corrupted by sin to warrant any hope of proving God's existence. The noetic (cognitive) effects of sin render such ambitions vain. This objection takes two basic forms. One is that human reason is too *weak* for such arguments to work. The other is that human reason is too *perverse* for the sinner to submit to an argument that concludes that God exists. These objections often appeal to Paul's statement in Romans that comes after the aforementioned claim that God reveals himself in nature: "Although they knew God, they neither glorified him as God nor

[9]Herman Bavinck, *The Doctrine of God*, trans. William Hendrickson (Grand Rapids: Eerdmans, 1951), p. 78, quoted in Alvin Plantinga, "Reason and Belief in God," in *Faith and Rationality*, ed. Alvin Plantinga and Nicholas Wolterstorff (Notre Dame, Ind.: University of Notre Dame Press, 1984), p. 64. Van Til thought there was essentially one argument for Christianity, the transcendental argument, but this is not a piece of classic natural theology as he understood it. For a discussion of this, see Greg L. Bahnsen, *Van Til's Apologetic: Readings and Analysis* (Phillipsburg, N.J.: P & R, 1998), pp. 516-29. I present a similar argument in chap. 17.

gave thanks to him, but their thinking became futile and their foolish hearts were darkened. Although they claimed to be wise, they became fools" (Romans 1:21-22).

There is no doubt that human reasoning and human reasoners have been adversely affected by the fall. However, reason itself—the logical structure of being and argument—is based on the eternal character of God as the Word (the *Logos* [John 1:1]), and on his bestowal of reason to creatures made in his image and likeness.[10] In that sense, reason is not fallen. Reason in itself cannot be fallen and remain reason. Users of reason, however, are corrupted and so are subject to multifarious errors of judgment based on ignorance, turpitude, sloth and even willful self-deception such that they become unreasonable and irrational.[11] Nevertheless, sound reasoning is the norm for people willing to follow truth wherever it leads. Few delight in obvious irrationality when it is seen for what it is: intellectual irresponsibility and infidelity to reality. Since the Bible advocates apologetics (see chap. 2), and since many of our contemporaries fail to believe in the existence of God, it makes good sense to offer persuasive arguments for the existence of God.[12]

4. Direct knowledge of God argument. Both Kierkegaard and Van Tillian presuppositionalists have argued that to attempt to argue for God's existence is radically inappropriate because people have a direct awareness of God that requires no proof. Van Tillians want to argue *from* God's existence rather than *for* God's existence. Kierkegaard believed that the knowledge of God should be coaxed out of people through "indirect communication," a manner of persuasion that challenges unbelief by means of psychological explorations, not rational arguments.[13]

---

[10]The meaning of *logos* in John 1:1 is wider than reason alone; it also indicates verbal communication. See Murray J. Harris, *Jesus as God: The New Testament Use of Theos in Reference to Jesus* (Grand Rapids: Baker, 1992), pp. 54-55. The apostle John uses *logos* in a manner that goes far beyond its use in Greek philosophy, since the *logos* is personal, moral and transcendent. For a thorough development of these themes, see Carl F. H. Henry, *God, Revelation, and Authority* (Waco, Tex.: Word, 1976-1983), 3:164-247.

[11]James Spiegel has done an excellent job in explaining the ultimate roots of atheism in immoral unbelief. Yet he does not therefore abjure natural theology or other forms of apologetics. See his *The Making of an Atheist: How Immorality Leads to Unbelief* (Chicago: Moody Press, 2010).

[12]For more on the noetic effects of sin with respect to natural theology, see Michael Sudduth, "The Dogmatic Model of Natural Theology," in *The Reformed Objection to Natural Theology* (Burlington, Vt.: Ashgate, 2009).

[13]On indirect communication, see Søren Kierkegaard, *The Point of View of My Work as an Author,*

Similarly, Paul Moser has argued for a "filial knowledge of God" that eschews natural theology. Moser's project is sophisticated and carefully nuanced, rightly emphasizing that the human knower needs to be properly related to God in order to know God in a personal manner. In this he is similar to Pascal. But Moser sees natural theology as unnecessary or even harmful to the cause of cultivating the proper response to God, given its impersonal or nonrelational nature.[14] What then should we make of natural theology?

Paul testifies in Romans that even the Gentiles have some knowledge of God through creation (Romans 1:18-20) and conscience (Romans 2:14-15). Therefore, all are culpable for their rebellion against God and for their idolatry. The text, however, does not tell us exactly by what means God makes himself known to all people such that they are responsible for this knowledge. Calvin claimed there was a sense of deity (*sensus divinitatus*) innate in all people.[15] This sense of deity probably has intuitive elements that are not based on arguments. We simply subjectively experience our creaturehood before God. Or we may simply infer from the material of creation that it was created. Otherwise, how did it get there? William Lane Craig makes the case that Romans 1:20 "could very well indicate that inferential reasoning is involved in the perception of God's invisible nature in creation, meaning something like, 'God's invisible nature is perceived through reflecting on the things that have been made.'"[16] The late Thomist scholar Etienne Gilson wrote that "quite apart from any philosophical demonstration of the existence of God, there is such a thing as a spontaneous natural theology." This is a "quasi-instinctive tendency, observable in most men," which invites "them to wonder from time to time

---

trans. Walter Lowrie (New York: Harper & Brothers, 1962). This form of apologetic interaction should not be rejected; my concern is that it should not replace a robust natural theology.
[14]See Paul Moser, "Cognitive Inspiration and the Knowledge of God," in *The Rationality of Theism*, ed. Paul Copan and Paul K. Moser (New York: Routledge, 2003), pp. 55-71; see also his larger treatment in *The Elusive God* (New York: Cambridge University Press, 2008). For a more in-depth critique of Moser's views, see Garrett DeWeese, "Toward a Robust Natural Theology: Reply to Paul Moser," *Philosophia Christi* 3, no. 1 (2001): 113-18.
[15]On the idea of the human sense of deity, see John Calvin, *Institutes of the Christian Religion* 1.3.1. His idea of the seed of religion is found in 1.4.1. This idea has been developed at great length in the religious epistemology of Alvin Plantinga, *Warranted Christian Belief* (New York: Oxford, 2000). I critique his approach in chap. 3.
[16]William Lane Craig, "Classical Apologetics," in *Five Views of Apologetics*, ed. Steven Cowan (Grand Rapids: Zondervan, 2000), p. 40.

if, after all, there is not such an unseen being as the one we call God."[17]

But even if Romans 1 refers to an intuitive knowledge, this does not rule out the propriety of theistic arguments, since the same thing (in this case God) can be known in various ways. For example, I may know that someone is a loving person by knowing him personally, by reading about his loving acts or by hearing about them from his friends. Moreover, a theistic argument might supplement the immediate knowledge of God.[18]

Despite this intuitive knowledge of God, there is also a suppression of that knowledge because of sin. Instead of glorifying God and being thankful for divine gifts, humans east of Eden share a universal propensity to exchange the transcendent reality of God for things ready at hand, things that can be manipulated and directly perceived: that is, idols. As Calvin noted, the human mind is a "perpetual forge of idols."[19] Although made by God and surrounded by the works of God, we become god-makers, substituting the finite for the infinite and losing our direction and wisdom in the process. Yet in the midst of this malaise, natural theology has a place and purpose. Solid arguments for the divine reality challenge the torpor and turpitude of the God-resisting and image-making mind. The idol-befogged creature of God may be reminded and chastened by evidences from nature that God is his or her Maker.[20]

5. Proofs lead to pride argument. Pascal has a further objection to natural theology. He claims that successful theistic arguments that have nothing to do with the incarnation would engender pride in those who engage in them. Such arguments could lead us to think that a sufficient knowledge of God is available apart from the work of the Mediator. Pride, or self-sufficiency, is the opposite of the condition Pascal wants to encourage in a religious seeker. The seeker ought to be humble and receptive before God. "It is not only impossible but useless to know God without Christ."[21]

[17]Etienne Gilson, *God and Philosophy* (New Haven, Conn.: Yale University Press, 1941), p. 115.
[18]I owe this insight to Michael Sudduth.
[19]Calvin, *Institutes of the Christian Religion* 1.11.8.
[20]Earlier Reformed thinkers recognized both the immediate and inferential knowledge of God. See Sudduth, *Reformed Objection to Natural Theology*, pp. 58-70. Many prominent thinkers who advocated the immediate knowledge of God in the nineteenth century (such as Charles Hodge, Augustus Strong and William Shedd) also endorsed natural theology (see ibid., pp. 70-75).
[21]Pascal, *Pensées* 191/549, p. 86.

Therefore, Pascal rejects these arguments as spiritually perilous.[22] Karl
Barth held a similar view.

Pascal's apologetic method focuses on Christ, not simply on providence
or a Creator. He passionately wants to convince people of their moral and
spiritual need for redemption offered by Jesus Christ. In light of this he
worries that natural theology proves a God without Christ, which might
undermine the sense of "wretchedness" that he seeks to demonstrate about
the human condition. He believes that God must be "hidden" to some
degree in order for creatures to feel their spiritual poverty.[23]

The Christian tradition teaches that pride is a vice that obscures our
need for spiritual redemption. However, it is not clear that a good argument for God's existence would necessarily or even likely encourage that
kind of pride in someone who accepts theistic arguments. If a good argument for a Creator or Designer or Lawgiver were produced and believed, a
person might well wonder about his or her status before this rather formidable being. Rather than fomenting pride, a winning theistic argument
may make a human being seem small in comparison to the metaphysical
grandeur of God. That might be the first step toward the humility so vital
to Pascal's approach to our knowledge of God.[24]

If Pascal means that, apart from Christ, one cannot know God *redemp-
tively,* he aligns with Scripture (John 14:6). However, natural theology
may help someone know that God exists, and if that person moves from
atheism to theism, he or she may then begin to investigate the claims and
credentials of Christian theism. If so, there are plenty of other apologetic
arguments that make a case for Christ as the only way of salvation.

6. Natural theology in competition with special revelation argument.
Karl Barth forcefully rejected natural theology because he took it to be in
competition with the revelation in Scripture.[25] For Barth, God's revelation
was found only in the Christ of the Bible. Any other revelation claim
would add something to the one true revelation and thus both usurp and

---

[22]Ibid., 352/526, p. 133; 190/543, p. 86.
[23]On Pascal's notions on skepticism and the hiddenness of God, see Douglas Groothuis, "Skepticism and the Hidden God," in *On Pascal* (Belmont, Calif.: Wadsworth, 2003).
[24]See Douglas Groothuis, "Proofs, Pride, and Incarnation: Is Natural Theology Theologically
Taboo?" *Journal of the Evangelical Theological Society* 38, no. 1 (1995): 67-77.
[25]Karl Barth, *Church Dogmatics: A Selection* (New York: Harper, 1961), pp. 49-64; see also Karl
Barth, *The Epistle to the Romans* (New York: Oxford University Press, 1977), p. 82.

corrupt it. Humans must receive revelation as stipulated by God and not try to fathom God apart from Scripture.[26] He thus denied general revelation (which is a necessary condition for natural theology). Barth wrote from his experience with Nazism, which had tried to supplant biblical revelation with its own counterfeit claims to destiny. He helped draft the Barmen Declaration, which denounced Nazi ideology and emphasized the centrality of the Bible for authentic Christian faith.

Although Francis Schaeffer was a strong and cogent critic of Karl Barth, he too criticized natural theology by claiming that it set up an "autonomous" realm of knowledge that eventually would pit itself against the deliverance of special revelation.[27] While Schaeffer believed in general revelation and used a kind of verificationist method in apologetics, he denied natural theology as classically understood.[28]

Barth was right to reject any external claim that would compromise the authority of Scripture and God's radical transcendence. He valiantly stood against Nazism. Schaeffer was a stalwart defender of Christianity, whose own apologetic incorporated general revelation. However, a right understanding of general revelation and natural theology is no threat to special revelation. Because the Bible itself claims that God is revealed in nature and conscience, belief in general revelation is rooted in special revelation. Further, a sound apologetic method attempts to verify the Christian worldview through various means, not merely by natural theology. Consider the touchstone proposition of the Christian worldview as mentioned in chapter four.

> The universe (originally good, now fallen and awaiting its divine judgment and restoration) was created by and is sustained by the triune God, who has revealed himself in nature, humanity, conscience, Scripture and supremely through the incarnation, that God may be glorified in all things.

---

[26]Barth, however, did not take the Bible to be without error. He held to higher critical views of Scripture, but thought God could still speak through the Bible supernaturally when he deemed fit.

[27]Francis Schaeffer, *Escape from Reason* (1968; reprint, Downers Grove, Ill.: InterVarsity Press, 2006), chap. 1.

[28]Schaeffer's exact method has been disputed, but Gordon Lewis best explains Schaeffer's approach as a kind of implicit verificationism, similar to that of Edward John Carnell. See Gordon R. Lewis, "Schaeffer's Apologetic Method," in *Reflections on Francis Schaeffer*, ed. Ronald W. Ruegsegger (Grand Rapids: Zondervan Academie Books, 1986), pp. 69-104.

This statement does not allow for the incorporation of data that fails to line up with its stipulations. If God is the author of the book of nature as well as the book of Scripture, these books will not conflict any more than God can deny himself. As the ancient saying goes, "All truth is God's truth." While Barth feared the claims of natural theology as a rival to special revelation, the danger of denying general revelation and its use for natural theology is even greater; for this tends to divorce Scripture from nature and faith from reason. Fideism or irrationalism is often the result, thus crippling apologetic endeavors.[29]

Having considered and rejected these six in-principle arguments against the propriety of natural theology, we will conclude by assessing three in-practice arguments against natural theology. These arguments claim that even if there is nothing wrong with natural theology per se, theistic arguments still fail to deliver what is necessary for the Christian apologetic cause.

7. Religious irrelevance argument. Some object that while the idea of natural theology is not wrong in itself, the arguments do not secure enough knowledge about the character of God. They are more about "the God of the philosophers" than "the God of Abraham, Isaac, and Jacob," as Pascal famously put it.[30] Even if the argument is rationally successful, it is thus apologetically and existentially moot.

It is true that one may grant that God exists and not be very moved by that fact, especially if God is regarded as performing merely a few metaphysical functions that fail to impinge on everyday life or to stir the conscience. On the other hand, a successful theistic argument (of whatever stripe) or a cluster of such arguments (a cumulative-case approach), while falling short of a full-orbed biblical theism, may move a skeptic or an atheist a bit closer to taking the distinctive claims of Christian faith more seriously. For instance, if Jane is argued out of atheism by one or more arguments from natural theology, she may become interested in evaluating the specifically Christian claims about God and Christ found in the Bible. Jane would have had less philosophical incentive to investigate Scripture

---

[29]For an overview and critique of Barth on natural theology, see Rodney Holder, "Karl Barth and the Legitimacy of Natural Theology," *Themelios* 26, no. 3 (2001): 22-37. Holder, however, makes the mistake of conflating general revelation and natural theology.
[30]Pascal, *Pensées* 913, pp. 309-10; see also 449/556, p. 169.

when she was an atheist, since that belief ruled out the possibility of a divine Author of Scripture. Natural theology in the Christian tradition has never been regarded as an end in itself (which could lead to deism) but rather as a prelude to other evidences and arguments pertaining to its creed.[31] Pascal, to his detriment as an apologist, seems to deny this potentially faith-enhancing tool of natural theology.[32]

8. Complexity of proofs argument. Pascal and others also complain about the complexity of theistic arguments. Even if they are logically successful, their conclusions have little existential effect on the philosophizer, who may doubt the warrant of the conclusion given the complexity of the argument.[33]

The philosophical debates over theistic arguments can be quite complex, involving the logic of possible worlds, the nature of causation, big bang cosmology and more. Nevertheless, if a metaphysical proof (a cosmological or design argument) is deemed more cogent than its denial, then it offers rational support for theism. These arguments may be complex and difficult, but if they are mastered they should be convincing.

Not all of these arguments need be intricate and intellectually taxing to be cogent. We may boil down a complex argument to several simple principles that remain convincing. For instance, someone impressed by a cosmological argument (that the universe requires a cause and explanation outside itself) may reason that either the universe (1) was created by God, (2) is eternal or (3) popped into existence without a cause a finite time ago. A person who takes (2) and (3) to be less plausible than (1) has an argument at hand that is not so "remote from human reasoning" as Pascal may have feared.[34] Craig, a leading proponent of natural theology, notes that as a boy when he gazed into the starry skies he believed in God because he "thought that it all had to come from somewhere," yet he had never heard of the cosmological argument. He surmises that "many people have rea-

---

[31]If the ontological argument is successful, a full panoply of theistic attributes would be established. See the discussion of this argument in chap. 10. I owe this point to David Werther. For more on the religious irrelevance argument, see Sudduth, *Reformed Objection to Natural Theology*, chaps. 10-11.

[32]See, Douglas Groothuis, "Do Theistic Proofs Prove the Wrong God?" *Christian Scholar's Review* 29, no. 2 (1999): 247-60.

[33]Pascal, *Pensées* 190/543, p. 86.

[34]See Douglas Groothuis, "Are Theistic Arguments Religiously Useless? A Pascalian Objection Examined," *Trinity Journal* 15 (1994): 147-61.

soned to themselves that God exists in ways that resemble rudimentary forms of the traditional theistic proofs.[35]

9. *Rational weakness argument.* One last criticism of theistic arguments is that they cannot compel belief; that is, they can be successfully resisted by rational people. If so, what worth are they in the overall case for Christian theism? Perhaps we should put our apologetic effort elsewhere or merely proclaim and live out the gospel instead.

In response, human reasoning is a complex thing. Theistic arguments may be quite strong in themselves (as I believe the best ones are) yet not be recognized as such by people for a variety of reasons. First, if an argument cuts sharply against an individual's worldview, the person will be (at least initially) reluctant to give up or significantly modify his or her beliefs. Second, someone may find such arguments threatening and simply avoid them for the sake of personal comfort in maintaining previously held beliefs. Third, a person may (for no good reason) raise the logical bar so high that no theistic argument can reach it. That is, he or she may insist that unless there is a deductively valid argument for God's existence that relies on clear premises known to be true by everyone, there is no good evidence for God. Yet there are very few arguments in metaphysics—or concerning important matters in general—that compel universal assent. Yet that is no reason to cease arguing entirely. Many surgeries fail to accomplish their ends, but that is no argument against surgery. More to the point, many evangelistic overtures are declined, but that is no argument against evangelism. As in all things, even after diligent labor, Christians leave the results in God's hands.

In the end, the proof of the theistic proofs lies in the proving, that is, in their validity and soundness, and not in theoretical musings about what they can and cannot or should and should not do. We must simply discover whether the arguments, singly and taken together, make belief in God more credible than otherwise. That is the robust goal of the next several chapters.

---

[35]William Lane Craig, "A Classical Apologist's Response," in *Five Views of Apologetics*, ed. Steven Cowan (Grand Rapids: Zondervan, 2000), p. 288.

10

The Ontological Argument

IMAGINE A PHILOSOPHICAL ARGUMENT that has been engaged by some of the most stellar minds in the history of thought about the greatest controversy ever engaged: the existence and nature of God. This line of reasoning requires no empirical premises; it works from sheer rational concepts. Now imagine that the conclusion of this argument announces that a Perfect Being exists—a superlative entity in whom rests all possible perfections and in whom no defect can be found. Is this an apologetic fantasy? No, it is the ontological argument.

The ontological argument claims that proper reasoning about the idea of a Perfect Being generates the conclusion that God exists.[1] For this argument, God's existence is not merely possible or probable or very likely, but is logically guaranteed. In this sense the ontological argument is "the king of the hill" of all the theistic arguments. It is a priori (depending on no debatable empirical conditions); it is deductive in form, thus making its conclusion certain and not merely probable; and its conclusion is metaphysically superlative: there must be a Perfect Being. If successful, the ontological argument is a masterpiece of a priori or rationalist reasoning and, as such, sharply and deeply cuts against the grain of the empiricism that dominates both the popular and the academic mind.

In his bestselling book *The God Delusion*, Richard Dawkins dedicates

---

[1]Stephen T. Davis points out that the ontological argument is often described as arguing from the concept of God to the existence of God. But this oversimplifies and subtly throws the argument into a bad light. The argument requires a particular concept of God, but then argues for God's existence based on other logical principles outside of the concept of God itself (see "The Ontological Argument," in *The Rationality of Theism*, ed. Paul Copan and Paul K. Moser [New York: Routledge, 2003], p. 94).

five pages to refuting the ontological argument.[2] Without prior knowledge of the history of this fascinating specimen of reasoning, we could conclude from Dawkins's treatment that the ontological argument was more of a joke than a serious work of philosophy. As a naive empiricist, he simply finds absurd the idea that an argument could prove God's existence without appeal to empirical evidence. But Dawkins's glib rejection never engages the richness or subtlety of the argument, a piece of reasoning that has intrigued some of the best minds in philosophy since the argument's inception by Anselm in the eleventh century. Noted philosopher of religion William Rowe has said, "Perhaps no other argument in the history of thought has raised so many basic philosophical questions and stimulated so much hard thought. Even if it fails as a proof of the existence of God, it will remain as one of the high achievements of the human intellect."[3]

While this argument has been extensively assessed in the philosophy of religion literature, most popular apologetics books omit it, and some of the more sophisticated texts do so as well.[4] Two purported reasons for this exclusion are that (1) the argument fails and (2) the reasoning employed is too difficult to understand or it somehow lacks the existential punch needed for dynamic apologetics. Granted, the argument is rationally demanding and trades on some esoteric metaphysical concepts, such as necessary existence (although the better design, moral, cosmological and religious experience arguments are also logically rigorous). Nevertheless, if the ontological argument is sound, it is fitting to include it in an apologist's tool bag.

Furthermore, the argument does pack existential punch. Anselm's version of the argument was offered as part of a prayer. He earnestly sought to offer an argument to God that would convince "the fool" of Psalm 14 that God must exist. So, the chapel and the study become the same room. The existence of the greatest possible being should compel our worship,

---

[2]Richard Dawkins, *The God Delusion* (Boston: Houghton Mifflin, 2006), pp. 80-85.

[3]William Rowe, *Philosophy of Religion: An Introduction* (Belmont, Calif.: Wadsworth, 1978), p. 46.

[4]The popular and well-done apologetics books by Lee Strobel fail to take up this argument, nor does J. P. Moreland's more sophisticated *Scaling the Secular City*. Ronald Nash's volume, *Faith and Reason* dedicates all of one paragraph to the argument, while giving entire chapters to the cosmological, religious experience and design arguments. The first two editions of *Reasonable Faith* (1984, 1994) by William Lane Craig lacked a developed treatment of this argument as well, although the third edition (2008) includes a bang-up version.

since no greater being is possible and we are far lesser beings than this being.[5] Moreover, the concept of God as a necessary being plays an important part in the cosmological argument and the moral argument, which we will address later in this book.

ONTOLOGICAL ARGUMENT 1: GREATEST POSSIBLE EXISTENCE

St. Anselm (c. 1033-1109) gives two versions of the ontological argument, as Norman Malcolm and Charles Hartshorne discovered in the 1960s.[6] Both are compelling once certain refinements and contemporary restatements are incorporated. The first argument is from chapter two of *Proslogium* and occurs within a prayer:

> We believe that you [God] are a being than which nothing greater can be conceived. Or is there no such nature, since the fool has said in his heart, there is no God? (Psalms xiv.1). But, at any rate, this very fool, when he hears of this being of which I speak—a being than which nothing greater can be conceived—understands what he hears, and what he understands is in his understanding; although he does not understand it to exist.
>
> For, it is one thing for an object to be in the understanding, and another to understand that the object exists. When a painter first conceives of what he will afterwards perform, he has it in his understanding, but be does not yet understand it to be, because he has not yet performed it. But after he has made the painting, he both has it in his understanding, and he understands that it exists, because he has made it.
>
> Hence, even the fool is convinced that something exists in the understanding, at least, than which nothing greater can be conceived. For, when he hears of this, he understands it. And whatever is understood, exists in the understanding. And assuredly that, than which nothing greater can be conceived, cannot exist in the understanding alone. For, suppose it exists in the understanding alone: then it can be conceived to exist in reality; which is greater.

[5]Thanks to David Werther for these insights on the existential punch of the ontological argument.
[6]Norman Malcolm, *Knowledge and Certainty: Essays and Lectures* (Englewood Cliffs, N.J.: Prentice-Hall, 1963), pp. 149-50; and Charles Hartshorne, *Anselm's Discovery: A Re-examination of the Ontological Argument for God's Existence* (Chicago: Open Court, 1965).

Therefore, if that, than which nothing greater can be conceived, exists in the understanding alone, the very being, than which nothing greater can be conceived, is one, than which a greater can be conceived. But obviously this is impossible.

Hence, there is no doubt that there exists a being, than which nothing greater can be conceived, and it exists both in the understanding and in reality.[7]

Anselm puzzles over the unbelief of "the fool" and labors to construct an argument to defeat this fool and, thereby, atheism. We may schematize the argument this way:

1. God is understood or defined as a being "than which nothing greater can be conceived." Even the fool possesses this concept of God.

2. A thing exists either in (a) the understanding only (such as the idea of a painting before it is painted) or (b) in both the understanding and reality, such as existing in the mind of the painter and then existing on the canvas.[8]

3. It is "greater" to exist in reality than to exist merely in the understanding.

4. If God exists merely in the understanding (existing only in the mind of the fool), then God is not the greatest possible being, since a being that existed in reality would be greater than a being that existed only in the understanding.

5. But God is by definition the greatest possible being (from 1).

6. Therefore, God exists not merely in the understanding (as the fool claims) but in reality as well. By reductio ad absurdum.

This argument is deductive and is formally valid. If the five premises are true, the conclusion follows necessarily from them. Concerning premise 1, contemporary reflection on the idea of a being "than which nothing greater can be conceived" has taken the concept to mean a greatest conceivable being or greatest possible being. This being is maximally perfect

---

[7]Anselm *Proslogium* 2, in *Internet Medieval Sourcebook* <www.fordham.edu/halsall/basis/anselm-proslogium.html#CHAPTER%20II>.

[8]A thing can also exist in reality but not exist in the understanding—at least in the understanding of any finite being—since there are many things unknown to finite knowers. But Anselm had no need to concern himself with this category.

and thus possesses every attribute that it is better to have than to lack.[9] Thus axiology (the theory or concept of value) plays a key role. Moreover, this being possesses each attribute to the highest degree possible. This *qualitative* concept of infinity should not be confused with the *quantitative* concept of infinity, which obtains, for example, with numbers (you can always add more numbers) or weight (you can always add more pounds).[10] Rather, God's perfections have an upper limit, a point of completion or "intrinsic maximum."[11] God possesses the maximal amount of power, goodness, knowledge and so on, with no admixture of their opposites. For example, one cannot bat higher than 1.000 in baseball, nor can one score higher than 300 in bowling. While these examples involve numerical *quantities*, they indicate *qualitative* perfection because of their upper limit. Thus, instead of having only some power, God is perfectly powerful (omnipotent); instead of being ignorant of anything, God is perfectly knowledgeable (omniscient); instead of being a mixture of good and evil, God is perfectly good (omnibenevolent); and so on. This qualification of possessing an absolute upper limit becomes important for defeating a criticism of the second version of Anselm's argument, which we will address shortly. Last, God possesses every desirable attribute in harmony with all his other attributes. Just as a being could not possess the property of being a good bachelor and of being a good married man, so God cannot possess properties that contradict each other. A collection of logically consistent properties is said to be *compossibile*.[12]

CRITIQUES OF THE ARGUMENT

If ontological argument 1 is valid, then the truth of the premises must be attacked in order to defeat it. The earliest critique of the argument, given by a monk named Gaunilo, charged that given God's unsurpassable greatness, we can form no concept of him. If so, the ontological argument founders at the first premise, since we have no intelligible concept from which to work.[13] While some still claim that the idea of a Perfect Being is

---

[9]Philosophers sometimes speak of this as possessing all "great-making properties" (see Thomas V. Morris, *Our Idea of God: An Introduction to Philosophical Theology* [Downers Grove, Ill.: InterVarsity Press, 1991], pp. 35-36).

[10]Technically, this is called "a potential infinite," a term to which we return in chap. 11.

[11]William Wainwright, *Philosophy of Religion*, 2nd ed. (Belmont, Calif.: Wadsworth, 1999), p. 8.

[12]Morris, *Our Idea of God*, p. 37.

[13]Gaunilo, "In Behalf of the Fool," in *St. Anselm: Basic Writings*, trans. S. N. Deane (Chicago: Open Court, 1962), p. 148.

unintelligible, this claim has lost much of its force, given all the rigorous philosophical work done on the concept of God.[14] We need not understand everything about this superlative being to have a proper apprehension of it; we simply need to understand the definition given by Anselm.[15] The notion of a Perfect Being is not opaque or swamped by mystery.[16] In fact, we can summarize the previous two paragraphs:

> A Perfect Being is a being who possesses every property it is better to have than to lack and who possesses this array of compossible excellent properties to the utmost degree (or to their intrinsic maximum value).[17]

Another famous criticism of the ontological argument comes from Kant. In *The Critique of Pure Reason*, Kant objects to the argument on the grounds that it requires that existence function as a predicate or attribute for a subject—in this case, God.[18] That is, in Anselm's first argument, one of the Perfect Being's perfections is existence, which functions as a predicate or property of God. This is found in premise 4:

> If God exists merely in the understanding (as in existing only in the mind of the fool), then he is not the greatest possible being, since a being that existed in reality would be greater than a being that existed only in the understanding.

Certainly the idea of existence functions *grammatically* as a predicate or

---

[14]For example, see part four, "The Theistic Concept of God," in *The Routledge Companion to Philosophy of Religion*, ed. Chad Meister and Paul Copan (New York: Routledge, 2007); Morris, *Our Idea of God*. Nevertheless, there is a book dedicated to the impossibility of God. Michael Martin and Ricki Monnier, eds., *The Impossibility of God* (New York: Prometheus, 2003). For a summary of these charges see Patrick Grim, "Impossibility Arguments," in *The Cambridge Companion to Atheism*, ed. Michael Martin (New York: Cambridge University Press, 2007). For a accounts of theism as internally coherent, see Richard Swinburne, *The Coherence of Theism* (New York: Oxford University Press, 1977); Ronald Nash, *The Concept of God* (Grand Rapids: Baker, 1983); and Stephen T. Davis, *Logic and the Nature of God* (New York: Palgrave Macmillan, 1983).

[15]Indeed, finite beings cannot know everything about anything, but that fact does not exclude knowledge of various sorts. As Francis Schaeffer often said, we can know God truly without knowing God exhaustively (Francis A. Schaeffer, *The God Who Is There*, 30th anniv. ed. [Downers Grove, Ill.: InterVarsity Press, 1998], p. 121).

[16]See Davis, *God, Reason, and Theistic Proofs*, pp. 27-28.

[17]This understanding is influenced by Morris, *Idea of God*, p. 35.

[18]Immanuel Kant, "The Impossibility of an Ontological Proof of the Existence of God," *The Critique of Pure Reason*, trans. Norman Kemp Smith (New York: St. Martin's Press, 1929). Kant was the first to apply the moniker "ontological argument" to this a priori theistic argument.

attribute when we say, "God exists." In this case, *God* is the subject and *exists* is the predicate.[19] Similarly, when we say "Abraham Lincoln was tall," *Abraham Lincoln* is the subject and *tall* is the predicate.

But Kant thought that existence cannot serve as a predicate or property of God; thus, the idea of *existing* added nothing to the concept of God. For Kant, existence is merely a *logical* predicate, not a *genuine* predicate. A genuine predicate adds significant information regarding the subject, as in, "The tree's leaves were dark green." But contrariwise, a logical predicate adds nothing significant to the subject, as in, "The tree's leaves are leaves."[20] Any grammatical statement can function as a logical predicate, but a real predicate "determines" a thing or "enlarges" the idea of the subject in Kant's terminology.[21]

If existence does not function as a genuine predicate, this is fatal to Anselm's argument, since he is arguing from the very concept of God (plus logical principles) to the existence of God. Kant claims that while being *almighty* is necessary to the idea of God, *existing* is not necessary to the idea of God. In the same way, *having three sides* is necessary to the idea of a triangle, but *existing* is not necessary for the idea of a triangle. That is, it might be the case that no triangles exist even if the very idea of a triangle requires that it have exactly three sides. One can conceive of God as non-existent, just as one can think of a triangle as nonexistent. The predicate of existence adds nothing to the concepts involved. The idea of existence is, in Kant's terms, merely "the copula of a judgment."[22] This means that existence is the link between the subject and the predicates in a proposition, as in "The barn is red." The word *is* here is the copula of a judgment. With this in mind, Kant claims that we either judge (or affirm) that something X exists or we don't. If we affirm that X exists, then we affirm that *all* the predicates of X exist. But if we do not affirm that X exists, *none* of its predicates obtain for it. If Kant is right, Anselm is wrong, since Anselm added the predicate of existence to the concept of God in the argument just laid out. Consider especially premises (3) and (4).[23]

---

[19]Ed L. Miller and Jon Jensen, *Questions that Matter*, 5th ed. (Boston, McGraw-Hill, 2004), p. 301.
[20]Davis, *God, Reason, and Theistic Proofs*, p. 32.
[21]Kant, *Critique of Pure Reason*, p. 504.
[22]Ibid.
[23]For a detailed exposition and criticism of Kant's objection that existence is not a predicate, see Alvin Plantinga, *God and Other Minds* (New York: Cornell University Press, 1967), pp. 26-47.

Although Norman Malcolm defends another version of the ontological argument (as we will see), he sided with Kant that existence is not a predicate. He perhaps put the matter more clearly through several examples, the absurdity of which Malcolm thought refuted Anselm. Consider this statement: "My future house will be better if it is air conditioned than if it is not." But what would it mean to say that it would be better if the home existed? The same holds true, mutatis mutandis, for children, automobiles, political figures and so on.[24] To say it would be better if they existed is bizarre. Malcolm accuses Anselm as having smuggled in the idea of existence as a real predicate, something that adds meaning to the concept of an entity.

CLARIFYING PREDICATION

Yet the matter of predication is more subtle and multiform than Kant and Malcolm conceive. Following Malcolm, we should grant that it is odd to add the idea of existence to that of a desired home or child. This oddness occurs because the existence of the home or child is *presupposed* in the context of the discussion (although we may wonder whether or not the desired object will ever exist).[25] However, it is not odd to use existence as a predicate in any number of other descriptive settings. For example, a young girl may be listening to a story read by her mother. The story includes a variety of animals, some found in zoology texts (real, such as a lion) and some not (unreal, such as a unicorn). The child may ask of any particular animal, "Mommy, is that animal real or just in the story?" The child is asking whether the animal described in the children's story exists in reality or only "exists in the understanding" (to use Anselm's phrasing).[26] The question is perfectly intelligible and intelligent and commits no fallacies. Existence is legitimately functioning as a predicate in this case and in cases of a similar sort. The same holds for the claims of cryptozoology. Do the Loch Ness Monster or Bigfoot exist or not? After James Frey's supposed memoir, *A Million Little Pieces* (2003), was revealed to be largely fictional, many wondered which of its accounts were factual and which were fic-

[24]Malcolm, *Knowledge and Certainty*, p. 144. I have altered his examples somewhat.
[25]Stephen T. Davis, *God, Reason, and Theistic Proofs* (Grand Rapids: Eerdmans, 1997), p. 34.
[26]The inspiration for this example comes from Frank Ebersole, *Things We Know* (Eugene: University of Oregon Press, 1967), pp. 240-43.

tional. In other words, did event X occur (exist objectively in reality) or not occur (exist only subjectively in Frey's mind)? Existence functions legitimately as a predicate here as well.

So, it seems that there is nothing wrong with existence functioning as a predicate for the subject God, since the matter of God's objective existence is a legitimate *question*, like the ontological status of the animals in the children's story or in matters of cryptozoology or James Frey's description of events. These things are *possibly existing things*, so existence is an appropriate and meaningful predicate concerning their ontological status.[27]

TO EXIST OR NOT TO EXIST

The last commonly made objection to the argument from the second chapter of *Proslogium* concerns the question of whether it is better to exist or not to exist, since Anselm claims that it is better for the Perfect Being to exist than not to exist.[28] Existence, he avers, is simply part of greatness. Anselm does not bother to define what he means by greatness, but we can sketch out the meaning in context. It is not a settled principle that for any possible being it is better for that being to exist than not to exist. Indeed, it is better for an unstoppable flesh-eating virus not to exist than to exist, and Anselm is not suggesting otherwise. Rather, he is specifically addressing a singular Perfect Being and nothing else—a being in a class by itself. An existing Perfect Being is certainly greater than the mere idea of one. This notion of greatness seems to consist in power—the ability to accomplish things in the world. Nietzsche granted that the *idea* of (a nonexistent) God was very powerful in the history of Western civilization—even if God had "died" in late-nineteenth-century Europe.[29] But an existing Perfect Being would be far greater—more powerful, able to accomplish things *as an existing agent*, not merely as a notion, idea or concept that exists only subjectively in the minds of people.[30] In this sense, we can affirm that the lowliest private investigator is *greater* than the comic book character Batman, since the latter only exists "in the understanding."

[27]Davis, *God, Reason, and Theistic Proofs*, p. 35.
[28]See E. J. Lowe, "The Ontological Argument," in *The Routledge Companion to Philosophy of Religion*, ed. Chad Meister and Paul Copan (New York: Routledge, 2007), pp. 331-32.
[29]Friedrich Nietzsche, "The Gay Science" 125, in *The Portable Nietzsche*, trans. Walter Kaufmann (New York: Viking, 1968), p. 95.
[30]See Davis, "The Ontological Argument," pp. 98-99.

Moreover, while ideas—both true and false—have consequences, ideas themselves are causally inert. Actual *agents* must believe ideas and act on them in order to bring about states of affairs in the world. Therefore, a false idea really has no power in itself. Rather, agents who hold false ideas act in accordance with their false beliefs and produce consequences. Likewise, agents who hold true ideas (about things that objectively exist) and act on them bring about states of affairs influenced by their true beliefs.

Thus it seems that the three most common objections to Anselm's first argument run aground because the following three propositions are sound: (1) The idea of a Perfect Being is conceivable. (2) Existence can function as a predicate for God. (3) It is better for a Perfect Being to exist than not to exist. But even if his first ontological argument fails, he has another argument that trades on the ideas of necessity and possibility (or modal logic).

ANSELM'S ONTOLOGICAL ARGUMENT 2

The argument of chapter three of *Proslogium* was routinely conflated with the argument from chapter two until Norman Malcolm and Charles Hartshorne distinguished them.[31] In the second argument, Anselm writes:

> God cannot be conceived not to exist. God is that, than which nothing greater can be conceived. That which can be conceived not to exist is not God.
>
> And it assuredly exists so truly, that it cannot be conceived not to exist. For, it is possible to conceive of a being which cannot be conceived not to exist; and this is greater than one which can be conceived not to exist. Hence, if that, than which nothing greater can be conceived, can be conceived not to exist, it is not that, than which nothing greater can be conceived. But this is an irreconcilable contradiction. There is, then, so truly a being than which nothing greater can be conceived to exist, that it cannot even be conceived not to exist; and this being you are, O Lord, our God.[32]

Here Anselm employs an argument strategy similar to the one in chap-

---

[31]William Rowe suggests that the discussion in chapter three may not have been meant by Anselm as a separate argument but rather as an elaboration on what he established in chapter two. Nevertheless, Rowe realizes that the ideas presented in chapter three (God's necessary existence) can be shaped into a distinct ontological argument. See William Rowe, "Modal Versions of the Ontological Argument," in *Philosophy of Religion: An Anthology*, ed. Louis Pojman (Belmont, Calif.: Wadsworth, 1987), pp. 69-73.

[32]Anselm, *Proslogium* 3 <www.fordham.edu/halsall/basis/anselm-proslogium.html#CHAPTER III>.

ter two. The difference with this argument is the employment of the concept of what later philosophers call "necessary existence."[33] God does not simply *happen* to exist as "a being than which nothing greater can be conceived to exist." Rather, God exists as a matter of logical necessity. God does not exist as a contingent state of affairs, something that might or might not have obtained—such as, for example, the saxophone. We can rightly conceive of a (sad) world in which saxophones were never invented. But since a necessary being must exist (just as a truth such as A = A must be true), its existence is not a matter of contingent fact (such as, for example, the saxophone). Therefore, the only way to deny the existence of a necessary being is to demonstrate that its existence is nonsensical or contradictory (such as a married bachelor).[34]

As Malcolm puts it, God's "existence must be logically necessary or logically impossible. The only intelligible way of rejecting Anselm's claim that God's existence is necessary is to maintain that the concept of God, as a being greater than which cannot be conceived, is self-contradictory or nonsensical."[35]

The argument for God as a necessary being can be put formally:

1. God is defined as a maximally great or Perfect Being.

2. The existence of a Perfect Being is either impossible or necessary (since it cannot be contingent).

3. The concept of a Perfect Being is not impossible, since it is neither nonsensical nor self-contradictory.

4. Therefore (a) a Perfect Being is necessary.

5. Therefore (b) a Perfect Being exists.

This deductive argument is valid. One must attack one of the three prem-

---

[33]This second argument does not depend on the controversial—but defensible—idea that existence is a predicate.

[34]In my discussion of Anselm's first ontological argument, I argued that existence can function as a genuine predicate in matters where the existence of a purported entity is a matter of dispute—even if that entity is God. One might object, however, that in Anselm's second ontological argument, he rules out the very question of whether or not God exists, since he says "God cannot be conceived not to exist." But Anselm is not denying the possibility of questioning God's existence philosophically, and this is all that is needed for existence to function as a genuine predicate. Rather, Anselm means that once we grasp the meaning of God's logically necessary existence, and argue for it, God "cannot be conceived not to exist."

[35]Malcolm, *Knowledge and Certainty*, pp. 149-50.

ises in order to discredit it. Premise 3 is the only premise worth attacking, but it is difficult to dislodge.

The idea of God as a necessary being is not nonsense, as is the sentence, "Tambourines reprise acidity." Nor is it likely at all that the idea of God as a Perfect Being is self-contradictory.[36] In order to ground such a claim, the objector would have to show either that (1) one or more attributes of God conflict with one or more other divine attributes, or (2) that one single divine attribute is incoherent. I will give a response to one example from each objection.

First, some have claimed that the idea of omniscience is incompatible with God being immaterial. Since God is intrinsically without a body, God cannot possibly know what it feels like to have a body with its attendant pains and pleasures. Since God lacks this knowledge, God cannot be omniscient.[37] Therefore, the idea of God is self-contradictory, and therefore no such God exists. The flaw with this argument lies in both its concept of omniscience and its failure to grasp a specifically Christian understanding of God.

The classical theological claim of omniscience is not that God has a first-person *experience* of all that occurs in any sentient being in the universe, but that God has *knowledge* (justified true belief) of all propositions, both true and false (believing the true to be true and the false to be false). Nevertheless, given God's unlimited power to know, God has access to the subjective states of finite and embodied creatures, human and nonhuman, experiencing what they experience by "seeing through their eyes," "hearing through their ears" and so on. So, while God is not a finite and embodied being, God is able to enter into the subjectivity of finite, embodied beings. This might be called "omnisubjectivity."[38] Nevertheless, since God is not himself a finite, embodied being, God

---

[36]The problem of evil claims that the idea of a perfect God combined with the existence of evil in the world yields a contradiction. This will be taken up in chap. 25.

[37]Michael Martin, *Atheism: A Philosophical Justification* (Philadelphia: Temple University Press, 1990), pp. 287-97. I have not explored all the objections given by Martin but rather one salient objection. I believe the response I will give defeats all of Martin's charges.

[38]See Linda Zagzebski, "Omniscience," in *Routledge Companion to Philosophy of Religion*, ed. Paul Copan and Chad Meister (New York: Routledge, 2008), pp. 264-65. Further, God could know counterfactual *qualia* by considering how an embodied, finite creature *would* experience a state of affairs that is, in fact, not experienced by any such being. On this account, God knows the scent of a rose that is never smelled by any creature.

cannot experience that kind of existence in a first-person sense. This does nothing to deny God's omniscience (classically understood); rather, it simply stipulates who God is qua God and God's relation to the not-God (the material and finite creation).

Moreover, Christianity (unlike any other religion) claims that the second person of the Trinity took on a human nature at the incarnation (John 1:14; Philippians 2:5-8). Therefore, God does know *something* of the embodied human condition in the first person. God knows what it is like to be a human being. (However, God would not know experientially those conditions outside of those experienced by Jesus, such as being married or committing sin.) Therefore, the claim that God is not omniscient fails because he does have knowledge of all things and is not a stranger to first-person human experience in Christ.

Second, the famous "paradox of the stone" claims that the divine attribute of omnipotence is self-contradictory. This objection is usually posed as a question: Can God make a stone so heavy that God cannot lift it? (A similar, nontheological question is, "What happens when the irresistible force meets the immovable object?") This sets up a dilemma:

1. If God cannot create the unliftable stone, then God is not omnipotent, since he cannot create the stone.

2. If God creates the unliftable stone, then God is not omnipotent, since he cannot lift the stone.

3. Therefore, God is not omnipotent, because the very concept of omnipotence is contradictory.[39]

This dilemma is fueled by a confusion concerning omnipotence and logic. Omnipotence cannot mean the ability to do anything, irrespective of logical coherence. As Aquinas put it, God's power only pertains to actualizing logically possible states of affairs; it does not apply to actualizing logically impossible conditions. God cannot make a square circle, simply because the very idea is contradictory and thus cannot possibly be instantiated. Likewise, for God to create something he could not lift would be a contradiction, and contradictions cannot possibly obtain. In other words,

---

[39]This argument does not rule out some subdeity of lesser strength, but we are not concerned with that here.

the same state of affairs cannot possibly contain both an unliftable stone and an all-powerful being.[40]

Craig adds more credibility to the coherence of the idea of a necessary being by arguing that even "if we cannot determine *a priori* whether maximal greatness is possibly exemplified, we may come to believe on the basis of *a posteriori* considerations that it is possible that a maximally great being exists."[41] While I think that through conceptual analysis of the idea of God we *can* determine a priori that a Perfect Being may exist (a premise needed for ontological argument 2), Craig submits three other non–a priori arguments to support this claim. First, Leibniz's cosmological argument, which trades on the principle of sufficient reason (PSR), argues for such a necessary being as the explanation for all contingent states (see chap. 11). Second, one moral argument for God concludes that God, as a morally maximal and necessary being, must be the source and explanation of morality (see chap. 15). Third, the conceptualist argument claims that the existence of abstract objects (or abstracta), such as propositions and numbers, requires an omniscient, metaphysically necessary mind (God) for their actuality.[42]

Craig summarizes his case that these other arguments lend credibility to the idea that God's existence is possible:

> Thus the [Leibnizian] cosmological argument leads to a metaphysically necessary being which is the ground of existence for any concrete [that is, contingent] entity, the moral argument to a locus of moral value which must be as metaphysically necessary as the moral values it grounds, and the conceptualist argument to an omniscient, metaphysically necessary intelligence as the foundation of abstract objects.[43]

---

[40]I am discussing the idea of a necessarily omnipotent being: a being that is necessarily omnipotent cannot lose that property. However, one might consider a being that is contingently omnipotent. That kind of being could create a rock too heavy to lift, but in so doing, it would lose omnipotence. The idea of a contingently omnipotent being is not biblical; moreover, it may be incoherent as well. See Joshua Hoffman and Gary Rosenkrantz, "Omnipotence," in *Routledge Companion to Philosophy of Religion*, ed. Paul Copan and Chad Meister (New York: Routledge, 2008), pp. 273-74. For more on the paradox of the stone and another way to resolve it, see Morris, *Our Idea of God*, pp. 74-76.

[41]William Lane Craig, "The Ontological Argument," in *To Everyone an Answer: A Case for the Christian Worldview*, ed. Francis Beckwith (Downers Grove, Ill.: InterVarsity Press, 2004), p. 131.

[42]Ibid., p. 135. Perhaps Craig should then refer to abstract objects as essential properties of the divine mind, since they do not exist on their own apart from God. David Werther pointed this out to me.

[43]Ibid.

If these arguments are sound, they show that the *idea* of a Perfect Being (or maximally great being) is logically possible. If so, given the previous ontological argument, then a Perfect Being exists necessarily. If so, logic has established the existence of a being with whom we have to do.

POSSIBLE WORLDS AND A NECESSARY GOD

The ontological argument that flows from chapter three of *Proslogium* has been further developed by Alvin Plantinga through the use of possible worlds conceptuality. Although this subject can involve complex metaphysics, a simplified understanding does the work required here.[44] A possible world is simply a way of considering possibilities. It is a logically possible state of affairs, which either exists (because it is actual as well as possible) or does not exist, but which might have existed.[45] To put it another way, a possible world is a description of the set of facts that would make up a hypothetical world; it is a maximally consistent set of propositions. Therefore, a possible world cannot contain people who are taller than they are, nor can it contain beings who need oxygen to survive but have none in their world.[46] In light of this basic understanding, we may move to Plantinga's possible-world ontological argument.

Plantinga's argument trades on Leibniz's idea that the existence of God is possible; that is, it is not a contradiction. From this, Plantinga argues that

1. It is possible that a maximally great being exists. (By this he means what we have described as a Perfect Being or greatest conceivable being.)

2. If it is possible that a maximally great being exists, then a maximally great being exists in some possible world. That is, God's existence is not impossible (logically contradictory), so we can conceive of a world in which God does exist.

---

[44]For an introduction to this thinking see Ronald Nash, "Possible Worlds," in *Ultimate Questions* (Grand Rapids: Zondervan, 1999).

[45]There are versions of possible-worlds theory that hold that every possible world is actualized (David Lewis and some multiverse theories in physics), but that need not be considered for our purposes here. The multiverse theory is taken up in chap. 12.

[46]The second example deals with the idea of *compossibility*. Some states of affairs may exist in some worlds but not in others. A compossible world contains only compatible states of affairs.

3. If a maximally great being exists in some possible world, then it exists in every possible world. (Otherwise, it would not be maximally great.)

4. If a maximally great being exists in every possible world, then it exists in the actual world.[47]

This argument trades on ideas of possibility and necessity. A possible state of affairs is logically consistent, whether or not it actually exists in the real space-time world. So, the idea of a unicorn is logically possible, since it is understood to be an animal that does not possess incompatible properties. Unicorns do not exist in our world. Nevertheless, they could exist; that is, they exist in a possible world. But a unicorn is not conceived as a necessary being, a being that *must* exist given its very nature. God is considered as such. And there is the rub metaphysically. If the concept of God is not *im*-possible, then God must exist in at least one *possible* world, and in that possible world God's existence is necessary. That is, God cannot *not* exist. So, if God exists as a logically necessary being in one world, he exists as such in all worlds.

Plantinga claims that the best versions of ontological argument "are just as satisfactory as most serious arguments philosophers give for important conclusions."[48] But Plantinga also grants that one can be rational in denying the argument if one denies that the existence of God is possible. So, we reach a kind of philosophical standoff wherein both denying and affirming the argument can be rational, even though God cannot both exist and not exist. However, it seems that the burden of proof weighs heavily on those who deny that God's existence is possible.[49] One can only demonstrate the impossibility of God's existence by showing a contradiction within the idea of God (as mentioned earlier).

Some, such as Gaunilo, have tried to reduce this argument to absurdity

---

[47]I have adapted Craig's formulation in "The Ontological Argument," p. 128. For Alvin Plantinga's more nuanced original version, see "The Ontological Argument," in *God, Freedom, and Evil* (Grand Rapids: Eerdmans, 1977). I have not addressed some disputes on the modal logic required for this ontological argument to work. On this, see Davis, "The Ontological Argument," pp. 105-8.

[48]Alvin Plantinga, "Self-Profile," *Profiles* 5, ed. James E. Tomberlin and Peter Van Inwagen (Dordrecht: D. Reidel, 1985), p. 71.

[49]See E. J. Lowe, "The Ontological Argument," in *The Routledge Companion to Philosophy of Religion*, ed. Chad Meister and Paul Copan (New York: Routledge, 2007), p. 339.

by setting up parallel or parody arguments that prove silly things, such as a perfect island.

1. It is possible that a greatest possible island exists.

2. If it is possible that a greatest possible island exists, then it exists in some possible world.

3. If a greatest possible island exists in some possible world, then it exists in every possible world.

4. If a greatest possible island exists in every possible world, then it exists in the real world.

5. But it is absurd that a greatest possible island exists in this world, since every extant island is less than perfect.

6. Therefore, this refutes the ontological argument, since it substitutes similar terms and uses the identical argument form, by reductio ad absurdum.[50]

This argument is valid, but it is not sound. The argument misfires at the first premise. There can be no greatest possible island for at least two reasons, either of which defeats the objection. First, a maximal being reaches or possesses the upper limit of greatness. God has all power; no power eludes his grasp. That is, there is "an intrinsic maximum value" to this power,[51] just as the best possible earned run average (ERA) for a baseball pitcher is 0.00—he never allows an earned run. But the idea of a maximal *island* is incoherent. There could always be more sand or palm trees or sweet fruits or dancing girls, and so on. Second, an island, by definition, is not *a necessary* being.[52] Its existence is *contingent* on all manner of things. We can easily conceive of a possible world in which there are no islands. What makes the ontological argument work is *the ontology of God as a necessary being.* Anything that is less than God necessarily (!) lacks this ontology (set of properties) and so cannot be the subject of an ontological argument. Therefore, this parallel/parody argument fails.

---

[50]This is a somewhat amplified version of Gaunilo's argument against Anselm (Gaunilo, "In Behalf of the Fool," pp. 150-51).

[51]Craig, "The Ontological Argument," p. 129.

[52]Ibid., pp. 129-30. This point holds even if there is such a thing as a perfect island.

Philosophers have proposed other ontological parody arguments for quasi-deities (gods something less than perfect) and for perfect devils. But in each case, the entity lacks the qualities possessed by a Perfect Being. A quasi-deity lacks perfection by definition.[53] A devil, by definition, is imperfect, since it is evil and not good.[54] Moreover, as William Wainwright points out, we know that quasi-deities and perfect devils do not exist; they are "cooked up" philosophical examples—as premise 5 grants. But this is not so in the case of God. God's existence is a real question of philosophical inquiry; it is not adventitious. As such, the ontological argument is a legitimate approach to God's existence.[55] Thus, these parody/parallel arguments also fail as reductio ad absurdum arguments.[56]

WHY THINK THE BIBLICAL GOD IS A NECESSARY BEING?

We should consider one last objection to this fascinating ontological argument. So far, I have claimed that it is proper to consider God as a necessary being: a being that possesses every great-making property to the highest degree possible. But some claim that there is no need to consider *the biblical God* in this way. The arguments are merely philosophical and are alien to the Hebrew-Christian mind. Is this right?

First, there are many texts that affirm God's uniqueness and unsurpassability. They boil down to this: There is no god like God. But could this not simply mean that God is the greatest *extant* being, not the greatest *possible* being? This seems highly unlikely. Although the Bible does not use sophisticated philosophical concepts for God, it does not lack conceptual resources for divine description. The testimony is that God lacks nothing; he is self-sufficient. Paul unambiguously grants self-existence to God when he declares this to the philosophers of his day in his Mars Hill sermon:

---

[53]For another criticism of the near deity argument, see Craig, "The Ontological Argument," pp. 130-31.

[54]This is not to say that there is no devil, biblically understood. Rather, one cannot use a priori ontological reasoning to infer the existence of the devil, who is not a Perfect Being in any sense. Since the devil is a contingent being, his existence must be argued for on the basis of a posteriori arguments. The primary evidence for his existence is the testimony of Jesus and the Scriptures as the best explanation for the origin and operation of evil in the world. See Michael Green, *I Believe in Satan's Downfall* (Grand Rapids: Eerdmans, 1981), esp. chap. 1.

[55]Wainwright, *Philosophy of Religion*, p. 41.

[56]See Craig, "The Ontological Argument," pp. 129-30; and Davis, "The Ontological Argument," pp. 100-103.

The God who made the world and everything in it is the Lord of heaven and earth and does not live in temples built by hands. And he is not served by human hands, as if he needed anything. Rather, he himself gives everyone life and breath and everything else. (Acts 17:24-25; see also John 5:26)

The idea that God could lack any perfection, while not explicitly stated in Scripture, seems quite alien to its manifold affirmations of the uniqueness and supremacy of God. Furthermore, it seems that worship—which the Bible commands creatures to engage in—requires a Perfect Being as its object. This is because unconditional adoration and service is due only to a Perfect Being, as Anselm himself claims.

A second problem bedevils the notion of a less-than-necessary God. If God is not necessary, then God exists in some possible worlds and not in others. That means, of course, that God might not have existed at all, and that in turn implies that God's existence is a brute fact—something that is the case and has always been the case (God is eternal), but might not have been the case in the first place. This further entails that nothing explains God's existence. God just is. This, however, violates the principle of sufficient reason (PSR), which claims (roughly) that for any positive state of affairs, that state of affairs is explained by something else or it explains itself. That is, there is a reason (sufficient explanation) for everything. In the case of God, according to the ontological argument, the reason for God's existence lies in God's very being, since he depends on nothing else. God exists necessarily. The reason for anything outside of God lies in God's creating and sustaining these beings as contingent creatures. We will address the PSR in more detail in chapter eleven (on the cosmological argument), but it is arguably a deep principle of reason. Not to apply the PSR to God seems ad hoc and counterintuitive.[57] But if we do apply the PSR to God, then God must be the greatest possible being.

WHO IS THE ONTOLOGICAL GOD?

If even one of the two ontological arguments given here is sound, then a superlative or maximal being exists. This being possesses every property that it is better to have than to lack and possesses these properties to the uttermost extent. This greatest possible being, therefore, must certainly be

---

[57]This connection of the PSR to the ontological argument was suggested to me by David Werther.

omnipotent, omniscient, omnipresent, self-existent (since noncontingent) and omnibenevolent.

What else could we know about God simply through the ontological argument? The answer to this depends on axiology (theory of value). If God is the greatest possible being, then what qualities are better to have than to lack? To put it another way, what are great-making properties? I will suggest several properties as great-making and, therefore, attributable to the greatest possible being.

First, a personal being is higher or greater than an impersonal being. This rests on the fact that a personal being is an *agent* who brings about states of affairs according to his thoughts and designs. An impersonal being would lack consciousness and so lack agency and the possibility of exemplifying love, justice, mercy, forgiveness and so on. Thus, there is little temptation to think of the greatest possible being as impersonal. We think of human persons as limited in power, knowledge and virtue. Yet the problem with humans is not their personality but the defects of their personality as sinners.[58] The ontological being, however, is unlimited and perfect. Therefore, it cannot be so limited in any of these areas. Thus, the ontological God is personal, not impersonal.[59]

Second, if a personal being is higher than an impersonal being, then a triune (or tripersonal) being is higher than a unipersonal being. Although there is nothing within the ontological argument that directly implies the existence of the Trinity, when we compare the biblical revelation of the Trinity to a unipersonal God, we can argue that the trinitarian conception of deity is more excellent; it is a great-making property. This is rooted in the concept that God as three-in-one establishes an eternal relationship of perfect interaction.[60] We esteem love and generosity to be higher than solitary, hermetic existence. If God is merely unitary, then God existed as a singular being, utterly devoid of relationships, until God created a universe with beings capable of concord with the divine being. On this view, relationality is only actualized through the creation of the contingent crea-

---

[58]Humans are, by definition and design, contingent beings, but this is not a defect.
[59]See also the argument against pantheism's impersonal god in Douglas Groothuis, *Confronting the New Age* (Downers Grove, Ill.: InterVarsity Press, 1988), pp. 107-13.
[60]We might argue that two members in the Godhead would be sufficient to establish love, but since there is no major world religion that teaches bitheism, this option seems historically and existentially strange.

ture. Accordingly, the statement "God is love" (1 John 4:8) could not be justified, since God would not be eternally engaged in love within God's own being. With respect to unitarianism, God could be described as loving, but this would be a contingent fact of his existence, since God would require creatures to exhibit love.

But if God is eternally loving within his own being, then the statement "God is love" has genuine, knowable and ontologically deep meaning. Human relationships would find their ultimate paradigm and source of original meaning in the Trinity. Given the concept of the Trinity, God is intrapersonal (within the Godhead) before God is interpersonal (interacting with creatures). Thus love has the deepest and most profound significance possible. The trinitarian view metaphysically and axiologically trumps a unipersonal account.[61] Additionally, the superlative love of a superlative God (who is, by nature, triune love) would make some provision for his erring creatures.[62] To this the Scriptures speak of the cross of Christ as the only remedy for God's lost but beloved human creatures.[63]

AN ONTOLOGICAL EXTRAVAGANZA

The rather abstruse reasoning of the ontological argument may make it intellectually inaccessible to many.[64] Nevertheless, it is not (Dawkins and others to the contrary) worthy of ridicule, nor is it lacking existential significance. This chapter has argued that both of Anselm's arguments (when augmented in light of contemporary discussions) are indeed successful. Anselm's ontological arguments may be enhanced by arguing that if the greatest possible being necessarily exists, then a personal God is greater than an impersonal one and a trinitarian God is greater than a unipersonal God. But since the ontological argument is an a priori argument, it does not directly speak to how exactly this Perfect Being may have revealed

---

[61]On the implications of the doctrine of the Trinity and its superiority to the unipersonal view, see Timothy Keller, *The Reason for God: Belief in an Age of Skepticism* (New York: Dutton, 2008), pp. 213-26. See also the discussion of the Trinity in relation to love in Richard Swinburne, *The Christian God* (New York: Oxford University Press, 1994), pp. 177-79.

[62]I will argue for the biblical doctrine of sin most explicitly in chap. 18.

[63]I discuss the significance of Jesus Christ in chaps. 20-22.

[64]For a much more technical and favorable treatment of the ontological argument (with lots of symbolic logic), see Robert E. Maydole, "The Ontological Argument," in *The Blackwell Companion to Natural Theology*, ed. William Craig and J. P. Moreland (Malden, Mass.: Wiley-Blackwell, 2009).

himself in history. However, if God is perfect, then we are warranted to believe that God will care about creation and reach out to his erring mortals in some way. Further, since the idea of the Trinity (which is supported by the ontological argument) is vouchsafed to us in Scripture, we have strong rational incentive to consider the scriptural claims that God was incarnated in the person of Jesus Christ for our redemption (John 1:1-18; 3:16-18; 14:1-6).

Yet even if the ontological argument ultimately fails philosophically, the apologist's quiver is not lacking in arrows. A host of other theistic arguments await our investigation, starting with the cosmological argument, to which we now turn.

11

Cosmological Arguments

A Cause for the Cosmos

DOES THE COSMOS STAND ALONE AND unsupported, or is its existence dependent on something outside of itself? This is the ultimate cosmological question. Cosmological arguments offer reasons to believe that the cosmos depends on something outside itself. These arguments take various forms. This chapter will engage the family of cosmological arguments, paying the closest attention to the kalam cosmological argument and the evidence for the beginning of the universe from big bang cosmology. Although some have challenged the claim that Scripture teaches that the universe came into existence a finite time ago out of nothing (ex nihilo), this view is well supported in the Bible and in the creeds and confessions of the church.[1]

Philosophers as diverse as Gottfried Leibniz (Christian theist) and Martin Heidegger (atheist) have claimed that the fundamental philosophical question is why there is something rather than nothing. Heidegger began his *An Introduction of Metaphysics* this way, "Why are there existents rather than nothing? That is the question. Clearly it is no ordinary question. 'Why are there existents, why is there anything at all, rather than nothing?'—obviously this is the first of all questions."[2] He

---

[1]See Paul Copan and William Lane Craig, *Creation Out of Nothing: A Biblical, Philosophical, and Scientific Exploration* (Grand Rapids: Baker Academic, 2005), chaps. 1-2; John Jefferson Davis, "Genesis 1:1 and Big Bang Cosmology," in *The Frontiers of Science and Faith: Examining Questions from the Big Bang to the End of the Universe* (Downers Grove, Ill.: InterVarsity Press, 2002), esp. pp. 19-25.

[2]Martin Heidegger, *An Introduction to Metaphysics* (New York: Anchor Books, 1961), p. 1. The translator coined the term *essents* to stand for "existents" or "things that art." I have used *existents* since it is not a neologism and conveys a straightforward meaning.

claimed that this question presents itself in moments of great despair, in times of rejoicing and even in boredom.[3] It is the deepest, broadest and most fundamental of questions.[4] Heidegger wrote that "anyone for whom the Bible is divine revelation and truth has an answer to the question." The answer is: "Everything that is, except God himself, has been created by Him."[5] However, Heidegger asserted that this answer has nothing at all to do with philosophy, since "a 'Christian philosophy' is a round square and a misunderstanding."[6]

Contrary to Heidegger, Christians may provide philosophical arguments for their theistic beliefs. Leibniz, a Christian philosopher—and not a round square—wrote, "The first question which should rightly be asked will be, *Why is there something rather than nothing?*"[7] For Leibniz there must be an answer, since "*nothing happens without a sufficient reason;* that is to say, that nothing happens without its being possible for him who should sufficiently understand things, to give a reason sufficient to determine why it is so and not otherwise."[8] Contemporary philosopher Russell Stannard essentially agrees: "It seems to be that as soon as something exists then it calls for an explanation, whereas a state of nothingness does not require explanation."[9]

TWO OBJECTIONS TO COSMOLOGICAL ARGUMENTS

Cosmological arguments come in several basic forms, but all argue from the fact of the universe to a cause of the universe. Before diving into the details, a fairly common misconception (and attempted refutation) of the argument must be eliminated.

Some have taken the argument from cosmos to God to be the following:

---

[3]Ibid.

[4]Ibid., pp. 2-3.

[5]Ibid., p. 6.

[6]Ibid.

[7]G. W. F. von Leibniz, "Principles of Nature and Grace" (1714), in *Leibniz Selections*, ed. Philip P. Wiener (New York: Charles Scribner's, 1951), p. 527, emphasis in the original. See also Leibniz, "Monadology" (1714), in ibid., p. 540. For an in-depth discussion of Leibniz, see Catherine Wilson, *Leibniz's Metaphysics: A Historical and Comparative Study* (Princeton, N.J.: Princeton University Press, 1990).

[8]Leibniz, "Principles of Nature and Grace," p. 527, emphasis in the original. We will return to this principle of sufficient reason shortly.

[9]Interview with Russell Stannard, "Science and Religion," in *What Philosophers Think*, ed. Julian Baggini and Jeremy Stangroom (New York: Barnes & Noble, 2003), p. 75.

1. Everything that exists must have a cause.

2. The universe exists and so must have a cause.

3. Therefore, the universe is caused by a first cause (a.k.a. God).

But if (1) is true, God himself must have a cause as well. This reduces the argument to absurdity, since God was introduced to be the first cause, not to be caused by another being, ad infinitum. No less a thinker than Bertrand Russell made this charge. "If everything must have a cause, then God must have a cause. If there can be anything without a cause, it may just as well be the world as God, so that there cannot be any validity in that argument."[10] This is a classic straw man fallacy. *No* cosmological argument claims that "*everything* must have a cause." Rather, these arguments (in their varied forms) have claimed that there is something about the universe itself—either its contingency and need for explanation or its finitude in time—that requires a cause beyond itself, a cause that is self-existent and *without need of a cause*. It is this self-existent being that explains the existence of the contingent universe. God is always understood to exist in and of himself (that is, to possess aseity). God is neither uncaused nor self-caused, but self-existent (see John 5:26; Acts 17:25). Nontheists may reject the idea of a necessary or noncontingent being for several reasons, but no cosmological argument dies the death that Russell pronounced.

One other dismissal of cosmological arguments should be nullified. In his *Critique of Pure Reason*, Kant argued that cosmological arguments presuppose the ontological argument's concept of God as a logically necessary being: a being who must exist and whose nonexistence is inconceivable because illogical. The ontological argument claims (as discussed in chap. 10) that the very concept of God as a perfect or maximal being, plus certain a priori logical principles, demands that God exists. This means that the statement "God exists" is logically necessary. But Kant denied that the ontological argument established the existence of a Perfect Being that exists as a matter of logical necessity. Kant reasoned that since the ontological argument fails as a proof for God, then cosmological arguments must fail as well, since they also attempt to prove the existence of a logically

---

[10]Bertrand Russell, *Why I Am Not a Christian and Other Essays on Religion and Related Subjects*, ed. Paul Edwards (New York: Simon & Schuster, 1957), pp. 6-7.

necessary being. If this criticism is successful, we need not trouble our minds with the various forms of cosmological argument, since we know their conclusions must be false.

First, it isn't clear that Kant refuted the ontological argument, as I argued in chapter ten. Second, even if the ontological argument fails, most cosmological arguments do not, in fact, presuppose the idea that God is a logically necessary being.[11] They reason that if the universe exists, God must exist as its cause. As the Creator of the universe, God does not depend on the universe (or on anything else) for the divine existence. But this argument does not yield the conclusion that God's existence is *logically* necessary. If God does exist, God is self-existent, but this is not the same concept as a being who must exist per se (or who exists in all possible worlds). The conclusion of a cosmological argument is not that God is a *logically* necessary being but that God is a *factually* necessary being; that is, God's original factuality is required to explain all the facts of the universe.[12]

However, the cosmological argument's conclusion that God exists as a factually necessary being (as the explanation or cause of the universe) is not incompatible with God being a logically necessary being as well. A logically necessary being may give evidence of his existence through the contingent cosmos.[13] Thus, cosmological arguments are undaunted by Russell's and Kant's criticisms. So let us proceed to explore three versions of cosmological argument, namely, the principle of sufficient reason, the kalam argument and big bang cosmology.[14]

THE PRINCIPLE OF SUFFICIENT REASON AND THE EXISTENCE OF GOD

Some cosmological arguments employ and adapt concepts formulated by

---

[11]Arguments from the principle of sufficient reason are the exception.

[12]See Ronald Nash, "Two Concepts of God," in *The Concept of God* (Grand Rapids: Zondervan, 1983); Anthony Kenny, *A New History of Western Philosophy* (New York: Clarendon, 2010), p. 744.

[13]On Kant's criticism of the ontological and cosmological arguments, see Michael Peterson et al., *Reason and Religious Belief*, 3rd ed. (New York: Oxford University Press, 2003), p. 89; and chap. 10 of this book.

[14]I am excluding Thomist cosmological arguments, not because I deem them inadequate but because I take the arguments that follow to be more cogent and pertinent to apologetics today. For a recent presentation of the Thomist argument, see Ralph McInerny, *Characters in Search of Their Author* (Notre Dame, Ind.: University of Notre Dame Press, 2001).

Leibniz—fundamentally, the principle of sufficient reason.[15] This principle has been given several forms, such as:

1. For any contingent entity, there is a sufficient explanation for why it exists.

2. "For everything that exists, there is a reason for its existence, either due to the causal efficacy of other beings or due to the necessity of its own nature."[16]

3. "By sufficient reason in the full sense I mean an explanation adequate for the existence of some particular being. An adequate explanation must ultimately be a total explanation, to which nothing further can be added."[17]

From this principle it is argued that the universe is not self-explanatory, but contingent. If everything in the universe can be explained in terms of other things in the universe, this leaves the universe as a whole unexplained. But God explains the existence of the entire universe. God himself, however, requires no explanation outside of himself, since he is an eternal and self-existent being.

The principle of sufficient reason has typically been used to support theistic arguments that are compatible with an eternally existing universe that has always depended on God for its existence. Richard Taylor, for instance, claims that while the universe needs an explanation outside itself, it may have always existed. But at every point, it depends on a necessary being for its existence.[18] Taylor has called the principle of sufficient reason "a presupposition of reason itself."[19] Bertrand Russell has affirmed that the universe was "just there" and in need of no explanation.[20] Stephen

---

[15]The best and most thorough treatment of this subject is Alexander Pruss, *The Principle of Sufficient Reason* (Cambridge, Mass.: Cambridge University Press, 2006). He goes into much more detail and addresses more problems than I can cover here. See also his chapter "The Leibnizian Cosmological Argument," in *The Blackwell Companion to Natural Theology*, ed. William Lane Craig and J. P. Moreland (Malden, Mass.: Wiley-Blackwell, 2009).

[16]Charles Taliaferro, *Contemporary Philosophy of Religion* (Malden, Mass.: Blackwell, 1998), p. 355.

[17]F. C. Copleston, "A Debate on the Existence of God: Bertrand Russell and F. C. Copleston," in *The Existence of God*, ed. John Hick (New York: Macmillan, 1964), p. 173.

[18]Richard Taylor, *Metaphysics*, 4th ed. (New York: Prentice Hall, 1992), p. 101.

[19]Ibid., p. 108.

[20]Copleston, "A Debate on the Existence of God," p. 175.

Davis has argued that he holds to the principle of sufficient reason because he is a theist. Theism justifies the principle, but not vice versa. Therefore, the principle itself could not be used as part of an argument from the cosmos to the cosmos-Creator.[21] Most, but not all, theists believe that if God exists, then everything has an explanation somehow traceable to God.[22]

However, one may hold to the principle of sufficient reason and not immediately discern its metaphysical implications. One may claim that any positive state can, in principle, be accounted for by antecedent reasons—nothing exists without reason—yet not apply this principle to the universe as a whole. Certainly some, like Russell, refuse to apply this principle to the universe as a whole, but this does not entail that the principle is inapplicable to the universe as a whole. It may simply indicate that some are obtuse on extending explanations beyond the natural realm.

Moreover, the metaphysical implication of rejecting the principle of sufficient reason with respect to the cosmos is that the cosmos is meaningless. It literally has no explanation. It is just there, as Russell stated. But this entails nihilism, a worldview claiming that nothing has any ultimate meaning and that everything is gratuitous.[23] This, however, is an unacceptable and unlivable worldview for most.[24] To hold, for example, that the universe has no explanation *and* that human beings have objective and intrinsic worth is incoherent, since, on the nihilistic account, existence is sterilized of any final explanation and of any objective or intrinsic meaning. Subjective meanings may abound, but these are not rooted in anything deeper than the individual self, which, along with everything else, is inexplicable and meaningless and will eventually expire. Furthermore, it seems arbitrary and ad hoc to search for explanations for anything and

---

[21]Stephen T. Davis, *God, Reason, and Theistic Proofs* (Grand Rapids: Eerdmans, 1997), p. 146. While Davis's concern in this book is worth considering, he himself reversed his view in "The Cosmological Argument and the Epistemic Status of Belief in God," *Philosophia Christi*, series 2, 1, no 1 (1999): 8-10.

[22]Exceptions might be those theists who believe God leaves the future open and does not know what will occur, and who further believe that there are gratuitous evils that do not further a greater good. These kinds of evils would not be explained on the basis of God's providence or foreknowledge—although the theist in this camp may argue that their occurrence is explicable given the overall worldview of open theism.

[23]C. Stephen Evans and R. Zachary Manis, *Philosophy of Religion*, 2nd ed. (Downers Grove, Ill.: InterVarsity Press, 2009), p. 75. The authors note that some atheists claim the question of ultimate meaning lacks intelligibility, so it can be put aside without experiencing angst.

[24]I address nihilism in chap. 15.

everything in the universe (as does science) but not to seek an explanation for the universe as a whole, especially when divine explanations are coherent and have been a staple of belief for so many intelligent people for so long.

An alternative to taking God as the explanation for the universe is to embrace the principle of sufficient reason and to posit that the universe (or Universe) itself is a necessary being, a being that explains itself. This metaphysical compliment, however, is entirely undeserved. The universe is just not the kind of thing we would expect of a necessary being—a being that is self-existent and self-explanatory. We can certainly conceive of the universe being different from what it is or of it not existing at all. Our question, Why is there something rather than nothing? pertains perfectly well to the universe. But if the universe were self-contained, self-explanatory and self-existent, such a question would be radically out of place—on the order of asking, Why is the law of noncontradiction true? Taylor argues:

> For we find nothing whatever about the world, any more than in its parts, to suggest that it exists by its own nature. Concerning anything in the world, we have not the slightest difficulty in supposing that it should perish, or even that it should never have existed in the first place. We have almost as little difficulty in supposing this of the world itself.[25]

So, we now must wrestle with this *modus tollens* argument:

1. If God is not the sufficient explanation of the universe, then either (a) it has no explanation or (b) it is self-explanatory.

2. The universe is not without explanation (which would entail nihilism).

3. The universe is not self-explanatory (pantheism).

4. Therefore, God is the sufficient explanation of the universe.

This argument is certainly valid, and premise 1 is beyond dispute, since it covers all the options. Premises 2 and 3 have been briefly defended, but more will be said in later chapters on the problems with nihilism and pantheism. While the principle of sufficient reason does not require that the universe have a beginning, it does offer God—as a necessary being—as the best explanation for the existence of the universe. God explains why

---

[25]Taylor, *Metaphysics*, p. 105; see also Evans and Manis, *Philosophy of Religion*, p. 69.

the universe exists moment by moment. As such, it lends support to theism and leaves the door open to a creation event as described in Genesis. Other cosmological arguments take up creation ex nihilo.[26]

THE KALAM COSMOLOGICAL ARGUMENT

The kalam cosmological argument was developed primarily by Muslim theologians in the Middle Ages, although the Christian St. Bonaventure endorsed it as well.[27] In recent decades Stuart Hackett, Ed L. Miller, William Lane Craig, J. P. Moreland and others have revived the argument, and it has become an item of intense philosophical debate.[28] This argument does not depend on the metaphysical notions of contingency or necessity, as do Thomist arguments. Unlike the Thomist and Leibnizian forms, the kalam argument, if successful, secures the biblical doctrine of creation ex nihilo. As stated by Craig, its form is simple and elegant:

1. Whatever begins to exist has a cause.

2. The universe began to exist.

3. Therefore, the universe has a cause.

This is a deductive argument. From this Craig then argues that

4. The cause of the universe is God.

But we must assess the argument one step at a time.

---

[26]I discuss the differences and overlap between the two types of cosmological arguments (original creation and eternal creation) in "Metaphysical Implications of Cosmological Arguments," in *In Defense of Natural Theology*, ed. James Sennett and Douglas Groothuis (Downers Grove, Ill.: InterVarsity Press, 2005).

[27]On the history of the kalam, see William Lane Craig, "Historical Statements of the Kalam Cosmological Argument," in *The Kalam Cosmological Augment* (1979; reprint, Eugene, Ore.: Wipf & Stock, 2000).

[28]Stuart Hackett, "The Cosmological Argument: The Argument from the Fact of Particular Existence," in *The Resurrection of Theism: Prolegomena to Christian Apology* (1957; reprint, Eugene, Ore.: Wipf & Stock, 2009); Ed L. Miller, *God and Reason: A Historical Approach to Philosophical Theology* (New York: Macmillan, 1972), pp. 47-49. Craig has defended the kalam in many writings and in public debates, but see *Reasonable Faith: Christian Truth and Apologetics*, 3rd ed. (Wheaton, Ill.: Crossway, 2009), pp. 111-56; and, in much more detail, William Lane Craig and James D. Sinclair, "The Kalam Cosmological Argument," in *The Blackwell Companion to Natural Theology*, ed. William Lane Craig and J. P. Moreland (Malden, Mass.: Wiley-Blackwell, 2009), pp. 100-201; J. P. Moreland, *Scaling the Secular City: A Defense of Christianity* (Grand Rapids: Baker, 1987), pp. 18-42; J. P. Moreland, "Yes: A Defense of Christianity," in J. P. Moreland and Kai Nielsen, *Does God Exist? The Debate Between Theists and Atheists* (1990; Amherst, N.Y.: Prometheus, 1993).

Craig takes the first premise to be a fairly noncontroversial concept: *ex nihilo nihil fit* ("out of nothing, nothing comes"). The alternative is that things pop into existence without a cause, which even the archskeptic David Hume denied in a letter he wrote: "But allow me to tell you that I never asserted so absurd a Proposition as *that anything might arise without a Cause.* I only maintan'd, that our Certainty of the Falsehood of that Proposition proceeded neither from Intuition or Demonstration, but from another Source."[29] We need not debate Hume's account of causation to understand that the notion of a causeless event is counterintuitive if not nonsensical. Some argue that such a thing is possible because it is conceivable or can be pictured. I can *imagine* a tenor saxophone appearing before me out of nothing at all. But this is just a series of possible *images* in the mind; it says little or nothing about the *ontological* possibility of *things* materializing out of nothing. In criticizing cavalier thought experiments, Elizabeth Anscombe comments that one could imagine a rabbit coming into existence without a cause, but this image would really be nothing more than, as it were, a title to a picture. "Nothing whatever follows about what is possible to suppose 'Without contradiction or absurdity' as holding in reality."[30] The mere ability to picture something certainly fails to establish its possibility or likelihood.

To say that something—saxophone or otherwise—comes from nothing (that is, begins to exist without a cause) is not to assign causal power to "nothing." "Nothing" lacks all causal power, because it has no properties at all. It is a linguistic device to indicate the utter lack of any essence, properties, qualities or attributes. Nothing is no thing. There are no causal powers at work here. In light of this, John Locke hits the mark: "Man knows by intuitive certainty, that bare nothing can no more produce any real being, than it can be equal to two right angles."[31]

But in discussing the origin of the big bang, physicist Paul Davies claims that matter may be created "from a state of *zero* energy. This pos-

---

[29]David Hume, "To John Stewart," Letter 91, in *The Letters of David Hume*, ed. J. Y. T. Greig (Oxford: Clarendon, 1932), 1:187

[30]Elizabeth Anscombe, "'Whatever Has a Beginning of Existence Must Have a Cause': Hume's Argument Exposed," *Analysis* 3, no. 4 (1974): 150.

[31]John Locke, *Essay Concerning Human Understanding: An Abridgment*, ed. John W. Yolton, bk. 4, chap. 10 (New York: J. M. Dent & Sons, 1961), p. 330.

sibility arises because energy can be both positive and negative."[32] Davies
is thinking of a state where negative and positive energy combine into a
state of zero energy. And from this zero state everything might have been
created! But his attempt to generate something from nothing confuses
nothing with something (positive and negative energy summing up to
zero). The nothing before the big bang (as we will see) is not a subject that
can have properties, but is rather the absence of all properties. There is no
subject in the ontological sense, but only a subject in the grammatical or
conceptual sense. The notion of "zero energy" reflects a subtle and fallacious ontologizing of nothingness.[33]

Even if "something from nothing" were possible, there would be no
possible evidence for such a thing, since we could always plausibly attribute
causes to events; as such we deem them as *effects*. We must go back to the
tenor saxophone. If this saxophonophany occurred, I would not assume
the instrument ontologized out of nothing. If I could rule out hallucination or hologram, I would infer that some new materialization device had
"beamed" it into my room. Or perhaps a supernatural being materialized
the saxophone.

In any event, the statement, "Something may begin to exist without a
cause," must fit one of the following four options concerning possibility.

1. Impossible (that is, necessarily false).

2. Possible, but highly unlikely.

3. Possible, but somewhat less likely than the first premise of the kalam
   argument (that whatever begins to exist must have a cause).

4. Inscrutable and therefore irrelevant as a criticism of premise (1) of the
   kalam. This is because the notion of things beginning to exist by way of
   a cause is entirely understandable (that is, not inscrutable) and is relied
   on in everyday observation.

---

[32]Paul Davies, *God and the New Physics* (New York: Simon & Schuster, 1984), p. 31.
[33]This paragraph is heavily indebted to Moreland, *Scaling the Secular City*, pp. 39-41. Moreland
goes into much more detail concerning the "is of identity" and the "is of predication," and
shows that Davies and others are essentially and erroneously thinking of the nothing before
the big bang as the "is of predication." For more on the fallacy of the ontologizing of nothingness, see Francis Schaeffer, *He Is There and He Is Not Silent*, 30th anniv. ed. (Wheaton, Ill.:
Tyndale House, 2001), pp. 6-7.

Some have claimed that just as subatomic particles pop into existence out of nothing, so too the entire universe might have simply popped into existence. John Jefferson Davis, however, criticizes this view thoroughly.

> Quantum-mechanical events may not have classically deterministic causes, but they are not thereby uncaused or acausal. The decay of a nucleus takes place in view of physical actualities and potentialities internal to itself, in relation to a spatiotemporal nexus governed by the laws of quantum mechanics. The fact that uranium atoms consistently decay into atoms of lead and other elements—and not into rabbits or frogs—shows that such events are not acausal but take place within a causal nexus and lawlike structures. Accordingly, it seems plausible to assume the validity of some causal principle in such cases. God, knowing both the states internal to the nucleus and its external environment and governing laws, can at any given moment "see what the nucleus is about to do."[34]

All we need for a legitimate and successful argument form is that the premise be more likely than its denial. So, while I favor premise 1, this cosmological argument will still move forward rationally if we opt for the less stringent premises 2, 3 or 4.

The second premise of the kalam argument is grounded on (1) the impossibility of there being an actual infinite, or (2) the impossibility of crossing (or traversing) an actual infinite. This premise denies that the universe comprises a beginningless series of linear events (which would require an actual infinite of events). An actual infinite must be distinguished from a potential infinite. The latter is a series that is always increasing but which never reaches an upper limit. A verse from "Amazing Grace" makes the philosophical point:

> When we've been there ten thousand years,
> Bright shining as the sun,
> We've no less days to sing God's praise,
> Than when we've first begun.[35]

Or think of a number line that keeps increasing endlessly. The endless bisection of a line of finite extension is another example of a potential in-

---

[34]Davis, *Frontiers of Science and Faith*, pp. 55-56. Thanks to Jeremy Green for bringing this quote to my attention. See also Craig, *Reasonable Faith*, pp. 114-15; and Moreland, *Scaling the Secular City*, pp. 38-39.

[35]John Newton, "Amazing Grace" (1772).

finite. The items of a potential infinite increase in number, but the total amount of items is always finite.[36]

An actual infinite, however, is complete and self-contained. According to J. P. Moreland, it "is a set considered as a completed totality with an actual infinite number of members."[37] No new members can be added to it. This is what distinguishes it from a potential infinite. But this concept generates problems. What if we attempt to divide or subtract from an actual infinite? For example, if a library with an actual infinite number of books is composed equally of red and blue books, the subtraction of all the blue books will still leave the same (infinite) number of books. The same is true if we subtract the red books from the total. But this is absurd. Similarly, if we subtract all the odd numbers from an actual infinite set of natural numbers, the amount of numbers remaining is still infinite. This seems logically unacceptable as well, since a particular subset cannot be equal in cardinality to the entirety of the set. In other words, a part of something must be less than the whole—or so it seems intuitively.[38]

But some dispute this premise by appealing to the notion of the infinite in Cantorian set theory, where the infinite plays a well-defined role and does not lead to absurdities. Two basic responses are in order. First, we may grant that the theoretical idea of an actual infinite in set theory has its proper functions but that this is disanalogous to situations in space and time where an actual infinite cannot obtain. The paradoxes generated by positing an actual infinite often involve spatial and temporal realities. Therefore, we cannot use set theory to validate the concept of an actual infinite in space and time. Craig claims that Cantorian theory is consistent but not applicable to extramental reality. To that end, he quotes the notable German mathematician David Hilbert who, while appreciative of Cantor's set theory, nevertheless claimed that "the infinite is nowhere to be found in reality. It neither exists in nature nor provides a legitimate basis for rational thought. . . . The role that remains for the infinite to play is solely that of an idea."[39]

---

[36]Moreland, *Scaling the Secular City*, p. 22.
[37]Ibid., pp. 20-21.
[38]Ibid.
[39]David Hilbert, "On the Infinite," in *Philosophy of Mathematics*, ed. Paul Benacerraf and Hillary Putnam (Englewood Cliffs, N.J.: Prentice-Hall, 1964), p. 151, quoted in Craig, *Reasonable Faith*, p. 117.

Second, even if an actual infinite might exist in some theoretical realm, kalam proponents argue that it could not be traversed through successive addition—that is, through incremental steps. A Chinese proverb says, "A journey of a thousand miles begins with a single step." But in this case, all the individual steps combined make up the entire length of the journey. In other words, the distance can be crossed in a determinate number of finite increments or steps. It is also true that a journey of thousand miles *ends* with a single step. But crossing an actual infinite is nothing like this, since the distance to be traversed is unlimited.

We can neither count from one to infinity nor count down from infinity to one. There is always an infinite distance to travel, so we never arrive. A thought experiment may help to explain this. Tristam Shandy is a very slow writer. It takes him one year to write one day of his autobiography. How far will this meticulous (and self-absorbed) soul get in writing his account of his life? Can he finish or even catch up, such that he is writing about the day he is experiencing at the time? He cannot, of course. Even if Mr. Shandy had been writing from eternity past, his autobiography would never catch up to his chronological age.[40]

I have already referred to the use of the infinite in set theory, but it is interesting and important to understand that set theory omits all temporal concepts. This is precisely because the actual infinite could never be achieved bit by bit or moment by moment. As Bertrand Russell put it, "Classes which are infinite are given all at once by the defining properties of their members, so that there is no question of 'completion' or of 'successive synthesis.'"[41]

If the actual infinite does not exist or cannot be traversed, this means that the series of linear events in the universe must be finite.[42] If the series is finite, it must have a beginning. If it has a beginning, the cause of the series must be outside of the universe. Moreover, this originating cause must not exist in an infinity of moments since that would introduce the problem of the actual infinite all over again. But the originator of the causal series is not subject to experiencing an actual infinity of moments if

[40]Moreland, *Scaling the Secular City*, p. 23.
[41]Bertrand Russell, *Our Knowledge of the External World*, 2nd ed. (New York: W. W. Norton, 1929), p. 170, quoted in Craig, *Reasonable Faith*, p. 124.
[42]That is, the series of events had a beginning, but the series does not have an ending. In that case, the series of events in the universe would be a potential infinite.

its existence does not involve a series of events. This can be understood in one of two ways. Craig argues that God exists atemporally without the creation and temporally with creation. (He is careful not to say "before creation" and "after creation" since these statements require linear sequence.) However, Craig's view seems problematic, since on this view time comes into existence at the creation and one cannot speak of time before creation. Instead, Craig speaks of God *sans* the universe (in which time does not exist) and God with the universe (in which time does exist).[43] Yet it seems most plausible to think that God, in some sense, existed in time *before* creation. In fact, Jesus speaks of his fellowship with God the Father "before the world began" (John 17:5).

To handle this problem we may opt for the view that God's existence before creation is "relatively timeless," in the words of Alan Padgett. God's existence before creation is not subject to any differentiation into moments (which would require an actual infinite to be traversed) because the necessary conditions of such temporal differentiation did not yet exist, namely, physical objects and natural laws. Before creation, God existed in a state of "pure duration."[44] God is not "in time" in the sense that we are, since God is not limited by time, does not run out of time and is not located in a specific time zone. The question What time is it for God? makes as much sense as Wittgenstein's trick question, "What time is it on the sun?" There is no coherent answer to that. Nevertheless, there is duration on the sun: it came into existence, experiences sunspots and so on. God's everlasting life would not be composed of discrete physical events such as that of the sun. God, nevertheless, existed in a state of pure duration before creation, and God continues to exist in a linear series events after the creation (which was a finite time ago).

On either Craig's or Padgett's view, God's life is not subject to the problem of the actual infinite.[45] However, if one argues that God exists in a

---

[43]See Craig's discussion of this in *God and Time: Four Views*, ed. Greg Ganssle (Downers Grove, Ill.: InterVarsity Press, 2001), chap. 4.

[44]See Alan Padgett, "Eternity as Relative Timelessness," in *God and Time: Four Views*, ed. Greg Ganssle (Downers Grove, Ill.: InterVarsity Press, 2001).

[45]Further, one could hold that God is atemporal *simpliciter* (with and without creation); that is, God never enters into temporal relationships. Although I am least attracted to this view, it too would eliminate the problem of the actual infinite backfiring on God himself. Paul Helm is a leading contemporary proponent of this view. See his essay in *God and Time: Four Views*, ed. Greg Ganssle (Downers Grove, Ill.: InterVarsity Press, 2001).

sequence of individuated moments, then God's "age," as it were, would be actually infinite. If we hold this view, we could not employ the kalam argument, since it would eliminate God himself. Nevertheless, someone who holds to divine temporality prior to creation—and rejects even "relative timelessness"—might appeal to other cosmological arguments or to the findings of big bang cosmology. The cosmological way of arguing for God's existence is not a solitary argument but rather a large and extended family of arguments.

Some might think, nevertheless, that since God is taken to be an infinite being (i.e., unlimited in power, knowledge and wisdom), the problem of the actual infinite arises with respect to these attributes, even if it does not arise concerning God's relationship to time. However, there is no real problem, as Craig explains:

> When we speak of the infinity of God, we are not using the word in a mathematical sense to refer to an aggregate of an infinite number of parts. God's infinity is, if you will, qualitative, not quantitative. It means that God is metaphysically necessary, morally perfect, omnipotent, omniscient, eternal, etc.[46]

ASSESSING THE KALAM ARGUMENT

One strength of this argument is that it may function somewhat independently of whatever cosmology may reign among scientists and philosophers at the time. This is because the kalam's second premise (that the universe began to exist) is derived from the logical problems with the actual infinite, and not on the basis of any current physical cosmology. At present, however, the second premise of the kalam argument receives considerable support from big bang cosmology. But if the kalam argument is sound, it does not *require* any outside endorsement from empirical science.[47] Another strength is that, unlike other cosmological arguments that are compatible with an eternal universe (which always depends on God), the kalam establishes the creation of the universe ex nihilo, which is a central biblical doc-

---

[46]Craig, *Reasonable Faith*, 119. For an extended discussion of the meaning of divine infinity, see Douglas Groothuis, *To Prove or Not to Prove: Pascal's Rejection of Natural Theology* (Ph.D. diss., University of Oregon, 1993), chap. 3.

[47]However, it does require the existence of the physical/temporal universe and certain notions of causation.

trine (Genesis 1:1; John 1:1). That the kalam argument has generated so much philosophical discussion and attention from world-class philosophers in the last twenty-five years is another feather in its cap.

But despite its elegant structure, the presentation of the kalam requires thinkers to wade into the deep and sometimes murky waters of metaphysics concerning the philosophy of mathematics (set theory and its relation to reality), and the nature of the infinite, variously understood. While the argument may "click" with some (Craig presents it very concisely in his many debates on God's existence),[48] handling its challenges profitably demands some sustained philosophical attention. This may reduce the psychological force of the argument, since many will not engage at this level for long. (Remember Pascal's worry that "metaphysical proofs" are too abstract to have much of an effect on the unbeliever's heart.)[49] Even those trained in philosophy may find their minds boggling at the contemplation of the infinite and its implications. Nevertheless, the kalam is very strong in its premise that whatever begins to exist must have a cause for its existence. Although atheist philosophers like Quentin Smith claim that everything can come into existence out of nothing without a cause (the universe is self-caused), this seems to be a rather desperate move forced upon atheists, who have had to bite the cosmic bullet on the big bang.[50]

But can the actual infinite exist in reality? The challenge of set theory poses a genuine problem for the kalam at this point. It would seem that if something is logically coherent in the abstract it could be instantiated, whereas impossibilities (such as square circles) cannot possibly be instantiated. Of course, we could oppose set theory in principle by attempting to create paradoxes in the mathematics of it. It does appear counterintuitive to claim that a proper subset (such as all the even numbers) can contain the same number of members as the entire set.[51] Craig admits that infinite sets function coherently in the world of mathematics. But with examples such as counting down or up to infinity and others, he challenges the claim that

---

[48]See the transcripts and videos of Craig's debates on his webpage <www.reasonablefaith.org>.
[49]Blaise Pascal, *Pensées* 190/593, ed. and trans. Alban Krailsheimer (New York: Penguin, 1966), p. 86. See my discussion in chap. 9.
[50]Quentin Smith, "The Uncaused Beginning of the Universe," in William Lane Craig and Quentin Smith, *Theism, Atheism, and Big Bang Cosmology* (Oxford: Clarendon, 1993).
[51]This is J. P. Moreland's strategy; see *Scaling the Secular City*, pp. 19-22.

the actual infinite could be part of the space-time world.[52]

Whatever hesitation we may have in ruling out the actual infinite, *traversing* an actual infinity of moments, piece by piece, seems much more problematic. Since the kalam aims at ruling out a universe of infinite *duration*, the crucial premise of this argument is that the universe began to exist. If the past is an actual infinity of linear events, the present can never arrive. It is akin to "climbing a ladder of water"[53] or "jumping out of a bottomless pit." We can also liken it to walking up a down escalator at exactly the same speed as the escalator. No progress can be made.

But progress *can* be made for the existence of God through scientific evidence gained from big bang cosmology. To this we turn.

SCIENTIFIC CONFIRMATION OF THE CREATION: THE BIG BANG

Craig and others have sought epistemic support for creation ex nihilo through the scientific evidence for big bang cosmology. Several converging lines of evidence have firmly established this cosmology, which is interpreted by most to require an absolute origination of the universe from nothing about fourteen billion years ago. Stephen Hawking, the renowned physicist, said that "almost everyone now believes that the universe, and *time itself*, had a beginning at the Big Bang."[54] Even the atheist Quentin Smith accepts that big bang cosmology entails that nothing at all existed before the first event of the universe.[55]

A detailed account of the ascent of big bang cosmology is not possible here, but a broad outline may be sketched.[56] Einstein's general theory of relativity (1917) had implications far beyond his imagination. His theory

---

[52]Craig, *Reasonable Faith*, pp. 116-24.

[53]"Climbing a ladder of water" comes from Cornelius Van Til, but was not used by him to defend a cosmological argument, since he forswore all natural theology, classically understood. See Cornelius Van Til, *The Defense of the Faith* (Philadelphia: Presbyterian & Reformed, 1972), p. 102.

[54]Stephen Hawking and Roger Penrose, *The Nature of Space and Time*, The Isaac Newton Institute Series of Lectures (Princeton, N.J.: Princeton University Press, 1996), p. 20, quoted in J. P. Moreland and William Lane Craig, *Philosophical Foundations for a Christian Worldview* (Downers Grove, Ill.: InterVarsity Press, 2003), p. 478. Science writer and astronomer Robert Jastrow concurs, *God and the Astronomers*, 2nd ed. (New York: Norton, 1992), p. 14.

[55]Smith, "Uncaused Beginning of the Universe," p. 120.

[56]I will be relying mostly on Jastrow, but also see Moreland and Craig, *Philosophical Foundations*, pp. 476-79.

of gravitation assumes an eternal universe existing in a steady state that is not expanding. However, Russian mathematician Alexander Friedmann found that Einstein had made an elementary mistake in his calculations when he divided by zero. When this was corrected, the theory predicted an expanding universe.[57] Independently of Friedmann, Belgian astronomer Georges Lemaitre found essentially the same thing.[58] The corrected theory then began to be verified by various strains of evidence.

In 1929, astronomer Edward Hubble picked up on observational data left by Vesto Slipher that about a dozen galaxies near earth were moving away from us at high speeds. This was indicated by "the red shift," which is "a change in the color of the light from . . . distant galaxies that indicated, to the trained eye, an enormously rapid motion away from earth."[59] Using large telescopes, Hubble, with the aid of Milton Humason, verified that the galaxies were moving away from each other in an isotropic fashion, thus further establishing the expanding universe. From this, Hubble formulated his famous law of the expanding universe, earlier predicted by Slipher, that *the farther away a galaxy is, the faster it moves."*[60] Hubble's law, taken by itself, does not prove that the universe has always been expanding but only that it is expanding now; in other words, it is a necessary condition, but not a sufficient condition, for the big bang.[61]

As the big bang was gaining ground, some scientists tried to take the ground out from under it. In the late 1940s, Fred Hoyle and two other scientists postulated the "steady state" universe, in which the universe is ever expanding yet eternal. This theory required that new material be created continuously out of nothing in the empty aspects of the universe (a dubious idea philosophically). Then another sky-shaking discovery further confirmed the big bang and rendered the steady state theory unsteady at best. At the end of World War II, three scientists calculated that if the universe came into being through a tremendous explosion, this event would have produced intense radiation that, while diminished, would still exist in the contemporary universe. In 1965, physicists Arno Penzias and Robert Wilson "detected the cosmic fireball radiation [that had been] pre-

---

[57]Jastrow, *God and the Astronomers*, pp. 18-19.
[58]Ibid., p. 32.
[59]Ibid., p. 18.
[60]Ibid., p. 32, emphasis in the original.
[61]Ibid., p. 54.

dicted and thereby made one of the greatest discoveries in 500 years of modern astronomy."[62] Their initial findings have been further confirmed.[63] Now both the necessary and sufficient conditions for the *occurrence* of the big bang have been established—although the *explanation* for it has not been. The implication is that everything in the universe can be traced to an original "singularity" from which it sprang. As two prominent physicists concluded, "At this singularity, space and time came into existence; literally nothing existed before the singularity, so, if the Universe originated in such a singularity, we would truly have a creation *ex nihilo*."[64] But there is yet more cosmic evidence for a beginning of the universe.

The abundance of helium in the universe also confirms what would be expected if the big bang occurred.[65] The fact that the formation and life of stars requires hydrogen also contributes to the evidence for an absolute beginning of the universe, since hydrogen is used up and not created in the process. From this astronomers infer that the further back in time one goes, the more hydrogen. "Turning back the clock still further, the astronomer comes to a time when the Universe contained nothing but hydrogen—no carbon, no oxygen, and none of the other elements out of which planets and life are made. This point in time must have marked the beginning of the Universe."[66]

Last, the second law of thermodynamics strongly indicates a beginning of the universe. Thermodynamics is the science of energy. Its second law states that closed systems incline toward a state of equilibrium or entropy. That is, the "universe is moving irreversibly toward a state of maximum disorder and minimum energy."[67] This endpoint is known as "heat death."[68] Entropy is an empirical and physical example of the philosophical concept of contingency. The present order of the universe (its assemblage of useable energy) is contingent on previous states of energy and is impossible without it. This contingency relation is strictly linear and irreversible.[69]

---

[62]Ibid., p. 69.

[63]Ibid., pp. 69-72.

[64]John Barrow and Frank Tipler, *The Anthropic Cosmological Principle* (Oxford: Oxford University Press, 1986), p. 442.

[65]For details see Jastrow, *God and the Astronomers*, pp. 79-81.

[66]Ibid., p. 85.

[67]Moreland, *Scaling the Secular City*, p. 34.

[68]For the two versions of this see Moreland and Craig, *Philosophical Foundations*, p. 478.

[69]That is, apart from supernatural intervention.

Entropy increases over time—and not the reverse. From these considerations, a *modus tollens* argument follows.

1. If the universe were eternal and its amount of energy finite, it would
   have reached heat death by now.

2. The universe has not reached heat death (since there is still energy available for use).

3. Therefore, (a) the universe is not eternal.

4. Therefore, (b) the universe had a beginning.

5. Therefore, (c) the universe was created by a first cause (God).

Or, more simply, what is winding down must have been wound up.

Writing in the influential, eight-volume *Encyclopedia of Philosophy*
(1967), G. C. Nerlich rejected this argument, as given by D. Elton
Trueblood,[70] in three sentences. "But this is far from lending support to
the theistic hypothesis. It simply means that the law leads us to a point
beyond which it will not take us. It gives no warrant for the conclusion
that the minimum entropy state has a supernatural cause."[71] But if a
natural law indicates a beginning of the universe and will not take us
beyond the beginning of the universe, then that beginning should be
explained on other, nonnatural grounds. A "supernatural cause" is a fitting candidate when natural explanations give out, as many scientists
and philosophers have begun to fathom. The only other alternative is
that everything came from nothing without a cause—an idea I challenged previously.

Others have disputed this argument by claiming that the universe as a
whole may not be entropic. As Whitrow put it, "It would seem that not
only is it difficult to formulate the concept of entropy for the whole universe but also that there is no evidence that the law of entropy increase
applies on this scale."[72] Put more philosophically, to extrapolate from items
in the universe that are running down to the conclusion that the entire
universe is running down is to commit the fallacy of composition. If one

[70]D. Elton Trueblood, *Philosophy of Religion* (Grand Rapids: Baker, 1957), pp. 102-5.
[71]G. C. Nerlich, "Popular Arguments for the Existence of God," *Encyclopedia of Philosophy*, ed.
   Paul Edwards (New York: Macmillan, 1967), 6:410.
[72]G. J. Whitnow, "Entropy," in *Encyclopedia of Philosophy*, ed. Paul Edwards (New York: Macmillan, 1967), 2:528.

feather is light, that does not imply that eighteen million feathers taken together are light. Similarly, although each individual brick is rectangular, a wall of bricks may be nonrectangular. The whole may take on new and contrary properties not shared by each of its parts. Therefore, parts of the universe may be running down, but not the whole show. If this is the case, then the argument that entropy entails a beginning to the universe fails. How might this objection be answered?

First, the second law of thermodynamics is purported to be a scientific law, that is, a universal or all-inclusive claim covering all cases of energy exchange. Although it relates to particular parts of the universe, the law is formulated to account for all the energy exchanges of the universe. If the scope of the law is universal, it is not "difficult to formulate the law for the whole universe" (as Whitrow claims) but entirely natural and appropriate.[73] Moreover, there is no positive evidence that the law is suspended or reversed in any part of the universe. Paul Davies puts this point clearly:

> Today, few cosmologists doubt that the universe, at least as we know it, did have an origin at a finite moment in the past. The alternative—that the universe has always existed in one form or another—runs into a rather basic paradox. The sun and stars cannot keep burning forever: sooner or later they will run out of fuel and die.

The same is true of all irreversible physical processes; the stock of energy available in the universe to drive them is finite and cannot last for eternity. The second law of thermodynamics, which, applied to the entire universe, predicts that it is stuck on a one-way slide of degeneration and decay toward a final state of maximum entropy or disorder. As this final state has not yet been reached, it follows that the universe cannot have existed for an infinite time.[74]

But does the entropy argument commit the fallacy of composition? The fallacy of composition is applicable to some, but not all, whole-part relations. This is because it is not a *formal* fallacy (such as denying the antecedent, which is fallacious *whenever* its form appears, independent of any material considerations) but rather an *informal* fallacy that only obtains when

---

[73]See Moreland, *Scaling the Secular City*, p. 37.
[74]Paul Davies, "The Big Bang—and Before," a paper presented at the Thomas Aquinas College Lecture Series, Thomas Aquinas College, Santa Paula, Calif., March 2002, quoted in Copan and Craig, *Creation Out of Nothing*, pp. 243-44.

particular material factors are present. In many whole-part relationships the fallacy of composition does not occur. If each individual playing card is made of paper, then one ton of playing cards will be made of paper. If each individual brick occupies space, then the whole wall will occupy space. In these kinds of cases a property of the parts distributes as a property of the whole. Therefore, no context-independent rule can be stipulated as to whether a fallacy of composition has been committed. We must consult individual cases.[75]

Additive factors may not cause a transmutation when applied to the whole. Adding up a million individually light playing cards will make the set of cards heavy, but it will not make the set of cards immaterial. There is no good reason to think that a universe consisting only of entropic beings will possess the property of nonentropy. But if the universe is universally entropic, it requires a source of original energy outside of itself. To avoid an infinite regress, we need to infer a first cause that is not itself subject to the entropic regress.

THE BIG BANG AND THE BIG PROTEST

Robert Jastrow notes that as the big bang theory was gaining ground, many physicists were reluctant to accept its implications because it placed limits on what naturalistic science could affirm. It also challenged the implicit naturalism of science. Arthur Eddington wrote in 1931, "I have no axe to grind in this discussion," but "the notion of a beginning is repugnant to me. . . . I simply do not believe that the present order of things started off with a bang . . . the expanding Universe is preposterous . . . incredible . . . it leaves me cold."[76] Walter Nernst, the German chemist, wrote, "To deny the infinite duration of time would be to betray the foundations of science."[77] Alan Sandage of the Carnegie Observatories, whose research helped confirm the theory, said, "It is such a strange conclusion . . . it cannot really be true."[78] The great Einstein himself, whose general theory of relativity paved the way for the development of the big bang, said that the idea of an expanding universe "irritates me" and to "admit such

---

[75]See Ed L. Miller, *God and Reason* (New York: Macmillan, 1972), p. 56.
[76]Arthur Eddington, quoted in Jastrow, *God and the Astronomers*, p. 104.
[77]Walter Nernst, quoted in Jastrow, *God and the Astronomers*, p. 104.
[78]Alan Sandage, quoted in Jastrow, *God and the Astronomers*, pp. 104-5.

possibilities seems senseless."[79] A more recent example is from the famous physicist Stephen Hawking. In reflecting on the standard or "hot big bang" model, he says, "It would be very difficult to explain why the universe should have begun in just this way, except as the act of a God who intended to create beings like us." He then speaks of Alan Guth's "inflationary model" as an attempt to "avoid this difficulty."[80] But there is no "difficulty" if we accept divine creation.

Jastrow reflects on these kinds of statements in a way that helps illuminate several apologetic issues.

> There is a strange ring of feeling and emotion in these reactions. They come from the heart, whereas you would expect the judgments to come from the brain. Why? I think part of the answer is that scientists cannot bear the thought of a natural phenomenon which cannot be explained, even with unlimited time and money. There is a kind of religion in science; it is the religion of a person who believes there is order and harmony in the Universe. Every event can be explained in a rational way as the product of some previous event; every effect must have its cause; there can be no First Cause. Einstein wrote, "The scientist is possessed by the sense of universal causation."[81]

This "religion of science"—despite its metaphysical naturalism—trades on the essentially Christian idea that the universe is an orderly and harmonious place, an idea that animated the scientific revolution.[82] However, as science became secularized after the scientific revolution, it dispensed with God as a credible scientific explanation for anything. In the case of big bang cosmology, however, the data leads to a primordial reality beyond the universe. A first cause is the best explanation of the facts at hand; yet this explanation is ruled out a priori if "every effect must have its cause; there can be no First Cause," as Jastrow says. For Hawking, a first cause is not an explanation but "a difficulty" to be overcome. Einstein, though a theist, did not believe in a Creator or first cause, but rather "Spinoza's

---

[79]Albert Einstein, quoted in Jastrow, *God and the Astronomers*, pp. 20-21.

[80]Stephen Hawking, *The Theory of Everything* (Beverly Hills, Calif.: New Millennium, 2002), p. 107.

[81]Jastrow, *God and the Astronomers*, p. 105. David Berklinski also notes this psychological unease with the implications of the big bang in *The Devil's Delusion: Atheism and Its Scientific Pretenses* (New York: Crown Forum, 2008), p. 81.

[82]See the discussion of this in chap. 5.

God, who reveals himself in the orderly harmony of what exists."[83] We will return to the methodologies and metaphysics of science in chapter thirteen, but suffice it to note this kind of illicit "metaphysical veto" that some scientists bring to their data.

THE STATUS OF BIG BANG COSMOLOGY

But how well-established is big bang cosmology? Some might claim that we are making Christianity hostage to fortune if we hitch apologetics to this—or any—scientific theory, because scientific theories may be falsified in the future. Three observations should diffuse these worries. First, since Scripture speaks to objective realities in the cosmos and claims that the cosmos itself bears witness to God (general revelation), Christians should consider how scientific theories relate to Christian theism. Second, big bang cosmology is not the only philosophical route from the cosmos to the Creator. Even when the steady state theory held court in cosmology, there were still solid *philosophical* arguments available for the existence of God. Even if big bang cosmology were to be replaced by some theory that does not entail that everything came from nothing, Christians (and other theists) could still appeal to other cosmological arguments—and arguments of other sorts—to establish the rationality of their theistic beliefs. Third, big bang cosmology is not a Johnny-come-lately theory of the universe. Its pedigree and credentials are stellar as macro scientific theories go (far better than Darwinism, for example). It was first predicted in esoteric equations and later confirmed through multiple layers of evidence. So, while the big bang cosmology is hardly Holy Writ, it is the prevailing incumbent, whose impeachment seems unlikely.

Furthermore, while there are a few competitors to the standard model of the big bang, they are highly speculative and lack significant empirical support. For example, the oscillating universe theory denies an absolute origination of the cosmos in favor of a cyclical process of creation and destruction. However, this view hasn't come close to displacing the big bang model for two outstanding reasons. First, it contradicts the known laws of physics by claiming that after the universe has used up all available energy it miraculously "bounces" back into a new fully loaded version. There is no

---

[83]Hawking, *Theory of Everything*, p. 21. Einstein was only partially right about Spinoza's theology. Spinoza believed that God and nature were one but that God was not a personal being.

known mechanism by which this could happen. Second, even if the universe could "bounce back," the model lacks empirical support with respect to the distribution of matter in the universe, which favors the big bang interpretation.[84]

Stephen Hawking has famously challenged the big bang's implication of an absolute origination, which would be entailed by an original singularity at the beginning of the universe. He says,

> So long as the universe had a beginning that was a singularity, one could suppose that it was created by an outside agency. But if the universe is really self-contained, having no boundary or edge, it would be neither created nor destroyed. It would simply be. What place, then, for a creator?[85]

Yet Hawking's no-singularity model is purely speculative and relies on very questionable notions such as "imaginary time."[86] Moreover, Hawking's theory, as articulated in *The Theory of Everything*, seems to be non-realist in its approach. After putting forth the question of whether "real time" (relied on for the big bang singularity) or "imaginary time" (invented by Hawking to avoid the singularity) is objectively real, Hawking claims that

> a scientific theory is just a mathematical model we make to describe our observations. It exists only in our minds. So it does not have any meaning to ask: Which is real, "real" or "imaginary" time? It is simply a matter of which is a more useful description.[87]

If Hawking is opting for a merely pragmatic or instrumental view of scientific theories, he exempts himself from any claim to know the objective reality of the universe. Certainly, most scientists engaged in these monumental matters do not take this route. Instead, they attempt to craft theories and interpret data to match or at least approximate objective reality. All theories "exist in our minds," but the interesting question is whether they accurately describe what they are purportedly about—the universe.[88]

---

[84]For the details of this argument, see Craig, *Reasonable Faith*, pp. 103-6.
[85]Hawking, *Theory of Everything*, p. 126.
[86]See Craig, *Reasonable Faith*, pp. 134-36.
[87]Hawking, *Theory of Everything*, pp. 124-25.
[88]For a critique of Hawking's views on God and creation, see William Lane Craig, "'What Place, Then, for a Creator?' Hawking on God and Creation," in William Lane Craig and Quentin Smith, *Theism, Atheism, and Big Bang Cosmology* (Oxford: Clarendon, 1993), pp. 279-300.

Several other theories to displace the big bang are on the table, including the quantum fluctuation model, the chaotic inflation model, quantum gravity model and the enkyroptic model. But after a detailed argument for the big bang and against its upstart rivals, Craig and Copan conclude:

> It can be confidently said that, with regard to the standard big bang model, no cosmogonic model has been as repeatedly verified in its predictions, as corroborated by attempts at its falsification, as concordant with empirical discoveries, and as philosophically coherent.[89]

As big bang cosmology becomes entrenched in modern physics, some scientists and philosophers are biting the cosmic bullet and granting that everything came from nothing. The steady state and oscillating universe cosmologies are left in shambles, and there is no sure-fire successor in the works for big bang cosmology. So, some are arguing that we can accept the fact that everything came from nothing—yet without conceding a first cause.

Unbelief in God as the originating cause of the universe results in a blind leap of faith in nothing at all at the source of everything whatsoever. Anthony Kenny discerns this problem, "A proponent of the big bang theory, at least if he is an atheist, must believe that the matter of the universe came from nothing, by nothing."[90] Unless one posits that everything came from nothing without a cause, one must concede that a supernatural Creator detonated the big bang. Yet some Christians are reluctant to accept the arguments just given.

CHRISTIAN RELUCTANCE TO ACCEPT THE BIG BANG

Christians have often ignored cosmology in favor of fighting battles over biology and evolution.[91] But if one can rationally establish divine creation as the original miracle, the defense of divine intervention later in earth history becomes more philosophically credible. If the universe began with a divine miracle (creation ex nihilo), could there not be more?[92] Some

---

[89]Copan and Craig, *Creation Out of Nothing*, p. 240.
[90]Anthony Kenny, *The Five Ways: St. Thomas Aquinas' Proofs of God's Existence* (New York: Schocken Books, 1969), p. 66.
[91]Craig Sean McDonnell, "Twentieth Century Cosmologies," in *Dictionary of Religion and Science in the Western World*, ed. Gary Ferngren (New York: Garland, 2000), p. 365.
[92]This is attributed to Norman Geisler, but I do not know where he wrote it.

Christians object that the big bang is the big bust, since the Bible teaches that the universe is far younger than the several billons of years indicated by big bang cosmology. Biologist Kurt Wise refers to the big bang theory as "the most popular atheistic theory for the origin of the universe" because it "leaves God totally out of the picture."[93] Given our argument, this assessment is wrong. The rejection of the big bang is fueled by two related concerns, both of which can be answered sufficiently.

First, some who want to preserve God's active agency in the formation of life and human beings see big bang cosmology as lending support to macroevolutionary theory, since it gives the universe so much time to evolve. Many Christians take big bang cosmology and macroevolution to be correlative: one implies the other. However, this reasoning is fallacious.

Big bang cosmology does not *establish* the truth of macroevolution. The evidence for macroevolution is quite weak and the evidence for God's intervention and guidance in creating life is quite strong, as I will argue in chapters thirteen and fourteen. A universe of vast antiquity is a *necessary* condition for macroevolution to be true, but it is not a *sufficient* condition. Chance and natural law (sans God) would require eons of time to kick up life and humans, but such a naturalistic theory would also have to supply some credible evolutionary mechanism to account for the specified complexity of life. The evidence, however, is squarely against this.[94]

Another objection to big bang cosmology is the belief that the Bible says the universe is only about ten thousand years old. I cannot canvass all the arguments, but several will suffice. First, the Hebrew word *day* in Genesis 1 can mean an indeterminate or long period of time. Second, the word *day* is used in Genesis before the earth and sun are even created, indicating that *day* is not a twenty-four-hour period (since what measures days was not yet in existence). Third, the seventh day of God's rest is not recorded in Scripture as having ended. If it is considerably longer than

---

[93]Kurt Wise, *Faith, Form, and Time: What the Bible Teaches and What Science Confirms About the Age of the Universe* (Nashville: Broadman & Holman, 2002), p. 89. Wise gives a scant three pages of criticism of the big bang, most of which hinges on the notion that the Bible teaches that the earth is only about six thousand years old and that the universe is not much older. Although the subtitle of his book claims that science confirms a young universe, he says, "Even though the Big Bang theory is wrong, no young-earth creationist theory has yet been forthcoming to provide an alternative explanation of its evidences" (ibid., p. 90).

[94]See William Dembski, *No Free Lunch* (New York: Free Press, 2002). I also take this up in chapter fourteen.

twenty-four hours, so may the other days be as well. Fourth, the amount of time following the six days of creation cannot be dated through the use of biblical genealogies because these genealogies are not meant to be detailed chronologies. This leaves considerable latitude in reckoning the amount of time that has passed in and since the "week" of creation.[95]

Therefore, if the Bible does not demand a young universe and earth, we should not press the point in the face of a well-established and large-scale scientific theory that also lends strong support to creation ex nihilo. There is good theological incentive for this strategy as well. God is the author of both Scripture (2 Timothy 3:15-16; 2 Peter 1:20-21) and nature (see Psalm 19:1-4; Romans 1:20). He is revealed through both "books." I am not claiming that the proper apologetic strategy is always to side with received or traditional views of the scientific establishment. (In fact, in chapters thirteen and fourteen, I will argue that the establishment is wrong with respect to the explanatory power of Darwinism.) However, (1) if Scripture leaves open the strong possibility of an ancient universe, and (2) if the evidence for the big bang is cumulative and impressive, and, most importantly, (3) if the theory lends support to the crucial biblical doctrine of divine creation from nothing, then the savvy apologist should endorse it.

THE GOD OF COSMOLOGICAL ARGUMENTS

If the universe has a beginning that was caused, what can be known about this cause on the basis of the cosmological arguments I have addressed? It is often claimed that even successful cosmological arguments land a million miles away from the God of the Bible. While I have developed this argument more fully elsewhere, I will here briefly set forth the claim that cosmological arguments substantiate a singular, personal, imperishable and all-powerful being.[96]

Some have claimed cosmological arguments allow for more than one uncaused being.[97] There appear to be two mutually reinforcing responses that

---

[95]See Moreland, *Scaling the Secular City*, pp. 214-20; and Hugh Ross, *Creation and Time* (Colorado Springs: NavPress, 1994).

[96]See Groothuis, "Metaphysical Implications of Cosmological Arguments."

[97]Dallas Willard, "The Three-Stage Argument for the Existence of God," in *Contemporary Perspectives on Religious Epistemology*, ed. R. Douglas Geivett and Brendan Sweetman (New York: Oxford University Press, 1992), p. 207. Willard fails to argue why there may be more than one uncaused being; he simply asserts it.

deflate this polytheistic possibility. First, on theoretical grounds, simplicity is typically preferred over complexity with respect to explanation, unless complexity is otherwise warranted. To invoke Ockham's razor, we should not multiply explanatory entities unnecessarily. Therefore, the conclusion that there is one cause of the universe is to be preferred to the idea that there are more than one, unless there is some overriding reason to posit multiple entities.[98] Second, the rejection of multiple creators can also find assistance in a successful design argument. Swinburne argues that Hume's objection that there may be many designers instead of one Designer seems to break on the rocks of the regularity and unity of the universe, which is more simply and better explained on the basis of one Designer, not many finite designers. The latter would be far less likely to cooperate to the degree required to produce the kind of universe we observe.[99]

But if there is a single cause of the universe, is it a personal being, such as the God of Abraham, Isaac and Jacob? The cause must be either personal or impersonal, since these categories exhaust the possibilities. An impersonal cause, whatever else it may be, would certainly not be the God of the Bible.[100] However, there is a strong case that the cosmological cause is personal. If the cause of the universe were an impersonal principle—that is, merely a set of necessary and sufficient conditions for creation—it could not *choose* to create but would automatically actualize the universe and "could not exist without its effect."[101] If so, the universe would be eternal, since the cause and the effect would coexist. Craig explains this with an example:

> Let's say the cause of water's freezing is sub-zero temperatures. Whenever the temperature falls below zero degrees Centigrade, the water freezes. Once the cause is given, the effect must follow, and if the cause exists from

---

[98]Some might worry here that this argument brings into question the Christian doctrine of the Trinity, which is more complex than a strict unipersonal view of monotheism. God is not three beings but one being in three persons. The logic and explanatory power of the Trinity was addressed in chap. 10. For some helpful thinking on the coherence of the Trinity philosophically, see Thomas D. Senor, "The Incarnation and the Trinity," in *Reason for the Hope Within*, ed. Michael J. Murray (Grand Rapids: Eerdmans, 1999), pp. 252-60.

[99]See Richard Swinburne, *The Existence of God*, rev. ed. (New York: Oxford University Press, 1991), pp. 141-42. I give several design arguments in chaps. 12, 14.

[100]For some of the philosophical and existential problems with the idea of an impersonal beginning of the universe (as opposed to the biblical God), see Schaeffer, *He Is There and He Is Not Silent*.

[101]Craig, *Reasonable Faith*, p. 153.

eternity, the effect must also exist from eternity. If the temperature were to remain below zero degree from eternity, then any water around would be frozen from eternity. But this seems to imply that if the cause of the universe existed eternally, the universe would also have existed eternally. And we know this to be false.[102]

Since the universe is not eternal, the cause of the universe is not impersonal but personal.

But someone might argue that abstract objects/entities (also called abstracta) existed before the advent of the universe, and that they are what created the universe. An abstract object/entity is timeless, spaceless and immaterial, as are "mathematical objects, such as numbers, sets, and geometrical figures, propositions, properties, and relations."[103] However, while abstract objects/entities are not part of the space-time material universe and could exist without it, they are also acausal, since they are not agents. Therefore, they cannot bring about the creation of the universe.[104]

Philosophers, even some Christian philosophers, often argue that the God supported by cosmological arguments cannot be taken to be omnipotent. All that the cosmological arguments can affirm is that God has the power to bring about our universe. But this falls short of establishing omnipotence.[105]

However, one can plausibly argue that if a being possesses causal necessity and self-existence, and has wrought creation ex nihilo, this being would very likely be unlimited in power. This follows from two considerations. First, it seems difficult to imagine a greater expenditure of power than the act of absolute origination or initiation (call it *exnihiliation*)—that of creating the entire universe out of nothing by one's unique action without external assistance. Thus, a fortiori, an exnihiliating being's power would admit of no limits, outside those of logic itself (which are not limits

---

[102]Ibid.

[103]"Abstract Entity" in *The Cambridge Dictionary of Philosophy*, ed. Robert Audi, 2nd ed. (New York: Cambridge University Press, 1999), pp. 3-4. For more on the existence and nature of abstract objects, see Moreland, *Scaling the Secular City*, pp. 80-82; and Paul Copan and William Lane Craig, "Creation Ex Nihilo and Abstract Objects," in *Creation Out of Nothing: A Biblical, Philosophical, and Scientific Exploration* (Grand Rapids: Baker, 2005).

[104]See Copan and Craig, "Creation Ex Nihilo and Abstract Objects," pp. 168-70.

[105]Stephen T. Davis, "The Cosmological Argument and the Epistemic Status of Belief in God," *Philosophia Christi*, series 2, 1, no. 1 (1999): 6; William C. Davies, "Theistic Arguments," in *Reason for the Hope Within*, ed. Michael Murray (Grand Rapids: Eerdmans, 1998), p. 25.

in a restrictive sense but are rather invariant conditions for intelligibility and actuality). Crudely put, if a weight lifter can bench-press three hundred pounds, all things being equal, he can bench press one hundred pounds. For instance, if a necessary being creates the universe in all its glory ex nihilo (and is personal, as I have already argued), and if exnihiliation is the unique and incomparable exertion of power, there seems to be no reason to believe this being could not perform miracles, bring about its desired ends in history or re-create the universe in the future—these being some of the more salient requirements of omnipotence.

A second consideration is that such an exnihilating being would be *uniquely* causally necessary and self-existent (or noncontingent), since it alone precedes the existence of the contingent universe and thus is unlimited by any external factors (although this being might freely place certain restrictions on itself). Such a noncontingent being would be incapable of losing its noncontingent status since, by definition, it depends on nothing outside itself for its existence. Nothing, then, could threaten its being. And if this incorrigibly noncontingent being has created ex nihilo, it seems there would be nothing logically possible that it could not accomplish at any point after creation, since an exnihiliating and self-existent being could suffer no diminution of the already maximal power it has demonstrated by the act of universe making.[106]

It should be granted, though, that in one sense omnipotence—which is a difficult concept to define in the first place—cannot be absolutely demonstrated or exemplified by any action, since we might at least imagine another action requiring more power, which the agent lacks. However, I think Craig's comments are on mark: "A being with the power to create the entire universe out of nothing not only meets the biblical requirements for being almighty, but the consensus of church theologians has also been

---

[106]But David Werther points out (in a personal conversation) that if God's existence is only causally necessary (as established by the non-Leibnizian cosmological arguments) and not logically necessary, then God's existence is a brute fact. That is, God might not have existed but does (happen to) exist as a self-existent being. Nevertheless, if God merely exists as a brute fact, God might cease to exist. "Even omnipotence cannot protect God from a causeless event," according to Werther. If this is so, it is possible that God could cease to exist if God's existence is not logically necessary. However, I argued in chap. 10 that God does exist by logical necessity, so there is no danger of God going out of existence. The kalam cosmological argument establishes that God's existence is necessary for the existence of the universe; the ontological argument, the Leibnizian cosmological argument, the moral argument and the conceptualist argument establish that God's existence is necessary in and of itself.

that *ex nihilo* creation is a power belonging to God alone."[107] Claiming
that this being is also omnipotent seems rationally justified, although it
may be too much to claim that omnipotence is logically *entailed* by ex nihilo creation. Nevertheless, it is a rationally warranted belief, given the
cosmological arguments marshaled here.

COSMOLOGICAL ARGUMENTS AND IMPLICATIONS FOR OTHER WORLDVIEWS

Several worldviews are in intellectual jeopardy if our cosmological conclusions thus far are sound. Obviously, atheism is refuted if the universe is
neither eternal nor sprung into existence out of nothing, since the only
other alternative is divine creation. If we have ruled out a committee of
deities as responsible for the creation, polytheism is eliminated as well.

Pantheism is also rejected, since it claims that the universe is a necessary being—an idea we found illogical given the contingent nature of the
universe. Pantheism also makes one of the two following claims, each of
which is refuted by the cosmological arguments given in this chapter: It
either (1) affirms the eternality of the universe, which develops and decays
in a cyclical fashion, or (2) it denies the reality of the physical universe as
entirely an illusion; only an impersonal god is real. When pantheism takes
cosmology seriously—and doesn't dismiss it as illusory (*maya*)—it is committed to an eternal universe composed of vast periods of time (*yugas*).
Carl Sagan, while irreligious, admired the unique Hindu concept that "the
Cosmos itself undergoes an immense, indeed an infinite, number of deaths
and rebirths. It is the only religion in which the time scales correspond, no
doubt by accident, to those of modern scientific cosmology."[108] (Sagan
does not mention the fact that the biblical cosmology allows for long periods of time as well.) Buddhist cosmology, though differing from Hindu
cosmology, similarly affirms an eternal universe without an absolute beginning, consisting of an infinite causal regress.[109] As such, it is also ruled

---

[107]William Lane Craig, "Closing Remarks," in *Five Views of Apologetics*, ed. Steven Cowan
(Grand Rapids: Zondervan, 2000), p. 323.
[108]Carl Sagan, *Cosmos* (New York: Random House, 1980), p. 258.
[109]The Buddhist cosmology is called "dependent origination." This (roughly) means that exis-
    tents (considered as nonsubstantial points that exist only evanescently) depend ultimately on
    other existents, but not on a Creator. This is explained and critiqued in David L. Johnson, *A
    Reasoned Approach to Asian Religions* (Minneapolis: Bethany House, 1985), pp. 133-136. See
    also Keith Yandell and Harold Netland, *Buddhism: A Christian Exploration and Appraisal*

out by successful cosmological arguments.

However, at this stage of our argument the nature of the Creator of the cosmos is not fully identified. We can liken the situation to receiving a letter with only a partial return address. We know someone has sent us a letter from somewhere, but there is more we want to know. Judaism, Christianity and Islam all affirm that one, personal, omnipotent and eternal being brought forth the universe out of nothing. Yet all these traditions make different claims about the Creator. Moreover, there is another worldview that has never solidified into a distinct religion, but which is nevertheless a philosophical possibility: deism. Historically, deism has usually been parasitic on Christianity for its notion of the Creator and for basic moral principles, but it has denied the incarnation, the Trinity, miracles or the need for special revelation. Deism accepts at least some of the deliverances of general revelation but calls it quits at that stage, relying on unaided human reason for the articulation of the rest of its theistic worldview.[110] Thus it is apparent that we cannot argue for something as rich as the entire Christian worldview simply on the basis of cosmological arguments.

(Downers Grove, Ill.: InterVarsity Press, 2009), pp. 121-28.

[110]For an explanation and critique of deism, see James W. Sire, "The Clockwork Universe: Deism," in *The Universe Next Door: A Basic Worldview Catalog,* 5th ed. (Downers Grove, Ill.: InterVarsity Press, 2009); Norman Geisler and William D. Watkins, *Worlds Apart* (Grand Rapids: Baker, 1989), pp. 147-86; John Henry Overton, *The English Church in the Eighteenth Century* (New York: Longmans, Green, 1906), pp. 75-112. A classic work is Joseph Butler, *The Analogy of Religion* (1736) <http://books.google.com/books?id=8YUBAAAAYAAJ&dq =intitle:Analogy%20intitle:of%20intitle:Religion%20inauthor:Butler>. For a short, scholarly exposition of deism see Stephen P. Weldon, "Deism," in *The History of Science and Religion in the Western Tradition: An Encyclopedia,* ed. Gary Ferngren (New York: Garland, 2000), pp. 158-60. Thanks to Tim McGrew for several of these references.

The Design Argument

Cosmic Fine-Tuning

ARE WE ORPHANS OR CITIZENS OF THE cosmos? Choruses of secular voices, many of whom shout loudly from the scientific academy, insist that humans and the rest of the cosmos are nothing but the result of time, space, matter/energy, impersonal laws and chance. This is our metaphysical pedigree. Our cosmic environment was not fashioned with us in mind. Many scientists proclaim this not as philosophical speculation but scientific fact. World-renowned physicist Steven Weinberg famously said, "The more the universe seems comprehensible, the more it seems pointless."[1]

On the contrary, the Christian worldview affirms that the universe is the handiwork of a designing agent. The Creator brought everything into existence ex nihilo and engineered the structure and function of the universe.

> God made the earth by his power;
> > he founded the world by his wisdom
> > and stretched out the heavens by his understanding. (Jeremiah 10:12)

God has left his fingerprints in creation for us to discern (Psalm 8:3). Human beings are symbols of the divine, being made in God's image and likeness.[2] God placed us in a world suited for us, ready for development and cultivation (Genesis 1–2). The universe is *teleological*.

But the universe was not made for human beings alone. The nonhuman

---

[1]Steven Weinberg, cited in James Glanz, "Scientist at Work: Steven Weinberg; Physicist Ponders God, Truth and 'Final Theory,'" *New York Times*, January 25, 2000 <www.nytimes.com/2000/01/25/science/scientist-at-work-steven-weinberg-physicist-ponders-god-truth-and-final-theory.html>.

[2]The apologetic significance of human beings will be taken up in chaps. 17-18.

creation—heavenly and earthly—was declared "good" by God before the creation of humans. All creation was made for the glory of its Creator, who calls it to praise its Maker (Psalm 148). Since humans are not the sole purpose of creation, there is no force to arguments by atheists that the vast amount of uninhabited space ("waste") in the universe argues against God's concern for humans. A vast universe is compatible with both God's care for us *and* his glory manifested in the rest of the universe.[3]

The ethos of modern science trades on the claim that the universe, our planet and our place on it is nothing special. This has been called "the Copernican Principle," based on the mythical idea that Copernicus's heliocentric theory displaced the earth from its privileged position in the larger scheme of things.[4] But this claim, made by Bertrand Russell and countless others, is false.[5] It is based on the legend that pre-Copernican cosmology granted the earth a privileged location at the center of the universe (geocentrism)—a view that was discarded when it became evident that the earth rotated around the sun (heliocentrism). In fact, the geocentric model did not flatter humans but viewed them as living far from the more perfect realm of the physical heavens.[6] Moreover, there is nothing in the Bible that correlates value or significance with location in the cosmos. Rather, human value is based on humans bearing the divine image.

DESIGNED BUT FALLEN

It is imperative to note that while the Christian account of reality claims that

---

[3]Victor Stenger, *God: The Failed Hypothesis* (New York: Prometheus, 2007), pp. 154-61. Job 38–41 speaks of God's glory being revealed in the nonhuman world, although it does not focus on the larger universe. Moreover, a vast universe was very likely necessary for life to exist anywhere in the universe. See Stephen Barr, "Why Is the Universe So Big?" in *Modern Physics and Ancient Faith* (Notre Dame, Ind.: University of Notre Dame Press, 2004); Guillermo Gonzalez and Jay Wesley Richards, *The Privileged Planet* (New York: Free Press, 2004), pp. 272-74; and Hugh Ross, "Why Such a Vast Universe?" in *Why the Universe Is the Way It Is* (Grand Rapids: Baker, 2008).

[4]In *Privileged Planet*, Gonzalez and Richards prosecute a sustained argument against the Copernican Principle, showing that its important scientific predictions have failed.

[5]Bertrand Russell, *Religion and Science* (1935; reprint, London: Oxford University Press, 1961), p. 216. Chapter 8 argues against any cosmic purpose.

[6]See C. S. Lewis, "Imagination and Thought in the Middle Ages," in *Studies in Medieval and Renaissance Literature* (1966; reprint, New York: Cambridge University Press, 1998). Thanks to Robert Velarde for this reference. The Bible itself grants no moral or spiritual significance to the physical location of earth in the universe. Human significance is based, rather, on the divine creation of humans in God's image and likeness (Genesis 1:26).

(1) the cosmos is designed, (2) signs of design are evident, and (3) these signs point toward the Designer, it does not claim that (4) all the structures and processes of this designed creation now exhibit perfection. If we take the Christian worldview to be a hypothesis to be confirmed or falsified, the hypothesis must be stated properly. Part of this hypothesis is that humans and the surrounding universe are *fallen as a result of human rebellion against God* (Genesis 3; Romans 3). Why God would create a world in which the fall would occur will be taken up in chapter twenty-five, but the point stands that while Christianity predicts that design in nature will be evident, it does not predict a flawless world untouched by sin and corruption.[7]

This chapter and chapter fourteen claim that there is enough design evident at multiple levels of nature to infer that there is a Designer. However, there is also evidence of deformity, decay and disease, indicating that the design is often less than optimal.[8] Thus there is enough evidence to believe in a Designer, but not enough to claim a perfect creation. There is enough deformity to warrant the idea of the fall, but not enough to deface the idea of design entirely. Hence, we have evidence for both creation and Fall in nature. The alternative would be no Designer (which explains nothing) or an imperfect designer who did what he could, but not enough. The success of cosmological, moral and ontological arguments, which yield a self-existent, maximal and moral being, eliminate this dispiriting possibility.[9]

One more point should be reiterated before we dive into design. All the theistic arguments work in tandem and should be assessed as such. The design argument does not bear the entire weight of establishing theism or Christianity. We have already given compelling reasons to believe that the universe was created by a personal and all-powerful being. This answers the question of cosmic origins, a titanic issue for any worldview. The design argument takes a closer look at what has been created and who designed it.

OTHER DESIGN ARGUMENTS

Philosophers such as Richard Swinburne have presented muscular induc-

---

[7]See especially Romans 8:20-23.
[8]However, some charges of bad design, such as the poor design of the eye or of so-called junk DNA, have been refuted (see chap. 13).
[9]I will say more about supposed design defects in chaps. 13 and 14.

tive arguments from design that do not depend on the fine-tuning argument that will be given shortly, but invoke long-known aspects of nature such as the cycles of the seasons, the orbits of planets, the spectrum of colors, the beauty of the natural world and so on.[10] He argues that the complexity (with respect to natural systems), regularity, simplicity (with respect to basic laws) and beauty of the universe is much more likely on the hypotheses of theism than that of naturalism. That is, these commonly observed aspects of nature are better explained by a creative mind than by mindless naturalistic processes.[11] While these arguments appeal to a broad variety of natural phenomena, are meticulously constructed and are quite convincing, this chapter will appeal to newer and rather spectacular findings in cosmology. I should note, though, that even if the fine-tuning argument for a cosmic Designer fails or is less than compelling, we may shift the ground back to the data that do not depend on it.[12]

DESIGN DETECTION

To the delight of theists and the horror of atheists, one of the twentieth century's leading atheist philosophers—a man not reluctant to debate Christians publicly—renounced atheism in 2007 on the basis of the evidence for a Designer and a Creator.[13] Antony Flew, with a coauthor, chronicled the reasons for this conversion to theism after half a century of atheism in his bestselling book *There Is a God*. The reason he came to believe in "a divine Source" is that the "world picture" that has "emerged from science" is best understood in these terms.[14] Flew made no leap of faith; he remained a philosopher who wanted to "follow the argument where ever it leads."[15] But the evidence led him to a Creator and Designer of nature.

---

[10]Swinburne also defends the fine-tuning argument in several places (see Richard Swinburne, "Teleological Arguments," in *The Existence of God*, 2nd ed. (Oxford: Oxford University Press, 2004); and Richard Swinburne, "How the Existence of God Explains the World and Its Order," in *Is There a God?* (New York: Oxford University Press, 1996).

[11]See J. P. Moreland, *Scaling the Secular City* (Grand Rapids: Baker, 1987), pp. 44-49.

[12]See the references in footnote 10.

[13]Antony Flew debated William Lane Craig on the existence of God in 1998; this was captured in book form (with various responses by philosophers) in *Does God Exist? The Craig-Flew Debate*, ed. Stan Wallace (Burlington, Vt.: Ashgate, 2003). Flew also debated Gary Habermas three times on the resurrection of Christ.

[14]Antony Flew with Ray Abraham Varghese, *There Is a God* (San Francisco: HarperOne, 2007), p. 88. Flew had not converted to Christian theism but only a kind of deism. He died in 2010.

[15]Ibid., p. 89.

To claim that anything—whether a computer, a living cell or the entire universe—is designed means that it cannot explain itself. Its features indicate an intelligent agent outside of itself who is responsible for those features. We readily and frequently make distinctions between what is and is not designed. We can discriminate between a nest that has fallen out of a tree and a clump of brush at the base of a tree.

This chapter and the following one will employ "the design inference" as the way of establishing design and ruling out other explanations. This has been rigorously developed by William Dembski.[16] He lays out an empirical strategy for detecting design in nature that makes use of careful criteria. This method of detecting intelligent causes is already accepted in several areas of science, namely, archaeology, forensic science, intellectual property law, insurance claims investigation, cryptography, random number generation and the search for extra terrestrial intelligence (SETI).[17] Intelligent design (ID) simply employs these methods of detecting or falsifying design and applies them to the natural sciences as well.

Design is detected or inferred through the use of an "explanatory filter" that filters out chance and necessity and checks for the marks of contingency, complexity and specificity. An event or object may be reckoned the result of an intelligent cause—as opposed to a nonintelligent, material cause—if it exhibits all three of these factors. Each factor by itself is a necessary but insufficient condition of design. But if all three factors are present, then this threefold cluster becomes a necessary and sufficient indicator of design.

For Dembski, an event or object is *contingent* if it is not explicable on the basis of natural law; that is, if it cannot be explained by automatic processes. For example, Dembski notes that a salt crystal can be explained on the basis of chemical processes described by chemical laws. Thus it is not contingent, in the sense in which Dembski uses the term. However, a complex setting of silverware is not explicable on the basis of automatically functioning natural laws. We infer from its properties that it was laid out by an intelligent agent. While natural laws act on contingent events (gravity affects the place set-

---

[16]William Dembski, *The Design Inference: Eliminating Chance Through Small Probabilities* (New York: Cambridge University Press, 1998). His ideas are further developed in *No Free Lunch* (Lanham, Md.: Rowman & Littlefield, 2002).

[17]Dembski, "Introduction," in *Design Inference*.

ting), natural laws cannot exhaustively account for them.[18]

Complexity is a form of probability. The greater the complexity, the less the probability that the event or object came about by chance—that is, without intelligent causation. But as Dembski notes:

> Complexity by itself isn't enough to eliminate chance and indicate design. If I flip a coin 1,000 times, I'll participate in a highly complex (or what amounts to the same thing, highly improbable) event. Indeed, the sequence I end up flipping will be one in a trillion trillion trillion, . . . where the ellipsis needs twenty-two more "trillions." This sequence of coin tosses won't, however, trigger a design inference. Though complex, this sequence won't exhibit a suitable pattern to detect design.[19]

Consequently, contingency and complexity are necessary but not sufficient indicators of design.

The last factor in design detection is *specificity* or *specification*. If an object or event is to pass successfully through the design filter, it must exhibit a pattern independent of its mere improbability. That is, the pattern of improbable and contingent factors must be *specified* ahead of time, not *fabricated* after the fact. If you randomly throw a dart against the side of a barn from twenty feet away, the place where the dart lands would be improbable in the sense that it might have landed in any number of places. If you were to paint a bull's-eye around the dart and then remark on what an accurate dart thrower you were, this would be what Dembski identifies as a *fabrication* and not a *specification*. However, if a bull's-eye is painted on the barn *before* the dart is thrown and the thrower hits the bull's-eye, the result is *specified*. This likely indicates skill instead of luck—especially if the results are repeated. On the other hand, chance and necessity can adequately explain the destination of the randomly hurled dart.[20]

---

[18]We can also argue that the very existence of natural laws calls for a design explanation, given that it might not have existed at all and given its universal scope and regularity (see Swinburne, "Teleological Arguments"). But Dembski's design filter is after a certain kind of design that is detectable through eliminative induction: when chance and/or natural law cannot adequately explain something, design is the remaining option. So, the design filter is a sufficient condition for recognizing design (there should be no false positives), but it is not necessary (since there will be false negatives).

[19]William Dembski, "Science and Design," *First Things*, October 1, 1998. Also available at the Discovery Institute's Center for Science and Culture <www.discovery.org/a/62>.

[20]The fact that an intelligent agent hurled the dart is irrelevant here, since the agent did not apply any specific intention to the throw with respect to hitting a specified target on the wall; that is, the agent was not trying to hit a particular part of the barn wall. We could change the

The design filter attempts to locate instances of "specified complexity" in the natural world. Specified complexity is a mark of intelligence; thus it cannot be reduced to the factors of chance and necessity. Both in the universe at large (the subject of this chapter) and in microsystems such as the cell and its information content (addressed in chap. fourteen), the design filter has this structure:

1. X is either designed, or the result of chance, or the result of natural law (often called necessity),[21] or the combination of chance and natural law.

2. X is not the result of chance or natural law or the combination of both.

3. Therefore: X is the result of design.

Thus we may reasonably conclude, or infer, that design accounts for all the relevant aspects of X (leaving out nothing important) better than does chance or natural law. Consider a simple example.

Upon visiting Mount Rushmore, we do not need to be informed that the faces of the American presidents did not appear through patterns of erosion caused by wind and rain. While natural law and chance explain the surrounding hillside, the faces of the presidents cannot be so accounted for, given (1) their contingency, (2) their complexity and (3) the independently specified pattern of the president's faces.

However, some reject design explanations in principle, claiming that they use the failed "God of the gaps" strategy—invoking the supernatural instead of working out a sufficient naturalistic explanation. Put another way, the God of the gaps brings in God only to cover our ignorance of the physical world as a kind of deus ex machina to explain certain phenomena. Isaac Newton famously postulated divine causation to explain some of the gaps in his theories of planetary motion. But this divine explanation was later dispensed with when more data and a better theoretical model were advanced to cover the previous ignorance. Stories like this have been used to construct a narrative for science in which a naturalistic scientific explanation always trumps any explanation depending on factors beyond the physical world. However, this narrative is

---

illustration by inserting a random, mechanical dart thrower.

[21]This is not *logical* necessity but *physical* necessity: what will happen according to laws governing nature; it must also be distinguished from natural law in the sense of moral truths known through conscience and apart from special revelation.

naive and often begs the question in favor of naturalism. While it has sometimes been shown that an explanation requiring divine intervention has been adequately replaced by one that appeals to natural laws, this does not rule out the possibility that a divine explanation may be a better explanation for some natural phenomena. In fact, as we will see, naturalistic explanations for cosmology and biology are becoming increasingly strained and untenable.

Although much more can be discussed about this issue, suffice it to say that the design inference is not based on *ignorance* of the natural world but on *knowledge* about it, especially given recent discoveries in physics (fine-tuning) and biology (the nature of the cell and DNA).[22] Those who reject all design explanations in principle have committed the logical fallacy of begging the question in favor of naturalism; if so, their naturalistic theories become unfalsifiable and impervious to counter-evidence—traits that are hardly theoretical virtues in the philosophy of science.

Chapters thirteen and fourteen will address, respectively, the attempt by Darwinists to delete design from living organisms and the arguments for and against the design inference applied specifically to biology. This chapter will investigate the fine-tuning of the universe as a whole, thus revealing God's existence, intelligence and wisdom.

FINE-TUNING DESIGN

The specific conditions of the universe at large reveal an intricate and finely tuned ensemble of factors that make embodied human life possible.[23] These are called "anthropic coincidences." These are necessary conditions for the existence of life as we know it, and all are balanced on a razor's edge.[24] Can these elements fit into a naturalistic worldview?[25]

---

[22]See John Lennox, *God's Undertaker: Has Science Buried God?* (Oxford: Lion, 2007), pp. 168-71; William Dembski, "Argument from Ignorance," in *The Design Revolution* (Downers Grove, Ill.: InterVarsity Press, 2004); Moreland, *Scaling the Secular City*, pp. 205-7.

[23]I emphasize *embodied* human life, since disembodied, rational life (angels, demons, God and the soul after death and before resurrection) is not at issue; such can exist without fine-tuned physical factors. Embodied *human* life is emphasized, since we are not concerned primarily with nonhuman life in this argument. If some of the features of the universe were different, some nonhuman forms of life may have been possible.

[24]Theistic evolutionists, such as Richard Swinburne, claim that these are necessary and sufficient conditions for life and species. I will critique this view in chap. 14.

[25]I will only briefly address whether pantheism can account for these factors at the end of the

Several decades after the big bang cosmology began to marshal its credentials for an absolute beginning of the cosmos, something with similar implications began to boil among scientists who study the basic physical conditions of the universe. Theistic apologists had often argued that the conditions on earth were uniquely fitted for all of life and for human beings.[26] But only fairly recently have scientists discovered just how many variables must be set precisely for human life to occur in the universe.[27] These discoveries fit in with the big bang scenario because they concern what the initial conditions of the universe must have been in order for the universe to be conducive to life at all. But first a preliminary objection needs to be faced.

Philosopher of science Bradley Monton notes that fine-tuning arguments are dogged by scientific technicality. Unlike some other arguments for the existence of God, unless a person is well-versed in physics, it is somewhat difficult to assess the claims made about cosmic fine-tuning by the experts.[28] This is true, but it need not disqualify the arguments. We often appeal to expert testimony in forming conclusions on controversial topics. Our rational certainty concerning the particularities of physics will vary in accordance with our knowledge of the subject, but scholarly opinion favors the claims that the universe is fine-tuned for life. The phrase *fine-tuned* is a neutral description that does not prejudice the issue toward a theistic or nontheistic interpretation; it simply means that many aspects of the universe are closely calibrated and make human life possible. Stephen Barr, a physicist, lists eleven very prominent physicists who have written in defense of fine-tuning, including Stephen Hawking, Martin Rees and Steven Weinberg.[29] Nevertheless, some disagree.[30] The fact that the preferred nontheistic explanation for fine-tuning is the highly speculative multiverse theory (explained later) gives credence to the claim that

chapter; this is because the leading competitor to theism is naturalism, not pantheism.

[26]Jimmy H. Davis and Harry Lee Poe, "The Custom-Designed Home," in *Designer Universe* (Nashville: Broadman & Holman, 2002).

[27]Especially significant was Brendon Carter, "Large Number Coincidences and the Anthropic Principle in Cosmology," in *IAU Symposium 63: Confrontation of Cosmological Theories with Observational Data* (Dordrecht: Reidel, 1974), pp. 291-98.

[28]Bradley Monton, *Seeking God in Science* (Boulder, Colo.: Broadview, 2009), p. 81.

[29]Stephen Barr, *Modern Physics and Ancient Faith* (Notre Dame, Ind.: University of Notre Dame Press, 2004), p. 139.

[30]See Victor J. Stenger, *God: The Failed Hypothesis: How Science Shows That God Does Not Exist* (Amherst, N.Y.: Prometheus, 2007), pp. 147-57.

physicists are in general agreement that the universe is carefully fine-tuned. Otherwise, they would not need to have recourse to such grandiose theorizing in hopes of explaining the universe without a Designer.[31]

Before inspecting the evidence for design, an analogy will help. Consider a self-enclosed habitat for life (biosphere) found on Mars. In the control room we find a panel of dials, each set exquisitely precisely for a life-permitting environment. There needs to be just enough heat, oxygen, moisture, air pressure and so on for the inhabitants to survive, since the outside environment would not allow it. No one would infer that this biosphere arose without intelligent thought and agency, that it could be explained by natural laws and chance events alone. If so, then how much more would we infer design if we found that our entire cosmos were finely tuned across a broad and deep range of physical values to support life? The basic argument states that without a Designer, given the odds, a life-forbidding universe would be much more likely than a life-permitting and human-friendly universe. Our universe is much better explained according to a Mind that fine-tuned it for life.[32] A deft summary of the anthropic situation is given by Patrick Glynn.

> The fine-tuning of seemingly heterogeneous values and ratios necessary to get from the big bang to life as we know it involves intricate coordination over vast differences in scale—from the galactic level down to the sub-atomic one—and across multi-billion year tracks of time.[33]

The various anthropic factors are numerous, and their explanation can become quite technical. However, we can summarize them by considering initial conditions, constants and laws.

THE PHYSICS OF FINE-TUNING

Let us begin at the beginning, with the big bang. The initial conditions of the universe are crucial for a human-friendly cosmos. Although Stephen Hawking resists the theistic implications of the big bang, he states:

---

[31]See William Lane Craig in *God? A Debate Between a Christian and an Atheist* (New York: Oxford University Press, 2004), p. 62.

[32]This illustration is from Robin Collins in "The Evidence from Physics," in Lee Strobel's *The Case for a Creator* (Grand Rapids: Zondervan, 2004), pp. 130-31.

[33]Patrick Glynn, *God: The Evidence: The Reconciliation of Faith and Reason in a Postsecular World* (Rockland, Calif.: Prima, 1997), p. 31.

If the rate of expansion one second after the big bang had been smaller by even one part in a hundred thousand million, million, the universe would have recollapsed before it ever reached its present size. On the other hand, if the expansion rate at one second had been larger by the same amount, the universe would have expanded so much that it would be effectively empty now.[34]

Hawking also notes that

if the electric charge of the electron had been only slightly different, stars would have been unable to burn hydrogen and helium, or else they would not have exploded. . . . [It] seems clear that there are relatively few ranges of values for the numbers (for the constants) that would allow for development of any form of intelligent life. Most sets of values would give rise to universes that, although they might be very beautiful, would contain no one able to wonder at that beauty.[35]

Considering what was built into the big bang, physicist Roger Penrose discusses the implications.

How big was the original phase-volume . . . that the Creator had to aim for in order to provide a universe compatible with the second law of thermodynamics and with what we now observe? . . . The Creator's aim must have been [precise] to an accuracy of one part in $10^{10^{123}}$. This is an extraordinary figure. One could not possibly write the number down in full in the ordinary denary notation: it would be 1 followed by 10^{123} successive "0"s! Even if we were to write a "0" on each separate proton and on each separate neutron in the entire universe—and we could throw in all the other particles as well for good measure—we should fall far short of writing down the figure needed. [This is] the precision needed to set the universe on its course.[36]

Concerning this number, Penrose has also written that "I cannot even recall seeing anything else in physics whose accuracy is known to approach, even remotely, a figure like one part in $10^{10^{123}}$."[37]

---

[34]Stephen Hawking, *The Theory of Everything* (Beverly Hills, Calif.: New Millennium Press, 2002), p. 104.

[35]Stephen Hawking, *Brief History of Time* (New York: Bantam Books, 1988), p. 125.

[36]Roger Penrose, *The Emperor's New Mind* (New York: Oxford University Press, 1989), p. 344, quoted in William Dembski, *Intelligent Design* (Downers Grove, Ill.: InterVarsity Press, 1999), p. 266.

[37]Roger Penrose, "Time-Asymmetry and Quantum Gravity," in *Quantum Gravity 2*, ed. C. J. Isham, R. Penrose and D. W. Sciama (Oxford: Clarendon, 1981), p. 249, quoted in J. P.

Astronomer Sir Martin Rees is also impressed by the numbers and argues that the mathematics required for human life boil down to "just six numbers." These numbers were built into the big bang and must have the precise values they possess for our world to be hospitable to humans. Rees notes that if any one of the numbers were different, "even to the tiniest degree, there would be no stars, no complex elements, no life." The numbers control both the smallest and largest aspects of the universe. Lemley summarizes the features of these "six numbers":

1. The strength of the force that binds atomic nuclei together and determines how all atoms on earth are made.

2. The strength of the forces that hold atoms together divided by the force of gravity between them.

3. The density of material in the universe—including galaxies, diffuse gas and dark matter.

4. The strength of a previously unsuspected force, a kind of cosmic antigravity, that controls the expansion of the universe.

5. The amplitude of complex irregularities or ripples in the expanding universe that seed the growth of such structures as planets and galaxies.

6. The three spatial dimensions in our universe—"Life could not exist if it were two or four," contends Rees.[38]

If each of the six numbers Rees has identified were dependent on the others—in the same sense that, say, the number of arms and fingers in a family depends on the number of family members—the fact that they allow for the existence of life would seem less of a shock. "At the moment, however," says Rees, "we cannot predict any of them from the value of the others." So unless theoreticians discover some unifying theory, each number compounds the unlikeliness of each of the other numbers.[39]

Moreland and William Lane Craig, *Philosophical Foundations for a Christian Worldview* (Downers Grove, Ill.: InterVarsity Press, 2003), p. 483.

[38]Martin Rees, quoted in Brad Lemley, "Why Is There Life?" *Discover*, November 2000, <http://discovermagazine.com/2000/nov/cover>.

[39]Ibid. I have omitted the explanation of the mathematical function of the numbers and some references to the margin of error allowed. See also Martin Rees, *Just Six Numbers* (New York: Basic Books, 2001).

Moreover, the strength of the various forces of nature fit into the very narrow window necessary for human life. These are mathematical constants that do not vary, but neither do they possess their values by any kind of necessity; they could have been otherwise. Consider only two. "If the strength of the strong nuclear force were even slightly weaker or stronger than it is, it would have been disastrous for the possibility of life," claims physicist Stephen Barr.[40] This force—one of the four basic forces in nature, along with gravity, electromagnetism and the weak interactions—is required for the way atomic nuclei are conjoined and, therefore, what kinds of atoms are possible. Barr notes that if this force were only 10 percent weaker, it would not be strong enough to produce the elements we now have, spare hydrogen. If so, no life could exist. Had it been only 4 percent stronger, stars would last for a much shorter time, thus imperiling life.[41] The same goes for gravity, the weakest of the four forces. Robin Collins notes that if the strength of gravity were changed by one part in ten thousand billion, billion, billion—relative to the "total range of the strengths of the forces of nature (which span a range of 10 to the 40th)"—there would likely be no humanly populated world.[42]

Although more anthropic coincidences could be cited, I will give just one more.[43] Collins is particularly impressed with the value of "the cosmological constant." He believes that the inference to design from fine-tuning can rest on the value of this factor alone if it cannot be explained naturalistically.[44] The cosmological constant is the part of Einstein's equation of general relativity that deals with the expansion rate of the universe. Physicist Stephen Weinberg, an atheist, notes that the cosmological constant "does seem remarkably well adjusted in our favor." Although it could have been any value, "first principles" suggest it would have been very large, either positive or negative. In fact, had this been so,

---

[40]Barr, *Modern Physics and Ancient Faith*, p. 119.
[41]Ibid., p. 121.
[42]Robin Collins, "The Teleological Argument: Fine-Tuning," in *Blackwell Companion to Natural Theology*, ed. William Lane Craig and J. P. Moreland (Malden, Mass.: Wiley-Blackwell, 2009), p. 214; for a more popular but still thoughtful version, see Lee Strobel, *The Case for a Creator* (Grand Rapids: Zondervan, 2004), pp. 131-32.
[43]See Barr, *Modern Physics and Ancient Faith*, chap. 15, which presents a total of eleven anthropic coincidences: a list which is not exhaustive. I have mentioned only two of his examples: gravity and the cosmological constant.
[44]Collins, "Evidence from Physics," p. 134.

life would not have been possible.[45] Collins states that if the "cosmological constant were not fine-tuned to within an extremely narrow range—one part in 10 to the 53rd or even 10 to the 120th of its 'theoretically possible' range of values—the universe would expand so rapidly that all matter would quickly disperse, and thus galaxies, stars, and even small aggregates of matter could never form."[46] According to Collins, the likelihood of this constant occurring by chance is that of randomly hurling a dart from outer space and hitting a bull's-eye on earth that is less than the size of one atom.[47] As Barr says, "This is one of the most precise fine-tunings in all of physics."[48]

Esteemed mathematician and astronomer Fred Hoyle provides an able summary of this diverse and amazing fine-tuning data, "A common sense interpretation of the facts suggests that a super intellect has monkeyed with the physics, as well as the chemistry and biology, and that there are no blind forces worth speaking about in nature."[49]

In *The Privileged Planet* (2004) Gonzalez and Richards augment the fine-tuning argument by making the impressive case that the earth in particular was designed not only for life but for the scientific discovery of the universe.[50] These findings contravene the commonly heard observation that the earth is really nothing special in the universe, just "a pale blue dot" when observed from far away, as the popular astronomer Carl Sagan (1934-1996) put it. But there is more to be said:

> The fact that our atmosphere is clear; that our moon is just the right size and distance from Earth, and that its gravity stabilizes the Earth's rotation; that our position in our galaxy is just so; that our sun is its precise mass and composition: all of these factors (and many more), are not only necessary for

[45]Stephen Weinberg, "A Designer Universe?" *New York Review of Books*, October 21, 1999 <www.nybooks.com/articles/archives/1999/oct/21/a-designer-universe>.

[46]Robin Collins, "The Teleological Argument," in *The Routledge Companion to Philosophy of Religion*, ed. Chad Meister and Paul Copan (New York: Routledge, 2007), p. 352.

[47]Collins, "Evidence of Physics," p. 134.

[48]Barr, *Modern Physics and Ancient Faith*, p. 130.

[49]Fred Hoyle, "The Universe: Some Past and Present Reflections," *Engineering and Science* (1981): 12.

[50]See Gonzalez and Richards, *Privileged Planet*. The authors are interviewed and the ideas of the book summarized in Lee Strobel, "The Evidence of Astronomy: The Privileged Planet," in *The Case for a Creator* (Grand Rapids: Zondervan, 2004). *The Privileged Planet* DVD (Illustra Media, 2004) is a magnificent illustration of the basic arguments culled from the book and is, like all Illustra Media productions, a superb educational tool.

Earth's habitability; they also have been surprisingly crucial for scientists to measure and make discoveries about the universe. Mankind is unusually well positioned to decipher the cosmos.[51]

The book argues that there is a staggering number of contingencies that must come together to make earth habitable, as well as an ideal place to observe the rest of the universe. This deepens and expands the fine-tuning argument to account not only for human life but also our role as discoverers and stewards of scientific knowledge.[52]

The fine-tuning of the universe suggests this argument:

1. The fine-tuning data are the result of either (a) chance, (b) natural law, (c) the combination of chance and natural law, or (d) design.

2. They are not the result of chance or natural law, or the combination of both, since the data are contingent, complex and specified.

3. Therefore, (a) the data are the result of design.

4. Therefore, (b) there is a Designer.

This argument will be filled out as we answer objections to it.

OBJECTIONS TO THE FINE-TUNING ARGUMENT

The staggering contingencies required for human life to exist in the universe have not led all observers to revere the wondrous work of God. There are five main naturalistic explanations of this data: (1) the truism objection, (2) the inscrutable odds objection, (3) the chance, one universe hypothesis, (4) the multiverse theory and (5) the more fundamental law objection. We will also consider a pantheistic explanation for fine-tuning.

Truism objection. The truism objection is sometimes called the weak anthropic principle (WAP). There is a panoply of finely tuned factors in the universe, all of which are necessary for our existence. But so what? If they weren't there, we would not be here to notice. This fact is sometimes

---

[51]This is taken from Illustra Media's promotional webpage for the *Privileged Planet* book and film <www.theprivilegedplanet.com>.

[52]Michael Denton deepens even further the fine-tuned factors necessary for life on earth by considering a plethora of chemical and biological factors that must be "just so" for life to exist (Michael Denton, *Nature's Destiny: How the Laws of Biology Reveal Purpose in the Universe* [New York: Free Press, 1998]).

called a "selection effect" or "selection principle."[53] That is, evolution selects for conscious beings who can know and adapt to the world.[54] After citing several features of the universe that are remarkably fine-tuned for life, Martin Rees notes that "some would argue that this fine-tuning of the universe, which seems so providential, is nothing to be surprised about, since we could not exist otherwise."[55]

It is undoubtedly true that unless the necessary conditions for life appeared we could not chart the necessary conditions for human life, because we would not be here as observers.[56] That is a mere tautology. But this does not describe the fine-tuning argument for design. The case for design argues that "what is *antecedently unlikely* is necessary for the very possibility of conscious beings knowing it."[57] It is this vast and overwhelming improbability—the tremendous odds against human life given all the possible worlds that would prohibit human life—that generates *an argument to the best explanation.* That is not a tautology.

Those who invoke the truism objection in order to reject fine-tuning as evidence of a Fine Tuner confuse two distinct but related ideas:

1. For humans to observe human-life-permitting conditions, those necessary conditions must obtain, otherwise humans could not observe the human-life-permitting world. (This is a truism or tautology; as such, it explains nothing.)

2. The necessary conditions for this human-life-permitting world themselves need to be explained. This is a world that must exist in order for humans to observe their human-life-permitting world. (This claim is not a truism or tautology, and as such, it raises fundamental philosophical questions that demand answers.)[58]

---

[53]Hawking, *Theory of Everything*, p. 104.
[54]Why even this would occur is not explained by Darwinism. See the discussion of Darwinism in chap. 13.
[55]Martin Rees, "Exploring Our Universe and Others," *Scientific American Special Issue: The Once and Future Cosmos* (2002): 87.
[56]I don't think that the fine-tuning provides *sufficient* conditions for life, but it does provide *necessary* conditions, which themselves require a sufficient explanation. The case will be made in chap. 14 that in addition to all the fine-tuning, divine involvement was also required to explain the world of biology.
[57]Michael Peterson et al., *Reason and Religious Belief*, 3rd ed. (New York: Oxford University Press, 2003), p. 93, emphasis added.
[58]See William Lane Craig, *Reasonable Faith*, 3rd ed. (Wheaton, Ill.: Crossway, 2008), p. 165.

Those who say that observing human-permitting conditions is no big deal and should prompt no philosophical questions should consider this illustration: You stand quaking before a firing squad of ten carefully trained veteran marksmen who have been ordered by their country's dictator to execute you for crimes against their country. You hear "Ready . . . aim . . . fire!" followed by the explosions of ten guns. However, this is not the last thing you experience. You see the ten executioners staring at you. You feel no pain. There are no wounds. The squad's commander locks onto your questioning eyes and exclaims, "Why be so surprised? If they had all hit you, you wouldn't be here to wonder why!"[59] True enough, but this is trivial and irrelevant to the query. It is only logical to conclude that there is some *reason* or *explanation* why all ten members of the firing squad missed their target. That they all missed is required for you to wonder why they missed, but the mere fact that they all missed is not *sufficient to explain* the fact that they missed you. The theory that they all missed by chance is far less likely than that they all missed for some particular reason (maybe they were bribed, for example). To seek that reason—the explanation for this remarkable fact—only makes sense. Similarly, given the antecedently unlikely vast configuration of finely tuned variables required for human life, an explanation is definitely in order.

The fact that these anthropic features occur is not comparable to the fact that *someone* must win the lottery, however unlikely it is that any one person who enters will win it. Any possible universe—with or without life—would be improbable. But a human-life-permitting universe contains a feature that conforms to *an independently discoverable pattern* (*specification*): the multitudinous requirements for life itself. Any gibberish pounded out by a chimp at a typewriter (random action) will be improbable. But if we enter the room where the chimp was typing and we find a long and beautiful sonnet, we would not infer that the randomly typing chimp was its author. The words and arrangement of words in the sonnet conform to a pattern (information) independent of mere proba-

---

[59]The inspiration for this example comes from John Leslie; the literary details are my own (see John Leslie, "How to Draw Conclusions from a Fine-tuned Universe," in *Physics, Philosophy and Theology: A Common Quest for Understanding*, ed. R. J. Russell, W. R. Stoeger and G. V. Coyne [Vatican City: Vatican Observatory Press, 1988], p. 304). For another example in this vein, see Swinburne, *Is There a God?* pp. 66-67; and Gonzalez and Richards, *Privileged Planet*, p. 267.

bility—the semantics, grammar and syntax of the sonnet. We would thus infer an intelligent author. As Craig notes:

> In the same way, physics and biology tell us independently of any knowledge of the early conditions of the universe what the physical conditions requisite for life are. We then discover how incredibly improbable such conditions are. It is this combination of a specified pattern plus improbability that serves to render the chance hypothesis implausible.[60]

Inscrutable odds objection. Walter Sinnott-Armstrong and Keith Parsons protest that the odds of a universe that is life-permitting are simply inscrutable, not low or high.[61] They reason that one can calculate probabilities for things *within the space-time world*, but not for *the world as a whole*. We know the odds of being dealt a royal flush, for example, since we know the number of cards and type of cards involved. But the odds of the universe having the unique features it possesses is something entirely different. This is inscrutable given the stark uniqueness of the situation. Therefore, no Designer can be inferred from the apparent fine-tuning, since the odds of the universe occurring by chance or by design are indiscernible.

Yet it seems that there are far more possible human-life-prohibiting universes than possible human-life-friendly universes. Consider this ratio:

A. The actual human-life-friendly universe (fine tuned) or possible other life-friendly universes (if other universe arrangements could permit human life)

B. Possible human-life-prohibiting universes (that is, not-A)

The ratio of A/B is extremely small. We obviously don't have various cases of universe-generation situations to compare, since our universe is one of a kind. But the uniqueness of our universe does not rule out the consideration of probabilities, since other universes are logically conceivable. Moreover, we rationally consider probabilities for singular events in other situations.[62]

---

[60]William Lane Craig, "Five Reasons God Exists," in William Lane Craig and Walter Sinnott-Armstrong, *God? A Debate Between a Christian and an Atheist* (Oxford: Oxford University Press, 2003), p. 11.

[61]Walter Sinnott-Armstrong, "There Is No Reason to Believe in God," in William Lane Craig and Walter Sinnott-Armstrong, *God? A Debate Between a Christian and an Atheist* (Oxford: Oxford University Press, 2003), p. 47. Keith Parsons, "Naturalistic Rejoinders to Theistic Arguments," in *The Routledge Companion to Philosophy of Religion*, ed. Chad Meister and Paul Copan (New York: Routledge, 2007), p. 437.

[62]See Moreland, *Scaling the Secular City*, p. 63.

An illustration from John Barrow is helpful. Put a red dot on a piece of paper, representing our (human-friendly) universe. Now vary the fine-tuning data slightly a very large number of times. When you get a human-friendly universe, assign another red dot; when you get a human-prohibiting universe, assign a blue dot. You will end up with a sea of blue dots and only a few pin points of red. Craig summarizes Barrow, "There are simply a vastly greater proportion of more life-prohibiting universes in our local area of possible universes than there are life-permitting universes."[63]

Chance, one universe objection. One might argue that this fine-tuning for life is simply the result of chance: an undirected random effect of the big bang. While this is mathematically possible, it is exceedingly unlikely, given the vast odds against it, as previously noted. For these reasons, naturalistic explanations seldom invoke chance as the explanation for fine-tuning. If there is only one universe, the chances of it containing the vast panoply of life-permitting features are amazingly infinitesimal. This has caused some thinkers to posit some version of the multiverse theory (sometimes called the many universe, multiple universe or world ensemble theory).

The multiverse theory. Faced with the evidence that the fine-tuning of the universe is best explained by a Mind, naturalists such as Steven Weinberg and Martin Rees have posited that our human-permitting universe is simply one of a vast (perhaps infinite) array of universes. While the odds of only one universe being life-permitting apart from design are extremely remote, the odds get better if we multiply actual universes mightily.[64] If you throw the cosmic dice enough times, an extremely improbable universe will eventually come up. As Moreland and Craig write, "The many worlds hypothesis is essentially an effort on the part of partisans of the chance hypothesis to multiply their probabilistic resources in order to reduce the improbability of the occurrence of fine-tuning."[65]

Davies claims that a growing minority of scientists support some version

[63]Craig, *Reasonable Faith*, p. 164. I take it that Craig means "human life-permitting." But if not, the basic point still stands, although there are more life-permitting possible worlds than *human* life-permitting possible worlds, since more fine-tuning is required for human life than just any life.

[64]The multiple universe theory should not be confused with possible worlds in metaphysics. The former posits actually existing worlds side by side, so to speak. Possible-worlds theory, generally speaking, concerns possible states of affairs that might have been. I also discuss possible worlds in chap. 10.

[65]Moreland and Craig, *Philosophical Foundations*, p. 487.

of the multiverse theory.[66] It comes in several subtheories, which can be put into two broad categories. First, the *many universes multiverse theory* claims that universes are completely isolated from each other, with no common ground in terms of physics. The number of universes is actually infinite, so everything logically possible happens in one universe or another. The second claim is that our universe is part of a *multidomain universe*, which is causally connected at a deep (and as yet unknown) level but in which each domain is isolated from the rest. The most popular of these theories recently is the inflationary theory, which claims that the big bang triggered an endless progression of universes, with one succeeding another.

The multiverse theory should not be confused with Hugh Everett's "many worlds interpretation" in quantum mechanics, "according to which, in addition to the world we are aware of directly, there are many other similar worlds which exist in parallel at the same space and time. The existence of the other worlds makes it possible to remove randomness and action at a distance from quantum theory and thus from all physics."[67] This is a controversial interpretation of the strange world of quantum events, but it was not formulated as an attempt to explain fine-tuning; rather, it was devised to solve the collapse of the wave-function problem. While it does seem to solve some problems in quantum theory, it generates significant others and is massively counterintuitive.[68] Even as such, it is not the favored theory in the difficult field of interpreting quantum mechanics. Moreover, as Barr notes, "even if the many worlds interpretation is correct it does not mean that different parts of the universe will have different effective laws; that is an added assumption."[69] But it is precisely these different laws that are needed to increase the probabilistic resources sufficiently to designate our universe a random "freak of the multiverse" fit for life. Thus, Everett's interpretation seems to provide little if any support to the multiverse theory.

The many universes multiverse theory is nothing more than metaphysical speculation, and very poor speculation at that. To posit that everything that could happen does happen (in some universe ontologically separated from all the rest) is bizarre and gratuitous. It is invoked without

---

[66]Paul Davies, *Cosmic Jackpot* (Boston: Houghton Mifflin, 2007), p. 263.
[67]Lev Vaidman, "Many-Worlds Interpretation of Quantum Mechanics," *Stanford Encyclopedia of Philosophy* <http://plato.stanford.edu/entries/qm-manyworlds>.
[68]See Barr, *Modern Physics and Ancient Faith*, pp. 248-52.
[69]Ibid., p. 152; see also pp. 154-57.

logical basis simply to avoid a Designer. There is no reason to conflate the actual and the possible in metaphysics. Moreover, "we could never know by any observation or inferences drawn from observations that the other universes existed." Therefore, as Barr notes, few physicists adopt it.[70]

The multidomain version of the multiverse theory is less extravagant than the many universes multiverse theory and commands its share of adherents. This is because, if true, it would help explain some unresolved problems in physics. Moreover, it is theoretically possible to confirm the existence of other domains indirectly if "the fundamental laws of nature are discovered, and experimentally proven to be correct, and it is found that they mathematically imply the existence of other domains."[71] The hottest domain theory recently is the inflationary model of Andre Linde. While this theory still lacks independent evidence, it would unite Einstein's theory of relativity with quantum mechanics, which is no mean feat. However, its success requires the truth of string theory, which itself is highly questionable.[72] At best, this theory is a popular postdated check. As such, unless one is a priori committed to naturalism, it does not give a better explanation than design. But there are other severe problems with the multiverse theory.

If a multiverse theory posits an *actual infinity* of existent universes, then it must face the objections to the existence of an actual infinite, which were given in chapter eleven, on the kalam cosmological argument. Let us label one-half of the universes A and the other half B. If we subtract A from the total number of universes, the result is still an infinite number of universes. But since a total cannot be both itself and half of itself, this is impossible. Therefore, there cannot be an actually infinite number of universes, either simultaneously or stretching forever into the past.

But even if an actual infinity of universes were not impossible, the existence of such an assembly is colossally improbable. There is as yet no independent evidence for multiple universes (although the multidomain version postulates *possible* evidence). These supposedly many universes are unobservable in principle; their existence must be inferred. But

---

[70]Ibid., pp. 153; see also Davies, *Cosmic Jackpot*, pp. 264-65.
[71]Barr, *Modern Physics and Ancient Faith*, p. 153.
[72]See Craig, *Reasonable Faith*, p. 163; David Berlinski, *The Devil's Delusion: Atheism and Its Scientific Pretensions* (New York: Crown Forum, 2008), pp. 116-23, 128, 131.

the overarching reason to infer their existence is the desire to deny a Designer and still explain the fine-tuning of physics. But by arguing from *what we know*, we observe that specified and improbable patterns evince a Designer. This inference to design is a "can do" principle used throughout life and in various scientific fields such as archaeology, cryptography, forensics and so on.[73]

As Collins points out, it is more rational to frame an explanation in terms of what we know, given independent evidence, than to appeal to unsubstantiated theories that, if true, would explain the data. Consider dinosaur bones. The best explanation for their existence in the fossil record is that dinosaurs died and left parts of their skeletons as fossils. We infer this because we know that other similar animals (which we have observed) have skeletons, die and leave fossils. However, if we appeal to a "dinosaur-bone-making field" to explain the strange remains, we invoke something utterly unknown as an explanation. There is no reason to do so, especially since a better explanation is close at hand. Similarly, there is no warrant to invoke esoteric theories of multiverses (all lacking a Designer) when (1) we know how to spot design and (2) the fine-tuning of the universe is most readily explained in terms of a Designer outside of the universe.[74] Barr notes that in order to "abolish one unobservable God," various multiverse theories require "an infinite number of unobservable substitutes."[75] A far simpler and more commonsensical explanation is that fine-tuning is due to the work of one Designer.[76]

In short, the multiverse theory appears to be flagrantly ad hoc, lacks experimental evidence and is exceedingly complex. All things being equal, a theory (scientific or otherwise) should be as simple as possible, so long as it explains the data in question adequately.[77] The multiverse theory seems more like an extravagant theory of metaphysics than anything dependent

---

[73]See Dembski's introduction to *Design Inference*.

[74]Collins, "Evidence from Physics," p. 148.

[75]Barr, *Modern Physics and Ancient Faith*, p. 157. Barr applies this principle not only to multiverse theory but also to other aspects of materialist explanations with respect to physics.

[76]This appeal to simplicity also rules out several finite designers. Moreover, each finite designer would require an explanation, since it would not be self-existent.

[77]Some have argued that materialism is simpler than theism, so it should be preferred in all explanations. But simplicity is only one virtue of a good theory. This book argues that materialism fails to explain adequately the origin and nature of the universe—no small defects. Therefore, a richer, more explanatorily robust theory is required: Christian theism.

on empirical science or responsible theorizing.

Undaunted by the evidence, Richard Dawkins claims that the multiverse theory trumps theism for two reasons. First, a designing God would be just as complex as the universe and would thus fail as an explanation for the universe, because the Designer itself would have to be explained. Second, the multiverse theory is simple, since each universe has a simple set of natural laws.[78]

In response, first, even if God were as complex as the one universe, this would not disqualify God as the explanation for fine-tuning. If we discover artifacts on Mars that evidence life (complicated telescopes or intricate statues, for example), we would rationally infer that these artifacts were designed by rational agents and are not the result of merely natural and unguided causes. The fact that these agents (Martian or otherwise) would themselves be complex does not foreclose their existence as the proper explanation for the advanced artifacts. Second, God, as classically conceived by monotheism, is not a collection of contingent physical states, unlike the Mars artifacts and their designers. God is, rather, an immaterial and self-existent being. Therefore, God is not subject to further explanation.[79]

Dawkins's claim that the multiverse is a simple explanation is absurd. The fact that each universe has natural laws does not make the overall—perhaps infinite—ensemble of universes (the multiverse) simple, since each universe could vary from all others in the nature of its laws, entities and processes.

More-fundamental-law objection. Another theory that accounts for fine-tuning without a Designer is the appeal to an as yet unknown and impersonal natural law that is more fundamental than any of the laws we now know. If *chance* cannot explain the fine-tuning of the one existing universe, and if multiple universes are impossible, unlikely or incompatible with design (as Collins argues), then an appeal can be made to the physical *necessity* of natural law. This explanation would eliminate the need to account for the contingencies of fine-tuning by invoking the necessity of

---

[78]Richard Dawkins, *The God Delusion* (New York: Houghton Mifflin Harcourt, 2006), pp. 146-47.

[79]This was also taken up in chap. 11 under "the principle of sufficient reason," which states that everything that exists needs to be explained or is the explanation for itself.

lawful behavior. If some superlaw is found, the universe had to be the way it is. However, no such grand natural law has been found, and any hope of finding it is only speculative—a cosmic postdated check. While physicists hope for "a theory of everything," it has not been found; thus, it cannot count against the design hypothesis.

But suppose a theory of everything were discovered that revealed one superduper natural law demonstrating that all that seems contingent is really physically necessary. Would this eliminate design as the best hypothesis for the resultant universe? No. The postulated natural law itself would be improbable and specified for life to exist. That is, it might have been otherwise. As Bernard Carr and Martin Rees have written, "even if all apparently anthropic coincidences could be explained [in terms of some grand unified theory], it would still be remarkable that the relationships dictated by physical theory happened also to be those propitious for CEL [conscious embodied life]."[80] The relationship between the purported law and the life-permitting features would still be remarkable because the concept of necessity that applies to a natural or scientific law is not that of *logical* necessity but of *physical* necessity. That is, if the law obtains, all the supposed contingencies of the universe are explained in terms of this law. But the law itself is not a necessary truth, as is the law of noncontradiction or the law of identity. The proposed physical law might not have existed at all (had there been no universe), or some other meta-law might have obtained (if there had been another universe instead of this one). That is, there are many logically possible worlds in which this law does not obtain.[81] Moreover, this supposed law is highly improbable in that it unites a plethora of seemingly disparate elements in a remarkable fashion. As Gonzalez and Richards note, it would be like making the opening shot in a game of pool and having all the balls directed into every available hole—except in this game, you would have far more balls than in a game of common pool.[82]

Pantheism and design. At the end of the day the case for theistic fine-tuning is more plausible than any appeal to chance (single universe or multiverse) or to a unified impersonal natural law without a Designer.

---

[80]Bernard Carr and Martin Rees, quoted in Collins, "The Teleological Argument," p. 356.
[81]For more on this idea, see Barr, *Modern Physics and Ancient Faith*, pp. 146-48.
[82]Richards and Gonzales, *Privileged Planet*, pp. 261-65.

The theistic interpretation also trumps a pantheistic one. The god of pantheism is not a personal creator, but an all-pervasive and impersonal substance, usually taken to be ineffable. The design evidence rules out this kind of deity for three main reasons.

First, the argument for fine-tuning by a Designer trades on the commonsense notion of the subject-object relationship; that is, we are subjects who evaluate the cosmos's nature. There is a distinction between the knowers and the known. By contrast, pantheism is typically nondualistic, which eliminates any distinction between God, the universe and the self; thus, it supposedly transcends the contingencies that the fine-tuning argument trades on and makes God/cosmos/self into a necessary being. However, the world is a very poor candidate for a necessary being, since (1) it came into existence a finite time ago (given the big bang and kalam cosmological argument) and (2) its contingent features take values that are not logically necessary.[83]

Second, the inference to a Designer contradicts the idea of an impersonal being, since design requires intelligence. A being who designed the universe for human life must be immensely intelligent (a mind) and have the power to bring about what this being intends (an agent).[84] In other words, this is a Person and is not impersonal. The god of pantheism cannot fit this theological profile.

Third, if pantheists claim that God is ineffable, and "known" only through nonrational mystical experiences, then no *rational argument* (fine-tuning or otherwise) can support this god's existence. A question mark explains nothing.

TUNED IN TO THE DESIGNER

We conclude that we live in a designer universe; it is not explicable by chance, by law, by a combination of chance and law, or by an impersonal God.[85] This Designer is thus singular, outside the universe (transcen-

---

[83]Davies explores the idea of the universe as a necessary being instead of God and doesn't seem to think that God is a better candidate (*Cosmic Jackpot*, p. 265)! See my discussion of God as a necessary being in chaps. 10-11.

[84]For example, nondualist theorist Ken Wilber disavows that the ultimate reality is a designer (see Ken Wilber, *The Integral Vision* [Boston: Shambhala, 2007], p. 153).

[85]I have not addressed every objection to the fine-tuning design argument, but I believe I have canvassed the most pertinent and significant ones for the thoughtful inquirer. The most exhaustive treatment of the argument and objections to it are given by Collins, "The Teleological

dent), a personal agent (having a mind to conceive the fine-tuning and the will to bring it about) and immensely powerful (given the complexity and scope of the universe). I argued that the seeming flaws in design (more evident in biology than cosmology) are due to the Fall, not to God's nature.[86] Moreover, the ontological argument rules out the idea that God is less than completely good (a maximal being must be perfectly good) or less than completely powerful (a maximal being must be perfectly powerful). The ex nihilo cosmological argument also allows for a being who is omnipotent, since creating everything out of nothing indicates limitless power.

If these arguments stand, we should fall in humility before this being, seeking further knowledge of who this God is, what God might give and what God wants.[87] But there is more evidence yet at hand, this time coming from a realm that naturalists tell us has been utterly fumigated of any design or objective meaning—the world of biology.

Argument." See especially his response on pp. 247, 249-52, to objections made by Timothy McGrew, Lydia McGrew and Eric Vestrup, "Probabilities and Fine-Tuning: A Skeptical View," in *God and Design: Theological Argument and Modern Science*, ed. Neil Manson (New York: Routledge, 2003), pp. 200-208. Elliott Sober has raised objections as well (see "Absence of Evidence and Evidence of Absence: Evidential Transitivity in Connection with Fossils, Fishing, Fine-tuning, and Firing Squads," *Philosophical Studies* 143 [2009]: 63-90). Sober's attempt to defeat the fine-tuning argument is critiqued in Troy Nunley, "Fish Nets, Firing Squads and Fine-Tuning (Again): How Likelihood Arguments Undermine Elliot Sober's Weak Anthropic Principles," *Philosophia Christi* 11, no. 2 (2010): 33-51; and Troy Nunley, "On Elliott Sober's Challenge for Biological Design Arguments," *Philosophia Christi* 9, no. 2 (2007): 443-58.

[86]More on the Fall can be found in chaps. 18, 25.

[87]I argue in more detail that cogent natural theology should have this existential effect in "Proofs, Pride, and Incarnation: Is Natural Theology Theologically Taboo?" *Journal of the Evangelical Theological Society* 38, no. 1 (1995): 67-76.

13

Origins, Design and Darwinism

THE MAJORITY OF AMERICANS BELIEVE in God or some higher power, while a smaller percentage holds to a fully naturalistic, Darwinian account of life.[1] Those in the media and the hard sciences, especially in biology, tend to be more secular than the general population. Consequently, certain cultural clashes are inevitable and predictable. Whenever Darwinism is challenged in a public setting—especially in a public school science curriculum—the scientific and media establishments join forces to lay out a prefabricated template:

> Fundamentalists are attempting to inject religion into the science curriculum again by censoring Darwinism in the public schools. This denial of church-state separation is being challenged by the ACLU. Parents and children have the right to believe whatever they want religiously, but the teaching of science leaves no room for personal and religious beliefs to be taught in the public classroom.

A second-level template argues that critics of Darwinism could make their case if they had the wherewithal to do so, but they have failed:

> If the creationists had scientific evidence for their position, they could have made their case in the professional peer-reviewed journals, which are the

---

[1]A 2009 Zogby poll showed that 52 percent believed that life was guided by an intelligence, 33 percent thought it was a purely naturalistic process, 7 percent said neither and 8 percent said other or not sure. The full report is available at the Discovery Institute website *Evolution: News & Views* <www.evolutionnews.org/zogby09poll063009%20 (2).pdf>. This data should be considered along with the fact that the majority of Americans are theists, however they relate God to the creation and the development of life. See Rodney Stark, *What Americans Really Believe*, (Waco, Tex.: Baylor University Press, 2009), pp. 75-78.

testing ground of theories. But they have not done so. Therefore, they have no claim on being scientific.[2]

The Darwinian templates do all the answering ahead of time by assuming that (1) Darwinism is scientifically established beyond a reasonable doubt; (2) any challenges to Darwinism are religiously based and are, therefore, unscientific and irrational; (3) any challenge to Darwinism in the public square violates the constitutional separation of church and state and must be legally opposed lest we turn into a theocracy; and (4) the scientific establishment is an open marketplace of ideas with little or no biases.

I take these four statements to be false, although space does not permit full discussion of points 3 and 4.[3] It should be noted, however, that historically some very significant scientific papers have been published in journals that were not peer-reviewed,[4] and a number of papers and books supporting intelligent design (ID) have also been published in peer-review journals, although the prejudice against them is strong.[5]

This chapter will argue two main theses: (1) Belief in Darwinism as a comprehensive explanation for the biosphere has become a deterrent to Christian faith; thus a cogent refutation is in order. (2) Darwinism suffers from fatal flaws both logically and evidentially. It is far less well-supported than commonly thought. Chapter fourteen will present positive arguments

---

[2]This was stated nearly word for word on a National Public Radio broadcast in 2004. Public pronouncements such as this seldom use the proper term *intelligent design* and instead use *creationism* for rhetorical purposes.

[3]On the constitutionality of teaching intelligent design, see Francis Beckwith, *Law, Darwinism, and Public Education* (Boston: Rowman & Littlefield, 2003); and Thomas Nagel, "Public Education and Intelligent Design," *Philosophy & Public Affairs* 36, no. 2 (2008). Thomas Kuhn's important work *The Structure of Scientific Revolutions*, 3rd ed. (Chicago: University of Chicago Press, 1996) challenges the pure objectivity of science, although he does not address intelligent design. For a sociological analysis of how the scientific establishment treats intelligent design, see Steve Fuller, *Science vs. Religion? Intelligent Design and the Problem of Evolution* (Malden, Mass.: Polity Press, 2007). For a detailed critique of how the scientific establishment persecutes those who challenge Darwinism, see Jerry Bergman, *Slaughter of the Dissidents: The Shocking Truth About Killing the Careers of Darwin Doubters* (Southworth, Wash.: Leafcutter Press, 2008). See also the 2008 film *Expelled*, starring Ben Stein.

[4]See Frank Tipler, "Refereed Journals: Do They Insure Quality or Enforce Orthodoxy?" in *Uncommon Dissent: Intellectuals Who Find Darwinism Unconvincing*, ed. William Dembski (Wilmington, Del.: ISI Books, 2004).

[5]For an updated list of these publications see "Peer-reviewed & Peer-edited Scientific Publications Supporting the Theory of Intelligent Design (Annotated)," Discovery Institute, August 26, 2010 <www.discovery.org/a/2640>.

for design as the best explanation for molecular machines and for the information content in DNA.

The entrenched Darwinian ideology is a formidable obstacle to the discussion and teaching of God's intervention in creating life and setting humans apart in nature. The de facto establishment of naturalism in science (and culture at large) has a vise-grip on most of the public discourse on science. Nevertheless, the ID movement, which challenges Darwinism scientifically, is calling the Darwinian establishment to account in constructive and creative ways. This movement consists of a variety of thinkers, of various religions or of none, who claim that nonhuman intelligent causes better explain certain aspects of nature than undirected, merely natural causes.[6] It thus opens a door for Christian apologetics that would otherwise be closed.

Many Darwinists reject all criticisms of Darwinism as religiously based and therefore unscientific and unworthy of serious attention. But this assumes that the deliverances of contemporary science always trump religiously based views. This is a questionable axiom, especially considering that scientific opinion in the past has favored eugenics.[7] It is false that all significant critiques of Darwinism come from religious sources.[8] Scientific criticisms of Darwinism were plentiful in the years following the publication of his theories.[9] In recent years a variety of thinkers have argued against Darwinism, yet without appealing to any religious sources. These include prolific philosopher Mortimer Adler (1902-2001), Harvard-trained lawyer Norman MacBeth, British novelist and science writer Arthur Koestler (1905-1983), social critic and science writer Jeremy Rifkin, British science writers Francis Hitching, Gordon Rattray Taylor (1911-

---

[6]For an excellent history and explanation of this movement, see Thomas Woodward, *Doubts About Darwin: A History of Intelligent Design* (Grand Rapids: Baker, 2003).
[7]The modern eugenics movement and social Darwinism in general was firmly rooted in Darwinian thinking. See John G. West, *Darwin Day in America* (Wilmington, Del.: ISI Books, 2008); and Benjamin Wiker, "What to Make of It All?" in *The Darwin Myth* (New York: Regnery, 2009).
[8]But, as atheist philosopher of science Bradley Monton points out, it is the arguments that count, not the religious viewpoints of those who make the arguments. To think otherwise is to commit the fallacy of "poisoning the well" (see Bradley Monton, *Seeking God in Science* [Boulder, Colo.: Broadview Press, 2009], pp. 12-14; and William Dembski, *The Design Revolution* [Downers Grove, Ill.: InterVarsity Press, 2004], pp. 45-49).
[9]See Benjamin Wiker, "One Long Argument, Two Long Books," in *The Darwin Myth.*

1981), and Richard Milton.[10] Very significantly because of his scientific
standing, Australian geneticist Michael Denton systematically critiques
the scientific inadequacy of Darwinism in *Evolution: A Theory in Crisis*
(1985).[11] Since 2001, over nine hundred scientists[12] of various worldviews
have signed a published statement questioning the legitimacy of Darwinism, which reads:

> We are skeptical of claims for the ability of random mutation and natural
> selection to account for the complexity of life. Careful examination of the
> evidence for Darwinian theory should be encouraged.[13]

But before wading into the turbulent waters concerning the origins and
development of life, we need to trace out what the Christian worldview
teaches concerning the origins of life, species and humanity, according to
the best understanding of the Bible.

ORIGINS AND THE BIBLE

Theological liberals take much of the Bible to be mythical, scientifically
ignorant (prescientific) and thus irrelevant.[14] They hold that the first
eleven chapters of Genesis should not be consulted for space-time history.

---

[10]Mortimer Adler, *The Difference of Man and the Difference it Makes* (New York: Holt, Rinehart
& Winston, 1967), esp. chap. 5. Norman Macbeth, *Darwin Retried* (New York, Dell, 1971).
This book was hailed by noteworthy philosopher of science Karl Popper, who said about it on
the back cover, "An excellent and fair, though unsympathetic retrial of Darwin. I regard the
book as most meritorious and as a really important contribution to the debate, . . . a truly valu-
able book." See also Norman Macbeth, *Darwinism: A Time for Funerals: An Interview with
Norman MacBeth* (San Francisco: Robert Briggs, 1985); Arthur Koestler, *Janus: A Summing Up*
(New York: Vintage Books, 1978), chaps. 9-11; Jeremy Rifkin and Ted Howard, *Entropy: A
New World View* (New York: Viking Press, 1980); Rifkin, the principal author, is a pantheist;
Francis Hitching, *The Neck of the Giraffe: Why Scientists Now Are Attacking Darwin's Theory of
Evolution* (New York: New American Library, 1982); Gordon Ratray Taylor, *The Great Evolution Mystery* (New York: Harper & Row, 1983); Richard Milton, *Scattering the Myths of Darwinism* (Rochester, Vt.: Park Street Press, 1997).
[11]Michael Denton, *Evolution: A Theory in Crisis* (Bethesda, Md.: Alder & Ader, 1985).
[12]The requirements to sign the list: "Signers of the Scientific Dissent From Darwinism must
either hold a Ph.D. in a scientific field such as biology, chemistry, mathematics, engineering,
computer science, or one of the other natural sciences; or they must hold an M.D. and serve
as a professor of medicine" (FAQ, *Scientific Dissent from Darwinism* <www.dissentfromdar
win.org/faq.php>).
[13]For a full list of signatories and other information, see *Scientific Dissent from Darwinism*
<www.dissentfromdarwin.org/index.php>.
[14]For an exposition of theological liberalism, see Donald E. Miller, *The Case for Liberal Christianity* (New York: Harper & Row, 1981). The classic older critique of liberalism is J. Gresham
Machen, *Christianity and Liberalism* (1923; reprint, Grand Rapids: Eerdmans, 2009).

Rather, these texts serve only as inspiring (fictional) narratives. The evangelical Christian cannot take this route, since evangelicalism holds to a high view of biblical inspiration and authority. This means, roughly, that the Bible, properly interpreted, is true in all that it affirms, whether statements about the nature of God, the way of salvation, morality, history or the cosmos.[15] Therefore, the evangelical should be loath to reject as mythological any biblical statement about the origin of life on earth. However, within the broad evangelical camp, three basic views on the relationship of the Bible and science have emerged. In order to proceed, we need to survey briefly the lay of the land and select an option.

First, some Christians claim that while the Genesis account is true, it was not meant to speak of science but only to the "who" and the "why" of creation. Science, on the other hand, speaks to the "how" and the "when" of creation. Therefore, Christians should embrace Darwinism, since Scripture is silent on scientific particulars. God could have used the Darwinian mechanism to bring about the various species and the eventual evolution of human beings. Accounts of the Garden and a literal first couple must be taken as metaphorical or poetic. The Fall is not a literal event but a failure of the first evolved humans to meet God's conditions for flourishing.[16] Theistic evolution teaches that God created the universe and let the inherent properties of the universe produce the first life and subsequent species naturally, without any direct evidence of a designing intelligence. As such, theistic evolutionists accept abiogenesis (the evolution of life from nonlife) and Darwinism as an adequate account of the development of species.[17] Broadly speaking, this is how theistic evolutionists approach science in relationship to the Bible.[18]

---

[15]For a carefully worded statement of biblical inerrancy, see *The Chicago Statement on Biblical Inerrancy* (Sunnyvale, Calif.: Coalition on Revival, 1978). The PDF of this booklet is online at the Coalition on Revival's website <http://65.175.91.69/Reformation_net/COR_Docs/01_Inerrancy_Christian_Worldview.pdf>. See also Carl F. H. Henry, *God, Revelation, and Authority* (Waco, Tex.: Word, 1976), vols. 1-4, esp. vol. 4, thesis 15: "The Bible as the Authoritative Norm," pp. 7-592.

[16]C. S. Lewis, who was so often a brilliant Christian apologist, took pains to explain a nonliteral Fall in evolutionary terms (see his "The Fall of Man," in *The Problem of Pain* [1962; reprint, New York: Touchstone, 1996]).

[17]Darwinism does not address abiogenesis, since Darwin's theory was concerned with the evolution of species, not the origination of life. If natural selection is to explain anything, it must begin with a replicating (living) organism. Thus, it cannot address how life developed from nonlife.

[18]See, for example, Bernard Ramm, *The Christian Approach to Science and Scripture* (Grand Rapids: Eerdmans, 1954), chap. 7; Francis Collins, *The Language of God* (New York: Free Press,

I deny this. First, the scientific evidence does not support Darwinian macroevolution or abiogenesis (addressed in chap. 14). Small changes within species (microevolution) can be explained by Darwinian mechanisms, but not the origin of all species (macroevolution or speciation). Second, theistic evolutionists' interpretations of the Bible seem strained. Although a creation week of six literal twenty-four-hour days is unwarranted, as argued in chapter eleven, Genesis 1–2 presents God *investing in* and *directing* the natural order, not merely letting it evolve on its own according to principles that can be explained without appeal to a designing intelligence.[19] God creates according to each animal's "kind," indicating a God-generated difference in nature or essence between discrete forms of life with determinate natures or essences, as opposed to a fluid development where one kind evolves into another.[20] (We do not know enough about the Genesis account's relation to the current categories of biology to say that *kind* is identical to *species*, but *kind* indicates a more general, but distinct, created ontological category that does not fit neatly into the total plasticity of living things required by macroevolution.)[21] More importantly, God's creation of human beings stands out from the rest of the living world because they are directly fashioned in the image of God. There are many theologically crucial passages of Scripture besides Genesis that refer to the first couple as a literal reality, and these have tremendous theological significance (such as Matthew 19:4-6; Romans 5:12-21; 2 Corinthians 11:3).[22]

2006); Alister McGrath, *A Fine-Tuned Universe* (Louisville: Westminster John Knox, 2009).

[19]Exactly how God invests in the creation through his creative design is a matter of some discussion. I will argue later that God's design is evident and does not hinder the progress of science, as critics claim. It may be best to understand God's intelligent investment in creation in terms other than that of a historical miracle. William Dembski thoughtfully addresses this in *The Design Revolution* (Downers Grove, Ill.: InterVarsity Press, 2004), chaps. 23-25; and William Dembski, "Moving the Particles," in *The End of Christianity* (Nashville: Broadman & Holman, 2009).

[20]See J. P. Moreland, *Love Your God with All Your Mind* (Colorado Springs: NavPress, 1997), pp. 35-36; Mortimer Adler, "The Possible Answers," in *The Difference of Man and the Difference It Makes*.

[21]On *kind* as a descriptive term useful in science, see J. P. Moreland, *Christianity and the Nature of Science* (Grand Rapids: Baker, 1989), p. 222.

[22]For a defense of this basic view see Francis Schaeffer, *Genesis in Space and Time* (Downers Grove, Ill.: InterVarsity Press, 1972); for a more rigorous exegetical and theological treatment see C. John Collins, *Genesis 1–4: A Linguistic, Literary, and Theological Commentary* (Phillipsburg: P & R, 2006), esp. pp. 166-67; 251-55; 257-60.

It also seems inconsistent for evangelicals to believe that God supernaturally intervenes in history after evolution has done its role but that
God fails to leave evidence of his design in life itself. In this, theistic evolution seems closer to deism than Christian theism.[23] Moreover, it is odd for
a theist to adopt a view of life that Darwin formulated specifically to *eliminate the need for a Designer*.[24] Darwin himself said, "There seems to be no
more design in the variability of organic beings, and in the action of natural selection, than in the course which the wind blows."[25] Darwin deemed
the natural world to be so cruel and wasteful that he wanted to get the
Creator out of the picture by accounting for the development of life according to natural law and chance.[26]

If God deigned to "use" Darwinian evolution to bring about the various
forms of life, including humans, then God strangely decided to employ a
system in which he would remain invisible.[27] Atheist and Darwinist William Provine rightly deems this kind of thinking to be deeply faulty.[28]
Michael Denton's assessment is on target:

> As far as Christianity was concerned, the advent of the theory of evolution
> and the elimination of traditional teleological thinking was catastrophic.

---

[23]See Phillip Johnson, *Defeating Darwinism* (Downers Grove, Ill.: InterVarsity Press, 1997), pp.
16-17; Michael A. Harbin, "Theistic Evolution: Deism Revisited?" *Journal of the Evangelical
Theological Society* 40, no. 4 (1997): 639-52.

[24]This is made clear in Benjamin Wiker's excellent biography of Darwin, *The Darwin Myth*
(Washington, D.C.: Regnery, 2009).

[25]Charles Darwin, *Life and Letters of Charles Darwin, Including an Autobiographical Chapter*, ed.
Francis Darwin (New York: Appleton, 1898), 1:278-79, quoted in Stephen Meyer, *Signature in
the Cell* (San Francisco: HarperOne, 2009), p. 19. Some are thrown off by Darwin's reference
at the end of the second and all following editions (there were six) of *The Origin of Species*, that
God breathed life into the first living form or forms. Darwin himself later wrote to his friend
Hooker, "I have long regretted that I truckled to public opinion & used [a] Pentateuchal term
of creation, by which I really meant 'appeared' by some whole unknown process" (Frederick
Buckhardt et al., *The Correspondence of Charles Darwin*, 11.278, quoted in Wiker, *Darwin
Myth*, p. 139).

[26]See Cornelius Hunter, *Darwin's God* (Grand Rapids: Brazos, 2002).

[27]For arguments against theistic evolution, see John Mark Reynolds, "Getting God a Pass: Science, Theology, and the Consideration of Intelligent Design," in *Signs of Intelligence: Understanding Intelligent Design*, ed. William A. Dembski and James M. Kushiner (Grand Rapids:
Brazos, 2001); Carl F. H. Henry, *God, Revelation, and Authority*, vol. 6 (Waco, Tex.: Word,
1976-1983), chap. 7; James S. Spiegel, "The Philosophical Theology of Theistic Evolutionism," *Philosophia Christi* 4, no. 1 (2002): 89-99; Jay Richards, ed., *God and Evolution* (Seattle:
Discovery Institute, 2010).

[28]William Provine, quoted in Lee Strobel, *The Case for a Creator* (Grand Rapids: Zondervan,
2004), p. 22.

The suggestion that life and man are the result of chance is incompatible with the biblical assertion of their being the direct result of intelligent creative activity.[29]

A second evangelical view is that of scientific creationism, championed by prolific writer Henry Morris (1918-2006), and Duane Gish, who both earned doctorates in science and debated hundreds of Darwinists over many decades. Their work continues largely through the auspices of the Institute for Creation Research. More recently Ken Ham has championed this idea through books, speaking and the Creation Museum in Petersburg, Kentucky. Creationism claims that Genesis teaches that God created the universe and all life in six twenty-four-hour days not more than about ten thousand years ago. Besides appealing to a literal view of the Bible, creationists find fault with Darwinism and cite support for a young earth and universe. They deem any deviation from the six-day model as both unbiblical and unscientific.

While creationists often do yeoman work to bring aspects of Darwinism into question, particularly regarding the lack of evidence for macroevolution in the fossil record,[30] their biblical literalism concerning a six-day creation is troublesome for two reasons. First, as mentioned in chapter eleven, the Genesis creation narrative does not insist on a set time period, but rather six creative periods or "days." Moreover, the genealogies in the Bible cannot be used as chronologies to fix exact time periods.[31] This leaves open the question of the amount of time that has transpired since the creation of the universe and of our first parents.[32]

Second, a coherent Christian worldview should attempt to bring together "the book of nature" (Psalm 19:1-6) and "the book of Scripture" (Psalm 19:7-10; 2 Timothy 3:15-17) as leaders of the scientific revolution understood it. Francis Bacon referred to them as "the book of God's Words" and the "the book of God's Works."[33] God is the Author of both

---

[29]Denton, *Evolution*, p. 66.

[30]Duane Gish, *Evolution: The Fossils Still Say No!* (Green Forest, Ark.: Master Books, 1995).

[31]See Norman Geisler, "Genealogies, Open or Closed," in *Baker Encyclopedia of Apologetics* (Grand Rapids: Baker, 1999), pp. 267-70.

[32]See Francis Schaeffer, *No Final Conflict: The Bible Without Error in All That It Affirms* (Downers Grove, Ill.: InterVarsity Press, 1975).

[33]Francis Bacon, *The Advancement of Learning* (1605; reprint, New York: Random House, 2001), bk. 1, p. 10.

the Bible and creation, and since God is the God of truth, these two books will not contradict each other. Therefore, both books need to be interpreted correctly according to the appropriate principles. There is overwhelming evidence that the universe is 13-15 billion years old and that the earth is ancient as well.[34] In chapter eleven we discussed the big bang cosmology and used this evidence to defend creation ex nihilo, a deeply biblical doctrine. Therefore, if the Bible does not clearly insist on a young earth or young creation, and if the evidence of the book of nature supports a much older universe, it is not necessary to defend a literal six-day creation and a universe that is only several thousand years old.[35]

The third view is the model that fits both Scripture and creation most consistently to my lights. It is what is called progressive creationism or day-age creationism.[36] This account is somewhat flexible on the specifics of the creation timetable and chronology (depending on how one interprets Genesis). But I take the following claims to be nonnegotiable biblically and theologically:

1. God created the universe ex nihilo.

2. God created each "kind" specially, not through a long naturalistic process of macroevolution. However, we cannot say with certainty that a biblical "kind" corresponds to what biologists call a "species" (although they may be very similar).

3. Species may change and adapt to their environment in various limited ways, given the natures God has given them (microevolution).

4. A considerable amount of time elapsed between the creation of other species and the creation of humans.

---

[34]See Hugh Ross, *Creation and Time* (Colorado Springs: NavPress, 1994), chaps. 9-12.

[35]For a debate on this topic, see J. P. Moreland and John Mark Reynolds, eds., *Three Views on Creation and Evolution* (Grand Rapids: Zondervan, 1999). I side most with the view of Robert C. Newman, "Old Earth (Progressive) Creationism." See also Robert C. Newman and Herman J. Eckelman Jr., *Genesis One and the Origin of the Earth* (Hatfield, Penn.: Interdisciplinary Biblical Research Institute, 1989). See also William Dembski, "Part II: Young- and Old-Earth Creationism," in *The End of Christianity: Finding a Good God in an Evil World* (Nashville: Broadman & Holman, 2009).

[36]The ID movement includes young earth creationists (who, nevertheless, do not make a young earth the hallmark of their arguments, unlike earlier creationists), day-age thinkers, those who hold to a common ancestor (but who reject Darwinian mechanisms as adequate explanations), and even agnostics. I am giving what seems to be the best fit between Scripture and nature.

5. God created human beings specially, not through a long process of naturalistic evolution.

6. The first human couple was specially created by God and experienced the Fall in space-time history.[37]

Although the exact timing of the events of Genesis 1 is left somewhat open, the general sequence is clear: first the inorganic world, then nonhuman life, then human life. While God created each "kind" specially, this does not rule out development within a kind, nor does it rule out extinctions of species. Walter Bradley has developed a plausible progressive creationist view that he believes corresponds nicely with the geological record.[38]

WHAT IS DARWINISM?

The history of evolutionary theory is a vast subject, but we can distill the essentials. Many entertained various evolutionary ideas prior to Charles Darwin, including members of his own family,[39] but Darwin's legacy was to advance a specific mechanism to explain how species originated (speciation). He called this mechanism natural selection.[40] In *artificial* selection, a breeder of animals or plants guides the development of a species through intelligent intervention (although this never results in a new species, only

---

[37]This account implies that animal death and suffering occurred before the Fall of humans. It interprets the Fall as bringing about human death and woes, as well as disruptions for the world as a whole. Some take this to be a denial of the Genesis record, but the text never says that all death began at the Fall. For an ingenious—but to my mind not fully convincing—way to reconcile an old universe with the idea that human sin is what brought about all death and suffering, see Dembski, "Part I: Dealing with Evil," in *End of Christianity*. Hugh Ross gives his account of this question biblically and scientifically in *The Genesis Question* (Colorado Springs: NavPress, 1998), pp. 93-100.

[38]Walter Bradley, "Why I Believe the Bible Is Scientifically Reliable," in *Why I Am a Christian*, ed. Norman Geisler and Paul Hoffman (Grand Rapids: Baker, 2001), pp. 161-81. For a theologically developed view of progressive creationism, see Gordon R. Lewis and Bruce A. Demarest, *Integrative Theology* (Grand Rapids: Zondervan, 1990), 2:17-68.

[39]See Wiker, "Hatching the Evolutionary Plot," in *Darwin Myth*.

[40]Alfred Russel Wallace developed a similar theory at nearly the same time but through a quirk of history never received the credit—and mythic status—that accrued to Darwin. See Martin Fichman, *An Elusive Victorian: The Evolution of Alfred Russel Wallace* (Chicago: University of Chicago Press, 2004); and Michael A. Flannery, *Alfred Russel Wallace's Theory of Intelligent Evolution: How Wallace's "World of Life" Challenged Darwinism* (Riesel, Tex.: Erasmus Press, 2008). The latter work indicates that Wallace, unlike Darwin, believed that evolution had an intelligent purpose. Flannery argues that while the metaphysics of naturalism compelled Darwin's science, Wallace's sense of science compelled him to see design in nature.

modifications of the original species). In *natural* selection, according to Darwin, this process is unintelligent and without purpose. Nature favors organisms that evolve adaptively and reproduce abundantly; it judges the unfit with sterility and death. The fittest survive and reproduce. Given enough time, this process of natural selection leads to the development of entirely new species, which appear through a gradual process of incremental change. This is called "descent with modification."

Darwin knew nothing of genetics or of the fantastically complex microscopic world of the cell (see chap. 14). Later Darwinists, appealing to the genetic discoveries of Gregor Mendel (not a Darwinist), filled out Darwin's theory by claiming that random genetic mutations supplied the means by which organisms changed into new species. After random mutations occur, natural selection kicks in to conserve beneficial mutational changes in offspring. This is called "the neo-Darwinian synthesis," the worldview that currently dominates the scientific establishment—despite some recent and cogent challengers. Darwinists sometimes refer to other factors driving evolution, such as genetic drift (another source of genetic variation), but natural selection working on random mutations is the dominant model for change at the deepest level.[41]

What is the significance of Darwinism for Christian apologetics? If Darwinism is true, it is much less likely that Christianity is true. Richard Dawkins said that Darwinism allows one to be "an intellectually fulfilled atheist."[42] That is, it gives strength to atheism because God is exorcised from biology. Many textbooks present Darwinism as an *alternative* to a Christian account of nature. Skeptics and atheists have employed Darwinism for well over a hundred years as a defeater of Christianity and theism, since they claim that undirected evolution replaces design. While King David said that he is "fearfully and wonderfully made" (Psalm 139:14) and the apostle Paul claimed that God has made himself known through nature (Romans 1:18-21; see also Psalm 19:1-6), Darwinism asserts that every aspect of the development of species and of the human body can be explained according to time, space, chance and natural law given the

---

[41]For a discussion of suggested Darwinian ways to augment genetic mutation and how these efforts fail to account for speciation, see Jonathan Wells and William Dembski, "The Origin of Species," in *The Design of Life: Discovering Signs of Intelligence in Biological Systems* (Dallas: Foundation for Thought & Ethics, 2008).

[42]Richard Dawkins, *The Blind Watchmaker* (New York: W. W. Norton, 1986), p. 6.

operations of nature, natural selection and the background conditions of the universe.[43]

Christian Darwinists assert that God created the universe out of nothing and then left it to evolve such that design is not evident from biology. The vast panoply of life on earth can be adequately understood sans Designer. Yet given the Darwinian view, the idea that "God used Darwinian evolution" is a bizarre claim, because this would mean that God would have used a process (that is, Darwinian evolution) that rendered God undetectable through his own works.[44] Worse yet, if a theist understands Darwinism as an undirected process of natural law and chance, there is no room for God's involvement at all.

But Darwinism is far more than a biological theory. It is integral to the secular worldview of the Western intellectual elite that wants to marginalize religious faith as having no claim on knowledge. The natural sciences and humanities are dominated by this naturalistic and secular worldview, and so they either ignore Christian claims or attack them forthrightly. Disputing Darwinism is, therefore, central in dislodging this secularist mindset that affects so much of elite intellectual life.[45]

BASIC FLAWS OF DARWINISM

The literature scientifically criticizing Darwinism is vast and respectable, despite the claim that Darwinism is beyond doubt. When a viewpoint becomes socially embedded (as has Darwinism), its opponents can be easily dismissed as ignoramuses (or worse). Proponents of the dominant view believe that they need not engage in rigorous argument. A quote by the late biologist Theodore Dobhansky is often invoked to silence the critics: "Nothing in biology makes sense except in light of evolution."[46] If so, to challenge Darwinism (which is what he meant by

---

[43]I argued in chap. 12 that these background conditions are fine-tuned for human life, but this is almost never brought up in discussions by Darwinists.

[44]On God's revelation in nature, see Psalm 19:1-6 and Romans 1:18-21 especially.

[45]See Philip Johnson, *Reason in the Balance* (Downers Grove, Ill.: InterVarsity Press, 1995); John West, *Darwin Day in America* (Wilmington, Del.: ISI Books, 2007). For influence of Darwin on Hitler see Richard Weikart, *From Darwin to Hitler: Evolutionary Ethics, Eugenics, and Racism in Germany* (New York: Palgrave Macmillan, 2004). Darwinism was a *necessary* but not *sufficient* condition for the origin and operation of Nazism, as David Berlinksi puts it in the film *Expelled* (2009).

[46]Theodore Dobzhansky "Nothing in Biology Makes Sense Except in Light of Evolution," *American Biology Teacher* 35 (1973): 125-29.

"evolution") means undermining all the achievements of biology. But Dobhansky was wrong. Most of the great disciplines of biology—such as anatomy, botany, microbiology, systematics and embryology—were founded before Darwin's theory and do not require it for them to flourish. Several notable pioneers in biology rejected Darwin's theory: embryologist Karl Ernst von Baer, comparative biologist Richard Owen, zoologist Louis Agassiz and the geneticist Gregor Mendel.[47] In a recent article in *The Scientist*, chemist Philip S. Skell, a member of the U.S. National Academy of Sciences, wrote that after considering the major biological discoveries of the twentieth century, he "found that Darwin's theory had provided no discernible guidance, but was brought in, after the breakthroughs, as an interesting narrative gloss."[48]

PHILOSOPHICAL COMMITMENT TO MATERIALISM

The contemporary Darwinian establishment is philosophically committed to naturalism (or materialism) as a worldview and modus operandi. This cannot be stated too strongly. The natural world is all that can be studied and must, by itself, provide all the answers to scientific questions. Darwinian naturalism takes two forms: metaphysical naturalism and methodological naturalism. Metaphysical naturalism is the philosophical claim that only material states exist; there is nothing immaterial, spiritual or supernatural. Methodological naturalism is the means of scientific inquiry given the presupposition of metaphysical naturalism. This methodology can also be stated in supposedly agnostic fashion. A scientist claims that he or she is not ruling out God and the supernatural, but that science qua science should not attempt to study such things. Therefore, only natural explanations are allowable; only materialistic explanations are christened "scientific."

While methodological naturalism appears modest and agnostic to the untutored, it is a ruse for metaphysical materialism. Methodological naturalism assumes that even if God or anything supernatural exists, this cannot be evident in the universe. It thereby issues a metaphysical veto against

---

[47]Jonathan Wells, *The Politically Incorrect Guide to Darwinism and Intelligent Design* (Washington, D.C.: Regnery, 2006), p. 79.
[48]Philip S. Skell, *The Scientist*, August 2005, <www.discovery.org/a/2816>. Wells gives several other quotes by significant scientists to this effect as well. See Jonathan Wells, *Icons of Evolution* (Washington, D.C.: Regnery, 2000), pp. 80-81.

any empirical evidence for the immaterial—such as the soul, God or the supernatural—regardless of the evidence that may be available. This is hardly a neutral strategy. If the mandate of science is to follow the evidence wherever it leads and then to select the best hypothesis for any given field of study, methodological naturalism betrays science itself.[49] The prevailing naturalism of biology is evident in this pronouncement by Richard Lewontin, an eminent biologist and defender of Darwinism:

> We take the side of science *in spite* of the patent absurdity of some of its constructs, *in spite* of its failure to fulfill many of its extravagant promises of health and life, *in spite* of the tolerance of the scientific community for unsubstantiated just-so stories, because we have a prior commitment, a commitment to materialism. It is not that the methods and institutions of science somehow compel us to accept a material explanation of the phenomenal world, but, on the contrary, that we are forced by our *a priori* adherence to material causes to create an apparatus of investigation and a set of concepts that produce material explanations, no matter how counterintuitive, no matter how mystifying to the uninitiated. Moreover, that materialism is an absolute, for we cannot allow a Divine Foot in the door.[50]

As Phillip Johnson has cogently argued in his pivotal book *Darwin on Trial*, if a person is committed to naturalism a priori, something like Darwinism *must be true*, since naturalism disallows the existence of any intelligence behind the origin and development of life.[51] Before this, but with less cultural impact, cultural critic Richard Weaver made the same essential claim, arguing that if naturalism is the only allowable worldview, then alternatives to Darwinism cannot be considered.[52] Even during Darwin's

---

[49]On methodological naturalism see Cornelius Hunter, *Darwin's Proof* (Grand Rapids: Brazos, 2003), p. 147; William Dembski, *The Design Revolution* (Downers Grove, Ill.: InterVarsity Press, 2004), pp. 171-72; Alvin Plantinga, "Methodological Naturalism," *Origins and Design* 18, no. 1 (1996): 18-27 <www.arn.org/docs/odesign/od181/methnat181.htm>; "Methodological Naturalism? Part 2: Philosophical Analysis" *Origins & Design* 18, no. 2 (1997): 22-34 <www.arn.org/docs/odesign/od182/methnat182.htm>. We will return to a proper sense of science in chap. 14.

[50]Richard Lewontin, "Billions and Billions of Demons," *New York Review of Books*, January 9, 1997, p. 31.

[51]Phillip Johnson, *Darwin on Trial*, 2nd ed. (Downers Grove, Ill.: InterVarsity Press, 1993). This point is made throughout the book, which, in many ways, launched the intelligent design movement.

[52]Richard Weaver, *Visions of Order: The Cultural Crisis of Our Time* (1964; reprint, Bryn Mawr, Penn.: Intercollegiate Studies Institute, 1995), pp. 139-40.

day, George Mitvart, a distinguished professor of biology, claimed that Darwin presupposed naturalism in order to explain away any religious realities.[53]

When Lewontin warns of "a Divine Foot in the door," he means that anything but "absolute materialism" will undo science itself by allowing haphazard divine interventions into the natural order that would subvert the regularities required for scientific observation and theorizing. That false claim will be taken up in chapter fourteen.

If empirical scientific study regarding the origins of life is separated from "absolute materialism," the possibilities for explanation expand tremendously. This "wedge" strategy—that is, introducing nonmaterialistic considerations into the investigation—is central to reopening the debate concerning the best explanation for the origins and development of life on earth.[54] As Phillip Johnson puts it, for naturalists, "In the beginning were the particles," and the particles had to do all the creating. This stands opposed to the biblical claim that "in the beginning was the Word" (John 1:1).[55]

Chesterton noted that the Christian need not be committed to a completely static creation, because natural development occurs in God's world. The materialist, however, must not allow any element of design to creep into his theory: "The Christian is quite free to believe that there is a considerable amount of settled order and inevitable development in the universe. But the materialist is not allowed to admit into his spotless machine the slightest speck of spiritualism or miracle."[56] The case for Darwinism hangs on some very questionable evidence. In fact, it hangs more on images than facts.

ICONS OF EVOLUTION

Jonathan Wells, who earned a Ph.D. in embryology from the University of California, Berkeley, argues that the support for Darwinism relies heavily on several deceptive "icons." These are taken-for-granted ideas

[53]See the discussion in Wiker, *Darwin Myth*, pp. 124-30.
[54]Phillip Johnson explains this strategy in depth in *The Wedge of Truth* (Downers Grove, Ill.: InterVarsity Press, 2000).
[55]Phillip Johnson, "Theistic Naturalism and Theistic Realism," in *Reason in the Balance* (Downers Grove, Ill.: InterVarsity Press, 1995).
[56]G. K. Chesterton, *Orthodoxy* (1908; reprint, New York: Image Books, 1959), p. 24.

put in pictorial form that often keep people from thinking critically about Darwinism.

The color of moths. Darwinists claim that natural selection occurs even now in the case of the peppered moth—"evolution in action." The peppered moth is clothed in various shades of gray. After the industrial revolution, over 90 percent of the moths near the industrial city of Manchester, England, were darker colored. As pollution darkened tree trunks, the darker moths that perched on trunks blended in better than the whiter moths. The lighter moths stood out and became easier targets for hungry birds. The darker moths produced through random genetic mutation were "selected" by the environment because they were safer from predation. It was a textbook case of natural selection. Or so it seemed.

Up until the 1980s the peppered moths were poster insects for natural selection. Then several discrepancies emerged. First, the darker moths did not replace the lighter moths in the most heavily polluted areas, which would have been expected by the theory. Second, in rural areas of England, which were less affected by pollution, the frequency of the darker moths was higher than anticipated, since the lighter months were expected to be favored by natural selection. Third, when pollution decreased in London, causing the tree trunks to become lighter, the proportion of dark moths increased in the northern part of London but decreased in the southern part.

Worse yet (for the Darwinists), these moths *do not normally rest on tree trunks*. Some readers may question this, because they have seen photographs in textbooks of peppered months on tree trunks. This is because the moths were placed there by hand.[57] Yet *even if* the peppered moths had had the good sense to go along with the Darwinian expectations, a change in the differential pigmentation tendencies of one species of moth (following a change in tree trunk color) would not explain how moths evolved from some previous species in the first place. Nor would it demonstrate that moths were in the process of evolving into a different species. Even if the pollution-predation theory were vindicated, this would only account for the pigmentation of moths, not "the origin of species."

The finch beak variations. Another supposed example of "evolution in

---

[57]Wells, *Icons of Evolution*, pp. 156-57.

action" is the finch beak. Darwin encountered various species of finches in the Galapagos Islands in 1835 while on a five-year sea voyage on the HMS Beagle. Legend has it that he took the different species, distinguished by their beak sizes, as strong evidence of natural selection. These birds are often called "Darwin's finches." Yet Darwin never mentions them in *The Origin of Species*, and he made only one small journal entry about them in his diary of the voyage.[58] Notwithstanding, after the rise of neo-Darwinism in the 1930s, finches became another "icon of evolution."

In the 1970s, Peter and Rosemary Grant and their team went to the Galapagos to study finches. During the drought year of 1977, there was a significant reduction in the seeds for the finches to eat. During this time the island's population of medium ground finches declined to about 15 percent of its previous size. The survivors tended to have slightly larger bodies and beaks than the casualties. Peter Grant got very excited: "If drought occurs once a decade, on average, repeated directional selection at this rate with no selection between droughts would transform one species into another within 200 years." But even if it took two thousand years for speciation to occur, this was nothing compared to "the hundreds of thousands of years the finches have been in the archipelago."[59] Natural selection is revealed in our time. Or so it seemed.

Grant's projection depended on unidirectional extrapolation with no setbacks (reversion to the norm) in beak size. After the 1982-1983 influence of El Niño's warmth and rain, finch food became plentiful again in the Galapagos and finch beaks devolved back to their previous average size. Instead of cumulative growth in finch beak size, an oscillation occurred. Thus, the finch beak variations proved nothing Darwinian. Nevertheless, numerous pro-Darwinist publications left out the awkward fact of finch beak reversion. As Wells notes, this is akin to "a stock promoter who claims a stock might double in value in twenty years because it increased 5 percent in 1998, but doesn't mention that it decreased 5 percent in 1999."[60] Darwinists routinely appeal to long stretches of time in order to allow evolutionary mechanisms to do their job of increasing complexity. But, as

[58]Ibid., p. 162.
[59]Peter R. Grant, "Natural Selection and Darwin's Finches," *Scientific American* 25 (1991): 82-87, cited in Wells, *Icons of Evolution*, pp. 167-68.
[60]Wells, *Icons of Evolution*, p. 175.

A. E. Wilder-Smith points out, long periods of time also allow for regression and devolution. Evolutionary epochs are not one-way tickets to radical change.[61]

Evolutionary extrapolation run amuck. The cases just mentioned underscore the Darwinian reliance on *extrapolation*. These examples, even if successful in demonstrating small adaptive changes in populations, provide scant evidence for one species developing into another species. In other words, microevolution (small changes within species that produce no major structural change and no new organs) does not logically establish macroevolution (the evolution of new species).[62] As Norman MacBeth pointed out, "Extrapolation is a dangerous procedure."

> If you observe the growth of a baby during its first months, extrapolation into the future will show that the child will be eight feet tall when six years old. Therefore, all statisticians recommend caution in extrapolation. Darwin, however, plunged in with no caution at all.[63]

Contemporary Darwinists also suffer from the same hyperactive tendency to find "evolution in action" (even when it isn't really there).

Natural selection itself does not provide the engine for speciation (macroevolution). Although it helps explain *the survival of species* (since species must adapt somewhat to environments if they are to survive over time),[64] it does nothing to explain *the arrival of species*.[65] Animal breeders who engage in artificial selection may change some of the basic features of particular species—such as horses, cows, pigs, peas or sugar beets—to some extent, but they cannot create new species. The beets may get sweeter, but they do not evolve into another species. In fact, Luther Burbank (1849-1926), deemed the greatest plant breeder in history and breeder of the

---

[61]A. E. Wilder Smith, *The Creation of Life: A Cybernetic Approach to Evolution* (Wheaton, Ill.: Harold Shaw, 1970), pp. 26-27. Many of Smith's insights—although largely ignored—were prophetic of later criticism of Darwinism.

[62]On the significance of this distinction, see L. Duane Thurman, *How to Think About Evolution and Other Bible-Science Controversies* (Downers Grove, Ill.: InterVarsity Press, 1978). Chapters 4 and 5 address microevolution (the factual side) and macroevolution (the theoretical side) respectively. See also Wells and Dembski, *Design of Life*, pp. 102-6.

[63]MacBeth, *Darwin Retried*, p. 31.

[64]This is more of a truism than an explanation, as many critics of Darwinism have pointed out.

[65]This winning locution was first offered a century ago by Darwin critic and Dutch botanist Hugh de Vries, *Species and Varieties: Their Origin by Mutation* (1904; reprint, New York: Garland, 1988), pp. 825-26, cited in Wells and Dembski, *Design of Life*, p. 108.

Idaho potato (1871) and of eight hundred documented new plants,[66] claimed that the proclivity for species to stay true to their type could be called "the law of Reversion to the Average." This "keeps all living things within more or less fixed limitations."[67] This, he argued, was true for "plant-breeding by design." How much more the case for what he called "plant breeding by chance"?[68]

Haeckel's fraudulent embryos. The claim has been made that evolution is evidenced right before our eyes in the developing embryo because "ontogeny recapitulates phylogeny." That is, the development of vertebrate embryos (ontogeny) revisits in visual form the development of life from one species to another species (phylogeny). The claim, according to a discredited principle called "the biogenic law," was that the human embryo passes through the stages of a one-celled marine organism, a worm, a fish, an amphibian, a mammal and then a human—thus recapitulating in miniature the entire evolutionary journey.[69]

Darwin knew that the evidence for macroevolution in the fossil remains was sketchy, so he put faith in embryology to support his theory. He had been informed that embryos of the most distinctive species belonging to the same class are very similar in their early stages and become different only later in development (a misconception embodied in drawings by Ernst Haeckel [1834-1919]). Darwin believed that "the embryo is the animal in its less modified state; and in so far it reveals the structure of the progenitor."[70] He considered this "by far the strongest single class of facts in favor of" his theory.[71] Biology textbooks relied on Haeckel's depictions

[66]Nara Schoenberg, "Luther Burbank Biography Salutes the Great Plant Breeder," *Chicago Tribune,* May 31, 2009 <http://articles.chicagotribune.com/2009-05-31/news/0905280271_1_Luther-burbank-gardener-mother-nature>.

[67]Luther Burbank, *Partner of Nature*, ed. Wilbur Hall (New York: D. Appleton-Century, 1939), p. 98. MacBeth cites several other sources on plant breeding to this effect in *Darwin Retried*, p. 39.

[68]Ibid., p. 107. The terms in quotes are Burbank's; the inference drawn is my own.

[69]See Richard Milton, *Shattering the Myths of Darwinism* (Rochester, Vt.: Park Street Press, 1997), p. 189.

[70]Charles Darwin, *The Origin of Species by Means of Natural Selection* (London: John Murray, 1935), pp. 449-50. Facsimile available at "The Complete Works of Charles Darwin Online," *Darwin Online* at <http://darwin-online.org.uk/content/frameset?viewtype=side&itemID=F373&pageseq=467>.

[71]Charles Darwin, "Letter to Asa Gray (September 10, 1860)," in *The Life and Letters of Charles Darwin*, ed. Francis Darwin (London: John Murray, 1887), 2:338. Available at <http://darwin-online.org.uk/content/frameset?viewtype=side&itemID=F1452.2&pageseq=354>.

for over a hundred years to promote Darwinism. Wells summarizes the three ways in which the drawings are misleading:

> (1) They include only those classes and orders [of embryos] that come closest to fitting Haeckel's [evolutionary] theory; (2) they distort the embryos they purport to show; and (3) most seriously, they entirely omit earlier stages in which vertebrate embryos look very different.[72]

Present-day depictions of embryos do not support the recapitulation theory. Neither Haeckel's drawings nor the facts of embryology lend any support to Darwinism's claim that life is traced to a common ancestor.[73]

Darwin's tree of life. Although Darwin admitted that the fossil record of his day provided scant support for his evolutionary theories, he did not find the problem insuperable. He acknowledged that

> just in proportion as this process of extermination has acted on an enormous scale, so must the number of intermediate varieties, which have formerly existed on the earth, be truly enormous. Why then is not every geological formation and every stratum full of such intermediate links? Geology assuredly does not reveal any such finely graduated organic chain; and this, perhaps, is the most obvious and gravest objection which can be urged against my theory.[74]

While his theory demanded incremental long-term change whereby one species evolved into another, he admitted that "several of the main divisions of the animal kingdom suddenly appear in the lowest known fossiliferous rocks." He took this to be a serious problem for his theory.[75] Nevertheless, Darwin hoped that the fossils would speak more loudly on his behalf for future paleontologists.

This hope has been deferred. The Darwinian model should show two broad patterns of fossil evidence. The first is Darwin's tree of life: the earliest strata of paleontological evidence should disclose simple and scarce organisms followed by more and more organisms of increasing complexity. The trunk should contain far fewer and far simpler forms

---

[72]Wells, *Icons of Evolution*, p. 102.
[73]Some still claim that the embryo has "gill slits," but this is merely apparent and has no genetic or structural basis (see ibid., pp. 105-6).
[74]Darwin, *Origin of Species*, p. 280, <http://darwin-online.org.uk/content/frameset?viewtype=side&itemID=F373&pageseq=298>.
[75]Ibid., p. 306, <http://darwin-online.org.uk/content/frameset?viewtype=side&itemID=F373&pageseq=324>. See also Wells, *Icons of Evolution*, pp. 35-37.

than the subsequent branches. Second, Darwin argued that evolution proceeds by very small increments; therefore, there should be a substantial record of transitions between species. Darwin noted that we cannot expect fossilization to preserve a perfect record (some organisms would fail to be fossilized or fail to be discovered), but if Darwin's theory is correct, there would have been abundant time and resources to unearth a heavy load of transitional forms. Nonetheless, the evidence is increasingly cogent that neither of these two broad patterns of evidence is supported by the rocks at hand.

Darwin's tree of life has been falsified by the fossil record. While it seems true that single-celled organisms occupy the earliest strata of earth history, many organisms appear in great numbers with no traceable ancestors.[76] This is particularly true for what is known as "the Cambrian explosion" or, more colloquially, "biology's big bang." During this period, dated at between 500 and 600 million years ago, the fossil record shows that the major animal groups appeared abruptly and completely formed. But according to Darwin, these animal groups—phyla—should increase in number gradually over time. "The fossil record, however, shows that almost all of the animal phyla appear at about the same time in the Cambrian explosion, with the number declining slightly thereafter due to extinctions."[77]

Some Darwinists counter that the fossil record is too fragmentary to preserve the pre-Cambrian ancestors who would surely have marched to the Darwinian drummer. This defense, however, is implausible and more ad hoc than based on evidence. Most paleontologists think the fossil record is complete enough to allow for the discovery of pre-Cambrian ancestors if they existed; yet none are forthcoming.[78] But another way to salvage Darwinian gradualism would be to claim that the ancestors to the Cambrian period were not fossilized at all, owing to their small, soft bodies. This fails to convince, however, because even more ancient small,

---

[76]There is no little dispute about the accuracy of various dating methods. See Milton, *Shattering the Myths of Darwinism*, chap. 5.

[77]Wells, *Icons of Evolution*, p. 43.

[78]Ibid., pp. 42-44; Stephen Meyer et al., "The Cambrian Explosion: Biology's Big Bang," in *Darwinism, Design and Public Education*, ed. Angus Campbell and Stephen C. Meyer (East Lansing: Michigan State University Press, 2003), pp. 354-58; Stephen C. Meyer, "The Cambrian Information Explosion: Evidence for Intelligent Design," in *Debating Design: From Darwin to DNA*, ed. William A. Dembski and Michael Ruse (New York: Cambridge University Press, 2006). See also the DVD *Darwin's Dilemma* (Illustra Media, 2009).

soft-bodied fossils have been preserved in other settings.[79] Thus, in the Cambrian explosion the major animal phyla are already present, fully formed, without the long branching-tree history required by Darwin's theory. The highest categories (phyla) are there at the start of animal history.[80]

WHAT ABOUT TRANSITIONAL FORMS?

Many evolutionists, let alone critics of evolution, have confessed that well over a century after *The Origin of Species*, the fossil record is still reticent to indicate a slow, gradual pattern of evolutionary development. The pattern is rather that of the abrupt emergence of organisms and of stubborn stasis (long periods of no organismic change). Further, as paleontologist David Raup comments, even though our knowledge of the fossil record has expanded considerably, ironically, "we have even fewer examples of evolutionary transition than we had in Darwin's time," since "classic cases of Darwinian change in the fossil record, such as the evolution of the horse in America, have had to be discarded or modified."[81]

Darwinists rely on two moves at this point. One is to claim that the transitional forms did exist, but we have no evidence of them because they failed to be fossilized because they were short-lived. In 1961, a hundred years after *Origin of Species*, Garrett Hardin answered the question of whether all the links in the evolutionary chain can be shown: "No, of course not; the geological record is imperfect and will always remain so, since it is highly improbable that short-lived intermediate species will be fossilized."[82] MacBeth comments that this response is "rather threadbare after a century of digging and collecting."[83] Besides, how can it be known that they were "short-lived" if there is no evidence for them? This fallaciously begs the question. On the standard theory of macroevolution, microchanges occur over tens of millions of years while macrochanges take hundreds of millions. That hardly seems short-lived. Of course, it is *possible*

[79]Wells, *Icons of Evolution*, p. 44.
[80]Ibid., p. 54.
[81]David Raup, "Conflicts Between Darwin and Paleontology," *Field Museum of Natural History Bulletin* 30, no. 1 (1979): 25, quoted in Dembski and Wells, *Design of Life*, p. 68.
[82]Garret Hardin, *Nature and Man's Fate* (New York: Mentor, 1961), p. 103, quoted in MacBeth, *Darwin Retried*, p. 32.
[83]MacBeth, *Darwin Retried*, p. 32.

that all the needed transitional forms somehow were not fossilized, but that bare possibility affords neither proof nor even likelihood that these forms actually existed.[84]

The second escape route for evolutionists is the way of the "saltation"— a new organism that suddenly (in geological time) arrives on the evolutionary scene without a long history of incremental change. The saltation theory was advanced by Richard Goldschmidt, a noteworthy geneticist, precisely because of the dearth of clear transitional forms. Goldschmidt was roundly rejected by his peers, but a similar theory was propounded by Niles Eldredge and the prestigious Stephen Jay Gould under the distinguished title of "punctuated equilibrium." The theory recognized long periods of species stasis combined with sudden emergence of new species.

> The history of most fossil species includes two features particularly inconsistent with gradualism: (1) Stasis—most species exhibit no directional change during their tenure on earth. They appear in the fossil record looking much the same as when they disappear; morphological change is usually limited and directionless. (2) Sudden appearance—in any local area, a species does not arise gradually by the steady transformation of its ancestors; it appears all at once and "fully formed."[85]

Rather than giving ad hoc reasons why the transitional forms are not available, the theory dispenses with them entirely by asserting that new forms developed very rapidly. This departs from Darwinian orthodoxy, which claims that all changes are slow and incremental. Leading Darwinists such as Richard Dawkins and Daniel Dennett have challenged the theory. Nevertheless, Gould's comments are telling concerning the fossil record.

> The extreme rarity of transitional forms in the fossil record persists as the trade secret of paleontology. The evolutionary trees that adorn our textbooks have data only at the tips and nodes of their branches; the rest is inference, however reasonable, not the evidence of fossils. . . . We fancy ourselves as the only true students of life's history, yet to preserve our favored account of evolution by natural selection we view our data as so bad that we never see the very process we profess to study.[86]

---

[84]Ibid.

[85]Stephen Jay Gould, "Evolution's Erratic Pace," *Natural History* 86 (1977): 14.

[86]Ibid., p. 14. See also Niles Eldredge's similar comment in "Missing, Believed Nonexistent," *Manchester Guardian (The Washington Post Weekly)* 119, no. 22 (November 26, 1978), p. 1.

Quotes to this effect by gradualists (the majority) and those favoring the punctuated equilibria theory (the minority) can be easily multiplied, although most writers do not think the problem brings down the Darwinian citadel.

The difficulty worsens, however, because genetics provides no proof that species derive their origins from other earlier species. The genetics of life preserves the basic structures and functions of organisms. When genetic mutations are observed, they are almost always deleterious, not adaptive—as even arch-Darwinist Richard Dawkins admits.[87] There is no known case where a genetic mutation has resulted in an increase in genetic information for an organism. But that is precisely what is needed for species to change into other species instead of remaining what they are. This poses a significant problem for both gradualists and saltationists, but especially for the latter, since a more radical and rapid change is postulated. As Paul Grassé put it:

> Mutations, in time, occur incoherently. They are not complementary to one another, nor are they cumulative in successive generations toward a given direction. They modify what preexists, but they do so in disorder. . . . As soon as some disorder, even slight, appears in an organized being, sickness, then death follows.[88]

Therefore, "No matter how numerous they may be, mutations do not produce any kind of evolution."[89] Mutation results in small changes in the organism; it cannot create major changes in organisms.

Italian geneticist Giuseppe Sermonti observes that natural selection (which relies on mutations for the internal change in organisms), far from generating new organisms, has a stabilizing effect, bringing populations back to the norm needed for survival. Some species may lose much through natural selection, such as the mole that loses the use of its eyes, but these "are species with no future; they are not pioneers, but prisoners in nature's penitentiary."[90] Species remain basically stable or die out. In fact, several

---

[87]Dawkins, *Blind Watchmaker*, p. 233. Dawkins wrongly thinks this is no problem for Darwinism.

[88]Pierre-Paul Grassé, *Evolution of Living Organisms* (New York: Academic Press, 1977), p. 97-98.

[89]Ibid., p. 88.

[90]Giuseppe Sermonti, *Why Is a Fly Not a Horse?* (Seattle: Center for Science & Culture, 2005), p. 51. This is a translation of the Italian *Dimenticare Darwin* ("Forget Darwin") from 1999.

species are known to have "remained virtually unchanged since the beginnings of multi-cellular animals about 550 million years ago." Species stability, not speciation, is "the real mark of life."[91]

Nevertheless, most Darwinists claim that the fossil record has vouchsafed a few strong transitional forms, particularly archaeopteryx, the missing link between reptiles and birds. Like a bird, archaeopteryx had wings, feathers and a wishbone, but like a reptile, archaeopteryx had a bony tail, forelimb claws and teeth. Christopher Hitchens's atheist apologetic confidently invokes the extinct species as proof positive.[92] However, "every one of its supposedly reptilian features can be found in various species of undoubted birds."[93]

Consider six facts: (1) The "bone and feather arrangements on a present-day swan shows striking similarities to Archaeopteryx."[94] (2) The hoatzin of South America and the ostrich have claws on their wings.[95] (3) Modern birds do not have teeth, but some ancient birds did. However, no one argues that these ancient birds were intermediates between reptiles and birds.[96] (4) It is argued that Archaeopteryx's shallow breastbone would have given it "a feeble wing beat and poor flight," thus supposedly making it a poor candidate for being bird. However, the present-day hoatzin has a similarly shallow breastbone, and there are many contemporary birds incapable of flight, such as penguins.[97] (5) Although Archaeopteryx's bones were once thought to be solid, like a reptile's, it is now known that they were hollow like a bird's.[98] (6) Recent discoveries indicate that bona fide bird fossils have been found that existed in the same fossil period as archaeopteryx. This, it appears, strips away its last credential as a Darwinian intermediary.[99]

[91]Ibid., p. 52. For a treatment of the unlikelihood of genetic mutation and natural selection producing new information for the formation of species, see William A. Dembski and Robert J. Marks Jr., "Conservation of Information in Search: Measuring the Cost of Success," *Man and Cybernetics, Part A: IEEE Transactions on Systems and Humans* 39, no. 5 (2009): 1051-61.
[92]Christopher Hitchins, *God Is Not Great* (New York: Twelve Books, 2007), pp. 281-82.
[93]Francis Hitching, *The Neck of the Giraffe* (New York: Signet, 1983), p. 21.
[94]Ibid.
[95]Ibid.
[96]Ibid., p. 22.
[97]Ibid.
[98]Ibid.
[99]See ibid., pp. 22-23; for a longer critique of the claim that archaeopteryx is a transitional form, see Wells, *Icons of Evolution*, pp. 111-36.

Human evolution: Do we have a common ancestor? Darwin's tree of life has not proven true, and the fossil record, while ancient, presents anything but a clear picture of biological change. Denton claims that while

> the rocks have continually yielded new and exciting and even bizarre forms of life, . . . what they have never yielded is any of Darwin's myriads of transitional forms. Despite the tremendous increase in geological activity in every corner of the globe and despite the discovery of many strange and hitherto unknown forms, the infinitude of connecting links has still not been discovered and the fossil record is about as discontinuous as it was when Darwin was writing the *Origin*.[100]

The data available from fossil remains to reconstruct the biological history, which supposedly leads to humanity from prehuman creatures, is scarce indeed. The ancestor-descendant relationship is a vexed problem since "no fossil is buried with its birth certificate."[101]

If one presupposes naturalism, then the fossil record will be interpreted as leading from prehuman to human, despite the categorical gaps that remain. These gaps are filled in not by the hard geological evidence—which is inadequate—but by the ideology of naturalism, which permits no hard breaks in the fossil record (or in any part of nature), given that there is nothing outside of nature to shape it. However, if we do not assume naturalism, but simply look at the evidence (contrasting Darwinism and design), a different picture develops.

Numerous prehistoric candidates have been advanced as the missing link between humans and their apelike ancestors, including some noteworthy frauds, such as Piltdown man and others.[102] Many people think that the prehuman-to-human evolutionary path has been cleared. This conviction is largely due to the often-seen icon that begins with a hunched apelike creature, then continues with more upright (and human-looking) creatures and ends with a bone fide human. But this is more image than reality. The fossil record itself hardly supports the iconography. Darwin and the early Darwinists knew that human evolution was not supported by

---

[100]Denton, *Evolution*, p. 162.

[101]Henry Gee, *In Search of Deep Time: Beyond the Fossil Record to a New History of Life* (New York: Free Press, 1999), p. 113, quoted in Wells, *Icons of Evolution*, p. 220.

[102]Wells, *Icons of Evolution*, p. 217. For a discussion of these failed candidates, see Marvin L. Lubenow, *Bones of Contention: A Creationist Assessment of Human Fossils*, rev. ed. (Grand Rapids: Baker, 2004), chaps. 6-12; and Dembski and Wells, "Human Origins," in *Design of Life*.

the fossil record, although it was demanded by their theory.[103] Subsequent finds have hardly vindicated Darwinian claims, despite overblown headlines about supposed "missing links."[104]

Moreover, there are numerous and substantial anatomical and physiological differences between humans and supposed prehuman ancestors, not to mention the uniquely human qualities of moral awareness, consciousness and rationality (see chaps. 15, 17-18). Marcel-Paul Schutzenberger, who was professor of the Faculty of Sciences at the University of Paris, argued in an interview in *La Rescherche* in 1996 that both classical Darwinian incrementalists and those that espouse punctuated equilibrium (saltationists) "alike are completely incapable of providing a convincing explanation of the near simultaneous emergence of a number of biological systems that distinguish human beings from higher primates."[105] These include bipedalism (walking exclusively on two feet), which requires a modification of the pelvis and the cerebellum; a more dexterous hand equipped with fingers "conferring a fine tactile sense"; the modification of the pharynx, necessary for phonation; and a modification of the central nervous system, "notably at the level of the temporal lobes, permitting the specific recognition of speech."[106] Natural selection, as a Designer substitute, provides no planning and no intelligent coordination of simultaneous changes required to explain the uniqueness of the human body and its workings.[107] Along these lines, the renowned biologist and Darwin defender Ernst Mayr wrote:

---

[103]Wells, "From Ape to Human: The Ultimate Icon," in *Icons of Evolution*.

[104]This was especially the case in the spring of 2009 when the "Ida" fossil was heralded as a great discovery. In fact, it lent no real evidence to Darwinism. See Casey Luskin, "What 'Ida' Give for a Missing Link," *Washington Examiner*, June 8, 2009, <http://washingtonexaminer.com/op-eds/2009/06/what-ida-give-missing-link>; Kate Wong, "Weak Link: Fossil Darwinius Has Its 15 Minutes: Skepticism about a fossil cast as a missing link in human ancestry," *Scientific American*, August 2009, <www.scientificamerican.com/article.cfm?id=weak-link-fossil-darwinius>.

[105]Marchel-Paul Schutzenberger, "The Miracles of Darwinism," in *Uncommon Dissent: Intellectuals Who Find Darwinism Unconvincing*, ed. William Dembski (Wilmington, Del.: ISI Books, 2004), p. 49.

[106]Ibid.

[107]Many argue the 98 percent similarity between human and chimpanzee DNA makes for strong evidence for common ancestry. However, the gaps between species in the fossil record remains, and the genetic similarity does not establish ancestry. More simply, it is the way the biological pieces are put together that makes the difference. On this see Dembski and Wells, *Design of Life*, pp. 6-8.

The earliest fossils of Homo, Homo rudolfensis, and Homo erectus are separated from australopithecus by a large, unbridged gap. How can we explain this seeming saltation? Not having any fossils that can serve as missing links, we have to fall back on the time-honored method of historical science, the construction of a historical narrative.[108]

Homology: Darwinian or designed? *Homology* means that similar structures can perform different functions in different organisms. Darwinists insist that the similarities in body structure between different species of life seal the deal for Darwinism, since it clearly indicates a common developmental lineage. The pattern of bones in a porpoise's flipper is similar to that of a bat's wing, although each is used for a very different function.[109] Wells notes that, along with the tree of life, homology "is probably the most common icon of evolution in the biology textbook."[110] Darwin viewed homology as significant evidence for macroevolution, and it is regarded as such by many today.

Nevertheless, all is not well with homology. First, the concept is often *defined* as similarity due to common descent. That is, homology indicates the ways various organisms evolved in different ways from a common ancestor. But if homology is defined as Darwinian evolution, the question of its truth is begged and no evidence is required.[111] While Darwin took homology as *evidence* of common descent, later Darwinists, such as Ernst Mayr, *assume* common descent as independently established by data outside of homology, and so homology becomes the result of that assumption.[112] Wells takes this to be circular reasoning: "Common ancestry demonstrates homology which demonstrates common ancestry."[113] If so, it is fallacious.

But Darwinists who do not beg the question about homology look for a biological basis for homology. They hope for an embryonic or genetic justification for homology—something that explains the different function but similar structure in terms of common descent. However, both ap-

---

[108]Ernst Mayr, *What Makes Biology Unique? Considerations on the Autonomy of a Scientific Discipline* (New York: Cambridge University Press, 2004), p. 198.
[109]Wells, *Icons of Evolution*, p. 59.
[110]Ibid., p. 61.
[111]Ibid., p. 62.
[112]Ibid.
[113]Ibid., p. 63.

proaches are problematic. As Denton points out, various organs and structures taken to be homologous "cannot be traced back to homologous cells or regions in the earliest stages of embryogenesis. In other words, homologous structures are arrived at by different routes."[114] Denton claims that while Darwin defined homology as that "relationship between parts which results from their development from corresponding embryonic parts," this does not answer to the facts of embryology as they came to be known through later scientific discovery.[115]

Another argument for homology is speculative and does not rely on empirical factors. It is a kind of fact-free reasoning. Darwinists claim that an intelligent Designer would never use similar structures in different organisms to accomplish different tasks (homology). Darwin says,

> What can be more curious, than that the hand of a man, formed for grasping, that of a mole for digging, the leg of the horse, the paddle of the porpoise, and the wing of the bat, should all be constructed on the same pattern, and should include the same bones, in the same relative positions?[116]

Therefore, according to Darwin, the unguided process of natural selection is the better explanation for homology than design.

This logic is flawed. Why should a Designer employ entirely different structures for different purposes when similar structures accomplish different goals quite well? Can the Darwinist read the mind of God? What exactly is the moral or logical principle that would forbid a Designer from doing this? Moreover, many human designers employ similar structures for divergent purposes. If this is the case for human designers, why could it not be the case for a nonhuman designer of the structures of living things? Or perhaps God likes to economize on structures and maximize on functions. In any case, this homology argument against design fails, given its unjustified assumptions concerning purported divine action.

Vestigial organs and systems. Vestigial organs do not quite have iconic status in Darwin lore, but they are often cited as evidence for Darwinism.

---

[114]Denton, *Evolution*, p. 146.
[115]Ibid., p. 149; see pp. 145-49 for the full argument.
[116]Darwin, *Origin of Species*, p. 434, <http://darwin-online.org.uk/content/frameset?viewtype=side&itemID=F373&pageseq=452>.

Supposedly the human body contains organs or structural remnants inherited from our animal predecessors that now serve no purpose. *The Structure of Man* (1895) by Ernst Wiedersheim listed eighty-six vestigial organs, but recent research has brought this into question.[117] The term *vestigial* is often used to cloak ignorance. The human coccyx (the tailbone) was viewed as a remnant of a tail that served no purpose. Yet a recent edition of *Gray's Anatomy* reveals that the coccyx is a crucial "point of contact with muscles that attach to the pelvic floor." The human appendix has also been shown to be a "functioning component of the immune system."[118] Many allegedly vestigial organs have been defrocked as such. The pineal gland, once thought to be a degenerate eye serving no function, is an endocrine gland with important functions.[119] The thymus and thyroid glands were formerly regarded by Darwinists as vestigial. It is now clear that the thymus gland helps in early infancy to develop the immune system and the thyroid is an endocrine gland that secretes two important hormones.[120] Those organs still on the vestigial list may yet come off the bench and get back into the game.[121]

This is also true for the so-called junk DNA, or aspects of DNA that seem to some to be vestigial because they contain no genetic information and so have no present purpose. However, supposedly vestigial and nonfunctional DNA serves very important purposes in the regulation of gene activity.[122] But Darwinists, including Francis Crick, originally believed

---

[117]Milton, *Shattering the Myths of Darwinism*, p. 187.
[118]Dembski and Wells, *Design of Life*, p. 132. See also "Evolution of the Human Appendix: A Biological Remnant No More," *Science Daily*, August 21, 2009 <www.sciencedaily.com/releases/2009/08/090820175901.htm>.
[119]Milton, *Shattering the Myths of Darwinism*, p. 187.
[120]Ibid., p. 188.
[121]One book claims that there are demonstrably no vestigial organs: Jerry Bergman and George Howe, *Vestigial Organs Are Fully Functional: A History and Evaluation of the Vestigial Organ Origins Concept* (Terre Haute, Ind.: Creation Research Society, 1990); see also, Dembski and Wells, *Design of Life*, pp. 131-36.
[122]See James A. Shapiro and Richard Sternberg, "Why Repetitive DNA Is Essential to Genome Function," *Biological Review* 80 (2005): 227-50; Richard Sternberg, "On the Roles of Repetitive DNA Elements in the Context of a Unified Genomic-Epigenetic System," *Annals of the New York Academy of Sciences* 981 (2002): 154-88; Richard Sternberg and James A. Shapiro, "How Repeated Retroelements Format Genome Function," *Cytogenetic and Genome Research* 110 (2005): 108-16. On the role of "junk DNA" in plants especially, see Jian Feng et al., "Coding DNA Repeated Throughout Intergenic Regions of the Arabidopsis Thaliana Genome: Evolutionary Footprints of RNA Silencing," *Molecular BioSystems* 5 (2009): 1679-87. On the uses of "junk DNA" see Stephen Meyer, *The Signature in the Cell* (San Francisco: HarperOne, 2009), pp. 125, 257, 367, 406-7, 454-55, 461, 464.

that this junk DNA had no current purpose, since they assumed that life was randomly cobbled together and thus filled with nonfunctional remnants of previous organisms. Richard Dawkins goads "the creationists" by citing junk DNA and asking them why a Designer would produce it. "Once again, creationists might spend some earnest time speculating on why the Creator should bother to litter genomes with untranslated pseudogenes and junk tandem repeat DNA."[123] But Dawkins had it wrong.

However, a few organs are vestigial, such as the "eyes" of some salamanders and fish. These animals inhabit totally dark regions. But this hardly proves Darwinian macroevolution. All it shows is that some of the ancestors of these creatures possessed a functioning organ that present-day species members have lost. Losing a function is not the same as evolving entirely new functions (or new species from previous species). It rather indicates a degenerative form of evolution. "It offers no insight into any mechanisms of evolution that might be responsible for creative innovations."[124]

Dissent on Darwin: An opening for design. The topic is vast, and our pages are limited. Nevertheless, I have argued that the Bible declares that our world is designed by a supernatural Mind whose imprint is scientifically observable. While we need not necessarily defend a "young earth" or six literal days of creation, the Bible does commit us to claims about God's hand in the creation of the major groupings (kinds) of life. Darwinism, on the other hand, presents a world alone and unguided by God. As such, it is not a wise option for Christians who want to stay true to biblical revelation and to good science. Darwinism itself runs more on evidential fumes and a commitment to philosophical materialism than it does on hard empirical evidence or good arguments. The "icons of evolution" are better taken as idols that hinder a sober investigation of biology. But simply criticizing Darwinism, while necessary, is not enough. It should not only be questioned and refuted, but replaced by another model.[125] Chapter fourteen marshals empirical evidence for design in nature from molecular machines and the information inherent in DNA.

[123]Richard Dawkins, "The 'Information Challenge,'" in *Intelligent Design Creationism* (Boston: MIT Press, 2001), p. 626.
[124]Dembski and Wells, *Design of Life*, p. 133.
[125]William Dembski, introduction to Neil Broom, *How Blind the Watchmaker?* (Downers Grove, Ill.: InterVarsity Press, 2002).

14

Evidence for Intelligent Design

DARWINISM, BOTH OLD AND NEW, FAILS to explain the development of major forms of life according to naturalism. Despite its social standing as the dominant model for institutional science, the "emperor has no clothes." Darwinism is the product of the psychologically and institutionally embedded presupposition of philosophical materialism. This, along with the attendant fear of the supernatural invading and infecting science, is what keeps the paradigm in power.[1]

INTELLIGENT DESIGN AS A SCIENTIFIC ALTERNATIVE TO DARWINISM

But if the well-coiffed emperor is propped up more by ideology than scientific demonstration, is there a genuine scientific alternative available to explain the origin, nature and development of life on the planet? The intelligent design (ID) movement claims that there is. Further, does ID have any significant apologetic implications for the Christian worldview? This chapter will investigate the intelligent design approach and will conclude by exploring the implications it has for Christian apologetics.

Darwinists often brush aside criticisms by claiming that even if their theory betrays some weaknesses (which, of course, will be worked out in time) it wins by default, since no other theory has replaced it. Thus, in order to discredit Darwinism (1) Darwinism must be brought into question by the evidence, and (2) another scientific model must be put in its place. The second condition is not necessary to bring Darwinism into

---

[1]For an explanation of how "plausibility structures" work with regard to the sociology of knowledge, see Peter Berger, *A Rumor of Angels* (New York: Anchor Books, 1969), pp. 34-38.

question, however, because this condition biases the case for Darwinism unfairly. In a court of law an attorney must merely exonerate his client in order for the client to be cleared of a crime. The attorney does not, in addition, need to find the real culprit. If a theory has sufficient problems (i.e., it cannot explain what it must explain), it should lose credibility. For example, noted philosopher Thomas Nagel avers that Darwinism cannot explain the achievements of human rationality, which he sees as an "enormous excess mental capacity, not explainable by natural selection."[2] Instead of assuming that natural selection can explain everything by appealing to unlikely explanations, Nagel rejects Darwinism on the basis of its inability to explain human mental capacity. He does so even though he does not offer an alternative theory.[3]

Nevertheless, large-scale and well-entrenched scientific theories such as Darwinism cast a wide net and don't release their long-held captives readily. In 1978, after mounting a considerable scientific case against Darwinism, Arthur Koestler lamented that Darwinism still commanded broad allegiance simply because there was no replacement in sight.[4] So the case against Darwinism is strengthened considerably when an alternative better explains the evidence. That is exactly what ID seeks to accomplish.

The salient feature of Darwinism—what Daniel Dennett calls a "universal acid"—is that life is shorn of *design*.[5] All intelligence has evolved from unintelligent material states without any antecedent plan. In Dennett's terms, there are no "sky hooks"—nothing above the earth that reaches down to produce or direct life. Instead, we have only earthbound cranes—unguided natural forces that produce life.[6] Richard Dawkins admits that biology "is the study of living things that give appearance of having been designed for a purpose,"[7] although he thinks they aren't. Francis Crick, codiscoverer of the double-helix structure of DNA, writes,

---

[2]Thomas Nagel, *The View from Nowhere* (New York: Oxford University Press, 1986), p. 80.

[3]Ibid., p. 81. Nagel says he does not offer "creationism" as an alternative. I suggest that intelligent design is the preferred alternative to a Darwinian understanding of biology; chap. 17 claims that theism best explains human rationality.

[4]Arthur Koestler, *Janus: A Summing Up* (New York: Vintage Books, 1978), p. 165.

[5]Daniel Dennett, "Universal Acid," in *Darwin's Dangerous Idea: Evolution and the Meanings of Life* (New York: Simon & Schuster, 1996).

[6]Ibid., pp. 73-80.

[7]Richard Dawkins, *The Blind Watchmaker* (New York: W. W. Norton, 1986), p. 1.

"Biologists must constantly keep in mind that what they see was not designed, but rather evolved."[8]

Is there solid empirical evidence for the design of living things? The Bible reveals that there is evidence for God's work in nature (Psalm 19:1-6; Romans 1:18-21). But does nature disclose design that science can detect? To answer this, we must first consider the nature of scientific explanation itself.

ORIGIN SCIENCE AND OPERATION SCIENCE

The older creationist literature often claimed that both creationism and Darwinism were not matters of science proper because they address what cannot be empirically tested in a laboratory—the origin of species. Because this topic cannot be settled by performing repeatable experiments, it is not truly scientific.[9] Therefore, both creationism and Darwinism are left to the realm of faith—faith in God or faith in godless nature. This approach, while highlighting the fact that Darwinism is not directly testable, is ill-advised for two main reasons.

First, science has long addressed issues that cannot be settled in the laboratory. Any time science treats a singularity—such as the creation of the universe, the origin of life and the origin of species—it considers events beyond direct experimental reach. Nevertheless, presently available evidence bears on these past singularities, as I noted in chapter eleven concerning the several lines of evidence confirming big bang cosmology. As we will see, the nature of molecular machines and the informational qualities in the living cell give strong evidence for design, even though we can neither observe the original formation of these entities nor create new ones. This kind of investigation is not a matter of blind faith but of principled inference from objective evidence. It is a *forensic* or historic discipline.

Norman Geisler and Kerby Anderson's distinction between *origin science* and *operation science* is helpful. Origin science addresses singularities and employs the forensic reasoning that is used by archaeologists and criminal investigators, who must explain past events in terms of present

---

[8]Francis Crick, *What Mad Pursuit* (New York: Basic Books, 1990), p. 139.
[9]See John Ankerberg and John Weldon, *Darwin's Leap of Faith* (Eugene, Ore.: Harvest House, 1998), pp. 248-49.

evidence. Intelligent design claims that with respect to singularities such as the origin of life, design is a better explanation than chance or natural law. On the other hand, operation science concerns the ongoing processes of nature, such as chemical reactions or embryology.[10] These processes are repeatable and observable; they are not singularities. There is a distinction between science as it treats matters of origins/singularities and science as it treats repeatable and directly testable aspects of nature. Both are scientific, but each uses somewhat different methods of investigation. In his investigation of the origin of genetic information, Stephen Meyer goes to great lengths to show that much of science concerns historical questions, the investigation of unique events that have testable effects in the present.[11]

Intelligent design proponents do not claim that a Designer contravenes the ongoing processes of nature in such a way as to make the study of regularities impossible, as theistic evolutionist Kenneth Miller has charged.[12] Rather, ID argues that key features of the regularly functioning natural world are best explained by the influence of design at some stage in the distant past.

A second reason that we should employ scientific evidence concerning origins is that since Christian theism makes objective claims about the visibility of design in nature, there should be some evidence available to back up these claims. The ID movement claims not only that Darwinism fails as a scientific theory to explain the biosphere in its totality, but that design is scientifically ascertainable in nature. But before giving the argument from ID to support this conclusion, we need to take up a handful of charges against ID, which, if cogent, would disqualify it in principle.

FIVE OBJECTIONS TO INTELLIGENT DESIGN

First, opponents of ID often use a "heads I win; tails you lose" strategy that has two prongs. The first states that ID is not science but merely masked religion. Therefore, it should be dismissed as unscientific, since religion has no bearing on scientific issues. But the second appeals to *sci-*

---

[10]See Norman Geisler and Kerby Anderson, *Origin Science* (Grand Rapids: Baker, 1987).

[11]See Stephen Meyer, *The Signature in the Cell* (San Francisco: HarperOne, 2009), pp. 166-70; 324-28; 343-44; 381-83; 408-10.

[12]See Phillip Johnson, *The Wedge of Truth* (Downers Grove, Ill.: InterVarsity Press, 2000), pp. 126-35.

entific evidence against ID. When both prongs are combined, they puncture each other. If ID is a religious belief and not scientific, then *no* scientific arguments are available for it—or against it. One cannot have it both ways.[13]

A second strategy is to define ID out of existence by appealing to a purely naturalistic understanding of science. Some claim that any explanation that appeals to a Designer is illegitimate for science. When it comes to living things, intelligent causes are ruled out in principle and a priori. This construal of science is deeply biased philosophically toward materialism, as mentioned in chapter thirteen's discussion of Darwinism. The common definition of science today is:

> S1: Science pursues materialistic explanations for natural phenomena through empirical observation and rational theorizing.[14]

This definition excludes any nonnatural explanations as unscientific in principle. It thus excludes intelligence as having causal primacy in any natural system. I propose a more neutral and fair definition of science:

> S2: Science pursues the best explanation for natural phenomena through empirical observation and rational theorizing.

Under this definition, the best explanation for some natural event or process may include intelligent causes. This debate over the definition of science is not a matter of philosophy of religion or of science proper; rather, it falls into the domain of the philosophy of science.[15]

A common justification for the materialistic understanding of science—when one is given at all—is that the introduction of intelligent causes is "a science stopper." When dealing with a hard scientific issue, people would simply say "God did it" and quit. Thereby, scientific explanations are eliminated and previous scientific achievements are dispar-

[13]Michael Behe, "Answering Scientific Criticism of Intelligent Design," in *Science and Evidence for Design in the Universe: The Proceedings of the Wethersfield Institute*, ed. Michael J. Behe, William A. Dembski and Stephen C. Meyer (San Francisco: Ignatius Press, 1999), pp. 144-45.

[14]This kind of understanding is given by Eugenie Scott, an avid opponent of ID. See Meyer's discussion in *Signature in the Cell*, pp. 146-47.

[15]I owe this insight to Anthony Lombardo. The question of the demarcation between science and other intellectual inquiries such as philosophy is a vexed one. Many leading thinkers believe that there is no one thing about scientific pursuits that definitely marks it off from other lines of inquiry (see Meyer, *Signature in the Cell*, pp. 400-401, 419, 430-31). Nevertheless, my proposed understanding seems to fit as a working and rough definition.

aged. In Richard Lewontin's words, "If we let a divine foot in the door," anything can happen—and science is doomed.[16]

The "science-stopper" argument fails for at least four reasons. First, Western science, since the Scientific Revolution and right up until Darwin, proceeded very well without methodological or philosophical materialism. Sir Isaac Newton, for example, was a theist who explained his laws of physics according to design. The metaphysic of Western culture was generally theistic, not naturalistic.[17] Second, ID is not advocating the direct intervention of intelligent causes in the orderly operations of chemistry or biology or physics (that is, in the domain of "operation science"). For example, chapter twelve contended that the fine-tuning of a plethora of factors in the universe makes life possible and reveals a Mind at work. However, no direct appeal was made to this Mind to account for the *ongoing* operations of nature. Rather, Mind was offered as the best explanation for the original constitution of our finely tuned universe. Therefore science, as it studies natural regularities, is not imperiled by a God who monkeys with regularities. Third, Christian theism affirms a God who insures the rational and regular patterns of nature, not randomness based on divine caprice.[18] Fourth, the search for intelligent causes—or the design inference—is alive and well in many areas of science outside of biology, such as archaeology, cryptography and the search for extraterrestrial intelligence (SETI).[19] Intelligent design extends this design inference into biology.

A third objection to ID made by Darwinists is that appealing to intelligent causes in biology is not testable. Intelligent design cannot make predictions—a necessary feature of genuine science.[20] But if we are concerned with origin science—the historical dimension of scientific questions—"predictions" are not primarily what we are after. Accounting for the constitution of the bacterial flagellum or the origin of life on earth is not about predicting

---

[16]Richard Lewontin, "Billions and Billions of Demons," *New York Review of Books*, January 9, 1997, p. 31.

[17]See the discussion of the Christian contribution to early science in chap. 5.

[18]God may intervene in history through miracles when God sees fit, but this does not jeopardize the intelligibility of any natural laws (see chaps. 19 and 22, which discuss miracles).

[19]William Dembski, "The Design Inference," in *The Design Revolution* (Downers Grove, Ill.: InterVarsity Press, 2004); and William Dembski, introduction to *The Design Inference* (New York: Cambridge University Press, 1998).

[20]See Niles Eldredge, *The Monkey Business* (New York: Washington Square Books, 1982), p. 39.

what will happen in the future; it is about *explaining* past events *historically* according to the best evidence and reasoning available.[21]

Nevertheless, ID does make certain testable empirical claims and predictions, and seeks out certain kinds of evidence. For example, ID proponents who do not hold to common ancestry claim that the fossil record will not support Darwinian gradualism. This, then, suggests that the basic kinds of life are designed by God with essential natures not subject to indefinite change.[22] It also predicts that human beings cannot be adequately explained on the basis of the propensities and behaviors of "lower" animals, since humans bear God's image (an objective design plan).[23] One who holds that life is designed will also question the authenticity of many so-called vestigial organs.[24] William Dembski predicted in 1998 that more DNA thought to be junk would be shown to be functional. He was correct.[25]

Fourth, some Darwinists disparage ID by claiming that anyone who wants to admit design into biology must base this view on religious authorities, which are not legitimate in science. This is empirically false. Thomas Nagel, David Berlinski and others who have questioned Darwinism or considered the possibility of design appeal to no religious authority to advance their critique.[26] Further, the ID movement in toto (which includes those of other religions and those of no religious belief) does not invoke Scripture or other religious authorities to challenge Darwinism. Intelligent design rather argues according to scientific evidence and models of reason now employed in the scientific community. That religious Scriptures speak of design in nature does not rule out the

---

[21]See Meyer, *Signature in the Cell*, pp. 166-70; 324-28; 343-44; 381-83; 408-10.

[22]Some ID theorists, such as Michael Behe, affirm common descent and would not support this claim, but I do not hold to common descent (see chap. 13), and so I do make this claim.

[23]This is a direct challenge to evolutionary psychology, as advocated by Steven Pinker and others.

[24]See the final section of chap. 13.

[25]William Dembski, "Science and Design," *First Things*, March 1998, pp. 21-27. Meyer gives several detailed predictions on the basis of ID in *The Signature in the Cell*, "Some Predictions of Intelligent Design," app. A. See also William Dembski, "Testability," in *The Design Revolution;* Hugh Ross, *Creation as Science* (Colorado Springs: NavPress, 2006), pp. 227-53. Ross compares predictions for the Reason to Believe Model (essentially an old-earth creation, ID perspective) with naturalism, six-day creationism and theistic evolution.

[26]Thomas Nagle, "Public Education and Intelligent Design," *Philosophy and Public Affairs* 36, no. 2 (2008); David Berlinski, *The Devil's Delusion: Atheism and Its Scientific Pretensions* (New York: Crown Forum, 2008). I mentioned other nonreligious critics of Darwinism at the beginning of chap. 13.

possibility of discovering design in nature *independently* of what these Scriptures affirm.

Moreover, scientists qua scientists are not exempted from unfair biases and prejudices. Although scientists claim to follow the evidence wherever it leads, they are just as susceptible to dogmatism, propaganda, egotism and authoritarianism as any religious believer supporting a religious cause. (And, of course, many scientists are religious believers themselves.) This is not to poison the well against the scientific establishment but simply to level the playing field. Holding religious beliefs about the origin and nature of life on earth does not disqualify someone from giving legitimate scientific arguments for these beliefs, which depend on no uniquely religious assumptions. For example, F. A. Kekule, the scientist who was instrumental in discovering the structure of the benzene molecule, reported that in 1865 he came up with the ring structure of benzene after having a dream of a self-devouring snake. However, he did not advance his claim on that basis by trying to get various scientists to have a similar vision. Rather, he argued the case scientifically and was vindicated.[27] As Moreland says, "It makes no difference whether a scientific theory comes from a dream, the Bible or bathroom graffiti. The issue is whether independent scientific reasons are given for it."[28]

Fifth, the preponderance of biologists believe that Darwinism already won the battle long ago, so ID is a moot point. This partially accounts for the condescending and irritated tone of many Darwinist responses to any challenge to its dominance.[29] But this modus operandi is ill-advised. First, scientific criticisms of Darwinism have persisted ever since Darwin published his theory in 1859. Darwinism has never held the unquestioned allegiance of the entire scientific community, as do the theories of heliocentrism and plate tectonics today.[30] Second, even well-established or "successful" scientific theories can be overturned.[31] In just four decades or so, plate tectonics overthrew the cylindrical column theory of mountain

---

[27]See J. P. Moreland, *Christianity and the Nature of Science* (Grand Rapids: Baker, 1989), p. 229.
[28]Ibid.
[29]See Nancy Pearcey, "You Guys Lost!" in *Mere Creation: Science, Faith and Intelligent Design*, ed. William Dembski (Downers Grove, Ill.: InterVarsity Press, 1998).
[30]In chap. 13 I noted that over nine hundred people with doctorates in science have signed a statement questioning Darwinism.
[31]See Moreland, *Christianity and the Nature of Science*, pp. 154-56.

formation. In fact, many widely held and deeply entrenched scientific theories have been shown to be false through developments in observation and theoretical reconstruction. The discerning student of science should therefore remain skeptical and be open to challenges to received orthodoxies—even to Darwinism.

MICHAEL BEHE AND MOLECULAR MACHINES

In *Darwin's Black Box* biochemist Michael Behe troubled the waters of Darwinism.[32] Darwin's "black box" refers to the fact that Darwin and his contemporary scientists knew nothing about the fantastically complicated nature of the cell. They, in fact, thought that the building blocks of life were relatively simple. But the black box has been opened in recent decades through high-powered microscopes, and molecular biology is now a well-established field. Darwinism, however, originated and was developed into neo-Darwinism before these revelations took place. But now, as Behe notes, "for the Darwinian theory of evolution to be true, it has to account for the molecular structure of life"—something Behe believes it cannot do.[33]

The argument for design in biology claims that "the molecular structure of life" cannot be explained on the basis of chance or necessity (natural law). The argument form is essentially the same one I used to argue for cosmic fine-tuning in chapter twelve:

1. Molecular machines evidence specified complexity (i.e., they are contingent, complex and specified).

2. Specified complexity cannot be explained on the basis of chance or necessity, or the combination of chance and necessity.

3. Intelligent agency is a known cause which produces specified complexity.

4. Therefore, the best explanation of the origin of specified complexity in molecular machines is intelligent design.

---

[32]Behe extends the argument with respect to other aspects of biology, particularly the limits of change possible through unguided genetic mutation, in *The Edge of Evolution* (New York: Free Press, 2007), but I will not consider these arguments here.
[33]Michael Behe, *Darwin's Black Box* (New York: Free Press, 1996), p. 25.

Behe's essential argument is that certain molecular machines could not have been brought about through undirected, gradualist Darwinian mechanisms. This is because their component parts are required to function at once and in conjunction with one another if they are to confer the function necessary for survival. Behe calls this "irreducible complexity."

> By *irreducibly complex* I mean a single system composed of several well-matched, interacting parts that contribute to the basic function, wherein the removal of any one of the parts causes the system to effectively cease functioning. An irreducibly complex system cannot be produced directly (that is, by continuously improving the initial function, which continues to work by the same mechanism) by slight, successive modifications of a precursor system, because any precursor to an irreducibly complex system that is missing a part is by definition nonfunctional. An irreducibly complex biological system, if there is such a thing, would be a powerful challenge to Darwinian evolution.[34]

Irreducible complexity can be contrasted with "cumulative complexity." The latter describes a system in which complexity is built up piece by piece, as in the founding and growth of a city. Thus any number of buildings and roads could be demolished without the city ceasing to be a city. Darwinian mechanisms might account for this kind of complexity in organisms, since it is built up gradually through slight modifications. But irreducible complexity is another animal altogether. Behe notes: "Since natural selection can only choose systems that are already working, then if a biological system cannot be produced gradually it would have to arise as an integral unity, in one fell swoop, for natural selection to have anything to act on."[35]

Behe aptly illustrates the concept of irreducible complexity with an everyday item far less complicated than molecular machines.

> In order to catch a mouse, a mousetrap needs a platform, spring, hammer, holding bar, and catch. Now, suppose you wanted to make a mousetrap. In your garage you might have a piece of wood from an old Popsicle stick (for the platform), a spring from an old wind-up clock, a piece of metal (for the hammer) in the form of a crowbar, a darning needle for the holding bar, and a bottle cap that you fancy to use as a catch. But these pieces, even though they have some vague similarity to the pieces of a working mousetrap, in

---

[34]Ibid., p. 39.
[35]Ibid.

fact are not matched to each other and couldn't form a functioning mouse-trap without extensive modification. All the while the modification was going on, they would be unable to work as a mousetrap. The fact that they were used in other roles (as a crowbar, in a clock, etc.) does not help them to be part of a mousetrap. As a matter of fact, their previous functions make them ill-suited for virtually any new role as part of a complex system.[36]

Thus the pieces of the mousetrap are nonfunctional as mousetrap parts unless all the pieces are put in their proper place. Just a few pieces provide no mousetrap function. Behe gives several examples of molecular machines he takes to be irreducibly complex, including the blood clotting cascade, the cilium and the bacterial flagellum. He claims that "examples of irreducible complexity can be found on virtually every page of a biochemistry textbook."[37] We will briefly consider only the bacterial flagellum.

Behe noted in 1996 that the available scientific literature on this motor—all written by Darwinists—fails even to attempt to explain how this could be formed in a gradualist manner. It is just assumed. The major journals that address molecular evolution—*Journal of Molecular Evolution, Proceedings of the National Academy of Science, Nature, Science, Journal of Molecular Biology*—contain no papers "that discuss the detailed models for intermediaries in the development of complex biochemical structures."[38] But Behe takes the assumption to be a presumption and proposes an alternative. These systems were designed ahead of time such that each part was intended to work with each other part to produce the end result. This notion of planning the relationship of parts to a whole to perform a function—so common in human experience—is utterly antithetical to Darwinism, which rejects any hint of antecedent intention.

The flagellum has become the poster child of the ID movement and a subject of great debate. Behe summarizes its workings:

> The flagellum is quite literally an outboard motor that some bacteria use to swim. It is a rotary device that, like a motorboat, turns a propeller to push against liquid, moving the bacterium forward in the process. It consists of a number of parts, including a long tail that acts as a propeller, the hook re-

[36]Ibid., p. 66.
[37]Michael Behe, "Design in the Details: The Origins of Biomolecular Machines," in *Darwinism, Design, and Public Education*, ed. John Angus Campbell and Stephen C. Meyer (East Lansing: Michigan State University Press, 2003), p. 298.
[38]Behe, "Design in the Details," pp. 298-99.

gion, which attaches the propeller to the drive shaft, the motor, which uses a flow of acid from the outside of the bacterium to the inside to power the turning, a stator, which keeps the structure stationary in the plane of the membrane while the propeller turns, and bushing material to allow the drive shaft to pike up through the bacterial membrane. In the absence of the hook, or the motor, or the propeller, or the drive shaft or most of the forty different types of proteins that genetic studies have shown to be necessary for the activity or construction of the flagellum, one does not get a flagellum that spins half as fast as it used to, or a quarter as fast. Either the flagellum does not work, or it does not even get constructed at all. Like the mousetrap, the flagellum is irreducibly complex.[39]

The flagellum's irreducible complexity is an example of Dembski's concept of specified complexity (see chap. 12). The flagellum is *contingent:* its constitution is not explicable on the basis of any natural law; it is amazingly *complex;* and it is *specified* in its functions. It is not merely improbable. The complexity fits a pattern that is independent of the components of the actual living system. That is, the key functions of the flagellum are found elsewhere, as in outboard motors. The complex functionality of the flagellum is a case of specified complexity, which is sufficient evidence for design.[40]

Darwin set up a possible refutation of his theory of gradual and undirected evolution: *"If it could be demonstrated that any complex organ existed, which could not possibly have been formed by numerous, successive, slight modifications, my theory would absolutely break down. But I can find out no such case."*[41]

---

[39]Michael Behe, "Answering Scientific Criticism," in *Science and Evidence for Design in the Universe*, ed. Michael Behe, William A. Dembski and Stephen C. Meyer (San Francisco: Ignatius Press, 1999), pp. 134-35. Behe gives a more in-depth description in *Darwin's Black Box*, pp. 70-73. To get a better sense of the machine's integrated complexity, consult one of the drawings in *Darwin's Black Box*, or, better yet, watch the video presentation of the flagellum contained in two DVDs: *Unlocking the Mystery of Life's Origins* (Illustra Media, 2002) or *A Case for a Creator* (Illustra Media, 2006).

[40]See William Dembski's explanation in *Intelligent Design: The Bridge Between Science and Theology* (Downers Grove, Ill.: InterVarsity Press, 1999), p. 149.

[41]Charles Darwin, *The Origin of Species*, chap. 6 (London: Langham, 1859), p. 189. Facsimile available at "The Complete Works of Charles Darwin Online," *Darwin Online*, <http://darwin-online.org.uk/content/frameset?viewtype=side&itemID=F373&pageseq=207>, emphasis added. I have chosen to cite the first of the five editions because later works incorporate some aspects of Lamarkianism, which are no longer favored by contemporary Darwinists. I owe this insight to William Dembski.

On the one hand, Darwin seems to be offering a possible means of falsifying his theory. If read this way, he is throwing down the gauntlet for possible falsification. That is, "If you can show that X is true, my theory is false." If read in this way, Behe's biochemical challenge (about which Darwin knew nothing) is pertinent and powerful, because Behe gives an impressive account of how irreducible structures could not—given the evidence we now have—be formed by "numerous, successive, slight modifications." With the biochemical black box no longer closed, scientists may look inside and find positive evidence for irreducible complexity. As Behe emphasizes, "We are not inferring design from what we do not know but from what we do know. We are not inferring design to account for some black box but to account for an open box."[42] Therefore, this is not an argument from ignorance or an appeal to the "God of the gaps." However, Behe leaves open the possibility that some Darwinian explanation might be forthcoming (see below).

On the other hand, many Darwinists have read Darwin's admission in such as way as to insulate Darwinism from Behe's criticism—or from anyone else's. This response trades on begging the question and writing a postdated check. Darwinists, such as Dawkins, respond to Behe by calling him "lazy" or by claiming that he has given up on genuine science by invoking design to account for irreducible complexity.[43] They claim that some Darwinian route from biological simplicity to extreme complexity *must* be out there, since they must deny the existence of genuine irreducible complexity. Nevertheless this Darwinian response merely assumes a naturalistic answer to the puzzle instead of advancing a credible alternative. The fact that some Darwinian biochemical narrative might account for the bacterial flagellum is no evidence that there is such a biochemical narrative, since possibility is not the same as credibility.

Behe can imagine ways of falsifying his own theory.

In fact, intelligent design is open to direct experimental rebuttal. Here is a thought experiment that makes the point clear. In *Darwin's Black Box* I claimed that the bacterial flagellum was irreducibly complex and so required deliberate intelligent design. The flip side of this claim is that the

---

[42]Behe, "Design in the Details," p. 301.
[43]See the account in James W. Sire, *Naming the Elephant: Worldview as Concept* (Downers Grove, Ill. InterVarsity Press, 2004), pp. 113-14.

flagellum can't be produced by natural selection acting on random mutation, or any other unintelligent process. To falsify such a claim, a scientist
could go into the laboratory, place a bacterial species lacking a flagellum
under some selective pressure (for mobility, say), grow it for ten thousand
generations, and see if a flagellum—or any equally complex system—was
produced. If that happened, my claims would be neatly disproven.[44]

However, Behe wonders if his Darwinian critics would accept any evidence for design as a falsification of their undirected, gradualist model.
The claim of the ID theorist is that no unintelligent process could produce
a system such as the flagellum. The claim of the Darwinist is that some
unintelligent process could produce the flagellum, and every other irreducibly complex living system. But, as Behe points out:

> To falsify the first claim [ID] one need only show that at least one unintel-
> ligent process could produce the system. To falsify the second claim [Dar-
> winism], one would have to show the system could not have been produced
> by any of a potentially infinite number of possible unintelligent processes,
> which is effectively impossible to do.[45]

This Darwinian immunity from disproof is hardly the mark of a mature scientific philosophy or methodology. Franklin Harold typifies this
mentality in *The Way of the Cell*. He writes, "We should reject, as a matter
of principle, the substitution of intelligent design for the dialogue of chance
and necessity; but we must concede that there are presently no detailed
Darwinian accounts of the evolution of any biochemical system, only a
variety of wishful speculations."[46] This is a kind of conceptual gerryman-
dering that pushes any design inference outside the bounds of acceptable
science. The place of falsification in the merits of a scientific theory is a
matter of debate in the philosophy of science, and it may not be that every
good philosophical theory must be falsifiable. Nevertheless, a heavily empirical science such as biology should be open to the possibility of counterevidence overturning a well-received theory, as long as that evidence fits

[44]Michael J. Behe, "Reply to My Critics: A Response to Reviews of Darwin's Black Box: The
Biochemical Challenge to Evolution," *Biology and Philosophy* 16 (2001): 697.
[45]Michael J. Behe, "Philosophical Objections to Intelligent Design: Response to My Critics,"
Discovery Institute, July 31, 2000, <www.discovery.org/a/445>. Behe makes a similar point in
"Reply to My Critics," p. 698.
[46]Franklin Harold, *The Way of the Cell: Molecules, Organism, and the Order of Life* (New York:
Oxford University Press, 2002), p. 205.

into a plausible alternative model. This is exactly what ID theory and its supporting counterexamples (such as the flagellum) is providing—if the Darwinists had but eyes to see and ears to hear.

Another objection to Behe is made by Kenneth Miller, who says that individual parts of irreducible structures may be used profitably for other things. This is sometimes called the cooption theory. One part of the flagellum—a cellular pump—is found in an organism outside of the flagellum. Therefore, the flagellum is not irreducibly complex. Its complexity is rather redundant, since one of its parts is used elsewhere. But this objection presents a straw man fallacy. Behe never claimed that each part of an irreducibly complex system must have no other function elsewhere in the living world. Certainly one part of a mousetrap could be used as a blunt object outside of a mousetrap.[47] Moreover, the cellular pump that Miller cites is likely another case of irreducible complexity in itself.[48]

Since ID critics cannot now argue that the flagellum by itself could have *directly* evolved its present irreducibly complex functions (given that there is no incremental pathway that will work), they must posit some *indirect* pathway from the simple to the complex that involves incorporating other organisms. However, no evidence for indirect pathways is forthcoming. Darwinian proposals must invoke the possible as opposed to the credible, since they eliminate every option but naturalistic explanations.[49] In *No Free Lunch*, Dembski has calculated the odds of the bacterial flagellum arising by an undirected, merely natural process. While the analysis is technical, Dembski calculates that the odds of the flagellum's many component parts assembling by luck are insurmountable; that is, the chance of this happening is virtually impossible, since the odds fall below the "universal probability bound."[50]

---

[47]See Michael J. Behe, "Irreducible Complexity Is an Obstacle to Darwinism Even If Parts of a System Have Other Functions: A Response to Sharon Begley's *Wall Street Journal* Column," Discovery Institute, February 18, 2004, <www.discovery.org/a/1831>.

[48]Stephen C. Meyer, "Verdict on the Bacterial Flagellum Premature: A Response to Begley's 'Evolution Critics Come Under Fire . . .' in the *Wall Street Journal*," Discovery Institute, February 19, 2004, <www.discovery.org/a/1843>. For responses to two other scientific criticisms of irreducible complexity, see Michael Behe, "Answering Scientific Criticisms of Intelligent Design," in *Science and Evidence for Design in the Universe* (San Francisco: Ignatius Press, 1999), pp. 133-49.

[49]Dembski, *Design Revolution*, pp. 294-95.

[50]William Dembski, "The Emergence of Irreducible Complex Systems," in *No Free Lunch* (New York: Free Press, 2002).

Many are outraged because Behe is breaking a rule promulgated by modern science. That rule is methodological naturalism: only undirected natural causes may explain anything in nature. Christian de Duve made it explicit in his 1995 book *Vital Dust:* "A warning: All through this book, I have tried to conform to the overriding rule that life be treated as a natural process, its origin, evolution, and manifestations, up to and including the human species, as governed by the same laws as nonliving processes."[51] But this rule, as I have argued here and in chapter thirteen, ends up stifling science by means of an illicit ideological exorcism: all intelligent causes must be banned! However, by using the scientific test of the design filter, we may infer design from empirical observations.

DNA: A LANGUAGE INDICATING DESIGN

The argument for ID does not end with molecular machines but penetrates even deeper into the unique structures of life. The argument given here is another example of the design inference. Schematically, it looks like this:

1. DNA contains genetic information in the form of language.

2. This genetic information is an example of specified complexity (i.e., it is contingent, complex and specified).

3. Specified complexity cannot be explained on the basis of chance or necessity, or the combination of chance and necessity.

4. Intelligent agency is a known cause that produces specified and complex information.

5. Therefore, the best explanation of the origin of specified complexity in DNA is intelligent design.

The genetic assembly instructions necessary for the construction and function of the amazing flagellum (and all other living things) are an in-

---

[51]Christian de Duve, *Vital Dust: Life as a Cosmic Imperative* (New York: Basic Books, 1995), p. xiv. De Duve rejects "creationism" as biblical literalism, not even considering the more sophisticated ID arguments available at the time of his writing, such as Walter L. Bradley, Roger L. Olsen and Charles B. Thaxton, *The Mystery of Life's Origin: Reassessing Current Theories* (New York: Philosophical Library, 1984); and A. E. Wilder-Smith, *The Scientific Alternative to Neo-Darwinian Evolutionary Theory: Information Sources and Structures* (Costa Mesa, Calif.: TWFT Publishers, 1987).

dication of specified complexity: highly improbable structures that fit a specified form (in this case, language). DNA has a tightly wound three-dimensional double helix structure that contains a wealth of closely packed information encoded as carefully sequenced chemicals represented with the letters A, C, T, G. These precisely arranged chemicals in the DNA form the instructions required to assemble the twenty amino acids into proteins through a process called protein synthesis. These proteins, in turn, form molecular machines in the cell, which carry out all the necessary functions within the cell.[52] As Bruce Alberts, a critic of ID, admits in the journal *Cell:*

> The entire cell can be viewed as a factory that contains an elaborate network of interlocking assembly lines, each of which is composed of a set of large protein machines. . . . Why do we call the large protein assemblies that underlie cell function protein *machines?* Precisely because, like machines invented by humans to deal efficiently with the macroscopic world, these protein assemblies contain highly coordinated moving parts.[53]

DNA thus contains the "genetic code" necessary for life and heredity, and has been referred to as "the language of life." The information content of DNA is vast. The A, C, T, G chemicals are arranged like a four-letter alphabet containing directions. Despite the simplicity of the alphabet, the complexity, volume and efficiency of the information conveyed is immense. All "the information needed to specify an organism as complex as a human being weighs less than a few thousand millionths of a gram and fits into less space than the period at the end of this sentence."[54]

Stephen Meyer, in his many articles and his massive and magisterial work *The Signature in the Cell*, has offered a compelling and rigorous case that the information content of DNA and RNA evidences specified complexity that indicates design.[55] Unlike physical structures such as crystals or tornadoes that can be explained without recourse to informa-

---

[52]The RNA is an information-rich molecule as well, the function of which is to bring the DNA message out of the nucleus and into the cell. But for simplicity's sake, I will not describe its role in the cell. See Meyer, *Signature in the Cell*, pp. 197-200.

[53]Bruce Alberts, "The Cell as a Collection of Protein Machines: Preparing the Next Generation of Molecular Biologists," *Cell* 92 (1998): 291-94.

[54]Charles Thaxton and Nancy Pearcey, *The Soul of Science* (Wheaton, Ill.: Crossway, 1994), p. 222.

[55]This significant work is a highly nuanced, thorough and readable account of the information argument, which I can only summarize here, along with other sources.

tion within them, living cells are an essential unit of life, possessing the ability "to store, edit, and transmit information and to use information to regulate their fundamental metabolic processes."[56] The specificity of the sequence of the DNA bears information. "The sequence specificity in the DNA begets sequence specificity in the proteins. Or put differently, the sequence specificity of proteins depends upon a prior specificity—upon information—encoded in DNA."[57] Therefore, the DNA exhibits specified complexity. It is not merely complex—involving many disparate and interlocking parts—but is specified in its complexity because the disparate parts communicate messages necessary for the functionality of organisms.[58]

The information strongly resembles human codes or languages. Just as the letters of the alphabet of a written language may convey a particular message depending on their sequences, so too the sequences of nucleotides or bases in the DNA molecule convey precise biochemical messages that direct protein synthesis within the cell.[59] DNA is not *analogous* to a language; it *is* a language, but not a language created by humans.

A common property of all languages, whether animal, machine, human or biological, "is that defined sets of symbols are used, and that definite agreed-upon rules and meanings are allocated to the single signs of language elements."[60] This is as true of DNA as it is of written or spoken English. The genetic code is just that, a symbol system (code) that represents other states of affairs. "Information is always an abstract representation of something quite different."[61] For example, the following sentence, "Ted Williams was the greatest hitter in baseball," is not itself Ted Williams or a baseball or a hitter. Rather, the string of words (using semantics and syntax) represents these things symbolically. So too is it for the DNA: "The genetic letters in a DNA molecule *represent* the amino acids which will only be constructed at a later stage for subsequent

---

[56]Stephen Meyer, "The Explanatory Power of Design," in *Mere Creation: Science, Faith and Intelligent Design*, ed. William Dembski (Downers Grove, Ill.: InterVarsity Press, 2000), pp. 113-14.

[57]Ibid., p. 122.

[58]Meyer, *Signature in the Cell*, pp. 364-69.

[59]Meyer, "Signature in the Cell," in *Signature in the Cell*.

[60]Werner Gitt, *In the Beginning Was Information* (Bielefeld, Germany: Christliche Literature, 2000), p. 72.

[61]Ibid., p. 84.

incorporation into a protein molecule."[62]

Such information is not reducible to its physical components. For example, the statement "Doug loves Rebecca" may appear on a computer screen, a printed page or be written in the sand with a stick. Moreover, the meaning of the simple sentence cannot be captured by giving an account (even an exhaustive one) of all the physical elements in the three media. Each of these three media is quite different in form and is made of different stuff; the message, however, is identical.

George C. Williams, a leader in gene selection theory, explains the difference between mere matter and information: While we can speak of physical objects as having "mass and charge and length and width," information cannot be so described. "Likewise, matter doesn't have bytes." This leads him to conclude that "matter and information [are] two separate domains of existence, which have to be discussed separately, in their own terms."[63] Gitt draws out the implication as a theorem: "There is no known law of nature, no known process and no known sequence of events which can cause information to originate by itself in matter."[64]

But the case for intelligent design is not based merely on a negation of the ability of natural processes to produce language or complex and specified information. Stephen Meyer argues that when we encounter an apparent artifact with high information content (a case of specified complexity) we infer an intelligent cause and design because chance and necessity are inadequate explanations. As Meyer put it in a peer-reviewed article in the journal *Proceedings of the Biological Society of Washington*:

> We have repeated experience of rational and conscious agents—in particular ourselves—generating or causing increases in complex specified information, both in the form of sequence-specific lines of code and in the form of hierarchically arranged systems of parts. . . . Our experience-based knowledge of information-flow confirms that systems with large amounts of specified complexity (especially codes and languages) invariably originate from an intelligent source from a mind or personal agent.[65]

---

[62]Ibid, p. 84, emphasis added.
[63]George C. Williams, "A Package of Information," in *The Third Culture*, ed. John Brockman (New York: Touchstone, 1995), p. 43.
[64]Gitt, *In the Beginning Was Information*, p. 107.
[65]Stephen C. Meyer, "The Origin of Biological Information and the Higher Taxonomic Categories," *Proceedings of the Biological Society of Washington* 117, no. 2 (2004): 232-33.

One would not infer that the markings on the Rosetta Stone (the key to
deciphering Egyptian hieroglyphics) could be accounted for on the basis of
natural laws and chance events. This is because the stone bears the marks of
intelligence, a complexity that specifies meaning.[66] Even Richard Dawkins
admits that the "machine code of the genes is uncannily computer-like.
Apart from differences in jargon, the pages of a molecular biology journal
might be interchanged with those of a computer engineering journal."[67]
Atheist Bill Gates remarks that "DNA is like a computer program, but far,
far more advanced than any software we've ever created."[68] Hubert Yockey
confesses that the "genetic code is constructed to confront and solve the
problems of communication and recording by the same principles found . . .
in modern communication and computer codes."[69] Neither Dawkins nor
Gates nor Yockey infer that a computer could be explained on the basis of
chance and natural laws. Yet they all claim that genetic information, in all
its specified complexity, does not require an intelligent cause to explain it.

   The design inference argues that the presence of specified complexity
indicates design, not chance or natural law (unintelligent causes). This
design inference is not based on *ignorance* but on (1) our *knowledge* of the
highly complex and informational nature of DNA (something only revealed since the early 1950s), and (2) our *knowledge* of how we detect design in other settings (the design filter) and the fact that intelligence is a
known cause of information. Hence, the God-of-the-gaps canard can be
dispensed with. On the other hand, naturalistic attempts to explain the
information-rich, information-bearing aspects of DNA must appeal to
unknown and unverified natural processes—a kind of naturalism (chance
and/or necessity) of the gaps. Naturalists must resort to some version of
abiogenesis to explain how life arose on earth without intelligent design,
but their task has been daunting and unsuccessful.

ABIOGENESIS

Darwin and his contemporaries knew precious little about the vast com-

[66]Myers, *Signature in the Cell*, p. 346, 351.
[67]Richard Dawkins, *River Out of Eden: A Darwinian View of Life* (New York: Basic Books,
   1995), p. 17.
[68]Bill Gates, *The Road Ahead*, rev. ed. (New York: Viking, 1996), p. 228.
[69]Hubert Yockey, "Origin of Life on Earth and Shannon's Theory of Communication," *Computers and Chemistry* 24 (2000): 105, quoted in Meyer, *Signature in the Cell*, pp. 368-69.

plexities of cellular life. They knew nothing of DNA or of molecular machines. Darwin reckoned life to be a fairly simple form of matter. On this assumption the transition from nonlife to life (abiogenesis) without a Designer did not seem farfetched. It was just another scientific problem to be solved by material explanation. This view was maintained to some degree into the twentieth century—that is, until the vast complexity of the cell was revealed through the microscope and the scientific breakthroughs regarding the structure of DNA.

But Darwin's concept of natural selection cannot apply to nonliving things since they do not reproduce themselves. There is no prebiological selection since natural selection requires replicating organisms. "Living systems distinguish themselves from nonliving ones by processing energy, storing information and replicating."[70] As Ludwig Bertalanffy says, "Selection, i.e., favored survival of 'better' precursors of life, already presupposes self-maintaining, complex, open systems which may compete; therefore, selection cannot account for the origin of such systems."[71] To assume otherwise is to commit a category mistake.[72]

Nevertheless, for some time it was commonly believed that an experiment producing amino acids (building blocks for life) from inorganic materials proved that something similar happened at the genesis of life on earth. In 1953 chemist Harold Urey and his graduate student at the University of Chicago, Stanley Miller, created an environment in a tube thought to be similar to that on earth before the arrival of life. This contained methane, ammonia, hydrogen and water. "He then heated the water and circulated the gasses past a high-voltage electric spark to simulate lightning."[73] Within a week the water had produced "glycine and alanine, the two simplest amino acids found in proteins. Most of the reaction products, however, were simple organic compounds that do not occur in living organisms."[74] This was hailed by many as evidence that life could develop from nonlife in a natural environment.

---

[70]Walter L. Bradley and Charles Thaxton, "Information and the Origin of Life," in *The Creation Hypothesis*, ed. J. P. Moreland (Downers Grove, Ill.: InterVarsity Press, 1994), p. 177.

[71]Ludwig Bertalanffy, *Robots, Men and Minds* (New York: Braziller, 1967), p. 82, quoted in Bradley and Thaxton, "Information," p. 177.

[72]Meyer explains this in rich detail in *Signature in the Cell*, pp. 272-77.

[73]Jonathan Wells, *Icons of Evolution* (Washington, D.C.: Regnery, 2000), p. 13.

[74]Ibid., p. 14.

However, the experiment assumes that the earth's early atmosphere was nonreducing (that is, it lacked oxygen). This is now widely rejected. Wells summarizes the scientific consensus: "The conclusion is clear: if the Miller-Urey experiment is repeated using realistic simulation of the Earth's primitive atmosphere, it doesn't work. Therefore, origin-of-life researchers have had to look elsewhere."[75] Furthermore, an amino acid is a million miles away from a functioning protein with respect to complexity and functionality. Nevertheless, as Wells documents, the discredited experiment remains an "icon of evolution" in many textbooks and in the popular mind.[76]

Since the failure of the Miller-Urey experiment, others have postulated that the first living "organism" was a molecule similar to RNA, since DNA requires a large number of complex proteins in order to replicate. If DNA requires proteins, it cannot come before proteins! But RNA also requires living cells to constitute it; it is by no means a simple molecule. Even if it were somehow produced from nonliving matter, it would have been unlikely to be produced in sufficient numbers or with sufficient strength to survive and serve as the backbone of all subsequent evolutionary development, given the earth's atmosphere at that time. Moreover, the "RNA world theory" does not explain the origin of biological information, but presupposes it. There is no materialist explanation of the "sequence problem," that is, how the base pairs in a hypothetical self-replicating RNA molecule might be ordered in the right sequence to allow for replication.[77]

Those who continue to defend abiogenesis, however, must defend the claim that the complex information contained in living things emerged from noninformational (nonliving matter) systems without design. Where we find a message in any medium ("Doug loves Rebecca"), we naturally infer the presence of a mind and a volition that issued the message. The materialist, however, has no such explanatory recourse in defending abiogenesis. If life comes from nonlife, then information comes from noninformation. The realm of matter, natural law, time, space and change—plus nothing—must explain the emergence of life and its rich informational structure.

Darwinism attempts to explain how living things develop into other living things. We found in chapter thirteen that it fares quite poorly in

---

[75]Ibid., p. 22.
[76]Ibid., pp. 24-27.
[77]Meyer, Signature in the Cell, p. 312.

this, but at least it may appeal to the continuity of life as one "domain of existence" (to use the language of George Williams a few pages ago). But when naturalists assert that information came out of noninformation without any intelligent causation, the claim is quite different. This is because information and noninformation are incommensurable "domains of existence." Yet, on the materialist account, material stuff somehow generates information. This is a kind of emergence ex nihilo, since the defining properties of information are entirely absent in nonbiological matter. If information cannot be reduced to the material components, then material components cannot explain the existence of information.

To complement this philosophical objection to abiogenesis (rooted in empirical observations) we can add a more specifically scientific objection. In 1967, Murray Eden, a noted mathematician from MIT, argued that the chance emergence of life from nonlife was statistically impossible.[78] The details of this case are fairly complex and cannot be canvassed here. But suffice it to say that even naturalistic scientists have admitted that the odds are astronomically against life developing on earth by chance.[79] This is because the assembling of all twenty amino acids for functional proteins by chance and natural law is fantastically improbable in the time frame allowable. Meyer explains that the chance thesis has been abandoned by most all theorists since the probabilistic resources of the entire universe for fourteen billion years cannot account for the features of even the simplest life form.[80] Noted scientist Fred Hoyle gave a memorable analogy for the likelihood of the naturalistic account of the origin of life: it is about as likely as the assemblage of a 747 by a tornado whirling through a junkyard.[81]

Some theorists have attempted to explain the origin of life (of which DNA is a vital part) on the basis of some possible natural law or laws. Yet these speculations are just that, speculations, since no known natural law of self-organization can account for specified complexity.[82] Michael

---

[78]Murray Eden, "Inadequacies of Neo-Darwinian Evolution as a Scientific Theory," in *Mathematical Challenge to the Neo-Darwinian Interpretation of Evolution*, ed. Paul S. Moorhead (Philadelphia: Wistar Institute, 1967), pp. 109-10.

[79]See Hubert Yockey, *Information Theory, Evolution, and the Origin of Life* (New York: Cambridge University Press, 2005).

[80]Meyer, "Chance Elimination and Pattern Recognition," in *Signature in the Cell*.

[81]Fred Hoyle, *The Intelligent Universe* (New York: Holt, Rinehart & Winston, 1984), pp. 18-19.

[82]Stuart Kaufman has argued that this complexity is intrinsic in matter, but his explanations

Polanyi demonstrated that DNA is not determined by any necessary chemical reaction—that is, by natural law. If it were so determined, the complex coding in DNA could not occur because codes require contingent conventions that specify meaning, not the simple repetitions wrought by laws. Polanyi wrote, "Whatever may be the origin of a DNA configuration, it can function as a code only if its order is not due to the forces of potential energy. It must be as physically indeterminate as the sequence of words on a printed page."[83] Since DNA is a code, a genetic language, its identity as a language cannot be accounted for on the basis of chemistry or physics alone, just as the message "Doug loves Rebecca" cannot be accounted for on the basis of physics or chemistry alone. We recognize an *author* of these words. For Polanyi, the information in DNA "cannot be explained by the lower level chemical laws or properties any more than the information in a newspaper headline can be explained by reference to the chemical properties of ink."[84]

Intelligence is the best explanation for the nature and origin of DNA. The design inference is a justified conclusion given the evidence at hand. But some refuse this explanation at all costs.

Hubert Yockey's approach illustrates the truculent commitment to materialism that dogs the contemporary scientific establishment. Yockey, a nuclear physicist and bioinformatician (one who applies information theory to biology), now retired, is a pioneering theorist on the origins of life and has drawn careful distinctions between living and nonliving matter. He criticized the once-popular "primordial soup" explanations for the origin of life on earth because they cannot account for the vast amounts of information encoded in living cells. Life necessarily contains these information-rich codes; nonlife does not. This yawning gap cannot be bridged by any materialistic explanation, he claims, since it is statistically impossible for life to have evolved from nonlife in the time allowable.[85]

However, Yockey refuses to consider ID as an alternative to abiogenesis.

---

always assume some extant information that is never explained on his naturalistic principles or is highly speculative and without empirical data (see Meyer, "Self-organization and Biochemical Predestination," in *The Signature in the Cell*).

[83]Michael Polanyi, "Life's Irreducible Structure," in *Knowing and Being*, ed. Marjorie Grene (Chicago: University of Chicago Press, 1969), p. 229.

[84]Meyer, *Signature in the Cell*, p. 240. Meyer is paraphrasing Polanyi, *Knowing and Being*, p. 229.

[85]Yockey, *Information Theory*, p. 93.

Instead, he affirms that the origin of life is unknowable. Life, for him, becomes an "axiom" (his term), not something that can be explained.[86] But axioms in mathematics are self-evident starting points that need no outside justification. They are not inferred from something else more obviously true. To make biological life axiomatic is to commit a deep category mistake. Life on earth is not a logical principle, nor is it a necessary state of affairs. It is, rather, a contingent, improbable and specified state of affairs. The ancient earth was once prebiotic; then it became biotic. This causal transition from prebiotic to biotic cannot be explained on the basis that life itself is an axiom. Therefore, life itself is in need of an explanation outside of itself. This is totally unlike the axioms of mathematics.

LIFE FROM SPACE

Things do not look at all promising for abiogenesis. Francis Crick, a co-discoverer of the double-helix structure of DNA and an atheist, confessed in *Life Itself* that "the origin of life appears to be almost a miracle, so many are the conditions which would have to be satisfied to get it going."[87] Crick, however, resorted to the theory of "directed panspermia"—the claim that the earth had been seeded for life by aliens who injected it by means of an unmanned probe. He realized that the odds of life accidentally coming to earth through an *undirected* process were far too small. But *directed* panspermia was the "miracle" he deemed necessary to explain the origin of life, since life cannot come from nonlife without intelligence. It is a design explanation. However, this appeal to design is a classic case of an ad hoc argument. When naturalism fails to explain the origin of terrestrial life, Crick appeals to an unknown and improvable alien source.

Astronomer Hugh Ross points out that this theory "collides with three insurmountable barriers." First, the laws of physics and the size of the universe prevent any aliens from "traversing the necessary interstellar distances in any reasonable time period." Either the spacecraft or the life onboard would be destroyed on the way by radiation, interstellar dust and debris, and general degeneration.[88] Second, given the received dating, the

---

[86]Ibid. For his rejection of ID see, "Does Evolution Need an Intelligent Designer?" in *Information Theory*.
[87]Francis Crick, *Life Itself: Its Origin and Nature* (New York: Simon & Schuster, 1981), p. 88.
[88]Hugh Ross, *Creation and Science* (Colorado Springs: NavPress, 2006), p. 120.

universe was only 9.9 billion years old when life appeared on earth—"far too young for an advanced physical species to have emerged and developed technological sophistication."[89] Third, Crick's far-fetched explanation merely pushes back the question of life's origin one step. If intelligent beings planted life on earth, where did they come from? Terrestrial abiogenesis is "solved," but extraterrestrial abiogenesis remains unresolved.[90] There is no known way that extraterrestrials (if they exist, which is unlikely)[91] could do such a thing. A nontheological miracle is required if a *divine* Designer is ruled out a priori.[92]

Others have argued that life may have been planted on earth accidentally, hitching a ride on meteors. This would be *undirected* panspermia. But this is even less plausible than the implausible scenario previously refuted since, in addition to the already-mentioned objections, any guiding intelligence would be absent.[93]

Therefore, if chance, aliens and natural law (or some combination of all three) are ruled out in explaining the specified complexity of the informational nature of the cell, the only remaining cause available is an intelligent cause or intelligent design. This argument rests on well-established biological data and a known cause of information-rich systems: intelligence. It begs no questions, writes no postdated checks and makes no appeal to ignorance.

BIOMIMICRY: NATURE AS MODEL FOR TECHNOLOGY

A new approach to biology has recently captured the imaginations and funds of many in the larger scientific establishment: biomimicry. This discipline studies the complex and specified structures of biology and uses these as models for humanly engineered technology. Recall Bill Gates's

---

[89]Ibid.

[90]See Richard Milton, *Shattering the Myths of Darwinism* (Rochester, Vt.: Park Street Press, 1997), p. 218. For further arguments against directed panspermia, see Massimo Pigliucci, "Where Do We Come From?" in *Darwinism, Design, and Public Education*, ed. John Angus Campbell and Stephen C. Meyer (East Lansing: Michigan State University Press, 2003), pp. 196-97.

[91]See Peter Ward and Donald Brownlee, *Rare Earth: Why Complex Life Is Uncommon in the Universe* (New York: Springer, 2003).

[92]See Phillip Johnson, *Darwin on Trial*, 2nd ed. (Downers Grove, Ill.: InterVarsity Press, 1991), pp. 110-11.

[93]See Pigliucci, "Where Do We Come From?" p. 196. Pigliucci is a critic of ID but also of panspermia theories.

statement made earlier that the information structure of DNA is far more complex than any computer. If so, that structure (and others like it) can provide ideas for various machines. Reuters reports that "International Business Machines Corp is looking to the building blocks of our bodies—DNA—to be the structure of next-generation microchips."[94] Microchips are obviously intelligently designed for a particular function. They evince specified complexity. Likewise, engineers in search of better information structures are looking to DNA and other aspects of biology for better models of efficiency in engineering.[95]

In light of biomimicry, consider this argument:

1. Scientists are mimicking naturally occurring mechanisms in nature (such as DNA) in order to develop *better design plans* for various human technologies.

2. If (1) is true, this assumes that these naturally occurring mechanisms are themselves designed, since they evince design plans *superior* to *human design plans*.

3. Therefore, these naturally occurring mechanisms (such as DNA) are designed, otherwise they would not be candidates for imitation by technologies.

AN OLD OBJECTION: DESIGN FLAWS

Darwinists invariably attempt to cripple the cause of ID by citing examples of design flaws in nature, such as the human eye (with its blind spot) or the "panda's thumb," which supposedly functions poorly. I briefly touched on this kind of criticism in chapter thirteen when we addressed homologous structures, but we need to address it in more depth. The argument is this:

1. If God, an all-powerful and all-knowing being, created life, then it would show no design flaws.

2. Life evidences design flaws. That is, it is not optimally designed because we can imagine another design improving on it.

---

[94]Claire Baldwin, "IBM uses DNA to Make Next-Gen Microchips," Reuters, August 16, 2009, <www.reuters.com/article/idUSTRE57F1K720090816>.

[95]See Bharat Bhushan, "Biomimetics: Lessons from Nature—An Overview," *Philosophical Transactions of the Royal Society of London* 367 (2009): 1445-86. The author does not advocate ID. The whole issue in which this paper appears is dedicated to biomimicry.

3. Therefore (a), life is not designed by God (by *modus tollens*).

4. Therefore (b), life is the product of Darwinian evolution (which is non-designed and nondirectional).

Stephen Jay Gould claims, following Darwin, that the best evidence for Darwinism is not "optimal design" (which he grants occurs) but the cobbled-together nature of the living world. He illustrates the principle by appealing to Darwin's discussion of orchids, claiming that the mechanisms that flowers employ to extract pollen from insects are merely the result of retooled mechanisms used for other purposes at earlier evolutionary stages. God would not work that way. "If God has designed a beautiful machine to reflect his wisdom and power, surely he would not have used a collection of parts generally fashioned for other purposes. Orchids were not made by an ideal engineer; they are jury-rigged from a limited set of available components."[96]

These orchids are not designed by God. Otherwise, their "intricate devices" would be sui generis. How did Gould gain the knowledge of this theological counterfactual? It is appropriate to assert that "if there are unicorns, they have exactly one horn" (a counterfactual claim, since there are no unicorns); but it is much more precarious to assert that "if God made the world, then the component parts of plants in an orchid would not be similar to other plants." Since Gould's remark trades on aesthetic values, we could as easily argue that God aesthetically values fewer basic structures (simplicity) and a largess of differing structures (multiplicity). Surely we are in no position to rule out this possibility if indeed God is the Designer.

Gould's criticism is aesthetic regarding the orchids. But considering the panda's thumb, he finds suboptimal design with respect to its *function*. Without giving the details of his presentation, here is Gould's conclusion:

> The panda's thumb provides an elegant zoological counterpart to Darwin's orchids. An engineer's best solution is debarred by history. The panda's true thumb is committed to another role, too specialized for the different function to become an opposable, manipulating digit. So, the panda must use parts on hand and settle for an enlarged wrist bone and a somewhat clumsy,

---

[96]Stephen Jay Gould, "The Panda's Thumb," in *Intelligent Design Creationism*, ed. Robert T. Pennock (Boston: MIT Press, 2001), p. 670.

but quite workable solution. The sesamoid thumb wins no prize in an engineer's derby.[97]

Gould reasons that if the panda's thumb is not as useable as a fully opposable thumb, it must not be designed. There are four responses to this.

First, Gould and many others claim that religion has no purchase on science whatsoever. Gould wrote a book on the subject of "nonoverlapping magisteria"—the notion that religion and science speak to entirely different realms and so do not "overlap" in their truth claims or methods of investigation.[98] This claim is false for many reasons, but it is clear that Gould believes that orchids and panda's thumbs *are evidence against a designing God*. Yet he cannot have it both ways.[99]

Second, even if there appear to be design flaws, that fact does not negate the presence of design in toto. Given the success of the design filter—by which we infer design by eliminating chance and natural law as capable of explaining the object in question—design remains the best inference. As Dembski says, "To find fault with biological design because it misses some idealized optimum" is off the mark. Not "knowing the objectives of the designer, Gould is in no position to say whether the designer has proposed a faulty compromise among those objectives."[100]

Third, many seemingly suboptimal systems are not truly suboptimal at all. Gould to the contrary, the Panda's thumb is not as dysfunctional as he claims. Hideki Endo and colleagues have argued that the "hand of the giant panda has a much more refined grasping mechanism than has been suggested in previous morphological models."[101]

Fourth, as mentioned in chapter twelve, the Christian worldview does not affirm the existence of a perfect creation given the Fall. Therefore, we should not expect life "east of Eden" to be without flaw. The notion of the

---

[97]Ibid., pp. 673-76.
[98]Stephen Jay Gould, *Rocks of Ages: Science and Religion in the Fullness of Life* (New York: Ballantine, 2002).
[99]See J. P. Moreland, *Scaling the Secular City* (Grand Rapids: Baker, 1987), pp. 200-202.
[100]Dembski, *Design Revolution*, p. 59. For a detailed discussion of how Darwinists presuppose certain theological ideas to support Darwinism and deny design, see Paul Nelson, "The Role of Theology in Current Evolutionary Reasoning," in *Intelligent Design Creationism*, ed. Robert T. Pennock (Cambridge, Mass.: MIT Press, 2001).
[101]Richard Thornhill, "The Panda's Thumb," *Perspectives on Science and Christian Faith* 55, no. 1 (2003): 31. Nor is the human eye badly designed. See Dembski, *Design Revolution*, pp. 59-60.

fall brings up several questions related to the problem of evil,[102] but Christianity predicts that the present world will show signs of stress fractures throughout. To list examples of creaturely imperfection hardly refutes the Christian worldview.

ID AND THE NATURE OF THE DESIGNER

We need to consider how these ID arguments contribute to Christian apologetics. Molecular machines and the informational nature of the cell offer strong evidence for a Designer who transcends the explanatory limits of naturalism. The design inference warrants this conclusion. But what can we know of the Designer given these arguments?

Dembski claims that ID is not necessarily a Christian, or even a theistic, hypothesis; it is also compatible with "the watchmaker-God of the deists, the demiurge of Plato's *Timaeus* and the divine reason (i.e., *logos spermatikos*) of the ancient Stoics. One can even take an agnostic view about the designer, treating specified complexity as a brute unexplainable fact."[103] This comment is offered to deflect the notion that ID is merely "stealth creationism." But the claim that ID is compatible with all these views may be casting the metaphysical net too widely. I will limit my comments primarily to pantheism of the nondualistic sort, which has been represented historically by Advaita Vedanta Hinduism or Zen Buddhism.

Contemporary nondualistic pantheistic philosophers such as Ken Wilber reject the naturalistic reductionism of Darwinism—Wilber calls it a "flatland" worldview—in favor of a "spiritual" worldview.[104] However, nondualistic pantheistic worldviews—for all their claims about "Mind-at-Large" (Aldous Huxley) and "Spirit" (Wilber)—cannot account for the design in the universe. This is because a pantheistic God is (1) impersonal and (2) exists beyond all dualities. The divine reality is taken to be identical with the totality of being. In other words, it is nondual (or monistic). Therefore, any subject-object relationship is unreal and must be transcended. There is no Creator-creation duality, as in theism.

---

[102]See chap. 25.
[103]William Dembski, *Intelligent Design* (Downers Grove, Ill.: InterVarsity Press, 1999), p. 252.
[104]See Ken Wilber, *A Brief History of Everything*, 2nd ed. (Boston: Shambhala, 2001).

Moreover, this god's impersonal nature eliminates conscious agency. Yet if there is a Designer, this being must be an intellectual *agent* who designs and brings about states of affairs. Furthermore, there must be a subject-object relationship between the Designer and the thing designed. The concepts of Designer and designed are correlative; they cannot be synonymous. Yet nondualism admits of no such distinction between Designer and designed, since there is but one divine reality. Therefore, according to nondualistic pantheism there can be no design at all, and thus no evidence for design. In addition, if "Spirit" is nondual, then the concepts of (1) the Designer planning among diverse possibilities and (2) the Designer actualizing the design among and through the diverse phenomena of nature are both ruled out in principle. There are no options (plural) among competing designs; there are no entities (plural) on which to implement the chosen design.

For these reasons (and others), ID is incompatible with any form of nondualistic pantheism. While ID provides some intellectual support for nonmaterialist worldviews outside of Christian theism, ID seems most clearly to provide epistemic support for a small cluster of *theistic* worldviews, including deism. Any impersonal, immaterial worldview—such as nondualistic pantheism—seems to lack the metaphysical components necessary for the concept of design to obtain. If this account is correct, arguments for ID are arguments against nondualistic pantheism, as well as against naturalism.

Intelligent design arguments are also incompatible with any other *impersonal, nontheistic* worldview. Therefore, Stoicism (a form of pantheism), panentheism and Neo-Platonism suffer defeat inasmuch as they deny the existence of a personal Designer distinct from what is designed.[105] Deism seems to survive the filter, since it affirms a personal Designer. But unlike theism, deism denies God's ongoing interaction with the creation.

We should add a second "design filter" argument, one that moves beyond the scientific detection of design and speaks to the nature of the Designer. The following argument summarizes material in this and previous chapters.

---

[105]There may be versions of panentheism and Neo-Platonism that adequately preserve the categories of an intelligent Designer distinct from what is designed, but we cannot address them here.

1. Design in nature is explained by either (a) extraterrestrial influence (accidental or intentional), (b) pantheism, (c) polytheism, (d) panentheism, (e) deism or (f) theism.

2. Design is not explained by accidental extraterrestrial influence because there is no good evidence that life could travel through the vast and hostile distances of space and sprout up on a fertile earth. But even if it could, this would still leave unexplained the evolution of all of life from one or several randomly seeded organisms.

3. Design is not explained by intentional extraterrestrial life. Even if this were the case, it would leave the design of the extraterrestrials unexplained.

4. Design is not explained by pantheism because (a) the pantheistic concept of God is not personal (a necessary condition for a Designer), and (b) pantheism views nature not as an orderly collection of teleological parts but as an undivided unity.

5. Design is not explained by polytheism because the multiplication of finite deities violates the principle that we should not multiply explanatory entities unnecessarily and because polytheism has no independent support philosophically.

6. Therefore, design in nature is best explained by deism, panentheism or theism.

The fact that the second design filter allows for deism need not derail Christian apologetics, since the chapters that follow will make the case that the Designer has revealed himself in Christ and the Bible, thus refuting the distant God of deism. We have not addressed panentheism in this book, not because it lacks adherents historically, but because it does not seem to be a live option for many today.[106] However, previous arguments have established creation ex nihilo, which refutes the panentheistic idea that the world and God are both eternal and that the world is part of God (see chap. 11).

The evidence for design in the universe should not be isolated from the other arguments in this book for God's existence. If solid arguments can

---

[106]For a critique of panentheism, see John Cooper, *Panentheism: The Other God of the Philosophers—From Plato to the Present* (Grand Rapids: Baker, 2006); Norman Geisler, "Panentheism," in *Baker Encyclopedia of Christian Apologetics* (Grand Rapids: Baker, 1999).

be presented for the existence of God based on cosmological arguments, ontological arguments and the fine-tuning design argument, the likelihood of design in biology is strengthened. With this background knowledge, ID should take its rightful place in the overall circle of evidence. Standing alone, it cannot provide a full apologetic for Christianity. Rather, ID provides strong evidence against the reigning naturalism in the realm of biology, as well as some support for theism as an overarching worldview. But there is much more evidence for theism worthy of our consideration, as we will find in the following chapters.

15

The Moral Argument for God

PHILOSOPHER PHILIP HALLIE WAS surprised by goodness. He had
written a book on cruelty, which investigated the manifold evils of the
Nazi Holocaust, including the Nazis' "medical experimentation" on de-
fenseless children.

Imagine an Aryan adult clothed in the professional authority of a doctor and supported by the terrible power of a triumphant Nazi Germany in
the first year of the 1940s. Then imagine a bone-thin Jewish or Gypsy
child lying naked on a metal table with a funnel built into it to drain off
the blood. Finally imagine the doctor bending over the child and cutting
the child's body to pieces.[1]

Haille's research was cutting his own soul to pieces. "I had learned that
you cannot go down into hell with impunity."[2] He became bitter and angry—uncharacteristically responding in rage or silence to his students.
When this behavior angered and frightened his own family, he left and
began walking to his office, entertaining thoughts of suicide. Once there,
Hallie discovered a book on the little-known story of the small Protestant
village of Le Chambon, situated in the Cenennes Mountains of southeast-
ern France. He read of a Huguenot pastor who refused to turn in Jews to
the Nazis and of villagers who courageously hid Jews. "When I got to the
bottom of the third page of the article my cheeks started itching, and
when I reached up to scratch them I found that they were covered with
tears. And not just a few tears—my cheeks were awash in them."[3]

---

[1]Philip Hallie, *Surprised by Goodness* (McLean, Va.: Trinity Forum, 2002), p. 10. The full story
 of his discovery is found in Philip Hallie, *Lest Innocent Blood Be Shed* (New York: Harper,
 1979).
[2]Hallie, *Surprised by Goodness*, p. 10.
[3]Ibid., p. 12.

Thus began Hallie's exodus from hell. He learned that a town of only 3,500 people managed to save about 6,000 Jews. Most of those saved were Jewish children whose parents had been killed by the Nazis in central Europe. The people of Le Chambon sheltered the children in their own homes or in homes the villagers established. They also spirited some children over the treacherous mountains to safety in Geneva, Switzerland. Under the leadership of Huguenot preachers, nearly all of them had deep religious convictions "that we are all children of God, and we must take care of each other."[4]

Two philosophical questions arise. First, why did the professor weep? Were his tears merely a symptom of an emotional release, or did they signal a deep moral response? Second, was the Christian worldview of these Huguenots necessary for a proper philosophical account of and response to good and evil? To offer a moral argument for the existence of God, we must (1) establish the existence of objective moral reality and (2) show that a personal and moral God is the best explanation for the existence and knowledge of objective moral reality. That is the task of this chapter.

TWO RED HERRINGS

Before beginning, however, I must dispense with two common (and malodorous) red herrings concerning the argument at hand. First, atheists, such as Paul Kurtz, often claim that atheists can be moral without believing in God; therefore, religion is not necessary for morality.[5] But the argument from objective morality to God is not concerned with this issue. Christians grant that non-Christians (including atheists) possess and act in accordance with true moral principles to some extent. The apostle Paul says as much (Romans 2:14-15). This is beside the point and entirely off topic, since the moral argument for God addresses the metaphysical foundation of goodness.

Second, John Arthur and others have claimed that God cannot be the source of morality since nontheists use moral terms such as *good*, *right* and

---

[4]Philip Hallie, "From Cruelty to Goodness," in *Virtue and Vice in Everyday Life*, ed. Christina Hoff Summers and Fred Summers, 7th ed. (Belmont, Calif.: Wadsworth, 2006), p. 22.

[5]See Paul Kurtz, "Opening Statement," in *Is Goodness Without God Good Enough? A Debate on Faith, Secularism, and Ethics*, ed. Robert K. Garcia and Nathan L. King (Lanham, Md.: Rowman & Littlefield, 2009), pp. 25-29.

wrong without referring to God's will to define them.[6] This is true but irrelevant to the argument. The moral argument has nothing to do with how people typically use or define moral terms; instead it addresses the *justification* of moral claims, which is one aspect of metaethics (the philosophical basis for moral claims).[7] A person may realize that stealing is morally wrong without knowing the ultimate reason why stealing is wrong. We can invoke the sense-reference distinction made famous by Gottlob Frege.[8] The "evening star" and "morning star" appear at different times of the day and so have different *senses*. However, they are the same star: the *referent* is identical even if the *senses* are different. Likewise, an atheist (or other nontheist) may have a *sense* about the meaning of morality yet fail to realize that the ultimate *referent* for morality is God's character and will.

ETHICAL RELATIVISM

The *New York Times* proclaimed that events like the September 11, 2001, terrorist attacks on America cry out for "a transcendent ethical standard" that is not available in the fashionable postmodern relativism of the academy.[9] Yet the fashionable option is still ethical relativism, which claims that moral judgments are dependent on contingent social and historical arrangements. Morality is merely human. One person's terrorist is another person's freedom fighter. Morality is contingent and revisable according to the postmodern mind.

Relativism comes in two broad forms: cultural relativism and individual relativism (sometimes called private subjectivism). Cultural relativism teaches that we should follow the moral principles of our culture. Cultural judgments are normative; yet these judgments are binding only for those within the culture. If culture A says that sex outside of marriage is wrong and culture B says that it is not always wrong, then societ-

[6]John Arthur, "Why Morality Does Not Depend on Religion," in *Vice and Virtue in Everyday Life*, ed. Christiana Hoff Summers and Sommers, 7th ed. (Belmont, Calif.: Wadsworth, 2006), p. 88.
[7]Metaethics is "the attempt to understand the metaphysical, epistemological, semantic and psychological presuppositions and commitments of moral thought, talk, and practices" (G. Sayre-McCord, "Metaethics," in *The Stanford Encyclopedia of Philosophy* <http://plato.stanford.edu/entries/metaethics>. Obviously, this chapter will not speak to all aspects of metaethics.
[8]Gottlob Frege, *Zeitscheift für Philosophie and philosophische Kritik* 100 (1892): 25-50.
[9]Edward Rothstein, "Attacks on U.S. Challenge Postmodern True Believers," *New York Times*, September, 22, 2001, p. A17.

ies A and B do not contradict each other. Rather, sex outside of marriage is wrong in culture A but is not necessarily wrong in culture B. Morality depends on location.

Individual relativism grants no favored moral status to one's culture. Moral judgments and obligations are based entirely on an individual's personal preference. Morality depends on what *you* think. I will argue that cultural relativism reduces to individualism relativism, but we must first explore the basic arguments for relativism in general.

The dependency and diversity theses. Relativists tend to support their view through two main claims: the dependency thesis and the diversity thesis. The dependency thesis asserts that morality inherently depends on cultural factors and no other factors. The culture determines the moral standards and sensibilities just as much as it determines what language will be spoken. The assumption at work is that cultures have no access to objective, universal, absolute and transcendent moral truths. So, in a widely anthologized essay, anthropologist Ruth Benedict claimed that her examples culled from various cultures "force upon us the fact that normality is culturally defined."[10] She claims that mores are selected from a wide possible range, just as language selects from a wide range of "phonetic articulations."[11] "The possibility of organized behavior of every sort, from the fashions of local dress and houses to the dicta of a people's ethics and religion, *depends* upon a similar selection among the possible behavior traits."[12] If humans depend on their culture for morality, morality cannot extend beyond or above their own culture.

The dependency thesis takes a half-truth and inflates it into a whole lie. It is incontestable that cultures affect moral codes. No one is acultural, a being from nowhere. The question is whether *morality itself* is nothing but cultural.

Benedict's argument from analogy is flawed. She claims that just as cultures choose from different phonetic possibilities for their speech, so also they choose from different mores in morality, each coming up with its own sense of what is normal. If we fail to deem one spoken language ob-

---

[10]Ruth Benedict, "A Defense of Ethical Relativism," in *Moral Philosophy: A Reader*, ed. Louis P. Pojman, 2nd ed. (Indianapolis: Hackett, 1998), p. 35.
[11]Ibid.
[12]Ibid., emphasis added.

jectively better than another,[13] then we cannot claim that one moral "language" is any better than another. However, different languages may express the same propositions and so refer to the same objects. We may utter or write "The earth is round" in English, Hindi or Spanish, but the meaning (that is, the propositional content) is identical. This is why translations between languages are possible.[14] Differing phonetic, syntactic and semantic elements do not render judgments like "The earth is round" relative to culture. Therefore, if varying nonmoral linguistic affirmations can successfully capture objective reality, so can varying moral affirmations capture—or fail to capture—objective realities.

Cultures use different semantics and grammars to refer to the sky as blue. They likewise use differing numerical symbols for doing mathematics. But this diversity of symbolic forms hardly renders the blueness of the sky "merely cultural" or the truth of mathematical equations "merely cultural." We depend on various cultural forms—the syntax and semantics of English, the deliverances of modern astronomy—to know that the earth is round, but this in no way jeopardizes the objective circularity of the planet.

Moreover, beliefs within cultures—no matter how well-established and embedded—may simply be mistaken. Consider the statement "All illness is caused by magic." Some tribes have (and may yet still) believe this; but we know it to be false. Or consider the astronomical opinions of the overwhelming majority of humans before the time of Copernicus concerning the placement of the earth relative to the sun. Geocentrism was a truism for centuries—and wrong the entire time. Similarly, there is no reason to believe that a culture's *moral judgments* are insulated from error.

The dependency thesis leads directly into the diversity thesis. If all morality is dependent on culture, and if cultures differ, then morality will differ from culture to culture. According to the diversity thesis, the possible range of selection for behavior and mores is vast, and the different cultures have selected various arrangements, judging different things as normal or abnor-

---

[13]Even this claim is disputable. Ideographic languages possess the resources to express abstractions better than pictographic languages (which is not to say that pictographic languages do not have some advantages of ideographic languages). Some languages are better versed to describe certain things than are others. For an example of this concerning Sanskrit, German and Chinese see Francis Schaeffer, *Art and the Bible* (Downers Grove, Ill.: InterVarsity Press, 2006), pp. 78-79.

[14]For more on propositions, truth and reference see Douglas Groothuis, "The Truth About Truth," in *Truth Decay* (Downers Grove, Ill.: InterVarsity Press, 2000), and chap. 6 of this book.

mal according to their specific situations. One society may stigmatize homosexuality while another condones it. And so on. Therefore, if different societies have made differing moral judgments (and if moral judgments depend inextricably on contingent cultures), then there can be no crosscultural and objective moral truths that apply to all cultures. What is moral is what is deemed "normal" by a culture; thus goodness is defined as normality. Postmodernism has expanded relativism to include language itself, thereby relativizing all truth (not just moral claims).[15]

The diversity thesis runs aground for two compelling reasons. The first is that even if cultures disagree radically on their most basic and central moral judgments, this does not lead to the conclusion that these judgments are all equally acceptable and no moral judgment is better than any other. The proposition "There is widespread disagreement over X" does not logically imply, "Any assessment of X is true and legitimate for the group that proposes it." Second, there is less diversity between cultures concerning fundamental human values than many imagine. Variations of the golden rule can be found throughout world history and amid various religions and ethical systems. Anthropologist Clyde Kluckhohn has discerned significant common ground on morality among cultures:

> Every culture has a concept of murder, distinguishing this from execution, killing in war, and other "justifiable homicides." The notions of incest and other regulations upon sexual behavior, the prohibitions upon untruth under defined circumstances, of restitution and reciprocity, of mutual obligations between parties and children—these and many other moral concepts are altogether universal.[16]

C. S. Lewis came to the same conclusion. After arguing for an objective moral order in *The Abolition of Man*, he surveyed the basic moral precepts of humanity through the ages. He divided "Illustrations of the Tao" into eight basic sections.

1. The law of general benevolence: (a) negative and (b) positive

2. The law of special benevolence

[15]For more on postmodernist ethics, see Douglas Groothuis, "Ethics Without Reality, Postmodern Style," in *Truth Decay* (Downers Grove, Ill.: InterVarsity Press, 2000), and chap. 6 of this book.
[16]Clyde Kluckhohn, "Ethical Relativity: '*Sic et Non*,'" *Journal of Philosophy* 52 (1955): 672.

3. Duties to parents, elders, ancestors

4. The law of justice: (a) sexual justice, (b) honesty, (c) justice in courts, etc.

5. Duties to children and posterity

6. The law of good faith and veracity

7. The law of mercy

8. The law of magnanimity[17]

These observations fit perfectly with Paul's claim that all people have "the work of the law written on their hearts" simply by virtue of being God's creatures (Romans 2:14-15). The same truth was affirmed by the Old Testament prophets who held the nations surrounding Israel accountable for their evil deeds even though these nations did not receive the law of Moses. They nevertheless possessed moral knowledge that rendered them accountable to God for their behavior (Jonah, Amos 1–2). Moral codes and moral awareness are never entirely the result of varying cultural influences.

A culture's metaphysical beliefs may affect its implementation of moral principles and produce contrasting moral behaviors. If a native tribe believes that putting one's parents to death before they get old and decrepit insures them a better afterlife than if they died in a compromised state, their putting the folks to death does not speak against their regard for their parents.[18] Of course, a Christian would never think of such a thing, because Christianity has an entirely different conception of the afterlife.[19] Nevertheless, people from both cultures share the same basic moral principle of respecting their elders. However, given their different worldviews, the application of this same moral *principle* may result in different *rules* (the principle applied to various situations).

Which culture decides morality? Another snag bedeviling cultural relativism is in determining the culture that authorizes norms for behavior.[20]

---

[17]C. S. Lewis, *Abolition of Man* (1944; reprint, San Francisco: HarperSanFrancisco, 1974), pp. 83-102.

[18]See William Frankena, *Ethics*, 2nd ed. (New York: Prentice-Hall), p. 109. See also James Rachels's *The Elements of Moral Philosophy*, 3rd ed. (New York: McGraw-Hill 1999), pp. 28-29.

[19]See N. T. Wright, *Surprised by Hope: Rethinking Heaven, the Resurrection, and the Mission of the Church* (San Francisco: HarperOne, 2008).

[20]J. P. Moreland, *Scaling the Secular City* (Grand Rapids: Baker, 1987), pp. 243-44.

This is an epistemic problem that in many cases makes finding the germane norms impossible. If one is a member of a remote Australian aboriginal tribe with a homogeneous culture, it is clear what culture determines his or her values. However, it is not clear which culture is normative if one lives in a cosmopolitan setting in which various subcultures coexist and often clash with each other in the larger society. For example, in America today, society is divided on the question of homosexuality. Many churches deem homosexual behavior sinful, but some liberal churches do not. The general population is divided. The legal system permits homosexual activity but has yet to sanction homosexual marriage in every state. If our "culture" determines the norms to which we are bound, all but those ensconced in closed communities will be left wondering what their defining culture might be.

Furthermore, even if the relevant culture can be ascertained, the notion of making the cultural consensus the moral arbiter leads to an absurdity, known as the reformer's dilemma. Many courageous moral reformers—such as Gandhi, the suffragists and Martin Luther King Jr.—opposed a cultural consensus that had been based on longstanding moral views. Their objections to injustices were not based on discerning a broad consensus, but rather by appealing to objective moral principles. King appealed to the ideals of the founders of America, but he also stood against the standing laws of Jim Crow. His "Letter from a Birmingham Jail" is a classic case of natural law argumentation. In explaining why he and his cohorts broke laws that led to his arrest and imprisonment, King wrote:

> A just law is a man-made code that squares with the moral law or the law of God. An unjust law is a code that is out of harmony with the moral law. To put it in the terms of St. Thomas Aquinas: an unjust law is a human law that is not rooted in eternal law and natural law.[21]

According to cultural relativism, King and all other laudatory moral reformers should be condemned as cultural and moral *deviants* who must be deemed immoral when judged by the extant standards of their societies. Their appeals to an objective moral law would be ruled out of court as false

---

[21]Martin Luther King Jr., "Letter from a Birmingham Jail," in *The Book of Virtues*, ed. William Bennett (New York: Simon & Schuster, 1993), p. 260.

absolutism. But this conclusion is absurd. If the reformer's arguments are accepted, cultural relativism must be rejected. If King is right, relativism is wrong by reductio ad absurdum.

Progress, tolerance and relativism. If various cultures determine what is moral and immoral apart from any objective moral standard, the concept of moral progress is impossible to apply. All we can claim is that cultures *change* with respect to their moral evaluations. But the very notion of moral progress assumes a standard or ideal that a culture seeks to approach. So, America's laws that give women the right to vote, own property and receive an education on a par with men are more progressive than what was legally stipulated in 1900. Conversely, the concept of moral decay assumes a standard from which a culture is retreating. C. S. Lewis writes:

> If "good" or "better" are terms deriving their sole meaning from the ideology of each people, then of course ideologies themselves cannot be better or worse than each other. Unless the measuring rod is independent of the things measured, we can do no measuring, For the same reason it is useless to compare the moral ideas of one age with those of another: progress and decadence are alike meaningless words.[22]

While we might abandon any use of the concept of progress with regard to cultures, this amoral resolve is difficult to maintain. Can we honestly claim that America has not progressed in its laws concerning African Americans since the Civil War? Worse yet, vetoing the concept of moral progress courts nihilism, which will be addressed later.

Still, one might protest that cultural relativism is a necessary condition for the toleration of differing moralities and religions. Claiming that there are transcendent moral principles encourages intolerance and dogmatism, since those so persuaded are incapable of tolerating those with whom they disagree.

This is erroneous for two reasons. First, cultural relativism cannot justify tolerance as a universal moral principle, although relativists often claim that relativism leads to tolerance. If culture A is radically intolerant concerning religion (as in Saudi Arabia), and culture B is not religiously intolerant (as in America), the relativist cannot claim that culture A is any

---

[22]C. S. Lewis, *Christian Reflections* (1967; reprint, Grand Rapids: Eerdmans, 1978), p. 73; see also G. K. Chesterton, *Orthodoxy* (1908; reprint, New York: Image Books, 1959), pp. 35-36.

better or worse than culture B. Yet cultural relativists typically do not tolerate intolerant cultures. They condemn their intolerance. But this is logically inconsistent given relativism. Therefore, cultural relativism cannot make tolerance an objective moral principle that is absolutely and universally normative.[23]

Second, a commitment to objective moral principles that stand over cultures does not necessarily endanger tolerance. The content of these moral principles makes the difference. The moral principles of Osama bin Laden contradict the Western sense of tolerance, but those based on the Bible do not contradict the Western sense of tolerance. Scripture never advocates violence in the cause of religious conversion. Nor does it encourage hatred toward unbelievers but rather calls for love—even for enemies (see chap. 5).

CULTURAL RELATIVISM LEADS TO INDIVIDUAL RELATIVISM

Cultural relativism cannot stand, but it at least attempts to maintain some moral authority on behalf of the determining culture. It claims a moral authority beyond individual choice in order to avoid anarchism. Yet cultural relativism reduces to individual relativism (or private subjectivism), which dispenses with any moral authority outside of the autonomous individual's views and choices. We have observed the impossibility of determining the defining "culture" for cultural relativism, at least in many modern cases. If there are no rules for finding our defining culture, then there seems to be no reason why individuals should be constrained by any sense of cultural authority over them. We could rather create our own values with or without any social group to back us up. Louis Pojman says: "But why can't I dispense with the interpersonal agreements altogether and invent my own morality—since morality, on this view, is only an invention anyway?" If there is no objective moral standard, it is left to the individual to decide what is right and wrong.[24]

---

[23]For a rich discussion of tolerance see Brad Stetson and Joseph G. Conti, *The Truth About Tolerance: Pluralism, Diversity and the Culture Wars* (Downers Grove, Ill.: InterVarsity Press, 2005). Os Guinness makes the case that tolerance is rather a debased notion and not sufficient for a pluralistic society. In its place he defends civility. See his *The Case for Civility* (San Francisco: HarperOne, 2008).

[24]Louis Pojman, "A Defense of Ethical Objectivism," in *Moral Philosophy*, 3rd ed. (Indianapolis: Hackett, 2003), p. 44.

Moreover, the moral claim "We should submit to the morality of our culture" is not culturally relative but crosscultural and absolute. Relativists thereby contradict themselves by their statements. Despite their relativism, they will issue universal and absolute moral imperatives, such as

1. We should *never* affirm our own moral views as universal and absolute.

2. Moral absolutists are *absolutely* wrong.

3. *Everyone* should be a relativist.

None of these imperatives survives the acid bath of relativism. The terms *never* (1), *absolutely* (2), *everyone* (3) do not cohere logically with the rules laid down by relativism itself. Therefore, on relativistic grounds, statements 1-3 cannot be true. Whenever relativists make such statements, they show that their moral system is unlivable and contradictory, and therefore false.

REFUTATION BY VISCERAL COUNTEREXAMPLES

Another blow against relativism is the visceral counterexample. Relativism, both cultural and individual, entails that no human act is intrinsically and always wrong. Yet consider these statements:

1. It is *always* wrong to torture the innocent merely for pleasure.

2. Rape is *always* wrong.

3. Female genital mutilation is *always* wrong.

If relativism is true, then statements 1-3 cannot be true, since they make absolute, universal and objective moral claims. Therefore, relativism is refuted by a simple *modus tollens* argument, which can be illustrated by using any one of the previous three statements. Consider statement 2:

1. If relativism is true, then rape is not always wrong, since a culture or an individual might allow for it under certain circumstances.

2. But rape is always wrong.

3. Therefore, relativism is false.

In a similar vein, this argument against cultural or individual relativism can be further developed by appealing to horrendous human evils such as

1. The terrorist apocalypse of September 11, 2001.

2. Joseph Stalin's planned famine in the 1930s, by which he killed six million peasants (mostly Ukrainian farmers) in order to punish resistance to the Communist system.[25]

Our immediate response to such events should be deep moral revulsion, not something like, "I wouldn't do that, but I cannot judge others." The profound moral loathing normally elicited by such events presupposes an objective moral order that has been transgressed.

THE ARGUMENT FROM DAMNATION

Horrendous evils call out for damnation, Peter Berger argues. Some acts are so desperately wicked that they demand a punishment greater than what earth has to offer. This "argument from damnation" is based on a class of human experiences "in which our sense of what is humanly permissible is so fundamentally outraged that the only adequate response to the offense as well as to the offender seems to be a curse of supernatural dimensions."[26] Countless people who witnessed two hijacked airplanes crash into the Twin Towers in New York City cried out, "Damn them!" These impassioned utterances were not examples of "taking the Lord's name in vain." Rather, they invoked God's prerogative to bring damnation. The damnatory utterances revealed a transcendent dimension in two senses.

First, this condemnation is "absolute and certain."[27] There are no qualifications or hesitations. The verdict has "the status of a necessary and universal truth."[28] While a social science analysis can give reasons why the hijackers did what they did in terms of politics, psychology and economics, these descriptions fall short of the proper and absolute moral judgment.

We are, then, faced with a simple alternative: Either we deny that there is here anything that can be called truth—a choice that would make us deny

---

[25]See Stephane Courtois et al., "The Great Famine," in *The Black Book of Communism: Crimes, Terror, Repression* (Cambridge, Mass.: Harvard University Press, 1999).
[26]Peter Berger, *A Rumor of Angels* (New York: Anchor Books, 1969), p. 65.
[27]Ibid., p. 67.
[28]Ibid.

what we experience most profoundly in our own being—or we must look beyond the reality of our "natural" experience for a validation of our certainty.[29]

Second, "Deeds that cry out to heaven also cry out for hell."[30] Given the unqualified condemnation of these evils, no earthly punishment suffices. The instant death of the nineteen hijackers of September 11, 2001, does not fit the enormity of their actions. This is because "the doer [of evil] not only puts himself outside the community of men; he also separates himself in a final way from a moral order that transcends the human community, and thus invokes a retribution that is more than human."[31] The argument from damnation centers on the fact that extreme evils cry out for supernatural justice.

Such unconditional evil shows its colors only against the backdrop of unconditional goodness. Thus we recall Philip Hallie's example of the praiseworthy actions of the Le Chambon villagers and the perdition-worthy actions of the Nazi doctors. But some have jettisoned the judgments of morality entirely—and nihilism darkly beckons us into the abyss.

FACING NIHILISM

Cultural relativism leads to individual relativism, and the autonomous self becomes the moral legislator. There is no rational basis for moral agreement or moral disagreement, since the self is supreme. Just as we cannot argue that vanilla ice cream is better than chocolate ice cream (since our evaluation is purely subjective), so we cannot argue that Nazi experimentation (read: torture) is any better or worse than the Huguenots' rescue of Jewish children from such a fate. Although relativism hides behind the makeup of commonly accepted social values, its true face is that of nihilism.

Nihilism has many dimensions, but its core is the denial of objective value of any kind: moral, aesthetic, intellectual and so on.[32] Nihilism as-

---

[29]Ibid. I have altered the punctuation slightly to make the quote more readable; the meaning is unaffected.

[30]Ibid.

[31]Ibid., pp. 67-68.

[32]See Karen L. Carr, *The Banality of Nihilism: Twentieth Century Responses to Meaninglessness* (New York: State University of New York Press, 1992). On nihilism in general see Eugene Rose, *Nihilism: The Root of the Revolution of the Modern Age* (Forestville, Calif.: Fr. Seraphim

serts moral meaninglessness. Since there is no objective moral meaning or value, there is no possibility of moral reasoning. Individuals are left to create "morality" on the basis of anything or nothing. People become, in Arthur Leff's term, "Godlets"—morally arbitrary agents who project values on the neutral screen of reality.[33]

A little-known German philosopher displays nihilism's visage: Max Stirner (1806-1856). Stirner was one of "the young Hegelians" and a contemporary of Karl Marx. In *The Ego and Its Own* (1845), Stirner argued that anything that is placed above the individual human being—such as a human essence, God, a moral ideal or political authority—robs each person of his or her unique individuality and agency. Therefore, it must die. He accused the atheists of his day of being "pious," since they inconsistently clung to Christian moral precepts.[34] But for Stirner, all such abstractions were illegitimate. We can only live for ourselves and on our own terms. "All things are nothing to me," exclaimed Stirner, emphasizing that nothing outside of himself had any claim on him. "I am nothing in the sense of emptiness, but I am the creative nothing, the nothing out of which I myself as creator create everything." Stirner goes beyond good and evil: "You think that the 'good cause' must be my concern? What's good, what's bad? Why, I myself am my concern, and I am neither good nor bad. Neither has meaning for me. . . . Nothing is more to me than myself."[35]

Stirner affirmed, "I decide whether it is the *right thing* in me; there is no *right* outside me."[36] All value is imputed by the self, for the self and through the self. The ego takes whatever it can; hence, the title of Stirner's lone work: *The Ego and Its Own*. No act is taboo.

> I secure my freedom with regard to the world in the degree that I make the world my own . . . by whatever might, by that of persuasion, or petition, of categorical demand, yes even by hypocrisy, cheating, etc.; for the means that I use for it are determined by what I am.[37]

Rose Foundation, 1994); Helmut Thielicke, *Nihilism: Its Origin and Nature—with a Christian Answer* (New York: Harper & Row, 1961).

[33]Arthur Leff's ideas will be developed later in this chapter.

[34]Max Stirner, *The Ego and Its Own* (New York: Libertarian Book Club, 1963), p. 185. In this, Stirner resembles Nietzsche.

[35]Ibid., p. 5.

[36]Ibid., p. 190. Stirner was exceptionally fond of the personal pronoun and the exclamation point.

[37]Ibid., p. 165.

The concept of rights, whether found intrinsically in the person or conferred by the state, is a fiction. The concept of right is just another unreal absolute placed above the individual ego. "What I can get by force I get by force, and what I do not get by force I have no right to."[38] Stirner follows this to the bloody end. "But I am entitled by myself to murder if I myself do not forbid it to myself, if I myself do not fear murder as a 'wrong.'"[39] Stirner fails to condemn neither incest between a man and his sister nor murder.[40]

Even the truth itself must yield to ego. Stirner understood that the concept of truth is closely aligned with the idea of God. Both stand over and above the individual and make demands on him or her. "As long as you believe in the truth, you do not believe in yourself, and you are a—a servant, a—religious man. You alone are the truth, or rather, you are more than the truth, which is nothing before you."[41] (I wonder if Stirner expected his readers to take his statement as truth for them.)

Stirner's pronouncements illustrate one truth: relativism is powerless to hold back nihilism. Of course, not all relativists will become *practicing* nihilists. Relativists might (arbitrarily) accept good morals: "Love works for me." But when moral standards are relative to the individual, nihilism is the result and "everything is permitted" (Dostoyevsky). The argument is a reductio ad absurdum:

1. Relativism leads to nihilism.

2. Nihilism is morally unacceptable.

3. Therefore, (a) relativism is morally unacceptable.

4. Therefore, (b) we need another moral theory to support objective morality.

The arguments of this chapter do not deny that moral principles may be applied somewhat differently from time to time. There is a difference between a deep moral *principle* and the application of that principle in a moral *rule*. For example, it is an objective and absolute moral *principle* that

---

[38]Ibid., p. 210.
[39]Ibid., p. 190.
[40]Ibid., pp. 45-46; 190.
[41]Ibid., p. 353 (the strange punctuation is in the original).

God should be worshiped, but the moral *rule* as to how God is worshiped changes from the Old Testament (the sacrificial system) to the New Testament (Christ fulfills the sacrifices). I have argued that ethical relativism is demonstrably false. If so, we are faced with an objective moral order of some kind. How can we best explain the existence of an objective moral order? A personal and moral God provides the best explanation for the existence of the moral values known to human beings.

FROM GOODNESS TO GOD

If Nazi experimentation on innocent children is unconditionally evil, and if the heroic actions of the Le Chambon villagers to save Jewish children are unconditionally good, we need to find a worldview that accounts for the origin, existence and knowledge of such good and such evil, and provides us sufficient moral motivation to pursue good and oppose evil. The basic argument from goodness to deity is fairly simple.

1. If a personal God does not exist, then objective moral values do not exist.

2. Objective moral values do exist.

3. Therefore, a personal God exists (by *modus tollens*).[42]

The truth of premise 2 has been established. Premise 1 has been affirmed by a number of atheists, although denied by others. We will first question whether or not an *impersonal* view of God (pantheism) can support moral values; then we will address the naturalist understanding of morality.

Pantheism and morality. Nondualistic pantheism claims that all that exists is divine and absolutely unitary.[43] The creed of one influential school of Hinduism (Advaita Vedanta) affirms that "Atman is Brahman." The

---

[42]William Lane Craig, "Five Reasons Why God Exists," in *God: A Debate Between a Christian and an Atheist*, ed. William Lane Craig and Walter Sinnott-Armstrong (New York: Oxford University Press, 2004), p. 19. I have added "personal" to the description of God, since there are impersonal concepts of God that Craig does not explicitly address.

[43]There are various metaphysical versions of pantheism, all of which are subject to philosophical problems. I have selected nondualistic pantheism because of its antiquity and popularity in the West. For a thorough critique of all major versions of pantheism see David Clark and Norman Geisler, *Apologetics in the New Age: A Christian Critique of Pantheism* (1990; reprint, Eugene, Ore.: Wipf & Stock, 2004).

individual self (Atman) is identical to Brahman (the impersonal and amoral universal self). In the Chandogya Upanishad, a father tells his son, "Believe me, my son, an invisible and subtle essence is the spirit of the whole universe. That is Reality. That is Atman. THOU ART THAT."[44] The phrase "THOU ART THAT" (some translations put it "THAT ART THOU") is repeated as the emphatic conclusion throughout the discourse. For Advaita Vedanta there is no distinction between the Creator and the creation; in fact, there is no Creator qua personal and moral agent who brought the universe into existence. This one (or nondual) Reality transcends the distinctions between good and evil. If "all is one," then there is no ontological space for any kind of diversity, even in morality. There are no objective moral values.

Hindu nondualism also affirms the reality of karma, an impersonal mechanism that makes judgments and assigns moral outcomes to people (and all living things) from lifetime to lifetime. So, pantheism attempts to give some place to moral evaluations as well as to moral rewards and punishments. However, the only way to defend such a doctrine is to hold a "two truth" view of reality, as the Hindu philosopher Sankara (788-820) attempted centuries ago.[45] Sankara said that morality is "real" on the lower level of reality (maya), but "unreal" on the higher level of absolute oneness (Brahman). It is a matter of perspective, but the enlightened being sees all things as pure Brahman. However, Sankara's attempt to rescue morality through a two-level view of truth fails because the ultimate reality of Brahman ends up negating and contradicting the appearance of moral duality (however real it may *seem*).

If there is but *one* supreme and nondual reality of Brahman, then duality cannot exist. Claims about moral duality (good and evil, kindness and cruelty) cannot describe objective conditions. Something cannot be both moral and amoral in the same respect at the same time. Yet this is exactly what the two-truth theory requires: reality is both moral (regarding the

[44]*The Upanishads*, trans. Juan Mascaro (Harmondsworth, U.K.: Penguin, 1965), quoted in James W. Sire, *The Universe Next Door: A Basic Worldview Catalog*, 5th ed. (Downers Grove, Ill.: InterVarsity Press, 2009), p. 150.

[45]Contemporary nondualist Ken Wilber attempts a similar philosophical rescue but adds nothing substantially to Sankara's strategy. See Ken Wilber, *A Brief History of Everything*, rev. ed. (Boston: Shambhala, 2000). See my review of this book, Douglas Groothuis, "A Summary Critique: *A Brief History of Everything*," *The Christian Research Journal*, <www.equipresources.org/atf/cf/%7B9C4EE03A-F988-4091-84BD-F8E70A3B0215%7D/DN267.pdf>.

individual self under the conditions of karma) and amoral (regarding its identity as one with Brahman). If so, the view is contradictory and therefore false. It fails the test of logical consistency.

Many nondualists, however, don't waste their energies trying to carve out some ontological space for moral distinctions. They simply deny the existence of objective moral values outright. In so doing they show a perverse logical consistency in the face of reality. In Robert Pirsig's popular novel *Zen and the Art of Motorcycle Maintenance*, he recounts a lecture he attended in India. The professor was expounding on the illusory nature of the world and Pirsig asked if it were true that the atomic bombs dropped on Hiroshima and Nagasaki were illusory. To this, "the professor smiled and said 'Yes.'" At this point Pirsig "left the classroom, left India, gave up."[46] To deny objective moral reality is illogical and unlivable. Unless an individual is a sociopath, he or she cannot live as if morality did not exist. So, nondualistic pantheism fails the test of livability or practicality.

We can approach the moral problem of nondualism from another angle: the propositional nature of moral knowledge. The deity of pantheism is not only impersonal and amoral but also unknowable in cognitive terms. If God is all and transcends all dualities, then the conceptual dualities required for propositions (moral and otherwise) must be negated as well. The simple affirmation S is P (a subject has a property) is dualistic to the core. The moral proposition "Murder is morally wrong" requires conceptual dualities that nondualism forbids. This simple and obviously true moral proposition is unacceptable given nondualism. If so, nondualism is false.

Therefore, nondualism is either internally contradictory (both affirming and denying morality) and therefore necessarily false, or it remains logically consistent and denies the existence of objective moral values. This leaves us with the following *modus tollens* argument:

1. If pantheism is true, then there are no objective moral values, either because (a) it overtly denies them or (b) it vainly attempts both to affirm and deny them on the basis of the two-level view of truth.

2. There are objective moral values.

3. Therefore, pantheism is false.

---

[46]Robert Pirsig, *Zen and the Art of Motorcycle Maintenance* (New York: William & Morrow, 1999), pp. 143-44.

Atheism and the denial of objective moral value. Most forms of atheism deny the existence of any nonmaterial form of reality. Reality is material and lacks any moral purpose or objective moral law. The atheist Bertrand Russell dramatically described this in his famous essay "A Free Man's Worship."

> That Man is the product of causes which had no prevision of the end they were achieving; that his origin, his growth, his hopes and fears, his loves and his beliefs, are but the outcome of accidental collocations of atoms; that no fire, no heroism, no intensity of thought and feeling, can preserve an individual life beyond the grave; that all the labours of the ages, all the devotion, all the inspiration, all the noonday brightness of human genius, are destined to extinction in the vast death of the solar system, and that the whole temple of Man's achievement must inevitably be buried beneath the debris of a universe in ruins—all these things, if not quite beyond dispute, are yet so nearly certain, that no philosophy which rejects them can hope to stand.[47]

Russell avers that morality is nothing more than a creation of human beings, who are themselves "the outcome of accidental collocations of atoms." He claims that the human herd, "being anxious that the individual should act in its interests, had invented various devices for causing the individual's interest to be in harmony with the herd. One of these is . . . morality."[48]

Therefore, despite their tragic condition, people should offer a noble but futile battle against the mindless cruelties of a world without design, meaning or hopeful destiny. Though the universe lacks purpose or meaning, humans have "ideals" in the face of it all.[49] These "ideals" do not come from the Creator or any realm of pure ideas (since omnipotent *matter* is all there is). And these human ideals are doomed to "extinction in the vast death of the solar system."

---

[47]Bertrand Russell, "A Free Man's Worship," in *Why I Am Not a Christian and Other Essays on Religion and Related Subjects*, ed. Paul Edwards (New York: Simon & Schuster, 1957), p. 107.

[48]Bertrand Russell, *Human Society in Ethics and Politics* (New York: Simon & Schuster, 1955), p. 125, quoted in Craig, "Five Reasons Why God Exists," p. 17.

[49]Russell, *Why I Am Not a Christian*, pp. 104-16. Some of Russell's language in "A Free Man's Worship" suggests that he may have believed in a realm of nontheistic objective values ("ideals") that exist above "the world of fact," but this is hard to interpret. If this was his position in this essay, he would fall under the category of "atheistic moral realism," which is critiqued below.

Morality thus reduces to physical and biological factors simply because this is all that exists. There is no independent sphere for moral realities that transcend the merely physical and cultural. Philosopher and arch-Darwinist Michael Ruse explains:

> Morality is a biological adaptation no less than are hands and feet and teeth. . . . Considered as a rationally justifiable set of claims about an objective something, ethics is illusory. I appreciate that when somebody says "Love thy neighbor as thyself," they think they are referring above and beyond themselves. . . . Nevertheless, such reference is truly without foundation. Morality is just an aid to survival and reproduction and has no being beyond or without this.[50]

Friedrich Nietzsche puts the matter dramatically in his well-known parable "The Madman," in which the madman claims that "God is dead." It is clear from the parable—and his other writings—that the "death of God" brought with it the death of objective value, meaning and significance; altruism had no basis in a universal moral law; the will to power was the essential fact in the struggle to thrive, and only a few specimens of humanity were worthy of existence. Nietzsche had no patience with Enlightenment philosophers who denied God yet retained Christian moral principles. Nietzsche hailed this deicide as the greatest of all deeds, but he knew—before many of his time—what the philosophical consequences would be.[51]

Like Nietzsche, existentialist Jean-Paul Sartre (1905-1980) rejected the notion that we could dispense with God and retain traditional morality, at least on the horizontal level.

> It [is] very distressing that God does not exist, because all possibility of finding values in a heaven of ideas disappears along with Him; there can no longer be an *a priori* Good, since there is no infinite and perfect consciousness to think it. Nowhere is it written that the Good exists, that we must be honest, that we must not lie; because the fact is we are on a plane where there are only men. As Dostoievsky said, "If God didn't exist, everything would be possible."[52]

---

[50]Michael Ruse, "Evolutionary Theory and Christian Ethics," in *The Darwinian Paradigm* (London: Routledge, 1989), pp. 262, 269.

[51]Friedrich Nietzsche, "The Gay Science," 125, in *The Portable Nietzsche*, trans. Walter Kaufmann (New York: Viking, 1968), p. 95.

[52]Jean-Paul Sartre, *Existentialism and Human Emotions* (New York: Philosophical Library, 1957), p. 22.

Sartre, Albert Camus and other atheistic existentialists attempted to transcend nihilism by heroically creating value in a valueless world. But even this existentialist imperative is without moral force if "all is permitted."[53] No human can create objective value; he or she might as well try to create a new primary color.[54] Sartre admitted as much when he lamented, "Man is a useless passion."[55] If all is meaningless and absurd, so is the creation of autonomous and individual value.

Arthur Leff: Law in the absence of God. In "Unspeakable Ethics, Unnatural Law," Arthur Leff argues that unless God is taken to be the unsurpassable moral authority behind human law, the law collapses into various arbitrary arrangements, none of which can survive the taunt, "But says who?" Leff begins by claiming that we moderns want to affirm two contradictory things:

1. [There is a] complete, transcendent, and immanent set of propositions about right and wrong, *findable* rules that authoritatively and unambiguously direct us how to live righteously.

2. We are wholly free, not only to choose for ourselves what we ought to do, but to decide for ourselves, as individuals and as a species, what we ought to be.[56]

Statements 1 and 2 are logically incompatible. Nevertheless, "What we want, Heaven help us, is simultaneously to be perfectly ruled and perfectly free, that is, at the same time to discover the right and the good and to create it."[57] This tension "between found law and made law" explains legal writers' recent suspicion that "we are able to locate nothing more attractive, or more final, than ourselves."[58]

To find authoritative law, we "must reach for a set of normative propositions in the form 'one ought to do X,' or 'it is right to do X,' that will serve" as the foundation for a legal system.[59] This found law "is not created by the

---

[53]For an excellent exposition and critique of existentialism, see James Sire, "Beyond Nihilism: Existentialism," in *Universe Next Door.*
[54]C. S. Lewis, "The Way," in *The Abolition of Man* (1944; reprint, New York: Touchstone, 1996).
[55]Sartre, *Existentialism and Human Emotions,* p. 90.
[56]Arthur Allen Leff, "Unspeakable Ethics, Unnatural Law," *Duke Law Journal* 1979, no. 6 (1979): 1229.
[57]Ibid.
[58]Ibid.
[59]Ibid., p. 1230.

finder, and therefore it cannot be changed by him, or even challenged."[60] If we imagine a legal system based on moral obligations that are absolutely binding, such as "Thou shalt not commit adultery," we must recognize that we need an *evaluator*, "some machine for the generation of judgments on states of affairs."[61]

> If the evaluation is to be beyond question, then the evaluator and its evaluative processes must be similarly insulated. If it is to fulfill its role, the evaluator must be the unjudged judge, the unruled legislator, the premise maker who rests on no premises, the uncreated creator of values. Now what would you call such a thing if it existed? You would call it Him.[62]

Such a "God-grounded system has no analogies." If God exists, "We are defined, constituted, as beings whose adultery is wrong, bad, sinful. Thus committing adultery in such a system is 'naturally' bad only because the system is supernaturally constituted."[63]

God's moral pronouncements would be "performative utterances"— statements that do not describe states of affairs but constitute them by the performance of the utterances. "There is no question whether I am accurately reporting on the world, because I am in the process of constituting it."[64] Consider, as well, the performative utterances by those officiating at weddings: "I now pronounce you husband and wife." Unlike the utterances of God, these words do not in themselves create the realities; rather, the utterances must be given according to certain rules and must be spoken by the appropriate persons.

But Leff moves beyond conventional performative utterances to the question of ultimate, objective moral authority. He claims that no one has this moral authority a priori to determine moral truth by fiat.

> There is no one who can be said a priori to have that power unless the question posed is also being begged. *Except, as noted, God.* It *necessarily* follows that the pronouncements of an omniscient, omnipotent, and infinitely good being are always true and effectual. When God says, "Let

---

[60]Ibid.
[61]Ibid.
[62]Ibid.
[63]Ibid., p. 1231.
[64]Ibid.

there be light," there is light. And when God sees that it is good, good is what it is.[65]

Leff then demurs that he cannot pronounce on whether God exists or not. He brought up the matter only to show why legal theorists despair of issuing legal or moral propositions without benefit of a "supernatural grounding."[66] Only God's will could survive "the cosmic 'says who?'" and remain authoritative, he claims. Legal and ethical theory must reckon with "the fact that, in the Psalmists words, there is no one like the Lord. If he does not exist, there is no metaphorical equivalent." This is because

> no person, no combination of people, no document however hallowed by time, no process, no premise, nothing is equivalent to an actual God in this central function as the unexaminable examiner of good and evil. The so-called death of God turns out not to have been just His funeral, it also seems to have effected the total elimination of any coherent, or even more than momentarily convincing ethical or legal system dependent upon authoritative extrasystemic premises.[67]

Only God, as the "final evaluator," could provide the moral premises that are outside of the merely human system.[68] In contrast, any surrogate evaluator "must be one of us, some of us, all of us—but it cannot be anything else."[69]

Without God any legal or moral system will be differentiated by its axiomatic choice of who serves as the moral evaluator. "Who among us, that is, *ought* to be able to declare 'law' that *ought* to be obeyed?"[70] Leff analyzes various social God candidates who serve as finite evaluators for law and morality.

First, he examines descriptivism, which takes legal systems as brute facts to be interpreted. This might be called "legal conventionalism," although Leff doesn't use that term. Descriptivism does not consider who generated the legal system but explores "what rules are actually obeyed" without trying to justify them or condemn them. "If law is defined as the

---

[65]Ibid., p. 1232, emphasis added.
[66]Ibid.
[67]Ibid.
[68]Ibid., p. 1233.
[69]Ibid.
[70]Ibid.

command of the sovereign, then the sovereign is defined as whatever it is the commands of which are obeyed."[71] There is no "extrasystemic" (or transcendent) principle available by which to judge the sovereign. So descriptivism "'validates' every legal system equally."[72] "Under Descriptivism, it is impossible to say that anything ought or ought not be."[73] God's role as final evaluator is given, ipso facto, to any and every legal system.

But, in the absence of God, why should the sovereign, or whoever generates law, "be entitled to final respect"?[74] Perhaps "each person is his own ultimate evaluative authority." This is called personalism. On this view, individuals now have the prerogative of determining good and evil through performative utterances: "What is said to be bad or good, wrong or right, is just that for each person, solely by reason of it being uttered."[75] The problem with descriptivism is that it validates any normative system, but the problem with "the 'God-is-me' approach is that it validates everyone's individual normative system, while giving no instruction in, or warrant for, choosing among them." How can a multiplicity of gods (or Godlets, as Leff calls them), all with identical moral rank, be morally regulated—in the absence of a final evaluator above them? When "Godlet preference" is the only basis for "interdivinity transactions," anything goes.[76] No appeal to a contract or treaty will rescue this sad situation, since on the personalist view, "a promise ought to be kept only if each promiser thinks it ought to be kept; the value of promise-keeping is no different from any other."[77]

Perhaps we can find some way to distinguish between individuals quantitatively or qualitatively. "One might choose to stand, that is, on the most evaluations or the best ones."[78] But majoritarianism fails as well, since the principle "the majority opinion should set the law" cannot be generated by any final evaluator.

Perchance logic will provide a solution for the problem of normative evaluation. The considered judgments of *rational* people whose moral systems are internally consistent should count more than the slapdash moral

---

[71]This is a tautology, but Leff does not note it.
[72]Ibid., p. 1234.
[73]Ibid.
[74]Ibid., p. 1235.
[75]Ibid.
[76]Ibid., p. 1236.
[77]Ibid., p. 1237.
[78]Ibid.

whims of the illogical. But here too the rational moralist can only be favored if "someone has the power to declare careful, consistent, coherent, ethical pronouncements 'better' than the sloppier, more impulsive kind. Who has that power and how did he get it"?[79]

Leff considers other possible sources of evaluations (including making a political constitution into a God), but all of them are subject to the same essential problem, which he refers to as "the cosmic 'sez who'" objection. A world without God is a world without objective moral authority.

Leff ends his essay with a compelling irony.

> All I can say is this: it looks as if we are all we have. Given what we know about ourselves and each other, this is an extraordinarily unappetizing prospect; looking around the world, it appears that if all men are brothers the ruling model is Cain and Abel. Neither reason, nor love, nor even terror, seems to have worked to make us "good," and worse than that, there is no reason why anything should. Only if ethics were something unspeakable by us, could law be unnatural, and therefore, unchallengeable. As things now stand, everything is up for grabs.
>
> Nevertheless:
> Napalming babies is bad.
> Starving the poor is wicked.
> Buying and selling each other is depraved.
> Those who stood up and died resisting Hitler, Stalin, Amin and Pol Pot—
> and General Custer too—have earned salvation.
> Those who acquiesced deserve to be damned.
> There is in the world such a thing as evil
> [All together now:] Sez who?
> God help us.[80]

While Leff claimed earlier that he would refrain from settling the question of God's existence, he now affirms God's nonexistence: "It looks as if we are all we have." Yet just a few words later Leff affirms the existence of objective good and evil regarding our response to tyrants and says, "There

---

[79]Ibid., p. 1238. To go beyond Leff, even if we make logical consistency a sufficient requirement for any plausible ethical system (since any system of thought must be logically consistent with itself), there could be two or more internally consistent ethical theories which, nevertheless, contradict each other. If so, we could not decide between them on the basis of logical consistency alone.

[80]Ibid., p. 1249. The brackets are in the original.

is in the world such a thing as evil." But even *this statement* is subject to the "sez who?" objection. In light of this conundrum: "God help us." He has argued himself into a corner, but from that corner he cries out for something he cannot reach, given his Godless presuppositions.

We can summarize Leff's dilemma through two arguments sharing the same conclusion. The arguments are structurally the same as the one given at the beginning of this chapter, but they emphasize *law* as well as objective morality.

1. If there is no God, then morality and law lose their foundations and there is no objective good and evil. (Leff is supported in this by Russell, Nietzsche, Stirner, Ruse, Sartre, Camus, Dostoyevsky and others.)

2. There is objective good and evil. (Illustrated by the examples Leff cites, as well as those I provided earlier in the chapter. Leff uses the "arresting counterexample" strategy that I mentioned earlier in my case against relativism.)

3. Therefore: (a) It is false that morality and law have no ultimate foundations and that there is no objective good or evil.

4. Therefore: (b) God exists as the ultimate Evaluator.

Leff's argument may be simplified as a *disjunctive syllogism:*

1. Either God exists (who provides the ultimate moral evaluation) or nihilism is true (all moral evaluations are arbitrary).

2. Nihilism is false because there is objective good and evil.

3. Therefore, God exists (as the ultimate moral evaluator).

For Leff to evade nihilism he must accept these arguments. But to do so, he must accept God as the "final evaluator" or the "evaluator-in-chief." Instead, Leff cries out to a God he denies. Despite the force of these arguments, nontheistic detractors have two lines of defense against this conclusion: the Euthyphro dilemma and atheistic moral realism. We will address each in turn.

The Euthyphro problem. First, many argue that making God the source of objective value solves nothing because it creates a dilemma fatal to theism. First raised by Plato in *Euthyphro*, this argument claims that (1) if something is good because God wills it good, God could will anything (even murder), and it would be, ipso facto, good. But this is absurd. (2) If God's will is not the source of the good, goodness lies outside of God's being and this robs him of his moral supremacy (an essential attribute of deity).

This dilemma is in fact a chimera since the theist can escape between the horns uninjured. The Euthyphro argument trades on a straw man (or straw god) that creates a false dilemma. Biblical theism—Islam is another matter (see chap. 24)—claims God as the source of all goodness on the basis of both God's character and God's will. God's moral will is based on God's changeless nature. The triune God, who has existed from eternity in a relationship of threefold love between the Father, the Son and the Spirit, cannot, for example, morally mandate rape. God's disposition forbids it. God's integrity abhors it. Objective moral values, according to the Bible, are not *created* in the sense that the contingent universe was created out of nothing (Genesis 1:1; John 1:1). Objective moral values have their source in the eternal character, nature and substance of a loving, just and self-sufficient God. Just as God does not create himself, so he does not create moral values, which are eternally constituent of his being. For that reason, when God creates humans in his own image and likeness, they need to know objective moral value and they must treat each other accordingly.

To hearken back to Leff, to say that God's moral utterances are "performative" does not mean that God brings something into being at a particular time that did not exist previously—as when a minister declares a couple now married as "husband and wife." Rather, God's character is eternally, changelessly good, so when God performs a moral utterance—as in the Ten Commandments or through the life and teachings of Jesus—he is speaking according to the eternal nature of his being. Herein is the warrant to declare the divine utterance unchallengeable and final. God's commands are not arbitrary, either in their relation to the divine character or in their relation to the divine creation, since the creation bears the mark of the Creator. Therefore, it is impossible for God to sanction adultery, stealing, murder, false witness and so on.[81]

---

[81]For a very illuminating treatment of this issue see James Hanink and Gary R. Marr, "What Euthyphro Couldn't Have Said," *Faith and Philosophy* 4, no. 3 (1987): 241-61. This also addresses the objection that God demanded murder when he commanded Abraham to offer his

Are moral values brute facts? A second attempt to reject God as the basis of morality is to view objective moral values as brute facts in a godless universe. There are objective moral values, but they are not related to God, because there is no God. This is called "atheistic moral realism."[82] The atheist resists both nihilism and theism thereby. This atheist argues that some things are morally despicable (rape) and other things are morally admirable (love). These are moral *facts* that cannot be reduced to contingent evaluations of individuals or societies. Thus, they are not reducible to any material properties, such as those addressed in biology. However, for various reasons—possibly because of the Euthyphro problem or the problem of evil—the atheist does not place these moral facts in God as the evaluator-in-chief. Sinnott-Armstrong claims that we know rape is wrong not because a God disallows it but simply because it hurts someone. That is sufficient. He sees no need to bring God into it, especially since he finds other reasons to disbelieve in God.[83]

But atheistic moral realism suffers from several philosophical problems. First, the ontological status of these moral facts is puzzling (at best). They simply exist without explanation as brute givens, part of the furniture of the universe. But as objective moral values, they are not reducible to physical states of affairs. Neither are they reducible to the subjective thoughts of any person's mind, since they are *objective*. These moral facts must be immaterial realities that are part of an otherwise totally material universe.[84] They are not personal beings or rooted in any personal being, so they lack consciousness or agency or feeling. Atheist philosopher J. L. Mackie argued that the existence of objective moral values was inconsis-

---

son Isaac as a sacrifice to God. See also William Alston, "What Euthyphro Should Have Said," in *Philosophy of Religion: A Reader and Guide*, ed. William Lane Craig (New Brunswick, N.J.: Rutgers University Press, 2002), pp. 283-98.

[82]See William Lane Craig and Walter Sinnott-Armstrong, *God? A Debate Between a Christian and an Atheist* (Oxford: Oxford University Press, 2003), pp. 19-20, 34, 67.

[83]See Walter Sinnott-Armstrong, "There Is No Good Reason to Believe in God," in *A Debate Between a Christian and an Atheist* by William Lane Craig and Walter Sinnott-Armstrong (Oxford: Oxford University Press, 2003), pp. 32-36. See also Iris Murdoch, *The Sovereignty of the Good* (1970; reprint, New York: Routledge, 1986).

[84]The atheist might grant the existence of other immaterial (but impersonal) entities such as propositions, numbers, etc., although thorough materialists will not grant any immaterial entities, since they need to explain *everything* in terms of the hard sciences. For a helpful discussion of this see Victor Reppert, *C. S. Lewis's Dangerous Idea: In Defense of the Argument from Reason* (Downers Grove, Ill.: InterVarsity Press, 2003), pp. 50-54.

tent with the atheist construal of reality; they were just too odd and out of place in a universe that is otherwise valueless and merely material. He denied their existence, since their existence would require that he—an atheist—enter the realm of theism.[85]

Second, moral facts would involve propositions, such as "Murder is wrong" or "Rape is wrong" or "Charity is better than cruelty." (They also involve the correlative imperatives, such as "Do not murder," "Do not rape," "Be charitable, not cruel." The significance of this imperatival aspect will be explained later.) So, if a human being thinks or speaks one of these moral statements, his or her statement is true if and only if the statement corresponds with some reality outside of the statement itself (given the correspondence view of truth). A moral statement made by a human (whether right or wrong) constitutes a *thought* in the human mind. How can a true statement (with normative force) exist apart from some kind of a mind? Yet according to atheistic moral realism, the objective moral facts required to rescue the atheistic worldview from relativism/nihilism are not located in any mind. They just are—mindless. This seems surpassingly strange metaphysically: there is propositional content without any mind proposing it.[86]

A far better explanation for the objective and normative existence of statements about morality would be that they are thoughts in a mind. The mind of God serves this function perfectly. However, atheistic moral realism has no such resource. Even if the concept of a brute moral fact can be made intelligible, theism provides the better explanation for moral truths.

British philosopher Hastings Rashdall argues that if we believe in an objective and absolute moral order, we must logically believe in God as well.

> Only if we believe in the existence of a Mind for which the true moral ideal is already in some sense real, a Mind which is the source of whatever is true in our own moral judgments, can we rationally think of the moral ideal as no less real than the world itself. . . . A moral ideal can exist only in a Mind from which all Reality is derived. Our moral ideal can only claim objective validity in so far as it can rationally be regarded as the revelation of a moral

[85]J. L. Mackie, *Ethics: Inventing Right and Wrong* (New York: Penguin, 1977), pp. 15-49.
[86]Moreland, *Scaling the Secular City*, pp. 124-25.

ideal eternally existing in the mind of God.[87]

Third, according to atheistic moral realism, there is no overall design of the universe that correlates brute moral facts with the human beings that fortuitously know them. That too is simply a happenstance. Because these moral facts are not personal, they cannot *communicate* their truths to humans through any kind of intentional cognitive agency. On this view, humans evolved for no purpose and simply happened to intuit brute moral facts through some faculty that transcends what was produced through natural selection and mutation, which is a purely material and unintelligent process.[88] Craig notes, "It is fantastically improbable that just that sort of creature would emerge from the blind evolutionary process which corresponds to the abstract existing realm of moral values."[89] But according to theism, moral knowledge is entirely explicable and expected. God, a moral and communicative being, created us to know moral truths.

Fourth, as Leff so ably argued, moral *evaluations*—whether they be about obligations, prohibitions, the moral status of institutions or whatever—are based on some *personal evaluating being*. But the atheistic moral realist simply posits the existence of objective moral values such as justice, fairness and love. These moral facts exist apart from any personal evaluator. We can imagine a person being just or issuing a just decree, but abstracting the concept of justice from anything personal vitiates it of its meaning.[90] To defend the existence of objective good and evil, we need the judgment of the evaluator-in-chief: a personal and moral God.

Fifth, how is moral obligation possible on the basis of impersonal, abstract and brute moral facts? Can we be obligated to a mere idea (which is not even in a mind)? The necessary and sufficient conditions for moral *obligation* depend on God. If, as Leff claims, "there is in the world such a thing as evil," we are obligated both to avoid and to oppose evil, as well as to promote good. The very concept of moral law implies a lawgiver to whom we are obligated. The nontheist philosopher Richard Taylor nails

---

[87]Hastings Rashdall, *The Theory of Good and Evil* (Oxford: Clarendon, 1903), 2:211-12, quoted in Ronald Nash, *Faith and Reason* (Grand Rapids: Zondervan, 1988), p. 161.

[88]Some atheists claim that an immaterial mind evolved from material antecedents, but this view is both rare and unsupportable. See my comments in chap. 17.

[89]Craig, "Five Reasons God Exists," p. 20. See also Greg Ganssle, "Necessary Moral Truths and the Need for Explanation," *Philosophia Christi* 2, no. 1 (2000): 105-12.

[90]See Craig, "Five Reasons There Is God," p. 19.

this down: "A duty is something that is owed. . . . But something can be owed only to some person or persons. There can be no such thing as duty in isolation."[91] Moral obligations make sense if understood as duties imposed by God, but if there is no "higher-than-human lawgiver," the very concept of moral obligation becomes "unintelligible."[92] This makes a simple *modus tollens* argument:

1. If God does not exist, there are no moral obligations.

2. There are moral obligations to parents, to children, to fellow citizens, to the truth itself and so on, which are more than socially constructed (relativism).

3. Therefore, God exists as the source of moral obligations.

Sixth, if God does not exist, it is impossible to hold a high moral view of human beings. If humans do not bear the divine image, their worth can only be determined on the basis of their differing abilities and empirical qualities.[93] Humans could not have "unalienable rights," as the Declaration of Independence states, if they have no objective value simply by being human. The moral traditions of the West, shaped significantly by Christianity, revolt against this kind of devaluation of human beings.[94] Yet when secular moral systems cling to this notion of equality, they illicitly depend on stolen capital from Christian theism.[95]

---

[91]Richard Taylor, *Ethics, Faith, and Reason* (Englewood Cliffs, N.J.: Prentice-Hall, 1985), p. 75; see also pp. 82-84. Interestingly, in Taylor's influential text *Metaphysics* (which has gone through four editions since its publication by Prentice-Hall in 1963), Taylor advocates two arguments for the existence of God. Apparently, he later changed his views or was presenting theistic arguments in *Metaphysics* that he himself did not believe. Elizabeth Anscombe also makes this point about moral obligation in "Modern Moral Philosophy," *Philosophy* 33, no. 124 (1958): 1-19.

[92]Craig, "Five Reasons God Exists," pp. 19-20.

[93]See Louis Pojman, *How Should We Live?* (Belmont, Calif.: Thomson, Wadsworth, 2005), p. 101. On the devaluing of human life and the need to reaffirm human beings as bearers of the divine image, see the prophetic book by Francis A. Schaeffer and C. Everett Koop, *Whatever Happened to the Human Race?* (New York: Fleming H. Revell, 1979).

[94]There are, of course, radical exceptions, such as Peter Singer, who realizes that without a Christian worldview there is no reason to give humans unique value. But since he rejects Christianity, he deems any preference of humans over others as "speciesism," which is in the same moral category as racism or sexism (see Peter Singer, *Rethinking Life and Death* [New York: St. Martin's Press, 1995]).

[95]I have in mind the *biblical* view of God. Hindu and Buddhist concepts of deity and humanity do not grant all humans inalienable rights, given their doctrine of karma. Islam teaches that humans are creatures of God, but it does not deem them made in the divine image. They are,

IS MORALITY SELF SUPPORTING?

There remains one last objection to the moral argument for God, which has been made by some theistic philosophers as well as by atheists.[96] The objectors claim that moral truths are necessary truths. This means that they cannot be false, just as a triangle must have only three sides. Moral truths are true in every possible world. A possible world, roughly, is a conceivable or logically coherent and maximal state of affairs.[97] So, in any possible world, either godless or theistic, moral truths obtain, such as "Murder is wrong." If so, the existence of God is not required to ground moral claims, since there are possible worlds in which no God exists but in which there is objective moral law. Much of what I have argued previously tackles this claim indirectly, since I've argued that moral truths cannot just exist as impersonal facts. Such putatative impersonal moral facts are too metaphysically attenuated to serve the functions that morality requires. But it can be added that even if moral truths are necessary truths, this need not dampen or defeat the moral argument for God.

A strong strain of Christian philosophy argues that God's existence is logically necessarily, as Anselm argued through the ontological argument. That is, God must exist. God exists in all possible worlds and is a logically necessary being. I defended two versions of the ontological argument in chapter ten. If God is logically necessary, then God's existence in every possible world entails the existence of moral truths in every possible world. So, there is no hindrance to arguing from morality to God, since they are correlative concepts, both occurring in every possible world. Moreover, necessary truths can "stand in relations of explanatory priority to one

---

rather, Allah's slaves. Therefore, Islam has never developed a tradition of human rights comparable to what emerged in the Christian West.

[96]See Richard Swinburne, *The Existence of God*, 2nd ed. (New York: Oxford University Press, 2004), pp. 212-15; Keith Yandell, "Theism, Atheism, and Cosmology," in *Does God Exist? The Craig-Flew Debate*, ed. Dan Wallace (Burlington, Vt.: Ashgate, 2003), p. 96. These theists could not use the kind of moral argument for God given in this chapter, but that would not foreclose other arguments for God. Thomas Nagel has given a sustained defense of the thesis that the necessary truths of logic and morality can exist without God (see *The Last Word* [New York: Oxford University Press, 1997], chap. 6). On this, see Douglas Groothuis, "Thomas Nagel's 'Last Word' on the Metaphysics and Rationality of Morality," *Philosophia Christi*, series 2, 1, no. 1 (1999): 115-22.

[97]For an introduction to possible-worlds thinking, see Ronald Nash, "Possible Worlds," in *Life's Ultimate Questions* (Grand Rapids: Zondervan, 1999). See the discussion in chap. 10 of this book.

another."[98] The statement "Murder is always wrong" is true in all possible worlds. But it is true in all possible worlds precisely because this statement is a thought in the mind of an omniscient and all-good being. "Murder is wrong" is necessarily true because "God exists" is necessarily true. In the same sense "addition is possible" is necessarily true because "numbers exist" is necessarily true.[99] We cannot have addition without numbers. The conception of the primacy of God in relation to necessary moral truths is found within the Augustinian tradition of understanding moral truths (and all other abstract objects) as necessarily true yet as also dependent on God's eternal intellection for their existence.[100]

NO MORAL MOTIVATION IN A GODLESS WORLD

Even if we were to grant the mind-independent existence of moral facts in a godless universe, this would hardly ennoble the moral life. Iris Murdoch, for example, calls us literally to be good for nothing.[101] By so doing, we are not pleasing a Perfect Being (there is none), nor fitting into the moral plan for the universe (there is none); neither can we expect any assistance in the moral life (since none is available), nor is it assured that good will ultimately triumph over evil (who knows?). Further, there is little or no incentive to do what is right when it counts against our own interests.[102] The call to altruism or self-sacrifice is decidedly strange in such a world; it seems not to fit a cosmos of impersonal moral facts that are impotent to reward virtue or punish vice.[103]

Yet if God exists as a personal and moral agent, morality rests secure on the divine character. The moral life, no matter how demanding, ultimately

---

[98]William Lane Craig, "A Reply to Objections," in *Does God Exist?* p. 169. See also Peter Van Inwagen, *Metaphysics* (Boulder, Colo.: Westview Press, 1993), p. 108.

[99]Craig, "A Reply to Objections," p. 169.

[100]I derive this insight significantly from Craig, *Does God Exist?* p. 170. On Augustine's view see Ronald Nash, *The Light of the Mind: St. Augustine's Theory of Knowledge* (Lexington: University Press of Kentucky, 1969).

[101]Murdoch, *Sovereignty of the Good*, p. 71.

[102]See Moreland, *Scaling the Secular City*, p. 127.

[103]On the strangeness of morality in a godless world see George Mavrodes, "Religion and the Queerness of Morality," in *Philosophy of Religion: An Anthology*, ed. Louis Pojman and Michael Rea, 5th ed. (Belmont, Calif.: Thomson, Wadsworth, 2008), pp. 578-86. Concerning the resources that Christian theism gives for moral motivation see Linda Zagzebski, "Does Ethics Need God?" *Faith and Philosophy* 4, no. 3 (1987): 282-93; and Moreland, *Scaling the Secular City*, pp. 128-32.

fits the contours of the divine creation and providential history—and eternity. God himself is available for both moral direction (through natural law and special revelation) and moral strength through the guidance and power of the Holy Spirit.[104]

THE GOD-HAUNTED CONSCIENCE

The moral argument has, for all its intricacies, an immediate existential bite. If objective moral truths bear witness to the existence of a good God as their source, we are then put in the dock before God. Our consciences reveal both a transcendent goodness and our own violation of this goodness through our pettiness, theft, cruelty, dishonesty, lust and a hundred other minor and major infractions. C. S. Lewis ends his moral argument for God in *Mere Christianity* by alerting the reader that Christianity has nothing to say to people "who do not know they have done anything to repent of and who do not feel that they need any forgiveness."

> It is after you have realized that there is a Moral Law and a Power behind the law, and that you have broken that law and put yourself wrong with that Power—it is after all this, and not a moment sooner, that Christianity begins to talk.[105]

---

[104]See Louis Pojman, *How Should We Live?* (Belmont, Calif.: Wadsworth, 2004), pp. 98-104. Pojman lists six factors that enrich morality if God exists, but he also makes some caveats concerning how religion can be used for evil.

[105]C. S. Lewis, *Mere Christianity* (1943; reprint, New York: Simon & Schuster, 1996), pp. 38-39.

16

The Argument from Religious Experience

THE CHRISTIAN WORLDVIEW CLAIMS THAT humans bear the image of God, a being who is personal, relational and communicative, and who created humans for relationships with himself based on knowledge. Being made in the divine image makes concourse with God possible and, in a sense, natural. Being God's image bearers establishes a created affinity between God and humanity, despite the fractures, fissures and stress points caused by sin. Moreover, we are creatures who may recognize God's actions in our midst or through the lens of history. This book has argued that God has revealed himself through rational reflection on the nature of God (the ontological argument), in the created order (the cosmological and design arguments) and the human conscience (the moral argument). The Bible and Christians through the centuries have also claimed that God reveals himself through various kinds of human experiences.

BASIC CONSIDERATIONS

The basic argument form for religious-experience arguments is inference to the best explanation. The ultimate question is whether the experience or experiences in question are veridical. A veridical experience is one that is truth-conveying and not deceptive. Veridicality relates experiences to truth claims. Hallucinations and mirages, for example, are not veridical. If a man dying of thirst in the middle of the desert hallucinates that there is a water fountain in front of him when none is there, he forms a false belief, and the experience is nonveridical. If I (a Miles Davis fan) hear a recording of Miles Davis at Starbucks and form the belief that "this is Miles," then that belief is true. Thus the experience is veridical.

Richard Swinburne's "principle of credulity" is a central key to determining veridicality. This principle claims that unless there is good evidence to the contrary, if person S seems to experience E, S should believe that E probably exists.[1] So, if I believe that I have encountered God in one way or another, all things being equal, I should suppose that I probably have encountered God. I may, of course, be mistaken. But this principle challenges the skeptical notion that all truth claims and experiences—especially truth claims and experience about God—are guilty until proven innocent. We usually don't apply this "guilty until proven innocent" line of reasoning in other cases. In fact, if every experience had to be justified on the basis of some other experience, we would fall precipitously into a bottomless pit of infinite regress; the result would be that no experience would be justified as veridical. So if there is no good reason to reject the existence of God, these experiences should be taken as providing some evidence for God's existence. The principle of credulity as applied to religious experience for Christianity could be annulled in principle if (1) the concept of God is incoherent, or (2) the existence of God is ruled out by a cogent case for naturalism. I have argued that neither of these conditions obtain; therefore, a religious experience argument may proceed. If successful, an argument from religious experience combines with natural theology, the reliability of the Bible and the uniqueness of Christ to contribute to the cumulative case for Christian theism.

A second principle from Swinburne further anchors religious-experience arguments. The "principle of testimony" claims that testimony is usually reliable.[2] That is, we typically do not assume people are lying or are deceived. This principle trades on the same idea as the principle of credulity: all things being equal, we typically do not doubt personal testimony. Of course, people may not be telling the truth, but the burden of proof lies on establishing guilt, not in establishing innocence. So, if someone claims to have experienced God in a particular way, we should not assume (before assessing the overall evidence) that this person has been deceived or is not telling the truth.

---

[1]Richard Swinburne, *The Existence of God*, 2nd ed. (New York: Oxford University Press, 2004), p. 303.
[2]Ibid., pp. 322-24.

But have mortals had experiences of God that can serve as evidence for God? Throughout history, a number of different kinds of religious experiences have been claimed by differing religions. I cannot assess all of them.[3] Nor will I address miracle claims reported outside of the Bible, which are thought to be signs of divine activity.[4] While some have argued that answered prayer provides empirical evidence for God or the supernatural, I will not address this either.[5]

Claims of religious experiences fall into four categories. First, an individual may deceptively claim to have had a religious experience that he or she never had. Given the principle of testimony, it is highly unlikely that all the reports of religious experience for Christianity through the centuries have been the result of conscious deception. Second, a person may have an experience that is completely subjective with no objective referent, such as an hallucination or mirage, yet believe that the experience is veridical. Third, someone may experience something out of the ordinary that is not divine, but wrongly claim that it is divine. This is false attribution. Fourth, a person may experience the divine reality. This, of course, is the category of explanation I want to argue for in this chapter.

To do so, I will address (1) the argument from emptiness and divine longing, (2) the argument from numinous experience and (3) nontheistic, mystical arguments.[6] Further, two naturalistic rejections of theistic arguments will be addressed as well: the projection argument and the reduction of religious experience to natural, physiological factors.

---

[3]For example, we will not address visionary experiences that concern angels, demons or supernatural personages. Phillip H. Wiebe deals with these sorts of phenomena (including visions of Jesus, who is taken by Christians to be the ultimate reality) in two books: *Visions of Jesus* (New York: Oxford University Press, 1997), and *God and Other Spirits* (New York: Oxford University Press, 2004).

[4]I discuss miracles in relation to the New Testament reports in chaps. 20, 22.

[5]See Paul C. Reisser, Dale Mabe and Robert Velarde, "Is God a Dependent Variable?" in *Examining Alternative Medicine: An Insiders Look at the Benefits and Risks* (Downers Grove, Ill.: InterVarsity Press, 2001). This addresses both New Age and more orthodox claims about empirically measuring the results of prayer. Their skepticism in no way demeans the importance of prayer in the Christian tradition. On this see Andrew Murray, *With Christ in the School of Prayer* (many editions).

[6]R. C. Zaehner divides mystical experiences into three categories: theistic, monistic and nature mysticism. I will address the first two but ignore the third, since it does not directly relate to the existence of God but rather the apprehension of nature (see R. C. Zaehner, *Mysticism: Sacred and Profane* [New York: Oxford University Press, 1957]).

THE ARGUMENT FROM EMPTINESS AND DIVINE LONGING

One argument for God's existence regards the aching absence of God in human experience. As St. Augustine famously said to God in the opening of *The Confessions*, "You have made us for yourself, O Lord, and our hearts are restless until they rest in You." There is, on the one hand, the pained longing for the transcendent and, on the other, the sense of the inadequacy of merely earthly goods to satisfy that longing. Blaise Pascal and C. S. Lewis have explored this in some depth. Combining their argument makes a strong case.

Part of Pascal's understanding of humans as "deposed royalty" (see chap. 18) is that people discern in themselves a wretchedness they cannot cure and a death they cannot escape. Unless people find solid solace in true religion, they will divert themselves from these realities to avoid despair. For Pascal the quest for diversion becomes a testimony to our fallen estate. If we were truly content with ourselves, we would have no need to distract ourselves. However, "being unable to cure death, wretchedness and ignorance, men have decided, in order to be happy, not to think about such things."[7] We escape through diversion.

But the very escape from our miseries testifies to our need of God. Diversion serves to distract humans from a plight too terrible to stare in the face, namely, our mortality, finitude and sinfulness. Pascal unmasks diversion for what it is—an attempt to escape unpleasant reality and an indication of something unstable and strange in the human condition. Interest in, or an obsession for, entertainment is more than silly or frivolous. It reveals a moral and spiritual malaise begging for explanation. Our condition is "inconstancy, boredom, anxiety."[8]

According to Pascal, the quest for diversion is rooted in the Fall. "There was once in man a true happiness, of which all that now remains is the empty print and trace."[9] All people seek happiness, but all complain endlessly of the inadequacies of life. Pascal argues that Jesus Christ uniquely answers the profound needs of humans, who cannot find adequate meaning and satisfaction in themselves or through worldly endeavors. Concern-

---

[7]Blaise Pascal, *Pensées* 133/169, ed. and trans. Alban Krailsheimer (New York: Penguin, 1966), p. 66.
[8]Ibid., 24/127, p. 36.
[9]Ibid., 148/428, p. 75.

ing this "God-shaped vacuum" (as the idea has often been summarized), Pascal explains:

> What else does this craving, and this helplessness, proclaim but that there was once in man a true happiness, of which all that now remains is the empty print and trace? This he tries in vain to fill with everything around him, seeking in things that are not there the help he cannot find in those that are, though none can help, since this infinite abyss can be filled only with an infinite and immutable object; in other words by God himself.[10]

Ecclesiastes observes that God "has made everything beautiful in its time. He has also set eternity in the human heart; yet no one can fathom what God has done from beginning to end" (Ecclesiastes 3:11). Pascal did not take this claim about inner emptiness to be merely a postdated check, cashable only in heavenly bliss (as much as this plays into Pascal's wager). A believer can experience something of spiritual renewal and ongoing spiritual empowerment in this life.[11]

C. S. Lewis developed his argument from yearning in his essay "The Weight of Glory." We all experience a deep sense of yearning or longing for something that the present natural world cannot fulfill—something transcendently glorious. In his autobiography he recounts several experiences of this throughout his life, in which he sensed something wonderful beyond his grasp. These were fleeting but invaluable moments, which he called the experience of "joy."[12] They were not encounters with God and did not directly result in his conversion. Instead, they were indicators that the everyday world was not a self-enclosed system; a light from beyond would sometimes peek through the "shadow lands." This thirst, which is intensified by small tastes of transcendence, indicates the possibility of fulfillment.

> Creatures are not born with desires unless satisfaction for those desires exists. A baby feels hunger; well, there is such a thing as food. A duckling wants to swim; well, there is such a thing as water. Men feel sexual desire; well, there is such a thing as sex. If I find in myself a desire which no experience in this world can satisfy, the most probable explanation is that I was

---

[10]Ibid.

[11]Ibid., 917/540, p. 312.

[12]See C. S. Lewis, *Surprised by Joy: The Shape of My Early Life* (New York: Harcourt Brace Jovanovich, 1955).

made for another world. If none of my early pleasures satisfy it, that does not prove that the universe is a fraud. Probably earthly desires were never meant to satisfy it, but only to arouse it, to suggest the real thing.[13]

Lewis argues that secularization and worldliness have deceived us into thinking that the satisfactions of earthly desires are adequate for our souls. We may, through our worldly ambitions and diversions, find our desires tamed and truncated when, in reality, something far greater is offered us. In our stupefaction, we

are half-hearted creatures, fooling about with drink and sex and ambition when infinite joy is offered us. Like an ignorant child who wants to go on making mud pies in a slum because he cannot imagine what is meant by the offer of a holiday at the sea. We are far too easily pleased.[14]

Ecclesiastes captures the hungry void of the human soul: "Everyone's toil is for their mouth, / yet their appetite is never satisfied" (Ecclesiastes 6:7). The spell of half-hearted obsessions is evident in the recent increase of all manner of plastic surgery for the alteration of outer appearance, even by those still in their thirties. Many attempt to spruce up the decaying earthen vessel at the expense of higher aspirations.

Lewis argues that this persistent yearning, or sense of *Sehnsucht*, reveals an elemental fact of the human personality, which alludes to another, higher reality.[15] It may be argued that being hungry does not mean that we will find bread, but Lewis thinks this misses the point.

A man's physical hunger does not prove that the man will get any bread; he may die of starvation on a raft in the Atlantic. But surely a man's hunger does prove that he comes of a race which repairs its body by eating and inhabits a world where eatable substances exist. In the same way, though I do not believe (I wish I did) that my desire for Paradise proves that I shall enjoy it, I think it a pretty good indication that such a thing exists and that some men will. A man may love a woman and cannot win her; but it would be very odd if the phenomenon called "falling in love" occurred in a sexless world.[16]

---

[13]C. S. Lewis, *Mere Christianity* (1944; reprint, New York: Simon & Schuster, 1996), p. 121.
[14]C. S. Lewis, *The Weight of Glory and Other Essays* (1949; reprint, San Francisco: HarperSanFrancisco, 1980), p. 26.
[15]*Sehnsucht* is a German word used by both C. S. Lewis and Sigmund Freud. On this, see Armand Nicholi, *The Question of God: C. S. Lewis and Sigmund Freud Debate God, Love, Sex, and the Meaning of Life* (New York: Free Press, 2002), pp. 41-47.
[16]Lewis, *Weight of Glory*, pp. 32-33.

This relation of desire to object is what Norman Geisler and Winfried Corduan call "fulfillability." It is a capacity for experience that may or may not be satisfied. Nevertheless, the capacity indicates the possibility of satisfaction and thus the probable existence of that object.[17]

Given the Christian hypothesis that humans are "deposed royalty"—both image bearers of God and fallen from grace—this desire for and limited sense of the transcendent must be viewed as marred by sin. The desire to transcend one's situation, to experience glory or joy, are not pure desires, but rather a mixture of the soul desiring its proper divine fulfillment and the flesh desiring to transcend a fallen world in any way possible.

Yet this yearning alone does not provide the answer to the human conundrum; it is neither a source of cognitive revelation from God nor a means of salvation. But it is a possible prelude to Christian fulfillment. At best, the argument from yearning renders credible some transcendent source of human satisfaction beyond the material world. Although it does not specify the exact nature of transcendence, it points toward a theistic worldview since it is based on the claim that humans desire a transcendent reality that can satisfy the human person. Buddhism, on the contrary, advocates the *cessation* of desire in order to experience nirvana, a condition in which personality is blown out. This is a prescription for transcendence, but one that eliminates desire instead of purifying and satisfying it. Similarly, the Advaita Vedanta Hindu's goal of intuiting Atman as Brahman (the individual self as the Universal Self) spells the end of personality, not its fulfillment.

NUMINOUS EXPERIENCE

How might a person more directly experience the divine in a personal sense? A standard category of religious experience is numinous experience. The term was coined by Rudolf Otto in *The Idea of the Holy*.[18] It refers to experiencing an object that is both transfixing and frightening. These experiences may be spontaneous or cultivated through religious disciplines. The numinous object is perceived as distinct from the person perceiving this object (unlike nondualistic experience). Phenome-

---

[17]Norman Geisler and Winfried Corduan, *Philosophy of Religion*, 2nd ed. (Eugene, Ore.: Wipf & Stock, 2003), pp. 74-76.
[18]Rudolf Otto, *The Idea of the Holy*, 2nd ed. (New York: Oxford University Press, 1958).

nologically, there is a triadic structure to the revelatory event, composed of (1) the subject who has the experience, (2) the experience or consciousness of the numinous itself and (3) the numinous object of the experience. These experiences are, philosophically speaking, *intentional:* they are about something objectively outside the self. They are also cognitive: features of the object are identified in the experience itself and later reported through the use of concepts.

This structurally resembles the normal experience of objects distinct from the self. Consider seeing a tree. (1) I am there to see it, (2) I have an experience of it and (3) the tree is there for me to have an experience of it. So, the *nature* or *structure* of these numinous experiences is the same as sense-experience claims. If we take these kinds of sense experiences as typically veridical (unless given some reason to question them), the door is open for numinous experiences to be regarded as veridical as well.

What singles out a *numinous* experience is the extraordinary nature of the object apprehended and, typically, the existential aftereffects of that experience. A classic numinous experience found in the Hebrew Bible is that of the prophet Isaiah after the traumatic death of King Uzziah.

> I saw the Lord, high and exalted, seated on a throne; and the train of his robe filled the temple. Above him were seraphim, each with six wings: With two wings they covered their faces, with two they covered their feet, and with two they were flying. And they were calling to one another:
>
>> Holy, holy, holy is the Lord Almighty;
>> The whole earth is full of his glory
>
> At the sound of their voices the doorposts and threshold shook and the temple was filled with smoke.

At this, Isaiah cried, "Woe to me! I am ruined! For I am a man of unclean lips and I live among a people of unclean lips, and my eyes have seen the King, the Lord Almighty" (Isaiah 6:1-5).

Isaiah's crisis is then resolved when God takes away his guilt and atones for his sin (Isaiah 6:6-7). Isaiah then receives his prophetic commission.

The structure of this account is triadic and has deep intellectual content.[19] There is subject, object and consciousness. Isaiah (who is the subject) reports what he has experienced (Isaiah's consciousness) of God (who

---

[19]I derive this triadic account from lectures by Keith Yandell.

is the object). Many truth claims issue from this experience: (1) God is maximally holy (indicated by the threefold use of *holy*). (2) God is worshiped by the angels. (3) The earth is filled with God's glory. (4) In response to this extraordinary phenomenon of God's appearance, the temple shook and filled with smoke. (5) In his own response, Isaiah sees that he is unholy along with his people, he laments over their sinful plight and then he is redeemed.[20]

Similar divine encounters occur throughout the Bible. These include God's revelation to Moses in the burning bush (Exodus 3),[21] Ezekiel's vision of God (Ezekiel 1–3), Job's vision of God (Job 38–42), the apostle Paul's experience of the risen Christ (Acts 9) and John's experience of the glorified Christ on the Isle of Patmos (Revelation 1:12-18). In each account the triadic structure is firmly in place, a structure identical to that of normal sense experience even if the object of that experience is not normal. However extraordinary these experiences may be, the framework of knowledge does not dissolve into mystical nonsense or illogic.

These kinds of experiences are not limited to biblical literature. After his death in 1662, among Pascal's personal effects was found a jacket that contained a parchment sewn into the inner lining. Apparently, Pascal had transferred these materials to every new jacket he acquired. He may have carried it with him constantly, literally next to his heart. Inscribed on the paper was a terse and poetic account of an experience dated November 23, 1654. This account is often referred to as "The Memorial." Pascal writes:

> From about half past ten in the evening until half past mid-night.
>
> Fire
>
> "God of Abraham, God of Isaac, God of Jacob," not of
> philosophers and scholars.
> Certainty, certainty, heartfelt joy, peace.
> God of Jesus Christ.
> God of Jesus Christ.
> *My God and your God.*

---

[20]For an excellent explanation of this account theologically, see R. C. Sproul, *The Holiness of God* (Wheaton, Ill.: Tyndale House, 1985).

[21]For a detailed epistemological account of the burning-bush event, see Douglas Groothuis, "Was Moses Rational After All?" *Philosophia Christi* 17 (1994): 31-44.

"Thy God shall be my God."
The world forgotten, and everything except God.
He can only be found by the ways taught in the Gospels.
Greatness of the human soul.
"Oh righteous Father, the world had not known thee, but I have known thee."
Joy, joy, joy, tears of joy.
I have cut myself off from him.
They have forsaken me, the foundation of living waters.
"My God wilt thou forsake me?"
Let me not be cut off from him for ever!
"And this is life eternal, that they might know thee, the only true God, and Jesus Christ whom thou has sent."
Jesus Christ.
Jesus Christ.
I have cut myself off from him, shunned him, denied him, crucified him.
Let me never be cut off from him!
He can only be kept by the ways taught in the Gospel.
Sweet and total renunciation.
Total submission to Jesus Christ and my director.
Everlasting joy in return for one day's effort on earth.
I will not forget thy word. Amen.[22]

The experience conveys many truth claims as well as Pascal's emotional response to the experience. The fact that Pascal kept this experience and the record of it secret lends credibility to the notion that he did not fabricate the event for some ulterior motive. After this experience, the re-created Pascal began to compose a defense of the Christian religion, a project he never completed. However, the *Pensées* has been eminently influential since its posthumous publication in 1669.

Numinous experiences are frequently noted in the history of Judaism and Christianity. As such, they provide good prima facie evidence for the existence of their object. Of course, similar experiences are found in Islam and in theistic versions of Hinduism and Buddhism as well. This fact, however, does not imply that (1) Islam, Buddhism, Hinduism and Christianity worship the same God or (2) that everyone who experiences the

---

[22]Pascal, *Pensées* 913, pp. 309-10.

numinous is redeemed thereby. A Muslim may experience God and mis-identify the object of the experience to some extent. For example, I may identify a hat on a table correctly but falsely claim that the hat is owned by my friend Bill, when it is owned by Tom. My experience of the hat is ve-ridical, but I have given qualities to the hat that are not true.[23] Moreover, a numinous experience need not be equated with salvation, although it might be. The companions of Paul on the Damascus Road experienced something of the supernatural appearance of Christ, but there is no indi-cation that this signaled their conversion (Acts 9:1-9).

All that can be claimed for veridical numinous experiences is that they involve an encounter with an external and personal being of transcendent significance. We cannot rest the entire case for Christianity on numinous experience. Nevertheless, the argument for veridical numinous experience is strong.[24]

TRANSFORMATIONAL EXPERIENCE

Another mode of monotheistic religious experience is transformational or causal. The focus here is not on the conversion experience but on the per-sonal transformation that accompanies Christian belief, repentance and religious commitment. Scripture is replete with promises to believers. A central promise was issued by Jesus after declaring his unique work as the Mediator between the Father and humans: "Come to me all you who are weary and heavy laden, and I will give you rest. Take my yoke upon you, and learn from me. For my yoke is easy and my burden is light, and you will find rest for your souls" (Matthew 11:28).[25]

Pascal had such a strong conversion (or reconversion) experience that it changed his life quite dramatically for the better. So too for the apostle Paul, who narrated his conversion twice in the book of Acts (Acts 22;

---

[23]This example and distinction is inspired by William Wainwright, *Philosophy of Religion*, 2nd ed. (Belmont, Calif.: Wadsworth, 1999), p. 136.

[24]For more on numinous experience as providing some evidence for God, see Keith E. Yandell, "Does Numinous Experience Provide Evidence That God Exists?" in *Christianity and Philoso-phy* (Grand Rapids: Eerdmans, 1984); and his *The Epistemology of Religious Experience* (New York: Cambridge University Press, 1994), pt. 4.

[25]For an in-depth treatment of the promises of the Bible and how they apply to Christians today, see Larry Richards, *Every Covenant and Promise in the Bible* (Nashville: Thomas Nelson, 1998).

26).[26] After speaking of his previous opposition to the Christian movement and recounting a blinding vision accompanied by the words of Jesus in Aramaic, Paul tells King Agrippa, "I was not disobedient to the vision [of Jesus] from heaven" (Acts 26:19). Rather, Paul made the gospel known far and wide after his conversion. "God has helped me to this very day" (Acts 26:22; see also Romans 1:16-17). Paul speaks often of the power of Christ working in his life even amid terrible difficulties and hardships (2 Corinthians 1:3-11). In these cases, Christians experience significant changes in their lives and attribute the cause of these changes to the influence of God.

These reports (if sincere) are, in fact, a necessary (but not sufficient) condition for the truth of the Christian faith, since many biblical passages predict that followers of Christ will experience "abundant life" subsequent to conversion (John 10:10). The nature and extent of these experiences in relation to Christian growth is a rich topic that cannot be fully addressed here.[27] Typically, Christians report a new moral awareness concerning good and evil in themselves and others (Hebrews 5:11-14), a sense of guidance and calling received primarily from the wisdom of the Bible (2 Timothy 3:15-17), as well as through Christian fellowship (Psalm 133), personal moral progress (adhering to moral principles and developing personal virtues through the agency of the Holy Spirit), and a deep sense of belonging to God through the work of Jesus Christ (Romans 8:14-16). Pascal found in Christ a vital balance and a third way between presumption and despair. "Jesus is a God whom we can approach without pride and before whom we can humble ourselves without despair."[28]

If such experiences as these were sparse or nil, a significant and necessary element of the Christian worldview would be missing. The Bible claims that believers will be divinely blessed with a new condition of being (Matthew 5:1-13) but will also be challenged and distressed by their own ongoing sinfulness and the opposition of forces hostile to their Christian

---

[26]John Stott explains the dynamics of Paul's conversion in *Why I Am a Christian* (Downers Grove, Ill.: InterVarsity Press, 2004), pp. 18-23.

[27]On basic Christian spirituality, see Francis Schaeffer, *True Spirituality* (Wheaton, Ill.: Tyndale House, 1972); Jerram Barrs and Ranald Macaulay, *Being Human* (Downers Grove, Ill.: InterVarsity Press, 1978); and J. P. Moreland, *Kingdom Triangle* (Grand Rapids: Zondervan, 2007).

[28]Pascal, *Pensées* 212/528, p. 98; see also ibid., 351/537, p. 133.

cause (Romans 7). These reports come not only from the Bible but from Christians around the world for the past two thousand years. This is to be expected if the Christian message is true. While they cannot stand on their own to defend the truth of Christianity, these accounts form a vital part of the confirmation of the Christian message. The witness of a transformed life may very significantly affect those close to the one transformed.[29] However, a life changed for the better after Christian conversion is not a *sufficient* argument for Christianity, as is sometimes claimed, since other religious traditions make similar claims about changed lives, and it is possible for positive change to be merely a placebo effect.[30]

However, reports abound from those who have fallen away from faith, some because of a perceived lack of religious experience. Yet this counterevidence need not be decisive against the positive apologetic from religious experience. First, Jesus and the apostles predicted that some would profess commitment to the Christian cause but fail to be true disciples. These will fall away. Jesus' parable of the sower and the three soils makes this clear (Matthew 13:1-23). The apostle John similarly warns of those who left Christian fellowship because they were never really a spiritual part of it to begin with (1 John 2:19; see also Hebrews 6:1-12).[31] Second, some people may embrace an aberrant form of Christianity in order to receive certain ecstatic experiences on a regular basis. When these experiences cease, they feel betrayed and cease to believe. Yet the Bible speaks of both the joy and the suffering of true believers, and never promises a life free of pain, hardship or sorrow (see 1 Peter 4:12-19; Psalm 88). Third, those not well-grounded in the rationality of Christianity may expect their religious experiences to carry them safely through all doubts about their faith. These people become disillusioned, not because biblical promises were tried and found to be wanting but because of their misunderstanding of the intel-

---

[29]See Walter Martin, "The Unanswerable Argument," in *Essential Christianity* (Ventura, Calif.: Regal, 1980).
[30]However, if these other religions fail the other tests of truth laid down in chap. 3, there would be no reason to take reports of positive change seriously.
[31]My understanding is that apostates were never regenerate in the first place. A strong case for the perseverance of the Christian (or eternal security, to use a less felicitous phrase) can be found in John Stott, *Men Made New* (Downers Grove, Ill.: InterVarsity Press, 1966), pp. 19-20; and, in more detail, in John Stott, "God's People United in Christ," in *Romans* (Downers Grove, Ill.: InterVarsity Press, 1994).

lectual foundations of faith itself.[32] Fideism is a weak reed to lean upon (see chap. 3).

OBJECTIONS TO RELIGIOUS-EXPERIENCE ARGUMENTS

One recurring objection is that religious experience cannot be checked or verified in any repeatable or objective way, as can be done with typical sense experiences or laboratory results. It is unreliable as a source of truth because of its subjective nature. However, this objection commits a category mistake and also begs the question regarding the claim against God's existence.

First, consider the category mistake. If I make the claim that there are two bushes outside of my study window, this can be easily verified or refuted by any interested observer. A person can come to my house and look at the bushes, or simply believe my testimony. But God is not a stationary physical object. While monotheism claims that God is omnipresent, God is not a perceptible material object physically located at one point in space. God is an invisible personal being who, in divine wisdom, reveals himself at different times and in different ways (Hebrews 1). Moreover, finite and fallible humans can only get partial glimpses of God, not the complete picture (1 Corinthians 13:9). This qualification is an integral part of the Christian hypothesis itself. Therefore, we should not expect God to be verifiable in the manner of physical objects. As George Mavrodes puts it:

> If Christian theologians are correct, then God will be experienced only when He chooses to reveal Himself. . . . The failure, then, of one person to apprehend God has very little significance against someone else's positive claim. For it is quite possible that the failure stems from the fact that the man is in some way yet unready for that experience, or from the fact that God—for reasons which we may or may not guess—has not yet chosen to reveal Himself to him.[33]

Suppose you spy a mountain goat through binoculars during a hike in

---

[32]For an excellent treatment of the relationship of faith, doubt and reason, see Os Guinness, *God in the Dark: The Assurance of Faith Beyond a Shadow of Doubt* (Wheaton, Ill.: Crossway, 1997); and Gary Habermas, *The Thomas Factor: Using Your Doubts to Draw Closer to God* (Nashville: Broadman & Holman, 1999).

[33]George Mavrodes, *Belief in God: A Study in the Epistemology of Religion* (New York: Random House, 1970), p. 79.

the Rocky Mountains, and you quickly hand the binoculars to your excited climbing partner. But after he receives the binoculars he cannot see the goat. What is a more reasonable response: that you lied or that the goat moved out of sight? This is analogous to experiences of God. God manifests himself as God wills. We cannot program religious experiences according to any formula.

Second, the skeptical objection begs the question against the manifestation of an immaterial and personal being. God *by definition* is not verifiable by simple empirical means. If we disallow reports of God on the basis that these reports do not fit the category of physical object reports (involving predictable measurement and repeatability), we simply beg the question as to whether religious experiences are veridical. But proper tests are available.

Religious experiences may be examined in various ways for veridicality. First, there is a long tradition of religious experiences within Christianity, starting with the religious experiences recorded in the Bible itself. We may test our experience or the claims of others against that basic tradition, realizing that there are variations within it. Second, for any religious experience we may ask if there might have been factors present that render the experience unbelievable. For example, various religious claims—but usually not by Christians—have been made by people under the influence of mind-altering drugs such as peyote or LSD.[34] Since these experiences are based on unusual and unnatural alteration of brain states, their veridicality is questionable in principle. Similarly, if a person has a history of hallucinating and gives a numinous report, this testimony could be brought into question. But to deem all numinous reports as hallucinations or deceptions begs the question. Put another way, to simply equate numinous experiences with mental illness poisons the well.

We should remember that religious experiences are only one avenue of evidence for a religious worldview. (Of course, in the nature of the case, there are no such positive, experiential arguments for atheism. So, this worldview lacks this type of evidence in its favor.) Worldviews must be evaluated and calibrated in relationship to other lines of evidence support-

---

[34]See Os Guinness, "The Counterfeit Infinity," in *The Dust of Death* (1973; reprint, Wheaton, Ill.: Crossway, 1994); and R. C. Zaehner, *Zen, Drugs, and Mysticism* (New York: Pantheon, 1972).

ing or questioning the seeming significance of the experience. For example, many Mormons claim that the Book of Mormon is divinely inspired, based on their experience of "the burning bosom" while reading it. But this experience, which is neither numinous nor transformational in and of itself, is hardly the kind of evidence that can support polytheism and the Mormon revision of key Christian doctrines regarding Christology and salvation. If, for example, one raises a question about the utter lack of historical or archaeological support for the Book of Mormon's many revisionist claims about American history and so forth, an appeal to the "burning bosom" is totally inadequate intellectually.[35]

Religious-experience claims need to be weighed against other germane sources of evidence for or against a worldview. This underscores the fact that religious experience forms only part of a cumulative case for Christian theism. It should not be made to shoulder the entire burden of apologetics. The phenomena of religious experience, however, form part of the Christian apologetic mosaic.

THE PROJECTION OBJECTION

Some object that religious experiences are merely projections of human thoughts and desires. The German philosopher Ludwig Feuerbach (1804-1872) claimed that the essence of theology was anthropology. All the concepts about God—omnipotence, omniscience, omnipresence—are merely objectified human attributes multiplied to infinity and then predicated to a nonexistent being. *"Man is the God of Christianity, Anthropology the mystery of Christian theology,"* claimed Feuerbach.[36] As this phantom deity is exalted, humans are debased. The more we worship a nonexistent God, the more alienated we become from ourselves. We should, therefore, leave deity behind and trust only in humanity.

Karl Marx (1818-1883) built on Feuerbach's foundation and added a political element, claiming that religion was "the opiate of the masses" and

---

[35]This is the common Mormon response, although some Mormon apologists may attempt to appeal (unsuccessfully) to revisionist historical claims outside the Book of Mormon. On Mormonism see Walter Martin, "Mormonism," in *The Kingdom of the Cults*, ed. Hank Hanegraff, rev. ed. (1967; reprint, Minneapolis: Bethany House, 1997); and Francis Beckwith et al., *The New Mormon Challenge* (Grand Rapids: Zondervan, 2002).

[36]Ludwig Feuerbach, *The Essence of Christianity*, trans. George Eliot (New York: Harper & Row, 1957), p. 336, emphasis in the original.

a false "haven in a heartless world."[37] The idea of God serves to pacify the masses, making them accept their exploitation by the owners. As such, the criticism of religion is the foundation of all criticism of society.

Sigmund Freud built on Feuerbach's thesis psychologically by adding that the ideas of God and religion are based on wish fulfillment.[38] In *The Future of an Illusion*, he argued that humans attempt to compensate for the often cruel and inexplicable universe they inhabit—a world that will kill them in the end—by projecting upon it a cosmic Father figure, God, who provides consolation and hope in the face of terror, trauma and trial.[39] Religious ideas also compensate for privations required for civilization.[40] Freud claimed that religious belief is an illusion. "What is characteristic of illusions is that they are derived from human wishes."[41] An illusion in Freud's sense is not necessarily a false belief.[42] Yet Freud argued that religious beliefs have no intellectual support beyond ancient tradition and present desires.[43] This is no harmless illusion: "Religion would thus be the universal obsessional neurosis of humanity."[44] Only science "can lead us to a knowledge of reality outside ourselves."[45]

These projection arguments are perennially pertinent in apologetics. Before pointing out their weakness, their strength should be saluted. The Bible condemns idolatry, which creates a god in the image of the finite creature. False religion is propelled by projection—as well as by repression of the truth. The Bible often warns its readers not to twist or distort its content for ulterior motives (Jeremiah 8:8; Matthew 15:1-9; 2 Peter 3:16).

But can all religious claims be reduced to merely human ideas and aspirations? There is good reason to deny this. First, Feuerbach, Freud and

---

[37]Karl Marx, *Critique of Hegel's Philosophy of Right*, quoted in Hans Küng, *Does God Exist?* (New York: Doubleday, 1980), p. 229. For an exposition and critique of Marx's view of religion, see ibid., pp. 217-61, and William Dryness, *Christian Apologetics in a World Community* (Downers Grove, Ill.: InterVarsity Press, 1983), pp. 172-80. For a theological critique, see Rousas John Rushdoony, *Freud* (Nutley, N.J.: Presbyterian & Reformed, 1965).

[38]Sigmud Freud, *The Future of an Illusion* (1927; reprint, Garden City, N.Y.: Anchor Books, 1961), p. 58.

[39]Ibid., pp. 23-24.

[40]Ibid., p. 24.

[41]Ibid., p. 49.

[42]Ibid.

[43]Ibid., p. 50.

[44]Ibid., p. 71.

[45]Ibid., p. 50.

Marx thought that the only basis for religious belief was superstition. Belief in God carried no evidential weight from science or philosophy or history, so they felt free to explain away belief in God as a mere psychological delusion. But, as this book argues, there is a host of arguments for the existence of God and for the Christian message.

Second, Feuerbach, Marx and Freud saw religion as morally degrading. This fueled their alternative explanation for religion. Feuerbach claimed that belief in God alienated humans from their own essence. Marx thought religion took the fight out of the proletariat. Freud saw religion as intrinsically neurotic, failing to provide individuals or society with emotional or moral health.[46] These charges cannot be addressed at length, but a few points suffice.

Concerning Feuerbach, although Christianity affirms the existence of an infinite God, it never denies the significance of finite human beings made in God's image. Humans were created to flourish under God and with each other and to develop and enjoy creation for the glory of God. As Irenaeus affirmed, "The glory of God is man fully alive."[47] Humans cannot rightly claim autonomy from God, but they can claim dignity under God and redemption in Christ, despite their sin. Marx's claim that religion pacifies the masses is a patently false generalization. Religion certainly did not pacify William Wilberforce from taking on the entire economic and cultural system of slavery in Great Britain in the name of God's justice. In fact, Christian ideals have been behind a plethora of positive social movements throughout history.[48] Despite Freud's zeal to be "scientific," his psychological investigations were quite speculative and based on very limited empirical evidence. The religious people he analyzed may have been neurotic, but this hardly condemns religion as neurotic in itself.[49]

Third, the presence of a strong wish for X to be true does not count against X being true, as Freud himself admitted.[50] In fact, a universal

---

[46]Ibid., pp. 60-62. For a thorough critique of Freud, see Küng, *Does God Exist?* pp. 262-339.
[47]Irenaeus *Against Heresies* 4.20.7.
[48]See Alvin Schmidt, *How Christianity Changed the World* (Grand Rapids: Zondervan, 2004); David Bentley Hart, *Atheist Delusions: The Christian Revolution and Its Fashionable Enemies* (New Haven, Conn.: Yale University Press, 2009). On how Christianity has a richer culture heritage than Islam, see Alvin Schmidt, *The Great Divide: The Failure of Islam and the Triumph of the West* (Salsbury, Mass.: Regina Orthodox Press, 2004).
[49]Paul Vitz, *Sigmund Freud's Christian Unconscious* (Grand Rapids: Eerdmans, 1993).
[50]Freud, *Future of an Illusion*, p. 49.

desire for transcendence may indicate that this wish may be fulfilled in some way, as argued by Pascal and Lewis. Hans Küng puts it well, "In a word, something real can certainly correspond in reality to my psychological experience; a real God can certainly correspond to the wish for God."[51] Someone may come to Christian faith for purely psychological reasons (say, to receive the love, acceptance and forgiveness never received from his or her father) and still hold a true belief. To dismiss this belief as false because it is psychologically motivated is a classic example of the genetic fallacy. The origin of a belief does not, in and of itself, disqualify the belief as being true. According to Moreland, "Where a belief comes from is a different matter than why one should believe it. The former involves the psychology of discovery, the latter the epistemology of justification."[52] If we have other reasons to believe that X does not exist (e.g., if X is the tooth fairy), then it would be appropriate to seek psychological (or neurotic) reasons why anyone would believe in X. But until and unless we have such reasons, such an intellectual autopsy would be premature and presumptuous.

Fourth, there are aspects of Christianity that are not good candidates for wish fulfillment. Most Christians are ill at ease with the doctrine of eternal punishment and may generally *wish* that the God of the Bible were less wrathful. I would not invent a religion that would have many of my friends and relatives ending up in hell. Nor would I create one in which God scrutinizes all my thoughts to the degree that he deems vicious thoughts tantamount to committing vicious acts (see Matthew 5:22). One mark of biblical revelation is that God continues to surprise and sometimes even scandalize people. Numinous experiences are often a shock to recipients and not something desired or expected at all. These shocking elements of Christianity don't render Christianity irrational. Rather, they mean that God is not subject to domestication. God is too untamed and holy for that.[53]

Fifth, we may reverse the projection argument in two ways. Theists may argue that atheists reject God because of a cosmic authority problem rooted in bad relationships with fathers or other authority figures. This

---

[51]Küng, *Does God Exist?* p. 210.
[52]J. P. Moreland, *Scaling the Secular City* (Grand Rapids: Baker, 1987), p. 229.
[53]See R. C. Sproul, *If There Is a God, Why Are There Atheists?* (Wheaton, Ill.: Tyndale House, 1988). Or as C. S. Lewis has one of his characters in *The Lion, the Witch, and the Wardrobe* say, "Aslan [the Christ figure] is not a tame lion."

rejection of authority figures in general then translates into the rejection of God, the ultimate authority. Thomas Nagel has admitted as much on his part.[54] Instead of projecting a religious figure above the universe, atheists erase the concept because of past psychological distress, possibly because of a desire to kill the father (Freud's Oedipus complex). In fact, Freud did have a strained relationship with his father,[55] as did several other notable Western atheists.[56] Prima facie, it seems more likely that atheists suffer from some psychological disorder that makes theistic belief difficult, since throughout history the vast majority of humans on the planet—including many who are quite brilliant—have believed in God or some form of the supernatural.[57] Moreover, as Moreland notes, "Conversions to Christianity fail to fit into some tight control groups, for converts come in all kinds of personality types, at different states in life (happiness, sadness), and different circumstance in time, place, culture, and education."[58] Explaining these conversions—or theistic belief in general—in terms of specifiable neuroses of a Freudian (or other) kind seems unlikely if not impossible.

A second form of turnabout is credible as well. The Christian may claim that God has placed within us a psychological mechanism that may produce true belief about God's existence based on the father-child relationship. John Hick makes this clear:

> For if the relation of a human father to his children is, as the Judaic-Christian tradition teaches, analogous to God's relationship to man, it is not surprising that human beings should think of God as the heavenly Father and should come to know him through the infant's experience of utter dependence and the growing child's experience of being loved, cared for, and disciplined within a family.[59]

Humans may gain an intimation of their relationship to God through the analogy of parent-child relationships. Unless we have ruled out theism on other grounds, we cannot foreclose the discussion of this possibility.

---

[54]Thomas Nagel, *The Last Word* (New York: Oxford University Press, 1998), p. 130. See the discussion of this in chap. 7.

[55]See Nicholi, *Question of God*, pp. 16, 23-24, 35, 47-48, 71, 117, 149, 223-24.

[56]See Paul Vitz, *Faith of the Fatherless: The Psychology of Atheism* (Dallas: Spence, 1999).

[57]Justin Barrett argues that it is natural to do so on the best evidence available from neuroscience (see *Why Would Anyone Believe in God?* [Lanham, Md.: Rowman & Littlefield, 2004]).

[58]Moreland, *Scaling the Secular City*, p. 229.

[59]John Hick, *Philosophy of Religion*, 4th ed. (Englewood Cliffs, N.J.: Prentice-Hall, 1990), p. 35.

NEUROTHEOLOGY: A CATEGORY MISTAKE

In recent years a host of brain researchers have been exploring and conjecturing as to the biological basis for religious beliefs. The basic thesis of many of these opinions is that beliefs in God or the sacred can be explained on the basis of certain functions in the brain. That is, neuroscience gives the answer to why we have religious beliefs, and it has nothing to do with any objectively real state of affairs that we perceive or discern.[60] Most of these accounts presuppose materialism and so beg the question philosophically: Since we know there is no God and no sacred realm (all is material), we need to explain (and explain away) why so many have religious experiences. Of course, this is not an argument, but a presupposition not argued for.

However, it is no threat to religious belief if certain brain states *correlate* with certain religious beliefs or experiences. We are material as well as spiritual beings. The mind interacts with the body, as Scripture teaches and our experience confirms. The threat to religious belief only appears when this correlation is understood as a reduction of the spiritual to the material (see chap. 17).

There is another problem for this reductive view: it works as a boomerang against itself. If religious beliefs can be explained away as illusory simply because their neurological components (physical states) are identified, we must, by the force of the same argument, explain away as illusory the belief that religious beliefs are illusory (there is no God) because they too are merely neurological states. This kind of reduction and refutation would extend to all beliefs that can be identified with brain activity.[61] But this conclusion results in an epistemological nihilism that is unsupportable logically and existentially.

It speaks volumes to note that while millions of dollars in grant money goes to explaining the neurological basis of religion, nothing goes to explain the neurological basis of atheism or skepticism. Apparently, atheism and skepticism are innocent until proven guilty, whereas religious beliefs are just plain guilty.

---

[60]See, for example, M. Alper, *The God Part of the Brain: A Scientific Interpretation of Human Spirituality and God* (New York: Rogue Press, 2000), p. 79.
[61]William James made essentially this same argument against those who dismissed religious beliefs on the basis of some kind of physical malady (see his *The Varieties of Religious Experience* [New York: Longmans, Green, 1902], pp. 10-18).

In conclusion, all the advances in the knowledge of the neurological workings of the brain and its relation to religious beliefs and experiences in no way refute the truth of these beliefs. That would be the work of philosophy. Here, as in so many other areas, naturalistic science (i.e., materialist explanation) is an unaccredited usurper of intellectual authority.[62]

DIVERSE RELIGIOUS EXPERIENCE CLAIMS: EASTERN RELIGIONS

We have thus far addressed only monotheistic and Mormon claims of religious experience. But what of the religious experiences found in religions such as Buddhism and Hinduism? This is a somewhat complicated topic, but a brief critique follows.

First, some thinkers, such as W. T. Stace, have tendentiously understood mystical experience as quintessentially nondualistic. In *Mysticism and Philosophy*, Stace arbitrarily stipulates nondualistic experiences as the norm for all mystical experience and simply relegates numinous experience to the margins.[63] This highly selective reading does not do justice to the wealth of theistic experiences throughout history and across cultures. Neither does it address the profound intellectual problems found in these kinds of experiences.

Claims of "enlightenment" found in the literature and testimonies of Buddhists and Hindus almost invariably involve notions antithetical to the nature of religious experiences as explained earlier. Despite the considerable differences between these two religions (and the pluralism within each religion), the enlightenment experience of both nirvana (Buddhism) and moksha (Hinduism) require the negation of individuality, personality and language. The ultimate reality that is purportedly experienced is taken to be ineffable, utterly beyond the realm of concepts. There is no personal encounter with another being of immense holiness and power. Rather, one ceases to experience reality as a human personality (with its volition, emotion and thought). Nirvana is what is left when a candle is extinguished, or

---

[62]For an excellent treatment of neurology in relation to religious belief, see Paul Copan, "Does Religion Originate in the Brain?" *The Christian Research Journal* 31, no. 2 (2008): 32-40.

[63]W. T. Stace, *Mysticism and Philosophy* (New York: Jeremy Tarcher, 1960).

literally, "to become extinguished."[64] It is a state beyond and without desire or personal, individual existence. Moksha, similarly, is reckoned to be a state in which the self ceases to exist and as such finds its identity with Brahman, which is an impersonal being without qualities.[65] Moksha speaks of the realization of a Universal Self (Brahman) and nirvana of no self at all (anatman), but both deny the reality of the separate and individual self and the ability of language to capture this state. Therefore, all the qualities that make numinous experiences similar to sense perception experiences vanish. There is no knower, knowing or known in any ordinary sense of these terms.

The possibility of *conceptual experience* vanishes as well, since these enlightened states leave concepts behind. Therefore, a mystical experience of this kind cannot communicate the knowledge needed to form an argument that moves from the mystical experience to the truth and rationality of *any* worldview. Worldviews are necessarily conceptual systems, which claim (rightly or wrongly) some important *knowledge of reality*. If I claim that experience X is beyond all the categories of normal human knowing—such as human selfhood, propositional language and so on—that experience cannot possibly serve as logical evidence for any worldview (or for any proposition, for that matter). The concept of evidence requires that propositions be ordered into premises leading to a conclusion based in some logical form (deduction, induction or abduction). But if mystical experience X is ineffable (having no intellectual content), it is forever barred from the proceedings of logic and evidence.

Reports of these experiences may nevertheless be couched in grandiose and appealing language—despite the fact that there is literally nothing to report in language. Ken Wilber often waxes ecstatic about experiencing the "Emptiness" that transcends personality, logic and language, yet he repeatedly describes this reality (in language, of course) as possessing positive properties, such as freedom, love, wholeness and more. He even writes of "the original Face," which is the oneness of the universe.[66] This emotive

---

[64]Bart Gruzalski, *On the Buddha* (Belmont, Calif.: Wadsworth, 2000), pp. 16-17.

[65]The concept of a being without qualities is deeply problematic. See Keith Yandell, *Philosophy of Religion* (New York: Routledge, 1999), pp. 102-9.

[66]Ken Wilber, *A Brief History of Everything*, rev. ed. (Boston: Shambhala, 2000), p. 39. The same problem besets the also nondualistic worldview of Joseph Campbell in his bestselling book *The Power of Myth* (New York: Doubleday, 1988). He refers to God as ineffable but then uses vari-

reference is intrinsically personal, whereas Wilber's worldview is impersonal; he specifically disavows the existence of a personal God. Poetic language, however, cannot paper over poor philosophy.

Yet some will claim that the practice of yoga (or a similar Eastern discipline) produces positive benefits that bespeak the truth of the worldview motivating the discipline. While it is often claimed that yoga is a neutral physical practice, its roots and structure are based on Hindu metaphysics. The point of yoga (which means to be united with the sacred) is to find the impersonal God within through posture, breathing and chanting mantras. These are means of neutralizing the body's power in order to escape its hindrances. Yet in the West, yoga has been repackaged as merely a physical discipline, a claim that Hindu yoga practitioners reject.[67]

Given this argument, whatever may happen in the practice of yoga, it cannot serve as *evidence* in a worldview in which the highest state of reality is deemed to be beyond logic, language, personality and individuality. Even if yoga makes a person more relaxed or tranquil, these effects contribute nothing to the rationality of a worldview in which human personality, logic, language and even the body itself are transcended in favor of a supposed higher state of consciousness that cannot be described coherently.

Yoga and related disciplines were never meant to contribute to human flourishing (a key promise of the Christian worldview); rather, their goal is to escape the limits of humanity so that a person may attain to a state beyond personality, individuality and relationality. There is nothing in this of the human (qua human) experiencing the divine through an encounter or transformation. Instead, personality (and its capacity for knowledge, relationships and rationality) is dissolved into the impersonal divine. Besides, no *impersonal* mystical experiences can provide *personal* satisfaction for the world-weary soul. The God-shaped vacuum is itself eliminated (along with the entire person) instead of being filled with "an infinite and immutable

---

ous concepts to describe God. For a critique of these ideas and others, see Douglas Groothuis, review of *The Power of Myth* by Joseph Campbell, *Christian Research Journal* (fall 1989) <www .iclnet.org/pub/resources/text/cri/cri-jrnl/web/crj0036a.htm>.

[67]Subhas R. Tiwari, "Yoga Renamed Is Still Yoga," *Hinduism Today*, January-February-March, 2006 <www.hinduismtoday.com/modules/smartsection/item.php?itemid=1456>. On the nature and dangers of yoga see Douglas Groothuis, *Confronting the New Age* (Downers Grove, Ill.: InterVarsity Press, 1988), pp. 77-80.

object; in other words by God himself," as Pascal put it.[68]

These nondualistic religious-experience reports have no parallel to common sensory or conceptual experience. They allow for no triadic structure of subject-object-consciousness as in numinous experience. Rather, the human personality is annulled and concepts are not available to form arguments. In nondualistic forms of mysticism (such as that espoused by Wilber, Advaita Vedanta and transcendental meditation), the categories of good and evil dissipate into the oneness of reality. But if the one true reality is amoral (beyond the dualities of good and evil), there is no basis for any personal transformation from poor to better through mystical experience. Nor could any purported transformation from poor to better serve as evidence for the veridicality of the experience, since the ultimate reality (Brahman) is beyond good and evil. Sainthood is no compliment for an amoral deity.

GOD IN HUMAN EXPERIENCE

Religious experiences of a personal kind—wherein neither God nor the person experiencing God dissolves into an impersonal oneness or void—are real and reoccurring across cultures and down through time to the present day. Many yearn for them, and many of us find them. This provides considerable evidence for the existence of a personal and relational being who is the ground of these experiences. But these accounts of divine encounters do not stand alone; they should be joined to the other arguments given in this book for the existence of a being who is the Creator, Designer and Lawgiver. Moreover, chapter seventeen avers that the human quest for the transcendent is best explained—in both its majesty and misery—by the Christian account of human nature.

---

[68]Pascal, *Pensées* 148/428, p. 75.

The Uniqueness of Humanity

Consciousness and Cognition

IF CHRISTIANITY IS TRUE, THEN humans stand in a unique relationship to both God and the rest of creation. They represent God as God's image bearers and so resemble God as moral and personal beings, but on a finite scale (Genesis 1:26). As God's regents, they exercise a sentient, logical and linguistic supremacy over the rest of creation (Psalm 8). This means that humans possess a unique awareness of themselves, creation and God (consciousness), are uniquely able to relate concepts rationally within their awareness (cognition), and can communicate their rational awareness through signs, both written and spoken (language). The Christian conception claims that these human capacities cannot be accounted for by any nontheistic worldview.[1] That is, humans cannot be reduced to the status of an evolved animal possessing nothing but natural properties. Nor can they be elevated to divine status (as pantheism asserts), since their finitude is always with them, despite their divinely endowed capacities.

Biblical anthropology explains these unique and distinguishing abilities in terms of the human person being an embodied mind or soul. We are a relational unity of body and soul. Philosophically, this is known as substance dualism. Each person has a material nature (explicable in terms of

---

[1]I will not take up the uniqueness of human language and the argument that theism better explains language than naturalism or pantheism. On this see Clifford Wilson and Donald McKeon, *The Language Gap* (Grand Rapids: Zondervan, 1984); and John W. Oller and John L. Omdahl, "Origin of the Human Language Capacity: In Whose Image?" in *The Creation Hypothesis*, ed. J. P. Moreland (Downers Grove, Ill.: InterVarsity Press, 1994). On how human language is significantly different from animal communication see Mortimer Adler, *The Difference of Man and the Difference It Makes* (New York: Holt, Rhinehart & Winston, 1967), chaps. 8-9; and Stephen R. Anderson, *Dr. Doolittle's Delusion: Animals and the Uniqueness of Human Language* (New Haven, Conn.: Yale University Press, 2004).

physics, chemistry and biology) and an immaterial nature (which interacts with but also transcends material states). Both of these natures compose the human person, although our immaterial substance is separated from the physical nature at death and before resurrection.

The concepts of *substance* and *property* need to be fleshed out a bit before developing an argument for substance dualism. First, a substance is a particular thing; it cannot be two places at once. (However, a universal, such as redness or circularity, can be two places at once.) A horse is a substance. Second, a substance can change its properties. A horse's coat may change color over time, but the horse remains a horse. Third, a substance is a basic or essential entity—unlike properties, which affix to substances. A horse is not a property of anything, although its color, age and size are properties of its substance. Fourth, a substance has causal powers. A horse can eat food and provides rides for people. Properties do not have such power.[2]

Applied to substance dualism, a person's soul or mind is not a property of his or her body, but a separate substance that bears properties (such as being alert) and interacts with the person's body. Neither is one's body a property of the soul or mind, but a separate substance that bears properties (such as weighing 200 pounds) and which interacts with the person's mind or soul.

This description of humans as both physical and mental is evident in the Bible. In Genesis 2, God created the first human out of the earth (matter) and breathed life into him by God's Spirit, thus giving him a mind or spirit. Moreover, Jesus' understanding of the person was dualistic. This is evident when Jesus assured the repentant thief on the cross next to him that the thief would be with Jesus in paradise that very day, even though their bodies would be lying dead in a grave (Luke 23:43).[3] The apostle Paul affirms dualism as well when he claims that to be "away from the body" is to be "at home with the Lord" (2 Corinthians 5:1-10). While some Christians have written off dualism as a hangover from Greek philosophy, the view is deeply biblical.[4] A materialist account of humanity, on

---

[2]This explanation is dependent on the discussion in J. P. Moreland, *Scaling the Secular City* (Grand Rapids: Baker, 1987), p. 79.

[3]See Douglas Groothuis, *On Jesus* (Belmont, Calif.: Wadsworth, 2003), pp. 40-42.

[4]For an in-depth biblical and theological defense of this thesis, see John Cooper, *Body, Soul, and the Life Everlasting: Biblical Anthropology and the Monism-Dualism Debate*, rev. ed. (Grand Rapids: Eerdmans, 2000); see also N. T. Wright, *The Resurrection of the Son of God* (Minneapolis: Fortress, 2003), chaps 5-10.

the other hand, fits far better with a Darwinian understanding than a biblical one. Moreover, as we will see, consciousness and cognition are better explained by dualism than by materialism, and dualism is better explained by theism than by any other worldview.

This chapter will argue that the Christian worldview best accounts for these distinctive human endowments. By wielding these arguments, I hope to use several aspects of the human condition as a colorful argument in the larger palette of Christian apologetics.

ACCOUNTING FOR CONSCIOUSNESS

Through his discovery of the incorrigible truth "I think, therefore I am," Descartes famously battled skepticism.[5] Even if Descartes were deceived about everything else, he knew he was thinking. And if he was thinking, he existed, since thoughts cannot exist apart from thinkers any more than a triangle can exist apart from having three sides.[6] Given this reality of thinking and thus thinkers, how can we philosophically explain the ability to think at all? Thinking, broadly understood, involves consciousness and cognition. We turn first to the most general category—human consciousness.

THE MATERIALIST PUZZLE

Consciousness is a puzzle to materialist philosophers. They have it, but they are not sure how they got it or why they have it. Materialist philosopher Colin McGinn argues in *The Mysterious Flame* that consciousness will forever remain a mystery, eluding explanation, because evolution keeps it under lock and key. "The bond between mind and the brain is a deep mystery. Moreover, it is an ultimate mystery, a mystery that human intelligence will never unravel."[7] This is a telling admission for a materialist, who attempts to account for *everything* on the basis of physics, chemistry and biology. Nevertheless, McGinn reaches this conclusion given the vex-

---

[5]It is less well known that this line of reasoning goes back to Augustine's critique of the skeptics in *The City of God* 11.26. See similar ideas in Augustine's *The Trinity* 9.6.9. On Augustine's treatment of skepticism see Gordon R. Lewis, "Immediate Knowledge," in *Faith and Reason in the Thought of St. Augustine* (Ph.D. diss., Syracuse University, 1959), pp. 117-24. I owe these references to Gordon Lewis.

[6]René Descartes, *Meditations on First Philosophy* (many editions); and *Rules for the Direction of Mind* (many editions).

[7]Colin McGinn, *The Mysterious Flame* (New York: Basic Books, 2000), p. 5.

ing problems inherent in accounting for consciousness materialistically. He claims—without much argument—that theistic accounts of nature have been usurped by Darwinism. (I argued against Darwinism and for intelligent design in chapters 13-14.) Thus, naturalism is the default mode—however inadequate it may be.[8]

One reason consciousness is deemed "the ultimate mystery" is that the materialist must describe reality in terms of material properties alone: size, weight, mass, motion and so on—the province of biology, chemistry and physics. These scientific descriptions presuppose consciousness, since scientists (as conscious beings) make them. But is consciousness itself susceptible to a purely materialistic description? Materialists have given several answers, and we cannot explore the complexities of what is known as "the mind-body problem."[9] However, the main conundrum is captured by G. K. Chesterton's philosophical quip:

> It is obvious that the materialist is always a mystic. It is equally true that he is often a mystagogue. He is a mystic because he deals entirely with mysteries, in things that our reason cannot picture; such as mindless order or objective matter becoming subjective mind.[10]

Similarly, atheist philosopher Raymond Tallis questions evolutionary theory's efforts to explain consciousness in material organisms. The evolutionary stories claim that

> every characteristic of living creatures has been generated by the operation of natural selection on spontaneous variation; that it is there because it has, or at the very least did once have, survival value or was a consequence of other things that had survival value.[11]

As a naturalist, Tallis assumes that the vast majority of cosmic history lacked any consciousness or intelligence and that there was no directing intelligence behind the universe. Then conscious beings appeared through unplanned evolution. Later still, conscious beings evolved intelligence and

---

[8]Ibid., pp. 80-85.
[9]For a very thorough treatment of this, see J. P. Moreland and Scott Rae, *Body and Soul* (Downers Grove, Ill.: InterVarsity Press, 2000), pt. 1.
[10]G. K. Chesterton, *Generally Speaking* (New York: Dodd, Mead, 1929), p. 106, quoted in *The Quotable Chesterton*, ed. George J. Marlin, Richard P. Rabatin and John L. Swan (Garden City, N.Y.: Image Books, 1987), p. 211.
[11]Raymond Tallis, "The Unnatural Selection of Consciousness," *The Philosopher's Magazine*, 3rd quarter (2009): 28.

the ability to deliberate. But Tallis asks what benefit consciousness and intelligence convey, since the universe did quite well for billions of years before these properties evolved. Much of the living world survives and reproduces through unconscious and nonrational means. Long before the higher functions of intelligence emerged, there would have been "a more promising alternative to consciousness at every step of the way: more efficient unconscious mechanisms, which seem equally or more likely to be thrown up by the spontaneous variation."[12]

Tallis thinks that unconscious mechanisms are more likely to evolve partially because of the fact that consciousness differs so radically from the nonconscious states that precede it in evolutionary history. The organ of sight (a collection of physical properties), for example, is vastly different from "the awareness of light" (which is not a collection of physical properties). We will address this issue—the qualia problem—shortly, but suffice it to say that Tallis's naturalistic worldview fails to explain how an unconscious universe evolved consciousness when consciousness was neither needed for survival nor can be explained in materialistic terms.

Before addressing the arguments against materialism and for mind-body dualism, we should retrace a few of our apologetic steps, because our argument does not appear in an intellectual void. I have argued from natural theology and science that materialism is false and that theism is true. If there were no good arguments for a personal-moral God, we would have more of a philosophical justification for claiming, in Chesterton's words, that "mindless order" and "objective matter" could "become subjective mind." As Moreland notes, "Much of the motivation for mind/body physicalism has been the desire to argue for physicalism at the worldview level. If physicalism at that level is false, then part of the reason for holding to mind/body physicalism is removed."[13] Theism provides a worldview framework for considering substance dualism. The reasoning for this is rooted in the character of God as the immaterial Creator and Designer and Lawgiver of the universe. Such a universe is surely friendly to dualism since God himself is an immaterial thinking and acting being who interacts with the material world.[14]

---

[12]Ibid., p. 32.
[13]Moreland, *Scaling the Secular City*, p. 82.
[14]See Charles Taliaferro, "The Project of Natural Theology," in *Blackwell Companion to Natural*

MIND AND MATTER: A DIFFERENCE IN KIND

There is a difference in *kind* between mental and physical states that has ontological implications. That is, a mental state is not a very refined or sophisticated physical state; it is not a physical state at all. A difference in kind involves two considerations. When two things differ in kind, one thing "possesses a defining characteristic not possessed by the other."[15] For instance, odd numbers cannot be evenly divided into whole numbers, while even numbers can be so divided. Second, there is no intermediate ground between two things that differ in kind. There is nothing "between" an odd number and an even number. A number is either one or the other. Mortimer Adler summarizes the distinction:

> The impossibility of intermediates constitutes the discontinuity or discreteness of kinds: the only things that differ in kind differ discretely or discontinuously. . . . Thus, for example, a whole number is either odd or even. There is no third possibility or *tertium quid*.[16]

A difference in degree, on the other hand, admits of intermediaries. Something may be more or less bright, dark, long, short, big or small. Two power hitters in major league baseball may differ from another *in degree* (of homerun-hitting proficiency) if one hits forty-one home runs in a season and the other hits thirty-nine home runs the same season. But both hitters differ *in kind* from the baseballs they belt out of the park. Adler notes that unlike difference in kind, "two things that differ in degree differ continuously, not discretely."[17]

DISCREPANT PROPERTIES

How do we explain ontologically the *unique* attributes of mental life—those features that seem to differ *in kind* from material states? It is only to consciousness that materialists ascribe states such as faith, hope, love, rational calculation, seeing blue, feeling blue and so on. A rock is not loving; a bed is not hateful. Love and hate are uniquely mental. As William

---

Theology, ed. William Lane Craig and J. P. Moreland (Malden, Mass.: Wiley-Blackwell, 2009). See also Charles Taliaferro, "God and the World," in *Consciousness and the Mind of God* (New York: Cambridge University Press, 1994).
[15]Adler, *Difference of Man*, p. 19.
[16]Ibid., p. 20.
[17]Ibid.

Hasker puts it, the materialist explanation makes no gain in simplicity over dualism if, after rejecting a mental substance, "we must then ascribe to the physical substance properties quite unlike those it is known to have *in all other contexts*."[18] Mental states and physical states differ in kind, not in degree. Thus they cannot be identical, given this very simple principle of identity: whatever differs *in kind* cannot be identical.[19] There is no metaphysical halfway house between mental and physical states. There is no graduated spectrum of states *between* the mental and the physical. In fact, mental states lack the *defining properties* of physical states, and physical states lack the *defining properties* of mental states. Contradictory properties cannot attach to the same thing. As Leibniz noted, if we liken the human brain to a factory, we could see any number of movable parts, but we could never see the thinking itself.

> One is obliged to admit that *perception* and what depends on it *is inexplicable on mechanical principles*, that is, by figures and motions. In imagining that there is a machine whose construction would enable it to think, to sense and to have perception, one could conceive it enlarged while retaining the same proportions, so that one could enter into it, just like into a windmill. Supposing this, we should, when visiting within it, find only parts pushing one another, and never anything by which to explain a perception. Thus it is in the simple substance, and not in the composite or in the machine, that one must look for perception.[20]

Or consider Pascal's probing question concerning the immateriality of the soul. "When philosophers have subdued their passions, what material substance has managed to achieve this?"[21]

Thoughts are not round or square, do not weigh a certain amount, smell like roses and are not colored. A thought about a rose isn't red; a thought

---

[18]William Hasker, *Metaphysics* (Downers Grove, Ill.: InterVarsity Press, 1982), p. 71, emphasis in the original.

[19]This is a version of Leibniz's famous law of the identity of indiscernibles, which states that if there is no difference between object A and B, they are really the same object. I have cast the difference in terms of kind to emphasize the kind of difference between mind and body.

[20]Gottfried Leibniz, *Monadology and Other Philosophical Essays*, trans. and ed. Paul Schrecker and Anne Martin Schrecker (New York: Bobbs-Merrill, 1965), sec. 17, emphasis in the original. Leibniz was not a substance dualist, but his point against materialism is still germane to my argument.

[21]Blaise Pascal, *Pensées* 115/349, translated by A. J. Krailsheimer (New York: Penguin Books, 1985), p. 59. See also ibid., 108/339b, p. 57.

about a rough road isn't rough; a thought about the smell of steak doesn't smell like steak. Yet materialists want to maintain that thoughts are, in some sense, identical to material states. Richard Taylor, for example, thinks we can, at least in principle if not in present-day science, find the physical state of affairs that explains the as-yet-mysterious referential mental states.[22] But does this notion make any sense?

PRIVATE ACCESS AND INCORRIGIBILITY

During delicate operations on the brain when the patient is awake, the surgeon literally sees the brain and knows the material nature of the brain far better than the patient. The surgeon can ask the patient what he feels in response to stimulation, and brain function can be accurately monitored.

Although the surgeon can see the brain (and has seen the brain previously through a CAT scan), she cannot see or hear the patient's emotions ("I am afraid"). Nor can she see or hear the thought the patient forms ("I feel the prod" or "I don't feel the prod"), although the verbal report of this thought is heard shortly after the feeling occurs. The point here is that these states of consciousness—feeling fear and forming thoughts—are not reducible to material descriptions. Even if some device could register every material property and process of the human brain, it could not capture consciousness itself. The fact that consciousness is affected by the brain and by other physical objects, such as the probe, in no way reduces consciousness to a physical property any more than a wooden oar that troubles water turns the water into wood.

Related to private access is the mind's incorrigibility concerning its own subjective states. An incorrigible criminal is one who cannot be reformed. An incorrigible belief is one that cannot be wrong. For example, if you feel a pain, you cannot be wrong about feeling that pain. This is true even if no physician can explain why you have this pain. It is also true when someone is experiencing "phantom limb pain." The claim "I am feeling pain *in my arm*" would be false if the person had lost the arm where the pain purportedly resides. But the claim "I am feeling pain" is true no matter what the

---

[22]See Richard Taylor, *Metaphysics,* 4th ed. (Englewood Cliffs, N.J.: Prentice-Hall, 1990), pp. 31-32. This is a kind of promissory note or postdated check for future science. This defensive move is common when naturalists run out of explanations.

physical situation is that accompanies it. Yet we do not have incorrigible knowledge of physical objects. We may be wrong as to why we have a pain. We may think we see water on the road when it is really a mirage. And so on. Therefore, incorrigible beliefs are another marker of immaterial consciousness.[23]

QUALIA: BEING THERE

The man's feeling the prod and phantom limb pain are but two of many examples of the experience of qualia. Qualia refer to the sensations that make up subjective feeling or the experience of being conscious. Some of the qualia I am experiencing as I type this argument include (1) minor pain in my left shoulder that often results from typing, (2) the feeling of a large stuffed animal propping up my left shoulder to reduce the pain in my shoulder and (3) the sound of a small fan aimed at me to keep me cool while I write. While all these qualia are *associated with* material states, they are not *reducible to* material states. I experience them. These subjective experiences are first-person accounts that are not reducible to or translatable into third-person accounts pertaining to material states. But on a materialist view, all experience should be reducible to third-person descriptions of physical states. Howard Robinson exposes the difficulty for the materialist in accounting for qualia:

> The notion of *having something as an object of experience* is not, prima facie, a physical notion; it does not figure in any physical science. *Having something as an object of experience* is the same as the subjective feel or the *what it is like* of experience.[24]

PROPOSITIONAL ATTITUDES AND INTENTIONALITY

In addition to sensations and perceptions, qualia also include propositional attitudes. A propositional attitude is the cognitive orientation one takes toward a proposition. One may either believe proposition P, fail to believe P or suspend judgment of P. But propositional attitudes do not fit easily under any material description. A computer works on a binary system of

---

[23]See J. P. Moreland and William Lane Craig, *Philosophical Foundations for a Christian Worldview* (Downers Grove, Ill.: InterVarsity Press, 2004), pp. 234-36.

[24]Howard Robinson, *Matter and Sense* (Cambridge: Cambridge University Press, 1982), p. 7, quoted in Moreland, *Scaling the Secular City*, p. 85, emphasis in the original.

zeros and ones, but it has no cognitive orientation toward the codes. It computes, but it does not think or experience anything, as even materialist John Searle has powerfully argued.[25]

Belief, disbelief, suspension of belief and confusion—as well as hoping, fearing, wishing and so on—are propositional attitudes *about* things in the world. They are directed at something. If you believe that the Cubs will win the World Series next year, that belief pertains to something outside of yourself. The same holds true for an equally delusional belief such as fearing the attacks of vampires. These beliefs have a direction, aim or focus. They identify and pick out a state of affairs in the world. Material- ists have had a whale of a time explaining this phenomenon, known as *intentionality*, which is an aspect of propositional attitudes. This is because intentionality is an irreducibly subjective state of mind; it is not amenable to natural properties. A cup may sit next to a fork, and both may rest on a table. These kinds of relationships pose no problem for the materialist. But the relationship of a person's belief to that purported belief's referent is something else entirely. However, a mind (an immaterial substance) may hold beliefs intentionally related to the world through thoughts.

TRUTH: A MATERIALIST PROBLEM

Materialism also founders when it attempts to account for truth, which is closely connected to the previous discussion of qualia, propositional atti- tudes and intentionality. First, I have the qualia (subjective state) of believ- ing that John Coltrane was the greatest jazz saxophonist of all time. Sec- ond, this example of qualia is a propositional attitude; I *believe* it to be true. Third, a propositional attitude entails a proposition. A proposition is what a declarative sentence expresses.[26] Similar sentences can express the same proposition, such as (1) "John Coltrane is the greatest saxophonist of all time," and (2) "No one equals or surpasses John Coltrane as a jazz saxo- phonist." The meaning of these two sentences is identical. But what, then,

---

[25]John Searle, "Can Computers Think?" in *Minds, Brains, and Science* (Cambridge, Mass.: Har- vard University Press, 1984).

[26]Other kinds of sentences, such as questions, exclamations and imperatives, are not proposi- tions, since they do not affirm positively a state of affairs. Nevertheless, they are in the neigh- borhood of propositions and are meaningless without propositions connected to them. For more on this, see Douglas Groothuis, "The Truth About Truth," in *Truth Decay* (Downers Grove, Ill.: InterVarsity Press, 2000).

is a proposition? It cannot be the sentence itself, since various sentences—even in different languages—may express the same proposition. A proposition is, rather, an intellectual unit of meaning not reducible to any of its physical manifestations. It is a thought consisting of concepts that compose an affirmation about reality. Propositions, which are at the heart of all human language, are out of step in a materialist universe, since they are not material things or states. Fourth, my belief is incorrigibly intentional; it is *about* John Coltrane. Intentionality is not a physical state, as I just pointed out.

But fifth, there is yet another problem for the materialist: the nature and knowledge of truth itself. Truth is the correspondence of a proposition with its referent. My statement "John Coltrane is the greatest jazz saxophonist of all time" is true if and only if John Coltrane possessed the properties I ascribe to him.[27] Truth, therefore, has a *relational* nature: a propositional belief *corresponds* to its object. A false proposition fails to match reality. But the relationships required for truth cannot occur in a materialistic world because beliefs and propositions are not reducible to material states. Therefore, according to materialism, the *relationship* between my belief (a truth claim) and the world to which it refers (what makes it true or false) cannot exist, since this relationship is not a material thing. C. S. Lewis captures this:

> We are compelled to admit that between the thoughts of a terrestrial astronomer and the behaviour of matter several light-years away that particular relation we call truth. But this relation has no meaning at all if we try to make it exist between the matter of the star and the astronomer's brain, considered as a lump of matter. The brain may be all sorts of relations to the star no doubt: it is a spatial relation, and a time relation, and a quantitative relation. But to talk of one bit of matter as being true about another bit of matter seems to me to be nonsense.[28]

For materialism, it seems that truth vanishes without a trace into matter. If so, we must turn a deaf ear to the materialist's pleas to believe that materialism—or anything else—is itself true (more on this problem below).

---

[27]For an argument that aesthetic qualities are objective and hierarchically ranked, see Groothuis, "True Beauty," in *Truth Decay.*

[28]C. S. Lewis, *Christian Reflections* (Grand Rapids: Eerdmans, 1987), pp. 64-65.

LOVE: THE MATERIALIST ACID

Imagine that I have the warm thought that "My wife loves me." For this instance of qualia to be *true*, several things must obtain in addition to the previous five points. First, I must exist as a substantial self that is the object of my wife's love. For my wife to love "me" as a person means that "I" exist over time without losing my essence or my defining properties. The dualist finds a person's defining personal properties in the soul, not in the body, since the body may undergo massive change (including major brain surgery) without the dissipation of the self. Unless the soul is a substantial entity with various properties inhering in it, this concept of the self is sunk. The materialist can only view the human being as a succession of discreet material states with no immaterial substance. Second, my wife must exist as a substantial self as well, in order to be an enduring center of consciousness that experiences intentional emotive states such as love.[29] Third, love itself must exist as an objective reality. For the materialist, any moral or emotive statement must be translatable without remainder into physical descriptions or must be rooted in them (epiphenomenalism). In that case, love is nothing more than a physical response aroused under certain material conditions and is on a physical par with a burp, sneeze or wheeze. Furthermore, when we love another person, we believe we are entering into a condition that is a moral ideal (assuming the love in question is not pathological, adulterous or otherwise vicious). It is a condition that many have experienced for thousands of years and have expressed in song, poetry, painting and prose. But if love is nothing but a collection of physical states in those persons feeling love, the existence of love as a moral ideal vanishes, because ideals are not material states.

Moreover, if the feeling of love is identical to and nothing more than a collection of a person's individual material states, then it is difficult to explain how another individual's very different collection of material states is also an instance of love.[30] However, if love exists as a moral ideal (rooted in

---

[29]For more on this, see Moreland and Craig, *Philosophical Foundations,* pp. 239-41.

[30]I have developed this argument with relation to love in a way that mirrors Gordon Clark's argument that materialism cannot account for two people having the same thought, since their thoughts are nothing but a collection of radically different physical states which are not identical (see Gordon H. Clark, *A Christian View of Men and Things* [Grand Rapids: Eerdmans, 1952], pp. 318-23; see also Jonah Haddad, *Leaving Dirt Place: Love as an Apologetic for Christianity* [Eugene, Ore.: Wipf & Stock, 2011]).

the eternal character of God, who is love), and we are substantial souls who can know and (to some extent) exemplify this ideal in our mental states (cognitive and affective), then love makes ontological sense and finds a sturdy place in reality. There is a metaphysic to support the songs, poetry, prose, laughter and tears. One need not resort to mystification instead.[31]

RESPONDING TO OBJECTIONS TO DUALISM

Materialists, despite the problems discussed, believe that the problems of substance dualism are far worse. So, we will briefly examine some of their core arguments.

First, materialists claim the high theoretical ground by invoking Ockham's razor on their behalf. Since we should never multiply explanatory entities beyond what is necessary to explain any phenomenon, we should explain human beings—consciousness and all—on the basis of only one substance (matter), not two (mind and matter).

But this principle does not insist on simplicity *at all costs for all explanations* (see the discussion in chapter three). That would be a theory simply for simpletons. Rather, according to this principle, a theory should be as simple as possible *given the nature of the (often complex) phenomenon to be explained or described.* On the one hand, heliocentrism is a simpler theory than geocentrism, since the latter required an elaborate system of epicycles to explain planetary motion. But heliocentrism also fits the facts at hand better than geocentrism. On the other hand, Newtonian mechanics (which works well for medium-sized objects) is simpler than quantum physics, but it fails to account for a broad range of phenomena at the microscopic and macroscopic levels. Newtonian mechanics' simplicity could not account for certain complexities, whereas quantum theory does account for them, however strangely.[32]

We have argued that the simplicity of materialism suffers from a paucity of categories. Materialism, simple though it is, cannot adequately explain first-person access and incorrigibility, qualia, propositional attitudes, intentionality, truth or love. No small failures, there! For these realities,

---

[31]On the rationale of mystification, see Os Guinness, *The Dust of Death*, rev. ed. (1973; reprint, Wheaton, Ill.: Crossway, 1994), pp. 42-46.

[32]For an introduction to quantum mechanics see John Polkinghorne, *Quantum Theory: A Very Short Introduction* (New York: Oxford University Press, 2002).

another explanatory category is required: the immaterial. Moreover, if we favor simplicity at all costs, we could just as easily opt for idealism (everything is mind) over materialism. But the arguments I've given in this chapter for dualism cut against idealism as well as materialism.

Second, materialists claim that since material states affect consciousness, consciousness must itself be a material state. Drugs may change a mood or induce a coma or even death. A good physical workout elevates the mood. But if the soul were immaterial, it would not be affected by material states. Therefore, there is no soul. However, this argument fails because the dualist does not claim that body and soul have no interaction. Rather, the body affects the soul and the soul affects the body. Besides the well-known fact that physical substances affect our consciousness, there is increasing evidence that certain mental states change the brain's physical configuration.[33] But even if a particular mental state is *correlated* with a particular brain state, this does not mean that the mental state is *identical* to the brain state.

But some argue that since scientists have found that certain brain functions are correlated with certain sections of the brain, consciousness is nothing but physical. Yet even if some future science finds that every mental state is correlated with a particular brain state or several brain states, this would establish no more than the *contingent* correlation of these two very different kinds of states. A complete scientific description would reveal that the bodily and mental states are *existentially inseparable*, but it would not show that they are *ontologically identical.* Jerome Shaffer remarks that if it were discovered that

> each particular mental event occurs if and only if some particular brain
> event occurs this would not establish the [materialist] identity theory, which
> holds not just that mental and neural events are correlated in some regular,
> lawful way but that they are one and the same event, and, moreover, that
> these events are, basically, physical.[34]

Third, materialists often object that mind and matter are too different

---

[33]See Jeffrey Schwartz and Sharon Begley, *The Mind and the Brain: Neuroplasticity and the Power of Mental Force* (New York: Harper Perennial, 2003); and Mario Beauregard and Denyse O'Leary, *The Spiritual Brain: A Neuroscientist's Case for the Existence of the Soul* (San Francisco: HarperOne, 2007).

[34]Jerome Shaffer, "The Mind-Body Problem," in *The Encyclopedia of Philosophy*, ed. Paul Edwards (New York: Macmillan, 1967), 4:339.

in nature to interact because they lack a common matrix or medium for that interaction to occur. But they must interact for substance dualism to be true. Therefore, substance dualism is refuted.[35]

This argument fails in at least two ways. First, we need not know how two substances interact in order to know that they both exist and that they interact. If a good case is made against materialism and for the objective existence of mind as an immaterial substance, then there is good evidence for dualism. As Adler points out, if there is reason to question materialism and to grant the immateriality of mental states, the problems of interaction should be considered after the fact. These kinds of puzzles should not disqualify interactionism if there are arguments and evidence in favor of it.[36] There are a number of puzzles and conundrums concerning the activity of subatomic particles, but their existence is nonetheless well established.

Second, this materialist criticism depends on a very questionable theory; moreover, we have plenty of evidence of two discrepant things interacting without any difficulty. Yandell explains:

> This is perhaps the only time in contemporary philosophy in which the causal likeness principle is invoked—the claim that in order for X to affect Y with respect to some property Q, X must have Q or something like Q. There is neither criterion for what degree of similarity is required nor reason to accept the principle. Dualists find it unclear why color experiences being caused by non-colored things, colds and the flu by bacteria and viruses, pain by unfeeling things, and the like somehow are unproblematic whereas mind-body interaction is problematic.[37]

Moreland and Craig also note that "a magnetic field can move a tack, gravity can act on a planet millions of miles away, protons exert a repulsive force on each other and so forth."[38]

Third, materialists claim that Darwinism entails materialism. Since they know that Darwinism is true, materialism follows as a matter of course. It is true that Darwinism logically leads to materialism (see chap. 13). But the case for Darwinism is feeble once the presupposition of materialism is with-

---

[35]Searle, *Minds, Brains, and Science*, p. 17; Richard Taylor, "Interactionism," in *Metaphysics*, 4th ed. (Englewood Cliffs, N.J.: Prentice-Hall, 1990).
[36]Adler, *Difference of Man*, pp. 198-99.
[37]Keith E. Yandell, *Philosophy of Religion* (New York: Routledge, 1999), p. 262.
[38]Moreland and Craig, *Philosophical Foundations*, p. 243.

drawn. Further, we may argue that because materialism has so many problems and dualism is a better theory, we are warranted in rejecting a Darwinian account of consciousness.[39] This turns the tables nicely.

Fourth, materialists aver that while matter may have very curious properties found only in humans, positing a separate soul or mind in order to explain mental events puts us in no better a position to explain consciousness than does invoking the mysteries of materialism. So we are on safer ground to say that mental and physical states are equivalent in some way yet to be discovered by science.[40] But, interestingly, several leading brain scientists specializing in brain function, such as Wilfred Penfield and Sir John Eccles, have concluded *on the basis of their scientific research* that there is more to consciousness than the physical brain. The existence of a distinct mind better explains, they think, the scientific findings.[41] This claim is in direct odds with the hope for a superscientific materialist explanation.

FROM MIND TO MINDFUL MAKER

The case has been made for substance dualism.[42] The human person is thus explained on the basis of its being made up of two substances: mind and body, neither of which is reducible to the other. But how do we then explain the existence of mind in the universe?[43] While dualism fits nicely with Christian theism, not all dualists are Christians or even theists.[44] So, it is imperative to consider which worldview best explains dualism.[45] There are only two basic options outside of theism, both of which are philosophically troublesome.

---

[39]Ibid.

[40]Taylor, *Metaphysics*, pp. 29-33.

[41]Karl R. Popper and John C. Eccles, *The Self and Its Brain* (London: Routledge & Kegan Paul, 1977); Wilder Penfield, *The Mystery of the Mind* (Princeton, N.J.: Princeton University Press, 1975), and Beauregard and O'Leary, *The Spiritual Brain*.

[42]For a much more in-depth treatment see J. P. Moreland, "The Argument from Mind," in *Scaling the Secular City;* and Moreland and Craig, *Philosophical Foundations*, chaps. 11-12.

[43]I am leaving aside the question of whether some animals have souls (although I think some do), since it is not pertinent to the argument here. C. S. Lewis discusses this in "Animal Pain," in *The Problem of Pain* (1962; reprint, New York: Touchstone, 1996).

[44]David Chalmers is a noteworthy example of a dualist who is not a theist (see *The Conscious Mind* [New York: Oxford University Press, 1997]).

[45]For a well-developed book-length treatment of this argument see J. P. Moreland, *Consciousness and the Existence of God* (New York: Routledge, 2008).

First, a nontheist may simply claim that mind originated from matter without any explanation at all. This is simply a brute fact about the universe. Mind comes out of matter without any antecedent mind acting as its designing cause. Jean-Paul Sartre held this position, claiming that human consciousness was a mysterious "upsurge of freedom" that could not be further explained.[46] Other philosophers have made similar claims. But this amounts to the belief that mind appeared ex nihilo at some point in earth history. Yet unlike the biblical doctrine of creation ex nihilo, this scenario lacks any creator, any designing agent who brought forth anything. There is only an upsurge, a cosmic hiccup, which is utterly inexplicable. Unless someone has extremely strong reasons to reject theism as an explanation (and Sartre did not), this account of mind is no more than a desperate move to preserve the soul at all costs. It violates the well-established principle, discussed in the chapter eleven on the kalam cosmological argument, that "from nothing, nothing comes" (*ex nihilo, nihil fit*). Worse yet, it is not an *explanation* at all. Minimally, an explanation needs to account for something (the *explicandum*) on the basis of some other factor or factors (the *explanans*). But the mind-without-mindful-cause argument cannot appeal to anything within matter or outside of matter to account for mind. Mind just is. This is not an explanation. It is an exclamation point casting about in a mindless void.

Second, a nontheist may argue that mind is latent or intrinsic in matter. When matter becomes complex enough through long periods of unguided evolution, consciousness emerges in the same way that hydrogen and oxygen combine to form water.[47] On this view, mind is not a separate substance but rather depends on matter for its existence in the same way that a shadow has no separate existence but depends on other factors for its

---

[46]Jean-Paul Sartre, "Conclusion," in *Being and Nothingness: An Essay on Phenomenological Ontology* (1943; reprint, New York: Routledge, 1994). Howard Mumma recounts an exchange with Sartre on this topic in *Camus and the Minister* (Brewster, Mass.: Paraclete Press, 2000), chap. 6, in which Sartre, when pressed, could give no answer to the origination of human freedom from the impersonal and deterministic world of physical causes.

[47]Even some theists have denied that mind is an immaterial substance, such as the late Donald M. MacKay, *Human Science and Human Dignity* (Downers Grove, Ill.: InterVarsity Press, 1977), pp. 26-34; and Joel Green, ed., *In Search of the Soul: Four Views of the Mind-Body Problem* (Downers Grove, Ill.: InterVarsity Press, 2005). See the different but overlapping views of Kevin Corcoran and Nancey Murphy, who both defend versions of physicalism.

406   Christian Apologetics

existence. This is often called epiphenomenalism or property dualism.

This view attempts to escape the problems of monistic materialism (there is nothing but matter) by granting the existence of mind as a *property* of matter. (Biblical dualism takes mind to be a *substance*, not a *property* of anything.) However, several problems follow from epiphenomenalism. First, it denies that the mind can act as an agent, since mind is dependent on matter for its very existence. Consequently, human thought never adequately explains any human action, since all thought is based on—and would not exist without—antecedent material factors. But since we typically regard ourselves as *agents*, this view falls short of convincing. That we are agents is an incorrigible or at least a properly basic belief. Second, epiphenomenalism has a hard time accounting for the unity of the self over time, since it reduces consciousness to a property.[48] On this view I am not a self that has experiences; I am a brain (which is not itself conscious) that has consciousness as a property. If I am not a self that has experiences but rather a material substance that has experiences, then the unity of the self through time cannot be sustained, since my physical states (the basis of consciousness) change radically over time. The soul, however, does not change with respect to its basic nature because it is a substance. Third, epiphenomenalism betrays the original impulse behind materialism, which was to explain everything without recourse to the immaterial. But this "does not fit naturally into a Darwinian understanding of our origins."[49] Physicalist Paul Churchland observes:

> The important point about the standard evolutionary story is that the human species and all of its features are the wholly physical outcome of a purely physical process. . . . If this is the correct account of our origins, then there seems neither need, nor room, to fit any nonphysical substances or properties into our theoretical account of ourselves. We are creatures of matter.[50]

J. J. C. Smart agrees:

> How could a nonphysical property or entity suddenly arise in the course of animal evolution? A change in a gene is a change in a complex molecule

---

[48]This was addressed above in the section on love in this chapter (pp. 400-401).
[49]Moreland and Craig, *Philosophical Foundations*, p. 263.
[50]Paul Churchland, *Matter and Consciousness* (Cambridge, Mass.: MIT Press, 1984), p. 21, cited in Moreland and Craig, *Philosophical Foundations*, p. 264.

which causes a change in the biochemistry of the cell. This may lead to changes in the shape or organization of the developing embryo. But what sort of chemical process could lead to the springing into existence of something nonphysical? No enzyme can catalyze the production of a spook![51]

Smart used this argument to defend a materialist philosophy of mind. But given the case against materialism, Smart's point rules out the emergence of mind from matter. If mind is real, as I have argued, we need a better explanation for its existence than emergence.

But if nontheists want to make consciousness somehow intrinsic in matter as a potential, they distance themselves very far from materialism and move toward panpsychism, the view that everything is fundamentally mental. Moreover, the notion of matter latent with consciousness is not easy to grasp. A seed is latently a tree, but a seed is a living thing that unfolds organically from a genetic blueprint. Mind and matter, however, are different substances—things that differ in kind, not in degree. Matter cannot be a property of mind or mind a property of matter (although as different substances, they may interact as they do in the human person).

Furthermore, the assertion that everything is fundamentally conscious—either latently or actually—does nothing to explain the structure of human consciousness and our ability to grasp truth. Even if we can make sense of the idea of a latent consciousness, it cannot be used as the explanation for more fully developed and complex structures of actualized human consciousness, which transcend any unconscious/latent forms of consciousness. This is because the lesser (latent consciousness) cannot be the designer of the greater (actualized human consciousness).

However, someone might abandon all of the above explanations and opt for a full-fledged pantheism to explain the reality of mind. On this worldview, mind is explained in terms of a Universal Mind or Consciousness that encompasses all of reality. Mind is not latent in matter: rather, it makes up all that is. There is one universal divine consciousness. Therefore, matter does not exist; it is merely an illusion of the unenlightened mind.

I have critiqued this worldview in previous chapters, but it should be evident that pantheism cannot explain the existence of matter. It can only

---

[51]J. J. C. Smart, "Materialism," *Journal of Philosophy* 22 (1963): 660.

explain it away as unreal. As such, it commits an equal and opposite error from materialism. Instead of reducing all to matter, it reduces all to mind. Yet to believe in matter is fundamental and justified, either as the best explanation of phenomena different from mind or as a properly basic belief. Thus, any worldview that denies the fact of matter fails to explain something extremely pertinent to human life.

Worse yet, pantheism cannot explain our *finite* consciousness, since it claims that only one *infinite* consciousness exists. But we experience life under cognitive constraints: our intellect, memory and perceptions are limited, not unlimited. This is the incorrigibility of the finite. Any worldview that claims we are really infinite must break upon these rocks, since something cannot be both finite and infinite in the same way at the same time.[52] Moreover, pantheism denies the subject-object consciousness relationship so common to our consciousness (see chap. 16), since it asserts that there is only one divine reality, which admits of no genuine ontological distinctions. Distinction is deception, on this view. Yet since we are warranted in believing that our typical consciousness of other people, trees and buildings are real (and not an illusion), we have good reason to deny pantheism. As Chesterton quipped, "If the cosmos is unreal, there is nothing to think about."[53] But we do rightfully think about things (plural); so pantheism is false.

Having eliminated monistic materialism, mind ex nihilo, epiphenomenalism, panpsychism and pantheism, we find ourselves before the throne of theism. According to theism an absolute, personal and self-existent Mind (God) is the original and fundamental reality. This consciousness is neither latent nor does it pop into existence unexpectedly. It is primordial: God is the great "I AM WHO I AM" (Exodus 3:14). God brought forth both the material and immaterial creation by his creative will ex nihilo, singling out but one species to bear his image and likeness (Genesis 1:26). Humans are thus the handiwork of an immaterial agent, who fashioned them out of created matter and spirit (or mind) for certain purposes. Hence, their materiality is explained on the basis of "the dust" God previously created. But their immateriality is not explained on the basis of dust, but through the

[52]Winfried Corduan, *Reasonable Faith: Basic Christian Apologetics* (Nashville: Broadman & Holman, 1994), pp. 93-94.
[53]G. K. Chesterton, *Orthodoxy* (1908; reprint, New York: Image Books, 1959), p. 34.

direct agency of God as Spirit (John 4:24). Moreover, the interaction between mind and body is explained by the design plan of God. Why certain physical states should have mental correlations and connections has puzzled materialists, but this need not puzzle theists who believe that we are—body and soul—"fearfully and wonderfully made" (Psalm 139:13-15) by a wise Designer.[54] The Christian worldview does not tell us which brain states will be correlated with which mental states, nor does it eliminate the need for brain research. Rather, it gives a metaphysical foundation for the very idea of brain-mind correlation, given the wise creation of God.

COGNITION: HOW CAN WE KNOW THE WORLD?

There is another unique feature of human nature that needs explanation: our ability to know the world through reason. This subject—epistemology—is vast. We addressed it in chapter three, which presented rational tests for worldviews. But there is an even deeper question: how can we account for our ability to know the world at all? We usually presuppose the trustworthiness of our basic rational inferences. All mentally competent humans use their reason—at various levels of achievement. This is constitutive of being human, a "rational animal" as Aristotle said. A rational mind uses proper argument forms (and avoids logical fallacies), exercises intellectual discipline and shows intellectual humility. This hardly covers the logical field but is sufficient to illustrate the commonality and necessity of sound reasoning.[55] Of course, we realize that we are error prone as well. We may reason fallaciously. Yet the very concept of *error* presupposes the concept of accuracy. We sometimes get it right and know it. It is difficult for us to image someone defending a viewpoint by exclaiming, "Well, it was irrational. That is why I did it."

There is nothing revolutionary in the previous paragraph, but the apologetic issue it raises is this: How do we *justify* our trust in our cognitive faculties? How did humans acquire the ability to know the world? Thus the question concerns which worldview best accounts for the existence of

---

[54]For more on the argument that only God can explain the relationship between physical and mental states, see Richard Swinburne, *The Existence of God*, 2nd ed. (New York: Oxford University Press, 2004), pp. 192-221; and Robert Adams, "Flavors, Colors, and God," in *The Virtue of Faith* (New York: Oxford University Press, 1987).

[55]For an excellent overview of basic inductive, deductive and modal reasoning, see J. P. Moreland and William Lane Craig, "Argumentation and Logic," in *Philosophical Foundations*.

reasoning and perceiving minds in the universe.

What follows is an abbreviated version of a kind of argument given by a variety of philosophers who argue from the existence of reason to the existence of God as the rational source of reason.[56] It is a *transcendental* argument in that it considers the conditions that must obtain if we are to trust our basic reasoning. Just as materialism and pantheism cannot explain the reality of mind as an immaterial substance interacting with material substances, neither can they explain the phenomenon of reason or its efficacy. First, we turn to materialism.

MATERIALISM AND REASON

Materialism is a mindless, matter-first worldview. Unconscious matter preceded consciousness and rationality, and serves as their only foundation and explanation. Here is the basic argument against materialism as an explanation for human knowing.

1. If materialism is true, we cannot trust our cognitive faculties because (a) they are not designed to know the world and (b) they are merely material organs with no ability to experience rational insight.

2. Our cognitive capacities are basically trustworthy.

3. Therefore, materialism is false (by *modus tollens*).

To make this argument work, we will assume that our cognitive faculties are basically reliable. If they were not, we could not even begin an argument! The real question is whether premise 1 is true. That is, does materialism rule out reliable cognitive faculties? We begin with the materialist claim that our rational faculties are *not designed*.[57] Then we address the materialist claim that our thoughts are completely determined by material causes.[58]

According to materialism, humans are the result of impersonal, nonrational and nonpurposive forces operating in a closed system of cause and

---

[56]This refers to a family of arguments, not to one argument. I will be drawing mostly from the arguments given or inspired by C. S. Lewis, "The Cardinal Difficulty of Materialism," in *Miracles* (1947; reprint, San Francisco: HarperSanFrancisco, 1996); and Alvin Plantinga in *Warranted Christian Belief* (New York: Oxford University Press, 2000), pp. 227-40.

[57]I am here relying somewhat on insights from Alvin Plantinga's version of this argument, often called "the evolutionary argument against naturalism."

[58]This will trade on insights mostly derived from C. S. Lewis in *Miracles*, chap. 3.

effect. Consider Nietzsche's statement: "How did rationality arrive in the world? Irrationally, as might be expected: by a chance accident. If we want to know what that chance accident was we shall have to guess it, as one guesses the answer to a riddle."[59] Our rational faculties have emerged only on the basis of natural selection, which is fueled by random genetic variation. Ophelia Benson and Jeremy Stangroom claim that humans may be the only beings in the universe "who have the capacity to make truth their object." Yet they claim we have this capacity "to conceptualize reality as existing independent of us, and the possibility of discovering what it is" by a "strange provocative contingent accident of natural selection."[60] Similarly, materialist and Darwinist Steven Pinkar claims that "our brains were shaped for fitness, not for truth."[61]

If this is true, then we have no certainty that this natural, nonrational process could evolve capacities to know truth through reason. Natural selection pertains to the utility of survival traits, not the knowledge of reality. Certainly, the capacity to know truth through reason and observation would lend toward survival, but the possibility of natural selection producing rationality is precisely what is in question. Consider Antony Flew's comments: "The dangers of Darwin's pointedly paradoxical expression 'natural selection'—and this danger has often been realized—is that it may mislead people to overlook that this sort of selection is blind and nonrational; precisely this is the point."[62]

J. P. Moreland expands on the implications of natural selection being blind and nonrational:

> Our capacities to accurately sense and think about the world cannot be explained by saying that they evolved over time because of their survival value.

[59]Friedrich Nietzsche, *Daybreak: Thoughts on the Prejudices of Morality*, trans. R. J. Hollingdale (New York: Cambridge University Press, 1985), p. 125. Nietzsche should have rather said that reason came forth *non*rationally instead of *ir*rationally, since only rational beings can be irrational. Mindless, purposeless nature cannot be irrational, only nonrational. Nevertheless, Nietzsche uses the antithesis of rational-irrational to good dramatic and philosophical effect in this suggestive fragment.
[60]Ophelia Benson and Jeremy Stangroom, *Why Truth Matters* (New York: Continuum, 2006), p. 21.
[61]Steven Pinker, *How the Mind Works* (New York: W. W. Norton, 1997), p. 305.
[62]Antony Flew, *Evolutionary Ethics* (New York: St. Martin's Press, 1967), p. 17. Flew's comment was made in connection with deriving *ethical* principles from natural selection. Nevertheless, the observation still holds for the epistemological realm: rationality rests on blind and nonrational foundations.

For one thing, it is not clear that the ability to know truth from falsity is necessary to survive. As long as the organism interacts consistently with its environment it need not interact accurately. For example, if an organism always saw blue things as though they were red and vice versa, or large things as small and vice versa, that organism and its offspring would adapt to its environment. It is hard to believe that an amoeba grasps the way the world is, but it does interact with the world consistently.[63]

In his much-used textbook *Metaphysics*, Richard Taylor gives an intriguing example to make the point that unless our cognitive capacities are designed, we have no reason to trust them to deliver facts about the outside world.[64] Consider a collection of stones on an English hillside which spells out the message "The British Railways Welcomes You to Wales." Taylor argues that while it is possible (although highly unlikely) that the stones came into this configuration by accident, we would have no reason to believe the meaning of the message unless they were purposely arranged. If you think that you are entering Wales, given the evidence of the sign, "then you could not . . . suppose that the arrangement of the stones was accidental."[65] Even stronger, it "would be irrational for you to regard the arrangement of the stones as evidence that you were entering Wales, and at the same time to suppose that they might have come to have that arrangement accidentally, that is as the result of the ordinary interaction of natural or physical forces."[66] Only if we assume that the message was designed can we believe that it communicates anything true *outside of itself*— that is, that someone is welcoming us to Wales.

Although Taylor claims (wrongly, I think) that the complexity of our brains and nervous systems can be explained on Darwinian grounds without any purpose behind their origin (see chaps. 13-14), he argues that if we consider our brains and nervous systems as arising from only purposeless processes, then we would have no reason to believe that they can tell us anything truthful about states of affairs beyond themselves. If our sensory and cognitive equipment "can be entirely accounted for in terms of chance variations,

---

[63]Moreland, *Scaling the Secular City*, p. 50; see also ibid., pp. 49-50. Plantinga develops this in more detail in *Warranted Christian Belief*, pp. 227-40.
[64]*Metaphysics* went through four editions in the influential Prentice-Hall series of introductory textbooks before Taylor's death in 2003.
[65]Taylor, *Metaphysics*, p. 111.
[66]Ibid.

natural selection, and so on, without supposing that they somehow embody and express the purposes of some creative being," then "we cannot say of them that they are, entirely by themselves, reliable guides to any truth whatever, save only what can be inferred from their own structure and arrangement."[67] I'm not sure how we could even infer anything from the sense organ's "own structure and arrangement" if they were not designed to ascertain truth, but Taylor's basic point stands: undesigned cognitive and perceptual capacities cannot tell us anything about the world around us.

Materialists themselves sometimes grant this point. Consider this damning statement by Richard Rorty, who admits that the Darwinian account of the evolution of life (naturalism's only available creation story)[68] makes no room for truth or "one true account of nature":

> The idea that one species of organism is, unlike all the others, oriented not just toward its own increased prosperity but toward Truth, is as un-Darwinian as the idea that every human being has a built-in moral compass—a conscience that swings free of both social history and individual luck.[69]

Rorty, the naturalist, impales himself on his own assumption, however, since he is presupposing his knowledge of the *truth* of Darwinism in order to undermine the notion that human animals apprehend any *truth*, moral or otherwise. He cannot have it both ways and make his peace with logic.

Therefore, if materialism is true, we have no basis to trust our reasoning. Our beliefs *might* be true (that is, by a cosmic fluke whereby nonrational forces cause us to hold true beliefs), but we would have no *reason* to hold these beliefs, and so they could not count as *knowledge*. If the materialist theory is true, we would have no reason to believe it to be true.[70] Patricia Churchland, an atheist and rigorous materialist, admits this:

> Boiled down to essentials, a nervous system enables the organism to succeed in . . . feeding, fleeing, fighting, and reproducing. The principle chore of nervous systems is to get the body parts where they should be in order

---

[67]Ibid.
[68]This is a phrase often used by Phillip Johnson, the architect of the intelligent design movement.
[69]Richard Rorty, "Untruth and Consequences," review of Paul Feyerabend's autobiography *Killing Time* in *The New Republic*, July 31, 1995, p. 36.
[70]See Richard Purtill, *Reason to Believe* (Grand Rapids: Eerdmans, 1974), pp. 38-47.

that the organism may survive. . . . Improvements in sensorimotor control confer an evolutionary advantage: a fancier style of representing [the world] is advantageous *so long as it is geared to the organism's way of life and enhances the organism's chances of survival.* Truth, whatever that is, definitely takes the hindmost.[71]

Charles Darwin himself, who labored so long and hard to develop and defend his naturalistic theory of evolution by natural selection, questioned his own rational abilities in light of the naturalism he confessed.

With me the horrid doubt always arises whether the convictions of man's mind, which has been developed from the mind of the lower animals, are of any value or at all trustworthy. Would any one trust in the convictions of a monkey's mind, if there are any convictions in such a mind?[72]

Notice that Darwin does not doubt the details of natural selection to explain speciation; he rather doubts his very ability to reason at all.

If materialism eliminates rationality as a way to know truth, then we must either deny our intuition that some truth can be known and become epistemological nihilists, or we must embrace a worldview that makes truth and knowledge possible. But few people will actually take the nihilistic step off the cliff. It contradicts common sense and would destroy scientific methods as truth-seeking procedures.[73]

There is another reason to reject materialism as an explanation for the reliability of our reason. If the world were made only of material things arranged in various causal patterns, our thoughts would not be exempt from this causal matrix. This means that all of our thoughts would be determined by various material processes, thoroughly determined or accounted for through some combination of determinism and randomness, and that our thoughts themselves would be material.[74] But when we reason

---

[71]Patricia Churchland, "Epistemology in an Age of Neuroscience," *Journal of Philosophy* 84 (1987): 548-49, emphasis in the original.

[72]Charles Darwin to W. Graham, July 3, 1881, in *The Life and Letters of Charles Darwin*, ed. Francis Darwin (1897; reprint, Boston: Elibron, 2005), 1:285.

[73]On the road from naturalism to nihilism through epistemology, see James W. Sire, *The Universe Next Door: A Basic Worldview Catalog*, 5th ed. (Downer Grove, Ill.: InterVarsity Press, 2009), pp. 103-7. For a book-length academic treatment of this topic, with an introductory essay and response by Alvin Plantinga, see James Beilby, ed., *Naturalism Defeated? Essay on Plantinga's Evolutionary Argument Against Naturalism* (Ithaca, N.Y.: Cornell University Press, 2002).

[74]I address the problem with a materialist sense of mind earlier in this chapter, so I will not revisit it here.

from a premise to a conclusion, we are not thinking in terms of material causes but rather in terms of rational inference. The truth of one or more premises is not the cause of the conclusion in the way that the rain is the cause of my lawn being wet. Rather, premises may lead to a conclusion through a rational inference: If P, then Q. P; therefore Q. The word *therefore* is a term of rationality, not of material causation.

C. S. Lewis distinguishes between causes for phenomena and reasons for holding beliefs. The former are nonrational, while the latter require an ability to have rational *insight* into truth. Consider how we use the word *because*. If we say "X moved because it was propelled by Y," we are using *because* in a causal fashion. Yet if we say "I believe X because of Y," we are using *because* not in a causal fashion but with regard to reasons or rational grounds for believing X. Lewis argued that if materialism were true, we could never grant *reasons* for holding beliefs since all our brain states would be rigorously determined in a materialistically *caused* fashion. Thought would be reduced to a mere reflex action on the order of a muscle twinge. But can glorified muscle twinges weigh evidence and reach warranted conclusions? There is no reason to think so. The notion that with our minds we can transcend material forces and discover the truth about reality would, therefore, be unwarranted.[75]

PANTHEISM AND REASON

The case against pantheism explaining human reason is similar to that against materialism, but shorter.

1. If pantheism is true, we cannot trust our rational faculties because (a) they are not designed to know the world, (b) there is no finite and material world to know, and (c) reason is not the organ to discern truth.

2. We can trust our rational faculties.

3. Therefore, pantheism is false (by *modus tollens*).

---

[75]For a developed version of this Lewis-inspired argument see Victor Reppert, *C. S. Lewis's Dangerous Idea* (Downers Grove, Ill.: InterVarsity Press, 2002); and Victor Reppert, "The Argument from Reason," in *Blackwell Companion to Natural Theology*, ed. William Lane Craig and J. P. Moreland (Malden, Mass.: Wiley-Blackwell, 2009).

A worldview could not be in worse shape to explain and justify reason. I will take each part of premise 1 in order.

First, while pantheists affirm a Universal or Supreme Mind, this entity is not a personal agent but rather some kind of impersonal consciousness. As such, this being does not design creatures to know the world, since design requires an intelligent personality. Thus our rational faculties are ungrounded. Second, pantheism eliminates the distinction between creation and Creator by asserting that all is divine. Therefore, no finite and material world exists to be known. But as argued earlier, it is intellectually proper to believe in a finite and material world that is accessible through reason. Third, pantheism typically claims that normal human reasoning, which trades so heavily on either-or logic, must be transcended in order to know reality as absolutely one or nondual. We have addressed the logical problems with this notion in chapter sixteen, but suffice it to say here that this undermines human rationality instead of justifying it.

THE CHRISTIAN ANSWER

Christianity provides the justification for our rational abilities through its doctrines of God, creation and humanity. God, the rational Creator of all things, created humans in his image and likeness. The divine image includes rationality. God created the world as an intelligible realm for humans to thrive in through dependence on him and the use of their rational faculties. Even after the Fall, knowledge is possible because God ensures it.

The theist is not committed to the view that reason is a comparatively recent development molded by a process of selection, which can select only the biologically useful. For the theist, reason—the reason of God—is older than nature, and from it the orderliness of nature, which alone enables us to know it, is derived. For the theist, the human mind in the act of knowing is illuminated by the divine reason. It is set free, in the measure required, from the huge nexus of nonrational causation; free from this to be determined by the truth known.[76]

Lewis speaks of "theism" in general, since the transcendental argument from reason to God is also compatible with non-Christian monotheisms,

---

[76]Lewis, *Miracles*, pp. 34-35.

such as Islam and Judaism, which also claim that a transcendent God created humans with the ability to know him and the universe. But given our apologetic thus far, we are moving more squarely into the Christian category. Further evidence for Christian theism will be given in the next chapters. This chapter has argued that neither consciousness nor reason can be explained by materialism or pantheism. But Christian theism gives us an adequate explanation for our very selves.[77]

---

[77]Some other form of theism may explain humans as having an immaterial soul, but none of them can explain the greatness and misery of humanity, as chap. 18 argues.

18

Deposed Royalty

Pascal's Anthropological Argument

The Bible is God's anthropology rather than man's theology.

ABRAHAM HESCHEL[1]

WE HUMANS OFTEN PUZZLE OVER OUR own humanity, scanning our heights and our depths, wondering about and worrying over the meaning of our good and our evil.[2] No other animal reflects on itself in this manner. Here, and in so many other ways, we are unique among living creatures. As G. K. Chesterton put it, "Every man has forgotten who he is. . . . The self is more distant than any star. We are all under the same mental calamity; we have all forgotten our names. We have all forgotten what we really are."[3] Along these lines, literary critic George Steiner observes that

> there is hardly a civilization, perhaps hardly an individual consciousness, that does not carry inwardly an answer to intimations of a sense of distant catastrophe. Somewhere a wrong turn was taken in that "dark and sacred wood," after which man has had to labor, socially, psychologically, against the natural grain of being.[4]

---

[1]Abraham Heschel, *God in Search of Man: A Philosophy of Judaism* (New York: Farrar, Straus and Giroux, 1976), p. 412.
[2]This chapter is a revised version of a paper called "Deposed Royalty: Pascal's Anthropological Argument," *Journal of the Evangelical Theological Society* 41, no. 2 (1998): 297-312.
[3]G. K. Chesterton, *Orthodoxy* (1908; reprint, Garden City, N.Y.: Doubleday, 1959), p. 54.
[4]George Steiner, *In Bluebeard's Castle: Some Notes Towards the Redefinition of Culture* (New

Why would a young student go on a homicidal rampage at Virginia Tech in 2008, murdering dozens of innocent people and then killing himself? Why does such evil strike so hard and so erratically? In spite of these upsurges of human evil, we are also struck by the beauty, courage and genius wrought by human minds, hearts and hands. After every tragedy heroes emerge who rescue the living, comfort the dying and put others above themselves in spontaneous acts of altruism. Humans make machines to torture others, and humans make music sublime in its ability to give pleasure.

The meaning of human existence is a question as perennial as it is perplexing. It haunts our songs and our poems, it stalks our relationships, and it troubles our philosophies and religions. As Shakespeare said in *King Lear*, "Who is it who can tell me who I am?"[5] This question also provides a strong clue for apologetics, since the Christian worldview can explain both our greatness and misery in ways unrivaled by other claimants on ultimate reality. Blaise Pascal gives us the inspiration for the anthropological argument. Pascal's antipathy toward classical natural theology—what he called the "metaphysical proofs"—did not hinder his apologetic endeavors.[6] In *Pensées* and elsewhere, Pascal develops several apologetic strategies, including an argument from human nature, in support of Christian revelation. He argues that the Christian doctrines of creation and the Fall best explain the paradoxes of the human condition and render Christianity worthy of respect. Pascal does not restrict his apologetic endeavors to this anthropological argument, but he does employ it skillfully in order to attract the attention of skeptics and other unbelievers.

The apologetic project of this book is wider than Pascal's, given the defense of several theistic arguments already covered in previous chapters. To the extent that these arguments are individually and conjointly successful, they form a cumulative case for a Perfect Being, a Creator, Designer

---

Haven, Conn.: Yale University Press, 1971), p. 4.

[5]William Shakespeare, *King Lear* 1.4.238.

[6]On Pascal's rejection of natural theology see Douglas Groothuis, "Are Theistic Arguments Religiously Useless? A Pascalian Objection Examined," *Trinity Journal*, n.s., 15 no 2 (1994): 147-61; Douglas Groothuis, "Proofs, Pride, and Incarnation: Is Natural Theology Theologically Taboo?" *Journal of the Evangelical Theological Society* (March 1995): 67-76; and Douglas Groothuis, "Pascal's Biblical Omission Argument Against Natural Theology," *Asbury Theological Journal* 52, no.2 (1997): 17-26.

(of fine-tuning and specific organisms, as well as human consciousness and reason), moral Lawgiver, and divine inspiration for theistic religious experience. Pascal's anthropological argument puts forth a uniquely Christian explanation for the human condition and, as I am employing it, depends on the previously established foundation of theism.[7]

This chapter focuses on *two uniquely biblical beliefs:* that humans are created in God's image and likeness, and that they have fallen into sin. No nonbiblical worldview makes these claims. While Islam has some affinities with the Bible, it denies that we are made in the divine image, thinking that this places humans too close to Allah, the utterly transcendent God. Likewise, Islam denies the doctrine that sin is a universal condition that disables humans from pleasing God through their own works.

Pascal's apologetic orientation is instructive for Western Christians today. Developing an apologetic argument from the point of the human condition is appealing in a psychologized and individualistic culture. While there is much theological illiteracy and philosophical naiveté today, there is also great interest in the soul, human potential and spirituality. People may doubt the existence of God, the reliability of the Bible or the deity of Christ, but they know that they exist, and they desire to understand themselves, their pain and their possibilities.[8] So, even if we could not interest an unbeliever in a theistic argument, we may be able to garner interest in an argument that focuses on the human condition. But it is all the better in establishing the Christian worldview if the anthropological argument is used in conjunction with natural theology.

By examining Pascal's treatment of the contradictions of humanity, his explanation for the human condition, and the form of argument he presents, we can discern the apologetic force of Pascal's anthropological argument for Christianity.

HUMAN GREATNESS AND MISERY

The true religion, Pascal argues, must be able to explain the human condition better than its rivals. "Man's greatness and wretchedness are

---

[7]Pascal used the argument in isolation from natural theology, given his suspicions of the latter. Given my endorsement of natural theology, I am using the anthropological argument in light of natural theology's rational cogency in arguing for the existence of God.
[8]On this see Millard Erickson, *Christian Theology* (Grand Rapids: Baker, 1983-1985), pp. 457-58.

so evident that the true religion must necessarily teach us that there is in man some great principle of greatness and some great principle of wretchedness."[9]

Humans are a curious mixture of widely divergent properties. Science and technology had made tremendous progress in Pascal's day, much of it at his hand. Yet, as Pascal notes, truth often escapes the ingenious inventors.[10] This causes Pascal to exclaim: "What sort of freak then is man! How novel, how monstrous, how chaotic, how paradoxical, how prodigious! Judge of all things, feeble earthworm, repository of truth, sink of doubt and error, the glory and refuse of the universe!"[11]

Pascal presses the incongruous juxtapositions of human life. He is not simply affirming the variety of human experiences but underscoring the painful condition of being situated between total skepticism and dogmatic rational assurance. As Francis Schaeffer put it, "Every man is in tension until he finds a satisfactory answer to the problem of who he himself is."[12] Many of the fragments of *Pensées* discuss the ironies and absurdities of this juxtaposition. This serves Pascal's purpose of showing from nature that nature is "corrupt," a word that implies a fall from divine grace.[13] But Pascal does not merely assume the fact of human fallenness; he explores the human condition in such a way as to suggest that it is a flawed version of an earlier model.

Pascal does not reject reason, experimentation or observation as vain or arrogant in all cases; yet he sees human finitude and cognitive corruption as severely circumscribing the powers of autonomous reason. He affirms that thought exalts humans over nature and says that "all human dignity consists in thought."[14] Yet he speaks of the fragility of reason, its lack of stamina in the face of external distractions. Though it confers dignity on humanity, reason is easily thrown off course. We are always subject to nature's ways of disorienting and even effortlessly eradicating us: "A vapor,

---

[9]Blaise Pascal, *Pensées* 149/430, ed. and trans. A. J. Krailsheimer (New York: Penguin, 1966), p. 76.

[10]For more on this, see Douglas Groothuis, "Bacon and Pascal on Mastery Over Nature," *Research in Philosophy and Technology* 14 (1994): 191-203.

[11]Pascal, *Pensées* 131/434, p. 64.

[12]Francis A. Schaeffer, *The God Who Is There*, 30th anniv. ed. (Downers Grove, Ill.: InterVarsity Press, 1998), p. 113.

[13]Pascal, *Pensées* 6/60, p. 33.

[14]Ibid., 200/347, p. 95.

a drop of water is enough to kill" us.[15]

Pascal makes much of this in connection with his argument that humans are fallen, east of Eden. By this he means that humans were once naturally in concord with themselves, others, nature and God. Yet through moral transgression against God, humans were banished from such harmonious arrangements and suffered a constitutional corruption that continues today.[16] All of our capacities are defaced yet not erased. We can conceive of their perfection but must endure their present inadequacies. Even the normal operations of human reason are easily derailed by factors beyond our control. As Pascal ironically observes:

> The mind of this supreme judge of the world is not so independent as to be impervious to whatever din may be going on near by. It does not take a cannon's roar to arrest his thoughts; the noise of a weathercock or a pulley will do. Do not be surprised if his reasoning is not too sound at the moment, there is a fly buzzing round his ears; that is enough to render him incapable of giving good advice.[17]

This observation does not undermine the capacity of reason to discern truth any more than inclement weather undermines the ability of an aircraft to fly in better conditions. It simply situates reason within the confines of human "wretchedness" and calls humans to ponder this limitation. What is dignified is also easily distracted:

> Man is obviously made for thinking. Therein lies all his dignity and his merit; and his whole duty is to think as he ought. Now the order of thought is to begin with ourselves, and with our author and our end.

---

[15]Ibid.

[16]Although Pascal undoubtedly believed in a literal first human couple specially created by a direct supernatural act of God, his insights about the Fall of humans can be accommodated by less literal interpretations. All that we need to conserve in Pascal's point is that the first humans (however they came about) in the distant past transgressed God's way of life, fell from grace into corruption, and that this corruption has been passed down to successive generations who experience the same alienation and disharmony recorded in Genesis 3. For a modern theistic evolutionary understanding of the Fall which is conversant with and appreciative of modern science (but one that I do not hold), see Bernard Ramm, *The Christian View of Science and Scripture* (Grand Rapids: Eerdmans, 1954), pp. 214-42. For the progressive creationist (old earth) view see Hugh Ross, *Creation and Time* (Colorado Springs: NavPress, 1994); and Gordon R. Lewis and Bruce A. Demarest, *Integrative Theology* (Grand Rapids: Zondervan, 1990) 2:17-68. I strongly favor the latter view, which should not be confused with theistic evolution or deism. See chapter 13 on this.

[17]Pascal, *Pensées* 48/366, p. 43.

Now what does the world think about? Never about that, but about dancing, playing the lute, singing, writing verse, tilting at the ring, etc., and fighting, becoming king, without thinking what it means to be a king or to be a man.[18]

Those crowned with dignity and honor misuse the very faculty that dignifies them; they divert their attention from ultimate matters by an infatuation with the mundane and the trivial. The greatness is abused yet still in evidence. The very awareness of wretchedness bespeaks greatness.

> Man's greatness comes from knowing he is wretched: a tree does not know it is wretched.
> Thus it is wretched to know that one is wretched, but there is a greatness in knowing one is wretched.[19]

For Pascal, the recognition of human limitation is a sign of excellence because it reveals a self-consciousness unknown in the nonhuman realm. Even some moral failings reveal a kind of ingenuity that inspires admiration:

> *Greatness.* Causes and effects show the greatness of man in producing such excellent order from his own concupiscence.[20]

> Man's greatness even in his concupiscence. He has managed to produce such a remarkable system from it and make it the image of true charity.[21]

Pascal does not in these fragments give any examples of what he means, but some come to mind. By "system" Pascal most likely means a culture in which avarice often masquerades as altruism. For instance, a large company may trumpet its contributions to charities (and thus its own virtue), not in order to lift up the poor but to exalt its own media image for the purpose of maximizing sales. The marketing (propaganda) plan may be ingenious, but the intention is ignoble. Greatness is used for a wretched purpose. An example from the incorrigible Rousseau is also apropos. Historian Paul Johnson notes that Jean Jacques Rousseau's rhetorical prowess was often employed deceitfully for self-justifying endeavors. Rousseau believed that his level of genius demanded that the world

---

[18]Ibid., 620/146, p. 235.
[19]Ibid., 114/397, p. 59.
[20]Ibid., 106/403, p. 57.
[21]Ibid., 118/402, p. 60.

provide him a living. To this end, he would sponge off various wealthy patrons until they found him intolerable and sent the pouting philosopher packing.

> Rousseau marked most of his major quarrels by composing a gigantic letter of remonstrance. These documents are among his most brilliant works, miracles of forensic skill in which evidence is cunningly fabricated, history rewritten and chronology confused with superb ingenuity in order to prove that the recipient is a monster.[22]

Rousseau showed intellectual greatness even in his concupiscence. He would have made a superb manager for political campaigns and administrations today.

Despite the greatness of human reason, the opportunities and modalities for deception are legion. Reason is both intrinsically debilitated through the Fall and hindered by extrinsic factors that frustrate its aims.[23] Reason can be adversely affected by imagination, illness, self-interest, diversion, misperception, custom, pride, vanity, contrariety (conflicting propensities), the follies of science and philosophy, and human injustice.

Human reason, according to Pascal, has always been limited in that humans are incorrigibly finite knowers who must depend on God's revelation for knowledge concerning matters of ultimate concern. This was true even in humanity's unfallen estate. However, since the Fall, humans do not naturally position themselves as finite knowers epistemically dependent on God as revealer. Rather, they confidently attempt to know the universe autonomously, or—realizing the vanity of this quest—they pessimistically succumb to utter skepticism.

Pascal's reflections on greatness and wretchedness (whether epistemic or otherwise) form an anthropology that appeals to the common facts of human experience, not to the Christian Scriptures. This anthropology does not yield a systematic and scientific assessment of the human species. Rather, Pascal intends to force an anthropological crisis, to point out that humans, when carefully considered, are mysteries even to themselves. He outlines how he desires to foment an anthropological crisis in this fragment.

---

[22]Paul Johnson, *Intellectuals* (New York: Harper & Row, 1988), p. 14.
[23]To explore Pascal's understanding of the corruption of reason, see Terence D. Cuneo, "Combating the Noetic Effects of Sin: Pascal's Strategy for Natural Theology," *Faith and Philosophy* 11, no. 4 (1994): esp. pp. 645-47.

If he exalts himself, I humble him.
If he humbles himself, I exalt him.
And I go on contradicting him
Until he understands
That he is a monster that passes all understanding.[24]

Pascal argues that the mystery of human nature can only be explained if we appeal to the Christian Scriptures, which are to be esteemed as propositional revelation from a personal God.

NO CONSOLATION FROM PHILOSOPHY

Pascal claims that merely human philosophies are unable to tell us who we are because they fall into two equal and opposite errors concerning humanity. They either exalt greatness at the expense of wretchedness or wretchedness at the expense of greatness. This is brought out clearly in a document called "Conversation on Epictetus and Montaigne," which narrates a conversation between Pascal and a spiritual leader at Port-Royal named M. De Saci.

The two representative philosophers under discussion are Epictetus and Montaigne, both of whom are admirable in one dimension but imbalanced overall. Epictetus, the Stoic, understands the duties of human beings, the importance of obedience to God and the virtue of humility. Yet Epictetus errs in thinking that people can live up to the standards he lays down and so falls into "diabolic pride" that leads him into such errors as thinking the soul is divine and suicide is permissible.[25]

Montaigne, on the other hand, is a skeptic and a tonic for "proud reason." His extended reflections on human ignorance and the quandaries of reason serve to deflate the hollow rationalism of the excessively confident. Pascal confesses his joy that Montaigne uses "proud reason" against itself to reveal its own insufficiencies.[26] Yet Montaigne advises that, in the face of skeptical considerations, we remain uncommitted and not search for an unattainable truth or good. He thus exalts human wretchedness by opting for unassailable skepticism.

Each system of thought contains a truth negated by the other. Stoicism

---

[24]Pascal, *Pensées* 130/420, p. 62.
[25]Blaise Pascal, "Conversation with M. De Saci on Epictetus and Montaigne," in Blaise Pascal, *Thoughts*, ed. Charles W. Eliot (New York: P. F. Collier, 1910), p. 392.
[26]Ibid., p. 400.

conserves greatness and rejects wretchedness, thus lapsing into presumption and pride. Skepticism conserves wretchedness and rejects greatness, thus lapsing into despondency. Even though it appears that "there would be formed from their alliance a perfect system of morals," the two systems of thought cannot be synthesized by selecting compatible elements from each system.[27] This is because Stoicism promotes certainty, while skepticism promotes doubt; Stoicism argues for the greatness of humanity, and skepticism argues for the weakness of humanity. Given this incompatibility, each system "would destroy the truths as well as the falsehoods of each other."[28] Neither system can stand alone because of its one-sidedness, nor can the two systems unite because of their mutually exclusive presuppositions. Each view contradicts the other while, nevertheless, offering partial truths reconcilable only through another anthropology entirely: that provided by the Christian doctrine of creation and the Fall. "Thus they break and destroy each other to give place to the truth of the Gospel."[29]

Pascal does not exhaust the philosophical options for anthropology, but calls into question two views that were very appealing to those in seventeenth-century France who were rediscovering pagan philosophy; variations of these views are with us today. Pascal's argument is twofold. First, neither view fully accounts for the human condition as one of both misery and greatness in both the ethical and epistemic dimensions. Second, a synthesis of the pagan views is not possible either, thus excluding another purely philosophical move. Pascal offers a *tertium quid*. He wants to open up the discourse to an explanation that transcends any human philosophical system—one that is beyond, but not against, unaided reason.[30]

TRANSCENDING HUMAN PHILOSOPHY

Pascal believes the Gospel harmonizes the contradictions "by a wholly divine act" that unites the respective truths and expels all falsehood;[31] it thus creates "a truly celestial wisdom in which these opposites" are brought together conceptually in a way unknown to merely "human doctrines."[32] The

---

[27]Ibid., p. 403.
[28]Ibid.
[29]Ibid.
[30]See Pascal, *Pensées* 173/273, p. 83 ; 174/270, pp. 83-84; 185/265, p. 85; 188/267, p. 85.
[31]Pascal, "Conversation," p. 403.
[32]Ibid.

problem with the philosophers is that they affirmed contrary descriptions of the same subject; one said human nature was great, the other that it was wretched. However, both predicates cannot obtain of the same subject universally. Yet biblical revelation (and not unaided reason) tells us that we should attribute all wretchedness to our fallen nature and all that is great to grace, which Pascal says in *Pensées* is dimly felt as our original nature. This is the innovation that only God could teach. We need not attribute contradictory predicates to the same subject. Humans have a *dual nature* of a kind not proposed by the philosophers. Human nature has fallen from a previous state that is now unattainable but is yet recognizable even in the ruins of humanity. We are not completely corrupted; we are not purely great. Yet neither do we have two souls: one good, one evil. Pascal observes:

> Man's dualism is so obvious that some people have thought he had two souls:
>
> > Because a simple being seemed to them incapable of such great and sudden variations, from boundless presumption to appalling dejection.[33]

This contradictory state of affairs has "amazed all mankind, and split them into such different schools of thought."[34] There is something deeply mysterious about human nature if it is capable of generating so many diverse—and sometimes logically incompatible—interpretations by philosophers. Although we seldom puzzle over the behavior of pets, though they might amuse us, we often find other people's actions to be unexpected if not indecipherable. A best friend may risk his life for you only to betray you for personal advantage at a later time. What accounts for such "contradictions"?

Pascal is offering a revelatory solution to this anthropological crisis. It is an answer that invokes ideas alien to autonomous thought; yet Pascal believes that these concepts better explain the human condition than do competing views. If we grant the theological concepts of creation and Fall, the human landscape is illuminated to a greater degree than if we deny them. To delineate the theological notion of the Fall, Pascal narrates from God's perspective:

> But you are no longer in the state in which I made you. I created man holy, innocent, perfect, I filled him with light and understanding, I showed him

---

[33]Pascal, *Pensées* 629/417, p. 236.
[34]Ibid., 149/430, p. 77.

my glory and my wondrous works. Man's eye then beheld the majesty of
God. He was not then in the darkness that now blinds his sight, nor subject
to death and the miseries that afflict him.

But he could not bear such great glory without falling to presumption.
He wanted to make himself his own centre and do without my help. He
withdrew himself from my rule, setting himself up as my equal in his desire
to find happiness in himself, and I abandoned him to himself. The creatures who were subject to him I incited to revolt and made his enemies, so
that today man has become like the beasts, and is so far apart from me that
a barely glimmering idea of his author alone remains of all his dead or flick-
ering knowledge.[35]

Pascal then speaks of humans retaining some "feeble instinct from the
happiness of their first nature" despite the "the wretchedness and concupiscence, which has become their second nature."[36] This dual nature explains the contradictions that the philosophers could not reconcile.

We can liken this condition to the batting swing of an aging Reggie
Jackson (b. 1946). The odds are that even years after retiring from baseball, his swing is still smooth and crisp—although probably incapable of
hitting a pitch by a major league pitcher. There are "rumors of glory" even
today; for Reggie was not always this age.[37] To say that he was always in
his present state is to emphasize misery at the expense of greatness; to say
that he is not now far beyond his prime is to emphasize greatness at the
expense of misery.

Of course, in the case of a Reggie Jackson we have more than a dim
recollection of former greatness; it is a matter of uncontroversial, historically verifiable fact. The case for human fallenness is not this kind of
claim; it cannot be verified historically (apart from the biblical texts). It is,
rather, a theological postulate used to explain historical phenomena. Pascal stipulates that the true religion must explain human nature if it is to be
credible. The principle of greatness is the original, unfallen state; the principle of wretchedness is the fall into sin and away from God. Pagan philosophies, Pascal proposes, founder at this point—and offer us no hope for
a solution, either philosophically or existentially.

---

[35]Ibid.
[36]Ibid.
[37]"Rumors of glory" is taken from Bruce Cockburn's "Rumors of Glory" on the album *Humans*
    (1980).

In advancing the Fall as an explanation for a perplexing situation, Pascal enlists the principle that we cannot miss what we never had. Our present state of corruption is only miserable because of a previous incorruption enjoyed by the species. He says,

> The point is that if man had never been corrupted, he would, in his innocence, confidently enjoy both truth and felicity, and, if man had never been anything but corrupt, he would have no idea either of truth or bliss. But unhappy as we are (and we should be less so if there were no element of greatness in our condition) we have an idea of happiness but we cannot attain it. We perceive an image of the truth and possess nothing but falsehood.[38]

> All these examples of wretchedness prove his greatness. It is the wretchedness of a great lord, the wretchedness of a dispossessed king.[39]

Pascal further asks, "Who would indeed think himself unhappy not to be king except one who had been dispossessed?"[40] No one, avers Pascal, is unhappy because he has but one mouth, but someone with only one eye is unhappy. No one is distressed at not having three eyes, but those with none suffer greatly. In other words, unhappiness comes from being deprived of what we are accustomed to having or what is natural to possess.

Yet people do complain about the lack of faculties they never had. Consider the wish to fly or the yearning to have political power that one has never known. Pascal might respond that the longing for what one never had is not as acute as the suffering associated with deprivation. But whether this is so may differ from person to person. One young man may suffer for years because he lacks the athletic prowess to become a professional basketball player, while a professional basketball player may suffer for only a short time after having to retire early because of a serious injury. One suffers badly over what he never had, and another suffers less severely over what is lost.

Pascal might also respond that the grandiose wish to fly or have other powers not possessed even by our first parents before the Fall is generated precisely because we are not content with the diminished capacities of our fallen nature. Adam and Eve in paradise were content not to fly because the

---

[38]Pascal, *Pensées* 131/434, p. 65.
[39]Ibid., 116/398, p. 59.
[40]Ibid., 117/409, p. 59.

prefallen earth was not so inhospitable. Pascal might credibly argue that if an individual's natural capacities are functioning without defect, there would be no yearning for the extranormal. In this case, the seemingly extravagant desires for superhuman powers can be seen as issuing from the loss of our original nature that did not involve superhuman powers at all.

What then is the force of Pascal's case? Pascal's observations concerning the reason for human misery should not be isolated from his total apologetic on human nature. He is merely emphasizing that people often suffer more acutely from goods lost than from the lack of goods never possessed. He then uses this as an illustration of the truth of his postulate about human fallenness: we retain some inkling of a former state of incorruption and we suffer over the loss of using our powers perfectly, even if we do not necessarily identify that situation in this manner.

PURSUING THE BEST EXPLANATION

To further defend his anthropological argument, Pascal must defend three claims: (1) that the construal of humanity as having a "dual nature" is intellectually cogent, (2) that the human condition even needs to be explained, and (3) that explanatory power is provided by the doctrine of humans being made in God's image and the doctrine of the Fall.

First, in order for his argument to get off the ground, Pascal needs to describe the human condition in a way that makes sense. I suggest that his analysis of the greatness and wretchedness of humanity rings true and that this, at least in part, explains the continuing interest in Pascal. He holds before us a mirror that reflects the whole person in its bewildering contrariety and in a wide range of circumstances. Martin Warner notes that the power of Pascal's

> fragments on the human condition lies partly in the precision of observation and partly in their range and scope that provide a cumulative effect. In epistemology, psychology, ethics, politics, the law, and even such matters as choice of career, Pascal attempts to show that an honest and accurate account of the facts requires concepts which invite interpretation in terms of man's "wretchedness" ("misere") or "greatness" ("grandeur") or, more often, of the tension between the two.[41]

---

[41]Martin Warner, *Philosophical Finesse* (Oxford: Clarendon, 1989), p. 176.

Pascal strikes several nerves that combine to register uncommon insights into human nature. These varied observations and judgments have a cumulative effect. No one reflection demonstrates the Christian position, but many mutually reinforcing reflections suggest a reevaluation of one's non-Christian perspective.

Second, even if we grant that Pascal's description of the human condition rings true, the intractable skeptic could simply say that human life is full of contradictions and conundrums that transcend our rational ability to explain. Why do we need to explain them at all, especially when this involves unverifiable metaphysics? Why should we force an anthropological crisis when life is difficult enough already?

Pascal wants to go beyond the nonchalant skepticism that is content to chronicle human folly and leave it at that. He wants to offer a compelling explanation that is both existentially appealing and rationally credible. Pascal asks if the subject matter at hand is worthy of reflection. It is the very marrow of our existence, as is highlighted when Socrates queries in the *Phaedrus:* "Am I a monster more complicated and swollen with passion than the serpent Typho, or a creature of simpler, gentler nature, partaking of something divine?"[42] Philosophers and sages throughout the ages have counseled us to know ourselves, and while their answers to the question of human nature have drastically differed, the burning question remains.

Pascal may in some sense agree with the skeptic that humans are great and miserable. The skeptic wants to end the discussion at this point. To this, Pascal argues that a mere survey of the anthropological and psychological facts is not sufficient. We need to push beyond this and seek to know something of our origin and nature if we are to have any hope of self-understanding, religious insight, spiritual renewal or moral improvement.

Pascal can also argue on the skeptic's grounds that the diversions into which he would flee are ultimately unsatisfying. They may temporarily distract us from grim realities, but the "hollow darkness" that remains cannot be healed on its own terms or according to its own resources.[43] This is why diversion never finally delivers peace. Furthermore, Pascal is not

---

[42]Plato *Phaedrus* 230a.
[43]"Hollow darkness" is taken from Bruce Cockburn's "Justice" on the album *Inner City Front* (1981).

describing the human situation as fallen without remedy; his analysis anticipates a solution to the problem through the incarnation, a doctrine that presupposes and addresses humanity's dual nature. Pascal's aphorism captures this: "Jesus is a God we can approach without pride and before whom we can humble ourselves without despair."[44]

This prospect of life and hope should further spark a person's prudential interest in the issue. There may be hope for restoration. But we must flee diversion to investigate that possibility. Diversion

> prevents us from thinking about ourselves and leads us imperceptibly to destruction. But for that we should be bored, and boredom would drive us to seek some more solid means of escape, but diversion passes our time and brings us imperceptibly to our death.[45]

Put metaphorically, "We run heedlessly into the abyss after putting something in front of us to stop us seeing it."[46]

> Know then, proud man, what a paradox you are to yourself. Be humble, impotent reason! Be silent, feeble nature! Learn that man infinitely transcends man, hear from your master your true condition, which is unknown to you. Listen to God.[47]

By speaking of the indications of human greatness and misery in a number of contexts, Pascal is inducing us to understand human nature from a different vantage point, to interpret it in a novel way. Through these ruminations he hopes that a new insight will flash upon us: that we are deposed royalty. This perspective does not force itself on us; it emerges through reflection. Pascal urges us to look into ourselves to observe the greatness and the misery: "Follow your own impulses. Observe yourself, and see if you do not find the living characteristics of these two natures."[48]

An example might clarify his project. Suppose you come across a perplexing painting in an art gallery. It is difficult to evaluate aesthetically because it shows marks of brilliance as well as serious defects. As long as you study the painting strictly according to appearances, you remain stymied. Why is there both brilliance and defect? Why would the painter

---

[44]Pascal, *Pensées* 212/528, p. 98.
[45]Ibid., 414/171, p. 148.
[46]Ibid., 166/183, p. 82.
[47]Ibid., 131/434, p. 65.
[48]Ibid., 149/430, p. 78.

combine such features so oddly? Later a guide in the art gallery informs you that this was painted by a great master but that it suffered corruption through mistreatment by thieves. You then begin to see the same painting from a new vantage point. The greatness of the original creation is now clearly revealed (even though you cannot see its original greatness), as is the corruption. The background information, *not deducible from the painting alone*, explains the mystery of the painting. You can now see the same picture with new insight, with a fuller awareness. Pascal is making a similar claim. To understand human nature truly, humans must ultimately see themselves in a theological framework.[49]

Pascal faces a third challenge to his anthropological argument. He is not unaware of the difficulties with the doctrines of the Fall and original sin. He embraces these difficulties in an interesting fragment that describes his anthropological angle quite clearly.

> Original sin is folly in the eyes of men, but it is put forward as such. You should not reproach me for the unreasonable nature of this doctrine, because I put it forward as being unreasonable. But the folly is wiser than all men's wisdom, it is wiser than men (1 Cor. 1:25). For without it, what are we to say man is? His whole state depends on this imperceptible point. How could he have become aware of it through his reason, seeing that it is something contrary to reason and that his reason, far from discovering it by its own methods, draws away when presented with it?[50]

Despite the "offensive" quality of this doctrine, Pascal embraces it because of its explanatory power.

> Certainly nothing jolts us more rudely than this doctrine, and yet, but for this mystery, the most incomprehensible of all, we remain incomprehensible to ourselves. The knot of our condition was twisted and turned in that abyss, so that it is harder to conceive of man without this mystery than for man to conceive of it himself.[51]

By "incomprehensible to ourselves," Pascal has in mind the "contradictions" of humanity, the strange juxtapositions and conflicts of greatness and misery. The doctrine of sin may leave us with unanswered questions

---

[49]See Geddes MacGregor, *Introduction to Religious Philosophy* (Boston: Houghton Mifflin, 1959), pp. 142-43. I have adapted his illustration somewhat.

[50]Pascal, *Pensées* 695/445, p. 246.

[51]Ibid., 131/434, p. 65.

about why God allowed corruption to enter his creation, but it neverthe-less fits the facts as we observe them: humans show signs of being both royal and wretched. In light of this, the doctrine is not intrinsically unrea-sonable but is the most reasonable way to explain the human condition.

Pascal himself calls the doctrine of original sin "an offense to reason." Yet he deems it a mystery that explains the puzzle of the human condition, because without this mystery we remain incomprehensible to ourselves. If we want to decrease the mystery, explain our lot and find hope for redemp-tion, Pascal claims that we should invoke the theological categories of creation, fall and incarnation.

This argumentative strategy chimes in with an observation by G. K. Chesterton that "the whole secret of mysticism is this: that man can un-derstand everything by the help of what he does not understand."[52] (By "mysticism" Chesterton means Christian theism, not mystical experience in any technical sense.) His point, although made in another connection, is that the mysterious can have great explanatory power. The fall of hu-manity is admittedly difficult to fathom; however, once it is admitted into our worldview, the enigmas of the human condition are explained and the human landscape is illuminated as never before. Chesterton compares this explanatory situation to our vision in relation to the sun: "The one created thing which we cannot look at is the one thing in the light of which we look at everything. Like the sun at noonday, mysticism explains every-thing else by the blaze of its own victorious invisibility."[53]

THE ABDUCTIVE ARGUMENT: THE BEST EXPLANATION

Pascal's reflections offer us an incentive to view the human condition from a different perspective. These reflections employ a particular logical form of argument. His argumentation is neither inductive nor deductive, nor is it merely a fideistic theological assertion. Rather, it is an appeal to a com-pelling explanation, a postulate that illuminates material that would not otherwise be as intelligible or significant. This is called abduction. C. S. Peirce, following a lead given by Aristotle, explains it this way: "The sur-prising fact, C, is observed. But if A were true, C would be a matter of

---

[52]Chesterton, *Orthodoxy*, p. 28. Chesterton does not iew mystery as absurdity.
[53]Ibid., p. 29.

course. Hence, there is reason to suspect that A is true."[54]

A deductive argument proceeds from the general to the particular; its conclusion must be true if its premises are true. The conclusion of an inductive argument is probable given proper inductive procedures that proceed from the particular to the general. An abductive argument, according to Peirce, "merely suggests that something may be."[55] In the case of Pascal's argument, the "surprising fact" is the contradictory nature of humanity. What renders this condition a "matter of course" is divine creation and human fallenness; we are deposed royalty vainly questing after a lost throne beyond our mortal grasp.

This kind of argument is often used in scientific theorizing and in courts of law. If astrophysicists are attempting to explain the origin of the moon or some other satellite or planet, they cannot conduct inductive experimentation to repeat the original process. Neither is deduction available. Instead, they attempt to survey the available data about the moon and its surroundings, and postulate an explanation for its existence and nature. In court cases various kinds of evidence are arrayed in support of a judgment concerning the guilt or innocence of the party on trial. A woman accused of larceny must give a better explanation of her whereabouts during the crime in question than does the prosecutor.

If this kind of reasoning is common, useful and acceptable in other contexts, its use in the philosophy of religion should not be excluded. In the claim about human fallenness Pascal adduces a wide array of factors that he argues are best explained by the postulate of original sin. This approach helps him avoid the fallacy of affirming the consequent, which states:

1. If A, then B.

2. B is true.

3. Therefore, A is true.

---

[54]Charles Peirce, *Collected Papers of Charles Sanders Peirce*, ed. C. Hartshorne and P. Weiss, 6 vols. (Cambridge, Mass.: Harvard University Press, 1931-35), B, 69a; quoted in Warner, *Philosophical Finesse*, p. 25. This abductive method was employed by the evangelical apologist Edward John Carnell throughout his writings. Gordon R. Lewis refers to this strategy as "verificationism." See his *Testing Christianity's Truth Claims* (Chicago: Moody Press, 1976), pp. 176-284.

[55]Ibid.

The following illustrates this fallacy:

1. If it rains, the grass will be wet.

2. The grass is wet.

3. Therefore, it rained.

Not necessarily. The grass might have gotten wet in a number of other ways, such as the morning dew, a water sprinkler or a fire hose. Although it may have rained, other explanations are also readily available. This error lies in failing to recognize a possible plurality of causes for one effect.

The logical situation changes, however, when a postulate helps explain a broad variety of relevant phenomena. If we say that A implies B1, B2, B3 and so on, and we find B1, B2, B3 and so on to obtain, then A becomes quite plausible. In other words, if we say that if it rains (1) the grass will be wet, (2) the sidewalk will be wet, and (3) the roads will be slippery, and we can verify these conditions, then the rain explanation becomes more tenable than if, say, only one possible implication of rain were to occur.[56] The explanation is not impregnable, however, because falsifying instances are imaginable, and other explanations might claim to better account for the facts more fully.

Rendering an explanation cogent through abductive reasoning and defending it against the fallacy of affirming the consequent is not a simple matter of multiplying the *quantity* of confirming instances. If this were so, we could argue:

1. If it rains, blades of grass 1 through 10,000 on my lawn will be wet.

2. Blades 1 through 10,000 are wet.

3. Therefore, it rained.

This argument is hardly convincing, because the items in the consequent (wet blades of grass) are not extensively distributed over a *relevant range* of confirmatory phenomena, as was the case in the previous example of diverse data confirming the occurrence of rain.

In making the abductive argument that his rendering of the human condition is the best explanation for the phenomena at hand, Pascal appeals to a wide and diverse variety of relevant anthropological confirmations.

---

[56]See D. Elton Trueblood, *Philosophy of Religion* (Grand Rapids: Baker, 1957), pp. 63-64.

CONCLUSION: A TREATMENT FOR UNBELIEF

Pascal argues that the claim of divine revelation solves the riddle of the human condition by providing a compelling theological explanation for a philosophical and existential conundrum. It states that humans are (1) wretched because fallen, (2) great because of their unfallen origin and the vestiges of it, and (3) redeemable through the incarnation. Pascal observes the human condition from a number of angles, crafts a cumulative and abductive case for his revelational anthropology, and challenges any other worldview to better explain the human condition. In a long fragment focused on the anthropological argument, Pascal throws down the gauntlet after specifying the need to explain the human condition and supply a concrete hope: "Let us examine all the religions of the world on that point and let us see whether any but the Christian religion meets it."[57] This chapter has not attempted such a systematic and comprehensive exercise in comparative anthropology (although mention was made of the problems of autonomous philosophy in this regard), but the rudiments of Pascal's case for Christianity can be applied to any potential rival on a case-by-case basis. When combined with a robust natural theology, the anthropological argument further strengthens the Christian apologetic by helping to explain human beings to themselves and to others.

---

[57]Pascal, *Pensées* 149/430, p. 76.

19

Jesus of Nazareth

How Historians Can Know Him and Why It Matters

Craig L. Blomberg[1]

JESUS OF NAZARETH HAS BEEN THE MOST influential person to walk this earth in human history. To this day more than two billion people worldwide claim to be his followers, more than the number of adherents to any other religion or worldview. Christianity is responsible for a disproportionately large number of the humanitarian advances in the history of civilization—in education, medicine, law, the fine arts, working for human rights and even in the natural sciences (based on the belief that God designed the universe in an orderly fashion and left clues for people to learn about it).[2] But just who was this individual and how can we glean reliable information about him? A recent work on popular images of Jesus in America alone identifies eight quite different portraits: "enlightened sage," "sweet savior," "manly redeemer," "superstar," "Mormon elder brother," "black Moses," "rabbi" and "Oriental Christ."[3] Because these depictions

[1]Craig Blomberg is Distinguished Professor of New Testament at Denver Seminary. This essay is copyright © 2008 by Christ on Campus Initiative (CCI), and used by permission of CCI, a nonprofit organization generously supported by the Carl F. H. Henry Center for Theological Understanding (a ministry of Trinity Evangelical Divinity School) and the MAC Foundation. CCI exists to prepare and circulate materials for college and university students, addressing an array of fundamental issues from a Christian perspective. Readers and organizations may circulate these essays without charge. Those wishing to contact CCI may email the secretary, Dr. Scott Manetsch, at smanetsc@tiu.edu.
[2]See esp. Jonathan Hill, *What Has Christianity Ever Done for Us? How It Shaped the Modern World* (Downers Grove, Ill.: InterVarsity Press, 2005).
[3]Stephen Prothero, *American Jesus: How the Son of God Became a National Icon* (New York: Farrar, Straus & Giroux, 2003).

contradict each other at various points, they cannot all be equally accurate. Historians must return to the ancient evidence for Jesus and assess its merits. This evidence falls into three main categories: non-Christian, historic Christian and syncretistic (a hybrid of Christian and non-Christian perspectives).

An inordinate number of websites and blogs make the wholly unjustified claim that Jesus never existed. Biblical scholars and historians who have investigated this issue in detail are virtually unanimous today in rejecting this view, regardless of their theological or ideological perspectives. A dozen or more references to Jesus appear in non-Christian Jewish, Greek and Roman sources in the earliest centuries of the Common Era (i.e., approximately from the birth of Jesus onward, as Christianity and Judaism began to overlap chronologically). These references appear in such diverse authors as Josephus (a first-century Jewish historian), several different portions of the Talmud (an encyclopedic collection of rabbinic traditions finally codified in the fourth through sixth centuries), the Greek writers Lucian of Samosata and Mara bar Serapion, and Roman historians Thallus, Tacitus, Pliny and Suetonius. Tacitus, for example, in the early second century, writes about Nero's persecution of Christians and then explains, "The founder of this name, Christ, had been executed in the reign of Tiberius by the procurator Pontius Pilate" (*Annals* 44.3). The Talmud repeatedly acknowledges that Jesus worked miracles but refers to him as one who "practiced magic and led Israel astray" (Babylonian Talmud *Sanhedrin* 43a; cf. Tosefta *Shabbath* 11.15; Babylonian Talmud *Shabbath* 104b). Josephus, in the late first century, calls Jesus "a wise man," "a worker of amazing deeds," "a teacher" and "one accused by the leading men among us [who] condemned him to the cross" (*Antiquities of the Jews* 18.3.3).

It is, of course, historically prejudicial to exclude automatically all *Christian* evidence, as if no one who became a follower of Jesus could ever report accurately about his life and teachings, or to assume that all *non-Christian* evidence was necessarily more "objective." But even using only such non-Christian sources, there is ample evidence to confirm the main contours of the early Christian claims: Jesus was a Jew who lived in Israel during the first third of the first century; was born out of wedlock; intersected with the life and ministry of John the Baptist; attracted great crowds, especially because of his wondrous deeds; had a group of particularly close followers called disciples (five of whom are named); ran afoul of the Jewish religious authorities because of his controversial teachings sometimes deemed heretical or blasphemous; was crucified during the time of Pontius Pilate's governorship in Judea (A.D. 26-36), and yet was believed by many of his followers to have been the Messiah, the anticipated liberator of Israel. This belief did not disappear despite Jesus' death because a number of his supporters claimed to have seen him resurrected from the dead. His followers, therefore, continued consistently to grow in numbers, gathering together regularly for worship and instruction and even singing hymns to him as if he were a god (or God).[4]

Contemporary reactions to this composite picture sometimes complain that this seems like a rather sparse amount of information. On the other hand, until the last few centuries, history and biography in general almost exclusively focused on the exploits of kings and queens (or their cultural equivalents), military conquests and defeats, people in official institutional positions of power in a given society, and the wealthy more generally, not least because it was primarily these people who could read or afford to own written documents. Jesus qualified for attention under none of these headings. Moreover, no non-Christians in the first several centuries of the Common Era had any reason to imagine that his influence would grow and spread the way it did in the millennium and a half ahead. So it is arguable that it is actually rather impressive that as much has been preserved outside of Christian circles as has been. And of course, most ancient testimony to *any* person or event has been lost over the centuries, so many other references to Jesus might have existed that we simply no longer know about.

---

[4]The most thorough and evenhanded presentation and assessment of these data appears in Robert E. van Voorst, *Jesus Outside the New Testament* (Grand Rapids: Eerdmans, 2000), from which the English translations of Tacitus, the Talmud and Josephus have been taken. Peter Schäfer is particularly helpful from a Jewish perspective on the clear references and various additional possible allusions in the rabbinic literature (*Jesus in the Talmud* [Princeton, N.J.: Princeton University Press, 2007]). What Josephus originally wrote has been disputed, but a reasonable consensus suggests that the only Christian interpolations were to affirm Jesus' messiahship and resurrection rather than simply note that his followers alleged that they occurred (see John P. Meier, "Jesus in Josephus: A Modest Proposal," *Catholic Biblical Quarterly* 52 [1990]: 76-103).

HISTORIC CHRISTIAN EVIDENCE FOR JESUS

By far the most important historical information about Jesus of Nazareth appears in the four Gospels of the New Testament. But chronologically, these are not the earliest Christian documents still in existence. Even most conservative scholars acknowledge that the Gospels were not written before the 60s, whereas Jesus was crucified in either A.D. 30 or 33. The majority of the undisputed letters of Paul, however, were all written at the latest by the 50s. These include Romans, 1–2 Corinthians, Galatians, 1 Thessalonians and Philemon. Thus, when they report on the deeds and sayings of Jesus, they cannot simply be following one or more of the written Gospels for their information. Rather, they must reflect the oral tradition that was preserving these details before the written accounts were produced. The letter of James contains about three dozen probable allusions to the teaching of Jesus, especially from his Sermon on the Mount, and it may well date to as early as the mid-40s.[5] But because this is more disputed, I will limit our focus here to the epistles of Paul just mentioned, before turning to the Gospels themselves.

The Apostle Paul

Readers of Paul's letters sometimes wonder why he does not refer back to the teachings and deeds of Jesus even more than he does. Several factors no doubt account for this silence. First, he is writing to Christian churches who have already heard considerable details about Jesus. Second, he is dealing primarily with specific issues reflecting the current situations of those congregations. Third, the genre of epistle was not designed primarily to retell the story of the life of Christ. The letters of John, written most likely by the same author as the Gospel of John, barely refer back to specific sayings and events from Jesus' life at all, even though the author had himself written about them in detail. Finally, Christians quickly recognized that the most important features of Jesus' life were his crucifixion and resurrection, and Paul has a lot to say about these in his letters.

But it is easy to underestimate the number of quotations and particularly allusions to the Jesus tradition in the epistles of Paul, precisely because ancient writers felt free to represent the gist of another person's

---

[5]Peter H. Davids, *The Epistle of James* (Grand Rapids: Eerdmans, 1982), pp. 22, 47-48.

teaching in their own words. Indeed, in some circles, good rhetoric demanded it.[6] Paul clearly knows the basic outline of Jesus' life.

> What Paul appears to know about Jesus is that he was born as a human
> (Rom. 9.5) to a woman and under the law, that is, as a Jew (Gal. 4.4), that
> he was descended from David's line (Rom 1.3; 15.12) though he was not
> like Adam (Rom. 5.15), that he had brothers, including one named James
> (1 Cor. 9.5; Gal. 1.19), that he had a meal on the night he was betrayed
> (1 Cor. 1.23-25), that he was crucified and died on a cross (Phil. 2.8; 1 Cor.
> 1:23; 8.11; 15.3; Rom. 4.25; 5.6, 8; 1 Thess. 2.15; 4.14, etc.), was buried
> (1 Cor. 15.4), and was raised three days later (1 Cor. 15.4; Rom. 4.25; 8.34;
> 1 Thess. 4.14, etc.), and that afterwards he was seen by Peter, the disciples
> and others (1 Cor. 15:5-7).[7]

More significantly, he knows very specific teachings of Jesus on a
wide range of topics. First Corinthians 11:23-25 quotes Jesus' words over
the bread and the cup at the Last Supper in considerable detail in language very close to what Luke later wrote in Luke 22:19-20. Earlier in
the same letter, Paul appeals to Jesus' principle that those who preach the
gospel should receive their living from the gospel (1 Corinthians 9:14; cf.
Matthew 10:10; Luke 10:7). He knows that Jesus opposed divorce (1
Corinthians 7:10; cf. Mark 10:2-12) but supported the paying of taxes
(Romans 13:7; cf. Mark 12:17). He taught about not repaying evil for evil
but rather loving one's enemies and praying for one's persecutors (Romans 12:14, 17-19; cf. Matthew 5:38; Luke 6:27-28, 36), and on not
judging but tolerating one another on morally neutral matters (Romans
14:13; cf. Matthew 7:1; Luke 6:37). Paul understands that Jesus declared
all foods clean (Romans 14:14; cf. Mark 7:18-19), that he warned of
God's imminent judgment on the leadership of the nation of Israel (1
Thessalonians 2:15-16; cf. Matthew 23:32-36) and that he predicted numerous specific events in association with his return at the end of the age
(1 Thessalonians 4:15-17; 5:2-6; see Christ's discourse on the Mount of
Olives in Matthew 24–25).

These are simply the clearest references in Paul's letters to Jesus' teach-

---

[6]Richard Bauckham, *Jesus and the Eyewitnesses: The Gospels as Eyewitness Testimony* (Grand Rapids: Eerdmans, 2006), pp. 333-34.
[7]Stanley E. Porter, "Images of Christ in Paul's Letters," in *Images of Christ: Ancient and Modern*,
ed. Stanley E. Porter, Michael A. Hayes and David Tombs (Sheffield, U.K.: Sheffield Academic Press, 1997), pp. 98-99.

ing. A much longer list of probable allusions can be compiled.[8] As a result, it just will not do to argue that Paul knew little or nothing about the historical Jesus or so distorted his picture of Jesus as to become, for all intents and purposes, the true founder of Christianity. But we may press the point further. In Paul's most detailed discussion of Jesus' resurrection, he writes,

> Now, brothers and sisters, I want to remind you of the gospel I preached to you, which you received and on which you have taken your stand. . . . For what I received I passed on to you as of first importance [or "at the first"]: that Christ died for our sins according to the Scriptures, that he was buried, that he was raised on the third day according to the Scriptures, and that he appeared to Cephas [that is, Peter], and then to the Twelve. After that, he appeared to more than five hundred of the brothers and sisters. (1 Corinthians 15:1, 3-6)

The language of "receiving" and "passing on" here is technical terminology for carefully memorized oral tradition. As central Christian doctrine, Saul of Tarsus (whom we know better as Paul) would have been taught these basic gospel facts not long after his conversion, which took place roughly three years after Jesus' death. Already in that very short period of time the belief that Jesus was bodily raised from death was entrenched as the heart of fundamental teaching new converts had to learn. It cannot be chalked up to the slow, evolutionary development of myth or legend decades after the original facts of Jesus' life had been left behind.[9]

The New Testament Gospels

Despite corroborating evidence outside the New Testament Gospels, the bulk of the evidence for Jesus comes from the three Synoptic Gospels (so-called because they are more alike than different and can be set next to each other in parallel columns for easy comparisons among them) and the Gospel of John, which is more different from than similar to any one of the Synoptics.

---

[8]See esp. David Wenham, *Paul: Follower of Jesus or Founder of Christianity?* (Grand Rapids: Eerdmans, 1995).

[9]Striking support for these claims appears in the work of atheist historian Gerd Lüdemann (with Alf Özen), *What Really Happened to Jesus? A Historical Approach to the Resurrection* (Louisville: Westminster John Knox, 1995), p. 15.

The Synoptics: Matthew, Mark and Luke. The various "quests for the historical Jesus" that have proved so influential in the last two centuries of New Testament scholarship have focused primarily on the three Synoptic Gospels. The upshot of all this research is that a significant cross section of current scholarship believes that at least the broad contours and most central items common to Matthew, Mark and Luke are likely to be historically reliable. Those central themes include such features as the following: Jesus was a Jewish teacher who was raised as a carpenter but who began a public ministry when he was around the age of thirty. He submitted himself to John's baptism, announced both the present and future dimensions of God's kingdom (or reign) on earth, gave love-based ethical injunctions to his listeners, taught a considerable amount in parables, challenged conventional interpretations of the Jewish law on numerous fronts but never broke (or taught others to break) the written law, wrought amazing signs and wonders to demonstrate the arrival of the kingdom, implicitly and explicitly claimed to be the Messiah or liberator of the Jewish people but only inasmuch as they became his followers, and counterculturally believed that he had to suffer and die for the sins of the world, be raised from the dead and return to his heavenly throne next to Yahweh, only to return to earth at some unspecified point in the future, ushering in Judgment Day. He called all people to repent of their sins and form the nucleus of the new, true, freed people of God led by his twelve apostles.[10]

A number of factors converge to make the assumption probable that a portrait relatively close to this one can be viewed as historically accurate.

1. Authorship and date. Many conservative scholars present plausible arguments for accepting the early church's unanimous attributions of these three documents. Mark is a relatively minor character on the pages of the New Testament, probably best known for deserting Paul and Barnabas on their first missionary journey for a reason we are never told (Acts 13:13; 15:37-38). He would not have been a likely person after which to name a Gospel if he did not actually write it, with many other more prominent and respected first-generation Christians available for such an ascription. The same is true of Luke, who was Paul's beloved doctor but who appears by name only three times in the New Testament, in each case tucked away

[10]See esp. N. T. Wright, *Jesus and the Victory of God* (Minneapolis: Fortress, 1996); and Ben Witherington III, *The Christology of Jesus* (Minneapolis: Fortress, 1990).

in the greetings at the end of an epistle (Colossians 4:14; 2 Timothy 4:11; Philemon 24). Matthew, on the other hand, *was* one of the twelve apostles—Jesus' closest followers during his lifetime—but, as a converted tax collector (Matthew 9:9-13), his background could easily have made him the least respected of the Twelve!

Many liberal New Testament scholars nevertheless doubt that Matthew, Mark and Luke wrote the Gospels bearing their names. But they almost all agree that they were written well within the first century by orthodox Christians in the orbit of apostolic Christianity. Typically suggested dates place Mark in the late 60s or early 70s, and Matthew and Luke in the 80s. Conservatives, accepting the church fathers' testimony concerning the composition of these Gospels, date all three to the early or mid-60s. On either set of dates, however, we are speaking of documents compiled about fifty years or less after the events they narrate. In our age of instant information access, this can seem like a long time. But in the ancient Mediterranean world, it was surprisingly short. The oldest existing biographies of Alexander the Great, for example, are those of Plutarch and Arrian, hailing from the late first and early second centuries C.E. Alexander died, however, in 323 B.C.! Yet classical historians regularly believe they can derive extensive, reliable information from these works to reconstruct in some detail the exploits of Alexander. This remains true despite various problems in harmonizing certain differences between these two sources and despite certain ideological grids through which each author filtered his information.[11] The words penned nearly half a century ago by A. N. Sherwin-White, the British historian of ancient Greece and Rome, remain as applicable today as then: "So, it is astonishing that while Graeco-Roman historians have been growing in confidence, the twentieth-century study of the Gospel narratives, starting from no less promising material, has taken so gloomy a turn . . . that [for some] the historical Christ is unknowable and the history of his mission cannot be written."[12] This gloom should be replaced by a much more optimistic spirit.

2. Literary genre. A second issue is that of Gospel genre. Did the Syn-

---

[11]Craig L. Blomberg, "The Legitimacy and Limits of Harmonization," in *Hermeneutics, Authority, and Canon*, ed. D. A. Carson and John D. Woodbridge (Grand Rapids: Zondervan, 1986), esp. pp. 169-73.

[12]A. N. Sherwin-White, *Roman Society and Roman Law in the New Testament* (Oxford: Oxford University Press, 1963), p. 187.

optic writers intend to produce works that would be viewed as serious history and biography by the conventions of their day? The evidence strongly suggests that they did. The clearest indication of what any of the three thought he was doing appears in Luke 1:1-4:

> Many have undertaken to draw up an account of the things that have been fulfilled among us, just as they were handed down to us by those who from the first were eyewitnesses and servants of the word. With this in mind, since I myself have carefully investigated everything from the beginning, I too decided to write an orderly account for you, most excellent Theophilus, so that you may know the certainty of the things you have been taught.

A careful reading of this prologue demonstrates that (1) Luke was aware of previously written sources that documented aspects of the life of Christ; (2) he interviewed eyewitnesses of Jesus' ministry, along with gleaning additional information from others through the oral tradition; and (3) he made his own selection and arrangement of material in order best to persuade his patron, Theophilus, of the validity of the Christian faith. These are precisely the kinds of details that we find, at times even in very similar language, in the lengthier prologues to volumes of that era which are generally viewed as among the most reliable works of history produced back then—most notably, in the histories of the Jewish author Josephus and the Greek writers Herodotus, Thucydides, Polybius and Lucian.[13] Even closer analogies appear in Greco-Roman "technical prose" or "scientific literature," including treatises on such topics as medicine, philosophy, mathematics, engineering and rhetoric.[14] This proves a far cry from the fictitious genres of literature to which modern skeptics often wish to assign the Gospels.

Of course, a historical intent by no means equates with success in accomplishing one's objectives. Indeed, three questions call out for an answer at this juncture of our investigation. (1) How carefully would the Gospel writers have wanted to preserve historical detail? (2) What ability did they have to do so? (3) How successful were they in their endeavors?

---

[13]A. W. Mosley, "Historical Reporting in the Ancient World," *New Testament Studies* 12 (1965-1966): 10-26; Terrence Callan, "The Preface of Luke-Acts and Historiography," *New Testament Studies* 31 (1985): 576-81.

[14]Loveday C. Alexander, *The Preface to Luke's Gospel* (Cambridge: Cambridge University Press, 1993).

With respect to the first question, it is often argued that the compilers of the Gospels would *not* have had a strong interest in meticulous preservation of accurate detail. Sometimes this conclusion is based on the conviction that words of the risen Lord spoken through early Christian prophets would have been intermingled with the sayings of the earthly Jesus. At other times it is alleged that a movement that thought that the world might end at any moment would have had no reason to chronicle the life of Jesus with great care. On still other occasions critics complain that an ideological (in this case, theological) ax to grind necessarily skews one's ability to report objective facts. Let us look at each of these objections in turn.

3. Authorial intent. It is true that in first-century Greco-Roman culture, would-be prophets sometimes felt no need to distinguish between the words of a great hero during his life and his later oracles to his followers, speaking (so it was believed) from beyond the grave. But in Jewish tradition, great care was exercised to preserve the correct name of a rabbi to whom a famous teaching was attributed and, if that information had been lost even though the saying outlived its author, attributions were left anonymous. In the New Testament, the only three explicit instances of an early Christian prophet's words (Acts 11:28; 21:10-11; Revelation 2:1–3:22) are all clearly distinguished, and distinguishable, from the words of the earthly Jesus. What is more, Paul insisted that all alleged manifestations of the gift of prophecy had to be evaluated by the other Christians present (1 Corinthians 14:29). From Old Testament days on, one of the central criteria for evaluating supposedly divine words was whether they cohered with previous revelation. So even if some of the teachings in the Gospels did in fact come from later Christian prophets rather than the historical Jesus, the overall portrait of his teaching could not have been materially altered.[15]

The argument about many Christians expecting the imminent end of the world at first glance seems more substantial. The Thessalonian epistles show how Paul had to walk a delicate tightrope between affirming that Christ was still coming back soon and yet there were signs of the end that had still to occur. But this was not a new problem for Jesus' followers. Jews, from the time of the first writing prophets in the eighth century B.C. on-

---

[15]See further Ben Witherington III, *Jesus the Seer: The Progress of Prophecy* (Peabody, Mass.: Hendrickson, 1999), pp. 293-328.

ward, had to wrestle with the declaration of Yahweh's spokesmen that the Day of the Lord was at hand in a rich variety of ways (e.g., Joel 2:1; Obadiah 15; Habakkuk 2:3), and yet the centuries continued to march by. The most common solution that pre-Christian Judaism adopted for this dilemma was to cite Psalm 90:4:

> A thousand years in your sight
>   are like a day that has just gone by,
>   or like a watch in the night.

Second Peter 3:8 shows that New Testament Christianity adopted the same strategy, so that the so-called delay in Christ's return was probably neither the all-consuming issue nor the history-erasing crisis that some have alleged. Moreover, the Essene Jews responsible for most of the Dead Sea Scrolls discovered at Qumran lived in the belief that they were seeing end-times events unfold before them, and yet they produced a prodigious literature, including enough information to enable us to chronicle a substantial history of their movement. It is unlikely that the first Christians would have behaved any differently.[16]

What then of the charge that an ideological agenda necessarily biased the Gospels' authors and prevented them from writing adequately objective history? There is no question that ideological bias can create severe historical revisionism: witness the one-line entry under Jesus Christ in the old Soviet encyclopedia that labeled him the mythological founder of Christianity.[17] In more recent days the overtly anti-Semitic president of Iran, Mahmoud Ahmadinejad, has seriously questioned whether the Holocaust occurred on anything like the scale it really did, despite the existence of warehouse-sized collections of records attesting the truth. Did the followers of Jesus do something comparable, changing him from a simple Jewish prophet into a cosmic Gentile god?[18] It is not likely. After all, sometimes the very ideology one wants to promote requires careful historical attestation. Holocaust survivors, like many Jewish historians, were passionately concerned that no comparable genocide ever

---

[16]See further Charles L. Holman, *Till Jesus Comes: Origins of Christian Apocalyptic Expectation* (Peabody, Mass.: Hendrickson, 1996).

[17]I. Howard Marshall, *I Believe in the Historical Jesus* (Grand Rapids: Eerdmans, 1977), p. 15.

[18]As is the thesis of Maurice Casey, *From Jewish Prophet to Gentile God: The Origins and Development of New Testament Christology* (Louisville: Westminster John Knox, 1991).

be perpetrated against their people (or any people) again, and for that very reason painstakingly chronicled atrocity after atrocity. First-century Christianity audaciously claimed that God had acted uniquely in the life, death and resurrection of Jesus of Nazareth to provide atonement for humanity's sins, reconciliation between those who became his followers and Yahweh the God of Israel, and the possibility of eternal life in a re-created and perfected universe in the future. If Christianity's opponents had been able to show that the central elements of the New Testament data did not closely resemble the true facts about Jesus, this fledgling religion would have crumbled at once. Or as Paul puts it quite simply, "If Christ has not been raised, your faith is futile; you are still in your sins" (1 Corinthians 15:17). In sum, the Gospel writers had every reason to want to preserve accurate history.

4. Compositional procedures. But were they able to do so? Even if a thirty-year oral tradition was remarkably short by ancient standards, it still leaves plenty of time for distortion to creep in, perhaps even unwittingly and undetected. Can we seriously believe that documents written no earlier than the early 60s accurately recounted the deeds and teachings of Jesus in the late 20s or early 30s? As it turns out, we can. Ancient Jews honed the art of memorization to an amazing extent. Some rabbis had the entire Hebrew Scriptures committed to memory. A few had quite a bit of the oral Torah (the oral law) under command as well. (For those who find these claims hard to believe, the popular twentieth-century Jewish writer Chaim Potok liked to tell of similar, verified feats of learning among orthodox Jewish students in the yeshivas of New York City.) A scribe who had recently completed a new copy of the Torah would often have the most gifted or venerated local rabbi proofread his manuscript by checking it against that rabbi's memory!

Nor were these feats limited to Jews in the ancient Mediterranean world. Greek schoolboys (and, unfortunately, with rare exceptions, it was only school*boys* in both Jewish and Gentile contexts) sometimes committed either the *Iliad* or the *Odyssey*—Homer's epic poems that functioned much like Scripture in Greek circles—to memory, with each containing roughly 100,000 words. How was such memorization possible? First, it was an oral culture not dependent on all the print media that dominate our modern world. Second, the main educational technique employed in schools was rote memorization. Jews even had a tradition that until a boy had memorized a passage of Torah, he was not qualified to discuss it lest he perhaps misrepresent it. Third, in Jewish circles, "Bible" was the only subject students studied during the fairly compulsory elementary education that spanned ages five to twelve or thirteen, and that took place at least wherever there were large enough Jewish communities to have a synagogue. Fourth, memorization thus began at the early ages when it is the easiest period of life to master large amounts of content. Fifth, texts were often sung or chanted; the tunes helped students remember the words, as they do with contemporary music too. Finally, a variety of other mnemonic devices dotted the texts that were studied so intensely. Especially crucial in the Jewish Scriptures were numerous forms of parallelism between lines, couplets and even larger units of thought.[19] In this kind of milieu, accurately remembering and transmitting the amount of material found in one Gospel would have been comparatively easy.

At the same time mere memorization cannot be the only factor that lies behind the transmission of the Gospel tradition. If it were, we would not have four different Gospels or, if we did, they would not vary in the precise way that they do. It has long been recognized that the Synoptic Gospels almost certainly reflect some kind of *literary* relationship among themselves. That is to say, one or more of these three documents utilized one or more of the others or other common sources. Only in this fashion can we account for the extensive verbatim parallelism between parallel accounts of the same event interspersed with utterly unparalleled or only slightly paralleled material. A few conservative scholars have argued for complete independence, leaving only divine inspiration to account for the current combination of similarities and differences, but this flies in the face of Luke's own testimony in Luke 1:1-4 and the standard Jewish and Greco-Roman practices of writing history and biography.

Most Gospels scholars therefore believe that, at least in the finished forms in which we now have them, (1) Mark came first, (2) Matthew and Luke each independently relied on Mark wherever they wanted to, and (3)

[19]For all these and related practices, see esp. Birger Gerhardsson, *Memory and Manuscript: Oral Tradition and Written Transmission in Rabbinic Judaism and Early Christianity* (1961, 1964; reprint, Grand Rapids: Eerdmans, 1998); Birger Gerhardsson, *The Reliability of the Gospel Tradition* (Peabody, Mass.: Hendrickson, 2001).

Matthew and Luke each utilized additional sources, both written and oral. One of these may well have been a common source, primarily of sayings of Jesus, to which both Matthew and Luke had access, in view of the approximately 250 verses in these two Gospels common to each other but not found in Mark. This hypothetical source has come to be called Q (from the German word *Quelle* for "source").[20]

Another factor comes into play here, too, which recent research has been particularly scrutinizing. Prior to a text becoming "canonical"—uniquely sacred and authoritative *in written form*—revered traditions in ancient Mediterranean cultures were transmitted orally with certain flexibility within fixed limitations. Even into the late twentieth century, preliterate or semiliterate communities or people groups in as diverse locations as Africa, the Balkan states, Lebanon and Palestine appointed certified "tradents"—oral storytellers (or singers) who were responsible for regularly rehearsing or performing the sacred traditions of that group of people. Yet, far from repeating every last word identically with each retelling of the epic, anywhere from 10-40 percent of the actual words could vary from one occasion to the next. This allowed for varying selections of episodes and portions of episodes to include abbreviation, explanation, application and paraphrase, in part for the storyteller to demonstrate some creative artistry and in part to keep the audience's interest fresh. At the same time, 60-90 percent of the information remained unvarying, including all elements deemed necessary for the lessons of the stories to remain intact. Tradents who left out or garbled any of these elements were to be interrupted and corrected by those in the audience who recognized the mistakes.[21]

Now turn back to the Synoptic Gospels. Choose all of the passages unambiguously appearing in at least two of these three books. That is to say, limit yourself to accounts that the various Gospel writers assign to the same time or place that cannot be dismissed as Jesus simply doing two

---

[20]An excellent introduction to Gospel source criticism, as this exercise is called, which presents the various hypotheses that have been proposed with the major rationales for each, is Robert H. Stein, *Studying the Synoptic Gospels: Origin and Interpretation*, 2nd ed. (Grand Rapids: Baker Academic, 2001). This volume also deals nicely with the features of oral tradition and final editing of the canonical Gospels.

[21]Two of the most important researchers and their most important works have been Albert B. Lord, *The Singer of Tales*, 2nd ed. (Cambridge, Mass.: Harvard University Press, 2000); and Jan Vansina, *Oral Tradition as History* (Madison: University of Wisconsin Press, 1985).

somewhat similar things twice or teaching the same basic teaching in different contexts. Count the words that are identical in the Greek in the parallel accounts. Rarely will you find less than 10 percent or more than 40 percent of the words differing! What has been called "informal controlled oral tradition" has almost certainly been at work in the production of the Synoptics and not just verbatim memorization and literary dependence on previously written sources.[22] This kind of tradition does not produce verbatim reproduction of every minor word but is true to the details that make a story or a teaching what its author intended it to be.

Nor dare we underestimate the power of the community in a culture that did not at all value individualism the way we do. Bart Ehrman likens the oral transmission of the Gospel tradition to the children's game of telephone, in which a long and complex message is whispered to one child who then has the responsibility of whispering what he or she thinks the message was to the next child, and so on.[23] After this "tradition" has been passed on to a number of participants, even over the span of a few minutes, the final child who then speaks out loud the last version of the message usually draws hilarious laughter because of how garbled the message has become. But Ehrman could hardly have chosen a more inappropriate analogy. The Gospel traditions were not whispered but publicly proclaimed, not to children but to adults, in the presence of knowledgeable tradents or with apostolic checks and balances (see, e.g., how Peter and John function in Acts 8:14-17). Indeed, a burgeoning field of research in the social sciences today is scrutinizing how "social memories" of various subcultures are formed through repetition and interpretation *in community*, creating certain fixed forms of oral tradition that might well not otherwise be established.[24] Even apart from this trend, Kenneth Bailey's research tellingly demonstrated that playing "telephone" with groups of his adult Middle-Eastern students did not yield garbled messages but extraordinarily well-preserved ones![25] This is exactly what we should expect

---

[22]Kenneth E. Bailey, "Informal Controlled Oral Tradition and the Synoptic Gospels," *Asia Journal of Theology* 5 (1991): 34-54.; reprinted in *Themelios* 20 (1995): 4-11.

[23]Bart D. Ehrman, *Jesus: Apocalyptic Prophet of the New Millennium* (Oxford: Oxford University Press, 1999), pp. 51-52.

[24]Nicely summarized and supplemented by Bauckham, *Jesus and the Eyewitnesses*, pp. 319-57.

[25]Kenneth E. Bailey, "Middle Eastern Oral Tradition and the Synoptic Gospels," *Expository Times* 106 (1995): 563-67.

of the Gospels too, given the culture in which they emerged.

5. Apparent contradictions. So the first Christian generation had plenty of reasons to want to preserve accurate information about Jesus. They certainly had the ability to do so as well. But did they succeed in accomplishing their objectives? The main obstacle to affirming that they did succeed involves the apparent contradictions between parallel accounts of episodes in Christ's life. Space does not permit us to look at anything like a comprehensive list of these seeming problems.[26] But the vast majority of them fall into predictable categories.

The largest group simply reflects the natural variations in storytelling and writing that characterize most partially independent accounts of the same event, without calling into question the historicity of the event itself. Many involve inclusion (or omission) of those details most relevant (or irrelevant) to a given Gospel writer's purposes, particularly his theological emphases. Only rarely do these create dramatic differences between two parallels, but even then we can understand how both perspectives may remain true. For example, were the disciples still misunderstanding Jesus due to hard hearts even after he walked to them on the water on the Sea of Galilee (Mark 6:52), or did they worship him and call him the Son of God (Matthew 14:33)? It takes only a little imagination to put ourselves in their position and see how acts of worship and titular acclamation, each without much understanding or truly empathetic hearts, would be a natural reaction. And once we learn that the disciples' failures and misunderstandings are a recurrent theme in Mark, while Matthew tends to portray their moments of greater faith and worship more often, we can see why each writer has chosen to narrate things the way he has.

Some of the most dramatic apparent contradictions simply involve different conventions for reporting events in the ancient world. Does the centurion himself come to ask for Jesus to heal his servant (Matthew 8:5-9), or does he send his friends (Luke 7:1-8)? Presumably the latter, because it was perfectly natural to speak of someone saying or doing something even if literally it occurred through duly appointed agents. The same is still true in certain modern contexts as, for example, when a press secretary reads to

---

[26]But see Craig L. Blomberg, *The Historical Reliability of the Gospels*, 2nd ed. (Downers Grove: InterVarsity Press, 2007), pp. 152-95; and Darrell L. Bock, *Jesus According to Scripture: Restoring the Portrait from the Gospels* (Grand Rapids: Baker Academic, 2002).

the media what a speech writer has composed, yet news reports maintain that "the President today said . . ." Does Jairus come to ask Jesus to heal his daughter while she is still alive only to find out later that she has just died (Mark 5:22-23, 35), or does he come only after her death (Matthew 9:18)? Because Matthew regularly abbreviates Mark's longer stories, he has probably also done so here, so that Mark gives the fullest, most accurate detail. But even if Matthew does not satisfy modern, scientific standards of precision, it is unfair to impose those standards on a first-century world that had not yet invented them. None of the differences affects the point of the story, which is the miraculous resurrection of the girl.

For some reason one of the more popular recurring charges of contradiction between Gospel parallels involves the identity of those individuals seen by the women who went to Jesus' tomb early on that Sunday morning we now celebrate on Easter. Mark 16:5 has them seeing a young man dressed in a white robe, Matthew 28:2-3 refers to an angel with clothing white as snow, while Luke 24:4 speaks of two men in dazzling apparel. Since angels are regularly depicted in the Bible as men, often in white or shining clothing, there is no reason that Mark or Luke needed to mention explicitly that angels were present. As for the number of them, if there were two it is hardly inaccurate to say that the women saw a young man who spoke to them, especially if one was the consistent spokesperson for the two. Only if Mark or Matthew had said that the women saw one person all by himself would there be an actual contradiction.[27]

Ehrman describes his own personal pilgrimage when, after writing a paper in graduate school trying to harmonize Mark's reference to Abiathar as the high priest in the account of David eating the sacred showbread (Mark 2:26) with the clear statement in the Old Testament that says it was Ahimelech (1 Samuel 21:1-6), his professor asked him why he couldn't just admit that Mark made a mistake. This, Ehrman claims, then opened the floodgates for him to recognize the Bible as nothing but a human book with errors all over the place.[28] Ironically, this "all-or-nothing" approach is exactly what some ultraconservatives have (illogically) insisted on as well.

[27]For an excellent analysis of all of the so-called contradictions surrounding the various accounts of Christ's resurrection, see John W. Wenham, *Easter Enigma: Do the Resurrection Stories Contradict One Another?* (Grand Rapids: Zondervan, 1984).
[28]Bart D. Ehrman, *Misquoting Jesus: The Story Behind Who Changed the Bible and Why* (San Francisco: HarperSanFrancisco, 2005), p. 9.

But no historian of any other ancient document operates this way. A document that has proved generally reliable is not suddenly discounted because of just one demonstrable mistake. At the same time, it is not at all clear that Mark *did* make a mistake. The expression he uses in the Greek is a highly unusual one if he meant to indicate time, since it is the preposition *epi* that he places before Abiathar's name, which normally means over, on top of, on, near, toward, or some other word denoting location.[29] But in Mark 12:26, when the identical construction appears in the context of Jesus' recounting the story of Moses and the burning bush, most translations render the Greek "in the passage" or "in the account" of the bush. Probably, in 2:26, Mark likewise intended Jesus to be understood as referring to the *passage* about Abiathar. Of course, this raises the follow-up objection that Abiathar doesn't appear in 1 Samuel until chapter 22. But ancient Judaism divided up Scripture into "passages" according to how much was read each week in the synagogues in order to get through all of the Law annually and all of the rest of the Old Testament once every three years. This required several chapters to be grouped together as a "passage" in most cases. Moreover, we know that each passage was given a brief title, often based on the name of a key character in it, and overall Abiathar was a better-known figure than Ahimelech. So it would not be unusual if a several-chapter stretch of 1 Samuel had been labeled "Abiathar." We cannot prove this, but it is plausible enough that we need not resort to assuming that Mark just made a mistake.[30]

We could continue giving numerous examples akin to these that we have treated briefly. Some of the proposed solutions seem more persuasive than others. Some seeming discrepancies have more than one possible solution, and different interpreters may opt for differing proposals as the most plausible. Occasionally, one runs across a problem where none of the proposed solutions seems free from difficulties. Much depends at this juncture on how much benefit of the doubt one is willing to give the Gospel writers. Completely apart from any prior convictions about whether a certain text is "inspired" or not, historians regularly seek for credible har-

---

[29]Not until the eighteenth and final cluster of definitions given by Walter Bauer et al., eds., *A Greek-English Lexicon of the New Testament and Other Early Christian Literature*, 3rd ed. (Chicago: University of Chicago Press, 2000), p. 367, does a temporal usage ("in the time of") appear.

[30]See esp. John W. Wenham, "Mark 2.26," *Journal of Theological Studies* 1 (1950): 156.

monizations along very similar lines as we have illustrated when they encounter seemingly contradictory testimony among ancient writers when they have established themselves elsewhere as reasonably competent and in a position to be "in the know."[31] And it is not as if any of the problem passages are new—Christians have been aware of them for two millennia. Both Augustine in the fifth century and Calvin in the sixteenth wrote detailed commentaries on harmonies of the Gospels and regularly addressed the texts that skeptics today find problematic. More conservative contemporary commentaries, along with scholarly monographs and articles, contain plausible solutions for every "error" that blogs can list. People whose faith is shaken as easily as Ehrman suggests his was over the supposed discovery of a solitary error must be fervently looking for reasons to abandon their faith, rather than engaging in dispassionate, historical investigation.

In sum, we may affirm that the Synoptic Gospel writers would have wanted to preserve accurate history according to the standards of their day, that they had every likelihood of being able to do so, and that the overall pattern of widespread agreement on the essential contours of Jesus' life and ministry coupled with enough variation of detail to demonstrate at least some independent sources and tradents on which each drew makes it very probable that they did in fact compose trustworthy historical and biographical documents. Certainly no insoluble contradictions appear.

The Gospel of John. But what about the fourth Gospel? Here the differences with the Synoptics appear to outweigh the similarities. Noticeably more passages in John than not find no parallel in Matthew, Mark or Luke. John contains no parables, no exorcisms and almost no teaching about the kingdom, and he fails to mention that Jesus was baptized by John or instituted the Lord's Supper during the last meal of his earthly life with his disciples. On the other hand, John contains two chapters about Jesus' ministry before the major period of popularity with the Galilean crowds that dominates the Synoptics (John 2–4). During that period of popularity he focuses primarily on Jesus' trips to Jerusalem at festival time, which are entirely absent from the Synoptics, and the claims he made for himself and conflicts he precipitated with various Jewish leaders there,

---

[31]See throughout my "Legitimacy and Limits of Harmonization," pp. 139-74.

along with his most spectacular miracle of all—the resurrection of Lazarus (John 5–11). Throughout his ministry, John's Jesus makes the most
explicit references to his own exalted nature, implying his deity, of anywhere in the canonical Gospels. For all these and related reasons, many
scholars, including those open to a fair amount of history in the Synoptics,
are often more skeptical of the historical trustworthiness of John. Is this
justified?

General considerations. For much of church history Christians simply
assumed that John, as the last and latest of the four New Testament Gospels, saw no need to repeat what was covered well in the Synoptics and
intended largely to supplement their narratives. In the early twentieth
century, however, in the heyday of biblical source criticism, scholars observed that even when John and the Synoptics did include parallel accounts of the same event, very few exact words were ever repeated, much
different from the results of a comparison of parallels among the Synoptics. So the pendulum swung to the opposite conviction: John was so
different from the Synoptics because he wrote independently of them,
whereas Matthew, Mark and Luke were related to each other at least
partly via some form of literary dependence. At the end of the twentieth
century a mediating perspective was being increasingly promoted that
may well do most justice to the most data. By the end of the first century,
most Christians around the empire would have been familiar with the
main accounts that the Synoptics retold, whether they had ever heard an
actual copy of Matthew, Mark or Luke read aloud to them in church or
not. So, while John does seem to be literarily independent of the Synoptics, the older argument about him not needing to repeat a lot of what
they treated well may be reinstated too.[32]

John's unique setting also accounts for much of his distinctive contents. Good early church tradition ascribes this Gospel to the aged apostle, brother of James and son of Zebedee, writing from Ephesus to the
Christian churches in and around that community, who were experiencing the twin challenges of an increasingly hostile Judaism that excom-
municated synagogue members who confessed Jesus as Messiah and of
an incipient Gnosticism (see p. 463) that had no problem affirming Jesus'

---

[32]See esp. Richard Bauckham, ed., *The Gospels for All Christians: Rethinking the Gospel Audiences*
(Grand Rapids: Eerdmans, 1998).

deity but denied his true humanity. Thus we should not be surprised to
see John stressing how Jesus was indeed the fulfillment of major Jewish
festivals and rituals (as in John 5–10), despite the conflict that it caused
with the religious leadership of his people. The loftier claims about his
deity may well have been John's way of establishing common ground
with those overly influenced by the Gnostics, with a needed corrective
emphasis on how "the Word became flesh and made his dwelling among
us" (John 1:14).[33]

A particularly intriguing phenomenon that demonstrates how much
more both John and the Synoptists actually knew and how complementary
rather than contradictory their Gospels are has sometimes been called
their "interlocking." This phenomenon involves instances in which John
refers to something so cryptically as to raise all kinds of questions that he
nowhere else answers but that the Synoptics do, or vice versa. For example,
John 3:24 refers in passing to the Baptist's imprisonment, but only the
Synoptists ever narrate that event (Mark 6:14-29 and parallels). John
knows Jesus was tried before the high priest Caiaphas (John 18:24, 28),
but only the Synoptics describe this trial's proceedings or its outcome
(Mark 14:53-65 and parallels). Conversely, the Synoptics claim that witnesses twisted Jesus' words to accuse him of claiming that he would destroy the temple and rebuild it in three days (Mark 14:57-58). But nothing
elsewhere in their narratives prepares the reader for this charge. John 2:19,
on the other hand, includes Jesus' allegation that if the Jewish leaders destroyed "this temple," he would rebuild it in three days, but it goes on to
explain that he was speaking of the temple of his body, that is, an allusion
to his death and resurrection. This, however, is a saying that could easily
be twisted into what the Synoptics claim the false witnesses declared. Or
again, why did the Jewish leaders enlist the help of the Roman governor
Pilate (Mark 15:1-3 and parallels), when their law was clear enough in
prescribing the death penalty—by stoning—for blasphemers? Only John
gives us the answer: under Roman occupation the Jews were forbidden
from carrying out this portion of their law (John 18:31). Many more ex-

---

[33]See further Craig L. Blomberg, *The Historical Reliability of John's Gospel: Issues and Commentary*
(Downers Grove, Ill.: InterVarsity Press, 2001), pp. 17-67; Paul N. Anderson, *The Fourth
Gospel and the Quest for Jesus: Modern Foundations Reconsidered* (London: T & T Clark, 2007).

amples of such interlocking, in both directions, can be adduced.[34]

Specific passages. We may also proceed sequentially through the fourth Gospel noting strong historical reasons for accepting at least a solid core of most of the main episodes as authentic, including those unique to this Gospel. Unique to John 1 is the period in which Jesus' ministry overlaps with John the Baptist before Jesus clearly "outshines" his predecessor. But the early church is unlikely to have invented a time when John needed to "become less" so that Christ could "become greater" (John 3:30), as concerned as they were to exalt Jesus over everyone. John 2 begins with the remarkable miracle of turning water into wine, yet it coheres perfectly with the little parable, regularly viewed as authentic, of new wine (Jesus' kingdom teaching) needing new wineskins (new religious forms). John 3 highlights Jesus' conversation with Nicodemus, a rare Jewish name that appears repeatedly in the rabbinic literature about the wealthy, powerful, Pharisaic ben-Gurion family. The story of Jesus' surprising solicitousness for the Samaritan woman in John 4 coheres closely with his compassion for outcasts throughout the Synoptics. The distinctive synagogue homily in John 6 on Jesus as the bread of life matches perfectly with a standard rabbinic exegetical form known as a proem midrash. Jesus' claims at the Festival of Tabernacles to be living water and the light of the world (in John 7–9) fit exactly two central rituals from that feast—a water-drawing ceremony and daily temple services with a giant candelabrum installed just for this occasion. And one could continue in similar fashion throughout the Gospel identifying key reasons for the probable authenticity of a key core of each main segment.[35]

What then of apparent contradictions between John and the Synoptics? Many of them may be dealt with via a similar cross section of the methods applied to the seeming discrepancies among the Synoptics. Quite a few have to do with Mark's choice to include only one visit of the adult Jesus to Jerusalem, at the Passover during which he was crucified, a choice that Matthew and Luke then followed. It is inherently probable that his min-

---

[34]See esp. Leon Morris, *Studies in the Fourth Gospel* (Grand Rapids: Eerdmans, 1969), pp. 40-63); D. A. Carson, *The Gospel According to John*, Pillar New Testament Commentary (Grand Rapids: Eerdmans, 1991), pp. 52-55.

[35]See esp. my *Historical Reliability of John's Gospel*, pp. 71-81; cf. Richard Bauckham, *The Testimony of the Beloved Disciple: Narrative, History, and Theology in the Gospel of John* (Grand Rapids: Baker Academic, 2007).

istry lasted longer than the few months it would have taken to do everything the Synoptics record, and, as a Jew who kept the written laws of Moses, Jesus would have surely attended the various annual festivals in Jerusalem prescribed in the Torah. Indeed, John appears more consistently chronological in the sequence of his accounts than do the Synoptics, who often group material together by theme or form, especially during Jesus' great Galilean ministry. Because Jesus' resurrection of Lazarus took place in Judea just before Jesus' final journey to Jerusalem, once the Synoptics had decided on their outlines, this miracle simply did not fit into them. Parables may have been omitted because they were a uniquely Jewish form less relevant in Ephesus, to which John's Gospel was written according to early church tradition. Exorcisms may have been left out because they were often viewed more as manipulative religious "magic" in the Greco-Roman world. The concept of the kingdom is largely replaced by the theme of eternal life, but this is a legitimate substitution because already in Matthew 19:16, 23-24, Jesus uses them interchangeably.

It is often alleged that John and the Synoptics contradict each other over the day of the Last Supper. The Synoptics reasonably clearly describe it as a Passover meal (e.g., Mark 14:12, 14, 16), whereas it is often alleged that John places it the day before the beginning of the Passover festival (esp. in light of John 13:1, 29; 18:28; 19:14, 31). But when John 13:1 explains, "It was just before the Passover Feast," and then a verse later refers simply to the evening meal in progress, it is at least as natural to assume that the Passover has now arrived than that this is a different, earlier meal. When Judas leaves the meal and the other disciples think he is going to buy "what was needed for the festival" (John 13:29), he could easily be thought to be securing provisions for the rest of the weeklong festivities, especially since some also thought he was going to give something to the poor, precisely a tradition central to the opening evening of Passover. That the Jewish leaders on Friday morning do not want to defile themselves because of the upcoming Passover meal (John 18:28) suggests that the midday meal is in view rather than that evening's dinner, since a new day started at sundown in Jewish reckoning and removed the defilement of the previous day. John 19:14 is often translated, "It was the day of Preparation of the Passover," but it could equally be rendered, "It was the day of Preparation during Passover week," that is, the Friday of Passover week, because Friday was the day of preparation for the Jewish sabbath, or Saturday. Verse 31 actually supports this interpretation since it explicitly declares that the next day was to be a sabbath. So again, a more careful reading of the text undermines the charge of contradictions.

What then of John's "high Christology"—his exalted view of Jesus which frequently equates him with God? We must always remember that statements from the lips of Jesus that sound so exalted to us with twenty-twenty hindsight, such as "I am the light of the world," "the true vine," "the sheep gate," "the good shepherd," "the way and the truth and the life" or "the resurrection and the life," were all metaphors that did not initially communicate without ambiguity. Even John's appeal to the divine "I am" of Exodus 3:14 (John 8:58) no doubt puzzled many. After all, even the Twelve could remark as late in Jesus' ministry as the last night of this life that only then was he finally "speaking clearly and without figures of speech" (John 16:29). And even then, Jesus' reply, anticipating their reaction to his death, suggests that they still do not fully understand (John 16:31-32). Conversely, only the Synoptics narrate the virginal conception, which surely represents high Christology. And they too have Jesus using the language of "I am," sometimes masked in translation by the English, "I am he" or "It is I." But in passages like Mark 6:50 in the context of his walking on the water or Mark 14:62 as he replies to the Sanhedrin concerning his messiahship, it is hard not to believe that a stronger self-revelation of his divinity is being at least hinted at.[36]

Topography and archaeology. Intriguingly, while John is the most overtly theological of the canonical Gospels, it also supplies the greatest amount of geographical information about the locations where events occur. Precisely because such references do not reflect John's main purposes in writing (see John 20:31 for those), they are all the more significant when they consistently turn out to be historically accurate. Most sites can still be visited today, and archaeological discoveries disproportionately illuminate John's Gospel compared to the Synoptics: the pool of Bethesda with its five porticoes near the Sheep Gate in Jerusalem (John 5:2), the pool of

---

[36]In addition to my writings elsewhere, for the kinds of interpretations of texts utilized in this subsection, see esp. Carson, *John*; Andreas Köstenberger, *John*, Baker Exegetical Commentary on the New Testament (Grand Rapids: Baker Academic, 2004); and Craig S. Keener, *The Gospel of John: A Commentary*, 2 vols. (Peabody, Mass.: Hendrickson, 2003).

Siloam in Jerusalem (John 9:7), Jacob's well at Sychar (John 4:5-6), the paving stones of Gabbatha (John 19:13), inscriptional evidence for Pontius Pilate (John 18:29), evidence of Roman use of nails through the ankles for crucified victims (cf. Luke 24:39 with John 20:25) and the like.[37]

Literary genre. There is no question that on a spectrum from bare, uninterpreted historical chronicle to total fiction, John stands a little further removed from the former extreme than do the Synoptics.[38] John uses his own linguistic style in recounting Jesus' words, so that at times it is almost impossible to know where Jesus stops speaking and John starts narrating (see, classically, John 3:13-21). In keeping with historiographical conventions of the day, he is often more overtly theological than the Synoptists. But in terms of literary genre, his work still remains closer to Matthew, Mark and Luke in form than to any other known writing of the ancient Mediterranean world. And a strong case has been made that this form most closely mirrored relatively trustworthy biographies.[39] A passage-by-passage comparison of John with the Synoptics points out conceptual parallels at almost every juncture, even if they do not reflect literary dependence and even if they are often narrated in a more dramatic fashion. The very emphasis of John's Gospel on providing trustworthy testimony to the truthfulness of the Christian message (John 21:24-25) makes its historical reliability that much more important and probable.

SYNCRETISTIC EVIDENCE

Recent blockbuster works of fiction like *The Da Vinci Code* have misled many readers because of fictitious claims that "all descriptions of ancient documents are accurate."[40] As a result, countless people around the world now believe that various noncanonical documents present an alternate story of Christian origins that has a greater historical likelihood of being reliable. In fact, nothing could be further from the truth. Particularly intriguing to

---

[37]For the Gospels overall, the state-of-the-art work is now James H. Charlesworth, ed., *Jesus and Archaeology* (Grand Rapids: Eerdmans, 2006). Emphasizing the Gospels' accuracy in light of archaeology is Bargil Pixner, *With Jesus Through Galilee According to the Fifth Gospel* (Collegeville, Minn.: Liturgical Press, 1996).

[38]See esp. Derek Tovey, *Narrative Art and Act in the Fourth Gospel* (Sheffield, U.K.: Sheffield Academic Press, 1997).

[39]See esp. Richard A. Burridge, *What Are the Gospels? A Comparison with Graeco-Roman Biography*, 2nd ed. (Grand Rapids: Eerdmans, 2004).

[40]Dan Brown, *The Da Vinci Code* (New York: Doubleday, 2003), p. 1.

many have been the Gnostic Gospels, so we will deal with them first and then turn to other post–New Testament apocryphal documents.

The Gnostic Gospels. Just after World War II, a cache of codices was unearthed in Egypt at a site known as Nag Hammadi. Ranging from the second to the sixth centuries in origin, a sizeable majority of these books reflected elaborate Gnostic reflection. Gnosticism was a collection of loosely related religious movements that combined significant elements of Greek philosophy and ritual with Christian characters and themes to create a hybrid, syncretistic mythology. At the heart of these various movements lay the conviction that matter is inherently evil and, thus, that only the spirit can be redeemed. Redemption, it was often believed, came through Jesus, but not through his atoning death and bodily resurrection. Rather, salvation came by knowledge—esoteric knowledge, to be more precise. Humans who recognized the spark of divinity deeply embedded in themselves and who fanned it into flame could then become initiates into a Gnostic sect, living as already somewhat free from the shackles of the body and the material world while looking forward to escaping this world and their bodies altogether upon death. Most Gnostics, therefore, were ascetics, trying to deny themselves normal bodily appetites, although a few swung the pendulum to the opposite extreme and became hedonists, indulging the body since they would soon be rid of it anyway. Most Gnosticism was anti-Semitic, rejecting the God of Israel as evil and the laws of the Israelites as perverse. It was also elitist, believing that no one in whom the gods had not already planted the spark of divinity could ever be saved.[41]

The Gospel of Thomas. If there is any Gnostic Gospel likely to preserve historical information about Jesus outside of texts that simply repeat information already found in the canonical Gospels, it is the so-called Coptic *Gospel of Thomas*. Though fourth century in origin in its Nag Hammadi form, second-century Greek fragments of it had already been discovered in nineteenth-century archaeological excavations at Oxyrhynchus. Thomas is not a connected narrative biography but a collection of 114 mostly independent sayings attributed to Jesus. A little

---

[41]Excellent recent introductions to Gnosticism include Riemer Roukema, *Gnosis and Faith in Early Christianity* (Harrisburg, Penn.: Trinity Press International, 1999); and Alastair H. B. Logan, *The Gnostics: Identifying an Early Christian Cult* (London: T & T Clark, 2006).

over a third find some reasonably discernible parallel in the canonical texts, roughly another third seem fairly clearly Gnostic in meaning and the remaining sayings are those that often fascinate scholars the most. Might there be authentic teachings of Jesus in this mix not preserved elsewhere? There certainly could be, but how would one ever discern which ones they are? After all, presumably *all* of Thomas's sayings could be interpreted in a Gnostic fashion, so it would be hard to develop fool-proof criteria for sifting the authentic from the inauthentic. Those who have made educated guesses as to which passages might go back to Jesus often include sayings 82 ("He who is near me is near the fire, and he who is far from me is far from the kingdom") and 77b ("Split a piece of wood, and I am there. Lift up the stone, and you will find me there"), or the little parables of the woman carrying a jar of meal (97) and the man who stuck his sword into the wall (98). They read, respectively,

> (97) Jesus said, "The kingdom of the [Father] is like a certain woman who was carrying a jar full of meal. While she was walking [on] a road, still some distance from home, the handle of the jar broke and the meal emptied out behind her on the road. She did not realize it, she had noticed no accident. When she reached her house, she set the jar down and found it empty."

> (98) Jesus said, "The kingdom of the Father is like a certain man who wanted to kill a powerful man. In his own house he drew his sword and stuck it into the wall in order to find out whether his hand could carry through. Then he slew the powerful man."

Accepting a few such sayings, however, hardly revolutionizes our portrait of Jesus. To argue that Gnosticism (or any other form of heterodoxy) actually predates orthodox, apostolic Christianity, requires dating *Thomas* (or other documents) into the mid-first century without any actual documentary evidence or external testimony supporting such a date. In fact, Nicholas Perrin has shown that the structure of *Thomas*, based on catchwords linking each saying to the next, appears most clearly in its Syriac form, which is dependent on a harmony of the Gospels written by a Syrian named Tatian in about A.D. 180. So Thomas may well not date to any earlier date than this.[42] Even if it does, the fact that it contains parallels to

---

[42]Nicholas Perrin, *Thomas, the Other Gospel* (Louisville: Westminster John Knox, 2007), pp. 73-106.

every one of the four canonical Gospels and all of the putative sources and layers of editing that scholars typically identify behind them strongly suggests that *Thomas* was not composed until the second century, by which time all four canonical texts were complete and had begun to circulate widely. Scholars like Elaine Pagels, Karen King and others often support a Thomasine or Gnostic form of Christianity over traditional forms because they believe that such religion proves more affirming of women.[43] Some texts do appear to promote a form of egalitarianism based on the belief that we will one day all become androgynous as we were, so it is asserted, in the beginning of human history. But this supports only the feminism of a generation ago, which blurred the distinctions between male and female in the name of equal opportunity rather than the currently dominant form that insists on equality *within difference*. Moreover, one has to read the Gnostic literature very selectively to get even a partial egalitarianism. Consider, for example, the final saying in Thomas:

> Simon Peter said to them, "Let Mary leave us, for women are not worthy of life." Jesus said, "I myself shall lead her in order to make her male, so that she too may become a living spirit resembling you males. For every woman who will make herself male will enter the kingdom of heaven." (*Thomas* 114)

The vast majority of women in any age do not consider this an attractive option!

Other Gnostic Gospels. Very few other Nag Hammadi documents even overlap in contents with the canonical texts at all. Those that are called Gospels are usually collections of lengthy, esoteric monologues attributed to Jesus after the resurrection in secret conversation with one or more of the disciples about the nature of heavenly beings and entities far removed from the down-to-earth practical ethics of Jesus of Nazareth. In keeping with Gnosticism's rejection of the full humanity of Jesus, little interest in his earthly life appears. Instead, the documents that are falsely ascribed to such writers as Philip, Mary, James and others devote almost all their attention to speculation about Jesus' heavenly origins and relationships, the nature of humanity in its fallenness and in redemption, parallel realities

---

[43]Elaine Pagels, *Beyond Belief: The Secret Gospel of Thomas* (New York: Vintage Books, 2003); and Karen L. King, ed., *Images of the Feminine in Gnosticism* (Harrisburg, Penn.: Trinity Press International, 1988).

between earth and heaven, and the like.[44]

A partial exception is the more recently discovered and quite recently published *Gospel of Judas*. It actually does appear in narrative form, though in its fragmentary condition it covers only select events from the last week of Jesus' life and, as we already knew from the writings of Irenaeus (the bishop of Lyons, France, at the end of the second century), it makes Judas the hero rather than the villain in betraying Christ. Despite his ignominious end on earth, he will be exalted in heaven, since *someone* had to turn Jesus over to the authorities so that he could atone for the sins of the world. Of course, the logic is flawed; there are countless ways Jesus could have been put to death. And it represents a tiny minority viewpoint even among ancient Gnostics. Despite the surprisingly sensationalized and occasionally inaccurate presentation of the contents of this Gospel by the National Geographic Society in 2006,[45] even very liberal and non-Christian biblical scholars quickly concede there is no chance that this reflects the original version of events.[46]

Other apocryphal Gospels. From the mid-second century of Christianity onward, other "Gospels" appeared as well. Many of these have survived, some only in partial form, while others are known only because various early Christian writers, or occasionally their opponents, make mention of them. Most of these appear to respond to the natural curiosity of readers of the New Testament about the "gaps" in the Gospel record. What was Jesus like as a child? The *Infancy Gospel of Thomas*, not to be confused with the Coptic *Gospel of Thomas*, portrays him as a "boy wonder," fashioning birds out of clay and breathing into them the breath of life so that they might fly away or, more ominously, withering up a playmate who refused to stop taunting him. The *Protoevangelium of James* describes Mary's "immaculate conception"—that is, the belief that her parents were completely free from lust when they conceived her, enabling her to become sinless. They also describe a *truly* virgin birth—even after Jesus came out of Mary's womb, the midwives confirmed that her hymen remained un-

---

[44]See esp. Majella Franzmann, *Jesus in the Nag Hammadi Writings* (Edinburgh: T & T Clark, 1996).

[45]Rodolphe Kasser, Marvin Meyer and Gregor Wurst, eds., *The Gospel of Judas* (Washington, D.C.: National Geographic Society, 2006).

[46]E.g., Bart D. Ehrman, *The Lost Gospel of Judas Iscariot: A New Look at Betrayer and Betrayed* (Oxford: Oxford University Press, 2006), pp. 172-73.

broken! At the other end of Jesus' life, the *Gospel of Nicodemus* contains a narrative of Christ's descent into hell, while the *Gospel of Peter* embellishes the resurrection account, with Christ emerging from the tomb accompanied by two angels, one on either side of him, whose heads reached up to the heavens, while Christ's even went through the heavens! Almost no true historians give these documents any chance to come from the people to whom they are ascribed or to reflect genuine, historical events not found in the New Testament.[47]

Still other documents are sometimes falsely put forward as being of ancient pedigree when in fact they were written in the Middle Ages or even more recently. The *Gospel of Barnabas* is a medieval Muslim composition that teaches explicitly Islamic doctrine and even contradicts the Qur'an in places (e.g., in denying Christ's messiahship).[48] More orthodox Christian texts purport to disclose never-before-seen documents written by Jewish and Roman leaders who participated in the proceedings against Jesus (most notably in a nineteenth-century composition called the *Archko Volume*, which is sheer modern fiction). The Book of Mormon addresses a particularly troubling theological issue of the early nineteenth century—the fate of the American Indians before their evangelization by European settlers—by claiming to be the long-hidden account of the exploits of Jews and their descendants who migrated to the Americas centuries before Christ and containing the story of the supposed appearance of Jesus to people on this continent not long after his death and resurrection in Israel. Per Beskow discusses the true origins of many of these and similar stories.[49] At the very least we may insist that those who are inclined to be suspicious of portions of the New Testament Gospels have no historical reason for placing *any* confidence in these extracanonical sources.

A quick exercise comparing the New Testament and Gnostic/apocry-

---

[47]The standard critical English translation of an introduction to all the noncanonical Gospels of which we know is Wilhelm Schneemelcher, ed., *New Testament Apocrypha*, vol. 1, 2nd ed. (Louisville: Westminster John Knox, 1991). Standing almost alone in defending part of the *Gospel of Peter* as older and more trustworthy than the canonical texts is John Dominic Crossan, *The Cross That Spoke: The Origins of the Passion Narrative* (San Francisco: Harper & Row, 1988).

[48]Oddbjørn Leirvik, "History as a Literary Weapon: The Gospel of Barnabas in Muslim-Christian Polemics," *Studia Theologica* 54 (2001): 4-26; Jan Joosten, "The Gospel of Barnabas and the Diatessaron," *Harvard Theological Review* 95 (2002): 73-96.

[49]Per Beskow, *Strange Tales About Jesus: A Survey of Unfamiliar Gospels* (Philadelphia: Fortress, 1983).

phal Gospels, using a number of standard historical criteria, proves remarkably telling. The canonical texts are all first-century in origin, no more than two generations removed from the eyewitnesses of Jesus' life; no other Gospel can be demonstrated to be earlier than the mid-second century at least two generations later. Most are one to five centuries later! The literary genres of the canonical Gospels closely resemble ancient historiography and biography, while not one of the Gnostic texts contains more than short bits of narrative in it, and most do not have any. The apocryphal texts *are* typically written in connected prose, but none purports to cover more than a tiny slice of Jesus' life or ministry. Except for some elements in the *Gospel of Thomas*, there are no problems of harmonization because the kinds of things that Jesus says or does in the apocrypha are so unlike the canonical Jesus that one must choose which one to accept (if either)—they cannot both be right! The canonical Gospels leave no doubt that Jesus of Nazareth was a human being; the issue his followers struggled with was how to account for his teachings and miracles, and they were increasingly compelled to use the language of deity. The Gnostic and at least some of the apocryphal Gospels have absolutely no question about the deity of a spirit-being called Christ, but whether that spirit ever was (or could have been) fully human is very much open to question. There is no archaeological corroboration for any distinctive parts of the Gnostic or apocryphal Gospels because, for the most part, their contents do not include events or sayings tied to any particular place. There is no testimony from non-Christian sources to support them, not least because they were not well enough known to command others' attention.[50] All of these observations prove crucial as we turn to two key remaining objections that often prove to be stumbling blocks for people in accepting the New Testament message.

REMAINING ISSUES

Considerations of text and canon. I often encounter questions along the following lines: How do we even know that we have what the authors of

---

[50]See Craig L. Blomberg, "Canonical and Apocryphal Gospels: How Historically Reliable Are They?" *From Athens to Jerusalem* 6, no. 3 (2006): 1-7. The one exception is a reference to one of the *Infancy Gospel*'s miracles in the Qur'an, attesting to the heterodoxy of at least some of the Christians with whom Muhammad came into contact.

the canonical Gospels first wrote? Haven't the texts been copied so many times, with so many errors having crept in, that what Matthew, Mark, Luke and John first wrote might have been quite different? Add to that all the different translations, especially in English, from the ancient Greek, and surely even more corruption has intruded, hasn't it? And even if this first cluster of questions can be dealt with, isn't it the case that the Gospels included in the New Testament canon are simply the product of ecclesiastical politics? Only because orthodoxy ultimately won out over Gnosticism do we have the Bible we have instead of a very different one. So how can anyone claim that these are uniquely inspired and authoritative sources for belief and behavior? The first of these clusters of questions deals with issues of text and translation; the second, with the formation of the canon. We shall consider each, briefly, in turn.

Text and translation. Over 5,700 handwritten Greek manuscripts of part or all of the pre-Gutenberg New Testament remain in existence. These range from a scrap of a few verses to entire copies of the New Testament. We have an unbroken sequence of ever growing textual resources (in both numbers and amount of text represented) from the early second century until the inventing of the printing press in the fifteenth century. Overall the texts were copied with remarkable care; the vast majority of changes that were introduced involved variant spellings, the accidental omission or repetition of a single letter, the substitution of one word for a synonym and the like. Textual critics of almost all theological stripes agree that we can reconstruct somewhere upwards of 97 percent of the New Testament text beyond a shadow of reasonable doubt. And it is certainly the case that no Christian belief or doctrine depends solely on a textually disputed passage. All these factors set the New Testament books off from every other known work from the ancient world in terms of our ability to have confidence that we know what the original authors wrote.[51] Bart Ehrman's *Misquoting Jesus* (see footnote 28) chooses to focus entirely on the tiny handful of more interesting and significant textual variants and could mislead the careless reader into thinking such changes occurred more

---

[51]For sample comparative statistics, see Darrell L. Bock and Daniel B. Wallace, *Dethroning Jesus: Exposing Popular Culture's Quest to Unseat the Biblical Christ* (Nashville: Nelson, 2007), p. 31; or J. Ed Komoszewski, M. James Sawyer and Daniel B. Wallace, *Reinventing Jesus: What The Da Vinci Code and Other Novel Speculations Don't Tell You* (Grand Rapids: Kregel, 2006), p. 71.

often than they did, but even Ehrman acknowledges that we have enough textual evidence that we can sift the most probable original readings from the later changes. As for translations, the differences among all the major English versions have to do merely with linguistic philosophy—how literal or periphrastic a rendering is (or, more technically, how formally or dynamically equivalent). A comparison of any dozen of the major Bible translations makes it clear how amazingly minor the overall differences are; again, all the fundamentals of the faith clearly appear in all of these versions.[52]

The formation of the New Testament canon. Already in the mid-second century, Christian writers began to compile lists of books they believed were canonical—that is, uniquely accurate and authoritative and worth putting on a par with the Hebrew Scriptures (what Christians would come to call the Old Testament). At first, this occurred largely in response to unorthodox teachings like those the various Gnostic sects promoted. But what is intriguing is that we have no record of the Gnostics themselves ever proposing any of their distinctive documents for inclusion in any canon, theirs or anyone else's. Instead, they tried to reinterpret New Testament writings in a fashion that would support their distinctives for the very reason that they recognized the unique authority attached to those documents. As the decades went by, the number of books for a New Testament on which there was agreement grew, until in A.D. 367, in his Easter encyclical, bishop Athanasius of Alexandria listed the twenty-seven books that have ever since composed the canon. Ecumenical councils in both Carthage and Hippo in North Africa at the end of the fourth century ratified this common consensus.

As far as we know, the four Gospels, Acts and the letters of Paul were never seriously in doubt. The only significant debates surrounded the letter of Hebrews, James, 2 Peter, 2–3 John, Jude and the book of Revelation. And the only books that were ever serious candidates for inclusion in the New Testament but omitted were also epistles, specifically, from the second-century collection of largely orthodox Christian writings known as

---

[52]See esp. Gordon D. Fee and Mark L. Strauss, *How to Choose a Translation for All Its Worth: A Guide to Understanding and Using Bible Versions* (Grand Rapids: Zondervan, 2007). The only exception to this principle is the Jehovah's Witnesses' *New World Translation,* which mistranslates the Greek at those places where the New Testament contradicts their doctrine, in order to hide this fact from their readers.

the Apostolic Fathers. Even then, there was considerably more enthusiasm for the most weakly supported of the letters that did "make it in" than for any of those that were left out. In no meaningful sense did these writers, church leaders or councils "suppress" Gnostic or apocryphal material, since there is no evidence of any canon that ever included them, nor that anyone put them forward for canonization, nor that they were known widely enough to have been serious candidates for inclusion had someone put them forward. Indeed, they would have failed all three of the major criteria used by the early church in selecting which books they were, at times very literally, willing to die for—the criteria of apostolicity (that a book was written by an apostle or a close associate of an apostle), coherence (not contradicting previously accepted Scripture) and catholicity (widespread acceptance as particularly relevant and normative within all major segments of the early Christian community).[53]

MIRACLES AND THE RESURRECTION

For some readers, potentially sympathetic to much of what we have already affirmed, the key sticking point remains the question of the supernatural. However strong the rest of the evidence may be, can we take seriously the historical claims of any documents as full of accounts of the miraculous as the canonical Gospels, and especially when so much hinges on the veracity of the most spectacular alleged miracle of all, namely, Jesus' resurrection? The largest part of an answer to this question lies outside the scope of this essay because it involves the much broader question of worldview. Is there reason to believe in a God who created the universe in the first place? If there is, then miracles arguably become a priori possible and perhaps even likely. Has science truly demonstrated that the universe is a closed continuum of cause and effect? If so, then we must exclude the miraculous, at least as normally conceived.[54] These issues must be thoroughly considered elsewhere.

What can be noted here as we near the conclusion of this study is that

---

[53]For full details on this history see esp. F. F. Bruce, *The Canon of Scripture* (Downers Grove, Ill.: InterVarsity Press, 1988). For the various lists and catalogs of New Testament collections from the early centuries, see appendix D in *The Canon Debate*, ed. Lee M. McDonald and James A. Sanders (Peabody, Mass.: Hendrickson, 2002), pp. 591-97.

[54]See Graham A. Cole, "Do Christians Have a Worldview?" Christ on Campus Initiative, 2007. Available at <http://henrycenter.org/files/cole.pdf>.

other ancient documents sometimes contain miracle narratives that don't preclude historians, whatever their views of the supernatural, from deriving sober historical detail from many other portions of those works. A striking example involves the four existing accounts of Julius Caesar's crossing of the Rubicon River, committing himself to the civil war that would lead to his becoming emperor and turning the republic into an empire. Often alluded to as one of the most historical (and historic) of events found in ancient Mediterranean sources, it is nevertheless accompanied in some accounts by miraculous apparitions (along with problems of harmonization and dating remarkably parallel to those among the New Testament Gospels). Yet classicists who reject the supernatural still confidently recover substantial historical information from all these accounts.[55]

Biblical scholars who are open to the supernatural are often accused of adopting a double standard: they will accept various miracles stories in the Bible but not in other works of ancient history. This would indeed be a double standard if their only rationale for such judgments were the sources in which the various accounts appeared. But often the corroborating evidence simply remains stronger for the biblical accounts.[56] On the other hand, there are a small number of claims of the miraculous at numerous junctures throughout history that do pass stringent criteria of authenticity, and there is no reason that Christian scholars should not accept them as well. God, in the Bible, often works through those who are not his people; human manufacture and diabolical influence are also possible sources for apparent miracle-working power.[57] It is telling, moreover, to observe how often the closest parallels to canonical Gospel miracles appear in *later* Jewish or Greco-Roman sources,[58] so that if any tradition influenced any other one, it would be Christianity being "copycatted" later. Demonstrably pre-Christian traditions do not present close

---

[55]Paul Merkley, "The Gospels as Historical Testimony," *Evangelical Quarterly* 58 (1986): 328-36.

[56]For the Gospels see esp. Graham H. Twelftree, *Jesus the Miracle Worker* (Downers Grove, Ill.: InterVarsity Press, 1999); and René Latourelle, *The Miracles of Jesus and the Theology of Miracles* (New York: Paulist Press, 1988).

[57]See further Joseph Houston, *Reported Miracles: A Critique of Hume* (Cambridge: Cambridge University Press, 1994).

[58]E.g., Philostratus's *Life of Apollonius of Tyana*, Talmudic accounts of Hanina ben Dosa or Honi the Circle-drawer, Gnostic Redeemer myths, Greco-Roman "divine men," and Roman Mithraism more generally.

parallels to the New Testament Gospels' miracles at all.[59]

As for the topic of the resurrection in particular, again an entirely separate essay would be needed to do it justice. But we may at least note here that several undisputed historical facts are very difficult to explain apart from Jesus' genuine, bodily return to life, including (1) how a small band of defeated followers of Jesus were transformed almost overnight into bold witnesses, risking death by proclaiming his bodily resurrection before many of the same people who fifty days earlier had participated in his crucifixion; (2) what motivated a group of devoted Jews to change what they believed to be the eternally immutable sabbath (or day of rest and worship) from Saturday to Sunday; (3) why they claimed in all versions of their testimony that women, whose witness was usually inadmissible in ancient law courts, were the first and primary witnesses to the resurrection; (4) what led them to declare Jesus to be both Lord and liberator despite his death by crucifixion, already interpreted, in light of Deuteronomy 21:23, to represent God's curse; and (5) how the Jewish expectation of all people being raised from the dead together at the end of time (Daniel 12:2) allowed them to declare Jesus to have been raised in advance of Judgment Day and separate from the general resurrection. It takes greater faith to believe in the various alternative accounts of the rise of the resurrection traditions in the first years of Christianity than to accept the accounts as retold in the New Testament.[60]

WHY IT MATTERS: THE ENDURING SIGNIFICANCE OF THE HISTORICAL JESUS

If the canonical Gospels remain our only source for more than just a bare-bones outline of the life and work of Jesus of Nazareth as a truly human figure, and if there are good reasons on sheer historical grounds apart from any religious faith to accept the main contours of their portraits of Jesus as historically trustworthy, then the "step of faith" involved in acknowledging Jesus as Lord and Savior and committing one's life in allegiance to him

---

[59]See Ronald H. Nash, *The Gospel and the Greeks: Did the New Testament Borrow from Pagan Thought?* 2nd ed. (Phillipsburg, N.J.: Presbyterian & Reformed, 2003); and Eric Eve, *The Jewish Context of Jesus' Miracles* (London: Sheffield Academic Press, 2002).

[60]See esp. N. T. Wright, *The Resurrection of the Son of God* (Minneapolis: Fortress, 2003); and Larry W. Hurtado, *Lord Jesus Christ: Devotion to Jesus in Earliest Christianity* (Grand Rapids: Eerdmans, 2003).

becomes the most reasonable response a person can make to his ministry.

History cannot corroborate everything in these Gospels, but it can provide enough support so that a spirit of trust rather than of suspicion remains natural in those areas where more difficult questions arise. The testimony of millions upon millions of Christians' lives transformed for the better, who often get far less press than the comparatively small number of believers responsible for the more shameful deeds done throughout history in Jesus' name, provides powerful experiential confirmation of the value of choosing to align ourselves with him. To receive forgiveness of sins, to be put into a right relationship with God, to understand one's vocation in this life as counting for all eternity, and to look forward to unending happiness in the life to come in the very presence of God in Christ and in all the company of his people throughout time all form powerful motivations for entrusting oneself to Jesus despite the ignominy, suffering and even martyrdom that such commitment can at times lead to in this world. The alternative, which is unending separation from God and all things good, precisely because God refuses to coerce belief or to give people that which they reject (including himself and his salvation), certainly makes any unpleasant aspects of this life pale in comparison.

The Claims, Credentials and Achievements of Jesus Christ

The people who hanged Christ never, to do them justice, accused him of being a bore—on the contrary, they thought him too dynamic to be safe. It has been left for later generations to muffle up that shattering personality and surround him with an atmosphere of tedium. We have very efficiently pared the claws of the Lion of Judah, certified him "meek and mild," and recommended him as a fitting household pet for pale curates and pious old ladies.

DOROTHY SAYERS[1]

FROM THE TIME HE FIRST BEGAN TO stir things up in ancient Palestine, the controversy over the identity of Jesus Christ has continued unabated.[2] Everyone has an opinion about Jesus, ranging from the traditional to the novel to the heretical. As Stephen Prothero claims, "In the book of Genesis, God creates humans in His own image; in the United States, Americans have created Jesus, over and over, in theirs."[3]

Jesus asked his disciples, "Who do people say the Son of Man is?" His

---

[1]Dorothy Sayers, "The Greatest Story Ever Staged," in *The Whimsical Christian: 18 Essays by Dorothy Sayers* (Grand Rapids: Eerdmans, 1978), p. 14.
[2]Some material from this chapter originally appeared in Douglas Groothuis, *Jesus in an Age of Controversy* (Eugene, Ore.: Harvest House, 1996).
[3]Stephen Prothero, *American Jesus: How the Son of God Became a National Icon* (New York: Farrar, Straus & Giroux, 2003), p. 298.

disciples reported that some said he was John the Baptist, others Elijah and others said he was Jeremiah or one of the prophets. Then Jesus asked, "But what about you? . . . Who do you say I am?" Peter replied, "You are the Messiah, the Son of the living God" (Matthew 16:13-16; cf. Mark 8:27; Luke 9:18-20). That question has reverberated ever since. As John Stott noted, we must *do something* with Jesus. We must personally respond in some way because Jesus presents himself to us as Lord and Savior (John 14:1-6).[4]

This chapter focuses on the story of Jesus and his unique and unparalleled identity as revealed in the New Testament as a whole. However, a strong case for the deity of Christ can be made through the "minimal-facts" approach championed by Gary Habermas and Royce Gruenler.[5] "Minimal facts" are a subset of the factual claims of the New Testament, consisting of texts that even the most radical New Testament critics believe to be authentic.[6] These texts alone attest that Jesus made extraordinary claims about himself. Gruenler isolated fifteen sayings of Jesus that are dissimilar to ideas common to the Jewish community at the time of Jesus or the early church. This criterion rules out many authentic sayings of Jesus, but even given this overly stringent filter, these sayings show that Jesus deemed himself greater than any previous or future religious figure, and that he believed he possessed the very authority of God to declare forgiveness of sins, to judge the world at the end of history and even to receive worship. A high view of Jesus was not invented by the later church but is rooted in the self-image of Jesus himself, even given an overly restrictive principle for authenticity.[7] But rather than cut to the bone to understand Jesus, I prefer to let the fuller story speak, since the beliefs and actions of Jesus are an apologetic in themselves. Many have become Christians simply by reading the accounts of his life found in the Gospels.[8] Chapter nineteen already argued for these documents' reli-

---

[4]John Stott, "The Hound of Heaven," in *Why I Am a Christian* (Downers Grove, Ill.: InterVarsity Press, 2002).

[5]See Gary Habermas, *The Risen Jesus and Future Hope* (Lanham, Md.: Rowman & Littlefield, 2003), chap. 3; and Royce Gruenler, *New Approaches to Jesus and the Gospels* (Grand Rapids: Baker, 1982).

[6]I will use the minimal-facts approach in the argument for the resurrection of Jesus in chap. 22.

[7]Gruenler, *New Approaches*, pt. 1.

[8]This happened to Mark Gabriel, who, after becoming disillusioned with Islam, read the Gospel of Matthew and immediately recognized Jesus as Lord and Savior (Mark Gabriel, *Jesus and Muhammad* [Lake Mary, Fla.: Charisma House, 2004]).

ability, so I am not citing texts without authority.

Each Gospel offers a distinctive portrait of Jesus.[9] After briefly discussing Jesus' early life, they present his teaching and ministry in detail and enter into great detail regarding the last few days of his earthly life leading to his crucifixion. The Gospels are thus focused biographies or distilled reports. Historical facts are never secondary to or removed from the theological message; rather, they fit hand in glove.

THE VIRGINAL CONCEPTION AND BIRTH OF JESUS

Matthew tells us that "Jesus was born in Bethlehem in Judea, during the time of King Herod" (Matthew 2:1), setting him squarely in history. Matthew 1:18-25 and Luke 1:26-38 report that Jesus was conceived without the intervention of a human father, when the Holy Spirit overshadowed his mother Mary.

Jesus' unique and supernatural human origin sets him off from all others.[10] He did not inherit a sinful human nature. His human genesis was not only natural but supernatural. Yet this supernatural conception was not an artificial invasion by an alien intruder. It was not out of place, since earth was the divinely ordained theater of redemption.[11] Jesus has both a supernatural origin and a truly human nature. He is one of us but also beyond us.

The virginal conception is a significant aspect of Jesus' uniqueness and should be defended (although many modern apologetics books omit it). This claim should not be confused with stories of divine-human propagation found in other religions and mythologies. John Frame notes:

> There is no clear parallel to the notion of a *virgin* birth in pagan literature, only of births resulting from intercourse between God and a woman (of which there is no suggestion in Matthew and Luke), resulting in a being half-divine, half-human (which is far different from biblical Christology).[12]

---

[9]While some have claimed that the Gospel accounts contradict each other, this is far from certain. In fact, biblical scholars have harmonized the Gospels persuasively. For example, see Craig Blomberg, *The Historical Reliability of the Gospels*, 20th anniv. ed. (Downers Grove, Ill.: InterVarsity Press, 2007), pt. 4.

[10]Similarly, the resurrection sets him apart from all others (see Bernard Ramm, *An Evangelical Christology: Ecumenic and Historic* [Nashville: Thomas Nelson, 1985], p. 69).

[11]See C. S. Lewis, *Miracles* (New York: Macmillan, 1960), p. 59.

[12]John Frame, "The Virgin Birth," in *Evangelical Dictionary of Theology*, ed. Walter A. Elwell (Grand Rapids: Baker, 1984), p. 1145.

Frame further notes that none of the pagan stories fix the event in specific history as do Matthew and Luke.[13] Shortly after Luke offers that he
has closely studied the historical facts about Jesus (Luke 1:1-4), he launches
into a discussion of the virginal conception and birth of Jesus. There is no
reason to think he would switch from fact to myth in this manner. Ben
Witherington notes that the narratives of both Matthew and Luke "collapse without the assumption of a virginal conception. Furthermore, the
arguments of both Evangelists about the theological significance of Jesus'
origins are predicated on the assumption of both writers of the historical
reality of the virginal conception."[14] Moreover, there is no reason for the
early church to invent this supernatural claim. Although Matthew speaks
of Jesus fulfilling the prophecy of Isaiah 7:14, "The virgin will conceive
and give birth to a son," Jews at that time were not expecting a virgin-born
Messiah. As N. T. Wright says,

> There is no pre-Christian Jewish tradition suggesting that the messiah
> would be born of a virgin. No one used Isaiah 7:14 this way before Matthew
> did. . . . The only conceivable parallels are pagan ones, and these fiercely
> Jewish stories have certainly not been modeled on them. Luke at least must
> have known that telling this story ran the risk of making Jesus out to be a
> pagan demigod. Why, for the sake of an exalted metaphor, would they take
> this risk—unless they at least believed the stories to be literally true?[15]

Christians would not borrow a pagan myth of virgin birth, since they
constantly defined themselves over and against the pagan thought of their
day (see, e.g., Acts 17:16-34; 1 Corinthians 1–2; Colossians 2:8).[16] The
pagan myths of supernatural births probably date after the Gospels. In any
event, the worldview of these myths is polytheistic, unlike the uncompro-

---

[13]Ibid. On the uniqueness of the biblical view of the virgin birth see Norman Anderson, *Jesus Christ: The Witness of History* (Downers Grove, Ill.: InterVarsity Press, 1985), pp. 74-75. Ben Witherington discusses several other New Testament passages that may suggest the virginal conception (see Ben Witherington III, "Birth of Jesus," in *Dictionary of Jesus and the Gospels*, ed. Joel Green, Scot McKnight and I. Howard Marshall (Downers Grove, Ill.: InterVarsity Press, 1992), p. 70.

[14]Witherington, "Birth of Jesus," p. 70. See his entire treatment in ibid., pp. 70-72.

[15]N. T. Wright, "God's Way of Acting," *Christian Century*, December 16, 1998, pp. 1215-17.

[16]For the classic book-length defense see J. Gresham Machen, *The Virgin Birth of Christ* (New York: Harper, 1930). For a defense that the virgin birth is predicted in the Old Testament, see Charles Lee Feinberg, *Is the Virgin Birth in the Old Testament?* (Whittier, Calif.: Emeth, 1967); see also Norman Geisler, "The Virgin Birth," in *Baker Encyclopedia of Christian Apologetics* (Grand Rapids: Baker, 1999), pp. 759-64.

mising monotheism of the New Testament. Jesus' supernatural conception is radically dissimilar to supernatural stories of the Buddha's birth, since these accounts do not feature a virgin mother and were written hundreds of years after the actual birth of Buddha (sixth century B.C.). During his lifetime, Buddha—unlike Jesus—was not considered a supernatural entity, but an enlightened sage.[17]

CHRISTHOOD IN A MANGER

Jesus' infancy also illustrates his distinctiveness. Joseph is told in a dream by an angel not to be afraid to take Mary as his wife because "what is conceived in her is from the Holy Spirit. She will give birth to a son, and you are to give him the name Jesus, because he will save his people from their sins" (Matthew 1:20-21). *Jesus* is a transliteration of the Hebrew *Joshua*, which means "Jehovah is salvation" or "is Savior."

An angel declares, "Do not be afraid. I bring you good news that will cause great joy for all the people. Today in the town of David a Savior has been born to you; he is the Messiah, the Lord" (Luke 2:10-11; cf. Matthew 1:18). The word *Messiah*, or *Christ*, is not a proper name but a title. *Christ* refers to being "anointed" by God and is used in the ancient Greek translation of the Old Testament (the Septuagint) to refer to God's favor toward those especially equipped by God. Jesus "is the Messiah, *the Lord*" from conception. None of the priests, prophets or kings of the Old Testament are hailed as "the Lord." This is why the wise men (magi) came from the East to worship him "who has been *born king* of the Jews" (Matthew 2:2, emphasis added).

Besides the infancy narratives and a few other events, the Gospels do not give us detailed descriptions of Jesus' childhood and early manhood. But there is reason to believe that he received religious instruction in the family, attended services and festivals, and learned the trade of his father, namely, carpentry (see Mark 6:3; cf. Matthew 13:55). Luke summarizes the time between Jesus' circumcision and his twelfth year by saying, "The child grew and became strong; he was filled with wisdom, and the grace

---

[17]Elmar R. Gruber and Holger Kersten make this claim (see *The Original Jesus: The Buddhist Sources of Christianity* [Rockport, Mass.: Element Books, 1995], pp. 82-83). It is refuted by Geoffrey Parrinder, *Avatar and Incarnation* (New York: Barnes & Noble, 1970), p. 135; and Machen, *Virgin Birth of Christ*, pp. 339-41.

of God was upon him" (Luke 2:40). The rest of Jesus' youth and early manhood are summed up with one sentence: "Jesus grew in wisdom and stature, and in favor with God and men" (Luke 2:52).[18]

JESUS IN THE PUBLIC EYE

After Jesus was baptized by John the Baptist, "Heaven was opened and the Holy Spirit descended upon him in bodily form like a dove. And a voice came from heaven: 'You are my Son, whom I love; with you I am well pleased'" (Luke 3:21-22; cf. Matthew 3:16-17; Mark 1:10-11). Although his baptism identified Jesus with the people, it also distinguished him from others because God the Father ratified him as "the Son" with a special mission.[19] "Jesus himself was about thirty years old when he began his ministry" (Luke 3:23).

Before Jesus began his public preaching, teaching and miraculous ministry, he fasted and was tempted in the wilderness by the devil, who tried to dissuade him from his destiny through a series of challenges, all of which invoked biblical passages out of context. Jesus emerged victorious through his reliance on the Holy Spirit and his expert knowledge of Scripture (see Matthew 4:1-11; Luke 4:1-13). Jesus engaged in person-to-person spiritual combat with Satan, and he retained his integrity. This insight is pivotal for understanding the nature and mission of Jesus. He is consistently presented as a spiritual liberator of those ensnared in the formidable powers of darkness, especially through his exorcisms and his death on the cross and subsequent resurrection.

JESUS: MASTER TEACHER

During his public ministry Jesus was hailed by many as a master teacher. As a boy, Jesus was "in the temple courts, sitting among the teachers, listening to them and asking them questions. Everyone who heard him was amazed at his understanding and his answers" (Luke 2:46-47). After the

---

[18]Some have erroneously claimed that Jesus traveled to the East during "the lost years" between about twelve and thirty. There is no evidence for this, and it is not seriously considered by scholars. Nevertheless, it is popular in New Age circles (see Douglas Groothuis, *Jesus in an Age of Controversy* [1996; reprint, Eugene, Ore.: Wipf & Stock, 2002], chaps. 7-8).

[19]For a refutation of the theory that Jesus became or was "adopted" as God's Son at his baptism, see Robert M. Bowman Jr. and J. Ed Komoszewski, *Putting Jesus in His Place: The Case for the Deity of Christ* (Grand Rapids: Kregel, 2007), pp. 87-88.

Sermon on the Mount "the crowds were amazed at his teaching, because he taught as one who had authority" (Matthew 7:28-29, cf. Mark 1:22; John 7:15). After Jesus spoke in the temple, the temple guards admitted to the chief priests and Pharisees, "No one ever spoke the way this man does" (John 7:46).

Eminent historian Paul Johnson takes Jesus to be a well-educated and articulate man:

> He was a civilized, cultured, educated man who chose his words with great care and precision, with delicacy, accuracy, and tact—all indications of wide reading in secular as well as religious literature. My belief is that he was familiar with Latin and Greek, as well as his native Aramaic and the Hebrew he spoke and read as an educated observant Jew.[20]

Jesus employed didactic teachings, dialogue and especially parables in order to impart truth to his hearers. Jesus' parables were masterful, powerful stories that confounded the hardhearted and illuminated the genuine seeker.[21] Jesus' use of parables connects him deeply with the Old Testament and also distinguishes him from contemporary teachers. The subject is substantial, but the upshot is that Jesus often referred to himself in parables, something never done by rabbis of his day. This is unique, but what is more remarkable is that "in the majority of the parables Jesus depicts himself through images which in the Old Testament refer to God. While these images occasionally allude to other objects, in most cases they picture God."[22] Philip Payne has found ten images of this sort in twenty of Jesus' parables.[23]

Although always on the theological hot seat, Jesus was never flummoxed by any questioner and often turned the tables on his opponents, exposing their poor logic or dishonesty. This is evident in Matthew 22, where Jesus is asked two very difficult theological questions: one about paying taxes to Caesar and one about the nature of the afterlife. After

---

[20]Paul Johnson, *Jesus: A Biography From a Believer* (New York: Viking, 2010), p. 28; see also ibid., p. 62.

[21]On the parables see Craig Blomberg, *Interpreting The Parables of Jesus* (Downers Grove, Ill.: InterVarsity Press, 1990).

[22]Millard Erickson, *The Word Became Flesh: An Incarnational Christology* (Grand Rapids: Baker, 1991), p. 442.

[23]Philip B. Payne, "Jesus' Implicit Claim to Deity in His Parables," *Trinity Journal*, n.s., 2, no. 1 (1981): 3-23.

exposing false dilemmas in both cases and providing a way to escape the intellectual trap that was set, the text records that his interlocutors were amazed at his teaching (Matthew 22:15-33; cf. Mark 12:13-17; Luke 20:20-26).[24] Pascal succinctly describes the genius of Jesus' teaching: "Jesus said great things so simply that he seems not to have thought about them, and yet so clearly that it is obvious what he thought about them. Such clarity together with such simplicity is wonderful."[25]

JESUS' BASIC WORLDVIEW

The following is only a synopsis of Jesus' worldview. However, it is crucial to understand his worldview in relation to his actions and the claims he made for himself.

God. Jesus articulated clear ideas about the reality of God, and he made this the core of his teaching. There is one God who is personal; knowable; worthy of adoration, worship and service; separate from the creation ontologically but involved with creation through providence, prophecy, miracle and supremely in the life of Jesus himself. But Jesus did not call for a blind leap of faith in the dark in order to believe in God. Instead, he spoke of God with conviction and certainty.

Jesus taught that the kingdom of God was being manifested in new and powerful ways through his life.[26] "Repent, for the kingdom of heaven has come near" (Matthew 4:17; cf. Mark 1:15). This is God's reign in history, the in-breaking of God upon a fallen order. Jesus said, "If it is by the Spirit of God that I drive out demons, then the kingdom of God has come upon you" (Matthew 12:28; cf. Luke 11:20). Jesus came as the very expression of the kingdom, "teaching in their synagogues, proclaiming the good news of the kingdom, and healing every disease and sickness among the people" (Matthew 4:23). Jesus inaugurated a new chapter in God's rule and will bring it to completion in the future. Millard Erickson notes, "And not only did he consider the wonders which he performed the signs of the presence or the coming of the kingdom (Matt. 12:28; Luke 11:20), but he made a positive response to himself the one real condition for entering the king-

---

[24]For more on Jesus' use of argument, see Douglas Groothuis, "Jesus' Use of Argument," in *On Jesus* (Belmont, Calif.: Wadsworth, 2003).

[25]Blaise Pascal, *Pensées* 309/797, ed. and trans. Alban Krailshemer (New York: Penguin, 1966), p. 125.

[26]See F. F. Bruce, *New Testament History* (Garden City, N.Y.: Doubleday, 1972), p. 173.

dom (Matthew 7:21-27; Luke 6:46-49; 22:28-30; 23:42-43)."[27]

Jesus intimated the notion of one God as triune when he authorized his disciples to baptize in the name (singular) of the Father, the Son and the Holy Spirit (Matthew 28:19).[28] Jesus prays to God the Father, speaks of the Holy Spirit in ontologically exalted terms (John 14:26), and affirms his own equality with God (John 8:58)—all without ever speaking of more than one God.[29] In the narrative of Jesus' birth, we find reference to God the Father, the Holy Spirit and the Son of God (Luke 1:26-80), as we do when Jesus was baptized (Matthew 3:13-17; Luke 3:21-22).

Humanity. Humans are God's creatures (Matthew 19:3-4; Mark 10:6), and Jesus placed them above the animals in value (Matthew 6:26; cf. Luke 12:6-7, 24-31). He considered humans spiritual beings with much to gain or lose spiritually (Matthew 16:26; Mark 8:36; Luke 9:25). While divinely created, humans are poisoned and plagued by the evil in their hearts: "For it is from within, out of a person's heart, that evil thoughts come—sexual immorality, theft, murder, adultery, greed, malice, deceit, lewdness, envy, slander, arrogance and folly" (Mark 7:21-22; cf. Matthew 15:19). Sin is not an occasional mistake but a deeply rooted disposition to disobey God and hurt others. Jesus warned, "Very truly I tell you, everyone who sins is a slave to sin" (John 8:34). Jesus informed the most scrupulously religious leaders of his day that "not one of you keeps the [moral] law" (John 7:19).

Ethics. Jesus' understanding of the moral law was revealed when he affirmed that the "greatest commandment in the law" is to

> "love the Lord your God with all your heart and with all your soul and with all your mind." This is the first and greatest commandment. And the second is like it: "Love your neighbor as yourself." All the Law and the Prophets hang on these two commandments. (Matthew 22:37-40; cf. Mark 12:28-33)

Jesus' ethical teachings are uncompromisingly elevated. Dietrich Bonhoeffer called them "extraordinary."[30] Cutting through the religious formalism

---

[27]Erickson, *Word Became Flesh*, p. 440.
[28]Robert L. Raymond, *Systematic Theology*, 2nd ed. (Nashville: Thomas Nelson, 1998), pp. 225-27.
[29]On the Trinity see comments in chap. 4. See also Millard Erickson, *God in Three Persons* (Grand Rapids: Baker, 1995).
[30]Dietrich Bonhoeffer, *The Cost of Discipleship* (New York: Touchstone, 1995), sec. 2.

and hypocrisy of his day, Jesus went to the root of God's commands, revealing their deepest meaning. Not only should we not externally murder, we should not internally assassinate another through anger and defamation (Matthew 5:21-26). Not only should we not commit adultery, we should not look lustfully at a person (Matthew 5:27-32).

However, Jesus commended people for faith that went beyond the law by saying to those who trusted in him: "Your faith has healed [or saved] you" (Mark 5:21-34; 10:46-52; Matthew 9:22; Luke 7:36-50; 8:48; 17:11-19). Their existential orientation toward Jesus—and not simply their adherence to the law—brought them physical and spiritual restoration. Jesus should not be interpreted as a stern moralist who demanded that people earn salvation through moral achievement. He viewed himself as the answer to humanity's inability to earn salvation. He said, "The work of God is this: to believe in the one he has sent" (John 6:29).[31]

JESUS: MIRACLE WORKER

Jesus was hailed as a worker of miracles, which singles him out as a master of circumstance and accredits him with unique authority.[32] The common Jewish expectation for the Messiah during the time of Jesus was not that of a wonder-working figure. Therefore, it is not likely that the record of Jesus' miracles is a later invention. As Craig Evans notes, "Messianic beliefs simply did not require a prospective Messiah to heal and exorcise demons. Therefore, one should hardly expect early Christians to find it necessary to create such a large number of miracle stories."[33]

His miracles centered on establishing his teaching, demonstrating his compassion and manifesting the kingdom of God. Jesus' miracles were never ostentatious demonstrations. He refused to perform miracles for those imperiously demanding a sign (Matthew 12:38-45; Mark 8:11-12; Luke 11:16-28). Nevertheless, Jesus' ministry explodes with supernatural demonstrations. The reach and depth of his miraculous activity is unpar-

---

[31]For more on Jesus' ethics see Douglas Groothuis, "The Ethics of Jesus," in *On Jesus* (Belmont, Calif.: Wadsworth, 2003).

[32]The rationality for believing in miracles was briefly defended in chap. 19. I come back to this issue in more depth in chap. 22, where I defend the grand miracle of Christianity: the resurrection of Jesus.

[33]Craig Evans, "Life-of-Jesus Research and the Eclipse of Mythology," *Theological Studies* 54 (1993): 28.

alleled. By calming the sea (Matthew 8:23-27; Mark 6:50-51; Luke 8:24-25), multiplying food for hungry crowds (Matthew 15:32-38; 14:15-21) and changing water into wine (John 2:11), Jesus demonstrated his power over nature.[34]

Jesus was also an extraordinary healer, supernaturally curing diverse physical infirmities—leprosy, dropsy, paralysis, fever, blindness, deafness, muteness, issues of blood. Jesus healed not only functional problems (in which the organism is intact but dysfunctional), but deep organic maladies involving physical degeneration, such as blindness (Luke 18:35-43). Jesus' healing power operated even at a distance, as when he healed a military officer's servant who was not present at the time. (Matthew 8:5-13).

Jesus' most spectacular displays of authority involved reversing death itself. The Gospels record three such cases, the most dramatic being the raising of Lazarus. When Jesus heard of Lazarus's illness he said, "This sickness will not end in death. No, it is for God's glory so that God's Son may be glorified through it" (John 11:4). Jesus mysteriously waited several days before reaching Lazarus. Upon arriving he found that Lazarus had expired four days earlier. After comforting Lazarus's sisters Jesus asked them where Lazarus was buried. He was deeply moved and wept with them.

> Then Jesus looked up and said, "Father, . . . I knew that you always hear me, but I said this for the benefit of the people standing here, that they may believe that you sent me." When he had said this, Jesus called in a loud voice, "Lazarus, come out!" The dead man came out, his hands and feet wrapped with strips of linen, and a cloth around his face. (John 11:38-44)

Many who had come to visit Mary, Lazarus's sister, "believed in him" (John 11:45). The mighty miracle validated Jesus' claim that he was sent from God (John 11:42).[35]

Jesus was "deeply moved" over human suffering. Yet he was not helpless in the face of death. Jesus raised the dead man to life, revealing the glory of God. The miracle provoked belief in him. Another even more miraculous

---

[34]For other nature miracles see Matthew 17:24-27; 21:18-22; Mark 11:12-14, 20-25.

[35]Some argue that since this miracle is only reported in John, it was probably an invention of John and not historical. Had it been an actual event, all the Gospels would have reported it. But this reasoning is faulty for several reasons (see Craig Blomberg, *The Historical Reliability of John's Gospel* [Downers Grove, Ill.: InterVarsity Press, 2002], pp. 165-72).

resurrection lay ahead (see chap. 22). The sheer number, variety, power and compassion of Jesus' miracles put him in a category by himself.[36]

JESUS: MASTER EXORCIST

Jesus freed a host of people from the torments of demons. Fallen angels (demons) are more evident in the ministry of Jesus than anywhere else in biblical history. Jesus began his ministry by being severely tempted by the devil (Matthew 4; Luke 4) and regularly addressed and dispatched demons, either one at a time or in groups.

In one of the more dramatic encounters, a demonized man fell on his knees before Jesus crying, "What do you want with me, Jesus, Son of the Most High God? In God's name don't torture me!" When Jesus asked him his name, he replied, "My name is Legion, for we are many." Jesus then cast out the demons, after which they entered a herd of pigs, causing the pigs to drown. A legion of demons was no match for Jesus. The once-possessed man, who was "sitting there, dressed and in his right mind," then begged Jesus to let him go with Jesus. But Jesus responded, "Go home to your own people and tell them how much the Lord has done for you, and how he has had mercy on you" (Mark 5:1-19).

In many other places Jesus identifies the presence of the demonic, casts it out and thus frees the one tormented. The apostle Peter connects Jesus' healings with his power over the devil, speaking of "how God anointed Jesus of Nazareth with the Holy Spirit and power, and how he went around doing good and healing all who were under the power of the devil, because God was with him" (Acts 10:38). All of these exorcisms prefigure Jesus' ultimate conquest of the devil, the demonic and death itself, which he won through his crucifixion (Colossians 2:14-15; Hebrews 2:14-15; 1 John 3:8).[37] In the book of Acts, Christ's followers continue his ministry of exorcism, casting out demons "in the name of Jesus Christ."[38] Moreover, demonic activity continues to this day, and followers of Christ around the world and throughout his-

---

[36]On the significance of Jesus' miracles for his identity as the divine Son of God, see Bowman and Komoszewski, *Putting Jesus in His Place*, pp. 198-206.

[37]For a detailed study of Jesus as an exorcist, see Graham Twelftree, *Jesus the Exorcist: A Contribution to the Study of the Historical Jesus* (Peabody, Mass.: Hendrickson, 1994).

[38]Graham Twelftree, *In the Name of Jesus: Exorcism Among Early Christians* (Grand Rapids: Baker Academic, 2007).

tory have invoked the authority of Jesus to free captives from demonic bondage.[39]

THE COMPASSION OF JESUS

Jesus practiced his own preaching by loving his neighbor. He found an especially attentive audience in the lowest class of his day, "the tax collectors and sinners," those who fell between the cracks of respectability. He was known as the friend of the downcast, and many of them believed in him. He loved both the down and out (prostitutes) and the up and out (tax collectors). Jesus also had a large following of women, whom he respected and to whom he taught doctrine. Dorothy Sayers memorably noted:

> Perhaps it is no wonder that women were first at the Cradle and last at the Cross. They had never known a man like this Man—there never has been such another. A prophet and teacher who never nagged them, never flattered or coaxed or patronized; who never made jokes about them, never treated them either as "the women, God help us!" or "The Ladies, God bless them!"; who rebuked without querulousness and praised without condescension; who took their questions and arguments seriously; who never mapped out their sphere for them, never urged them to be feminine or jeered at them for being female; who had no ax to grind and no uneasy male dignity to defend; who took them as he found them and was completely unself-conscious. There is no act, no sermon, no parable in the Gospel that borrows its pungency from female perversity; nobody could possibly guess from the words and deeds of Jesus that there was anything "funny" about woman's nature.[40]

JESUS: A MAN OF AUTHORITY

Jesus yearned for people to *believe in him*. He is the object of faith for healing. He commands nature with a word. He casts out demons with a word. He raises the dead. His disciples cast out demons in Jesus' name, not their own

---

[39]Francis McNutt discusses the historic reality of Christians' supernatural power over demons and for healing and its loss in *The Nearly Perfect Crime: How the Church Almost Killed the Ministry of Healing* (Grand Rapids: Chosen Books, 2005); see also J. P. Moreland, *Kingdom Triangle* (Grand Rapids: Zondervan, 2007).

[40]Dorothy L. Sayers, *Are Women Human?* (Grand Rapids: Eerdmans, 1971), p. 47. For more on Jesus' revolutionary treatment of women see Douglas Groothuis, "Jesus' View of Women," in *On Jesus* (Belmont, Calif.: Wadsworth, 2003).

(Luke 10:17). Jesus Christ has unique authority—even to forgive sin.

In Capernaum some resourceful people lowered a paralytic through an opening they made in the roof above Jesus. When Jesus recognized their faith, he said to the paralytic, "Son, your sins are forgiven." Some of the religious teachers responded, "Why does this fellow talk like that? He's blaspheming. Who can forgive sins but God alone?" Jesus countered:

> "Why are you thinking these things? Which is easier: to say to this para-lyzed man, 'Your sins are forgiven,' or to say, 'Get up, take your mat and walk'? But I want you to know that the Son of Man has authority on earth to forgive sins." So he said to the man, "I tell you, get up, take your mat and go home." He got up, took his mat and walked out in full view of them all. (Mark 2:2-12)

Jesus did not deny that God alone can forgive sins. He rather backed up the claim that he could forgive sins by healing the paralyzed man. He was, thus, implicitly claiming for himself a uniquely divine prerogative to for-give sins.[41]

At a dinner in a Pharisee's house, a woman of ill repute came to Jesus and anointed his feet with perfume and her own tears. When the Phari-see objected to this behavior, Jesus told a parable to the effect that this woman loved Jesus much because she was forgiven much. "Then Jesus said to her, 'Your sins are forgiven.' The other guests began to say among themselves, 'Who is this who even forgives sins?' Jesus said to the woman, 'Your faith has saved you; go in peace'" (Luke 7:48-50). In word and deed, Jesus claimed to have the authority to forgive sins, a uniquely di-vine prerogative.

Jesus valued people who put their faith in his name. He also provoked faith in many by the confidence with which he spoke of himself. As E. Stanley Jones said, "He never used such words as 'perhaps,' 'may be,' 'I think so.' Even his words had a concrete feeling about them. They fell upon the soul with the authority of certainty."[42] This is manifest in the fact that he never apologized or hesitated. He issued challenging moral abso-lutes, such as "love your enemies" (Matthew 5:44), without reservation. He

---

[41]See Bowman and Komoszewski, *Putting Jesus in His Place*, p. 211.
[42]E. Stanley Jones, *The Christ of the Indian Road* (New York: Grosset & Dunlap, 1925), p. 191.

made grand promises without caution, such as "Blessed are those who hunger and thirst for righteousness, for they will be filled" (Matthew 5:6) and "If you hold to my teaching, you are really my disciples. Then you will know the truth, and the truth will set you free" (John 8:31-32). He confidently asserted, "Heaven and earth will pass away, but my words will never pass away" (Matthew 24:35). He warned his hearers that their eternal destiny depended on their response to him (Mark 8:38). He foretold the future without reservation (Matthew 24).[43]

Jesus not only warned his hearers of Judgment Day, he proclaimed himself the Judge of the world. In warning of false prophets to come in his name, Jesus declared that he will say to them on the Day of Judgment, "I never knew you. Away from me, you evildoers!" (Matthew 7:23). Jesus stated, "Whoever hears my word and believes him who sent me has eternal life and will not be judged but has crossed over from death to life" (John 5:24). Jesus has authority to judge the world:

> When the Son of Man comes in his glory, and all the angels with him, he will sit on his glorious throne. All the nations will be gathered before him, and he will separate the people one from another as a shepherd separates the sheep from the goats. (Matthew 25:31-32)[44]

He added that the goats "will go away to eternal punishment, but the righteous to eternal life" (Matthew 25:46), all on the basis of how they respond to Jesus during their life on earth. When Jesus makes reference to "sitting on his throne" and rendering final judgment he is indirectly claiming deity, since these prerogatives belong only to God according to the Jewish Scriptures. In the Hebrew Bible, no angel, prophet, king, priest or anyone else sits on a "heavenly throne" or makes an ultimate evaluation of people's life after their death. Only God does that. Jesus also refers to "his

---

[43]See John Stott, *Basic Christianity*, 2nd ed. (Downers Grove, Ill.: InterVarsity Press, 1971), p. 31. On the claim that Jesus falsely predicted his second coming as occurring just a few years after his death, see Paul Copan, *When God Goes to Starbucks* (Grand Rapids: Baker, 2008), chaps. 15-16. For a more in-depth treatment of Jesus and eschatology, see Charles L. Holmes, *Till Jesus Comes: Origins of Christian Apocalyptic Expectation* (Peabody, Mass.: Hendrickson, 1996).

[44]For the theological significance of Jesus' title as "the Son of Man" and for his other titles, see Ramm, *An Evangelical Christology*, pp. 107-16; David Wells, *The Person of Christ* (Westchester, Ill.: Crossway, 1984), pp. 67-81; I. Howard Marshall, "Son of Man," in *Dictionary of Jesus and the Gospels*, ed. Joel B. Green, Scot McKnight and I. Howard Marshall (Downers Grove, Ill.: InterVarsity Press, 1992), pp. 775-81.

angels." Biblically, only God has authority to command angels. Again, Jesus implicitly claims to be divine.

THE UNIQUENESS OF JESUS CHRIST

Jesus' sense of authority, sincerity and certainty are demonstrated in his frequent use of *amen* before making a statement. This form of address is found in all the Gospels but is never used by anyone but Jesus. Of all the English translations, only the King James Version and the New King James Version use the word *amen*. It is usually translated as "verily" or "truly" or "solemnly," or is not translated directly but put as "Believe me," "I tell you this," "Remember this," and so on. This "amen" preface signals that Jesus is speaking prophetically for God and as the unique messenger of God.[45] Although other New Testament writers use *amen* at the end of statements to affirm strong agreement, no "other person—apostle or prophet—of the early church felt a liberty to follow his example by making use of this very formula."[46] These emphatic utterances by Jesus addressed matters such the kingdom of God or heaven (Matthew 13:17; 18:3; Mark 10:15; John 3:3-5), the end times (Matthew 10:23; 16:28), the Judaism of Jesus' day (Matthew 6:2, 5, 16; 8:10), faith (Matthew 17:20; John 5:24) and more.[47] The truth of these utterances is based squarely on Jesus himself as the source of authority.[48]

Jesus professes to have a unique knowledge of God. In a passage widely regarded as authentic even by many who are generally skeptical of much in the Gospels, Jesus says: "All things have been committed to me by my Father. No one knows the Son except the Father, and no one knows the Father except the Son and those to whom the Son chooses to reveal him" (Matthew 11:27). No prophet, priest, king, angel or anyone else in the Hebrew Scriptures made this kind of claim. Jesus establishes a unique and exclusive relationship between himself—as "*the* Son," not merely "*a* son"— and the Father. He also equates the Father's knowledge of the Son with the Son's knowledge of the Father. This implies an equality of divine knowledge. Further, Jesus claims unique ability as the absolute and exclu-

---

[45]G. F. Hawthorne, "Amen," in *Dictionary of Jesus and the Gospels*, ed. Joel B. Green, Scot McKnight and I. Howard Marshall (Downers Grove, Ill.: InterVarsity Press, 1992), p. 7.
[46]Ibid.
[47]Ibid.
[48]Erickson, *Word Became Flesh*, p. 434.

sive revealer of the Father and as mediator between the Father and those who receive the revelation of the Father through the Son.[49]

Jesus' statement about the Son's singular relationship to the Father closely parallels many claims in the Gospel of John, particularly his controversial answer to Thomas's question, "Lord, we don't know where you are going, so how can we know the way?"

> Jesus answered, "I am the way and the truth and the life. No one comes to the Father except through me. If you really know me, you will know my Father as well. From now on, you do know him and have seen him." (John 14:5-7; see also John 1:18)

As in Matthew 11:27, Jesus claims to be the sole and exclusive mediator between humans and God the Father, and to be the sole and exclusive revelation of God to humans. To know Jesus is to know the Father as well. Not to know Jesus is not to know the Father. Jesus' singular role as mediator was an early item of attention and declaration in the early Christian movement. In Jesus' response to challenges about his activities on the sabbath,

> Jesus said to them, "My Father is always at his work to this very day, and I too am working." For this reason they tried all the more to kill him; not only was he breaking the Sabbath, but he was even calling God his own Father, making himself equal with God. (John 5:17-18)

Jesus healed on the sabbath on several occasions and used the opportunity to proclaim, "The Son of Man is Lord even of the Sabbath" (Mark 2:28). It is one thing to teach about the sabbath. It is another to claim to be "the Lord of the sabbath." Such a person must be no less than the Lord of creation—that is, God Almighty, who himself created and blessed the sabbath (Genesis 2:2).

When Jesus' disputants said, "Who do you think you are?" he concluded his response by saying, "Very truly I tell you, before Abraham was born, I am!" John observes, "At this, they picked up stones to stone him, but Jesus hid himself, slipping away from the temple grounds" (John 8:53, 58-59). Jesus thus affirmed his preexistence as God.[50] Jesus also expressed his uniqueness by saying, "For God so loved the world that he gave his one

---

[49]See William Lane Craig, *Reasonable Faith*, 3rd ed. (Wheaton, Ill.: Crossway, 2008), pp. 311-12. This saying is also recognized by liberal scholars to be very ancient and authentic.
[50]Bowman and Komoszewksi, *Putting Jesus in His Place*, pp. 96-97.

and only Son, that whoever believes in him shall not perish but have eternal life" (John 3:16). He affirmed that he alone is the agent of redemption as God's "*only* Son."

Jesus' claims could be uttered by anyone (with enough nerve). But these claims could only be *substantiated* by Jesus through his acts and by his character. For the Gospel writers, God is focused in Jesus of Nazareth.[51] John declares that Jesus has made the Father known by coming into the world (John 1:18).

Jesus glorified the Father as no one else could. Therefore, he can make strong demands on God's creatures. We hear the ring of exclusivity in Jesus' warning:

> Enter through the narrow gate. For wide is the gate and broad is the road that leads to destruction, and many enter through it. But small is the gate and narrow the road that leads to life, and only a few find it. (Matthew 7:13-14; see also John 10:7-10)

The Gospel of John catalogs seven of Jesus' "I am" statements that accentuate his uniqueness: (1) "I am the bread of life" (John 6:48) and "I am the living bread that came down from heaven. Whoever eats of this bread will live forever. This bread is my flesh, which I will give for the life of the world" (John 6:51). (2) "I am the light of the world. Whoever follows me will never walk in darkness, but will have the light of life" (John 8:12). (3) "I am the gate" (John 10:7, 9). (4) "I am the good shepherd. The good shepherd lays down his life for the sheep" (John 10:11). (5) "I am the resurrection and the life. The one who believes in me will live, even though they die" (John 11:25). (6) "I am the way and the truth and the life" (John 14:6). (7) I am the "true vine" (John 15:1, 5).[52]

After his resurrection and before his ascension, Jesus affirmed without qualification the mission he left for his disciples:

> All authority in heaven and on earth has been given to me. Therefore go and make disciples of all nations, baptizing them in the name of the Father and of the Son and of the Holy Spirit, and teaching them to obey every-

---

[51]On the idea of Jesus as "God in focus," see J. B. Phillips, *Your God Is Too Small* (New York: Macmillan, 1979), pp. 63-66.

[52]See Erickson, *Word Became Flesh*, pp. 27-29. It has been argued that Jesus' "I am" statements were spoken such that they were claims to deity as well (see Ethelbert Stauffer, *Jesus and His Story* [New York: Alfred A. Knopf, 1974], pp. 174-95).

thing I have commanded you. And surely I am with you always, to the very end of the age. (Matthew 28:18-20)

He spoke with an unrelenting sense of confidence in both his beliefs and his task.

While Jesus was at times called a blasphemer, out of his mind and even demon possessed (see chap. 21), he and others made some remarkable claims about his moral character. Pontius Pilate found no basis for convicting him as a criminal (Luke 23:4). A centurion who witnessed his death on the cross said, "Surely this was a righteous man" (Luke 23:47). The criminal crucified next to Jesus declared, "This man has done nothing wrong" (Luke 23:41). The testimony of his disciples is telling. John refers to him as "full of grace and truth" (John 1:14) and as "Jesus Christ, the Righteous One" (1 John 2:1) in whom there is no sin (1 John 3:5). Peter praised Jesus as "a lamb without blemish or defect" (1 Peter 1:19) who never spoke deceitfully (1 Peter 2:22). Paul confessed that Jesus "had no sin" as the spotless sacrifice for sinners (2 Corinthians 5:21). Even Judas confessed, "I have betrayed innocent blood" (Matthew 27:4). Hebrews speaks of the greatness of Jesus as the perfect high priest "who has been tempted in every way, just as we are—yet he did not sin" (Hebrews 4:15; see also Hebrews 7:26-28). Jesus contrasts himself with one who speaks on his own to gain honor for himself, by saying that "he who seeks the glory of the one who sent him is a man of truth; there is nothing false about him" (John 7:18). Jesus also asked, "Can any of you prove me guilty of sin?" (John 8:46).

Jesus received worship during his earthly ministry, beginning at his birth (Matthew 2:11). We must remember that faithful Jews worshiped God alone, as God had commanded (Exodus 20:1-3). Yet Jesus receives worship on several occasions. After Jesus calmed a storm while on a boat with his disciples, they "worshiped him, saying 'Truly you are the Son of God'" (Matthew 14:33). The risen Jesus is worshiped first by "Mary Magdalene and the other Mary" (Matthew 28:1, 9) and then the eleven disciples (Matthew 28:17; see also Luke 24:52).[53]

JESUS THE CHRIST

Christ is the Greek equivalent of the Hebrew word *Messiah*. So whenever

---

[53]Bowman and Komoszewski, *Putting Jesus in His Place*, pp. 37-45.

Jesus is called "the Christ" he is being referred to as the Messiah. He admitted this to the Samaritan woman, who said to him, "'I know that Messiah' (called Christ) 'is coming. When he comes, he will explain everything to us.' Then Jesus declared, 'I, the one speaking to you—I am he'" (John 4:25-26). Jesus likewise admitted to being the Christ when he said to his disciples, "Truly I tell you, anyone who gives you a cup of water in my name because you belong to the Messiah will certainly not lose their reward" (Mark 9:41; see also Matthew 23:10; John 17:3). Originally in the Old Testament *Messiah* could refer to various people specially "anointed" by God for specific tasks performed in his service. Through various prophecies the concept was narrowed down to the person of the Messiah, one uniquely equipped by God for a divine mission.

Several strands made up the messianic expectation of the Old Testament. One was political. The Messiah would rule on David's throne in righteousness. Another was apocalyptic: the "son of man" would come from heaven to judge evil (Daniel 7:13-14). "Son of Man" was Jesus' most frequent self-reference and it carried a strong divine and messianic connotation.[54] The last was that of the Suffering Servant who bears the sin of his people (Isaiah 52:13-15; 53).[55]

Jesus of Nazareth fulfilled all three expectations, although in ways not expected by many. In so doing he fulfilled scores of prophecies concerning his mission.[56] There are several prophetic references in the Hebrew Bible specifically to the deity of the Messiah.

1. God's Son is to rule on the throne at God's right hand, equal in power with the Father (see Psalm 2:7-12; 110:1-2).

2. The promised Messiah will be Immanuel (i.e., "God with us") (see Isaiah 7:14; Matthew 1:23).

3. The promised Messiah will be "Mighty God" ruling eternally (see Isaiah 9:6-7).

---

[54]For the theological significance of Jesus' title as "the Son of Man" and for his other titles, see Ramm, *Evangelical Christology*, pp. 107-16; Wells, *Person of Christ*, pp. 67-81; Marshall, "Son of Man," pp. 775-81.
[55]On the Suffering Servant in the Hebrew Bible and the New Testament, see Richard Bauckham, "God Crucified," in *Jesus and the God of Israel: God Crucified and Other Studies on the New Testament's Christology of Divine Identity* (Grand Rapids: Eerdmans, 2008).
[56]For a careful, developed treatment of this see Walter Kaiser, *The Messiah in the Old Testament* (Grand Rapids: Zondervan, 1995).

4. The ruler born in Bethlehem has his origin from all eternity (see Micah 5:2).

5. The righteous Branch of David is called "The LORD Our Righteous Savior" (see Jeremiah 23:5-6).

6. The one who will appear in the temple is "the Lord" (see Malachi 3:1).[57]

Jesus did not set up an earthly political rule, but nevertheless viewed himself as King and Lord of the universe. He did not bring apocalyptic judgment at his incarnation but promised that it will come when he returns at the end of the age. As the Suffering Servant, the Christ must go to the cross.

THE DEATH OF CHRIST

Jesus explained to the disciples that he must go to Jerusalem to suffer many things, be killed and be raised to life on the third day (Matthew 16:21). Jesus faced his crucifixion not as an accident or a mistake, but as a necessary part of his mission. The great theologian B. B. Warfield has aptly commented that

> He came into the world to die, and every stage of the road that led to this destiny was determined not for Him but by Him. He was never the victim but always the Master of circumstance, and pursued His pathway from the beginning to the end, not merely in full knowledge from the start of all its turns and twists up to its bitter conclusion, but in complete control of them and of it.[58]

Without his death the ministry of Jesus is meaningless. Throughout the Bible death is required for life. In Genesis 3:15, after the Fall, the first promise of the Messiah says that he will be struck even as he crushes Satan's head. God then clothes Adam and Eve in animal skins, which re-

---

[57]I have slightly adapted this material from "Passages Indicating the Deity of Christ," in Kenneth L. Barker and John Kohlenberger III, *Zondervan NIV Commentary*, vol. 2, *New Testament* (Grand Rapids: Zondervan, 1994), p. 570. For more on the argument from biblical prophecy, see Robert C. Newman, *The Evidence of Prophecy* (Hatfield, Penn.: Interdisciplinary Biblical Research Institute, 2001), esp. pt. 3. The fulfillment of these and other prophecies lends credence to the divine inspiration of Scripture.

[58]B. B. Warfield, *The Person and Work of Christ* (Phillipsburg, N.J.: Presbyterian & Reformed, 1950), p. 17.

quired the animals' death. God provides a sacrificial animal for Abraham in place of his son's death (Genesis 22). The Passover lamb is killed so that the Israelites can be saved (Exodus 12). The entire sacrificial system of the Hebrew Bible looks forward to Jesus, "the Lamb of God, who takes away the sins of the world." This was proclaimed by John the Baptist (John 1:29), and by the prophecy of the suffering servant (Isaiah 53). As Schaeffer writes, "The center of the Christian message is the redemptive death of Jesus Christ."[59]

As the hour approached Jesus became more explicit about his death:

> We are going up to Jerusalem, and the Son of Man will be delivered over to the chief priests and the teachers of the law. They will condemn him to death and will hand him over to the Gentiles to be mocked and flogged and crucified. On the third day he will be raised to life! (Matthew 20:18-19)

About one-third of Matthew, one-third of Mark, one-fourth of Luke and one-half of John focus on the last hours of Jesus' life. Approximately one-third of the material making up the four Gospels relates to the last week of Jesus. We will sample a few key events and statements to understand the death of Jesus.

Jesus' sense of his impending death harmonizes with his sense of mission. We noted that he said, referring to himself, "The good shepherd lays down his life for the sheep" (John 10:11). When explaining that his disciples should not jockey for power and prestige but rather serve their neighbors, Jesus used himself as the supreme example by saying "the Son of Man did not come to be served, but to serve, and to give his life as a ransom for many" (Matthew 20:28).

Shortly before his betrayal, Jesus was in great agony over his coming death and prayed, "*Abba*, Father, everything is possible for you. Take this cup from me. Yet not what I will, but what you will" (Mark 14:36). Soon after this, when Jesus was arrested, someone tried to protect him by the sword. Jesus responded by rebuking the deed and saying, "Do you think I cannot call on my Father, and he will at once put at my disposal more than twelve legions of angels? But how then would the

---

[59]Francis Schaeffer, *True Spirituality*, 30th anniv. ed. (Wheaton, Ill.: Tyndale House, 2001), p. 20.

Scriptures be fulfilled that say it must happen in this way?" (Matthew 26:53-54).

Later the Jewish religious leaders said, "Tell us if you are the Messiah, the Son of God." "'You have said so,' Jesus replied. 'But I say to all of you: From now on you will see the Son of Man sitting at the right hand of the Mighty One and coming on the clouds of heaven'" (Matthew 26:63-64). In just a few words Jesus affirmed that he was the promised Messiah, the Son of Man, who was equal to ("sit at the right hand of") almighty God, who was coming in divine judgment ("the clouds of heaven"). The high priest understood. He ripped his clothes, crying out, "He has spoken blasphemy" (Matthew 26:65). Jesus was then beaten and handed over to the Roman political officials, who further beat him, taunted him, spit on him and had him crucified.

Jesus was savagely scourged before being crucified, and he carried the cross part way to Golgotha before another man was constrained to shoulder it the rest of the way (Mark 15:21; John 19:17). He was nailed between two common criminals. In the midst of the suffering of the cross, Jesus cried, "Father, forgive them, for they do not know what they are doing" (Luke 23:34). Jesus loved his enemies, even to the end, but affirmed their need for forgiveness.

Jesus' last words on the cross were, "My God, my God, why have you forsaken me?" (Mark 15:34). After this

> with a loud cry, Jesus breathed his last.
>
> The curtain of the temple was torn in two from top to bottom. And when the centurion, who stood there in front of Jesus, saw how he died, he said, "Surely this man was the Son of God!" (Mark 15:37-39)

The crucifixion and its meaning were revealed hundreds of years before the fact. Jesus himself often quoted from Isaiah 53 that said of the Messiah:

> He poured out his life unto death,
>> and was numbered with the transgressors.
> For he bore the sin of many,
>> and made intercession for the transgressors. (Isaiah 53:12)

It was fulfilled to the letter.

Isaiah speaks of one

despised and rejected by mankind;
   a man of suffering, and familiar with pain. . . .
Surely he took up our pain
   and bore our suffering,
yet we considered him punished by God,
   stricken by him, and afflicted.
But he was pierced for our transgressions,
   he was crushed for our iniquities;
the punishment that brought us peace was on him,
   and by his wounds we are healed. (Isaiah 53:3-5)

Although "we all, like sheep, have gone astray, . . . the LORD has laid on him the iniquity of us all." He was "like a lamb" led to the slaughter, "for the transgression of my people he was punished." And although "he had done no violence nor was any deceit in his mouth," the Lord "makes his life an offering for sin" (Isaiah 53:6-10). Isaiah concludes the chapter by saying, "For he bore the sin of many, / and made intercession for the transgressors" (Isaiah 53:12). Jesus Christ is this Suffering Servant. [60]

But Jesus' death, while necessary, was not the end. There would be no Christianity without his resurrection, which is central to the entire New Testament. As Paul proclaims, Jesus was declared the Son of God with power through his resurrection (Romans 1:4). We return to this stunning and stellar credential in chapter twenty-two.

OTHER TESTIMONY TO JESUS

We have examined primarily the claims and credentials of Christ made by Jesus himself as found in the four Gospels (leaving the resurrection to chap. 22). This hardly exhausts our knowledge of Jesus. We find the themes of the Gospels repeated and amplified throughout the rest of the New Testament. I will only cite a trickle of the great stream of high Christology to be found there.

The preface to John's Gospel declares:

In the beginning was the Word, and the Word was with God, and the Word was God. He was with God in the beginning. Through him all

---

[60]The argument that Jesus messianically fulfilled Isaiah 53 is made in detail by Michael L. Brown, *Answering Jewish Objections to Jesus* (Grand Rapids: Baker, 2003), 3:40-85.

things were made; without him nothing was made that has been made. In him was life, and that life was the light of all mankind. The light shines in the darkness, but the darkness has not overcome it. (John 1:1-5)

The word John uses for "Word" is the Greek *logos*. While the term has been used in Greek philosophy to mean the *impersonal* ordering principle of the universe, John uses it to refer to the *personal* God of the universe who has taken on human nature to conquer sin.

In his letter to the early church John writes, "That which was from the beginning, which we have heard, which we have seen with our eyes, which we have looked at and our hands have touched—this we proclaim concerning the Word of life" (1 John 1:1). He later says, "He is the atoning sacrifice for our sins, and not only for ours but also for the sins of the whole world. We know that we have come to know him if we keep his commands" (1 John 2:2-3).

After Jesus' resurrection and ascension, Peter became a great preacher and the evangelist that Jesus promised he would be (Mark 1:17). When standing before the rulers and elders of the Jews in Jerusalem, Peter, filled with the Holy Spirit, proclaimed, "Salvation is found in no one else, for there is no other name given under heaven to mankind by which we must be saved" (Acts 4:12). The apostle Paul also accentuates the uniqueness and supremacy of Jesus. "For there is one God and one mediator between God and mankind, Christ Jesus, himself human, who gave himself as a ransom for all people" (1 Timothy 2:5-6).

While the New Testament presents Christ as exalted over all as the crucified, risen and ascendant Lord, he achieved this only by becoming the servant of all, by being the Lamb who was willing to be sacrificed on the cross to give life to those who come to him in faith (2 Corinthians 8:9).[61] The apostle Paul writes that Christ Jesus was "in very nature God," but took on a human nature and humbled himself to die on a cross. Because of this

> God exalted him to the highest place
>   and gave him the name that is above every name,
> that at the name of Jesus every knee should bow,

---

[61]For an excellent study of both the transcendence and condescension of Jesus Christ, see Jonathan Edwards, "The Excellency of Christ," in *The Puritan Sage* (New York: Library Publishers, 1953), pp. 326-32.

in heaven and on earth and under the earth,
and every tongue acknowledge that Jesus Christ is Lord.
   (Philippians 2:6-11; cf. Isaiah 45:23)

The author of Hebrews places Jesus at the pinnacle of God's revelation
to humanity:

> In the past God spoke to our ancestors through the prophets at many times
> and in various ways, but in these last days he has spoken to us by his Son,
> whom he appointed heir of all things, and through whom also he made the
> universe. The Son is the radiance of God's glory and the exact representa-
> tion of his being, sustaining all things by his powerful word. After he had
> provided purification for sins, he sat down at the right hand of the Majesty
> in heaven. (Hebrews 1:1-3)

JESUS AND OTHER RELIGIOUS LEADERS

In a religiously pluralistic setting, it is not rude or imperious to compare
and contrast the teachings of religions and their leaders; it is apologetically
necessary. I will return to the question of how Christianity relates to religious pluralism in chapter twenty-three. Given my argument thus far for
the identity of Jesus as God incarnate, Lord and Savior, it is fitting to
compare his life and claims to those of other significant religious founders
or key persons. (I will further argue for Jesus' uniqueness and supremacy
in chapters twenty-one and twenty-two.) These leaders can be classified as
sages, avatars or prophets.

SAGES, NOT SAVIORS

Buddhism teaches that Siddhartha Gautama (563-479 B.C.) attained enlightenment through self-effort and thus became "the Buddha" (enlightened one). He then began teaching "The Four Noble Truths" about suffering and its transcendence. The Buddha never claimed to be divine, a
prophet or a mediator between God and humans. He is an enlightened
sage who sought to lead others to nirvana.

Lao-Tze (sixth century B.C.) is the founding sage of Taoism. He is considered by some the author of the *Tao Te Ching*, a book of enigmatic epi-
grams offered to find "the watercourse way" of wisdom. The existence of a
historical person named Lao-Tze is disputed, but he is taken to be a sage,

not a savior, a mystic or a prophet. His purpose was to show the Tao (or the way) not to *be* the way.

Mahavira (599-527 B.C.) was the founder of Jainism, but little is known about him. He is viewed as a heroic figure who had insights into reality and taught a strict asceticism. Since Jainism is atheistic or polytheistic (depending on the interpretation), he is in no way viewed as an emissary of the divine being or as a savior figure.

Confucianism venerates Confucius (551-479 B.C.) as its ethical sage, but without the mystical elements found in Taoism and Buddhism. He spoke of "the way of Heaven" but never advanced himself as the go-between. Confucius had little to say about the transcendent realm, although there is some intimation of monotheism in his teaching. He rather focused on principles of conduct for the family and the state.[62]

AVATARS, NOT INCARNATION

Hinduism teaches that the God Vishnu appeared on earth at least ten times in the form of avatars. The principal avatar is Krishna, the hero of the *Bhagavad-Gita*. The avatar, however, is not usually considered to be a personal manifestation of a personal God. Rather, the avatar takes on human form only to be reabsorbed into Brahman, which is often viewed as an impersonal oneness. The avatar does not secure redemption through its efforts, because redemption requires many lifetimes of effort (reincarnation and karma). The historical basis for any of the ten avatars is exceedingly thin and, in the final analysis, not important for Hinduism, which does not stress the reality of space-time history.[63]

PROPHETS, NOT MESSIAHS

The leading figure of Judaism has long been considered Moses, since he received the law and led God's people out of Egypt and toward the Promised Land. Moses himself spoke of another prophet who would come after him who would be greater (Deuteronomy 18:18). This, according to the New Testament, is Jesus himself (Acts 3:17-23). Moses,

---

[62]See Thomas I. S. Leung, "Confucianism," in *The Compact Guide to World Religions*, ed. Dean Halverson (Minneapolis: Bethany House, 1996).

[63]On Hinduism and avatars see Dean Halverson, "Hinduism," in *The Compact Guide to World Religion*, ed. Dean Halverson (Minneapolis: Bethany House, 1996), pp. 87-10; and Parrinder, *Avatar and Incarnation*.

though flawed, communicated God's law to his people and provided remarkable leadership. Though a prophet, Moses was unlike Jesus; he
never claimed to be sinless, nor did he ever suggest anyone should put
their faith in him. The Messiah was yet to come. As John put it, "For the
law was given through Moses; grace and truth came through Jesus
Christ" (John 1:17).

Zoroastrianism, an originally monotheistic religion of ancient Persia,
claims Zoroaster (628-551 B.C.) as its prophet, the one who made known
the will of the god, Ahura-Masda. Zoroaster preached against priestly
elitism, animal sacrifice and polytheism. He adjured his followers to follow the truth and avoid lies in order to accrue for themselves a blessed
afterlife. In no way did he offer himself as the way of salvation, nor did
he accept worship or perform miracles.[64]

"Allah is God and Muhammad is his prophet," affirm all Muslims.
Muhammad (A.D. 570-632) is deemed the last and greatest prophet.
Through the reception of the Qur'an, he is said to correct the errors of
Christians and Jews, who have distorted their own Scriptures. Islam denies any mediator between Allah and his creatures, and denies salvation by
grace alone through Jesus, whom it deems an exalted prophet but not divine. Muhammad is not presented as sinless and in the Qur'an is never
credited with performing miracles.[65]

The Baha'i faith is the newest of the world's major religions and claims
to be in continuity with all of them. Its prophet, or "manifestation of God,"
Bahaullah (A.D. 1817-1892), claimed to be the second coming of Jesus and
God's prophet for a thousand years. Yet he performed no miracles and is
not deemed a mediator. Rather, he calls people to believe that all religions
are from God and culminate in his own teachings. The Baha'i faith deems
Jesus another manifestation of God, but not God incarnate. Jesus is revered but considered outmoded as a "manifestation of God."[66]

Whether a religious leader is considered a prophet, sage or avatar, his
(or her) status differs radically from what is ascribed to Jesus in the Bible.

---

[64]For more on Zoroastrianism see Winfried Corduan, *Neighboring Faiths* (Downers Grove, Ill.:
InterVarsity Press, 1998), pp. 113-34; and Sir Rustom Masani, *Zoroastrianism: The Religion of
the Good Life* (New York: Macmillan, 1968).
[65]I will offer a more in-depth treatment of Islam in chap. 24.
[66]On the Baha'i faith see Francis Beckwith, "Baha'i Faith," in *New Religious Movements*, ed.
Ronald Enroth (Downers Grove, Ill.: InterVarsity Press, 2005).

No other religion so highly esteems its founder or makes such titanic claims about him. Away, then, with all baseless claims about Jesus being reducible to some general religious category along with Buddha, Muhammad and so on. He did not present us with that pallid option.

JESUS: ONE OF A KIND

The evidence for the uniqueness and supremacy of Jesus presented in this chapter is far from complete.[67] However, the cumulative evidence singles Jesus out from all other religious figures.[68] He entered the world supernaturally, accredited himself with unparalleled signs and wonders, possessed an impeccable character, made claims only befitting God himself, and died with the purpose of redeeming humanity. The best account of the historical facts is that he was who he said he was. If this is so, we should respond to him on his terms.

JESUS AND THE AUTHORITY OF THE BIBLE

This chapter has thus far argued for the uniqueness and supremacy of Jesus as Lord and Savior based on the historical reliability of the New Testament (see chap. 19). Chapters twenty-one and twenty-two will argue further for Jesus as the God-man who was raised from the dead never to die again. If these combined arguments prove successful, this warrants our belief in both the reality of Jesus' deeds and the truth of his words, including his understanding of the Bible.[69] Although we cannot here address the subject in great detail, we can, on the basis of Jesus' well-established authority, argue for the divine inspiration of both the Old and New Testaments.[70]

---

[67]See Groothuis, *Jesus in an Age of Controversy;* Groothuis, *On Jesus;* Erickson, *Word Became Flesh;* Bowman and Komoszewski, *Putting Jesus in His Place;* Murray Harris, *Three Crucial Questions About Jesus* (Eugene, Ore.: Wipf & Stock, 2008).

[68]On the uniqueness of Jesus' claims in relation to the teachings of Buddha, Socrates, Muhammad and Confucius, see C. S. Lewis, "What Are We to Make of Jesus Christ?" in *God in the Dock* (Grand Rapids: Eerdmans, 1970), pp. 157-58; see also, Edwin Yamauchi, *Jesus, Zoroaster, Buddha, Socrates, Muhammad*, rev. ed. (Downers Grove, Ill.: InterVarsity Press, 1972).

[69]For a thorough contemporary treatment of Jesus' understanding of the Old Testament, see Craig L. Blomberg, "Further Reflections on Jesus' View of the Old Testament," in *The Scripture Project: The Bible and Biblical Authority in the New Millennium*, ed. D. A. Carson, vol. 1 (Grand Rapids: Eerdmans, forthcoming). For Jesus' view of the entire Bible, see John Wenham, *Christ and the Bible*, 2nd ed. (1972; reprint, Grand Rapids: Baker, 1984).

[70]See footnote 15 in chap. 15. We can further argue for the Bible's inspiration and total truthfulness on the basis of its fulfilled prophecies, its historical corroboration by extrabiblical sources, its unity (although written over a long period of time by diverse authors not all in contact with

In all of his teaching and interactions as recorded in the Gospels, Jesus affirmed that the Jewish Scriptures were divinely inspired. The books to which Jesus referred are the same ones we find in the Hebrew Bible today (although they were ordered somewhat differently). The concept of inspiration means that God, who cannot err, directed the writers of the Bible to write what God intended them to write, and to do so without any kind of error—logical, historical, scientific or moral.[71] Jesus confidently quotes and interprets the Old Testament as a settled matter of his worldview. He asserts that "the Scripture cannot be broken," which means that it cannot be nullified or contravened: it is true and enduring (John 10:35; see also John 17:17). Christ came not to abolish the Scripture in any way, but rather to fulfill its ultimate purpose (Matthew 5:17-19; cf. Luke 16:7). These sacred writings find their completion in his own person and ministry, because they testify to him (John 5:39; Luke 24:25-27). When tempted in the wilderness by the devil, Jesus confidently affirmed and properly interpreted Scripture in order to repel Satan's attack (Matthew 4:1-11; Luke 4:1-13).[72] Jesus equated the Hebrew Bible with the very words of God, as when he said that David's writing in Psalm 110 was through the Holy Spirit (Mark 12:35-36). He also spoke of the religious leaders of his day as nullifying "the word of God" through their human tradition (Matthew 15:1-6).[73]

In light of Jesus' unmatched credentials, there is no reason to doubt his judgment about the Old Testament. If he is indeed the miracle-working master teacher and philosopher, who made incomparable claims about his divine mission and backed them up by his impeccable and incomparable life, death, resurrection and ascension, then we can trust his

---

one another), its moral and spiritual wisdom, and so on—as I have done in various ways throughout this book.

[71]See 1 Peter 1:20-21; 2 Timothy 3:15-16, which teach that both the authors and the writings are thus divinely inspired. These passages refer to the Old Testament, but, as we will see below, the concept of inspiration can be extended to the New Testament as well.

[72]For details on Jesus' endorsement of the Hebrew Bible, see John Stott, *The Authority of the Bible* (Downers Grove, Ill.: InterVarsity Press, 1974), pp. 9-17; and John Frame, "Jesus' View of the Old Testament," in *The Doctrine of the Word of God* (Phillipsburg, N.J.: P & R Publishers, 2010).

[73]For more on Jesus' (and the rest of the New Testament's) employment of the Old Testament, see B. B. Warfield, "The Terms, 'Scripture' and 'Scriptures' as Employed in the New Testament," and Warfield, "'It Says:' 'Scripture Says:' 'God Says,'" in *The Inspiration and Authority of the Bible* (1948; Philadelphia: P & R Publishers, 1970).

assessment of the sacred Scriptures of his day. By his authoritative teachings, we can know that the Old Testament itself bears a unique authority. This does not deliver us from the various historical and moral questions about the Old Testament (some of which are addressed in appendix two), but it should give us a strong confidence that since these writings have received the imprimatur of God incarnate, these problems are neither insurmountable nor insufferable.[74]

But what of the inspiration of the New Testament, which was not yet written during Jesus' earthly ministry? As Craig Blomberg argued in chapter nineteen, the canon of the New Testament was determined by its adherence to the coherent and ancient teachings of the apostles of Jesus Christ.[75] The books selected as part of the biblical canon (combined with the Jewish Scriptures, thus forming the entire Bible) were not chosen for partisan or political reasons (as many irresponsibly and ignorantly claim), but ultimately because of their anchorage in the peerless person of Jesus Christ himself. This is illustrated by Jesus' choice and authorization of the apostles as his unique representatives in the world. As Stott says, the "apostle was a specially chosen emissary, the bearer of another and higher authority, the herald of a given message."[76] The apostles were personally commissioned by Jesus (Luke 6:13; Acts 9; Galatians 1:1), had unique historical experience with Jesus (Mark 3:14; John 15:27) and were given special inspiration by the Holy Spirit (John 14:25-26; 16:12-13).[77] One finds many references in the New Testament to the apostles' sense of authority and inspiration as specially designated emissaries of Christ (e.g., 1 John 1:1-3; 2:7, 24; 1 Peter 1:22-25; 2 Thess. 3:6-15). This authority was recognized by the ancient church as the basis of their beliefs and practices (see Acts 2:42).[78]

---

[74]Some have implausibly argued that Jesus' incarnation involved a limitation of his knowledge; thus he mistakenly believed the Hebrew Bible was inspired. For a thorough refutation of this claim, see Norman Geisler, *Systematic Theology* (Minneapolis: Bethany House, 2002), 1:273-80.

[75]The New Testament books were either written by an apostle (such as the Gospels of Matthew and John, the letters of John, Peter, and Paul), or by close associates of an apostle (such as the Gospels of Mark and Luke), or in accordance with apostolic doctrine (such as Hebrews, if it was not written by Paul himself).

[76]Stott, *Authority of the Bible*, p. 17.

[77]Ibid., pp. 17-19.

[78]The apostles also recognized the divine authority of the Hebrew Bible; see Frame, "The Apostles' View of the Old Testament," in *The Doctrine of the Word of God;* and Wenham, "The New

While much more could be elaborated on this rich topic, our argument from Jesus to the inspiration and authority of the Bible can be thus distilled:

1. The New Testament is historically reliable.

2. The New Testament accredits Jesus as one with unsurpassable authority.

3. Jesus endorses the divine inspiration of the Hebrew Bible and anticipates the divine inspiration of the New Testament through his authorization of the Apostles, whose teachings inform and ratify the entire New Testament.

4. Therefore, on the basis of Jesus' authority, we can accept the divine inspiration of the Hebrew Bible and the New Testament.

This argument does not commit the fallacy of circular reasoning or begging the question: "We know the Scripture is inspired because the divine Lord Jesus said so, and we know the Lord Jesus is divine because the inspired Scripture says so."[79] Nor does it maintain that the Bible's only credential is its self-authenticating nature wherein one simply reads it and "knows" that it is true (although this often happens through the work of the Holy Spirit). Rather, this simple and direct argument is *linear* because we argued *from* the reliability of the New Testament (and especially the Gospels) *to* the authority of Jesus and then *to* the truthfulness of his teachings about Scripture as inspired by God. From this reasoning, we conclude (not presuppose or assume or take on blind faith) the authority of the Bible.[80]

Testament Writers and the Old Testament," in *Christ and the Bible*.
[79]Stott, *Authority of the Bible*, 23.
[80]Ibid., p. 25.

21

Defending the Incarnation

HAVING MADE A CASE FOR JESUS' impeccable character, miraculous credentials and claims to deity, we must now assess two fundamental issues. First, should we believe the testimony of Jesus concerning his deity, or are there other plausible explanations for his claims? Second, does the concept of a person who is both divine and human cohere logically? If it does not, then Jesus' claims must be false; but if it is logically coherent, then the evidence marshaled for Jesus' divine claims becomes very persuasive.[1] In this chapter we will pursue the best explanation for the identity of Jesus. The best explanation will be internally consistent, will avoid ad hoc claims, will genuinely match the facts at hand and will omit nothing of significance.

Before assessing the logical coherence of the concept of the incarnation, we need to work through the logical possibilities for interpreting Jesus' implicit and explicit claims to deity. The argument for the deity of Jesus is quite ancient and can be put into the form of a disjunctive syllogism.

1. If Jesus claimed to be divine (in addition to being human), but was not divine, he was a bad man and merely human: that is, he was deceived or a deceiver.

2. Jesus was not a bad man and merely human: that is, he was *neither* (a) deceived nor (b) a deceiver.

3. Therefore, Jesus was divine (in addition to being human).

---

[1]Logically speaking, it is possible that the concept of incarnation is logically coherent but not instantiated, such as the concept of a unicorn or a satyr. But we claim that the concept is both coherent and instantiated, since God has come into the world uniquely through Jesus Christ.

C. S. Lewis famously put it this way:

A man who was merely a man and said the sort of things Jesus said would not be a great moral teacher. He would either be a lunatic—on the level with the man who says he is a poached egg—or else he would be the Devil of Hell. You must make your choice. Either this man was, and is, the Son of God: or else a madman or something worse. You can shut Him up for a fool, you can spit at Him and kill Him as a demon; or you can fall at His feet and call Him Lord and God. But let us not come with any patronizing nonsense about His being a great human teacher. He has not left that open to us. He did not intend to.[2]

This claim is put in rhetorically charged terms, but it can be fleshed out carefully. While popular atheist author Christopher Hitchens summarily and caustically rejects this argument, it is extremely strong when presented carefully.[3] It is called the "God or a bad man" argument. The argument trades on the claims and character of Jesus, and seeks to eliminate the possibilities of Jesus being something other than God incarnate.

LEGENDARY CLAIMS

Before assessing the logical options available given that Jesus claimed deity, we must consider two different arguments to the effect that he never claimed to be God incarnate. The first argument can be disposed of quickly, considering the previous two chapters. Some insist that Jesus' divine claims are merely *legendary*, the stuff of pious fiction and not of historical fact. Jesus himself never claimed deity. Rather, this claim was foisted on him by overly zealous disciples who wanted to give him a posthumous metaphysical compliment.

It is true that some merely human religious teachers—who claimed to be nothing more—have been deified or otherwise valorized over time by their rambunctious followers. The Buddha is the prime example, since texts attributing to him any supernatural elements come hundreds of years after his

---

[2]C. S. Lewis, *Mere Christianity* (1943; reprint, New York: Touchstone, 1996), p. 56. Lewis made this basic argument in a few places, but this is the most well-known and well-stated example. See also C. S. Lewis, "What Are We to Make of Jesus Christ?" in *God in the Dock*, ed. Walter Hooper (Grand Rapids: Eerdmans, 1970), pp. 156-60.
[3]Christopher Hitchens, *God Is Not Great: How Religion Poisons Everything* (New York: Twelve Books, 2007), pp. 118-22.

death.[4] However, this process takes many decades or even centuries to occur. As noted in chapter nineteen, the primary documents concerning Jesus were written only a few decades after his death by eyewitnesses or those who consulted eyewitnesses and other reliable sources. We cannot find an original teaching of Jesus in which he is shorn of divine claims, either implicit or explicit. Therefore, the legend option is untenable.

JESUS AS A GURU

Others deny Jesus' claims of incarnation not by questioning the historicity of the Gospels (although they typically find some fault with them) but by reinterpreting them according to a nondualistic or pantheistic worldview. To them, Jesus was a guru, adept or avatar, but not uniquely God incarnate, since the concept of incarnation requires a distinction between God and the creation not allowed by pantheism. Rather, Jesus was a man who awoke to the divinity that was within him and in everyone. As such, he was part of a long line of enlightened beings who transcended their ignorance and affirmed their oneness with a universal and impersonal force, power or consciousness. Popular spiritual writer Deepak Chopra expresses it this way: "Once we see Jesus as a teacher of enlightenment, faith changes its focus. You don't need to have faith in the Messiah or his mission. Instead, you have faith in the vision of higher consciousness."[5] By "higher consciousness," Chopra means an awareness of the universal deity. I have written a book refuting this view, but two broad points will suffice here.[6]

First, pantheistic gurus typically use an esoteric method of teaching that shrouds the meaning of their beliefs in mysteries, paradoxes and riddles. Their words have veiled meanings, and they only reveal the inner secrets to a small group of the initiated, usually through a nonrational mystical experience. But Jesus, on the contrary, taught openly and clearly to all who "had ears to ear." At his trial, Jesus declared:

> "I have spoken openly to the world," Jesus replied. "I always taught in synagogues or at the temple, where all the Jews come together. I said nothing in

---

[4]I addressed this in chap. 20 in connection with mythological stories of Buddha's supposedly miraculous birth.
[5]Deepak Chopra, *The Third Jesus* (New York: Harmony Books, 2008), p. 62.
[6]Douglas Groothuis, *Jesus in an Age of Controversy* (1996; reprint, Eugene, Ore.: Wipf & Stock, 2002). See also Ron Rhodes, *The Counterfeit Christ of the New Age Movement* (Grand Rapids: Baker, 1991).

secret. Why question me? Ask those who heard me. Surely they know what I said." (John 18:20-21)

While the God of Eastern mysticism is beyond thought and language, the God of the Bible speaks and makes himself known through actions and language. It was true that the hardhearted could not fathom his teaching, but he declared the message of the kingdom openly and discussed his beliefs with others freely. There were some cases where people did not understand Jesus' message, but the Gospels went on to explain the meaning to the reader. In no case were the misunderstood teachings pantheistic.[7] Unlike gurus who must initiate their followers through arcane and often noncognitive means (chanting mantras, staring at blank walls), Jesus taught his disciples rationally. When his teachings are propagated by his disciples (in the Acts and the Epistles), they line up with what he himself is recorded as teaching in the Gospels. There is no hidden or secret meaning that must be deciphered by an inner circle. If Jesus really meant to teach an esoteric message that differs completely from what Christianity has always taken it to mean, he was one of the worst teachers in the history of humanity, since for two thousand years he has been taken by his followers (and his critics) to teach monotheism.[8] Any other interpretation is highly unlikely.[9]

Second, Jesus was a rigorously monotheistic Jew.[10] His teaching is steeped in the Hebrew Scriptures, which brook no other God than the one personal, moral and transcendent Creator of heaven and earth. The great creedal affirmation of the Jews was (and is), "Hear, O Israel, the LORD our God, the LORD is one" (Deuteronomy 6:4). God's oneness means that God is the one Lord over creation. God is not one with the universe. Jesus taught his disciples to pray, "Our Father in heaven" (Matthew 6:9), thereby emphasizing God's personality and relationality. Jesus never affirmed that God is the only reality, that all is divine.

---

[7]See Douglas Groothuis, *Unmasking the New Age* (Downers Grove, Ill.: InterVarsity Press, 1986), pp. 146-48.

[8]Peter Kreeft and Ronald K. Tacelli, *Handbook of Christian Apologetics* (Downers Grove, Ill.: InterVarsity Press, 1994), pp. 165-66.

[9]On the fallacies of "esoteric interpretation" see Douglas Groothuis, *Confronting the New Age* (Downer Grove, Ill.: InterVarsity Press, 1988), pp. 87-91.

[10]On Jesus as a monotheist see Douglas Groothuis, *On Jesus* (Belmont, Calif.: Wadsworth, 2003), pp. 37-39, and the discussion in chap. 20 of this book.

JESUS AS A BAD MAN: DECEIVER

We now must consider the various possibilities that Jesus' claims to be God incarnate were false. Perhaps Jesus knew full well he was not "one with the Father" (John 10:30) but claimed to be such nevertheless. If so, Jesus would be a liar of the highest magnitude. He would also have been a very effective liar, since his immediate disciples ended up believing his claims—as have all orthodox Christians ever since—and many went on to be persecuted (John was exiled to Patmos [see Revelation 1]) or killed as a result of confessing Christ without renunciation (see Acts 7, the martyrdom of Stephen). If this were the case, Jesus would have been a colossal moral failure.[11] To explore this option, we need to focus on two questions. First, what possible motive would Jesus have to make such grandiose claims that he knew were false? Second, does this supposed metaphysical lie about his own being comport with what else we know of Jesus from the Gospels?

It is difficult to assign a reason for Jesus to claim deity if he knew himself to be merely mortal. Yet lies are usually told to achieve certain ends. The greater the lie, the greater must be the reason for the lie. To claim oneself divine in ancient Israel was no public relations formula for a successful career. No religious culture in the history of the world has been more militantly monotheistic than the Jews.[12] While there were intimations and clues in the Hebrew Bible that the Messiah would be divine (as pointed out in chap. 20), this was not common knowledge. Worse yet, the Jewish legal penalty for blasphemy was stoning, and we find several instances in the Gospels where people try to stone or otherwise kill Jesus even before his crucifixion (see John 8:58-59).

Moreover, if Jesus' claim to deity was a ruse, it was not very successful for Jesus in terms of money, sex or power. As he said, "The Son of Man has no place to lay his head" (Luke 9:58). As an itinerant rabbi, Jesus was supported by others outside the religious establishment. He had no land or possessions to speak of. He was not even married—which was unusual but not unheard of for religious leaders in that day—and there is no credible

---

[11]David Horner, *"Aut Deus Aut Malus Homo*: A Defense of C. S. Lewis's 'Shocking Alternative,'" in *C. S. Lewis as Philosopher*, ed. David Baggett, Gary R. Habermas and Jerry L. Walls (Downers Grove, Ill.: InterVarsity Press, 2007), p. 73.

[12]Larry Hurtado, *Lord Jesus Christ* (Grand Rapids: Eerdmans, 2005), pp. 27-53.

record of him having any romantic associations.[13] His followers were not, by and large, those of great repute; many of them were infamous for being of low repute (prostitutes, tax collectors and various women, including a Samaritan). The claims and actions of Jesus eventually lead to a scourging and a gruesome cross, not to fame, fortune or hedonistic indulgence. Therefore, the claim that this stupendous lie was told for some ulterior motive fails.

But someone might argue that Jesus simply failed to achieve his goal of becoming famous through lying. He wrongly thought that making a claim to have the authority to forgive sins or to have existed before Abraham as God, or making similar claims, would propel him into fame, fortune, honor or hedonistic reward. But this supposition is at odds with the rest of Jesus' teachings in two ways. First, he was intensely intelligent, reasoning well and never being bested by the best minds of the day.[14] Could someone that bright also be so utterly dense with respect to his self-promotion plan? This is highly implausible. Second, Jesus emphasized truth-telling, honesty and humility in his teachings (see Matthew 5–7). These emphases, however, are absolutely at odds with any theological prevarication about being Yahweh when one is not. Could Jesus be both a great (many would say the greatest) moralist as well as the greatest liar of all time? The question answers itself.

JESUS AS DECEIVED: IDIOSYNCRATIC OR MAD

The idea of Jesus as a liar breaks down into too many pieces of psychological rubble. But another alternative is possible: Jesus was sincere in his theological beliefs about himself, but sincerely wrong. Those who claim this option believe either that (1) he was merely mistaken but otherwise sane or (2) that he was totally insane. In both cases, Jesus would have been a psychological failure.[15] We first take up option 1.

A person might claim that certain geniuses hold very bizarre beliefs in some areas to the point of being delusional yet remain generally sane and

---

[13]This is contrary to the outlandish claims made by Dan Brown in *The Da Vinci Code* (New York: Doubleday, 2003). See Ben Witherington III, *The Gospel Code: Novel Claims About Jesus, Mary Magdalene, and Da Vinci* (Downers Grove, Ill.: InterVarsity Press, 2004), pt. 2.

[14]See Groothuis, *On Jesus*, esp. chaps. 1, 3.

[15]Horner, "*Aut Deus Aut Malus Homo*," p. 74.

competent otherwise.[16] An extremely idiosyncratic genius scientist may hold ridiculous beliefs about himself yet retain the other faculties needed to maneuver through life without being institutionalized. Perhaps Jesus was in the same category. He was a brilliant teacher and reasoned well with his interlocutors. He just happened to be colossally wrong about his own identity, thinking he was divine when he was merely human.

But we need to consider the magnitude of this supposed error. We certainly acknowledge that fallible people—with all their idiosyncrasies—can be good moral teachers. Someone may teach and exemplify virtue and still be *minimally deceived* about minor things, but not about the things that directly impinge on their teaching. However, we would not take someone to be a good *moral* teacher if, for example, she considered Africans and African Americans to be of less moral worth than other races, no matter how brilliantly the teacher may reason on other matters. A fortiori, if a mere man took himself to be almighty God in human form, this would be no small mistake, but a case of *maximal deception*. This magnitude of deception would certainly spill over into many areas, introducing erroneous beliefs and practices across the board.[17]

The scientist's strange beliefs do not affect his focus of intellectual concern. Jesus, on the other hand, focused his teachings (whether moral or theological) on himself, either directly or indirectly. As mentioned in chapter twenty, he spoke with great authority and conviction about matters of ultimate concern, including his own identity and how people responded to his claims. Therefore, if Jesus spoke falsely about himself, it would not be analogous to the scientist's idiosyncratic beliefs. Jesus' claim to have unique authority and supremacy in and over the universe is central to his beliefs and teachings and actions. For example, at the end of the Sermon on the Mount, Jesus claims to be the Lord of history who will determine people's eternal destiny (Matthew 7:21-23). Jesus' teaching cannot be separated from his personhood as the Lord of history.[18] Likewise,

---

[16]This illustration was given to me by a student of mine who heard it from someone she was interviewing for an assignment. I had never considered it before.

[17]I derive the distinction between minimal and maximal deception from Horner, *"Aut Deus Aut Malus Homo,"* p. 77, although I have changed the terms somewhat.

[18]J. Gresham Machen makes this point in "Christ," in *Christianity and Liberalism* (1923; reprint, Grand Rapids: Eerdmans, 2009) against those who want to keep the ethics of Jesus but scuttle his supernatural dimensions.

he affirms that unless we build our lives on his teachings we will not hold up under the stresses of life (Matthew 7:24-29). Jesus offers himself as the source of comfort and rest—not abstract principles—when he says,

> Come to me, all you who are weary and burdened, and I will give you rest. Take my yoke upon you and learn from me, for I am gentle and humble in heart, and you will find rest for your souls. For my yoke is easy and my burden is light. (Matthew 11:28-30)

If Jesus were wrong about this all-encompassing fact of his own identity, his entire worldview would be skewed, thus revealing that he was radically out of touch with reality. As John Montgomery puts it, "What greater retreat from reality is there than a belief in one's divinity, if one is not in fact God?"[19] But Jesus' teaching on love, mercy, justice and character are not radically out of touch with reality.[20] He has been the most influential moral teacher in the history of the world.[21] As the eminent Yale historian Kenneth Scott LaTourette said, "no other life ever lived on this planet has been so potent in the affairs of men."[22] Moreover, he backed this up with a life of radical compassion and courage through multiple miracles that are well-attested.[23] Even non-Christians resonate with many of his claims, as did Gandhi. Therefore, the idea that Jesus was wrong about his deity but right about most all other things—even brilliant on moral matters—is extremely unlikely.

A related objection is that Jesus' moral teaching is all that counts; the question of his divinity is irrelevant. John Beversluis argues that Jesus could be both a good moral teacher and quite wrong about his identity. This is because good moral teaching is independent of the person teaching it.[24] Therefore, the basic disjunction we have been explicating, "God or a bad man," would be a false dichotomy. Jesus could have falsely claimed to

---

[19]John Warwick Montgomery, *History and Christianity* (Downers Grove, Ill.: InterVarsity Press, 1965), p. 64.

[20]Some, like Bertrand Russell, argue that Jesus' belief in hell made him a bad person. I take this up in appendix 1.

[21]See Jaroslav Pelikan, *Jesus Through the Centuries: His Place in the History of Culture* (New Haven, Conn.: Yale University Press, 1985).

[22]Kenneth Scott LaTourette, *The Unquenchable Light* (New York: Harper and Brothers, 1941), p. xi.

[23]See chaps. 19 and 22 on the credibility of Jesus' miracles.

[24]John Beversluis, *C. S. Lewis and the Search for Rational Religion*, 2nd ed. (Amherst, N.Y.: Prometheus Press, 2007), pp. 133-35.

be God and been an otherwise good man (with sound moral teaching). He says that whether or not Jesus was God, "the content of his teachings would be exactly the same."[25]

While it is true that moral teaching (considered as a set of propositions or imperatives) is good or bad independent of who offers the teaching, Beversluis misses the point. The question is not whether we can assess the legitimacy of moral principles apart from those who teach them but whether Jesus could hold to a set of good moral teachings *and* be so deceived about his identity. That is, the *conjunction* of (1) Jesus' false claims to divinity and (2) Jesus' moral teaching is unlikely because Jesus' teaching about morality (and everything else) was so closely tied to his self-understanding. Jesus did not merely teach the golden rule (many moralists have taught something similar, as C. S. Lewis noted). Jesus also affirmed that his teaching was the foundation on which we should build our lives (Matthew 7:24-29) and that he himself was the way to life (Matthew 11:27; John 14:1-6; see also Acts 4:12). So, Beversluis's claim that Jesus' moral teaching would be the same whether or not he were God is false. If he were not God and he taught with the moral authority reserved for God, he would not be a good moral teacher overall, since he would lack the intellectual and moral integrity required of a good moral teacher.

Certainly one can be a mere human and give good moral teachings. What is highly questionable, however, is that one could be a mere human, think oneself divine and still give good moral teaching at the level of Jesus' teaching, and also exhibit all the other strengths of character we find in Jesus: compassion, intelligence, courage, wisdom and so on. Beyond this, people who encountered Jesus in the New Testament never took him to be *merely* a good moral teacher. They had met those before. Jesus occupied another category altogether. As Lewis said, Jesus "was never regarded as a mere moral teacher. He did not produce that effect on any of the people who actually met Him. He produced mainly three effects—Hatred—Terror—Adoration. There was no trace of people expressing mild approval."[26]

The idiosyncratic thesis is itself too idiosyncratic. But perhaps Jesus was deceived about his identity such that it rendered him *fundamentally insane*—radically out of touch with reality. Could he have been a certifi-

---

[25]Ibid., p. 135.
[26]Lewis, "What Are We to Make of Jesus Christ?" p. 158.

able lunatic? Some sad people do make outrageous claims about being
Christ, God or some notable historical figure, such as Napoleon. But
given what I just argued about Jesus' sanity, this option appears even
more unlikely than the idiosyncrasy thesis. Those who suffer from a "divinity complex" exhibit unhealthy character traits that accompany their
metaphysical self-congratulation. These include "egotism, narcissism,
inflexibility, dullness, predictability, inability to understand and love
others as they really are and creatively relate to others."[27] Peter Kreeft
and Ronald Tacelli note that these traits have nothing in common with
Jesus, who was wise, loving and creative.

> He wisely and cannily saw into people's hearts, behind their words [see
> Matthew 12:25; Mark 2:8]. He solved insolvable problems [see Matthew
> 22:15-33]. He also gave totally to others, including his very life [see Mark
> 10:45]. Finally he was the most creative, interesting, unpredictable man
> who ever lived. No one—believer, unbeliever or agnostic—was ever bored
> by him. The common verb predicated of those who met Jesus was *thaumazo*,
> "to wonder" [see Matthew 7:25; Mark 1:22]. Lunatics are not wonderful,
> but Jesus was the most wonderful person in history. If that were lunacy,
> lunacy would be more desirable than sanity.[28]

On one occasion, however, members of Jesus' family doubted his sanity. "Then Jesus entered a house, and again a crowd gathered, so that he
and his disciples were not even able to eat. When his family heard about
this, they went to take charge of him, for they said, 'He is out of his
mind'" (Mark 3:20-21). The crush of circumstance and the controversy
stirred up by Jesus may have overwhelmed his family. They likely feared
that Jesus was exhausted and overwhelmed, being pressed upon on all
sides. So they wondered if he might be on the verge of a nervous breakdown. Besides, they did not yet fully understand his messianic mission.
Jesus said that a prophet is not without honor except in his own country
(Matthew 13:57; Mark 6:4), so this kind of response would not be
unexpected.

---

[27]Kreeft and Tacelli, *Handbook of Christian Apologetics*, p. 159.
[28]Ibid. I have added the Scriptures. On the mental health of Jesus see also Gary Collins's (a
psychologist) interview, "The Psychological Evidence," in Lee Strobel, *The Case for Christ*
(Grand Rapids: Zondervan, 1998), pp. 144-54; and Jon A. Buel and O. Quentin Hyder, "Delusions or Grandeur?" in *Jesus: God, Ghost, or Guru?* (Grand Rapids: Zondervan, 1978).

We do not know with certainty why his family questioned his sanity at this time. However, we do know that this charge is reported only once in Jesus' ministry, and likely near the beginning of it. Moreover, this worry does not represent the settled conviction of any of his family members; Jesus' brother James eventually became a follower of Christ. Mary the mother of Jesus was faithful to Christ at the crucifixion. Therefore, the family's concerns about Jesus' sanity can be seen as a premature and ignorant assessment of a remarkable and unpredictable family member.

John reports that after Jesus had given a teaching, many disputed him and said, "'He is demon-possessed and raving mad. Why listen to him?'" (John 10:20). In Matthew 12:22-29, Jesus is accused of being in league with the devil.[29] The Pharisees attempt to discredit his reputation as an exorcist by charging him with driving out demons by the agency of Beelzebub, the prince of demons. That is, what seem to be godly miracles really issue from a demonic being. In response, Jesus employs a reductio ad absurdum argument. Jesus takes their premise and derives an absurdity:

> Jesus knew their thoughts and said to them, "Every kingdom divided against itself will be ruined, and every city or household divided against itself will not stand. If Satan drives out Satan, he is divided against himself. How then can his kingdom stand? (Matthew 12:25-26)

Put formally:

1. If Satan were divided against himself, his kingdom would be ruined.

2. But Satan's kingdom is not ruined (since demonic activity continues). To think otherwise is absurd.

3. Therefore, (a) Satan does not drive out Satan.

4. Therefore, (b) Jesus cannot free people from Satan by satanic power (by *modus tollens*).

In his own defense Jesus marshals a powerful reductio argument.[30] Further, those who were demon-possessed in the Gospels were invariably sick,

---

[29]In Mark 3:20-30, the accusation of being demon possessed follows the accusation of insanity by family members. In Matthew's account there is no mention of the family's charge of insanity. Matthew probably omitted this charge for some reason, since he relies on Mark quite often.

[30]In fact, in verse 27 he gives another reductio argument that I have not mentioned. See *On Jesus*, pp. 34-35.

self-injuring or out of their minds in some other way. Jesus was nothing like that.[31]

It is also worth noting that the Gospel writers do not shy away from reporting that some thought Jesus was insane. They had such confidence in his overall character that they were willing to record these contrary opinions without fear of tarnishing Jesus' reputation. Historian Will Durant makes this point about the Gospel writers' honesty.

> Despite the prejudices and theological preconceptions of the evangelists, they record many incidents that mere inventors would have concealed—the competition of the apostles for high places in the kingdom, their flight after Jesus' arrest, Peter's denial, the failure of Christ to work miracles in Galilee, *the references of some auditors to his possible insanity*, his early uncertainty as to his mission, his confessions of ignorance as to the future, his moments of bitterness, his despairing cry on the cross; no one reading these scenes can doubt the reality of the figure behind them.[32]

I have set forth a case that Jesus indeed claimed deity and meant it literally. In light of the failed alternatives (myth, guru, liar, deceived or insane),[33] I conclude that Jesus is Lord and God based on the logic of his own testimony, not to mention the witness of those nearest to him.[34]

THE RATIONAL COHERENCE OF THE INCARNATION

Even if we grant the argument for the deity of Jesus, some still complain that the very notion of Jesus as divine and human is logically incoherent. This was the concern of a caller to "The Bible Answer Man" when I was a

---

[31]Some have attacked Jesus' character on other grounds, such as his harsh judgments, his cursing of the fig tree and so on. On this see Benjamin B. Devan and Thomas W. Smythe, "The Character of Jesus Defended," *Christian Apologetics Journal* 5, no. 2 (2006), pp. 109-40.

[32]Will Durant, *Caesar and Christ*, vol. 2, *The Story of Civilization* (New York: Simon & Schuster, 1944), p. 557, emphasis added.

[33]I have not taken seriously the claims made by some UFO cults that Jesus was a space alien. This claim has no support intrinsic to the Bible and lacks any extrabiblical reasoning as well. Nevertheless, some hold this view. For a refutation of this see Kenneth Samples, *Without a Doubt* (Grand Rapids: Baker, 2004), pp. 116-17.

[34]Stephen T. Davis (pro) and Daniel Howard-Snyder (con) have debated the merits of this argument in considerable detail (see Stephen T. Davis, "Jesus: Mad, Bad, or God?" in *Christian Philosophical Theology* [New York: Oxford University Press, 2006]; Daniel Howard-Snyder, "Was Jesus Mad, Bad, or God . . . Or Only Mistaken?" *Faith and Philosophy* 21 [2004]: 456-79; Stephen T. Davis, "The Mad/Bad/God Trilemma: A Reply to Daniel Howard-Snyder," *Faith and Philosophy* 21 [2004]: 480-92).

guest some years ago. While John Hick denies the incarnation, he rightly says that "the orthodox task is to spell out in an intelligible way the idea of someone having both a fully divine nature, i.e. having all the essential divine attributes, and at the same time a fully human nature, i.e. having all the essential human attributes."[35] Hick believes that classical orthodoxy cannot meet the challenge and therefore ends up with an incoherent doctrine.[36] What can be said about this and the related claim that the Trinity is logically incoherent?

The specific metaphysics of Jesus as God incarnate was worked out over several centuries through the creeds and councils of the church. The most mature formulation of the doctrine is contained in the statement of the Council of Chalcedon in A.D. 451. All three branches of Christendom (Orthodox, Roman Catholic and Protestant) affirm this creed. Before we consider whether the notion of the incarnation is logically coherent, we need to consider this creed:

> Therefore, following the holy fathers, we all with one accord teach men to acknowledge one and the same Son, our Lord Jesus Christ, at once complete in Godhead and complete in manhood, truly God and truly man, consisting also of a reasonable soul and body; of one substance with the Father as regards his Godhead, and at the same time of one substance with us as regards his manhood; like us in all respects, apart from sin; as regards his Godhead, begotten of the Father before the ages, but yet as regards his manhood begotten, for us men and for our salvation, of Mary the Virgin, the God-bearer; one and the same Christ, Son, Lord, Only-begotten, recognized in two natures, without confusion, without change, without division, without separation; the distinction of natures being in no way annulled by the union, but rather the characteristics of each nature being preserved and coming together to form one person and subsistence, not as parted or separated into two persons, but one and the same Son and Only-begotten God the Word, Lord Jesus Christ; even as the prophets from earliest times spoke of him, and our Lord Jesus Christ himself taught us, and the creed of the fathers has handed down to us.

---

[35]John Hick, *The Metaphor of God Incarnate: Christology in a Pluralistic Age* (Louisville: Westminster John Knox, 1994), p. 48.

[36]Ibid., p. 178. For a critique of Hicks's specific charge, see Paul D. Adams, "The Mystery of the Incarnation," in *The Mystery of God Incarnate: An Analysis and Critique of John Hick's Christology* (master's thesis, Denver Seminary, 1994).

Chalcedon responded to a variety of christological options in order to preserve the biblical teaching in a conceptually tight and rich manner. We cannot explore all the details of this affirmation.[37] What is important to note is that Chalcedon affirmed the true humanity and true deity of Jesus in one person. In so doing, a variety of heresies were avoided.[38] The relationship of Jesus' divine and human natures is called the *hypostatic union*, which essentially means that Jesus is one person with two natures.

THE INCARNATION AS PARADOX

However, some, such as Hick, have argued that the properties of deity and the properties of humanity could never be conjoined in one person. Consider the differing natures of God and humans:

1. God is eternal (having no beginning), self-existent, immaterial, not limited in power (omnipotence), knowledge (omniscience) or presence (omnipresence).

2. Humans are temporal (having a beginning), contingent, material (or at least partially so) and limited in power, knowledge and presence.

The charge is that one being cannot possess both divine and human attributes, since these attributes are antithetical. To oversimplify somewhat: humans are finite and God is infinite. The infinite cannot be united in one being with the finite because this would produce contradictory properties in one subject. Therefore, the idea of Jesus as equally divine and human is necessarily false. It is as contradictory as a square circle.

Some Christian thinkers, such as Søren Kierkegaard in *Philosophical Fragments*, have embraced the incarnation as an irresolvable paradox. He called it "the absolute paradox" and a necessary offense to human reason.[39]

---

[37]For a fascinating study on the wide-ranging implications of Chalcedon, see Rousas John Rushdoony, *The Foundations of Social Order: Studies in the Creed and Councils of the Early Church* (Vallecito, Calif.: Chalcedon, 2003). For a detailed theological assessment of Chalcedon and developments leading up to it, see Millard Erickson, "The Development of Incarnational Christology. (1) To the Counsel of Chalcedon," in *The Word Became Flesh: An Incarnational Christology* (Grand Rapids: Baker, 1991).

[38]For a handy summary of the Christological heresies, see Kenneth Samples, *Without a Doubt* (Grand Rapids: Baker, 2004), pp. 130-31. On the "metaphysics of Chalcedon," see Erickson, *Word Became Flesh*, pp. 513-16.

[39]Søren Kierkegaard, *Philosophical Fragments*, trans. Edna Hong and Walter Hong (Princeton, N.J.: Princeton University Press, 1985).

We hold to it by passionate faith, not because it is reasonable. If it were reasonable, there would be no occasion for faith, given Kierkegaard's fideism. I heard a preacher declare that "Jesus was a hundred percent God and a hundred percent man. Don't try to understand it. Just believe it." We rejected fideism in chapter three, but two comments are forthcoming.

First, if we allow ourselves to affirm what appears to be a logical contradiction (Jesus is both finite and infinite), labeling it a *paradox* is too kind. A paradox appears contradictory, but need not be. When Jesus said that "many who are first will be last, and many who are last will be first" (Matthew 19:30), he was not affirming a contradiction such that a person possesses incompatible properties. Rather, those who pridefully put themselves first have no moral priority. But those who are humble take moral priority over the proud. Jesus often employed paradoxes as a pedagogical tool. However, to literally predicate both A and non-A of anything with no resolution in sight is another matter. Unless some possible resolution is available, the charge of *contradiction* rings true. As Gordon Clark said, a paradox is "a charley horse between the ears."[40] It needs to be worked out, not lived with.

If we affirm a hopeless paradox (which amounts to a contradiction) at the very heart of Christian faith, we lose more than a coherent account of the incarnation; we also lose noncontradiction as a necessary and negative test for evaluating *other* worldviews (see chap. 3). If Christians confess an utter paradox that is exempt from logical analysis, then they have no basis to criticize other worldviews as contradictory, which is a necessary element of negative apologetics. Such apologetic suicide must be rejected if we yearn to outthink the world for Christ.

Second, if we affirm apparent contradictions, we jeopardize the possibility of acquiring any knowledge of God. The laws of logic are necessary preconditions for all knowledge (justified, true belief). If God can reveal himself as being both A and non-A, God has revealed nothing at all, because nothing can possess incompatible properties, given the law of noncontradiction. Without the knowledge of God, apologetics becomes impossible—as does theology, biblical ethics and more. Therefore, we must resist this entailment.

---

[40]Gordon Clark, quoted in John Robbins, *Trinity Review*, March-April 1986, p. 8.

The paradox of the God-man is better taken as a hopeful paradox—or perhaps as a puzzle, a unique and arresting claim about a being whose identity has no clear analogy with anything else in existence. This sense of Christ's uniqueness comports with the biblical affirmation that the incarnation is singular, unrepeatable, unparalleled and awe-inspiring. That God Almighty would visit earth as a fetus who became an infant who "grew in wisdom and stature, and in favor with God and man" (Luke 2:52) is remarkable indeed. To quote Chesterton: "Omnipotence and impotence, or divinity and infancy, do definitely make a sort of epigram which a million repetitions cannot turn into a platitude. It is not unreasonable to call it unique."[41] The incarnation is no commonplace. When speaking to a non-Christian man about Christianity many years ago, he asked, "Why would God reveal himself in such an awkward way?" The word *awkward* captures the disarming and striking nature of the incarnation quite well, and it stimulated further apologetic discussion.

Instead of seeing an irresolvable paradox (or even absurdity), Christian philosophers and theologians have attempted to erase the apparent contradiction while retaining a sense of holy mystery regarding Jesus as the God-man. Before considering these efforts, we should note that establishing a truth claim as contradictory is no easy matter. So long as there is any *possible* way to defend against the charge of contradiction, the charge fails. This is because a contradiction is *necessarily* false. Therefore, if one can affirm Chalcedonian orthodoxy and provide a possible way of logically reconciling Jesus' divinity and humanity, the charge of contradiction fails. Let us consider this.

While some think that the gap between God and humans is too great for an incarnation to occur, we should understand that the Bible never presents God as "totally Other" (as do Kierkegaard and Karl Barth). God is transcendent in his omnipotence, omniscience and omnipresence, but God is also personal: a moral agent who knows, intends, feels and acts. In this sense we are like God with respect to personality, but in a finite way.[42] We are finite agents who know, intend, feel and act. This helps lay the foundation for the incarnation because it is not unseemly for a personal

[41]G. K. Chesterton, *The Everlasting Man* (New York: Image Books, 1925), p. 173.
[42]See Francis A. Schaeffer, *The God Who Is There*, 30th anniv. ed. (Downers Grove, Ill.: Inter-Varsity Press, 1998), pp. 118-22.

God, who made humans in his own image, to take on that very image for his once-for-all mission for his creation.[43] But we need to elaborate on how the incarnation could be coherent.

THE METAPHYSICS OF THE INCARNATION

The incarnation does not mean that Jesus possesses *only* divine attributes and *only* human attributes. These claims are contradictory and are, therefore, necessarily false. For example, an object cannot be only spherical and only square. However, an object could be a circle and have a square within it. As Gordon Lewis and Bruce Demarest write:

> As a circle encompasses a square the two figures together form a more complex geometrical design. The whole complex pattern has two natures with both the attributes of the circle and the attributes of the square. We need not contradict ourselves in reference to the complex design if we affirm that some of the attributes of the complex design are those of a circle and some those of a square. The holistic unity of the design is not thereby divided. The two "natures" need not be confused. The circle remains a circle; the square within it remains a square. The one "circle-square design" has two distinct natures.[44]

The relationship between Jesus' deity and humanity is better understood as a subcontrary relationship of assertions, not a contradictory relationship of assertions (which would be necessarily false). In subcontrary relationships between statements, neither the denial nor the affirmation is universal. If we claim that (1) "all of Jesus' attributes are divine" and (2) "some of Jesus' attributes are not divine," statements 1 and 2 contradict each other. They cannot both be true. But the two statements (3) "some of my students are from Africa" and (4) "some of my students are not from Africa" cohere with each other because they stand in a subcontrary—and not a contradictory—relationship. Given this background we can argue that Jesus possesses divine and human attributes in a coherent and subcontrary arrangement.

> In a subcontrary relationship neither the affirmation nor the denial is universal, hence both may be true. For example: "Some of the attributes of a person are physical" and "Some of the attributes of a person are nonphysi-

---

[43]See Erickson, *Word Became Flesh*, pp. 554-58.
[44]Gordon R. Lewis and Bruce A. Demarest, *Integrative Theology* (Grand Rapids: Zondervan, 1990), 2:349.

cal." Similarly, "Some attributes of the person of Jesus Christ are divine and some are human." Neither the divine set of attributes nor the human set of attributes is said to be all that he has, and so neither affirmation is necessarily false.[45]

Let me expand on the idea that human beings are both material and immaterial, since it helps explain the logic of the incarnation.[46] Humans have both a material and an immaterial nature, but they are not thereby two persons. My brain weighs a certain amount, but my mind weighs nothing. This is not a contradiction, because I am speaking of two different aspects of my personhood.[47] This analogy is not perfect, since the incarnation is a singular and unparalleled fact that differs from the merely human relationship of body and mind (substance dualism). Both my body and mind are finite. There is no union of the divine and the human in my person, as in the case of the incarnation, since I am entirely human. Nevertheless, this analogy helps explain how Jesus' deity and humanity can coexist in the same person without contradiction. I am two substances (mind and body) that nevertheless make up my one person.

A few more qualifications may be of assistance. We can speak of the incarnation with respect to each distinct nature (divine or human) without contradiction. That is, Jesus qua human got tired, but Jesus qua God did not. Jesus qua human was born of Mary, but Jesus qua God was not (having existed eternally). Yet there is no contradiction herein since two distinct natures are being referred to (which, nonetheless, are hypostatically united in one person). Consider again the mind-body relationship: If I consider myself qua body, I have a certain skin and hair color; if I consider myself qua mind, I do not, since immaterial substances do not have color.

In pondering the coherence of the incarnation, it is also useful to distinguish between being *merely* human and being *fully* human with respect to Christ's identity. To be *merely* human is to possess the properties necessary and sufficient to humanity—some of which were adumbrated earlier—and to possess nothing but properties attributable to a human nature. But Jesus was *fully* human, not *merely* human. That is, in addition to having a genuine human nature (with its defining properties), he pos-

---

[45]Ibid., p. 350.
[46]I dealt with this issue at length in the first half of chap. 17.
[47]These are, in fact, two different *substances*.

sessed a divine nature (with its defining properties).

We may also distinguish *common properties* from *essential properties*. For example, it is *common* (in fact, universal as of 2010) for humans to be born on earth or in its atmosphere (such as on an airplane). But this property of *being earth-born* is not *essential* to being a human. A human might be born on a space station or on another planet. Yet he or she would still be human. While it is *common* for a human to possess only human properties, it is not *essential* to possess only human properties to be human. Apart from Jesus it is *common* (in fact, universal) for humans not to have a divine nature. Yet it is not *essential* to being a human not to have a divine nature. But, of course, possessing both a divine and human nature is exemplified only in Jesus Christ.[48]

We now need to consider how Jesus could retain his divine attributes while becoming a truly human being. For the incarnation to be "God with us," Jesus could not have relinquished his divine attributes, as some have claimed (extreme kenoticism). In Philippians 2:5-11, Paul speaks of Jesus' being willing to "empty himself" ("made himself nothing" NIV) in order to take the form of a human servant. This is referred to as the "kenosis," taken from the Greek word *ekenōsen* in Philippians 2:7 ("emptied himself"). Jesus did not forfeit his divine *attributes* in the incarnation. If he had, there would have been no incarnation, because deity would have been left behind. Rather, Christ left behind his preincarnate *position*—the full manifestation of his divine power and glory with the Father and the Spirit. And in so doing, Christ temporarily suspended *the employment* of some of his divine attributes, but without ontologically *losing* these attributes. For example, during his prime as a basketball player, Michael Jordon might play a pickup basketball game with some junior high children in Chicago. In order to have fun with lesser players, he would voluntarily *suspend the use* of some of his exemplary basketball skills. He would continue to *possess* those powers, but they would be held in check in order to play basketball with the children. However, at times Jordan might decide to dazzle the kids by showing his true

---

[48]The distinctions of this paragraph are most fully developed in Thomas V. Morris, *The Logic of God Incarnate* (Ithaca, N.Y.: Cornell University Press, 1986). These ideas are summarized in Thomas V. Morris, "Rationality and the Christian Revelation," in *Christian Faith and Practice in the Modern World*, ed. Mark A. Noll and David F. Wells (Grand Rapids: Eerdmans, 1988), pp. 120-31; and Thomas V. Morris, *Our Idea of God: An Introduction to Philosophical Theology* (Downers Grove, Ill.: InterVarsity Press, 1991), pp. 159-65.

stuff. Similarly, Jesus would sometimes declare that he had forgiven a person's sins (Mark 2:1-10) or would receive worship from his followers (John 20:24-28). These are both uniquely divine prerogatives.[49]

The debate over the coherence of Christ's identity as divine and human has generated some very sophisticated philosophical and theological perspectives.[50] But for our purposes it is sufficient to note that there is nothing necessarily contradictory in the idea of the incarnation; that is, there are plausible ways of resolving the paradox. To resolve the charge that the incarnation is logically incoherent we need only offer an account of the incarnation that is both biblically orthodox (Chalcedonian formulation) and logically possible. Further, we should not be repulsed by the idea of the incarnation, because it is, when received humbly, the best news possible. God himself descended to earth as one of us to rescue us from our fallen plight. This is no mere philosophical puzzle, calling out to logicians for resolution. This is God among us, full of grace and truth (John 1:14).

CONCLUSION: LOGIC AND THE LOGOS

This chapter has set forth the case that the most rational assessment of Jesus' claim to deity is that he was correct in his titanic assertion. As the Gospel of John reveals, "The Word [Logos] was with God and the Word was God" (John 1:1). Some still cavil that the very notion of the incarnation is logically incoherent or hopelessly paradoxical, since deity and humanity could never conjoin. But when carefully stated and explained, the idea of the incarnation is shown to be logically coherent, awe-inspiring, unique and wonderful for errant mortals in need of divine rescue. There is, then, good reason to accept Jesus' deity as the best explanation for his words and behavior, and no reason to reject the incarnation as logically impossible.

But there is yet one more christological credential to consider that further elevates Jesus above all of the players on history's stage—his resurrection from the dead. To this we now turn.

---

[49]I have not addressed the interesting question of the consciousness of Jesus as the God-man, but coherent and biblical models are available (see Richard Swinburne, *Was Jesus God?* [New York: Oxford University Press, 2008], pp. 41-47; and Morris, *Logic of God Incarnate*, p. 102-7).

[50]For more on the metaphysics of the incarnation, see Erickson, *Word Became Flesh*, pp. 507-76, and David Werther, "Incarnation," in *The Internet Encyclopedia of Philosophy* (2009) <www.iep.utm.edu/incarnat>.

The Resurrection of Jesus

THUS FAR, IN ADDITION TO THE PREVIOUS apologetic for rational theism, we have argued that the New Testament books that speak of Jesus are historically trustworthy given reasonable standards of evidence. We have also inspected the claims and credentials of Jesus, arguing that he singles himself out of the crowd as the God-man. Yet a necessary and crowning credential of Christ remains to be considered: his supernatural resurrection from the dead in space-time history.

THE SIGNIFICANCE OF THE RESURRECTION

Of all the world's religions Christianity alone purports to be based on the resurrection of its divine founder. No other religion or worldview makes such an audacious and consequential claim. Throughout the Gospels, Jesus himself predicts his own betrayal, death and resurrection: "From that time on Jesus began to explain to his disciples that he must go to Jerusalem and suffer many things at the hands of the elders, the chief priests and the teachers of the law, and that he must be killed and on the third day be raised to life" (Matthew 16:21; see also Matthew 12:40; John 2:19-22).

While some assert that Christianity stole the idea of resurrection from various mystery religions featuring a dying and rising figure, the Gospel accounts breathe a far different air—the air of factual actuality, of datable, verifiable history.[1] The heroes or gods of the mystery religions are tied to

---

[1]A recent case is the film *The God Who Wasn't There* (2005), which claims that Jesus did not exist and that all the Gospels' themes (including the resurrection) were stolen from mystery religions. For a thorough response to this line of attack—more thorough, indeed, than the attack itself deserves—see Paul Rhodes Eddy and Gregory Boyd, *The Jesus Legend* (Grand Rapids: Baker, 2007); and Gary R. Habermas, "A Summary Critique: Questioning the Existence of Jesus," *The Christian Research Journal* 22, no. 3 (2000): 54-56.

vegetative patterns, a mythologizing of nature rather than the events of history. They occur in a kind of dream world. The deities are, according to Bruce Metzger, "nebulous figures of an imaginary past."[2] They were plainly not even meant to be historical. J. N. D. Anderson observes, "There is all the difference in the world between the rising or re-birth of a deity which symbolizes the coming of spring (and the re-awakening of nature) and the resurrection 'on the third day' of an historical person."[3] The early church could have drawn no inspiration from such stories in their accounts of the risen Christ and the empty tomb, nor were mystery religions well established during the time of Jesus or the early church.[4]

The resurrection of Jesus is at the center of the Christian worldview and Christian devotion. The Gospels do not end with the death of Jesus but speak of an empty tomb, of his appearances and of a commission by the risen Jesus.[5] Without Easter there is no Christianity, as Paul makes abundantly plain in a letter that took up a dispute in the church at Corinth about the resurrection of the dead.

> If Christ has not been raised, our preaching is useless and so is your faith. More than that, we are then found to be false witnesses about God, for we have testified about God that he raised Christ from the dead. But he did not raise him if in fact the dead are not raised. For if the dead are not raised, then Christ has not been raised either. And if Christ has not been raised, your faith is futile; you are still in your sins. Then those also who have fallen asleep in Christ are lost. If only for this life we have hope in Christ, we are of all people most to be pitied. (1 Corinthians 15:14-19)

If Christ has not been raised (1) Christian preaching is useless; (2)

---

[2]Bruce Metzger, *Historical and Literary Studies: Pagan, Jewish, and Christian* (Grand Rapids: Eerdmans, 1968), p. 13, quoted in James R. Edwards, *Is Jesus the Only Savior?* (Grand Rapids: Eerdmans, 2005), p. 136.

[3]J. N. D. Anderson, *Christianity and Comparative Religion* (Downers Grove, Ill.: InterVarsity Press, 1971), p. 38.

[4]See Edwards, *Is Jesus the Only Savior?* pp. 135-36. Although I cannot develop it here, C. S. Lewis held that the incarnation fulfilled not only the prophecies of the Hebrew Bible but the mythological yearning for redemption intimated by the tales of dying and rising gods in pagan literature. He held that the incarnation and resurrection were truly historical but that in Jesus Christ "myth became fact" (C. S. Lewis, "Myth Became Fact," in *Christian Reflections* [Grand Rapids: Eerdmans, 1970]). On the events in Lewis's life that led him to this conclusion, see David Downing, *The Most Reluctant Convert: C. S. Lewis's Journey to Faith* (Downers Grove, Ill.: InterVarsity Press, 2002), pp. 146-47.

[5]The Gospel of Mark ends with the women wondering over the empty tomb. The verses concerning Christ's resurrection (Mark 16:9-20) are of questionable textual integrity.

Christian faith is useless; (3) Christians are false witnesses about God; (4) Christian faith is futile; (5) Christians are unforgiven and left in their sins; (6) those who have died in Christian hope are lost; and (7) those who hope in Christ are supremely pitiable, since their hope ends with this life.[6] In other words, Christianity without a risen Christ is pointless.

The resurrection of Christ, if true, insures that life under the sun is not meaningless, that death is not the end and that humans who rightly relate themselves to God in Christ can become agents of the kingdom of God now and eventually thrive in a restored universe without curse and without end (Matthew 6:33; Revelation 21–22). Rather than appealing to vague hopes of some "survival" after death, Christianity roots its hope for the future in an event in the past: the resurrection of Jesus. This give the Christian confidence for today and tomorrow. In fact, the entire world has been transformed through the resurrection, as N. T. Wright highlights:

> The resurrection of Jesus offers itself, to the student of history or science no less than the Christian or the theologian, not as on odd event within the world as it is but the utterly characteristic, prototypical, and foundational event within the world as it has begun to be. It is not an absurd event within the old world but the symbol and starting point of a new world.[7]

The earliest preaching after the death of Jesus made the resurrection its lynchpin, its fulcrum and center of gravity (see Acts 2:22-24). What was unique and consequential about the first Christian witness is not so much its ethical teaching, but an event that exalted its founder and gave his followers new meaning and new mission for life.[8] N. T. Wright observes, "There is no evidence for a form of early Christianity in which the resurrection was not a central belief. Nor was this belief, as it were, bolted on to Christianity at the edge. It was the central driving force, informing the whole movement."[9] When Paul preaches to Greek philosophers in Athens, he first speaks of the nature of God as Creator and

---

[6]The inspiration for this itemization comes from Peter Kreeft and Ronald Tacelli, *Handbook of Christian Apologetics* (Downers Grove, Ill.: InterVarsity Press, 1994), pp. 176-77.

[7]N. T. Wright, *Surprised by Hope: Rethinking Heaven, the Resurrection, and the Mission of the Church* (San Francisco: HarperOne, 2008), p. 67.

[8]C. S. Lewis, *Miracles: A Preliminary Study* (1947; reprint, San Francisco: HarperSanFrancisco, 1996), pp. 233-35.

[9]N. T. Wright, *The Challenge of Jesus* (Downers Grove, Ill.: InterVarsity Press, 1999), p. 133.

Lord of the universe, and of some points of contact between Christianity and Greek thought. He then cites the resurrection as the decisive factor in God's relationship to humanity: God commands everyone to repent and "has set a day when he will judge the world with justice by the man he has appointed. He has given proof of this to everyone by raising him from the dead" (Acts 17:30-31).

Paul attests that Jesus' resurrection was "proof" of God's authority and the judgment. The resurrection is the unifying doctrine of New Testament theology.[10] But our concern is with its apologetic significance. While many have claimed that this event can only be believed by faith apart from any historical evidence, this chapter will marshal arguments for the reality of this event and will take seriously any claims to the contrary. As such, we will pursue the best explanation for the biblical data: the account that makes the most sense of all the germane facts at hand.

THEISM AND THE RESURRECTION OF JESUS

The resurrection of Jesus is part of a theistic worldview. It is the supremely significant event in providential history. Jesus' resurrection from the dead is explained on the basis of a supernatural event brought about by God. This is the repeated affirmation in the preaching in Acts and elsewhere: God raised Jesus from the dead (Acts 2:24; 3:15, 26; 5:30; 10:40; 13:30, 34; see also Romans 4:24; 7:4; 10:9; 1 Corinthians 15:15; Ephesians 2:6; Colossians 2:12; 1 Peter 1:21).

If a convincing case can be given for theism, the probability of miracles in general, and the resurrection in particular, is increased. If a supernatural Perfect Being, Creator, Designer and Lawgiver exists, that being could intervene in history miraculously. In other words, if our background belief is a well-established theism, we will come to the historical evidence for the resurrection of Jesus with a more open attitude than would an atheist or agnostic. Antony Flew admitted as much when he wrote, "Certainly given some beliefs about God, the occurrence of the resurrection does become enormously more likely."[11]

---

[10]See Gary Habermas, *The Risen Jesus and Future Hope* (Lanham, Md.: Rowman & Littlefield, 2003), pp. viii-xiii. See also Richard Swinburne, "The Significance of the Resurrection," in *The Resurrection of God Incarnate* (New York: Oxford University Press, 2003).

[11]Antony Flew, quoted from personal correspondence to Gary Habermas in *Did Jesus Rise from the Dead? The Resurrection Debate*, ed. Terry L. Miethe (New York: Harper & Row, 1987), p. 39.

It is possible for an atheist to be so impressed with the historical evidence for Jesus' resurrection that he converts from theism and believes in the resurrection all at once. The apologetic methods of John Warwick Montgomery and Gary Habermas emphasize the resurrection as the main line of evidence for Christianity (although neither of them denies the legitimacy of natural theology).[12] However, I have here tried to make a cogent case for theism before staking out particular Christian claims.[13] As Richard Swinburne says, if there is "evidence giving substantial probability to the existence of God," then we have antecedent evidence for an incarnation. He rightly chides biblical scholars for approaching New Testament texts without taking this background evidence into account.[14] We shall find that even though a majority of critical New Testament scholars agree on several basic facts that are best explained by the resurrection, they typically pull back from affirming the resurrection. This is not because the evidence is weak but because of a precommitment to methodological naturalism in historical explanation—that is, the position that historians qua historians must never admit a supernatural explanation for anything.[15] Yet, if theism is well established philosophically and scientifically, then this conceptual discrimination is uncalled for.

ARE MIRACLES CREDIBLE?

Before we look at the claim that Jesus rose from the dead in history, we need to address some of the arguments that miracle claims are untrustworthy in principle. To do this, we will discuss the biblical meaning of miracle and rebut charges by David Hume that miracle stories are never believable.

---

[12]John Warwick Montgomery, *Tractatus Logico-Theologicus* (Bonn: Verlag für Kultur und Wissenschaft, 2002); and his *Where Is History Going? A Christian Response to Secular Philosophies of History* (Minneapolis: Bethany Fellowship, 1969), chaps. 2-3. See Habermas, *Risen Jesus*, chaps. 1-2.

[13]In this respect, the overall strategy is more similar to the massive apologetic project of Richard Swinburne, who wrote several volumes defending theism before publishing his entire book on the incarnation and resurrection. His apologetic strategy is summarized in Richard Swinburne, "The Vocation of a Natural Theologian," in *Philosophers Who Believe*, ed. Kelly James Clark (Downers Grove, Ill.: InterVarsity Press, 1994).

[14]Swinburne, *Resurrection of God Incarnate*, p. 30; see also, Douglas R. Geivett, "The Epistemology of Resurrection Belief," in *The Resurrection of Jesus: Dominic John Crossan and N. T. Wright in Dialogue*, ed. John Dominic Crossan, N. T. Wright and Robert B. Stewart (Minneapolis: Fortress, 2006), pp. 93-105.

[15]This parallels the dogma of methodological naturalism that infects biology as well, as was noted in chap. 13.

A biblical miracle is an act of divine agency whereby a supernatural effect is produced for the purpose of manifesting God's kingdom on earth.[16] Biblically, miracles are signs of the in-breaking of God's kingdom. They are never merely extravagant or spectacular episodes, but rather reveal God's supernatural character.

Deists have argued that belief in miracles is tantamount to claiming that God botched the original version of creation and now must monkey with it in order to bring it up to speed. This would not be worthy of God.[17] But this reductio ad absurdum argument fails. Biblically, God ordained a good world that operated according to natural laws. Yet that world fell into rebellion and sin against God and his good gifts. As part of God's strategy to reestablish contact and fellowship with humans, God sometimes intervenes miraculously. Yet this too was part of God's plan and is executed with infinite wisdom. Miracles do not compensate for an original plan gone wrong; rather, they are part of God's unfolding providence. The world is not a defective machine that God needs to fix; it is more like an instrument that he plays and retunes when necessary.[18]

The philosophical discussion over the laws of nature is a somewhat vexed topic.[19] But we can cut to the chase by highlighting what is at issue. A law of nature describes the normal pattern of events in the universe, which can be described in terms of physics, chemistry and biology.[20] A law of nature describes the basic properties of physical objects in relationship to one another.[21] A miracle is an event that is inexplicable on the basic of natural laws but

---

[16]I do not take up the issue of miracles occurring outside those recorded in the Bible, although I believe that they have continued to occur through history and today by the power of God. See Craig Keener, *Gift and Giver: The Holy Spirit for Today* (Grand Rapids: Baker Academic, 2001).

[17]See James W. Sire, *The Universe Next Door: A Basic Worldview Catalog*, 5th ed. (Downers Grove, Ill.: InterVarsity Press, 2009), pp. 51-52.

[18]William Dembski, *The Design Revolution* (Downers Grove, Ill.: InterVarsity Press, 2004), p. 149. The retuning may be to put the world back in tune, given the results of the Fall, or to specially tune it for a different kind of music, as when guitars use special tunings.

[19]See William Lane Craig, *Reasonable Faith*, 3rd ed. (Wheaton, Ill.: Crossway, 2008), pp. 259-63.

[20]This does not rule out the detection of intelligent causes, which do not fit under the category of either chance or natural law (see chap. 12).

[21]But even these natural regularities are the normal ways in which God upholds and governs the universe. On divine conservation see Frank McCann, "Divine Conservation," in *Guide to the Philosophy of Religion*, ed. Phillip L. Quinn and Charles Taliaferro (New York: Blackwell, 1997), pp. 306-12.

is attributable to a supernatural cause. As Flew says, "A miracle is something which would never have happened had nature, as it were, been left to its own devices."[22] Objects act in ways not possible, given the existence of natural forces working by themselves. When Jesus raised Lazarus from the dead (John 11), he performed an act otherwise impossible, since those who are dead stay dead—*all things being equal*. But if there is a God who is able to intervene supernaturally in history, all things are not always equal. God may act in ways that transcend the causal powers of nature.

The formulation of this last claim is important. I did not say that God may *contradict* or *overturn* or *suspend* or *violate* the laws of nature. Miracles are often defined in this way, but this prejudices the case against them, since it seems to undermine the validity of natural laws. David Hume famously defined a miracle as "a violation of the laws of nature."[23] But miracles do not break natural laws. The day Christ raised Lazarus, people all over the world were still dying and staying dead. The law of nature had not changed. But natural laws speak only to natural events. Supernatural events are outside of their purview.

Another example may help clarify this point that miracles do not break natural laws. The Bible speaks of an ax head that floated at the command of a prophet (2 Kings 6:1-7). Given the laws of gravity and buoyancy, iron ax heads do not float; they sink. In fact, given the configuration of the cosmos, it is *physically* impossible for an ax head to float. But it is not impossible for a supernatural agent to exercise power outside of the natural realm to make the ax head levitate (as it were) and so have the appearance of floating.[24] As C. S. Lewis put it, "The divine art of miracles is not an art of suspending the pattern to which events conform but of feeding new events into the pattern."[25]

HUME'S ARGUMENT AGAINST MIRACLES

David Hume famously argues against miracles in two basic ways.[26] First,

---

[22]Antony Flew, "Miracles," in *The Encyclopedia of Philosophy*, ed. Paul Edwards (New York: Macmillan, 1967), 5:346.

[23]David Hume, "Of Miracles," in *Writings on Religion*, ed. Antony Flew (Chicago, Ill.: Open Court, 1992), p. 68. This was first published in *An Enquiry Concerning Human Understanding* (1751).

[24]I owe the germ of this example to Keith Yandell, who mentioned it in a lecture many years ago.

[25]Lewis, *Miracles*, p. 81

[26]Hume, "Of Miracles," pp. 63-88. I address a third way below.

he gives an in-principle argument against miracles by claiming that belief in miracles is never intellectually justified because it is always more probable that the purported miracles can be explained naturally. Hume does not argue that miracles are metaphysically impossible, but that no amount of evidence could ever ground belief that a miracle occurred. Second, Hume argues that all miracle claims are based on the superstitious misunderstandings of "ignorant and barbarous nations."[27] Their testimonies are not credible, so they should not be believed.

Hume's critique, long (but not universally) hailed as definitively nailing the coffin shut on miracles, has been subjected to intense philosophical scrutiny in recent years and has lost much of its previous prestige.[28] I cannot exhaustively critique Hume here, but a few comments suffice.

Hume's in-principle argument—that we should never believe a miracle claim—would render unknowable a very important class of events, if indeed these events occur. The claim "X may occur, but we are never justified in believing X" is not axiomatic; it needs special support to be sustained. But if God exists, miracles are then possible, although infrequent. The question is whether there is reliable evidence by which to determine that a miracle has occurred. The fact that a miracle is initially improbable does not render all testimony to miracles moot and mute. It is improbable that anyone will be dealt a perfect poker hand three times in a row, but if we have evidence that this has occurred, there is no reason to deny it simply because it is improbable.

The *general* probability that a miracle will occur is low, since they are infrequent. However, we must consider the *conditional* probability in order to assess a miracle claim rationally.[29] Conditional probability assesses all the pertinent evidence for a claim. Consider a nonmiraculous claim. It is vastly improbable that any given person will run a four-minute mile, since this feat of athleticism is rare. However, it is not improbable that an American Olympian runner will run a four-minute mile, since he has the ability

[27]Hume, *Writings on Religion*, p. 72. There was racism inherent in Hume's remarks about the incredulity of ancient folk (see Charles Taliaferro and Anders Hendrickson, "Hume's Racism and His Case Against the Miraculous," *Philosophia Christi* 4, no. 2 [2003]: 427-42).
[28]See, for example, John Earman, *Hume's Abject Failure* (New York: Oxford University Press, 2000). The author is an atheist.
[29]See C. John Collins, *The God of Miracles: An Evangelical Examination of God's Action in the World* (Wheaton, Ill.: Crossway, 2000), pp. 147-50.

to do so, has done so before and has focused his life on running the fastest mile possible (which is now under four minutes). The same holds true for miracles. The likelihood of occurrence of a miracle occurring is generally quite low. Yet if we (1) have good evidence for the existence of a supernatural God who could work a miracle and (2) have a constellation of evidence supporting a miracle claim (as we do with Jesus' resurrection), the likelihood increases considerably.

Hume's in-principle argument simply begs the question against the identification of a miracle. If there is a God who can intervene in creation, then miracles may occur and be identified. Nevertheless, many biblical critics presuppose that miracles do not happen or can never be verified, despite the critics' claims to neutrality.

Hume's argument against the character of the witnesses to miracles raises a significant objection. A believer in biblical miracles may gladly grant that most miracle claims—even many of those made by Christians today—are spurious or at least dubitable because the quality of evidence in their support is substandard. We need a higher level of evidence to substantiate a miracle claim than we do for a nonmiraculous event. If I tell you that my sprained leg is finally healed after six weeks, and you see me walking on it, there is no reason to doubt my report. But if I you tell you that God healed my severely sprained leg only one day after the injury, you might want to look into the matter more closely and require more corroborating evidence before believing me. The most reasonable initial response might well be that I am lying or joking or am somehow deluded.

For Christianity, the canonical miracle reports, especially the resurrection of Jesus, are constitutive of the religion itself and cannot be separated from it. The church's institutions of baptism and the Lord's Supper presuppose the resurrection of Christ and the Gospel accounts. These sacraments have been used to instruct and disciple new believers since the middle to later first century and are primary to the story of Jesus. (We return to the significance of this later in the chapter.) These are miracle claims around which a persecuted new religious movement developed, a movement that thrived even against the odds of a hostile initial environment.

Miracle claims are frequent in history, but many can safely be disregarded as hoaxes, misunderstood natural phenomena or mysteries resolvable according to natural explanations. But our attention is here focused on the miracle claims within the Bible, particularly the Gospels and Acts.[30] So, the question becomes whether we can trust the reports of miracles *in these sources*.

Some, such as Hume and more recent writers, have written off all of these reports because they were made by prescientific men and women who routinely misinterpreted natural events as supernatural actions.[31] These benighted souls, the objection runs, had no understanding of science and natural law. So, their superstitious minds were ripe for manifold deceptions taken to be divine interventions. But as Lewis argued, an ancient Jew such as Joseph, whatever his scientific naiveté, could recognize that his fiancée's virgin pregnancy was not caused by natural means. Moreover, if

> there ever were men who did not know the laws of nature at all they would have no idea of a miracle and feel no particular interest in one if it were performed before them. Nothing can seem extraordinary until you have discovered what is ordinary. Belief in miracles, far from depending on an ignorance of the laws of nature, is only possible insofar as those laws are known.[32]

So the claim that the ancients merely misidentified natural occurrences loses plausibility. Moreover, the biblical accounts of miracles do not read as embellished tales, especially when compared to miracle stories found in other religions or even in later treatments of the Christian Gospel accounts.[33]

The cancellation argument. Hume also claims that even if miracles could be verified in connection to religion, the various miracles of various religions would cancel each other out. That is, if miracle A verified the truth claims of religion X, and miracle B verified the truth claims of religion Y, then neither religion could claim superiority on the basis of miracles. Yet the purpose of miracles in religion is to authenticate one's own religion over other religions and over irreligion. Therefore, the religious

---

[30]For a complete listing of all the miracles in the Bible, see Norman Geisler, "Miracles in the Bible," in *Baker Encyclopedia of Christian Apologetics* (Grand Rapids: Baker, 1999), pp. 480-88.
[31]Hume, *Writings on Religion*, pp. 71-74.
[32]Lewis, *Miracles*, p. 65.
[33]See the mythologized account of the feeding of the five thousand from the *Hayat al-Qulub*, quoted in Thomas Baldwin Thayer, *Christianity Against Infidelity* (Cincinnati: John A. Gurley, 1849), p. 368. I owe this reference to Timothy McGrew.

appeal to miracles loses its evidential force.[34]

This argument is quite overrated. First, different religions relate miracle claims to their core doctrines in different ways. Miracles do not directly support the truth claims of all religions. There are many miracle stories surrounding the birth and life of the Buddha, but these are not central to the teachings of Buddhism, which focuses on the dharma (or the Four Noble Truths). Likewise, Taoism makes no essential miracle claims, although supernatural stories are told of Lao Tze, its founder. The truth or falsity of these tales is irrelevant to the metaphysics and ethics of Taoism. The many sacred texts of Hinduism are filled with miraculous encounters between gods and humans, but these occur in realms inaccessible to historians. For the Hindu, a historical inquiry into the life of Krishna and his miracles would be taken as a category mistake. The stories have spiritual power and speak of extranormal dimensions, but they are not concrete claims about historical events.[35]

Let us consider the great monotheistic religions. The miracles claims of theologically conservative Judaism are not denied by Christians but viewed as a part of God's revelation to the Jews. Concerning Islam, the central miracle claim concerns the divine inspiration of the Qur'an. If it could be established that this book was supernaturally received by Muhammad (supposedly an illiterate) through the angel Gabriel, then Islam would be powerfully supported. However, there is insufficient evidence for this claim given that the Qur'an contradicts well-established facts of history such as the crucifixion and resurrection of Jesus. Furthermore, no miracle claims are made for Muhammad in the Qur'an. For Christianity the miracles of Jesus (particularly his resurrection) are central and are taken to exalt him above all others. Further, the commonly made arguments made for the Qur'an's divine inspiration fail.[36]

I cannot possibly relate all the miracle claims made by all the major (and minor) religions here. But two points are sufficient. First, the case for Jesus' resurrection is far stronger historically than for any miracle claim

[34]Hume, *Writings on Religion*, p. 75-76.
[35]See Norman Anderson, *A Lawyer Among the Theologians* (Grand Rapids: Eerdmans, 1974), pp. 29-30. This lack of concern for historical detail is related to Hinduism's devaluing of history in itself, which is taken as something to escape from through enlightenment.
[36]See Norman Geisler and Abdul Saleeb, "An Evaluation of the Qur'an," in *Answering Islam*, rev. ed. (Grand Rapids: Baker, 2002). See also chap. 24 of this book.

made by non-Christian religions.[37] Edwin Yamauchi, a professor of ancient history, observes that no founder of any other world religion has miracles attributed to him in its early and primary documents.[38] Second, if the apologetic case made thus far for monotheism is successful, then religions that are not monotheistic (such as Buddhism, Hinduism and Taoism) are out of the running—miracle claims notwithstanding. Further, the miracle claims made by Buddhism, Hinduism and Taoism are historically unverified and not significant to the religion's central affirmations. The miracle claims of Judaism are compatible with Christianity, but those of Christianity are not compatible with Judaism. While Islam accepts some of the miracle claims of the Bible, it denies the grand miracle of the resurrection. So the competition really boils down to whether the miraculous acts of Jesus can be substantiated in ways that defeat both Judaic and Islamic arguments to the contrary.[39]

JESUS' CHARACTER AND THE RESURRECTION

Richard Swinburne has argued that we need to consider what kind of person God might raise from the dead. The New Testament does not merely assert that a random person was dead, buried and brought back to life never to die again. We are speaking of Jesus of Nazareth, who, as Peter preached, "was a man accredited by God to you by miracles, wonders and signs" (Acts 2:22). Even apart from considering his resurrection, Jesus was "accredited by God" in numerous ways.[40] As pointed out in chapter twenty, the Gospels portray him as a master teacher who spoke with authority on all matters and was never out-argued, who taught things that humans could not have otherwise known, a man of compassion and strong and sterling character, a worker of miracles, whose life fulfilled many Old Testament prophecies and promises. Jesus articulated a clear and compelling worldview, placing himself at its vital center as God incarnate. As part and parcel of his teachings he predicted

---

[37]Gary Habermas, "Resurrection Claims in Non-Christian Religions," *Religious Studies* 25 (1989): 167-77.

[38]Edwin Yamauchi, *Jesus, Zoroaster, Buddha, Socrates, Muhammad*, rev. ed. (Downers Grove, Ill.: InterVarsity Press, 1972), p. 40.

[39]For more on the cancellation argument, see David K. Clark, "Miracles in the World Religions," in *In Defense of Miracles: A Comprehensive Case for God's Action in History*, ed. R. Douglas Geivett and Gary Habermas (Downers Grove, Ill.: InterVarsity Press, 1996).

[40]See Swinburne, *Resurrection of God Incarnate*, chaps. 2-3, for his full argument.

his own death and resurrection, and explained something of its meaning (although the fuller explanation is given through the apostolic witness). As James Sire put it, "If anyone were to be raised from the dead, it would be a person like Jesus."[41]

In assessing the arguments for the resurrection, our first consideration harks back to previous chapters concerning the essential reliability of the New Testament. On this basis we have reason to trust these reports in a general sense. As Schaeffer said, the naturalistic investigation into the life of Jesus failed, "for the supernatural was so intertwined with the rest [of Jesus' life] that, if they ripped out all the supernatural, . . . no historical Jesus remained; if they kept the historical Jesus the supernatural remained as well."[42] But since the idea that Jesus never existed is absurd, given the biblical evidence and extrabiblical evidence, the most rational approach is to accept the supernatural accounts.[43]

Moreover, N. T. Wright has provided the most thorough investigation of all the New Testament texts regarding the resurrection in his magisterial work *The Resurrection of the Son of God* and has found them to be reliable.[44] In an interview in which Antony Flew spoke with Gary Habermas about his abandonment of atheism for a minimal form of theism (or deism), Flew, while not a believer in the resurrection, made this telling point about Christianity's claim of resurrection with respect to other miracle claims: "The evidence for the resurrection is better than for claimed miracles in any other religion. It's outstandingly different in quality and quantity, I think, from the evidence offered for the occurrence of most other supposedly miraculous events."[45]

MINIMAL FACTS AND MAXIMAL RESULT: RESURRECTION

Another argument, ably and often employed by William Lane Craig, Gary

---

[41]James Sire, *Why Should Anyone Believe Anything at All?* (Downers Grove, Ill.: InterVarsity Press, 1994), p. 152. Sire realizes that the Bible claims that others have been raised from the dead besides Jesus. What he means is that Jesus uniquely fits the role of one to rise from the dead as the Lord of life, never to die again.

[42]Francis A. Schaeffer, *The God Who Is There*, 30th anniv. ed. (Downers Grove, Ill.: InterVarsity Press, 1998), p. 72.

[43]See footnote 1 of this chapter.

[44]N. T. Wright, *The Resurrection of the Son of God* (Minneapolis: Fortress, 2003), pt. 2.

[45]Antony Flew and Gary Habermas, "My Pilgrimage from Atheism to Theism: A Discussion Between Antony Flew and Gary Habermas," *Philosophia Christi* 6, no. 2 (2004): 209.

Habermas and Richard Swinburne, appeals to particular claims in the Gospels and the rest of the New Testament. Instead of attempting to argue for the reliability of the *entirety* of the New Testament, this strategy enlists a set of "minimal facts" contained in the New Testament that are accepted by the majority of critical New Testament scholars, both liberal and conservative, on the basis of certain criteria. It is then argued that these minimal facts are best explained on the basis of the resurrection of Jesus and not according to any rival hypothesis. I will begin by considering four facts that are very broadly agreed on by New Testament scholars of all stripes. I will then move to consider other factors that also enjoy considerable support by scholars.

1. Death by crucifixion. It is a well-established fact of history that Jesus died by crucifixion in the early 30s. New Testament scholars of all persuasions find no reason to doubt the biblical and extrabiblical material witness that Jesus was crucified. However, some, such as Friedrich Schleiermacher, suppose that he survived his crucifixion (the swoon theory), and Islam claims he was never was crucified.[46] Some even claim he survived crucifixion and is buried in India.[47]

As a general point, we have to wonder why those who trust the Gospel accounts enough to affirm that Jesus was put on a cross then depart from the same narratives that tell them that Jesus died. Why believe at one point (the cross) and doubt at another (death by crucifixion)? If critics do not provide grounds for their doubts, their rejection of Jesus' death is simply ad hoc.

Nevertheless, some argue that there are indications that Jesus did not die. These typically include two factors: that there was not enough time for Jesus to die, or the drink he received on the cross was a drug that simulated death (Mark 15:36).[48] These objections can be dealt with summarily.[49]

There *was* sufficient time for Jesus to die on the cross. We must not view the crucifixion in isolation from what preceded it. As Michael Green notes:

---

[46]We will discuss the key points of disagreement between Islam and Christianity in chap. 24.

[47]I address some of the New Age–oriented theories that Jesus survived the cross and went to India in *Jesus in an Age of Controversy* (1996; reprint, Eugene, Ore.: Wipf & Stock, 2002), pp. 147-51.

[48]This kind of argument was famously made a generation ago in Hugh Schonfield, *The Passover Plot* (New York: Bantam Books, 1966), and gets resurrected from time to time.

[49]It is interesting to note that while the swoon theory receives almost no attention in scholarly circles, it continues to be influential in the culture at large; hence, I will give it more space than would be warranted by the scholarly literature.

It is incredible that Jesus, who had not eaten or slept before his execution, who was weakened by a loss of blood through the most brutal flogging [see 1 Peter 2:24], who was pierced in both hands and feet, could have survived unaided had he been alive when taken down from the cross.[50]

Jesus was so weakened from his beatings that he was unable to carry his cross all the way to Golgotha, the execution site (Matthew 27:32). Dr. Alexander Metherell, a renowned pathologist who holds both an M.D. and Ph.D., argues that given what the Gospel accounts say of Jesus' brutal treatment before the crucifixion, he would have gone into hypovolemic shock due to extreme blood loss. This involves a racing heart attempting to pump missing blood, severe blood-pressure drop, kidney malfunction and extreme thirst.[51] Metherell says, "There is no doubt that Jesus was already in serious to critical condition even before the nails were driven through his hands and feet."[52]

The authors of a technical article titled "The Physical Death of Jesus Christ," in *The Journal of the American Medical Association*, remarked that the time of survival for Roman crucifixions "ranged from three or four hours to three or four days and appears to have been inversely related to the severity of the scourging."[53] This kind of death was horrific. As Craig notes,

> As the victim hangs on the cross, his lung cavity collapses, so that he can no longer exhale. In order to breathe, he must pull himself up on those nail-pierced hands and push with his feet until he can catch a breath. He cannot remain in this position for long. So he has to let himself drop back down.[54]

And on it went until the sufferer died of asphyxiation.[55]

Pilate showed surprise that Jesus died so rapidly (Mark 15:44), but he did

---

[50]Michael Green, *The Empty Cross of Jesus* (Downers Grove, Ill.: InterVarsity Press, 1984), p. 93. On the speed of Jesus' death, see also James Charlesworth, *Jesus Within Judaism* (New York: Doubleday, 1988), pp. 122-23.

[51]Alexander Metherell, interviewed in Lee Strobel, *The Case for Christ* (Grand Rapids: Zondervan, 1998), p. 196.

[52]Ibid.

[53]William D. Edwards, Wesley J. Gabel and Floyd E. Hosmer, "On the Physical Death of Jesus Christ," *Journal of the American Medical Association* 255, no. 11 (1986): 1460.

[54]William Lane Craig, *Knowing the Truth About the Resurrection* (Ann Arbor, Mich.: Servant Books, 1988), pp. 32-33.

[55]Metherel interview, pp. 198-99.

not question that Jesus was, in fact, dead. The Romans were no beginners when it came to crucifixion. The squad of four soldiers broke the legs of the two men crucified with Jesus (a practice that would hasten death) but did not bother to break Jesus' legs because they knew he had already expired.

One version of the swoon theory, championed in Hugh Schonfield's *The Passover Plot* (1967), argues that Jesus arranged to be given some potion to feign death. But this is problematic in several ways. The Gospel of John reports that Jesus was given a drink *in full view of the Roman guards* before he expired (John 19:28-29). It was their job to be executioners, not accessories to a hoax. They had a vested interest in being accurate coroners. "Had the centurion, had the governor made a mistake over the execution of a messianic pretender, their jobs and probably their lives would have been on the line."[56] Surely they would have been wise to such a ploy. Moreover, if we assume that Jesus somehow arranged for his last-minute rescue, he would be a grand impostor and not worthy of any respect, because he preached the necessity of his own death. The high morality preached by Jesus would be severely violated by any such ruse; it would be radically incongruous with the Gospel accounts of his character (see chap. 20).

The fact that blood and water came from his side is positive evidence for his death. The Roman soldiers pierced his side because they wanted to make doubly sure he was dead; this was standard practice to insure death.[57] What followed confirmed Jesus' death, as explained in the aforementioned article in the *Journal of the American Medical Association*. Here is the conclusion of the authors:

> Clearly, the weight of historical and medical evidence indicates that Jesus was dead before the wound to his side was inflicted and supports the traditional view that the spear, thrust between his right ribs, probably perforated not only the right lung but also the pericardium and heart and thereby ensured his death. Accordingly, interpretations based on the assumption that Jesus did not die on the cross appear to be at odds with modern medical knowledge.[58]

---

[56]Michael Green, *The Empty Cross of Jesus* (Downers Grove, Ill.: InterVarsity Press, 1984), p. 93.

[57]Craig, *Knowing the Truth of the Resurrection*, p. 33.

[58]Edwards et al., "On the Physical Death of Jesus Christ," p. 1463. See also Metherell's comments in Strobel, *Case for Christ*, p. 199.

Last, even if Jesus somehow survived the intense scourging, as well as the agonies of the cross—an idea that Metherell calls "impossible"—this would leave completely unexplained why Jesus' disciples ended up hailing him the resurrected Lord of life.[59] As Metherell says, "After suffering that horrible abuse, with all the catastrophic blood loss and trauma, he would have looked so pitiful that the disciples would never have hailed him as a victorious conqueror of death; they would have felt sorry for him and tried nurse him back to health."[60] This kind of criticism has dogged the swoon theory ever since it was first advanced by H. E. G. Paulus in 1828.[61] The upshot is that anyone who claims that Jesus survived his attempted execution bears a crushing burden of proof. Critical scholarship has long left this dead theory in its grave.

2. Burial in a known tomb. Besides his death, scholars agree that Jesus was buried in a tomb owned by Joseph of Arimathea, a member of the Jewish court that sentenced Jesus (Matthew 27:57-61; Mark 15:42-47; John 19:38-42). Craig notes that this is important because it gives the exact location of Jesus' burial. The disciples could not have later confidently claimed in Jerusalem that Jesus' tomb was empty if its location had not been known. For several reasons, there is no warrant to doubt Jesus' burial in this tomb. First, no other burial tradition exists as a competitor. Second, the account is well established through multiple attestations in Mark (probably the earliest written Gospel), Matthew and John. Third, that Jesus was buried is also corroborated by Paul's early report in 1 Corinthians 15:3-5. Fourth, as Craig notes, "As a member of the Jewish court that condemned Jesus, Joseph of Arimathea is unlikely to be a Christian invention."[62] The early Christians would not have created a story in which Jesus sentenced to death and given a proper burial and dignified tomb. The very liberal scholar John A. T. Robinson states that the burial of Jesus is "one of the earliest and best attested facts about Jesus," being attested to in 1 Corinthians 15, in all four Gospels and in the preaching of Acts.[63]

---

[59]Metherell, in Strobel, *Case for Christ*, p. 201.
[60]Ibid., p. 202.
[61]See Craig, *Knowing the Truth About the Resurrection*, pp. 31-34.
[62]William Lane Craig, "Opening Statements," in *Jesus' Resurrection: Fact or Figment?* ed. Paul Copan and Ronald Tacelli (Downers Grove, Ill.: InterVarsity Press, 2000), p. 32.
[63]John A. T. Robinson, *The Human Face of God* (Philadelphia: Westminster Press, 1973), p. 131.

John Dominic Crossan, once a member of the Jesus Seminar, made headlines by claiming that Jesus was probably buried in a shallow grave and that
his body was eaten by dogs. Crossan affirms this because executed criminals
were commonly buried in common graves. However, Crossan must disregard all the evidence we find in the Gospels to make this claim, and he can
adduce no countervailing evidence to the contrary besides the custom of the
day. Jesus was certainly no *common* criminal, and the best records available
to us claim he was buried in a special grave by Joseph of Arimathea. Accordingly, Crossan's controversial claim may be dismissed.[64]

3. The empty tomb. The four Gospels are unanimous in reporting that
on the Sunday after Jesus' crucifixion and burial, his tomb was found
empty by several women, Peter and another disciple (probably John)
(Matthew 28:1-7; Mark 16:1-8; Luke 24:1-8; John 20:1-9). This is reliable for several reasons. First, it is found in Mark, probably the oldest
Gospel material. Second, it is assumed in Paul's report in 1 Corinthians
15. Third, the stories are basic and lack fictional embellishments. Fourth,
the fact that all four Gospel accounts mention that women beheld the
empty tomb gives this story credibility, since the witness of women in
that day was held in very low regard. If the Gospels invented convincing
stories, they would not include women as primary witnesses.[65] Fifth, the
early Jewish polemic against the Christians was that Jesus' disciples stole
the body of Jesus—an allegation that presupposes that Jesus' tomb was
indeed empty (Matthew 28:11-15).[66] In a debate with Gary Habermas,
philosopher Antony Flew, though not a Christian, admits that the tomb
was empty.[67]

A vacant tomb is a necessary but not a sufficient condition for establishing Jesus' resurrection. If Jesus had been bodily raised from the
dead—the only kind of resurrection the Jews of that day believed in—
there is no way his body could be decomposing in a tomb (or anywhere
else). Nevertheless, the tomb might be empty for some reason other than

---

[64]William Lane Craig, "Evidence for the Empty Tomb," in *In Defense of Miracles*, ed. Gary
  Habermas and R. Douglas Geivett (Downers Grove, Ill.: InterVarsity Press, 1997), pp.
  248-51.
[65]See N. T. Wright, *Resurrection of the Son of God*, pp. 607-9.
[66]That the Jews made this claim is also affirmed by Tertullian and Justin Martyr (Tertullian *On
  Spectacles* 30; Justin Martyr *Dialogue with Trypho* 108).
[67]See Gary Habermas and Antony Flew, *Resurrected? An Atheist and Theist in Dialogue*, ed. John
  Ankerberg (Lanham, Md.: Rowman & Littlefield, 2005), p. 28.

resurrection, such as the theft of his body by some interested party. I will address this alternative explanation shortly, but the point here is that the tomb *must* be empty for the claim of Jesus' resurrection to have the remotest possibility of being true.

Luke, whom we have found to be historically reliable, tells us that the early church began to preach the resurrection in Jerusalem about seven weeks after Jesus' death. The preaching was heard by those familiar with Jesus and his crucifixion. If Jesus' tomb had not been empty, the apostles' preaching could have been stopped simply by producing Jesus' dead body for public display or by taking people to the tomb where Jesus was buried. Both the Jewish religious leadership and the Roman political leadership would have had a vested interest in doing so in order to stop a threatening movement. But we have no evidence that anything of the kind occurred. The apostles feared nothing of the sort and boldly proclaimed a risen Jesus as the central theme of all the sermons recorded in Acts.[68] A Jesus with rigor mortis was not a resurrected Jesus, wherever his spirit might be.

Gerd Lüdemann has tried to undermine the idea that Jesus' body could have been produced as counterevidence to the resurrection by claiming that Jesus' corpse would have been too decomposed at that point to be recognizable.[69] But this is far from certain. Even if Jesus' face were decomposed at this point to some degree (and how much he would be disfigured is hard to know), his physique, hair color and crucifixion wounds would still be visible and recognizable. Moreover, the burden of proof would have been placed on the disciples to show that this was not Jesus. But we have no indication that anything like this ever occurred.[70]

If Jesus had in fact been killed and buried and was in the tomb, it would be very likely that his tomb would be venerated as that of a saint, as was the custom in that day. In the Palestine of Jesus' day there were at least fifty such venerated tombs (see Luke 11:47-48).[71] Luke tells us that women followed Joseph of Arimathea to the tomb of Jesus, probably to mark the spot for later tribute. We know that Jews of that day preserved the bones of their loved ones in ossuaries, in anticipation of a resurrec-

---

[68]Lewis, *Miracles*, pp. 188-89.

[69]Lüdemann, "Second Rebuttal," in *Resurrection: Fact or Figment?* p. 61.

[70]I owe this insight to a July 2006 e-mail from William Lane Craig.

[71]Edwin Yamauchi, "Easter—Myth, Hallucination, or History? Part Two," *Christianity Today*, March 29, 1974, p. 13.

tion at the end of history. Yet the church commemorated an empty tomb, not an occupied one.[72]

4. The postmortem appearances of Jesus. Another set of facts is paramount in the case for the resurrection. "On multiple occasions and under various circumstances, different individuals and groups of people experienced appearances of Jesus alive from the dead."[73] The New Testament lists twelve separate appearances over a forty-day period.[74] Jesus appeared to

1. Mary Magdalene (John 20:10-18)

2. Mary and the other women (Matthew 28:1-10)

3. Peter (Luke 24:34; 1 Corinthians 15:5)

4. two disciples on the road to Emmaus (Luke 24:13-35)

5. ten apostles (Luke 24:36-49)

6. eleven apostles (John 20:24-31)

7. seven apostles (John 21)

8. all of the apostles (Matthew 28:16-20)

9. five hundred disciples (1 Corinthians 15:6)

10. James (1 Corinthians 15:7)

11. again to all the apostles (Acts 1:4-8)

12. the apostle Paul (Acts 9:1-9; 1 Corinthians 15:8; 9:1)[75]

The nature of these appearances must be explicated in order to avoid confusion. First, the accounts speak of visitations of an embodied person, not a disembodied spirit. Jesus returns from the dead as a living man who takes up space, can be seen, heard and touched. He walks with his disciples, teaches them and dines with them. About this, the New Testament vouchsafes no doubts.[76]

---

[72]Ibid., pp. 15-16.

[73]Craig, *Knowing the Truth About the Resurrection*, p. 33.

[74]All critical New Testament scholars may not accept all of these accounts as historical, but they nevertheless generally consider the experience of postmortem appearances to be well-founded historically.

[75]I owe this list to Kenneth Samples, *Without a Doubt* (Grand Rapids: Baker, 2004), p. 137.

[76]For a full account of all the appearances and their physical nature, see Norman Geisler, *Baker Encyclopedia of Christian Apologetics* (Grand Rapids: Zondervan, 1999), pp. 651-56; see esp. the chart on p. 655.

Second, throughout history and in Jesus' day, there have been reports of the living seeing or otherwise experiencing the dead. These are apparitions or visionary experiences. But these claims are made about those who are dead and buried. They should not be confused with reports of the resurrected Jesus. As Wright amply documents, the Second Temple Judaism of Jesus' day had no concept of disembodied resurrection.[77] Those Jews who believed in the afterlife (unlike the Sadducees, see Mark 12:18) believed in a general resurrection of all people at the end of history. (See, for example, Jesus' dispute on the nature of the resurrected life in Matthew 22:23-33; see also Daniel 12:2.) Therefore, Jesus' resurrection differed from the prevailing view in that (1) it happened in history, not at the end of history, and (2) it happened to one individual, not to the entire human race. Given this, the early church could not have derived their idea of Jesus' singular resurrection in history from prevailing Jewish ideas.

Thus if Jesus' followers (or others) had only visionary or apparitional experiences of Jesus, these would not have supported the claim that he was alive from the dead. They could at best claim that Jesus' disembodied spirit was making various appearances on earth. But the New Testament nowhere makes this claim, since it emphasizes the physical resurrection of Jesus and the empty tomb. As Wright notes, "if a first-century Jew said that someone had been 'raised from the dead,' the one thing they did *not* mean was that such a person had gone to a state of disembodied bliss, there either to rest forever or to wait until the great day of re-embodiment."[78]

Moreover, the claim that Jesus was alive in a heavenly realm from whence he was appearing to various people at various times cannot explain the unambiguous and multiply attested *interval* between Jesus' death and his ascension. The sequence is death, burial, resurrection and then ascension. The resurrection and ascension are not elided but unmistakably distinguished.[79]

We should again note that women are listed as witnesses of the resurrected Jesus, as they were of the empty tomb. This gives the ring of truth for

---

[77]Wright, *Resurrection of the Son of God*, chaps. 3-4.

[78]N. T. Wright, "Christian Origins and the Resurrection of Jesus: The Resurrection of Jesus as a Historical Problem," *Sewanee Theological Review* 41, no. 2 (1998), <www.ntwrightpage.com/Wright_Historical_Problem.htm>.

[79]N. T. Wright, "Jesus' Resurrection and Christian Origins," *Gregorianum* 83, no. 4 (2002): 615-35, <www.ntwrightpage.com/Wright_Jesus_Resurrection.htm>.

the same reason as cited concerning the empty tomb: the testimony of women was not highly regarded in that day.[80] If the church were going to invent a resurrection story (for some strange reason), it would not have listed women as primary witness of the empty tomb and resurrected Jesus.

But we have another, perhaps the strongest, witness of the resurrection: the apostle Paul. In handling a dispute in the church at Corinth over the resurrection of the dead, Paul speaks of the various appearances of the risen Jesus.

> Now, brothers and sisters, I want to remind you of the gospel I preached to you, which you received and on which you have taken your stand. By this gospel you are saved, if you hold firmly to the word I preached to you. Otherwise, you have believed in vain.
>
> For what I received I passed on to you as of first importance: that Christ died for our sins according to the Scriptures, that he was buried, that he was raised on the third day according to the Scriptures, and that he appeared to Cephas, and then to the Twelve. After that, he appeared to more than five hundred of the brothers and sisters at the same time, most of whom are still living, though some have fallen asleep. Then he appeared to James, then to all the apostles, and last of all he appeared to me also, as to one abnormally born. (1 Corinthians 15:1-8)

This passage, while a confession of doctrine, is also rich in evidential force and detail. First, Paul is affirming the physical nature of the resurrection: the same Christ that was buried was raised. Paul assumes the empty tomb; what he relates makes no sense without it. Second, Paul's authorship of 1 Corinthians is never disputed, even by liberal scholars who question the authorship of some of the other epistles traditionally attributed to him.[81] Third, Paul's language in this passage indicates that he is invoking an already-existing creed of the early church.[82] Paul's letter was written in the middle 50s, thus making it most likely the earliest

---

[80]See the Talmud, e.g., *Rosh Hashana* 1.8c and Babylonian *Mas. Sotah* 31b ; and N. T. Wright, *Resurrection of the Son of God*, p. 317, 322-26; C. Cetzer, "Excellent Women: Female Witnesses to the Resurrection," *Journal of Biblical Literature* 116 (1997): 259-72.

[81]For further discussion of Pauline authorship of epistles attributed to him see the introductory material on all the Pauline epistles in D. A. Carson and Douglas Moo, *Introduction to the New Testament*, 2nd ed. (Grand Rapids: Zondervan, 2002).

[82]There are a number of such creeds or hymns distributed in the New Testament (see W. J. Porter, "Creeds and Hymns," in *Dictionary of New Testament Background*, ed. Craig Evans and Stanley E. Porter [Downers Grove, Ill.: InterVarsity Press, 2000]).

written testimony to the resurrection of Jesus. The words "What I received I passed on" refer to an earlier statement about Jesus' life, death,
burial and resurrection that Paul is reiterating for the purposes at hand.
This may not be very obvious in English, but the words are easily translated into Aramaic, the spoken language of Jesus' first Jewish disciples.
Jewish New Testament scholar Pinchas Lapide lists eight separate "linguistic items" that "speak in favor of the fact that Paul in this oldest faith
statement about the resurrection does not pass on his own thoughts
but indeed delivers what he himself has 'received' from the first
witnesses."[83] Fourth, since Paul here mentions Peter and James as witnesses of the resurrection, and since Paul speaks in Galatians and Acts
of his meeting with them, it is very likely that Paul received this creed
from these eyewitnesses of the resurrection, thus firmly connecting him
to ancient witnesses.

These features of Paul's passage would date the original creed for the
burial and resurrection of Jesus during the 30s, considerably before the
writing of Paul's letter at approximately the mid-50s.[84] The affirmation of
the death and resurrection of Christ was so firmly established just a few
years after his death that it was formulated in a creed, a brief summary and
confession of the community's essential beliefs. This disproves the notion
of the resurrection as a legendary development of a later period, especially
when we remember that Paul speaks of those *now living* who had seen the
resurrected Jesus. These witnesses were alive and available. This is either
one of the greatest bluffs in the history of religion or a confident assertion
of substantiated fact.

The witness of Paul is extraordinary, not only given the early date of his
letter but because we know more about him from his writings (and what
was written about him in Acts) than we do of the writers of the Gospels.
Richard Swinburne writes,

> Paul is different from any other person who appears on the pages of the
> New Testament in that we can judge his character as a witness for ourselves
> by reading those of his letters that are without dispute genuine, and he

---

[83]Pinchas Lapide, *The Resurrection of Jesus* (Minneapolis: Augsburg Publishing, 1983), pp. 98-99.

[84]Gary Habermas and Antony Flew, *Did Jesus Rise from the Dead?* ed. Terry L. Miethe (San Francisco: Harper & Row, 1987), p. 23.

comes over as a totally honest person. If Paul endorses a creedal formula, above all on this all-important matter, he believes it.[85]

Paul not only bears witness that others had seen the risen Christ, but he lists himself as a witness to the resurrection as well (see Galatians 1:15-16). Paul's conversion is recounted by Luke in Acts 9:1-19 and is retold by Paul twice in Acts 22:1-11 and Acts 26:9-18. In Galatians, Paul writes of his convocation with the apostles James and Peter in which they agree as to the meaning of the gospel (Galatians 1–2). Jesus appeared to Paul last, after the appearances he lists in 1 Corinthians 15, but this was still a physical appearance. Paul heard Jesus speak to him and saw Jesus' form. Paul's companions at the time also saw physical manifestations and heard something.[86] This was not a subjective vision, however different it may have been from the other appearances narrated in the New Testament.[87]

These are the four facts commonly accepted by most all New Testament scholars: (1) Jesus' death on the cross, (2) burial in a known tomb, (3) the empty tomb and (4) Jesus' followers' experience of Jesus as resurrected. The last claim is put phenomenologically, since these experiences need to be interpreted as veridical or not. I believe that a solid case for the resurrection can be made from just these facts, as many have done.[88] But I will go on to cite some other well-established evidence in favor of the resurrection.

---

[85]Richard Swinburne, *The Resurrection of God Incarnate* (New York: Oxford University Press, 2003), p. 148.

[86]Some have argued that there is a contradiction between two of Paul's accounts of his encounter with Jesus. In Acts 9:7, Paul says his companions saw the light and heard a voice. But in Acts 22:9, Paul says that those with him did not hear the voice. Gleason Archer explains that what seems contradictory in English is not so in Greek. What Paul means in both cases is that they heard something but could not make out its meaning. So, they did hear *a sound*, but they could not hear *in the sense of understanding the message*, as Paul himself did. For the Greek specifics, see Gleason Archer, *Encyclopedia of Biblical Difficulties* (Grand Rapids: Zondervan, 1982), p. 382.

[87]In his debate with Habermas, Flew tries to argue that since Paul's companions did not have the exact same experience of the risen Christ as Paul did, the event was not truly physical. But as Habermas responds, "If you take the three texts in Acts (9:7, 22:9; 26:13-14), Paul's companions saw a light. We are told they all fell down. They heard a voice but they didn't understand what the voice was saying. . . . So plainly there's an objective effect on them" (*Resurrected?* p. 35). Certainly a physical event may occasion differing responses from different perceivers.

[88]Such as the many debates and books on this topic by Gary Habermas and William Lane Craig. See earlier notes for bibliographic details.

THE TRANSFORMATION OF THE DISCIPLES

The evidence for the various appearances of Jesus to different people at different times is tightly associated with another line of evidence for the resurrection of Jesus: the transformation of the disciples. These men went from dejected, dispirited and grieving followers of a crucified rabbi to apostles, those who had beheld the risen Christ and who, on that basis, preached him as the Lord of life and the Judge of history. The Gospels report that the disciples could not stay awake for one hour of prayer on the night before Jesus' arrest; one of their own betrayed him (Judas), and they fled when he was arrested (Mark 14:32-50). Jesus' disciples failed to pray faithfully for Jesus shortly before his resurrection, Peter denied his master, and the disciples were shocked and incapacitated at Jesus' arrest. Peter later disowned Jesus publicly (Mark 14:66-72). Besides some of Jesus' female followers, only John was at the crucifixion. Further, the male disciples refused to believe the women's early report that Jesus was raised from the dead (Mark 16:11; Luke 24:11).

Although Jesus had alluded to his resurrection, his disciples did not understand what he meant. No Jews of that day "had the belief in a dying, much less rising, Messiah."[89] Moreover, according to Jewish law, Jesus' execution as a criminal signaled that he was a heretic and under the curse of God (Deuteronomy 21:23; see Galatians 3:13).[90] Yet Christianity, as Paul so clearly affirms (1 Corinthians 15), is premised on the resurrection of just this Jesus who was crucified. The actual resurrection of Jesus is the best explanation for the disciples' transformation from cowardice, despair and confusion to confident proclamation and the willingness to suffer persecution, hardship and even martyrdom for the sake of Jesus and his gospel.

If this resurrection did not actually occur, how can we account for the origin and rapid spread of Christianity across the face of the ancient world? How did the same disciples—who could not pray one hour for their Lord before his crucifixion and who scattered after his capture—be the same evangelists who braved persecution and martyrdom for a resurrected Jesus?

---

[89]Craig, *Knowing the Truth About the Resurrection*, p. 34.

[90]Ibid. Muslims deny that Jesus was crucified, because God (that is, Allah) would not allow a prophet such an ignominious death. Yet the Bible predicts and records that Jesus, God's prophet, priest and king, had to die such a death (Isaiah 53; Acts 8:32-35).

Christianity was born out of the afterglow of the resurrection of Jesus. This was the fire of its motivation and the fiber of its courage. The infant Christian message was rooted in the resurrection. "In the Book of Acts, it is consistently the resurrection that forms the central hope of early Christian preaching (e.g., 2:22-36; 17:18; 26:6-8)."[91] Noting that the origin of Christianity cannot be explained without the resurrection, C. F. D. Moule affirmed that "the birth and rapid rise of the Christian church *therefore remain an unsolved enigma for any historian who refuses to take seriously the only explanation offered by the Church itself.*"[92] Lapide has called the resurrection "the birth certificate of the church."[93]

The church's belief that people can be forgiven of their sins, justified and adopted into God's family by faith in Christ assumes that Christ has been raised. Paul says that Jesus was "raised to life for our justification" (Romans 4:25). Peter preached that because of the resurrection, everyone who believes in Jesus receives forgiveness of sins (Acts 10:43). The death of Christ would have no meaning without the resurrection of Jesus. An early confession of the church, mentioned by Paul, makes this clear: "If you declare with your mouth, 'Jesus is Lord,' and believe in your heart that God raised him from the dead, you will be saved" (Romans 10:9).

THE EARLY WORSHIP OF JESUS

Another essential element of the transformation of the disciples and the practice of the early church is its worshiping of Christ as divine. In the past twenty-five years Larry Hurtado has done extensive research on the early church's esteeming of Jesus as a divine being worthy of worship.[94] While he shies away from drawing strong apologetic conclusions, his arguments establish that the worship of Jesus—not merely the belief that he was resurrected—was central to the devotional life of the earliest church. For example, in Philippians, Paul cites an early Christian creed— which predates Philippians itself, probably by several decades—that

---

[91]Craig L. Blomberg, *Jesus and the Gospels: An Introduction and Survey*, 2nd ed. (Nashville: B & H Academic, 2009), p. 409.

[92]C. F. D. Moule, *The Phenomenon of the New Testament* (Naperville, Ill.: Alec R. Allenson, 1967), p. 13, emphasis in the original. See pp. 1-20 for his entire argument.

[93]Lapide, *Resurrection of Jesus*, p. 46.

[94]Larry Hurtado, *Lord Jesus Christ* (Grand Rapids: Eerdmans, 2005); and his *How on Earth Did Jesus Become a God?* (Grand Rapids: Eerdmans, 2006).

speaks of Jesus' preexistence, his incarnation and exaltation (Philippians 2:5-11).

In a well-known text, Pliny the Younger, governor of Pontus/Bithynia from A.D. 111-113, wrote to emperor Trajan concerning the activities of Christians. He reported that some disavowed the faith under pressure and worshiped other gods. Pliny notes that the defectors admitted "that the sum and substance of their fault or error had been that they were accustomed to meet on a fixed day before dawn and sing responsively a hymn to Christ as to a god."[95]

As Hurtado repeatedly emphasizes, it is extremely odd and unlikely that the zealously monotheistic Jews of Jesus' day would be found worshiping a human being. Yet if Jesus had in fact claimed to be God incarnate and had supremely vindicated these claims by his resurrection, such beliefs and worship would then be explained by the very fact of his resurrection. Such beliefs and practices are extremely difficult to explain apart from Jesus' resurrection. Jesus' resurrection is, in fact, the best explanation for why ancient monotheistic Jews would worship him as divine.

CIRCUMSTANTIAL EVIDENCE

Thus far, we have dealt with *documentary evidence* for the resurrection, namely, various written sources claiming to present accurate information about the primary events of Jesus' crucifixion and resurrection. Yet there is also strong *circumstantial evidence* for the historicity of the resurrection, namely, the practice of the early church in observing baptism, the Lord's Supper and Sunday worship.

The symbol of baptism is based on the analogy that just as Jesus died and was raised to life, so the believer dies to sinful ways and is raised to a new life in Christ (see Romans 6:3-4). Baptism presupposes and is meaningless without the resurrection; moreover, it is original with and intrinsic to the practice of Christianity. Another sacrament is the Lord's Supper as a symbol of Jesus' life given for the believer. Michael Green notes that this was no "memorial feast in honor of a dead founder." Believers "broke bread with *agalliasis*, exultation (Acts 2:46) because they believed the risen Lord was in their midst as they took the tokens of His

---

[95]Pliny *Letters* 10.96-97.

death for them."[96] Both practices, he adds, "would have been a complete travesty had the earliest Christians not believed that Jesus rose from the dead."[97] And, again, the best explanation for why they believed it was that it was a fact.

Very quickly after the death of Jesus the early church began meeting on Sunday, the first day of the week (Acts 20:7; 1 Corinthians 16:1-2). This went against the religious grain of Jewish observance that honored Saturday, the seventh day, as the sabbath ordained by God (Genesis 2:1-3; Exodus 20:8). The Gospels do not record Jesus advocating a new holy day for Sunday, yet the church began to meet on Sunday in honor of the risen Lord.[98] In this, the early church challenged a core doctrine of their original Jewish faith and the faith of those unconverted Jews around them. Such a transformation would not occur for frivolous reasons. This deep change in spiritual observance is best explained by their belief in the resurrection of Jesus on Sunday, which, in turn, is best explained by the resurrection itself.

SPIRITUAL EXPERIENCES IN HISTORY AND TODAY

Although it may be discounted as merely subjective, it should be remembered that Jesus and his apostles promised his followers abundant life (John 10:10), spiritual victory (Ephesians 6:10-18) and the advance of his kingdom through history on the basis of his life, death and resurrection (Matthew 19:18; 28:18-20). Without the death-defeating and life-conferring reality of the resurrection, these realities would not be available (1 Corinthians 15:14-19). The fact that millions of Christ's followers around the globe for the last two thousand years have testified to the reality of their risen Savior's claims lends credibility to the reality of the resurrection. Without this line of evidence in the confirmation of the resurrection, all the historical evidence for the resurrection would be of little account, since one necessary consequence of the resurrection of Jesus is the salvation, empowerment and success of the church throughout history (see chap. 16).

---

[96]Green, *Empty Cross of Jesus*, p. 94.

[97]Ibid.

[98]See D. A. Carson, ed., *From Sabbath to Lord's Day: A Biblical, Historical and Theological Investigation* (Eugene, Ore.: Wipf & Stock, 2000); and Willy Rordorf, *Sunday: The History of the Day of Rest and Worship in the Earliest Centuries of the Christian Church* (Philadelphia: Westminster Press, 1968).

When taken together, these multiple lines of evidence, both documentary and circumstantial, lead us to a Christless tomb, a dead man found supernaturally alive and a dynamic group of followers who turned the ancient world upside down.[99]

ALTERNATIVE NATURALISTIC THEORIES

Several naturalistic theories argue that the resurrection claim made in the New Testament does not prove a historical resurrection. However, none of these theories explain the key facts previously noted. They end up multiplying improbabilities or canceling each other out. Moreover, multiple natural explanations are needed to cover the basic facts agreed on by the scholars, and none of these explanations are very plausible. However, the resurrection itself neatly accounts for all the facts according to one theory. Antony Flew tellingly admitted in a debate with Gary Habermas that no naturalistic explanations adequately account for the confirmed facts on which Habermas based his case for the resurrection.[100] It seemed that Flew resisted the resurrection more on the basis of his philosophical commitment to naturalism than on the basis of the evidence.[101] Nevertheless, we will investigate a few of the more prominent naturalistic claims. Pascal presents the essential dichotomy: if Christ be not raised, the disciples were either innocently deceived or culpable deceivers.

> The apostles were either deceived or were deceivers. Either supposition is difficult, for it is not possible to imagine that a man has risen from the dead. While Jesus was with them he could sustain them, but afterwards, if he did not appear to them, who did make them act [as if Jesus were resurrected]?[102]

Is it likely that despite these lines of evidence, the purported eyewitnesses of the risen Jesus were sincerely deceived? The most common

---

[99]Bernard Ramm argues that those who deny Jesus' resurrection face more difficulties than those who affirm it (*Protestant Christian Evidences* [Chicago: Moody Press 1967], pp. 195-207). John Warwick Montgomery argues that according to legal reasoning, the burden of proof lies on those who deny the credibility of the witnesses (*Human Rights and Human Dignity* [Grand Rapids: Zondervan, 1986], pp. 139-56).

[100]Flew, *Resurrected?* p. 31.

[101]Since this debate, Flew converted to deism because of the arguments for a Designer but did not embrace Christianity. See Antony Flew with Roy Abraham Varghese, *There Is a God* (San Francisco HarperOne, 2007). He died in 2010.

[102]Blaise Pascal, *Pensées* 322/802, ed. and trans. Alban Krailsheimer (New York: Penguin, 1966), p. 127.

argumentation in defense of this notion is that the resurrection appearances were hallucinations of some kind and not objectively real. Habermas notes that contemporary critical scholarship is in broad agreement that Jesus' disciples believed that he was raised from the dead and made claims to have seen him.[103] So, this visionary encounter needs to be explained supernaturally (Christ is risen) or naturally (the disciples were deceived). Given that the disciples perceived some kind of visionary events (although more than visual experiences were involved), the most promising explanation outside of what the New Testament itself offers, is that of a hallucination. The hallucination theory has experienced a bit of a renewal in recent years.[104]

HALLUCINATED OR RESURRECTED?

It is extremely difficult to defend the idea that such a diversity of persons, at different times and places, were all subject to the same hallucination of a physically risen Jesus, especially since they perceived Christ through multiple modes of perception: sight, hearing and touch. Hallucinations are not a group phenomenon but individual aberrations. Further, they are usually occasioned through intense wish fulfillment. But we should remember that the original disciples had given Jesus up for dead and were quite shocked at the first reports of his resurrection (Luke 24:1-11; John 20:24-26).[105] Those Jews who believed in the coming resurrection[106] believed it would come for everyone at the end of history, but not to one person before the end.[107] Although Jesus repeatedly predicted his resurrection, his disciples did not understand him (Matthew 16:21-23).

This sense of surprise at the resurrection and the unlikelihood of it being a hallucination based on wish fulfillment applies even more forcefully to Paul and James.[108] James, though Jesus' brother, did not believe in

[103]Gary Habermas, "Resurrection Research 1975 to the Present: What Are Critical Scholars Saying?" *Journal for the Study of the Historical Jesus* 3, no. 2 (2005): 135-53.

[104]Gary Habermas, "Explaining Away Jesus' Resurrection: The Recent Revival of Hallucination Theories," *The Christian Research Journal* 23 (2001): 26-31.

[105]Swinburne, *Resurrection of God Incarnate*, pp. 170-72; Craig, *Truth About the Resurrection*, pp. 109-10.

[106]The Pharisees affirmed this; the Sadducees denied it. For the beliefs of the Jews at the time of Jesus, see Wright, "Time to Wake Up (2): Hope Beyond Death in Post Biblical Judaism," in *Resurrection of the Son of God*.

[107]Wright, *Resurrection of the Son of God*, chaps. 2-3.

[108]The very liberal New Testament scholar Reginald Fuller admits that even if we did not have

him before the resurrection (John 7:5) but subsequently became a witness of the resurrection and an apostle (Acts 13:13-14; 1 Corinthians 15:7; Galatians 1:19).[109] Paul was a notorious persecutor of the church, who consented to the death of the first Christian martyr, Stephen (Acts 7:54–8:1). Until his own conversion (Acts 9:1-19), Paul was not originally inclined to view Jesus favorably at all, as he himself admits in several places.

The hallucination theory also leads to the unlikely conclusion that the very existence of Christianity is based on multiple mental illnesses and that its earliest converts (including those who claimed to be eyewitness of the resurrection) preached, quite literally, a message of madness.[110] Lapide tellingly comments:

> If the defeated and depressed group of disciples overnight could change into a victorious movement of faith, based only on autosuggestion or self-deception—without a fundamental faith experience—then this would be a much greater miracle than the resurrection itself.[111]

Lapide says that "the resurrection belongs to the category of the truly real and effective occurrences, for without a fact of history there is no act of true faith."[112]

Moreover, if so many had (somehow) been deceived by hallucinations, they would have been easily cured of their hallucinations by a visit to the occupied tomb of Jesus. Both the antagonistic Jews and the Roman establishment had ample animus against this young "cult," so they would have refuted the resurrection claims quite swiftly by producing the body of Jesus or taking people to his known gravesite.[113] The hallucination theory fails given the nature of hallucinations, but it also fails to explain the empty tomb. In a debate with Gary Habermas on the resurrection, Antony Flew attempts

---

James's name listed here, "we should have to invent" an appearance to James in order to account for his conversion and his subsequent prominence in the church at Jerusalem (*The Formation of the Resurrection Narratives* [New York: Macmillan, 1971], p. 37).

[109]Josephus writes that James was stoned for his Christian faith in A.D. 57 (Josephus *Antiquities of the Jews* 20.200).

[110]See Norman Anderson, *Jesus Christ: The Witness of History* (Downers Grove, Ill.: InterVarsity Press, 1985), pp. 140-44; Craig, *Knowing the Truth About the Resurrection*, pp. 109-13; and Green, *Empty Cross of Jesus*, pp. 113-19.

[111]Lapide, *Resurrection of Jesus*, p. 126.

[112]Ibid., p. 92.

[113]The claim that the body would not have been recognizable was addressed on p. 545 in this chapter.

to use various hallucination theories as a way to explain the early disciples' belief in Jesus. Tellingly, after intense interrogation by Habermas, he reluctantly lets them go by the end of the debate and says that no naturalistic theories explain the resurrection. Nevertheless, he deems the resurrection "impossible," thus revealing his philosophical commitments at that time.[114]

A CHRISTIAN CONSPIRACY?

Some attempt to deny the resurrection by accusing the early church of perpetuating a belief they knew to be a lie (although this is not offered in scholarly circles in modern times).[115] They were not deceived but willful deceivers. What logical motive could account for such a lie? Blaise Pascal puts the lie to the lie theory:

> The hypothesis that the apostles were knaves is quite absurd. Follow it out to the end and imagine these twelve men meeting after Jesus' death and conspiring to say that he had risen from the dead. This means attacking all the powers that be. The human heart is singularly susceptible to fickleness, to change, to promises, to bribery. One of them had only to deny this story under these inducements, or still more because of possible imprisonment, tortures and death, and they would all have been lost.[116]

In order to set up an alternative theory such as conscious deception, one needs first to establish a credible *motive* for such a ruse. Second, one must consider if those so motivated had the *means* by which to pull off the fakery. The disciples had neither. They could have possessed no motive for deception because there was no benefit in cooking up a religion based on a lie. The book of Acts and ancient history tell us that early Christians were often persecuted and martyred.

As William Paley long ago pointed out in his classic work *A View of the Evidences of Christianity* (1794), a dangerous life lived for a noble cause has its enjoyment, but only if it is a sincere life.[117] Craig writes, "With the consciousness at bottom of hollowness and falsehood, the fatigue and strain would have become unbearable."[118] As Pascal noted, the human

---

[114]Flew, *Resurrected?* p. 67.
[115]Craig, *Knowing the Truth About Jesus*, p. 31.
[116]Pascal, *Pensées* 310/801, p. 125.
[117]William Paley, *A View of the Evidences of Christianity* 1.1.1 (London: John W. Parker, 1859), p. 38.
[118]Craig, *Knowing the Truth About Jesus*, p. 23.

heart is too weak to perpetuate a known falsehood under such intense pressures to recant. Hume himself admitted as much: "We cannot make use of a more convincing argument, than to prove that the actions ascribed to any person are directly contrary to the course of nature, and that no human motives, in such circumstances, could ever induce him to such a conduct."[119]

Moreover, even if the disciples had some motive for their resurrection schemes, they would have lacked the *means* by which to deceive enough people to start a mass movement that continues to this day. The disciples were not the movers and shakers of ancient Palestine, but a bedraggled assemblage of tax collectors, fishermen and other commoners. Convicted Watergate felon and Christian convert Charles Colson makes a telling comparison. He recounts the desperate efforts made by himself and Nixon's inner circle to try to cover up the Watergate break in. "With the most powerful office in the world at stake, a small band of hard-picked loyalists, no more than ten of us, could not hold a conspiracy together for more than two weeks."[120] Despite their power and their loyalty to a corrupt president, "after just a few weeks the natural human instinct for self-preservation was so overwhelming that the conspirators, one by one, deserted their leader."[121]

Colson argues a fortiori that if the Watergate lawbreakers defected at the risk of ruined careers and possible imprisonment, there would have been far more incentive for Jesus' disciples to confess their fraud in the face of even worse consequences, such as social rejections, beatings, poverty and even death. Nor would they have had the social means to deceive that was possessed by the Watergate conspirators. However, there is no record of any such confession of fraud by the disciples. Colson sums this up:

> Take it from one who was inside the Watergate web looking out, who saw firsthand how vulnerable a cover-up is: Nothing less than a witness as awesome as the resurrected Christ could have caused those men to maintain to their dying whispers that Jesus is alive and Lord.[122]

---

[119]David Hume, *An Enquiry Concerning Human Understanding*, ed. T. Beauchamp (Oxford: Oxford University Press, 2001), p. 65.
[120]Charles Colson, *Loving God* (Grand Rapids: Zondervan, 1983), p. 67.
[121]Ibid.
[122]Ibid., p. 69.

WAS IT A CORPSE HEIST?

Over the years some have averred that Jesus' tomb was empty not because
he rose from the dead but because someone stole his body. It is often
claimed that Jesus' disciples stole the body, but sometimes other candidates are proposed.

The early Jewish argument against the Christians presupposed an
empty tomb. The New Testament itself records that the Jews spread the
word that the disciples stole the body (Matthew 28:11-15). This is corroborated by Tertullian and Justin Martyr.[123] The notion of a corpse heist
was highly implausible because of the skilled guard set around the tomb
(according to Matthew, the very same Gospel that mentions the heist
thesis),[124] the difficulty in identifying the disciples as the thieves if they
somehow sneaked past the guards without getting caught, and it is ludi-
crous to think that these thieving disciples would then take on the whole
world by preaching a blatant lie seven weeks later in Jerusalem.[125] Last, it
would make no sense for the disciples of Jesus Christ—who is acknowledged even by non-Christians as one of the greatest ethical teachers of
history—to break the law by stealing the body and then claim that the
empty tomb indicated a resurrection which they know did not occur.

Some have argued that the tomb was raided by unknown grave robbers,
since this was fairly common at that time. This theory would also have to
overcome the guarding of the tomb. Moreover, grave robbers focused their
attention on the graves of the wealthy, since they could steal expensive
material left on the body of a rich corpse. Jesus, of course, had no such
endowments materially on his person, having died naked and unadorned
without any regalia.[126]

Moreover, none of these heist theories can account for the well-established fact that, as I have argued at length, many people over a significant

[123]Tertullian *On Spectacles* 30; Justin Martyr *Dialogue with Trypho* 108.
[124]Most critical scholars reject the account of the guard at Christ's tomb as a fictional addition
by Matthew (who alone mentions it). However, Swinburne (who thinks that some legendary
material made its way into the Gospels) argues otherwise, claiming that the Romans would
have had reason to secure Jesus' tomb, since they viewed him as a potential political threat.
Hence, they would not want his disciples to take the body, which might give the disciples
some motivation to continue their supposed political insurrection (*The Resurrection of God
Incarnate*, pp. 177-78; see also N. T. Wright, *Resurrection of the Son of God*, pp. 636-40).
[125]See Craig, *Knowing the Truth About the Resurrection*, p. 21.
[126]For more against this theory, see Swinburne, *Resurrection of God Incarnate*, pp. 182-83.

amount of time encountered the risen Jesus (Acts 1:1-3; 1 Corinthians 15:5-8). Even if theft could explain the empty tomb (which it cannot), the appearances of Jesus still demand a sufficient explanation. And I have argued that the best explanation is the resurrection itself.[127]

ARE THERE DISCREPANCIES IN THE RESURRECTION ACCOUNTS?

Some might be troubled that the resurrection accounts in the Gospels do not seem to agree perfectly. At the extreme, Michael Martin argues that this provides strong evidence that they are fictional, not factual.[128] But this does not follow logically. With a little patience and some careful reconstruction, the events narrated in the Gospels can be harmonized with one another. The accounts of virtually any multiply attested event of secular history display discrepancies as great as or greater than those in the Gospel narratives. For example, Greek historian Polybius and the Roman historian Livy seem to disagree in their description of Hannibal's route in crossing the Alps in Italy during the second Punic War. Yet ancient historians do not question whether Hannibal made this trek.[129] Harris notes that historians use two basic principles to harmonize seemingly discrepant accounts: (1) The "assumption of innocence" principle claims that accounts about an event given by two independent writers, or even one writer at two different occasions, "are bound to exhibit some differences." Moreover, these differences of description give "a priori evidence of noncollusion." Thus, an "innocent until proven guilty" (and not vice versa) approach is in order.[130] (2) The "complexity of truth" principle affirms that

> where two or more accounts of the same incident or phenomenon seem to
> differ or actually do differ in matters of detail or substance, the truth is as
> likely to be found in both accounts as in one, for "truth" in the realm of

---

[127]For a very thorough refutation of all the naturalistic theories to explain away the resurrection, see Gary Habermas and Michael Licona, *The Case for the Resurrection of Jesus* (Grand Rapids: Kregel, 2004), pt. 3.

[128]Michael Martin, *The Case Against Christianity* (Philadelphia: Temple University Press, 1993), pp. 78-81.

[129]See Murray Harris, *From Grace to Glory: Resurrection in the New Testament* (Grand Rapids: Zondervan, 1990), pp. 158-59. Harris discusses the strategies that ancient historians use in this case and also gives another example of discrepancies concerning Nero's location while Rome burned (see ibid., p. 159).

[130]Ibid., pp. 159-60.

history as in the realm of thought is more often complex than simple.[131]

Yet even if there might be some irreconcilable differences in the accounts, this would not prove that the resurrection itself did not occur, since all the accounts agree that

> Jesus was dead, that he was buried in a tomb near Jerusalem supplied by a man named Joseph of Arimathea, that early on the day after the Sabbath certain women in the company of Jesus (among them Mary Magdalene) went to the tomb, that they found the tomb mysteriously empty, that they met an angel or angels, that the women were either told or else discovered that Jesus had been raised from the dead, and that Jesus subsequently appeared a number of times to certain of the women and certain of the disciples. There seem to be no resurrection texts that question any of these items.[132]

In fact, some minor differences in the telling of this story indicate authenticity, not substantial error. If each account perfectly mirrored the rest, this would likely be a sign of collusion, not accurate history told from differing (but equally truthful) perspectives.[133] An apologetics text from the early 1800s explains why minor disagreements in accounts of the same event should not rule out the credibility of these accounts.

> It is here to be observed, that partial variances in the testimony of different witnesses, on minute and collateral points, although they frequently afford the adverse advocate a topic for copious observation, are of little importance, unless they be of too prominent and striking a nature to be ascribed to mere inadvertence, inattention, or defect of memory.
>
> It has been well remarked by a great observer, that "the usual character of human testimony is substantial truth under circumstantial variety." It so rarely happens that witnesses of the same transaction perfectly and entirely agree in all points connected with it, that an entire and complete coincidence in every particular, so far from strengthening their credit, not infrequently engenders a suspicion of practice and concert.

---

[131]Ibid., p. 160.

[132]Stephen T. Davis, *Risen Indeed: Making Sense of the Resurrection* (Grand Rapids: Eerdmans, 1993), p. 181.

[133]Many writers have attempted to harmonize the resurrection accounts. See, e.g., Harris, *Raised Immortal*, pp. 157-63; and George Eldon Ladd, *I Believe in the Resurrection of Jesus* (Grand Rapids: Eerdmans, 1975), pp. 91-93. For a book-length treatment, see John Wenham, *Easter Enigma* (1984; reprint, Eugene, Ore.: Wipf & Stock, 2005).

The real question must always be, whether the points of variance and of discrepancy be of so strong and decisive a nature as to render it impossible, or at least difficult, to attribute them to the ordinary sources of such varieties, inattention or want of memory.[134]

CHRIST IS RISEN INDEED!

In a theistic universe miracles are not impossible but possible, since a transcendent, morally impeccable, immensely powerful being exists who could perform them. Whether any miracles have occurred becomes a historical question; they cannot be ruled out a priori according to methodological (or metaphysical) naturalism. This chapter has argued that the resurrection of Jesus is well established. The alternative naturalistic theories of the resurrection fail to account for commonly agreed-on facts relating to Jesus and the early church. This unparalleled divine intervention in history is the Rock on which the church stands.[135]

---

[134]Thomas Starkie, *A Practical Treatise of the Law of Evidence* (London: n.p., 1833), pp. 488-89. I owe this citation to Timothy McGrew.

[135]Some claim that the evidence for the resurrection cannot move beyond agnosticism, neither affirming nor denying that it occurred. On this see Gary Habermas, "The Resurrection of Jesus and Recent Agnosticism," in *Reasons for Faith: Making a Case for the Christian Faith*, ed. Norman L. Geisler and Chad V. Meister (Wheaton, Ill.: Crossway, 2007), pp. 281-95.

PART THREE

Objections to Christian Theism

23

Religious Pluralism

Many Religions, One Truth

THE VAST MAJORITY OF AMERICANS BELIEVE in God or some higher power. The 2008 Religious Landscape Report by the Pew Forum, which addressed the religious beliefs of Americans, claimed that 71 percent of Americans were absolutely certain of the existence of "God or a universal Spirit." Seventeen percent were "fairly certain."[1] The First Amendment guarantees freedom of religion, and a plurality of religions have flourished on American soil. Increasing globalization is bringing goods, services *and religions* from around the world to our shores in unprecedented ways.[2] Yet this diversity of faiths—still dominated by Christianity—often leads American Christians and others to adopt a stance toward religion in general that ill comports with a biblical view of Christianity and other religions. The Pew Forum found that 57 percent of evangelical Christians believed that "Many religions can lead to eternal life," while 70 percent of the general public held this belief.[3]

Adherents of these different religions routinely declare that their beliefs are both objectively true and essential for spiritual liberation. The dizzying plethora of religious pluralism has led many to believe that no religion can claim to be the only way of salvation. Religions should succumb to a more humble estimation of themselves in order to avoid religious dogma-

---

[1]*U.S. Religious Landscape Survey* (Washington, D.C.: Pew Research Center, 2008), p. 116, <http://religions.pewforum.org>.
[2]For an informed and wise discussion of globalization with respect to religion, see Harold Netland, *Encountering Religious Pluralism* (Downers Grove, Ill.: InterVarsity Press, 2001), pp. 80-89.
[3]*U.S. Religious Landscape Survey*, p. 58.

tism, controversy and strife. When Christians as well as others adopt the view that religion in general is good and no one religion should claim that it alone offers truth and salvation, then the biblical worldview will not be taken seriously. Religious pluralism therefore poses a significant challenge to historic Christian apologetics, which claims that Christ alone is the way of eternal salvation and that other religions cannot reconcile sinful humans to God. The Bible endorses no polyglot heaven, but a heaven alive and aglow in worship of the Lamb of God.

It is a daunting task to commend the Christian worldview as the *one* thing that matters most. To esteem Jesus as the unique and supreme revelation of God is taken by many to be theological chauvinism. The most powerful apologetic for Christianity will be ignored by anyone who simply—and probably ignorantly—accepts all religions as equally spiritual. This chapter challenges that notion and argues for a biblical view of other religions.

THE ELEPHANT AND THE BLIND MEN

A popular parable about an elephant and several blind men illustrates a common idea about the relationship among the world's religions. The story promises that religious intolerance and even violence can be overcome through mutual understanding and humility.

Several blind men were feeling an elephant. The man who felt the tusk said the beast was smooth and hard. Feeling the tail, another described the elephant as thin and wiry. One who touched the ear believed the animal to be a soft and flexible creature. The man rubbing his hand over the hide said the elephant was hard and rough like clay. Each man had but a limited exposure and understanding of the elephant. Because of his ignorance of the whole truth, each man assumed the entire elephant matched a very limited description. Of course, the elephant is made of all the things the blind men described. The tusk is smooth, the ear is soft, the hide is rough and the tail is wiry.

The moral is that each religion has only partial knowledge of the divine reality, but each mistakenly thinks it has captured the essence of religious truth. From an enlightened vantage point, one sees that all religions are part of the one divine reality (the same elephant). This parable has captured much of the popular sentiment.

RELIGION AND TRUTH CLAIMS

We will return to our elephant and his friends later. First, we need to consider the nature and function of religion in order to evaluate the claim that all religions are one in some significant sense. Defining religion is notoriously difficult. We know that Buddhism, Islam, Christianity, Judaism and Hinduism are religions, but what essential attribute do they share that makes them religions? For our purposes, a religion is defined as a set of beliefs that attempts to explain the nature of the sacred and how humans can become in harmony with it.[4] While religions involve many elements related to morality, ritual, experience and so on, all the world religions make truth claims about ultimate reality, the human condition and how humans can find spiritual liberation. A truth claim purports to represent reality accurately (see chap. 6). This is the doctrinal dimension of religion, which is indispensable to its identity.[5] Religious founders, whether Buddha or Jesus or Muhammad, purport to have received knowledge of objective truth—truth that all need to know in order to find spiritual liberation.

Religions are embedded in cultures and serve a number of social and psychological functions. They serve to unite a community, to give hope and to challenge or sanction secular powers. As William James pointed out in *The Varieties of Religious Experience* (1902), despite the vast differences between religions, "there is a certain uniform deliverance in which religions all appear to meet. This common element has two parts: (1) an uneasiness; and (2) its solution. (1) The uneasiness, reduced to its simplest terms, is a sense that there is *something wrong about us* as we naturally stand. (2) The solution is a sense that *we are saved from the wrongness* by making proper connexion with the higher powers."[6]

---

[4]On this discussion see Winfried Corduan, "Religion: Study and Practice," in *Neighboring Faiths* (Downers Grove, Ill.: InterVarsity Press, 1998), chap. 1; and Ian Markham, *A World Religions Reader*, 2nd ed. (Oxford: Blackwell, 2000), pp. 3-7.

[5]On truth claims and religion see Mortimer Adler, *Truth in Religion: The Plurality of Religions and the Unity of Truth* (New York: Macmillan, 1990); and Harold Netland, *Dissonant Voices: Religious Pluralism and the Quest for Truth* (Grand Rapids: Eerdmans, 1991); Ian Markham, "Truth and Religion," in *Routledge Companion to Philosophy of Religion*, ed. Chad Meister and Paul Copan (New York: Routledge, 2008).

[6]William James, *The Varieties of Religious Experience: The Works of William James*, ed. Frederick Burkhardt (Cambridge, Mass.: Harvard University Press, 1985), p. 400, emphasis in the original.

However, the nature of the problem and the manner of the solution proposed have been defined in widely differing ways. Religions may be similar in form and function, but they claim contradictory things about ultimate reality, the human condition and spiritual liberation. G. K. Chesterton made this point in his classic work *Orthodoxy* when he countered the idea that "the religions of the earth differ in rites and forms, but they are the same in what they teach." This idea, he maintained,

> is false; it is the opposite of the fact. The religions of the earth do *not* greatly differ in rites and forms; they do greatly differ in what they teach. . . . The truth is that the difficulty of all the creeds of the earth is not as alleged in this cheap maxim: that they agree in meaning, but disagree in machinery. It is exactly the opposite. They agree in machinery; almost every great religion on earth works with the same external methods, with priests, scriptures, altars, sworn brotherhoods, special feasts. They agree in the mode of teaching; what they differ about is the thing to be taught. . . . Creeds that exist to destroy each other both have scriptures, just as armies that exist to destroy each other both have guns.[7]

When Chesterton says that creeds exist to destroy each other, he does not mean that religions should take up arms against each other but that every religion issues truth claims that cannot be squared with the truth claims of other religions.

One way to ascertain whether all religions are one is to compare the core teachings of three major religious traditions. If all the major world religions were ultimately expressions of the same reality, we would expect them to agree on matters of ultimate reality, the human condition and spiritual liberation. At the very least we would expect to find some strategy by which to unify their apparently contradictory teachings, as with the elephant story.

Therefore, I will compare the teachings of Christianity, nondualistic Hinduism and Buddhism concerning (1) ultimate reality, (2) the nature of humanity and (3) spiritual liberation.[8] My point is to show that these world religions are not united in their basic *truth claims*. My discussion of Christianity will be very brief, since the Christian worldview was explained in chapter four.

---

[7]G. K. Chesterton, *Orthodoxy* (1908; reprint, New York: Image Books, 1959), pp. 128-29.
[8]As mentioned in chap. 16, nondualistic Hinduism is only one school of Hinduism, but has significantly influenced Western thinking in recent decades.

ULTIMATE REALITY: TRINITY, BRAHMAN OR NIRVANA?

Christianity. God is the unique and supreme Creator of the universe (Genesis 1:1), who cannot be identified with the cosmos because he is transcendent. God is a self-existent being upon whom the universe depends (Acts 17:25); he is a self-reflective, personal being (Exodus 3:14) who acts in the world. Isaiah describes God this way:

> Turn to me and be saved,
>   all you ends of the earth;
>   for I am God, and there is no other. (Isaiah 45:22)

Jesus taught his disciples to address God as their "Father" in prayer (Matthew 6:9). This personal language refers to God's very character; it is not a poetic accommodation used to describe a being beyond personality, as in some forms of Hinduism.

Christianity is also trinitarian, which distinguishes it from other forms of theism (see chap. 4). Jesus, the second person of the Trinity, is God incarnate, the promised Messiah of the Old Testament. Jesus said, "I and the Father are one," which his audience identified as a claim to deity (John 10:30). Paul affirmed that Jesus suspended some of his divine prerogatives by becoming a human servant for the purpose of redeeming his erring creatures (2 Corinthians 8:9; Philippians 2:6-11).

Nondualistic Hinduism. Hinduism is a religion of great variety, with six major schools and plenty of theological disagreements. I have chosen one school as representative of pantheistic monism (or nondualism), a worldview that has influenced the West largely through transcendental meditation and the New Age movement.[9] As taught by Sankara (A.D. 788-820), nondualistic Hinduism claims that reality is ultimately one (monism). All apparent distinctions, dualities and diversities are not real but illusory (*maya*) and due to our ignorance (*avidya*) of ultimate reality. This ultimate reality of great oneness or nonduality is called Brahman, the supreme deity of Hindu scripture. Brahman is the totality of reality (pantheism); there is nothing but Brahman.

Monism cannot become a partner with monotheism. Nondualism de-

---

[9]On the relationship between pantheistic monism and New Age perspectives, see Douglas Groothuis, *Unmasking the New Age* (Downers Grove, Ill.: InterVarsity Press, 1986); and *Confronting the New Age* (Downers Grove, Ill.: InterVarsity Press, 1988).

nies the duality of the Creator-creature distinction affirmed by Christianity. While Christianity teaches that the creation is not divine, nondualistic Hinduism teaches that there is nothing but the divine, and the self itself is divine in essence. In the Chandogya Upanishad a son asks his father about the nature of God. He is told, "That art thou."[10] The self is identical with God.

The God of nondualistic Hinduism is not a personal being but an impersonal principle or essence. Although nondualists may accommodate popular sentiment by allowing worship of a personal God (*saguna Brahman*), this is deemed a lower and inadequate understanding of God. Rather, a person should graduate to a higher knowledge of God as impersonal (*nirguna Brahman*).[11] Brahman is not a personal agent who enters into relationship with his creatures.[12]

Buddhism. Buddhism has many branches with different teachings, but I will deal with what we can know of the teachings of the Buddha himself. The Buddha did not deem theological or metaphysical speculations important, but rather unedifying and irrelevant to attaining spiritual liberation. He challenged key features of the Hinduism of his native India (such as the existence of Brahman) but did not embrace monotheism. Buddha never considered himself a revelation of God, but rather an enlightened teacher. (*Buddha* means "the enlightened one.") The ultimate reality cannot be put in positive terms, because it is unlike the impermanent and insubstantial world and can only be experienced to be known. This is nirvana, which literally means what is left when a candle is blown out. It is described in negative terms such as *cessation, the unconditioned* or *absence of craving.* It may be put positively as *freedom from rebirth.* Nirvana is not a person or a place, but a condition. This state beyond the human can only be achieved through rigorous discipline.

---

[10]Swami Prabhavananda and Frederick Manchester, *The Upanishads: Breath of the Eternal* (New York: Mentor, 1957), p. 70.

[11]For an insightful discussion and critique of this distinction, see Stuart Hackett, *Oriental Philosophy: A Westerner's Guide to Eastern Thought* (Madison: University of Wisconsin Press, 1979), pp. 145-67; and Douglas Groothuis, "Sankara's Two Level Theory of Truth: Nondualism on Trial," *Journal of the International Society of Christian Apologetics* 1, no. 1 (2008): 105-12.

[12]For a good general treatment of pantheistic monism see James Sire, "Journey to the East: Eastern Pantheistic Monism," chap. 5 in Sire, *The Universe Next Door*, 5th ed. (Downers Grove, Ill.: InterVarsity Press, 2009); Os Guinness, "The East No Exit," chap. 6 in *The Dust of Death* (1973; reprint, Wheaton, Ill.: Crossway, 1994).

HUMAN NATURE: SINFUL, IGNORANT OR DIVINE?

Christianity. Humans are made in the image and likeness of God for the purpose of having fellowship with God and each other, and in order to cultivate and develop God's good creation (Genesis 1–2). However, humans disobeyed the wise will of God and fell into disobedience and sin (Genesis 3). Ever since, people have suffered from the effects of this rebellion. "All have sinned and fall short of the glory of God" (Romans 3:23). Sin is a force that has corrupted every aspect of human nature and all areas of life. It is a moral offense against a morally perfect God, and it severs the divine-human relationship (Psalm 51:4).

Nondualistic Hinduism. Human beings are inherently one with Brahman. The individual self (sometimes referred to as Atman) is not a creature of Brahman or distinct from Brahman. The sense of separation comes from ignorance of one's true identity. Since God is impersonal and all-encompassing, nondualism has no notion of sin as a moral offense against a holy God. The flaw in humanity is a lack of awareness of one's essence as divine. Sankara said, "The difference between the individual self and the highest Lord is owing to wrong knowledge only, not to any reality."[13]

Buddhism. The Buddha did not speculate about human origins but focused on the human condition as (1) suffused with suffering and (2) brought about through unfulfilled desires (the first two of the Four Noble Truths, the essence of Buddhism). People cannot satisfy their souls with anything because they do not have souls (i.e., enduring substances). Just as a chariot has no essence but is only a collection of individual parts, so the human person has no essence; it is only a collection of states called *skandas*. Because there is no soul, there is no personal afterlife. While the Buddha did not deny the Hindu idea of reincarnation, he denied that there is any individual soul that comes back in another form, animal or human.

SPIRITUAL LIBERATION: FAITH OR ENLIGHTENMENT?

Last, we come to the vital matter of spiritual liberation. As William James

---

[13]Sankara, quoted in *A Sourcebook in Indian Philosophy*, ed. Sarvepalli Radhkrishnan and Charles A. Moore (Princeton, N.J.: Princeton University Press, 1957), p. 515.

observed, all religions offer purported solutions to the human condition. Just what is wrong? How can it be corrected?[14]

Christianity. Christians hail Jesus as the Lord and Savior of humanity and as God incarnate (John 1:14). He lived a perfect life, died a sacrificial death on the cross so that people could be reconciled to a holy God and rose from the dead to vindicate his mission (Romans 1:4). There is one mediator between God and humanity, Christ Jesus (1 Timothy 2:5-6). Spiritual liberation bestows on the believer the forgiveness of sins and a righteous standing before God. This is received by faith alone in Christ alone through God's grace alone (Ephesians 2:8).[15]

Nondualistic Hinduism. Spiritual liberation (*moksha*) is achieved through the proper yoga (spiritual practice). Sankara taught that *jnana* yoga (the yoga of knowledge) was the means to realize the self's identity as Brahman. He said that "the man who has once comprehended Brahman to be the Self does not belong to this transmigratory [reincarnational] world as he did before. "On the other hand, he who still belongs to this transmigratory world as before has not comprehended Brahman to be the Self."[16] The person who experiences *moksha* is released from the wheel of reincarnation and finds his or her divine identity. Everyone is Brahman itself (whether one knows it or not).

Buddhism. Buddha taught that spiritual deliverance was found by letting go of desire—the quest to satisfy the nonexistent soul—and by detaching oneself from impermanent things. This is the Third Noble Truth. The Fourth Noble Truth is that salvation is achieved through proper effort called "the eightfold path." It requires wisdom (right understanding and thought), ethical conduct (right speech, action and livelihood) and mental discipline (right effort, awareness and meditation). Those who succeed transcend the realm of karma and rebirth, and attain nirvana. Buddha did not bestow this state on others; he simply pointed toward it.

Table 23.1 summarizes the religious teachings we have been discussing.

---

[14]James, *Varieties of Religious Experience*, p. 400.
[15]For the biblical doctrine of justification by faith alone, see R. C. Sproul, *Faith Alone: The Evangelical Doctrine of Justification* (Grand Rapids: Baker, 1995); and Charles Hodge, *Justification by Faith Alone* (Hobbes, N.M.: Trinity Foundation, 1995).
[16]Sankara, quoted in Radhkrishnan and Moore, ed., *Sourcebook*, p. 513.

Table 23.1. Major Teachings of Christianity, Hinduism and Buddhism

Religion	Ultimate Reality	Human Condition	Spiritual Liberation
Christianity	Triune, personal God	In God's image but fallen, sinful	Found through faith alone in Jesus Christ alone
Nondualistic Hinduism	Impersonal God (Brahman)	Divine but ignorant	By knowledge of inner divinity
Buddha (Theravada Buddhism)	Impersonal state of being (nirvana)	Nonsubstantial (no soul), ignorant	The path of knowledge leading to nirvana

ASSESSING THE DIFFERENCES

Recall the elephant and the blind men. The story puts all the world's religions in the position of blind men. No world religion would accept this assessment, because each claims to reveal ultimate and universal truths, not partial insights needing elaboration from other religions. Even Hinduism, which claims tolerance and universality, denies the absolute claims of other religions and reinterprets other religions according to its own worldview.[17] Those who employ the elephant story claim to look down on all the religions from an elevated vantage point. In essence, the interpreter is creating a new religion that denies the particular claims of the actual religions he or she is assessing.[18] Moreover, the parable tells us that the blind men are touching the same elephant, which represents the reality of all religions. But the claim that all religions (blind men) are part of a greater whole (the elephant) is what needs to be proved. The parable merely asserts this without evidence.[19] Can the supposedly elevated view of religion really reconcile the divergent claims we have discovered?

Although an elephant can be rough in one spot and smooth in another, it cannot be smooth all over and rough all over simultaneously. Likewise, the ultimate reality cannot be both nirvana and the personal God of the Bible. Nirvana is neither a personal nor a divine being, but rather an impersonal state of being. Neither can we align the nondualistic views of impersonal Brahman with the thoroughly personal notions of deity found in Christianity. God's nature cannot be both personal and impersonal,

---

[17]See S. Radhakrishnan, *The Hindu Way of Life* (New York: Macmillan, 1964), chap. 2, particularly p. 34.

[18]On this see Lesslie Newbigin, *The Gospel in a Pluralist Society* (Grand Rapids: Eerdmans, 1989), pp. 9-10.

[19]Thanks to Professor Harold Netland for this point.

because personality cancels out impersonality and vice versa. The biblical God is thoroughly and purely personal, with no admixture of impersonality. While both nirvana and Brahman are impersonal accounts of ultimate reality, they are contradictory as well, since Brahman is the Absolute Self and nirvana is the absence of any self. In fact, early disputes between Buddhists and Hindus focused on just these debates. Buddhists critiqued the Hindu doctrine of Brahman, and Hindus returned the favor by arguing against the Buddhist doctrine of no self (anatman).[20]

The same logical difficulties in harmonizing these religions emerge in their teachings on human nature and liberation. Buddha taught that salvation was found by leaving the world of craving through a rigorous life of discipline. Jesus taught that salvation was found not in human effort but through faith in his own unique achievements. Humans cannot be both one with Brahman (nondualism) and distinct from their Creator (Christianity).

Differing descriptions of ultimate reality lead to differing descriptions of the human problem and to different prescriptions for its solution. It seems that the elephant and its benighted observers have let us down.

PERENNIALISM: A WIDE PATH AND A DEAD END

In his popular book *Living Buddha, Living Christ*, Buddhist monk Thich Nhat Hanh describes the Christian ceremony of Communion as a way in which Christians reflect on their interconnections with the earth, represented by the wine and the bread. He says: "If we allow ourselves to touch our bread deeply, we become reborn, because our bread is life itself. Eating it deeply, we touch the sun, the clouds, the earth, and everything in the cosmos. We touch life, and we touch the kingdom of God."[21] Hanh straps Christian Communion onto the Procrustean bed of Zen Buddhism. By doing so, he denies the Christ-centered practice of remembering and celebrating Jesus' broken body (the bread) and shed blood (the wine), which were offered through his death on the cross. Hanh has a "personal shrine" containing images of Buddha and Jesus, both of whom he deems spiritual

---

[20]Richard King, *Indian Philosophy: An Introduction to Hindu and Buddhist Thought* (Washington, D.C.: Georgetown University Press, 2007).
[21]Thich Nhat Hanh, *Living Buddha, Living Christ* (New York: G. P. Putnam's, 1995), p. 31. Hanh redefines Christianity in Buddhist terms.

brothers. But Hanh does nothing to bring greater understanding to religious discussion, because he does not honor the intrinsic meaning of the religion being described. The kingdom of God, biblically understood, is not a matter of oneness with the cosmos but of God's personal reign and redeeming presence.[22]

Hanh is not alone in this disingenuous endeavor. Perennialism teaches that certain core truths are perennially evident in the great world religions. All the major religions disagree only on peripheral matters. The unenlightened are those who consider only the outer or *exoteric* elements of the religion and thus never reach the core *esoteric* reality. The wise, however, realize that at the esoteric level, all religions teach the same thing. This thesis has been advanced by Aldous Huxley, and more recently by Joseph Campbell (1904-1987) in the bestselling book and popular television series *The Power of Myth* and in the writings of the prolific nondualist author Ken Wilber.[23] Wilber chastises Christians for remaining at the exoteric level and failing to realize that when Christ said that "I and the Father are one" this "was the same revelation that the [Hindu] Upanishads brought in India: Tat tvam asi, 'Thou art that,' you and God are ultimately one."[24] Although Jesus was only an adept who recognized the reality of nondualism, the church mistook him to be uniquely God incarnate.[25]

Celebrated religion writer Huston Smith has long taught perennialism, as presented in his popular 1958 textbook, *The Religions of Man* (later retitled *The World's Religions*). More recently he summed up his view of Christianity in *The Soul of Christianity*. Smith's definition of Christianity excludes any reference to Jesus, and he redefines every cardinal and historic doctrine of Christianity according to his pantheistic presuppositions. For example, he writes that at Jesus' baptism his "third eye" was opened.[26] This indicates that Smith sees Christianity through a Hindu lens. In Hin-

---

[22]On the kingdom of God see Craig Blomberg, *Jesus and the Gospels*, 2nd ed. (Nashville: Broadman & Holman, 2009), pp. 448-52.

[23]Aldous Huxley, *The Perennial Philosophy* (1944; reprint, New York: Meridian Books, 1969). Joseph Campbell, *The Power of Myth* (New York: Anchor Books, 1988). For a critique of Campbell see Douglas Groothuis, "Myth and the Power of Joseph Campbell," in *Christianity That Counts* (Grand Rapids: Baker Books 1994), pp. 150-62. Ken Wilber, *Up from Eden* (New York: Anchor Books, 1981).

[24]Wilber, *Up from Eden*, p. 244.

[25]Ken Wilber, *Sex, Ecology, Spirituality: The Spirit of Evolution*, 2nd ed. (Boston: Shambhala, 2000), pp. 362-65.

[26]Huston Smith, *The Soul of Christianity* (San Francisco: HarperSanFrancisco, 2005), p. 41.

duism the third eye is considered one of the chakras (energy centers) of the human body. Awakening the third eye through yoga means that one has intuited one's own innate spiritual power, if not deity. Hinduism teaches that this is possible for anyone who goes through the right yogic practices. Despite this, Smith's book was endorsed by two purportedly evangelical writers.[27] But, as ex-Hindu guru and Christian convert Rabi Maharaj says, "Jesus was not enlightened. He is the light of the world!"[28]

For Hanh, Huxley, Campbell, Wilber, Smith and others, the esoteric religion is not a form of theism (and especially not orthodox Christianity, which they abhor), but nondualistic pantheism.[29] The unavoidable problem for perennialism of all stripes is that it lacks justification for its project of redefining all religions according to one underlying worldview (nondualism). The burden of proof is certainly on the perennialists, since they must refute the longstanding understandings of the fundamental teachings of all religions outside of nondualism.[30]

JOHN HICK'S RELIGIOUS PLURALISM

Nevertheless, several modern thinkers—of whom John Hick is the most prominent—have tried to harmonize the world's religions without resorting to perennialism.[31] If Hick is correct, we can move beyond both perennialism and particularism (the view that one religion is uniquely true and uniquely salvific). Hick's theory of religious pluralism is too involved to be adequately criticized here.[32] However, we can assess some important elements of his approach.

---

[27]See my review of *The Soul of Christianity* in *Christian Research Journal* 29, no. 4 (2006): 48-49.

[28]I heard this remark in a lecture by Maharaj. See his remarkable book *Death of a Guru* (Eugene, Ore.: Harvest House, 1984), which records his conversion from Hindu guru to evangelical Christian.

[29]This book argues that nondualism cannot account for the creation of the universe out of nothing, cannot answer the problem of evil, cannot give significance to the individual human person and cannot find any support through arguments from religious experience. As such, it fails to be a rationally convincing worldview.

[30]For a brief and cogent refutation of perennialism see Netland, *Encountering Religious Pluralism*, pp. 106-10; see also Keith E. Yandell, "On the Alleged Unity of All Religions," *Christian Scholar's Review* 6 (1976): 140-55.

[31]The most developed statement of Hick's position is *An Interpretation of Religion* (New Haven, Conn.: Yale University Press, 1989).

[32]For more thorough critiques see Netland, *Dissonant Voices*, esp. chaps. 5-7; Netland, *Encountering Religious Pluralism*, esp. pp. 158-77, 218-26; and Ronald Nash, *Is Jesus the Only Savior?* (Grand Rapids: Zondervan, 1995), chaps. 1-6.

Hick is one of the major philosophers of religion in the last fifty years, contributing to discussions of religious language, religious experience and, most recently, religious pluralism. He believes that all the major religions produce saintly people with roughly the same success rate. His encounters with saintly non-Christians were a key factor in his conversion from conservative Protestantism to his present view.[33] Therefore, he believes that salvation cannot be restricted to one religion because this rules out too many saints from other religions. But he realizes that religions teach very different things and that they cannot be distilled to some hypothetical essence (perennialism).

Hick's strategy for reconciling conflicting truth claims involves creating an all-encompassing category called "the Real," which signifies the ultimate reality that is the source of the diverse manifestations of the major world religions. Hick knows that religions disagree on key truth claims. He does not claim that all religions are one in essence, and he is not a relativist. Rather than siding with one religion against the others, he claims that all express "the Real" in different, culturally bound, but equally salvific, ways.

Hick's theory depends on three very questionable assumptions, all of which have already been challenged in this book. First, he believes that knowledge of God comes only through religious experience and cannot be informative about the very nature of God. That is, he denies that *objective* knowledge of God is possible through religious experience. Nevertheless, he does not deem religious experience as merely subjective or nonrealist, since he claims that these experiences can warrant various (and even contradictory) beliefs concerning the Real, which does objectively exist. However, there is no knowledge of the Real as it is in itself. Hick also denies the category of propositional revelation as given in the Bible. Second, because of this, Hick claims that the universe is "religiously ambiguous"—it may be rationally interpreted in many different ways: either as theistic, polytheistic or even atheistic. Therefore, one major worldview cannot rationally rule out others through philosophical argument. Third, Hick denies that the New Testament is historically reliable. He takes its accounts of Jesus to be largely mythical and metaphorical. Therefore, he finds no reason to

---

[33]See Netland, *Encountering Religious Pluralism*, chap. 5.

take seriously the New Testament claim that Jesus is the only Lord and Savior of the universe.[34] In light of these presuppositions, he states his hypothesis this way:

> [There is an] ultimate ineffable Reality which is the source and ground of everything, and which is such that in so far as the religious traditions are in soteriological alignment with it they are contexts of salvation/liberation. These traditions involve different human conceptions of the Real, with correspondingly different forms of experience of the Real, and corresponding different forms of life in response to the Real.[35]

This removes the Real from any meaningful intellectual content, since it is "ineffable." It is beyond any substantial description. Hick claims that the Real is equally represented by *personae* (personal understandings of God, as in Judaism, Christianity, Islam and so on) and as *impersonae* (impersonal understandings of God as in Hinduism, Taoism and so on). Yet, for Hick, the Real is neither personal nor impersonal.

> [The Real] cannot be said to be one or many, person or thing, conscious or unconscious, purposive or nonpurposive, substance or process, good or evil, loving or hating. None of these descriptive terms apply literally to the unexperienceable reality that underlies that realm.[36]

We cannot say the Real is personal because this would oppose pantheism and Buddhism; neither can we say it is impersonal, because this would oppose monotheism. We cannot even say the Real is divine, since Theravada Buddhism is atheistic or agnostic. Hick must drain the concept of ultimate reality of all substantial meaning in order to inflate it into a metaphysical and epistemological category capacious enough to serve as the source and basis for all religions. The Real is beyond the reach of concepts. Hick is forced into this position because he must defend the equality of mutually contradictory religious claims.

However, this appeal to the unknowable solves nothing and triggers an avalanche of problems. If all Hick can say of the Real is that it exists and is the source of the world's religions, he can say nothing specific about its

---

[34]Netland presents and discusses Hick's presuppositions astutely in *Encountering Religious Pluralism*, pp. 158-77.

[35]John Hick, *A Christian Theology of Religions* (Louisville: Westminster John Knox, 1995), p. 27.

[36]John Hick, *An Interpretation of Religion* (New York: Oxford University Press, 1989), p. 350.

nature. Hick admits that we cannot refer to the Real as having knowledge, as being powerful, or as being good or loving. The proverbial blind men knew more about the elephant than Professor Hick says religions know about the Real. But if the Real is unknowable, it cannot adequately explain the nature of the world's religions, since knowledge is required for explanation. If I claim to explain a mysterious death by saying, "I have no idea who or what did it," I have explained nothing. If our concept of the Real can never capture its essential nature, then why should we believe that the Real is the source of all genuine religious manifestations, especially when these traditions explicitly contradict each other on fundamental doctrines? The Real, therefore, becomes mute—and meaningless.

Moreover, the description of the Real itself appears to be logically incoherent. As such, it cannot serve to explain anything. This problem can be disclosed by a close analysis of Hick's basic statement about the nature of the Real.

In the previous quote Hick sets up a series of seven contradictory predicates, neither of which may be predicated of the Real. If two predicates have a contradictory relationship to each other, both cannot be true in the same way and in the same respect (given the law of noncontradiction). However, one or the other of the predicates must be true, because there is no other alternative. That is, for contradictory relationships the following three statements are true.

1. Either X or Y.

2. Not neither X nor Y. It has to be one or the other.

3. Not both X and Y.

This is also called *exclusive disjunction*. To make this concrete, consider this statement, which involves contradictory predicates.

O1: Object O at time T1 is either transparent (can be seen through) or opaque (cannot be seen through).

We can either see through the object to some extent or we cannot (assuming normal human vision and adequate light). But consider this statement:

O2: Object O at time T1 is *neither* transparent *nor* opaque.

But what else could this object be? The alternatives—we can see through it or we cannot—exhaust all the possibilities. Therefore, this statement is false, since there is no third alternative to opacity or transparency as I have described them.

Consider again Hick's description of the Real, "which cannot be said" to have positive descriptions. He claims the Real is

1. Neither one nor many

2. Neither person nor thing

3. Neither conscious nor unconscious

4. Neither purposive nor nonpurposive

5. Neither substance nor process

6. Neither good nor evil

7. Neither loving nor hating

Consider statements 1-5. These polarities exhaust the logical possibilities. The qualities described in statements 1-5 are all negated; there are no predicates remaining for an entity to possess. Any entity, the Real or otherwise, would have to possess one or the other of the dichotomistic alternatives specified in statements 1-5. Therefore, Hick appears to be defining the Real out of existence altogether.

But now consider statement 6, which concerns moral qualities. If an entity were impersonal (that is a thing, not a person—the alternative specified in statement 2), then it could be neither good nor evil (statement 6); it would also be neither loving nor hating (statement 7). For example, a rock is neither good nor evil (in a moral sense).[37] Therefore, Hick could only affirm statements 6 and 7 if he were to affirm that the Real is impersonal. But affirming the Real as impersonal is precluded by statement 2, which excludes the Real being a "person or *thing*"—*thing* means something *impersonal*. As Netland notes, "It seems that although the Real is the foundation of both personal and nonpersonal conceptions of the religious ultimate, in itself the Real is neither personal nor non-

---

[37]I say "in a moral sense" because Genesis 1 teaches that the entire creation was "good," rocks included. But it is not moral goodness in the sense that moral agents can be good.

personal. It transcends such distinctions."[38]

But Hick is in a pickle if he cannot make the idea of the Real intelligible. His statements 1-5 seem to eliminate any kind of existence. Yet the Real must exist to serve Hick's purposes. Statements 6-7 could only apply to an impersonal reality, but Hick claims he cannot attribute impersonality to the Real either, since it transcends the "person or thing" dichotomy (statement 2). (He is not supposed to take sides on the question of the personality or impersonality of the Real, given his metaphysical agnosticism about the religious ultimate.) Thus Hick's set of seven negations are not internally consistent; thus, the set cannot be affirmed as true, and his very concept of the Real fails; thus it explains nothing.

In the introduction to the second edition of *An Interpretation of Religion*, Hick briefly responds to this kind of criticism, which has been made by William Rowe and Alvin Plantinga.[39] He argues that just as the concept of "clever" or "not clever" does not apply to a molecule, neither does "personal" or "non-personal" relate to the Real. Hick simply reaffirms that it "would importantly infringe on the principle of divine transcategoriality" to affirm substantial predicates to the Real. Quite so, but it is just that principle that Plantinga, Rowe and myself have subjected to philosophical criticism. Hick ignores this criticism more than responds to its substance.[40]

Yet there are three other problems with Hick's pluralistic hypothesis. First, a strong motivation for Hick's religious pluralism is the moral goodness of non-Christians. He took this to be commendable and remarkable, given his previous evangelical belief that only Christians were redeemed. However, a conservative Christian worldview can account for moral goodness on a horizontal level apart from granting such people salvation on that basis. God's image remains in all people (Genesis 1:26), and because of that they may, to some degree, live by the light of their God-given conscience (Romans 2:14-15). But all fall short of the perfect righteousness

---

[38]Netland, *Dissonant Voices*, p. 217.

[39]John Hick, *An Interpretation of Religion*, 2nd ed. (New Haven, Conn.: Yale University Press, 2004), pp. xx-xxi. The main text and pagination of this edition are identical to the first edition. The only difference comes with the addition of a new introduction.

[40]Ibid., p. xxii. It is odd that Hick used the term *divine transcategoriality*, since he emphasizes that the Real must incorporate or encompass both theistic and nontheistic understandings. Thus to call it "divine" prejudices the matter toward theism, a category the real is supposed to transcend. This is no small inconsistency for Hick.

that God requires (Matthew 22:37-40; Romans 3:23). Nevertheless, this concern over salvation pushed Hick away from Christian particularism and into pluralism. Hick's pluralism claims that the Real—purportedly the transcendent source of all religion—"cannot be said to be good or evil." This puts Hick in the strange position of claiming that

1. The Real generates saints (morally exemplary people) who *as such* bear witness to the reality of the spiritual world and the legitimacy of their own varying religions.

2. The Real itself cannot be said to possess any moral properties.

But if the Real is barren of moral properties, then it has no moral properties to impart to the various "saints" in the world's religions. This undercuts a key reason for adopting Hick's pluralistic hypothesis in the first place. Since statements 1 and 2 are both required for his system, and because they contradict each other, his system cannot be true.

Second, Hick affirms that we cannot "say that the Real is either purposive or non-purposive." But remember "saint *production*" is vital to his hypothesis. All the major religions of the world produce saints with roughly the same degree of success. This commits Hick to affirming the following two statements:

1. The Real produces saints (morally exemplary people) that bear witness to the reality of the spiritual world and the legitimacy of their own religions.

2. The Real cannot be said to be purposive or nonpurposive.

However, statement 2 contradicts statement 1, which itself requires that the Real be the *purpose* behind the production of saints. Since these statements are both required for his system, and because they contradict each other, Hick's system cannot be true.

Third, Hick attempts to conserve the reality of all the world's major religions. It is, after all, a *pluralistic* hypothesis, not an exclusionary one. Yet, ironically, Hick's hypothesis ends up negating the cardinal doctrines of all the major religions, which end up being only culturally dependent responses to the Real. Hick tries to handle the disagreements between religions by claiming that whenever a religion makes exclusive claims about reality (as they all do in one way or another), the religion over-extends itself. The enlightened perspective sees all religions as partial expressions of the Real—even if the religions themselves allow no such category. But in so doing, Hick creates a new religious (and ultimately irreligious) category in order to harmonize religions.

ACCOUNTING FOR JESUS CHRIST

The ideas of Hick and other religious pluralists collapse in the face of Jesus Christ. They cannot accept him as he is presented in the New Testament and still claim that all religions are one. Hick knows this. "If Jesus was literally God incarnate, and if it is by his death alone that men can be saved, and by their response to him alone that they can appropriate that salvation, then the only doorway to eternal life is Christian faith."[41]

Although the monotheistic religions claim that God influences the world in some way, Christianity is unique in claiming that God became a human being in history for the purpose of our redemption (chaps. 20-22). Hinduism teaches that the impersonal Brahman sometimes takes a personal form as an avatar to help enlighten the ignorant. But avatars are historically shadowy (or nonexistent) figures, having little in common with Christ.[42] Although the Buddha and Christ are often compared, the Buddha made no divine or even prophetic claims.[43] Muhammad, for all he is revered in Islam, claimed only to be a prophet, not an incarnation (see chap. 24).

CHRISTIANITY AND THE UNEVANGELIZED

The attempt to take the particularity out of Christianity, whether through the perennialist or pluralist strategy, fails. Nevertheless, a daunting question remains for Christian apologetics. What is the fate of the countless souls throughout history who either had no contact with God's covenanted people in the Old Testament period or who never had access to the gospel in the New Testament period? The question can be formulated into a

---

[41]John Hick, "Jesus and the World Religions," in *The Myth of God Incarnate*, ed. John Hick (London: SCM, 1977), p. 180, quoted in Netland, *Dissonant Voices*, p. 241.

[42]On the avatar doctrine in relation to the incarnation, see Geoffrey Parrinder, *Avatar and Incarnation* (New York: Barnes & Noble, 1970).

[43]For an insightful comparison between Buddha and Jesus, see Russell Aldwinkle, *More Than a Man: A Study in Christology* (Grand Rapids: Eerdmans, 1976), pp. 211-46.

modus tollens argument against Christianity.

1. If Christianity is true, then those who have not had the opportunity to respond to God's saving revelation (either during the old covenant or during the new covenant) cannot be redeemed.

2. It would ill befit a God of love and justice to punish people so severely for what they could not have known.

3. Therefore, Christianity is not true, since it teaches that (a) God is loving and just, and that (b) most people are damned.

Before responding to this charge, there is another way to disarm it—or at least soften its force. The previous argument may be stood on its head by a *modus ponens* argument.[44]

1. If there is good reason to believe that Christianity is true (considering the cumulative case argument made here and elsewhere), then *however* God relates to his creatures who did not have access to covenantal revelation, God will demonstrate his just, holy and loving character.

2. There is good reason to believe that Christianity is true given the manifold evidence in its favor.

3. Therefore, the fate of those outside of covenantal revelation is in the hands of a just and loving God, however God works this out.

This argument could especially trade on the goodness and justice matchlessly evidenced through the life, death and resurrection of Jesus Christ (see chaps. 20-22). If Christ is the Lord, Savior and Judge of the universe, we can rest assured that his judgments will be righteous.

Although it may appear that this is an evasion, it is not. The issue of the fate of the unevangelized remains, but it is now framed by the apologetic arguments already established in this book. We can, however, build a detailed and positive case that God's treatment of the unevangelized is just. The topic of the fate of the unevangelized in particular, and the relationship of Christianity to other religions in general, has generated a considerable literature among evangelicals in recent decades, which I

---

[44]Some may note this argument employs what the philosophical literature calls the "G. E. Moore shift." A short but clear discussion of the history and nature of this argument can be found in Ronald H. Nash, *Faith and Reason: Searching for a Rational Faith* (Grand Rapids: Zondervan, 1988), pp. 112-13.

cannot canvass.[45] Instead, I will pinpoint several key concerns as they pertain to the issue at hand.

THE DEBATE ON THE UNEVANGELIZED: BASIC POINTS

Before directly addressing the fate of the unevangelized, we need to consider eight crucial concerns. First, the Bible should not be twisted in order to synthesize its revealed teachings with those of non-Christian religions. This is the failed program of perennialism. To adopt perennialism would be to engage in an ad hoc and illegitimate readjustment of Christianity (as well as other religions).[46] As highlighted in our earlier discussion, Christianity is antithetical to nondualistic Hinduism and Buddhism at crucial points. The same antithesis is evident when Christianity is compared with other religions such as Islam, Taoism, animism and Confucianism.[47]

Second, Christianity's veins pump pure and strong with the lifeblood of world evangelization. The church has been commissioned by its Lord to take the gospel to all the nations (Matthew 28:18-20; Luke 24:44-47; Acts 1:8). This is nonnegotiable and essential. God is a missionary God; Christ is a missionary Christ; the church is a missionary church.[48] This presupposes that the gospel needs to be made known to those who are ignorant of it. Any approach to Christianity or other religions that undermines or mitigates this evangelistic thrust is incompatible with genuine, revealed religion.[49]

Third, although Christianity cannot be reduced to a common core that it shares with other religions, it can still find *some* common ground with respect to the *individual beliefs* held by other religions. Other religions are not completely false, even though their teachings cannot offer salvation and even though they must be rejected as inadequate religious *systems* or *worldviews*.[50] This issue is richly explored in Winfried Corduan's study *A*

---

[45]See Veli-Matti Kärkkäinen, *An Introduction to the Theology of Religions: Biblical, Historical and Contemporary Perspectives* (Downers Grove, Ill.: InterVarsity Press, 2003).

[46]See the discussion of infelicitous ad hoc readjustments in worldviews in chap. 3.

[47]See Dean Halverson, ed., *The Compact Guide to World Religions* (Minneapolis: Bethany House, 1996).

[48]I owe these turns of phrase to a lecture by John Stott.

[49]For the larger theology of mission see Christopher Wright, *The Mission of God* (Downers Grove, Ill.: InterVarsity Press, 2006).

[50]On this distinction see David Clark, *To Know and Love God* (Wheaton, Ill.: Crossway, 2003), p. 323.

Tapestry of Faiths.[51] The Christian must not cavalierly dismiss other religions, saying they contain no truth.

Human beings, while fallen and needing redemption, still bear God's image, have a conscience and live in God's world. These facts make general revelation possible (Psalm 19:1-6; Romans 1–2). Therefore, we should expect that other religions contain some truth about morality, humanity and the sacred. For example, Buddhism affirms the value of compassion and releasing people from suffering. The more conservative forms of Judaism affirm much of what Christians believe, since they take the Hebrew Scriptures to be authoritative. Nevertheless, they still need the promised Messiah for their salvation.[52] We might liken the relationship of Christianity and other religions to a group of people beginning to walk through a maze. Since it is the narrow path that leads to life, Christianity alone makes it through the twists and turns all the way to the center of the maze. However, other religions make it part way there, before running into dead ends where their worldview is false. So, the two other major monotheistic religions, Judaism and Islam, share the journey to the point of monotheism but hit a wall at the point of Christ as the Mediator and Lord.[53]

Fourth, because of the Fall, human beings, apart from special revelation and regeneration, will twist the deposit of truth knowable through general revelation into false religions and philosophies. Paul explains this devolution carefully in Romans 1:18-32. He begins by declaring that "the wrath of God is being revealed from heaven against all the godlessness of people, who suppress the truth by their wickedness" (v. 18). This bodes ill for the natural person. Paul then notes that all people are responsible for the knowledge that they have, since "what may be known about God is plain to them, because God has made it plain to them. For since the creation of the world God's invisible qualities—his eternal power and divine nature—have been clearly seen, being understood from what has been made, so that people are without excuse" (vv. 19-20). But despite the revelation given, it is taken wrongly: "For although they knew God, they

---

[51]Winfried Corduan, *A Tapestry of Faiths* (Downers Grove, Ill.: InterVarsity Press, 2002).
[52]Of course, as Paul lamented, when they read the Old Testament they do so as if the had a veil over their hearts (2 Corinthians 3:15).
[53]I owe this illustration to J. P. Moreland and Tim Muehlhoff, *The God Conversation* (Downers Grove, Ill.: InterVarsity Press, 2007), pp. 50-52.

neither glorified him as God nor gave thanks to him, but their thinking became futile and their foolish hearts were darkened" (v. 21). They thus became foolish by exchanging "the glory of the immortal God for images made to look like a mortal human being and birds and animals and reptiles" (v. 23). Idolatry eclipsed the truth known through nature and the result was judgment (vs. 24-32).

Neither Paul nor any other biblical writer has any faith in pagan religiosity. When Paul writes to the Ephesians concerning the fact that Christ has broken down the wall that separates Jews and Gentiles, he in no way downplays the lostness of the Gentiles apart from Christ. Paul reminds them that before their conversion they were "separate from Christ, excluded from citizenship in Israel and foreigners to the covenants of the promise, without hope and without God in the world" (Ephesians 2:12). This alienation was overcome not through their godly response to general revelation or through their inherent virtues, but "by the blood of Christ" (Ephesians 2:13), which they took as their own. Similarly, when Jesus was speaking to the Samaritan woman at the well, he affirmed unequivocally that the Samaritans worshiped in ignorance, but the Jews had the proper knowledge of God, since "salvation is from the Jews" (John 4:22).

Fifth, the Bible nowhere claims that people will be judged according to what they do not know or could not have known. Rather, God holds people accountable for the knowledge that is made available to them and how they have responded to it. (This is why we always find some common ground with the unbeliever, religious or otherwise.) In building his case against the human race in the first three chapters of Romans, Paul never affirms or even intimates that people are held accountable for knowledge they could not have gained. He rather argues that through the witness of the created order God can be known to exist and to be worthy of thanksgiving (Romans 1:18-32; see also Psalm 19:1-6). Additionally, all people have been given a conscience that connects them to an objective moral order rooted in God himself (Romans 2:14-15). Various Hebrew prophets (Amos, Isaiah, Jonah) spoke against the immorality of the pagan nations surrounding Israel, even though these nations were not beneficiaries of the law of Moses. This assumes that the pagan nations had sufficient knowledge of moral truth to render them accountable before God. Whatever evaluation is to be made of those outside the divine covenants will be leveled on the basis of this available knowledge.

Sixth, no one is morally or spiritually worthy of redemption, nor can anyone claim it as a right or entitlement. Humans are too mired in sin and rebellion, as I argued in chapter eighteen ("Deposed Royalty") and in chapter twenty (based on Jesus' teachings about humanity's sinfulness). This is pertinent to the objection that it is unfair for God to condemn so many "good people" who were not recipients of special revelation. The image of God in all people explains unbelievers who exhibit significant obedience to the second table of the law (Exodus 20:12-17). Nevertheless, all our deeds are "filthy rags" (Isaiah 64:6) in comparison to God's perfect standard and the luminous example of Jesus Christ himself (Romans 3:14-26). Salvation is a divine gift to the undeserving, which is offered by a gracious, just and holy God.

Seventh, whatever position we hold on the fate of the unevangelized, given the truth and rationality of the Christian worldview it is impossible that anyone can be redeemed except through the mediation of Jesus Christ (Matthew 11:27; John 14:6; Acts 4:12; 1 Timothy 2:5). He alone is the source of reconciliation with God, atonement for sin, forgiveness of sin, justification before God, adoption into God's family and the bestowal of eternal life.

Eighth, Christians cannot sidestep the biblical insistence that some will incorrigibly resist and rebel against the knowledge of God provided to them, whether they are privy to special revelation or not. Those who are finally unrepentant are beyond redemption and will be consigned to eternal punishment. Those who search the Scriptures for support for universalism (that Christ will eventually save all people) labor in vain. There are several biblical passages that clearly affirm that some will suffer this loss. After the parable of the sheep and the goats, Jesus speaks of those who served him by serving the "least of these." These receive "eternal life." Those who failed to serve him by failing to serve the "least of these" go into "eternal punishment" (Matthew 25:31-46). The same Greek word for "eternal" is used in both cases, and the constructions are identical. Therefore, if the life given by Christ is eternal and conscious, so is the punishment eternal and conscious. This doctrine, however difficult to swallow for the believer or unbeliever, is an essential part of the Christian message and should be part of a faithful Christian apologetic.[54]

PARTICULARISM AND INCLUSIVISM

In light of these eight points, we can begin to answer the question of what happens to those of other religions who never hear the gospel. Evangelicals are divided on this issue. Although various categorical schemes have been used, I will simply divide the field into the particularists (exclusivists) and the inclusivists. Both camps believe that Christ alone is the only *agent* of salvation. The two camps differ over how much a person needs to know about the salvific plan of God in order to be redeemed. Inclusivists believe that salvation is possible for those who have never heard the gospel proper. Particularists deny this and assert that redemption requires the particular knowledge of the gospel, hence the term *particularists*.[55] The latter term is less inflammatory than *exclusivist*, so it will be used.

Of course, if non-Christians can be saved apart from hearing the gospel, the question becomes, "What must they do?" On this, inclusivists take a variety of positions. The more liberal evangelical inclusivists, such as Clark Pinnock, believe that people *may* be redeemed even within their non-Christian religions, since faith *itself* is more important than the *object* of faith.[56] This approach, however, cuts against the grain of our argument thus far. If Paul said that the Gentiles were "without hope and without God in the world" (Ephesians 2:12), this does not bode well for their redemption apart from the reception of the gospel. Moreover, the manifold references to saving faith in the New Testament focus on the *object of faith*, *Jesus Christ*, not on a general belief in God. As Paul told the jailer, "Believe in the Lord Jesus, and you will be saved" (Acts 16:31). Moreover, the exigency for evangelism is diminished if God can mediate saving faith

---

[54]I take up the justice of hell in appendix 1.

[55]This discussion also considers how those who have reached the age of moral accountability respond to general revelation. Both exclusivists and inclusivists may claim that salvation is possible for the unborn, infants and the severely retarded. For a particularist view of the salvation of the unborn and children, see Ronald Nash, *When a Baby Dies* (Grand Rapids: Zondervan, 1999). For an inclusivist view see Millard Erickson, "The Salvation of Those Incapable of Faith," in *How Shall They Be Saved?* (Grand Rapids: Baker, 1996).

[56]See Clark Pinnock, *A Wideness in God's Mercy: The Finality of Christ in a World of Religions* (Grand Rapids: Zondervan, 1992). Pinnock, however, thought that God could redeem adherents of non-Christian religions in spite of their specific teachings and practices. See pp. 110-11.

through religions that Paul claims "suppress the truth by their wickedness" (Romans 1:18). Therefore, liberal inclusivism is brought into question because it excludes too many biblical truths in its attempt to include more people in salvation.

However, other inclusivists argue that if an unevangelized person is to be redeemed, more is required than some general and sincere theistic faith. Those such as Norman Anderson and Millard Erickson claim that people may respond rightly to general revelation by realizing that their own religion cannot save them, that they cannot save themselves and that they must cast themselves on the mercy of God. Neither Anderson nor Erickson offer any guesses as to how many non-Christians may rightly and salvifically respond to general revelation, but they leave open the possibility. Of the two versions of inclusivism, this formulation is the more plausible biblically.

Entire books have been written on this controversy.[57] However, I will chart the view that seems the most biblical and apologetically astute. The evidence of Scripture leans strongly toward particularism, which has been, generally speaking, the historic position of the church until fairly recently.[58] The missionary mandate of the church seems to presuppose that ignorance needs to be overcome with *the knowledge of the truth of the gospel* and that human beings are God's primary instrument for communicating this truth. A verse from the Psalms highlights this: "The LORD is near to all who call on him, / to all who call on him *in truth*" (Psalm 145:18; emphasis added). The apostle Peter highlights this when he and John are brought before the Sanhedrin. Having been "filled with the Holy Spirit," Peter claims that he is on trial for healing a man through the power of Jesus Christ, who is

> the stone you builders rejected,
> which has become the cornerstone.
> Salvation is found in no one else, for there is no other name given under heaven given to mankind by which we must be saved. (Acts 4:11-12)

---

[57]Dennis L. Okholm and Timothy R. Phillips, eds., *Four Views of Salvation in a Pluralistic World* (Grand Rapids: Eerdmans, 1996). This collection includes essays by John Hick, who falls outside the evangelical circle.

[58]Netland, *Dissonant Voices*, pp. 10-14. The argument from tradition does not decide the case, since "there may yet be more truth to break forth from God's word," as is often said. Nevertheless, it does contribute to the overall case and place the burden of proof on another view.

Nothing less than eternal salvation is at stake. No one other than Jesus Christ of Nazareth is the agent of salvation. The fact that Peter mentions the "name" of Jesus is significant. Salvation comes through this particular person, whose name is "Jesus Christ of Nazareth" (Acts 4:10). The implication is that Jesus is not only the sole agent of salvation but that salvation comes only through the knowledge of who he is and what he has done; that is, by his "name."[59]

Another text that strongly implies particularism is found in Romans, a book that carefully stipulates the nature and plan of God's salvation. While discussing salvation for the Jews and Gentiles, Paul affirms:

> If you declare with your mouth, "Jesus is Lord," and believe in your heart that God raised him from the dead, you will be saved. For it is with your heart that you believe and are justified, and it is with your mouth that you profess your faith and are saved. As Scripture says, "Anyone who believes in him will never be put to shame." For there is no difference between Jew and Gentile—the same Lord is Lord of all and richly blesses all who call on him, for, "Everyone who calls on the name of the Lord will be saved."
>
> How, then, can they call on the one they have not believed in? And how can they believe in the one of whom they have not heard? And how can they hear without someone preaching to them? And how can anyone preach unless they are sent? As it is written: "How beautiful are the feet of those who bring good news!"
>
> But not all the Israelites accepted the good news. For Isaiah says, "Lord, who has believed our message?" Consequently, faith comes from hearing the message, and the message is heard through the word about Christ. (Romans 10:9-17)

Notice that Paul, like Peter, speaks of the specific "name" of the Lord, which is Jesus. Paul teaches that the knowledge of the gospel is required for faith, and faith is required for salvation. That seems to rule out the salvation of those who have not known of the gospel.[60]

---

[59]For a fuller explanation of this verse see Douglas Geivett and W. Gary Phillips, "A Particularist View," in *Four Views of Salvation in a Pluralistic World*, ed. Dennis L. Okholm and Timothy R. Phillips (Grand Rapids: Eerdmans, 1996). pp. 230-33.

[60]See ibid., pp. 236-37. Some believe that this (and similar passages) only stipulate sufficient conditions for salvation, not necessary conditions. That is, if a person responds along the lines of these passages he or she is saved, but others may be saved who do not respond in just this way. This is possible but seems unlikely given the force and flow of the contexts in which these passages occur.

Some inclusivists, like Pinnock, appeal to the account of Cornelius in Acts 10 as evidence that there are "righteous Gentiles" who can be saved apart from the knowledge of "the name of Jesus."[61] Cornelius was a God-fearer who, though not a Jew, worshiped the God of the Jews as best he could without becoming a Jewish proselyte. He was told by an angel in a vision that his prayers had been heard and that he should call Peter to come and speak with him. However, the text unambiguously affirms that although Cornelius prayed to God and served him as best he knew how, salvation came only *after* Cornelius responded to the gospel *message* given by Peter. Peter's statement that God accepts those from every nation who fear him and do what is right (Acts 10:35) cannot, in context, be meant to apply to those who do not hear the gospel, since Peter addresses it to Cornelius's situation. However, this text does provide reason to believe that people who respond to what they know about God in good faith will be given more light.[62]

Others have argued that since believers in the Hebrew Bible were saved apart from the knowledge of Jesus Christ (who had not yet come), so too can faithful monotheists be saved who just happen to be *informationally* but not *chronologically* before Christ. However, this argument breaks down. The Jews were God's covenant people and had unique access to saving truth as demonstrated through the law, the prophets and the sacrificial system of worship. This revelation anticipated a Messiah to come, both in its Scriptures (Psalm 22; Isaiah 53) and through its practices, such as animal sacrifices, which had to be "without blemish." So the intellectual content of ancient Jewish faith was far richer than mere monotheism and was sufficient for salvation even though it was received prior to the incarnation. As Jesus said, "Salvation is from the Jews" (John 4:22). Therefore, the parallels required for the argument to work do not seem to obtain.[63]

HOW MANY WILL BE SAVED?

One issue remains concerning the relationship of Christianity to other religions. What seems to drive many to unbiblical views of salvation is the

---

[61]Pinnock, *Wideness in God's Mercy*, p. 165.
[62]Ajith Fernando, *Sharing the Truth in Love* (Grand Rapids: Discovery House, 2001), pp. 222-24.
[63]Ibid., pp. 224-27.

notion that the Bible teaches that more will be lost than saved. This idea repulses many and causes them to accept annihilationism, universalism or to renounce Christianity entirely (see appendix 1). I will here raise the strong possibility that more will be saved than will be lost. This is a tall order, and we cannot canvass all the pertinent issues. However, several considerations should be faced.

First, Jesus' statements concerning the exclusivity of salvation through himself (Matthew 11:27; John 14:6) are taken by many to demand that the majority of humankind is doomed. For example, Jesus said, "Enter through the narrow gate. For wide is the gate and broad is the road that leads to destruction, and many enter through it. But small is the gate and narrow the road that leads to life, and only a few find it" (Matthew 7:13-14). There is, however, a parallel text in Luke 13:22-30 that gives more context for Jesus' statement and thus opens up other possibilities. Jesus is asked, "Lord, are only a few people going to be saved?" (v. 23), but he refuses to answer the question and turns it back on the hearer.

> Make every effort to enter through the narrow door, because many, I tell you, will try to enter and will not be able to. Once the owner of the house gets up and closes the door, you will stand outside knocking and pleading, "Sir, open the door for us." But he will answer, "I don't know you or where you come from."
>
> Then you will say, "We ate and drank with you, and you taught in our streets."
>
> But he will reply, "I don't know you or where you come from. Away from me, all you evildoers!"
>
> There will be weeping there, and gnashing of teeth, when you see Abraham, Isaac and Jacob and all the prophets in the kingdom of God, but you yourselves thrown out. People will come from east and west and north and south, and will take their places at the feast in the kingdom of God. Indeed there are those who are last who will be first, and first who will be last.

Jesus speaks of "the narrow door" and the fact that "many . . . will try to enter and not be able to" (v. 24). Here the context seems to address the Jews of his day, those who dined with Jesus and saw him teach (v. 26). Many of these Jews will fail to recognize their Messiah (v. 28). But in verse 28, the tenor of the passage changes radically. Jesus now affirms that people from "east and west and north and south" will feast in the kingdom of God. This reversal of what was expected—after all, the Jews were God's chosen race—is evident in Jesus' statement, "There are those who are last who will be first [Gentiles], and first who will be last [Jews of Jesus' day]" (v. 28). Few Jews of Jesus' day would "enter the kingdom," but later many others would enter—Jews and Gentiles—from around the world. So, the restriction found in Matthew 7:13-14 should probably be taken to refer to the Jews of Jesus' day, not to all who would ever live. When Jesus affirmed that "many are invited, but few are chosen" (Matthew 22:1-44; Luke 14:15-24), he likely meant what he said in Matthew 7:13-14—that few of those in Jesus' *own time* were chosen.

The large number of the redeemed seems to be underscored by other references in the New Testament. Jesus himself proclaims that "the Son of Man did not come to be served, but to serve, and to give his life as a ransom for *many*" (Matthew 20:28, emphasis added). Hebrews proclaims, "In bringing *many sons and daughters to glory*, it was fitting that God, for whom and through whom everything exists, should make the pioneer of their salvation perfect through what he suffered" (Hebrews 2:10, emphasis added). In discussing the death that came through Adam and the life that came through Jesus Christ, Paul affirms, "For just as through the disobedience of the one man the many were made sinners, so also through the obedience of the one man the *many* will be made righteous" (Romans 5:19, emphasis added). Further, in Jesus' encounter with the Roman centurion, Jesus exclaimed, "I say to you that *many* will come from the east and the west, and will take their places at the feast with Abraham, Isaac and Jacob in the kingdom of heaven" (Matthew 8:11, emphasis added). Moreover, Revelation depicts a vast multitude "who have come out of the great tribulation; they have washed their robes and made them white in the blood of the Lamb" (Revelation 7:14).[64]

> After this I looked, and there before me was a great multitude that no one could count, from every nation, tribe, people and language, standing before the throne and before the Lamb. They were wearing white robes and were holding palm branches in their hands. And they cried out in a loud voice:
> "Salvation belongs to our God,

---

[64]This does not exhaust the biblical references to "many" being saved, but is indicative of this kind of passage.

who sits on the throne,

and to the Lamb." (Revelation 7:9-10)

Revelation is notoriously difficult to interpret, but this vision of the vastness of the redeemed may refer to all the redeemed throughout history, since Jesus said his followers would experience tribulations and trials (John 16:33).

Passages taken to restrict the number of the redeemed to a small percentage of the overall population of the world may be plausibly interpreted otherwise, and several passages suggest a large number of those redeemed, perhaps a majority. As a general theological principle it would seem strange for God to create more beings who fail to be redeemed than who experience God's redeeming love.

However, someone may argue that the percentages of those saved up until now do not justify this conclusion. Christians have been in the minority throughout history, and even though the percentage of Christians has been increasing dramatically in the last hundred years, this is still true today.[65] Three responses are forthcoming. First, those that die in the womb, at childbirth or at a very young age are likely redeemed by God's mercy.[66] God alone knows how many have died in this way, but the total throughout history must be very large, especially given ancient rates of miscarriage and infant mortality. Second, history is not over. Although some subscribe to a very pessimistic eschatology and are assured that the end is near, there may yet be a great harvest of souls before the second coming.[67] Third, particularists need not assume that humans are the only messengers to bring the gospel to the lost. While the New Testament emphasizes the need for the human witness to bring people to saving faith, there is a reference to an angel preaching the everlasting gospel (Revela-

---

[65]See David B. Barrett, George Thomas Kurian and Todd M. Johnson, eds., *World Christian Encyclopedia: A Comparative Survey of Churches and Religions in the Modern World*, vol. 1, *The World by Countries: Religionists, Churches, Ministries*, 2nd ed. (New York: Oxford University Press, 2001).

[66]See Nash, *When a Baby Dies*.

[67]A person's views on this are, to some extent, governed by his or her millennial views. The most optimistic concerning the total number of the redeemed is postmillennialism (see B. B. Warfield, "Are There Few That Be Saved?" in *Biblical and Theological Studies*, ed. Samuel Craig [Phillipsburg, N.J.: Presbyterian & Reformed, 1968]). But amillennialism and premillennialism (particularly of the historic version) allow for optimistic possibilities concerning the number of the redeemed.

tion 14:6). Outside of the Bible there are many credible reports of non-Christians hearing the gospel through dreams and visions before being evangelized by Christians.[68] Further, Jesus himself directly evangelized Paul on the road to Damascus (Acts 9). He may have evangelized others as well, and may do so in the future as also.[69] The scope of evangelism may be broader than what can be accomplished by human witnesses alone.

JESUS CHRIST: THE END OF RELIGION

Religion is wide, but truth is narrow. Truth captures reality in statements, and any statement that fails that task is erroneous. Error in religion is no small thing, and it can be a matter of eternal consequence if that error be egregious enough. The end of true religion must be truth, saving and flaming truth. According to Christianity, Jesus Christ is the eternal cornerstone of reality and truth incarnate (John 14:6). This is no idle claim, but is backed up by considerable philosophical and historical arguments. Christ is, therefore, the only source of undying liberation. To err at this point is catastrophic. While other religions contain elements of truth, they reject the most important truth of all: Christ crucified, resurrected and offered for the redemption of the cosmos. Therefore, all religions are not created equal. While God will judge every human being justly, neither logic nor Scripture allow us to endorse all religions as one or to justify any path to salvation except that carved out by the crucified and risen Nazarene.

---

[68]See Brother Yun and Paul Hattaway, *The Heavenly Man* (Grand Rapids: Monarch, 2002), p. 50. For a discussion of the role dreams and visions play in a conversion from Islam to Christianity, see Bilquis Sheikh and Richard H. Schneider, *I Dared to Call Him Father: The Miraculous Story of a Muslim Woman's Encounter with God* (Lincoln, Va.: Chosen Books, 2003); for this phenomenon more generally, see Joel C. Rosenberg, *Inside the Revolution: How the Followers of Jihad, Jefferson, and Jesus are Battling to Dominate the Middle East and Transform the World* (Carol Stream, Ill.: Tyndale House, 2009), pp. 387-88. See also the many testimonies of former Muslims who became Christians in "Truth, Love, and Newness of Life," AnsweringIslam.org, <www.answering-islam.org/Testimonies/index.html>.

[69]See Phillip Weibe, *Visions of Jesus: Divine Encounters from The New Testament to Today* (New York: Oxford University Press, 1997).

24

Apologetics and the Challenge of Islam

NEARLY THE ENTIRE WORLD IS enmeshed—in one way or another—in "the war on terrorism." When emotions burn hot and fears run high, it is difficult for many to get an accurate fix on the realities of Islam as a religion and as a geopolitical force. It is a simple truth that while all terrorists are not Muslims and that most Muslims are not terrorists, it is nevertheless also true that the majority of terrorists worldwide are Muslims who wage jihad in pursuit of punishing infidels—principally Jews and Christians—and establishing Islam globally.

For several reasons, Americans in particular struggle to accurately assess Islam. First, the United States government has taken great care to affirm that military actions taken against certain countries are not part of a war on Islam. To underscore this, President George W. Bush repeatedly said that "Islam means peace" and that it is "a religion of peace." President Barack Obama delivered an address in Egypt in 2009 that went even further in its unqualified praise for Islam. Many others have said that Jews, Christians and Muslims "all worship the same God."

Second, there is tremendous pressure in American culture to be nonjudgmental and affirming when it comes to religious particularities. (The exception to this is the supposedly objective, neutral and scientific attack on Christian claims waged largely by "the new atheists," such as Sam Harris, Richard Dawkins and Christopher Hitchens.) Rather than attempting a rational evaluation of religion, one should cultivate a benign indifference to religious diversity. This is especially the case with respect to Islam when tensions are already so high. It is sometimes deemed un-American to criticize the religion of one who has immigrated to this country.

Nevertheless, this clutter must be swept away in order to evaluate Islam in relation to the truth claims of Christianity. Yes, Muslims in America are rightly protected by the First Amendment as much as Christians or Jews or anyone else and thus possess all of its freedoms, including freedom of speech and religion.[1] Yet a political right—which in this case is also a moral right—does not insure that one's beliefs are correct. They may, in fact, be very wrong—and even dangerous. Whatever may be politically expedient in discussing Islam should take a back seat to evaluating rationally Islam's worldview and its relationship to Christianity. In chapter twenty-three we discussed the claim that all religions are one and found it wanting.

Islam is the second largest religion on the planet, claiming approximately 1.3 billion adherents. If the present trends of Western secularism,[2] multiculturalism and Muslim migration into Europe continue, Europe is likely to be a largely Muslim continent within several decades.[3] Islam is the fastest growing religion in existence, owing largely to the high birth rate among its followers, its global vision for the expansion of Islam and the intense social pressure to remain a Muslim. In traditional sharia law, the penalty for apostasy from Islam is death.[4] When Mark Gabriel (his adopted name after having converted to Christianity) began to question the ethics of Islam as a professor of Islamic history at the most prestigious Muslim seminary in Egypt, he was arrested by the secret police and thrown in jail, where he was tortured.[5] When Gabriel confessed his

---

[1]However, if the practice of religion leads to the attempt to undermine the constitutional system of the United States (especially regarding freedom of religion and speech), the practice of that religion should be carefully monitored and even restricted insofar as it becomes treasonous to the nature of the American system itself. Many Muslims in America want to establish Islamic (sharia) law in America (see Robert Spencer, *Stealth Jihad* [New York: Regnery, 2008]; and Nonie Darwish, *Cruel and Usual Punishment: The Terrifying Implications of Islamic Law* [Nashville: Thomas Nelson, 2008]).

[2]On the secularization of Europe and its unwillingness to even recognize its Christian history, see George Weigel, *The Cube and the Cathedral: Europe, America, and Politics Without God* (New York: Basic Books, 2005).

[3]See Bat Ye'or, *Eurabia* (Madison, N.J.: Fairleigh Dickinson University Press, 2005). See also the passionate condemnation of expansionist and anti-European Islam by the veteran Italian journalist Oriana Fallaci, *The Rage and the Pride* (New York: Rizzoli, 2002), and *The Force of Reason* (New York: Rizzoli, 2006). On the increasing influence of Islam on Britain see Melanie Phillips, *Londonistan* (New York: Encounter Books, 2007).

[4]Robert Spencer, *Religion of Peace? Why Christianity Is and Islam Isn't* (New York: Regnery, 2007), p. 174.

[5]Mark Gabriel, "Leaving the University," in *Jesus and Muhammad* (Lake Mary, Fla.: Charisma House, 2004).

Apologetics and the Challenge of Islam
601

belief in Christ to his father, the man pulled out a handgun and attempted to shoot him on the spot.[6] Moreover, in some Islamic nations a person can be penalized or even put to death for blaspheming "the prophet" (Muhammad).[7] These are surely disincentives to investigating other religious claims, voicing doubts or criticisms of Islam or defecting from Islam to Christianity (its 1,400-year and most significant rival). Unlike postmodernists in the West, Muslims believe in objective truth and the divine universal revelation found in the Qur'an. This philosophical backbone helps explain much of the Islamic success historically and today.[8]

This chapter will challenge the Muslim claim that Islam has replaced and usurped Christianity as the only legitimate monotheistic religion. We will consider five specific charges leveled by Muslims against Christianity. But before beginning the apologetic interaction, we need to fill out Islam's doctrinal skeleton, emphasizing its beliefs more than narrating its history. Islam claims to be the final revelation to humanity from God as given to Muhammad. Six key doctrines constitute the worldview of Islam, which are found in sura 2:177 of the Qur'an.[9]

BASIC MUSLIM DOCTRINE AND PRACTICE

1. God. Islam insists that there is but one God, whose name is Allah. Allah, a personal God, is the creator, lawgiver and judge of the universe. In Arabic, *Allah* is grammatically incapable of the plural construction: Allah is the one and only God. The utter transcendence and oneness of God is repeatedly and militantly affirmed by Islam. Islam thus insists that God has no son or cohort.

> Certainly they disbelieve who say: Surely Allah, He is the Messiah, son of Marium; and the Messiah said: O Children of Israel! serve Allah, my Lord

---

[6]Gabriel, *Jesus and Muhammad*, p. 131.

[7]Historic Islam cannot support a Western doctrine of religious and political tolerance. On this see Nezir Hyseni, "Tolerance and the Qur'an: Understanding the Unavoidable Islam," Answering-Islam.org <www.answering-islam.org/Quran/Themes/tolerance.html>.

[8]See Irving Hexham, "Evangelical Illusions: Postmodern Christianity and the Growth of Muslim Communities in Europe and North America," in *No Other Gods Before Me?* ed. John Stackhouse (Grand Rapids: Baker Academic, 2001).

[9]I am presenting orthodox Islam. However, these ideas and practices are often compromised through the practice of "folk Islam," wherein other worldviews are incorporated into Muslim belief and practice. For example, much of Islam in Africa is affected by animistic beliefs.

and your Lord. Surely whoever associates (others) with Allah, then Allah has forbidden to him the garden, and his abode is the fire; and there shall be no helpers for the unjust.

Certainly they disbelieve who say: Surely Allah is the third (person) of the three; and there is no god but the one God, and if they desist not from what they say, a painful chastisement shall befall those among them who disbelieve. (surah 5:72-73)[10]

2. Angels and demons. Islam affirms the reality of finite, immaterial beings. These are angels who are under Allah's control. Two angels list all the deeds of humans, both good and bad, and these deeds are produced on the Day of Judgment (Qur'an 50:17-18; 53:5-10; 81:20). In addition to angels, there are spirits known as jinn, both good and evil. The Qur'an itself was supposedly revealed through the angel Gabriel to Muhammad. Muslims also believe in the existence of a chief evil spirit known as Satan.[11]

3. Prophets. Allah inspires prophets to declare his message of submission to humanity. The first prophet was Adam, the first human. There are many others, including Moses, David, John the Baptist and Jesus (Qur'an 3:84), who is also known as the Messiah, sinless and a worker of wonders. (I will have more to say about Islam's view of Jesus later.) About twenty-five prophets are named in the Qur'an, but Muslim tradition affirms as many as 124,000 prophets.[12] However, the last prophet, "the seal of the prophets" (Qur'an 33:40), is Muhammad, who received God's final and perfect revelation, the Qur'an. This was received by Muhammad over about a twenty-two-year period (A.D. 610-632) and was collected and edited after his death. Another large group of writings, known as the Hadith, record events from the life of Muhammad. While these are not as authoritative as the Qur'an, they are consulted for doctrine and practice by Muslims and are thus very important for Islam.

---

[10]*The Holy Qur'an*, trans. M. H. Shakir (Elmhurst, N.Y.: Tahrike Tarsile Qur'an, 1983) <http://quod.lib.umich.edu/k/Koran>. The translations that follow use this source for the Qur'an.

[11]Mark Gabriel points out that in Islam, Muhammad, unlike the Jesus of the Gospels, was not considered to have special power or authority over the realm of evil spirits (see Gabriel, *Jesus and Muhammad*, chap. 12).

[12]Abdul Saleeb, "Islam," in *To Everyone an Answer*, ed. Francis Beckwith, William Lane Craig and J. P. Moreland (Downers Grove, Ill.: InterVarsity Press, 2004), p. 351.

4. The holy books. Muslims believe that some of the prophets received divinely inspired books. Thus they accept the Torah (*Taurat*) as from Moses, the Psalms (*Zabur*) from David, the Gospel (*Injil*) from Jesus and the Qur'an from Muhammad as divinely revealed holy books.[13] The Qur'an, however, is deemed the final and ultimate authority, having been directly revealed to Muhammad and flawlessly preserved since its inception. Where the Bible contradicts the Qur'an—as it often does—the Qur'an is deemed to be correct and the Bible in error.

5. The judgment of God. Nearly every chapter of the Qur'an speaks vehemently of the last judgment of Allah, and speaks far more often of hell than of paradise. If a person's good deeds outbalance the bad deeds (the score is kept by angels), he or she may hope for paradise as a reward. However, since Allah is regarded as utterly sovereign and free, an individual cannot know whether he might receive mercy or severity in the afterlife (Qur'an 36:54; 53:38). However, it is certain that a man cannot be certain of his eternal condition—unless he dies in a genuine jihad. Then his destiny is certain: endless life in the company of multiple, heavenly virgins.[14]

6. Divine decrees and predestination. Allah is absolutely sovereign and views humans as his slaves, not his friends or his servants (Qur'an 17:16; 59:23; 74:31; 35:8). While Christianity and Judaism stress the providence of God, Islam does so to the extent that petitionary prayer is excluded. Prayer involves reciting parts of the Qur'an and invoking Allah's power, but does not include personal requests to affect his will.[15]

On these six doctrines are placed the five pillars that make up the practices of Islam. The first is the confession of Allah as God and Muhammad as his prophet (*shahada*). On the basis of this belief one is considered a Muslim—that is, one who submits to Allah. This act does not change the being of the person, however. One has simply confessed a belief, which implies a commitment to live accordingly. Second, Mus-

---

[13]Of course, Jesus himself did not write or deliver a book to the world. That was left to the apostolic witness, according to the New Testament (see Qur'an 19:30).

[14]I write of males intentionally to exclude women. There are no depictions of women from earth in the Islamic paradise. The women who are mentioned, the houris, are dark-eyed virgins who supply the men with erotic pleasures (see Qur'an 56:12-39).

[15]Ergun Mehmet Caner and Emir Fethi Caner, *Unveiling Islam: An Insider's Look at the Muslim Life and Beliefs* (Grand Rapids: Kregel, 2002), pp. 109-10. This does not deny that Muslims may, nonetheless, pray in that way—even if it ill fits Islamic doctrine.

lims must engage in five daily prayers, facing Mecca (*salat*). These prayers are highly ritualized and physical, and require ablutions and proper postures. There is little sense of spontaneous prayer and no personal petition. Third, Muslims are required to give alms (*zakat*), which amount to 2.5 percent of their profits to an Islamic charity. Fourth, a yearly month-long fast during daylight is required (Ramadan). Fifth, if at all possible every Muslim is to make one pilgrimage to Mecca, the birthplace of Islam (*hajj*).

ISLAM AND CHRISTIANITY

While Islam refers to Christians as "people of the book" along with Jews and Zoroastrians (as opposed to polytheists and animists), it denies that Christianity is the final and permanent revelation of God and speaks quite negatively of Christians as "the infidels" (*kaffur*).[16] This is because Muhammad, "the seal of the prophets," is the last and greatest of the prophets of Allah (Qur'an 48:27-28). He alone corrects the errors of the past, including the aberrations of Christianity. Islam abrogates Christianity (Qur'an 48:27-28); it is Christianity's replacement. The argument for abrogation is rooted in five major claims made by Islam against Christianity. This is a significant apologetic challenge that Christians today need to face intelligently, given the global reach of Islam and its growing influence in the West.

Claim 1: The original holy book has been distorted. Since there are distinct differences between Christianity and Islam concerning the nature of God, humans and salvation (as well as devotional practices), Muslims need to account for these discrepancies while affirming that Moses, David and Jesus were bona fide prophets of Allah. Therefore, Muslims charge that the original revelation to the Jewish and Christian prophets (who were all prophets of Allah) has been altered and distorted. This charge takes two forms. Either it is claimed that (1) the writings of the Bible even in their original form were distorted, or (2) the original Christian documents supporting Islam were tampered with after the fact. The second claim provides the better argument for the Muslim since the Qur'an endorses the

---

[16]Much of the inspiration for what follows comes from Kevin Bywater's essay "Islam as the 'End' of Christianity: Assessing the Arguments for Abrogation," AnsweringIslam.org, <http://answering-islam.org/Intro/replacing.html>.

divine authority of the Old Testament and the Gospels (Qur'an 4:48, 136; 5:47-51, 68-71; 10:94).

But as we have seen in chapter nineteen, the New Testament has been transmitted with integrity. Moreover, the Old Testament texts from Muhammad's day are substantially similar to what we read in our Bibles today.[17] The claim that Jews or Christians had radically changed the original documents is logically unsupportable. First, the magnitude of the change would have been enormous. All references from the Bible that contradict Islam would had to have been inserted into the documents. That would have included the Trinity, the incarnation, the crucifixion of Jesus, salvation through faith alone and more. Second, given the rapid dissemination of the New Testament in the ancient world, it would have been impossible for any group to seize and alter all the texts at hand. Third, we know of no early Christian texts of the New Testament that lack these distinctively Christian doctrines.

Islam faces another obstacle in establishing its accusation that the Bible has been radically altered such that it no longer teaches the truths of Islam. The Qur'an, supposedly received from Allah by Muhammad from 610 to 632, tells the reader to consult the Christian Scriptures to corroborate the veracity of Muhammad's message and his status as a prophet.

> But if you are in doubt as to what We have revealed to you, ask those who read the Book before you; certainly the truth has come to you from your Lord, therefore you should not be of the disputers. (Qur'an 10:94; see also 5:47-51, 72; 19:29-30; 21:7; 29:46-47)

Gleason Archer summarizes the Qur'an's teaching by noting first that "the author of the Quran firmly believed in the full inspiration of the Old Testament and the Gospels of the New Testament as containing the authoritative Word of God, and secondly that the Hebrew-Christian Bible should be appealed to in confirmation that what is revealed in the Qur'an is the very truth of God."[18]

---

[17]See E. Tov, *Textual Criticism of the Hebrew Bible*, 2nd ed. (Minneapolis: Fortress, 2001), p. 27; and more generally, Kenneth Kitchen, *On the Reliability of the Old Testament* (Grand Rapids: Eerdmans, 2003).

[18]Gleason Archer, "Confronting the Challenge of Islam in the 21st Century," in *Contend for the Faith: Collected Papers of the Rockford Conference on Discernment and Evangelism*, ed. Eric Pement (Chicago: Evangelical Ministries to New Religions, 1992), p. 96.

Yet manuscripts of the Bible from this time period are in substantial agreement with what we read in our Bibles today. Archer observes:

> It is completely out of the question to discredit the text of Holy Scripture as no longer conforming to what was current in Muhammad's time, from A.D. 610-632. Complete manuscripts of the New Testament copied out in the fourth century (Codex Vaticanus and Codex Sinaiticus) and the fifth century (Codex Alexandrinus), antedate the revelation of the Qur'an by three centuries.

Therefore, when the Qur'an says to consult the Christian Scriptures for the verification of the truth of Islam, it contradicts itself. The extant Christian Scriptures of Muhammad's day teach that God is a Trinity, that Christ is the incarnation of God, and that salvation is through faith in Jesus Christ—all doctrines that Islam rejects.

Furthermore, Jesus, whom the Qur'an esteems as a prophet, endorsed the Old Testament as God's revelation (Matthew 5:17-20; John 10:35). He deemed his own teaching to be in accordance with that previous disclosure from God. Yet, as we will see, Islam denies crucial claims about Jesus.

Claim 2: Jesus was not crucified. The Qur'an states that Jesus (Issa or Isa) was not crucified.

> And their saying: Surely we have killed the Messiah, Isa son of Marium, the apostle of Allah; and they did not kill him nor did they crucify him, but it appeared to them so (like Isa) and most surely those who differ therein are only in a doubt about it; they have no knowledge respecting it, but only follow a conjecture, and they killed him not for sure.
>
> Nay! Allah took him up to Himself; and Allah is Mighty, Wise.
>
> And there is not one of the followers of the Book but most certainly believes in this before his death, and on the day of resurrection he (Isa) shall be a witness against them. (4:157-59)

While Chawkat Moucarry points out the difficulties in understanding this text in the original Arabic, this text has been taken by Muslims worldwide to mean that Jesus was not crucified but was delivered somehow by Allah. To the Islamic mind, it is unthinkable that a true prophet should be subject to such humiliation. Thus, if Jesus was a prophet, he must not have been crucified. However, another verse from the Qur'an claims that Jesus would be killed (Qur'an 3:54-55). Most Muslims interpret this to mean that Jesus will die after he returns from heaven some time in the future. But when he was on earth the first time, he was taken directly back to Allah.[19]

A quick glance at the Gospels and the rest of the New Testament indicates that the death of Jesus on the cross is the ineradicable center of the Christian message. As I argued in chapter twenty, the Hebrew Scriptures prophesy Jesus' death (Isaiah 53). Jesus himself spoke of his impending death with his disciples (Matthew 12:39-40; John 10:11), his death on the cross is recorded in all four Gospels, and it is either assumed or expressed in every New Testament book. These are the most ancient and reliable documents available about Jesus of Nazareth. In Paul's summary of the gospel, Jesus' death is foundational: "For what I received I passed on to you as of first importance: that Christ died for our sins according to the Scriptures, that he was buried, that he was raised on the third day according to the Scriptures" (1 Corinthians 15:3-4).

Moreover, contemporary historians agree that Jesus was executed through crucifixion. Even the archliberal New Testament scholar Rudolf Bultmann believed this. For over six centuries before Muhammad, Christians (and Jews) believed that Jesus had died on a cross. While secular historians may reject the biblical *meaning* of Jesus' death as atoning for human sin, they do not question the *factuality* of his death by crucifixion. Therefore, any claim to the contrary bears the burden of proof to refute the universal claim of the Christian church and the testimony of the vast majority of ancient historians (see chap. 22).

Claim 3: Jesus is not divine. Muslims are repulsed by the confession of Jesus as divine. The Qur'an affirms concerning Allah, "Say not three" (4:171) and "Allah has no son" (72:3). Thus they reject a trinitarian God by insisting that Allah has no partner.

> Surely Allah does not forgive that anything should be associated with Him, and He forgives what is besides this to whom He pleases; and whoever associates anything with Allah, he indeed strays off into a remote error. (Qur'an 4:116)

---

[19]For an excellent exposition of the Islamic view, see Chawkat Moucarry, *The Prophet and the Messiah: An Arab Christian's Perspective on Islam and Christianity* (Downers Grove, Ill.: InterVarsity Press, 2001), pp. 128-44.

According to Islam, Jesus is Allah's prophet, born of a virgin, sinless and the Messiah (in a scaled down sense from the biblical view); he will come again, but he is emphatically not divine. As the Qur'an declares:

> O followers of the Book! do not exceed the limits in your religion, and do not speak (lies) against Allah, but (speak) the truth; the Messiah, Isa son of Marium is only an apostle of Allah and His Word which He communicated to Marium and a spirit from Him; believe therefore in Allah and His apostles, and say not, Three. Desist, it is better for you; Allah is only one God; far be It from His glory that He should have a son, whatever is in the heavens and whatever is in the earth is His, and Allah is sufficient for a Protector. (4:171).

> Certainly they disbelieve who say: Surely Allah, He is the Messiah, son of Marium; and the Messiah said: O Children of Israel! serve Allah, my Lord and your Lord. Surely whoever associates (others) with Allah, then Allah has forbidden to him the garden, and his abode is the fire; and there shall be no helpers for the unjust. (5:72)

In response, one must appeal to the most reliable documents: the New Testament. As these documents attest in multiple ways, Jesus claimed deity, and his apostles affirmed this repeatedly, as argued in chapters twenty and twenty-one. If so, the claims of the Qur'an can be dispensed with on purely historical grounds.

Muslims sometimes employ philosophical arguments against the deity of Jesus (although the Qur'an does not) by claiming that Jesus cannot be divine given that he prayed to his Father, said that the Father was greater than he was and so on. These objections have received sustained treatment in recent decades by philosophers, which I surveyed earlier. As argued in chapter twenty-one, the concept of the incarnation is not contradictory and has not been affirmed as such in Christian creeds or confessions. Therefore, this charge is without bite.

Claim 4: God is not triune. Islam denies that God is triune, affirming that Allah is absolutely one, without son or partner. Any other doctrine is abominated as polytheism.

> Certainly they disbelieve who say: Surely Allah is the third (person) of the three; and there is no god but the one God, and if they desist not from what they say, a painful chastisement shall befall those among them who disbelieve. (Qur'an 5:73)

The Qur'an misunderstands the nature of the Trinity as presented in Scripture (see chap. 4). While the Bible speaks of one God (Deuteronomy 6:4) and three persons who are divine—Father, Son and Holy Spirit—the Qur'an's interpretation of the Bible leaves out the Holy Spirit and deems Mary one of the divine persons.

> And when Allah will say: O Isa son of Marium! did you say to men, Take me and my mother for two gods besides Allah he will say: Glory be to Thee, it did not befit me that I should say what I had no right to (say); if I had said it, Thou wouldst indeed have known it; Thou knowest what is in my mind, and I do not know what is in Thy mind, surely Thou art the great Knower of the unseen things. (Qur'an 5:116)

This threesome has never been affirmed as the divine Trinity by any branch of Christianity before, during or after Muhammad. The Qur'an is simply wrong on this and thus should not be taken seriously on this issue. The Muslim, however, may press the purely logical point that God cannot be three and one (although the Qur'an does not do so). To this we respond in the same spirit and with the same logic as when the incarnation is rejected as illogical. The orthodox formulation of the doctrine is not that of a contradiction, and there are various ways of understanding God's oneness and God's triunity without contradiction. The backbone of any approach is to argue that God is one in one respect (the divine essence of substance) and three in another respect (the personhood of each member).

Claim 5: Jesus was a prophet of Islam. Islam teaches that Jesus' "gospel" (*injil*) was no different from the teaching of Old Testament prophets: one must worship Allah and obey his law. All the prophets or messengers have declared essentially the same thing, but Muhammad is the final and greatest prophet. However, this simple message of Jesus, the prophet of Allah, was lost and replaced by the Christian gospel, which is a perversion.

Our counterclaim has been made in the preceding arguments. The New Testament witness is far better established historically than the revisionism of the Qur'an. We know of no earlier documents concerning the nature of Jesus' person and message than the Gospels and the rest of the New Testament. In none of these books do we find a prophet of Allah who exhorts weak humans to know and live up to the divine law.

Instead, the figure that illuminates every book of the New Testament is the Lord and Savior of a deeply flawed humanity (Mark 7:20-23), who never called people to work harder at obeying the law in hopes of salvation but rather called people to himself for the forgiveness of their sins and eternal life (John 3:16-18). Jesus' message was crucially about himself as God's Son, Savior and Lord (John 3:16-18; 14:1-6; Matthew 11:27). Only Jesus perfectly obeyed the will of God through his virtuous life and obedient death on the cross. This matchless life was crowned by his resurrection, as Paul highlights at the commencement of Romans:

> Paul, a servant of Christ Jesus, called to be an apostle and set apart for the gospel of God—the gospel he promised beforehand through his prophets in the Holy Scriptures regarding his Son, who as to his earthly life was a descendant of David, and who through the Spirit of holiness was appointed the Son of God in power by his resurrection from the dead: Jesus Christ our Lord. (Romans 1:1-4)

On the basis of the preceding five claims, Islam esteems itself as the replacement of Christianity: the one true religion for all of humanity. Before Allah, all must submit. However, given the credentials of the New Testament and supremacy of Jesus himself, none of these assertions hold up. There is no reason to believe that Islam is the successor to Christianity, given the respective qualifications of these two religions.

Since Jesus' lordship is perpetual and universal (Matthew 28:18-20; Acts 4:12; Ephesians 1:15-23), all who deny it have denied Christ himself and have excluded themselves from the only way of salvation. As Jesus warned, "Watch out for false prophets. They come to you in sheep's clothing, but inwardly they are ferocious wolves. By their fruit you will recognize them" (Matthew 7:15-16). Islam denies that Jesus is the Christ, rendering him a merely human prophet. As such it denies the gospel, the only way of salvation in time and eternity. Thus, it falls under the warning issued by the apostle Paul to an early church in Galatia that had betrayed the gospel: "But even if we or an angel from heaven should preach a gospel other than the one we preached to you, let them be under God's curse!" (Galatians 1:8).

Jesus Christ is the final and supreme revelation of God. He cannot be succeeded by another prophet. Jesus commissioned his followers to make disciples of the nations, baptizing them in the name of the Trinity and teaching to others all that Christ had taught them. The foundation for this work was Jesus' own unimpeachable and perpetual authority. He possesses "all authority in heaven and on earth" and will be with his followers "until the end of the age" (Matthew 28:18-20). Paul amplifies this in writing to the Ephesians when he waxes ecstatic about the grandeur of the resurrected and ascended Christ, who is

> far above all rule and authority, power and dominion, and every name that can be invoked, not only in the present age but also in the one to come. And God placed all things under his feet and appointed him to be head over everything for the church, which is his body, the fullness of him who fills everything in every way. (Ephesians 1:21-23)

Christ's perpetual and perennial supremacy cannot be assailed by the statements of a seventh-century religious leader.

ISLAM AND THE HUMAN CONDITION

Islam claims that the Qur'an replaces the Bible (as we now have it) as God's revelation. I cannot address the arguments made for the authority of the Qur'an here, but suffice it to say that given its erroneous claims about Christ and the Bible, there is no reason to deem it divinely inspired.[20] Inasmuch as I have made a case for the Christian worldview, I have refuted those points of Islamic monotheism that disagree with the Bible. But the case against Islam includes not only the historical reliability of the biblical documents but also an understanding of Christianity as a conceptual system that better explains salient aspects of reality. I shall draw attention to two aspects of Christianity that contrast sharply with Islam concerning our relationship to God.

First, the human condition is not that of mere weakness and ignorance of the law, but of radical depravity and corruption. If humans are born innocent, as Islam teaches, why is the world so full of evil?[21] Unlike Islam, Christianity teaches that humans are made in God's image and likeness. However, this original greatness has been horribly defaced by sin such that only a rescue from above, from God himself in Christ, is necessary and

---

[20]See Norman Geisler and Abdul Saleeb, "An Evaluation of the Qur'an," in *Answering Islam*, rev. ed. (Grand Rapids: Baker, 2002).

[21]On this, see the argument from a former Muslim Jerry Rassamini, *From Jihad to Jesus: An Ex-Muslim's Journey of Faith* (Chattanooga: Living Ink, 2006), chap. 3.

sufficient to forgive our sins, put us right with God and grant us eternal life (see chaps. 18 and 20).

Second, Christian faith offers confidence that humans are loved by God, given the work of Christ on our behalf. Unlike Islam, which teaches salvation through works, the gospel teaches that salvation is entirely through the loving grace of God as demonstrated in the life, death and resurrection of Jesus Christ. The Christ follower is thus freed to love God, receive love from God and love his or her neighbor (or enemy). This deep-seated emphasis on divine and human love is absent from the Qur'an.[22] Unlike Islam, Christians are not considered the mere slaves of God, but God's beloved friends (John 15:16). Yes, Christians must submit to God in all things (James 4:7-8). He is Lord. However, this submission is based on the knowledge of God's glory and his compassion toward his children.

Christians often speak of their *relationship* with God, and rightly so. God, while often inscrutable (Romans 11:33-36), is available to his redeemed children as a Father, Counselor and Friend. Moreover, God gives strength to his beloved servants to accomplish God's will (1 Peter 4:11). Allah, on the contrary, does not reveal his character to the creation, but rather his will as known in the Qur'an. Muslims submit to Allah's absolute authority, yet do not speak of fellowship with Allah or of a living relationship with Allah, since they believe this would compromise Allah's otherness and supremacy.

Yet God calls us into a family relationship with himself in terms unheard of and anathema to Islam:

> The Spirit you received does not make you slaves, so that you live in fear again; rather, the Spirit you received brought about your adoption to sonship. And by him we cry, *"Abba,* Father." The Spirit himself testifies with our spirit that we are God's children. (Romans 8:15-16)

CHRISTIANITY: UNDEFEATED BY ISLAM

While Islam commands the allegiance (and often violently so) of over a billion souls worldwide, its case that it has succeeded in annulling Chris-

---

[22]See Mark Gabriel, "Teachings About Love," in *Jesus and Muhammad* (Lake Mary, Fla.: Charisma House, 2004).

tianity fails for all the reasons given in this chapter. It cannot bear the burden of proof in contradicting the Bible's claims about God, Christ and salvation. Christians do well to keep this in mind as they endeavor to challenge Muslims with the truth and rationality of the Christian worldview.[23]

---

[23]This chapter has focused on defending Christianity against the charges of Islam. It has not given specific strategies for Muslim evangelism. On evangelizing Muslims see Abdiyah Abdul-Haqq, *Sharing Your Faith with a Muslim* (Minneapolis: Bethany House, 1980); Anne Cooper and Elsie Maxwell, *Ishmael My Brother: A Christian Introduction to Islam* (London: Monarch Books, 2004); and Phil Parshall, *Muslim Evangelism: Contemporary Approaches to Contextualization* (Waynesboro, Ga.: Gabriel Publishing, 2003).

The Problem of Evil

Dead Ends and the Christian Answer

LONG AFTER THE CIVIL WAR SUPPOSEDLY abolished slavery in America, a Saudi Arabian man living in Denver was convicted for keeping an Indonesian woman in his home as a slave. She had been taken to the United States from Saudi Arabia when she was a teenager. In Denver, she was required to do manual labor in the home and to sleep on a mattress in the basement. She was also sexually abused by this man.[1] Moreover, slavery and human trafficking are on the rise nationally and globally. More people are enslaved today than at any other time in history.[2]

This, along with so many other things in this broken and bleeding world, is evil. Relativism rings hollow here. "Man's inhumanity to man" is writ large on the face of history, giving us the most graphic and gut-wrenching exhibits of death camps, torture, poverty, rape, racism and terrorism. Dogs howl at the moon, a mother polar bear lingers and wails over the corpse of her dead cub, but humans wonder, lament and protest evil. They cry out to heaven for the rectification of wrongs, for justice for the oppressed, for a sense of hope in a world often stripped of hope. But in the smothering grip of evil, humans also turn on heaven. The wounded often move from questions to accusations, from accusations to rebellion and from rebellion to disbelief.

The presence of evil in the face of a good God has classically been called the problem of evil. Simply put, if God exists, there should not be

---

[1] Kieran Nicholson, "Saudi Gets 28 Years to Life in Nanny Abuse," *Denver Post*, September 1, 2006 <www.denverpost.com/search/ci_4269856>. His sentence was later reduced for good behavior.
[2] See David Batstone, *Not for Sale* (San Francisco: HarperOne, 2007). See also Kevin Bales, *Ending Slavery: How We Free Today's Slaves* (Berkeley: University of California Press, 2007).

such evil, since God would have the power and desire to stop it. Therefore, the existence or goodness or power of God is brought into question. Before engaging the issue in more detail, I must articulate the meaning of evil.

What is evil? This vexing question has no simple answer, though this hardly stops us from recognizing evils. Evil frustrates human goods, as well as goods befitting the nonhuman world (animals and larger environments). The avoidable suffering of both man and beast is evil. Even deforestation can be evil. Evil comes in a plethora of types and instances, but the field divides into two categories: natural evil and human evil.

Natural evil is the natural world turned savage: tornadoes, earthquakes, tidal waves, hurricanes, floods. Diseases and deformity fill out this category, since they are not usually instigated by humans. This includes both deadly diseases (birth defects, cancer, strokes) as well as disabling diseases (lupus, fibromyalgia, irritable bowel syndrome).[3]

Then there is evil from human hands. It comes from the gun, the knife, the bomb, the pen and the tongue. We tell lies, murder and steal; we are lied to, killed and stolen from. Human cruelty is all around us; we will find it within ourselves as well. In his historical novel *Night*, Holocaust survivor Elie Weisel describes his time as a boy in Hitler's death camps. He saw a Jewish child hanged for a petty infraction. But the child's light weight did not snap his young neck quickly, as with the grown men hanging next to him. Instead, the boy dangled in mid-air, half-alive and half-dead for several hours. One of the prisoners watching cried out, "Where is God? Where is God?" Another answered, "God is hanging on that noose." Weisel concludes his hellish account by saying, "That night the soup tasted of corpses."[4]

These are intentional evils. Yet there is another category of human evils that are unintentional, such as death and injury through "friendly fire" in war; car, plane and train accidents; medical mishaps and more. These may include human culpability through negligence, but the harm is not brought about intentionally.

Although humans philosophize over evil, and animals (presumably) do

---

[3]On understanding and coping with chronic illness, see Jeffrey Boyd, *Being Sick Well* (Grand Rapids: Baker, 2005); and James Rotholz, *Chronic Fatigue Syndrome, Christianity, and Culture* (Binghamton, N.Y.: Hayworth Medical Press, 2002).

[4]Elie Weisel, *Night* (New York: Avon Books, 1969), p. 76.

not, we cannot exclude animals from the company of suffering. Without lapsing into the pathetic fallacy (wherein we attribute human emotions to animals), we acknowledge that some mammals show signs of sorrow and fear; they certainly feel pain.[5] It is tragic when a pod of whales mysteriously beaches itself, when a beloved pet dies at a young age or when animals are mistreated by the factory-farm system.[6]

FORMULATING THE PROBLEM OF EVIL

What exactly is the problem of evil? The problem was classically stated by Epicurus:

> God either wishes to take away evils, and is unable; or he is able and unwilling; or he is neither willing nor able, or he is both willing and able.

He then tries to work out each possibility.

1. If God is willing and is unable, he is feeble, which is not in accordance with the character of God.

2. If he is able and unwilling, he is envious [meaning: evil], which is equally at variance with God.

3. If he is neither willing nor able he is both envious [meaning evil] and feeble, and therefore not God.

4. If he is both willing and able, which alone is suitable to God, from what source then are evils or why does he not remove them?[7]

I will spell out the specific problem for *Christian* theism later in this chapter.

DEVELOPING A STRATEGY

The problem of evil is often flashed before Christians as a trump card. One need not state it as eloquently as Epicurus (or David Hume) in order

---

[5]On animal suffering and how it differs from human suffering, see Michael Murray, *Nature Red in Tooth and Claw* (New York: Oxford University Press, 2008), pp. 41-72.
[6]For the record, I am not a vegetarian, but I cannot deny the cruel profit-driven way that many factory-farm animals are treated.
[7]Epicurus, quoted in William Dyrness, *Christian Apologetics in a World Community* (Downers Grove, Ill.: InterVarsity Press, 1983), p. 153. I have adapted the quote a bit by using enumerated claims. It is fascinating to note that while Epicurus lived before Christ and probably had no contact with the ancient Jews and their monotheism, he nevertheless clearly conceived of God as all-powerful and all-good.

to wield the argument in an intimidating way. There is evil; therefore, there is no God. But there is much more to be said.

This chapter is placed near the end of the book because we should not take up the problem in a philosophical vacuum. We have contended that the case for Christian faith is multifaceted and cumulative. Christianity is rationally supported by a number of arguments. If so, then the biblical worldview cannot prima facie be refuted by one particular problem. The problem of evil is a heavy weight for Christianity (and for any worldview, as we shall find), but a strong constitution can bear a heavy load. Therefore, the problem should be debated in light of the evidence for a personal and moral Creator of the universe, who created humans in his image and who pursued them even in their fallen state through his revelation to Israel, culminating in the life, death and resurrection of Jesus Christ. We should consider *all the arguments* given thus far for the Christian worldview and against its competitors when considering the problem of evil.

But does the existence of evil count decisively against the existence of an all-good and all-powerful God? Before answering this directly, we must consider five pertinent non-Christian options for explaining evil.

FIVE UNSATISFACTORY ANSWERS TO EVIL

The problem of evil is not limited to the Christian scheme of things. Any worldview worth its salt must give an account of evil and how to cope with it wisely.

1. Atheism. Given the surfeit of evil, atheism advances itself as intellectually and morally superior to Christianity (and any religion). Atheism is not burdened with attempts to explain evil in relation to God. Evil just exists in a godless world. The problem vanishes.

But it does not so vanish, for two main reasons. First, in order to speak of the problem of evil, a person must believe that objective evil exists.[8] To justify this claim, the person needs to adequately explain the existence and nature of evil. In order for objective evil to exist, objective goodness must exist as well, and good must exist in a more fundamental way. This is because evil is a corruption or twisting of the good. Evil does not exist in and

---

[8]See Mark T. Nelson, "Naturalistic Ethics and the Argument from Evil," *Faith and Philosophy* 8, no. 3 (1991): 368-79.

of itself. C. S. Lewis observed that no one does evil simply because he or she takes it to be evil. The badness of an action "consists in pursuing [good things] by the wrong method, or in the wrong way, or too much." Although the person doing so may be "desperately wicked," that "wickedness, when you examine it, turns out to be the pursuit of some good in the wrong way."[9]

> You can be good for the mere sake of goodness; you cannot be bad for the mere sake of badness. You can do a kind action when you are not feeling kind and when it gives you no pleasure, simply because kindness is right; but no one ever did a cruel action simply because cruelty is wrong—only because cruelty was pleasant or useful to him. In other words badness cannot succeed even in being bad in the same way in which goodness is good. Goodness is, so to speak, itself; badness is only spoiled goodness. And there must be something good first before it can be spoiled. We call sadism a sexual perversion; but you must first have the idea of a normal sexuality before you can talk of its being perverted; and you can see which is the perversion, because you can explain the perverted from the normal, and cannot explain the normal from the perverted.[10]

Lewis follows the Augustinian tradition that evil is "privation" of the good; it is parasitic on the good, and not a substance in and of itself. The privation view is revealed in both the psychology of evil and the metaphysics of evil, as Lewis shows. Evil is the rust on the iron or the hole in the roof.[11] While a person or an event may be truly evil (the evil is not illusory), that evil could not have existed without an antecedent and original good.

This discussion harks back to our argument for God from the existence of morality, where we argued for the existence of objective moral goods. These goods eliminate both relativism/nihilism and pantheistic monism, since neither can rationally support the existence of objective moral goodness. Neither is objective moral goodness a brute fact in a godless world. Objective moral goodness, therefore, is best explained by the character of a Creator God who made the universe good and gave us the capacity to

---

[9]Augustine makes the same point in his account of stealing pears as a youth. See his *Confessions* bk. 2.

[10]C. S. Lewis, *Mere Christianity* (1952; reprint, New York: HarperCollins, 2001), p. 44.

[11]See also Winfried Corduan, *No Doubt About It* (Nashville: Broadman & Holman, 1994), pp. 131-33.

recognize the good as such, even now in our fallen state.

Second, atheism fails to give a sufficient answer to the problem of evil because several strong theistic arguments—besides the moral argument—have refuted it. The cumulative case for theism has likewise been a cumulative case against atheism (and any other worldview opposing theism). Therefore, the God-denier cannot declare victory over theism by merely stating the problem of evil.

2. A finite god. God is not to blame for evil, some argue. This is not the claim that God has mysterious reasons for allowing evil he could have prevented; rather, God is powerless to stop evil.[12] This was popularized in the bestselling book *Why Bad Things Happen to Good People* by Rabbi Harold Kushner. After his young son tragically died of a rare and cruel disease, Kushner concluded that God was unable to interfere with the laws of nature and the free will of humans.[13]

I cannot give a complete critique of this finite concept of god, but a few points suffice. The first is psychological, but still germane. Such a limited deity could not be worshiped or even trusted. This god would be more powerful than humans but would be bested by chance and the will of his own besotted creatures. This argument has sometimes been called the *religious inadequacy* of the finite god theology.[14] Second, there are good philosophical reasons to believe that God is unlimited in power. Chapter eleven argued that creation ex nihilo is the sine qua non manifestation of metaphysical strength, supporting God as omnipotent. Further, the ontological argument in chapter ten insures that God possesses maximal power, since God possesses all perfections. Additionally, if God raised Jesus Christ from the dead in space-time history, as I have argued (in chap. 22), even death cannot defeat God's designs, thus assuring us of his goodness and power.

3. God as not omnibenevolent. While no major religion or school of

---

[12]This was held by John Stuart Mill in *Three Essays on Religion* (1874), as well as by Alfred North Whitehead in *Process and Reality* (1929; reprint, New York: Free Press, 1982), the fount of process philosophy and theology. For a critique of process thought see Carl F. H. Henry, "The Resurgence of Process Philosophy," in *God, Revelation, and Authority* (Waco, Tex.: Word, 1983), 6:52-75; Ronald Nash, ed., *Process Theology* (Grand Rapids: Baker, 1987).

[13]Harold Kushner, *When Bad Things Happen to Good People* (New York: Schocken, 1981). For a critique of Kushner see Norman Geisler, "Harold Kushner," in *Baker Encyclopedia of Christian Apologetics* (Grand Rapids: Baker, 1999), pp. 411-13.

[14]See Corduan, *No Doubt About It*, pp. 128-29.

thought propounds that God is only partially good, it remains a possibility and is embraced by some.[15] Events and actions in the world seem cruel and unfair. Perhaps God sponsors them with evil intent. Life sometimes feels that way, but does this reflect reality?

Alan Carter raised the possibility of an evil or not fully good God in his attempt to refute Pascal's wager.[16] Why wager on the existence of a God who might not be trustworthy and not agree to your bet? God might not care whether you believe in him or not. However, the monotheistic concept of God renders the notion of a less than morally impeccable God incoherent. If God is omnipotent and omniscient, he cannot produce evil through some accident. Moreover, if God is omniscient God knows what is good and what will produce desired outcomes. In fact, the good is rooted in God's eternal character (and cannot exist otherwise), as I argued in chapters ten and fifteen. God is self-existent (Acts 17:25) and therefore impervious to random change or devolution, as argued in chapter eleven. Since evil is a defection from good and parasitic on an antecedent good (as argued earlier), it is impossible that God could defect from the good.

4. The nonexistence of evil. One way to dispense with the problem of evil is to dispense with evil itself. This route is taken by various forms of pantheism, such as Advaita Vedanta Hinduism, Zen Buddhism, assorted New Age worldviews and mind-science churches such as Christian Science, Religious Science and Unity. Since all is ultimately divine, evil is unreal; it is only a problem of perception, and not a problem of objective reality. Pantheists hold that God "is beyond good and evil." The difference between good and evil is apparent and not real.[17] The more a person approximates the divine Mind, the more these distinctions drop out of view. A sixth-century Zen poem puts it this way:

> If you want to get to the plain truth
> Be not concerned with right and wrong.

---

[15]One reflective account of this view is given by John K. Roth, "A Theodicy of Protest," in *Encountering Evil*, ed. Stephen T. Davis (Louisville: Westminster John Knox, 2001), pp. 1-19.

[16]Alan Carter, "On Pascal's Wager: Or All Bets Are Off?" *Philosophia Christi,* series 2, vol. 3, no. 2 (2001): 511-16. I respond to Carter's argument about an evil God (and other charges) in Douglas Groothuis, "Are All Bets Off? A Defense of Pascal's Wager," *Philosophia Christi,* series 2, 3, no. 2 (2001): 517-24.

[17]See Lewis, *Mere Christianity,* p. 36.

The conflict between right and wrong
Is the sickness of the mind.[18]

But consider this poem. It advocates "the plain truth," which must be taken as objectively good. Otherwise, there is no reason to *get* the plain truth." The poem then offers an imperative: "Be not concerned with right and wrong," because "the conflict of right and wrong is the sickness of the mind." The imperative is a *moral* one, an injunction to "get the plain truth" by being unconcerned with the sick idea of moral conflict. The poem reduces to this:

1. There is no right and wrong that are in conflict with each other.

2. One should not be concerned with right and wrong, since to be concerned with right and wrong is a "sickness," which must be taken as wrong.

But statements 1 and 2 contradict each other and yield:

3. If statement 2 is true, then statement 1 is false.

4. If statement 1 is false, then there *is* a conflict between good and evil.

Despite its insistence that good and evil are illusions, pantheism still issues moral judgments and makes moral commands. As such, it is logically and existentially inconsistent. These considerations should lead us to reject the idea that no objective evil exists.

5. Karma and reincarnation. Many believe that karma and reincarnation answer the problem of evil. The evils of this life cannot be justified if we have only one life to live. However, if we have lived before and will live again (reincarnation), the scales will balance out because karma (a law of moral assessment and administration) assigns rewards and punishments from lifetime to lifetime.[19] Nevertheless, multiple problems dog this attempted response.

First, most forms of Buddhism and Hinduism, the two leading religions that advocate karma and reincarnation, deny the existence of a

---

[18]Quoted in Alan Watts, *The Way of Zen* (New York: Vintage Books, 1957), p. 115. See also pp. 107, 147 on the Zen's denial of objective morality. Given my argument for objective morality in chap. 15, this fact alone is enough to disqualify Zen Buddhism as a true and rational worldview. See Harold Netland, *Dissonant Voices* (Grand Rapids: Eerdmans, 1991), pp. 189-92.

[19]However, the goal of religions that hold to karma is not a world of perfect justice sometime in the future but the escape from the world of space and time and personality entirely.

substantial and personal soul (an individual, spiritual substance that endures through time, whether of a human or nonhuman being). Buddhism has many different schools, but all claim that the individual self does not exist (see chap. 23). The self is nothing but a name for a collection of separable parts (*skandas*)—like a chariot that has no essence. There is no substance that binds the parts together in an essence. At death, the parts—which combined to form the *illusion* of a self—separate. If so, no personal self is available to be reincarnated, since there was no self to begin with. But if there is no personal being who exists from lifetime to lifetime, then there is no way for that being to experience either good karma or bad karma, since the karma has nothing to work on.[20]

Hinduism displays a dizzying diversity of schools, but the form most popular in the West (Advaita Vedanta) also denies the existence of an individual self.[21] The one reality is Brahman, or the Absolute Self. Finite, individual selves are illusions of the unenlightened mind. Therefore—although its metaphysics of the self differs from that of Buddhism—Hinduism faces the same problem concerning reincarnation. Because it claims that Brahman is the sole reality, there are no individual selves available to endure from lifetime to lifetime on which karma might attach with its various outcomes.

For there to be reincarnated subjects of karma, there must be individual, personal selves that endure and *continue as themselves* from lifetime to lifetime. But Buddhism and Advaita Vedanta Hinduism do not affirm the existence of individual, personal selves. Therefore, these religions cannot logically support the existence of selves that endure from lifetime to lifetime or which are subjects of karma. Therefore, these Eastern religions cannot logically support reincarnation. If this argument succeeds, it not only demonstrates that they cannot solve the problem of evil, it further shows that both religions propose essential truth claims that contradiction each other: (1) there is no self, and (2) reincarnation and karma. Thus, both religions fail the test of internal logical

---

[20]See Paul Griffiths, "Apologetics in Action: Buddhists and Christians on Selves," in *An Apologetic for Apologetics* (Maryknoll, N.Y.: Orbis, 1991).
[21]On the various schools, see R. C. Zaehner, *Hinduism* (New York: Oxford University Press, 1983).

consistency and are necessarily false.

Second, Buddhism and Hinduism cannot explain the system of karmic evaluation and administration. Both religions affirm that karma is a universal system that *evaluates* the moral conduct of human beings and *administers* rewards and punishments appropriately. Even those versions of Buddhism and Hinduism that grant a personal deity do not claim that this deity administers the karmic system, which is deemed a brute fact. The system is thoroughly impersonal.

But how can an impersonal (meaning unconscious and nonagentive) system morally evaluate the worth of actions by human persons? Karma is a law akin to a natural law of science. G. R. Malkani, a Hindu, claims that karma "automatically produces the appropriate results like any other law in the natural domain. Nobody can cheat the law. It is as inexorable as any natural law."[22] But this law is nothing like any law of nature described by science. The law of gravity, for example, explains the regular behavior of physical objects. It has nothing to say about objective moral values; rather, it predicts the automatic reactions of material entities. But moral states are very different from material states because they are nonphysical and related to human agents, who are not reducible to the physical realm, as argued in chapter seventeen. When considering the moral value of an act (or attitude), we necessarily think of judgment or evaluation. Moral judgments require an evaluator, as argued in a chapter fifteen. However, the idea of karma does not include a moral evaluator of any kind. Therefore, the notion of karma is logically unsupportable. In addition, this problem rationally disqualifies the worldviews of Hinduism and Buddhism in toto, since both affirm reincarnation and karma as essential religious doctrines that turn out to be irrational and thus false.

But problems continue to mount because reincarnation and karma also require moral administration. The impersonal karmic system must meet out rewards and punishments universally and for all time to all sentient beings—a fantastically complex process of cosmic government. But it is government without a governor—a vast system of karmic coordination and implementation, but all without the benefit of a *mind* to plan the ad-

---

[22]G. R. Malkani, *Philosophical Quarterly* (1965): 43, quoted in Paul Edwards, *Reincarnation: An Examination* (New York: Prometheus, 1996), p. 39. This reference is to an Indian publication, not the more well-known Scottish journal of the same name.

ministration or a *will* to implement it. Yet surely a personal and moral agent would be required for such a grand scheme of administration.

The Hindu and Buddhist doctrine of karma and reincarnation cannot solve the problem of evil, nor is their central teaching rationally warranted. Therefore, these religions are disqualified as rational worldviews.

Third, the doctrines of reincarnation and karma do not solve the problem of evil because they cannot explain the reality of evil. One of the engines of the problem of evil is innocent suffering. This is a vexing conundrum for any worldview, but karma does nothing to solve or allevi-ate it. According to karma, there is no unjust suffering. Everyone gets what he or she deserves, even supposedly innocent children. This should strike us as counterintuitive. As Paul Edwards points out, it would hardly be consoling to a mother grieving over a severely deformed child to be told by a reincarnationist minister that this death was morally deserved because of an evil committed in a previous life.[23] Edwards suggests that if he were the mother and a baseball bat were available, he would clunk the person over the head and say, "You deserve your pain not because of a sin in a previous life but because you are a monster right now. You see that justice has prevailed."[24]

Fourth, karma and reincarnation are not adequate responses to the problem of evil because they cannot insure that good wins out over evil in the end. The goal in Hinduism and Buddhism is to escape the realm of karma and reincarnation (samsara) and to attain enlightenment in an inef-fable realm beyond personality, individuality, morality and history (nir-vana for Buddhism; moksha for Hinduism). There is no final vindication of the cosmos and its beleaguered pilgrims. The cosmos and humanity it-self must be left behind because both are trapped in an endless cycle of futility. Life will not be redeemed; it must be obliterated. The contrast with the new heavens and new earth promised to Christians could not be more striking (see Revelation 21–22).

In conclusion, the Eastern systems of karma and reincarnation do noth-ing to solve the problem of evil. We must look elsewhere.

Thus far, I have eliminated five alternative strategies for explaining the problem of evil: atheism, a finite god, a morally impaired god, a world

---

[23]Edwards, *Reincarnation*, p. 45.
[24]Ibid.

without evil and karma/reincarnation. We now explore ways to approach the problem from a Christian worldview.

THE ORIGIN AND NATURE OF EVIL

Since the biblical worldview is rooted inextricably in the themes of creation, fall and redemption, the problem of evil must be addressed according to all three themes.

Creation. Unlike Eastern religions or atheism, both of which lack the doctrine of creation, the Bible affirms that God created the universe according to his matchless wisdom (Proverbs 8) and untrammeled will (Ephesians 1:11), and then pronounced it "good" (Genesis 1; see also 1 Timothy 4:4). God then created human beings in his image and likeness, declaring them "very good" (Genesis 1:26, 31). He gave them dominion over the creation, urging them to cultivate and develop it.

Several philosophical points stand out. First, the universe and humans are objectively valuable to God because he created them and declared them good. The universe is not deficient either because it is separate from God or because it is material.[25] God created a vast quantity of matter and made the first human from "the dust of the earth," after which he breathed his spirit into him (Genesis 2:7). Second, the universe has a structure and purpose, since it was created by and is sustained by a personal and moral God. Third, God gave humans moral responsibility and instructed them on how to live. In the beginning, the road to life was broad and the road to death was narrow (do not eat of *one* tree). Of course, Jesus later claimed that the opposite was now true (Matthew 7:13).[26] The question then becomes, what happened?

The Fall. The doctrine of the Fall explains our present condition and gives hope for redemption, now and in the future. We visited this topic in chapter eighteen, but we should remember that the specific theological concept of the Fall is unique to the Bible and significant in understanding the problem of evil. No other worldview explains our condition in light of a space-time defection from the original intention of the Creator.

However, certain mythologies speak of a "golden age" or of "Pandora's

---

[25]In the fullness of time (Galatians 4:4; John 1:14), God himself would take a human body in the incarnation without thereby polluting himself.

[26]I owe this insight to a taped lecture by Rousas John Rushdoony.

box," which brought vice and strife into the world. The biblical doctrine of the Fall, however, accounts for the abnormality or dysfunction of humans and the world in a deeper and more systematic way than is possible through either mythology or philosophical speculation. In chapter eighteen we explored the meaning of the sin of our first parents and its transference to humanity. Here I develop several themes specifically related to the problem of evil.

First, unlike other worldviews, Christianity claims that vice and natural evil are not intrinsic to or necessitated by human nature or the universe. Evil was not built into creation by God. Our first parents rebelled against the known law of God and thus fell into sin (Genesis 3). This was not on account of God misleading them (the serpent did that) or of God coercing them (they deliberated and acted against God's instructions). Nor was the Fall due to their own finitude (creatures are finite by God's good design, and the unfallen angels remain finite and sinless). As Francis Schaeffer put it, human beings are now discontinuous with their original condition, not because God created them vicious or because God coerced them against their will, but because humans changed themselves by rebelling against God. "In this case we can understand that man is now cruel, but that God is not a bad God. This is precisely the Judeo-Christian position."[27]

Moreover, evil is not metaphysically necessitated; in fact, evil is dependent on a prior and original goodness. This point was made a few pages back, but we need to return to it. Evil is a lack or privation of goodness. It is not evil for a rock not to be able see, since it is not in the nature or purpose of a rock to possess vision. But it is an evil for a human being to be blind, since seeing is part of the original purpose for human beings. Evil is dependent on goodness in a parasitic way. Evil is not a thing or a substance in and of itself, but the warping and twisting of an antecedent good, which results in a lack of proper goodness. For example, Hitler's temporary successes stemmed from his oratorical and strategic abilities. These abilities were not evil in themselves, since a person may inspire goodness through oratory and lead others into righteous endeavors through proper strategies. But Hitler misused his gifts and lacked virtue, particularly love. Hence, he was dominated by evil.

---

[27]Francis Schaeffer, *He Is There and He Is Not Silent*, 30th anniv. ed. (Wheaton, Ill.: Tyndale House, 2001), p. 127.

The upshot is that God is not the author of evil. He did not directly cause or create evil in the same way he created the universe. There are several biblical passages that claim God brought evil upon some person or group (Isaiah 45:7), but these do not mean God created something evil ex nihilo. On the contrary, God brings judgment against evildoers by thwarting their plans and punishing them. Their own evil is the cause of God's actions. God is responding to the spoilage of his creation by bringing judgment.

Second, the discontinuity between original and fallen humanity means that humanity as it now stands has hope for recovery. Our present abnormality—"cruelty" as Schaeffer aptly abbreviated it—is not part of our original created essence, which is good. As Rushdoony says, "Man is *naturally* good and *historically* and *presently* fallen, sinful, and depraved."[28] There would be little hope for human (or cosmic) improvement if people and the world had always been a wreck (the position of Eastern religions, Gnosticism and naturalism). The defects would be hardwired and probably permanent. However, if human and natural evil is the result of a descent into abnormality (which does not involve a loss of human uniqueness and objective value), there may be hope for a substantial recovery or healing of humanity and the cosmos. Evil is then an injury to a healthy body for which there is a cure, at least for those who consult the Great Physician.

This puts the Christian view on an entirely different footing from that of naturalists who try to explain human behavior—the virtuous and the vicious—on the basis of supposed evolutionary antecedents, as is done so often in the evolutionary psychology practiced by Steven Pinker and others. In a *New York Times Magazine* article, Pinker spoke of a teenager who delivered her baby at her prom and then stuffed it into the garbage. Pinker minimized the evil of infanticide by claiming that new mothers in the animal world sometimes kill their offspring if they think their prospects are poor. So, while we do not condone the actions of this young woman, we should not label it "murder."[29] In fact, on Pinker's naturalistic account, her actions could be condoned (given that we are no

---

[28]Rousas John Rushdoony, *Revolt Against Maturity: A Biblical Psychology of Man* (Fairfax, Va.: Thoburn Press, 1977), p. 14.
[29]Steven Pinker, "Why They Kill Their Newborns," *New York Times Magazine*, November 2, 1997, pp. 52-54.

more than evolved animals). But his conscience evidently knew more than his worldview allowed.[30]

Third, if the abnormality that results in moral and natural evil is rooted in the Fall, then we have a philosophical basis for opposing all manner of evils without thereby opposing God himself. We can even fight against evils in ourselves without viewing ourselves as worthless. We are all damaged goods that need radical repair. As Schaeffer says, "God did not make man cruel, and he did not make the results of man's cruelty. These are abnormal, contrary to what God made, and so we can fight the evil *without fighting God*."[31] The Bible never teaches that God is to be morally blamed for human evil and its effects. Jesus' reaction to the death of his friend Lazarus indicates that even the Son of God resisted evil in this fallen world. Jesus showed both sorrow and outrage over death, the death of his friend. Jesus was "deeply moved in his spirit and troubled" (John 11:33). The Greek indicates not mere sorrow but intense anger.[32] *The Message* paraphrase states that "a great anger welled up within him." Death had marred God's good creation, and Jesus, God incarnate, was incensed by it. Jesus expressed these emotions even though he would soon supernaturally raise Lazarus from the dead.

Fourth, with the doctrine of a historic space-time fall of God's good creation in place, the Christian affirms the reality of an objective moral order based on the character and commands of an absolutely good God. The doctrine of the Fall preserves both the original goodness of creation and the goodness of God as the Creator. This is because the Fall explains evil, not on the basis of the intrinsic properties of creation nor on the bad intent of God, but according to the rebellious wills of God's human creatures. Our present abnormality is not the final word. Ethics is not rooted in the fallen nature of human beings but in God's own character and in the created telos of creation, which has been defaced but not erased by the Fall.

Redemption. But what of God's redeeming work in a fallen world? This subject is so vast it fills the entire Bible and would require a systematic

---

[30]C. S. Lewis discusses this in *The Abolition of Man* when he notes that some people are "better than their principles" (1944; reprint, New York: Touchstone, 1996), p. 34.

[31]Schaeffer, *He Is There and He Is Not Silent*, p. 28, emphasis in original.

[32]The inspiration for these comments comes from B. B. Warfield, "On the Emotional Life of Our Lord," in *Biblical and Theological Studies* (New York: Scribners, 1912), pp. 35-90.

theology to do it justice. However, we can sketch God's strategy to accomplish his design in a broken world by saying that God has not left the world to itself; while it is broken, it is not ruined beyond repair. Immediately after the Fall, God promised redemption through "the seed of the woman" (Genesis 3:15-16) and continued to reveal himself through nature, the prophets, his providential workings through his special people (the Jews). God's revelation culminated in the incarnation of himself in Jesus of Nazareth (Hebrews 1:1-3), an event that makes possible the redemption of individuals, cultures and every area of life (Colossians 1–2).

FACING THE PROBLEM

It is important to note that a biblical approach to the problem of evil differs in significant ways from a generic answer to the problem of evil given on behalf of some nameless monotheism. The approaches will overlap at some points, but they are not identical. My basic strategy will be to defeat the charge that God has no reason for allowing or using evil in the world.

I begin with the problem as classically stated. How can this triad be made consistent?

1. God is omnipotent and omniscient.

2. God is omnibenevolent.

3. There is objective evil.

Some have argued that this triad is logically inconsistent because it entails a contradiction. If so, that would mean that any form of theism is necessarily false because three of its defining doctrines fail to cohere logically. This has been called "the deductive problem of evil."

1. God's power means God can prevent any evil, since God can do absolutely anything.

2. God's goodness means he would prevent any evil.

3. But there is evil.

4. So, God *cannot* exist.

This follows deductively; given the truth of the premises, the conclusion necessarily follows.

But in the past several decades very few philosophers have advanced the argument in this form, due to the work of several philosophers to defeat it, principally Alvin Plantinga. I will summarize only the basic points.[33]

The argument given above assumes that (1) God can prevent any evil, since God can do absolutely anything, and that (2) there is never a sufficient reason for God to allow evil. But these premises are highly debatable within the philosophical context of theism itself. It may be that God can only bring about certain goods by letting some evils exist, and that God therefore cannot just do *anything*. For example, God's omnipotence does not mean God can bring about contradictions, since a contradiction (such as a square circle) is not a possible thing. It is impossible, not because no being has the requisite power to do so, but because there is literally nothing to do. Likewise, God cannot create a world in which people learn valuable moral lessons through pain—that are not learnable otherwise—in a world in which there is no pain.[34]

The seeming contradiction stemming from the theistic triad stated earlier can be dissolved fairly easily by introducing another proposition, one that is logically consistent with the triad itself. I will restate the triad and add the qualifying proposition:

1. God is omnipotent and omniscient.[35]

2. God is omnibenevolent.

3. There is objective evil.

4. For any evil that God allows, God has a morally sufficient reason for allowing this evil, even if we do not know what this morally sufficient reason is in some cases.

All that is needed to resolve the purported contradiction in the theistic

---

[33]For an excellent and lucid treatment of the deductive problem of evil and its demise, see Ronald Nash, *Faith and Reason* (Grand Rapids: Zondervan, 1988), pp. 177-94.

[34]Plantinga's argument trades on the idea that libertarian freedom puts some constraints on God and that God would rather instantiate a world with libertarian freedom than one without it. I deny this, so I have changed the example to fit the view that I will defend. However, all that is needed to defeat the deductive problem of evil is a possible way to dissolve the contradiction. Plantinga's strategy, as it stands, does accomplish this purpose.

[35]I take it that omnipotence entails omniscience, since knowing is a power that God possesses to the maximal degree.

triad (1-3) is a proposition that is *possibly* true. This is because contradictions are *necessarily* false. The proposition does not need to be proven true. It simply needs to fit within a theistic worldview and to be logically possible. The deductive problem of evil says the existence of God and evil is *impossible*. If we can show a *possible* way for God and evil to coexist, then it is no longer *impossible*. We can elaborate on statement 4 by stating the following statement by Plantinga: "A good God will eliminate evil as far as he can without either losing a greater good or bringing about a greater evil."[36]

Given this premise, the triad can be reformulated in a perfectly consistent manner:

1. An omnipotent, omniscient, omnibenevolent God created the world.

2. God created a good world in which evil was possible and became actual and had a good reason for doing so.

3. Therefore, the world contains evil.[37]

This strategy has come to be known as a *defense*, as opposed to a *theodicy*. A defense defeats an attack on theism by laying out a possible solution that renders theism rational. But a defense fails to give any specifics on what God's sufficient reasons might be for allowing evil. As Nash notes, a theodicy "on the other hand, attempts to show that God *is* justified in permitting evil; the Christian thinker attempts to show that his reasons as to why evil exists are true, not just possibly true."[38]

It has been said that the best defense is a good offense, and this applies to the problem of evil as well. As I have repeatedly emphasized, the most effective strategy for defending and commending Christianity is to argue that it best explains what matters most. Accordingly, I take up several reasons why God indeed has morally sufficient reasons for the amount of evil that he has permitted in his creation. In so doing, I am tackling the inductive or evidential problem of evil. Unlike the deductive problem of evil, the evidential argument claims that while some evil may be compatible with God's existence, there is too much evil (quantity) and too many

---

[36]Alvin Plantinga, *God, Freedom, and Evil* (Grand Rapids: Eerdmans, 1974), p. 19.
[37]Nash, *Faith and Reason*, p. 189.
[38]Ibid., p. 188.

kinds of evil (quality) for this claim to be plausible. The best way to counter this charge is to advance ways in which God may use evil to further his ends while remaining impeccably good in himself.

FREE WILL

Many notable Christian philosophers, from the early Augustine to C. S. Lewis to Alvin Plantinga and Richard Swinburne, have championed the premise that genuinely free moral agents may err in their choices.[39] Therefore, if God creates beings that control their own actions and are not constrained by forces outside of themselves, they may abuse their power of choice to turn against God himself. Even God, if he decides to create such beings, cannot stop them from so doing without violating their free will.

Another premise of this argument is that it is better to create free beings who may fail than to create beings who are "robots" or "automata" or "puppets" or such. Appeals to free will such as this trade on a libertarian view of agency.[40] For the libertarian, an action A is free if and only if the agent could have refrained from action A or performed action A solely on the basis of his choice. Nothing in the agent's environment or in God himself or even in the agent's character compels the agent from dong A or not doing A. This is sometimes more simply called "the power of contrary choice." Libertarians believe that the conjunction of (1) freedom of the will and (2) determination of the will from factors outside of the will are *incompatible*. Thus, they are also known as *incompatibilists*. For the libertarian or incompatibilist, the power of contrary choice is a *necessary condition* for moral agency. This is free will, on their account.

The apologetic benefit of such an approach is that moral evil is rooted in the autonomy of humans. God is off the hook. Natural evil, however, becomes more problematic, since it does not appear to be caused by the free action of agents, although freewill defenders have addressed it.

The metaphysics of agency (human or otherwise) is a vexed and hoary

---

[39]C. S. Lewis, "Divine Omnipotence," in *The Problem of Pain* (New York: Touchstone, 1966). Plantinga famously gives "the freewill defense" and not a theodicy (see *God, Freedom, and Evil* [Grand Rapids: Eerdmans, 1974]). However, other philosophers, such as Lewis, use the freewill claim as part of their positive theodicy (see Lewis, *Problem of Pain*). Richard Swinburne, *Providence and the Problem of Evil* (New York: Oxford University Press, 1998).

[40]This view of human agency should not be confused with the political philosophy of libertarianism.

subject, both philosophically and theologically. Although many people assume the libertarian account of agency, a strong philosophical case can be made for another view, usually called compatibilism. According to compatibilists, finite agents do not have the power of absolute origination. That is, they cannot bring about states of affairs ex nihilo.[41] Nonetheless, genuine agency is compatible with the determination of the agent's actions by factors outside of the agent. Power of contrary choice, therefore, is not a necessary condition for agency. What is necessary is that the agent deliberates over choices—that a person makes his or her own decision according to his or her own reasons.

Agents are affected significantly by nature, God and their own character. Their choices do not occur in a causal vacuum. However, their character is *their* character, not someone else's. It is not a subset of the larger causal nexus that renders them a set of mere reactions. The choices that issue from deliberative reasoning are genuinely free and responsible choices. (Of course, some human actions are not responsible choices. A tick is different from a gesture; a seizure is different from a lecture—or at least it should be.)

Although compatibilism has been the source of heated debate philosophically and theologically, it is sometimes simply ignored or dismissed. In *The Problem of Pain*, C. S. Lewis assumes the libertarian position and never considers compatibilism. He takes compatibilism to be logically contradictory and does not consider the problems inherent in libertarianism. Some of the most sterling defenders of Christian theism today are libertarians, such as Alvin Plantinga and William Lane Craig. They employ the libertarian-freewill strategy quite brilliantly concerning the problem of evil, especially through their use of middle knowledge. Nevertheless, I take libertarianism to be false. Rather than giving a developed philosophical case for compatibilism,[42] I will offer a biblical argument for compatibilism. By so doing, I am affirming the traditional Reformed or

[41]For a development of this idea, see R. K. McGregor Wright, "The Incoherence of the Free Will Theory," in *No Place for Sovereignty* (Downers Grove, Ill.: InterVarsity Press, 1996); see also Gordon Clark, *Religion, Reason, and Revelation* (Philadelphia: Presbyterian & Reformed, 1961), pp. 199-206, for a discussion of free will.

[42]See R. E. Hobart, "Free Will as Involving Determinism and Inconceivable Without It," in *Metaphysics: The Big Questions*, ed. Peter Van Inwagen and Dean W. Zimmerman (Malden, Mass.: Blackwell, 1998), pp. 343-55. See also John Frame, "Human Responsibility and Freedom," in *The Doctrine of God* (Phillipsburg, N.J.: P & R Publishers, 2002).

Calvinist concept of human agency and God's sovereignty, and denying the traditional Arminian view, which is libertarian.

Some claim that the Bible teaches both libertarian freedom and God's comprehensive rule over all creation, including human choice. This cannot be true because the two claims contradict each other and the Bible does not contain contradictions. If it did, we could not believe it. The Bible affirms human responsibility from Genesis to Revelation. Human evil is never excused on the basis that someone "couldn't help it" or was forced into it by God against his or her will. Human choices and actions are always put in the framework of God's ordination and "meticulous providence."[43]

D. A. Carson claims that the Bible "presupposes or teaches that both of the following propositions are true":

> 1. God is absolutely sovereign, but his sovereignty never functions in such a way that human responsibility is curtailed, minimized, or mitigated.
> 2. Human beings are morally responsible creatures—they significantly choose, revel, obey, believe, defy, make decisions and so forth, and they are rightly held accountable for such actions; but this characteristic never functions so as to make God absolutely contingent.[44]

Carson cites and summarizes many key biblical texts to this effect, but a few must suffice. Consider God's absolute sovereignty.

The psalmist affirms that "our God is in heaven; / he does whatever pleases him" (Psalm 115:3; see also Psalm 135:6). God sets the agenda for the cosmos. What pleases him is to work "out everything in conformity with the purpose of his will" (Ephesians 1:11).[45] "In the Lord's hand the king's heart is a stream of water / that he channels toward all who please him" (Proverbs 21:1). This divine direction is true for all: "In their hearts humans plan their course, / but the LORD establishes their steps" (Proverbs

---

[43]I take this term from Paul Helm, *The Providence of God* (Downers Grove, Ill.: InterVarsity Press, 1994). For a strong view of God's providence, see also James Spiegel, *The Benefits of Providence: A New Look at Divine Sovereignty* (Wheaton, Ill.: Crossway, 2005).

[44]D. A. Carson, *How Long, O Lord?* (Grand Rapids: Baker, 1991), p. 201. I am not sure why Carson wrote "absolutely contingent." He seems to be saying that God is not contingent on our responses in any sense. The concept of contingency is an either-or concept; there are not degrees of contingency.

[45]See John Feinberg's exegesis of this passage and his case for compatibilism in "A Case for a Compatiblist Specific Sovereignty Model," in *No One Like Him* (Wheaton, Ill.: Crossway, 2001).

16:9; see also Jeremiah 10:23). While God "does not willingly bring affliction or grief to anyone" (Lamentations 3:33), God says,

> I am the LORD, and there is no other.
> I form light and create darkness,
> > I bring prosperity and create disaster;
> > I, the LORD, do all these things. (Isaiah 45:6-7)

Several other texts speak of God's hardening people and using evil inten-
tions for his own purposes (Genesis 50:20; Romans 9:18; 1 Samuel 2:25;
2 Samuel 16:10; 1 Kings 22:21). Carson explains that in these passages and
many others like them "at no point is the human agent exonerated of responsibility just because God is in some way behind this or that."[46]

Carson also cites many passages that ratify the reality of human volition
and moral accountability. Joshua famously declares, "Choose for yourselves
this day whom you will serve. . . . But as for me and my household, we will
serve the LORD" (Joshua 24:14-15). Many passages explain our relationship to God on the basis of "if . . . then" statements that enjoin human
action. For example, "If you declare with your mouth, 'Jesus is Lord,' and
believe in your heart that God raised him from the dead, you will be saved"
(Romans 10:9).

In all of this the Bible resolutely affirms God's perfect and faultless
goodness. "God is light; in him there is no darkness at all" (1 John 1:5; see
also Deuteronomy 32:4; Habakkuk 1:13). The heavenly chorus cries out,

> Just and true are your ways,
> > King of the nations.
> Who will not fear you, Lord,
> > and bring glory to your name?
> For you alone are holy. (Revelation 15:3-4)

"God is never presented as an accomplice of evil, or as secretly malicious,
or as standing behind evil in exactly the same way he stands behind
good."[47]

The cross of Christ is the focal point for God's absolute sovereignty,
God's incomparable goodness and human responsibility for evil. This is
especially salient in a prayer in the book of Acts. After their release from

---

[46]Carson, *How Long, O Lord?* p. 203.
[47]Ibid., p. 205.

prison, Peter and John join fellow believers in praise for God's deliverance (Acts 4:24-30). In this prayer, the believers affirm four things:

1. God is the sole Creator of everything (v. 24).

2. The opposition by the leaders of the world, and particularly of Herod and Pilate, against the Messiah (vv. 25-27) is a fulfillment of biblical prophecy (Psalm 2:1-2).

3. Those who opposed and killed the Messiah "did what your power and will had decided beforehand should happen" (v. 28).

4. Believers must petition the Lord for strength to speak the word with boldness and to see signs and wonders manifested "through the name of your holy servant Jesus" (vv. 29-30).

God did not intervene at the last moment to save a sinking Savior. It was all "decided beforehand." Neither did God use human agents like pawns on a chessboard. Herod and Pilate conspired "against [God's] holy servant, Jesus" (v. 27). Carson comments:

> Christians who may deny compatibilism on front after front become compatibilists (knowingly or otherwise) when they think about the cross. There is no alternative, except to deny the faith. And if we are prepared to be compatibilists when we think about the cross . . . it is only a very small step to understanding that compatibilism is taught or presupposed everywhere in the Bible.[48]

Since everything in creation is centered on and summed up in the person and work of Christ (Colossians 1:15–2:15), compatibilism applies to every area of creation. The *Westminster Confession of Faith* presents this view adroitly in the third chapter:

> 1. God from all eternity did by the most wise and holy counsel of his own will, freely and unchangeably ordain whatsoever comes to pass; [nevertheless,] neither is God the author of sin; nor is violence offered to the will of the creatures, nor is the liberty or contingency of second causes taken away, but rather established.

---

[48]Ibid., p. 212. For further development of the compatibilist position, see Mark R. Talbot, "True Freedom: The Liberty That Scripture Portrays as Worth Having," in *Beyond the Bounds: Open Theism and the Undermining of Christianity*, ed. John Piper, Justin Taylor and Paul Kjoss Helseth (Wheaton, Ill.: Crossway, 2003).

2. Although God knows whatsoever may or can come to pass, upon all supposed conditions; yet hath he not decreed any thing because he foresaw it as future, as that which would come to pass, upon such conditions.

Although the argument rages about the relationship of God's providence to human actions, I will approach the problem of evil from this broadly Reformed or Calvinistic position. I do not dismiss the other view lightly, but I am giving the apologetic that seems to me to be the most biblical and fruitful.[49]

THE GREATER-GOOD DEFENSE

Is this the end of the explanation? Happily it is not, although some Reformed thinkers wrongly believe that a strong view of God's sovereignty rules out developing a positive theodicy.[50] In light of God's goodness and sovereignty, it is still possible and fruitful to consider how evils might be used in accord with God's infinite wisdom to bring about God's desired ends—even in and through a fallen world.

Evil has a secondary status in the universe; it is not a direct creation of God but comes about through human mismanagement of people and their environment. Nevertheless, some moral goods are impossible apart from responding to particular evils. Therefore, the Fall (while based on human rebellion against a holy God) opens up possibilities for virtue not possible otherwise. That is, evil serves an instrumental, good purpose in the providence of God. This line of defense has historically been called "the greater-good defense." William Wainwright explains: "This defense at-

---

[49]I have not addressed directly the middle knowledge position, which claims that God scans all possible worlds and chooses the best libertarian world. In this sense God exercises precognition, but not foreordination, since he passively sees what would occur (counterfactually) in these libertarian worlds. There are significant problems for this position philosophically (primarily "the grounding objection"), but I have rejected it for two basic biblical reasons: (1) The biblical view of agency is compatibilist, not libertarian. (2) The biblical view of foreknowledge is not simply precognition but preordination. On this see Carson, *How Long, O Lord?* pp. 219-20. Another less theologically mainstream school advocates libertarian agency and denies that God knows all that will happen in the future. This is called "open theism" and is advanced by Greg Boyd, John Sanders, Clark Pinnock, William Hasker and others. I take this view to be unbiblical and so not worthy of a biblical consideration as a possible response to the problem of evil. For an exposition of this view see Greg Boyd, *Satan and the Problem of Evil* (Downers Grove, Ill.: InterVarsity Press, 2001). For a critique of open theism see Piper et al., *Beyond the Bounds.*

[50]See John Frame, *Apologetics to the Glory of God* (Phillipsburg, N.J.: Presbyterian & Reformed, 1994), chaps. 6-7; and Clark, "God and Evil," in *Religion, Reason, and Revelation.*

tempts to show (roughly) that (1) evil . . . is logically necessary to some good, that (2) this good outweighs the evil, and that (3) there are no alternative goods not involving those evils that would have been better."[51] All evils serve some justifiable purpose in God's economy. I will address the human element first.

This approach is sometimes called the soul-making strategy and was advanced by the early church father Irenaeus.[52] Another church father, Origen, said, "Virtue, if unopposed, would not shine out nor become more glorious by probation. Virtue is not virtue if it be untested and unexamined." Apart from evil, "there would be no crown of victory in store for him who rightly struggled."[53] Augustine gave this classic response:

> For the Almighty God, who, as even the heathen acknowledge, has supreme power over all things, being Himself supremely good, would never permit the existence of anything evil among His works, if He were not so omnipotent and good that He can bring good even out of evil.[54]

Considering how souls might be perfected through struggle and suffering opens the door to the classic understanding of "the greater-good defense." God uses certain evils to actualize a good greater than would be possible otherwise. While the first and prototypical humans were without sin, they lacked difficult experiences that could help produce virtue. For example, virtues such as courage, heroism and self-sacrifice require some element of risk or danger. After the Fall the world became dangerous, and these kinds of virtues became possible. The virtue of patience likewise requires that certain obstacles be dealt with over time in a peaceful and loving fashion. You cannot be patient with my impatience in an unfallen world. More generally, humans could never triumph over adversity without there being adversity of various kinds. We could never demonstrate the "extraordinary" life that Christ calls us to if there were no enemies to love or pray for.[55] This fact by no means exonerates evildoers, since their inten-

---

[51]William Wainwright, *Philosophy of Religion*, 2nd ed. (Belmont, Calif.: Wadsworth, 1999), p. 75.

[52]John Hick is well known for developing this in *Evil and the God of Love*, rev. ed. (New York: Palgrave Macmillan, 2007). Hick, however, is not orthodox in his theological views.

[53]Origen, quoted in Henry Bettenson, ed., *The Early Christian Fathers* (London: Oxford University Press, 1956), p. 264.

[54]Augustine, *Enchiridion on Faith, Hope, and Love*, trans. J. F. Shaw (Chicago: Henry Regnery, 1961), p. 11.

[55]See Dietrich Bonhoeffer on Christianity as an "extraordinary" way of life in *The Cost of Dis-*

tion is to harm, not to help. No understanding of the role of evil in God's world should result in what Bertrand Russell claimed was the effect of Leibniz's teaching on the queen of Prussia: "Her serfs continued to suffer evil, while she continued to enjoy the good, and it was comforting to be assured by a great philosopher that this was just and right."[56] While evils serve larger instrumental ends orchestrated by God, they are not to be praised as moral in themselves, since this would obliterate the distinction of good and evil (see Isaiah 5:20).

Evils should provide possibilities for virtuous responses to vicious behavior. The classic biblical account is the story of Joseph, whose brothers unjustly sold him into slavery. Yet because God was with him, Joseph could say to his brothers many years later, "You intended to harm me, but God intended it for good to accomplish what is now being done, the saving of many lives" (Genesis 50:20).

While evils often befuddle and depress us, we can sometimes find good things left in their wake. Even while he was dying of an inoperable brain tumor that severely restricted his speech, I saw Clyde McDowell, the young president of Denver Seminary, continue to love, minister to and pray for others even in the midst of suffering and deep disappointment. He was close to heaven and radiated it. Similarly, Marshall Shelley says that the greatest evangelist he ever knew never spoke a word. This was his profoundly disabled daughter, who lived only several weeks. Through her short life, she drew love out of people in remarkable ways and caused several to come to terms with the deeper matters of life.[57] Through it all, the family kept faith even while they suffered. Love may cause great suffering, and suffering may occasion great love.

C. S. Lewis writes of God's rigorous and demanding love for his erring creatures in a fallen world in his *The Problem of Pain*.[58] A perfectly loving being may use painful means to perfect less than perfectly loving creatures. Given our fallen condition, what we take to be good may only reinforce our

---

cipleship (New York: Touchstone, 1995).

[56]Bertrand Russell, *History of Western Philosophy* (1945; reprint, New York: Simon & Schuster, 1972), p. 590. Russell was giving a rather caricatured view of Leibniz's theodicy.

[57]Marshall Shelley, "Wordless, Sightless, Helpless Theologian," *Christianity Today*, April 26, 1993, pp. 34-36.

[58]While I do not share Lewis's libertarian view of human agency, his insights can still be applied to a compatibilist account of agency.

own God-forsaking and God-avoiding ways. We think of God's goodness as a sort of sentimental kindness, not a blazing holy desire that the beloved be radically transformed to better represent its Maker and Redeemer.

> We want, in fact, not so much a Father in Heaven as a grandfather in heaven—a senile benevolence who, as they say, "likes to see young people enjoying themselves," and whose plan for the universe was simply that it might be truly said at the end of each day, "a good time was had by all."[59]

After discussing several modes of love (that of the artist for the artifact, the master for the pet and the father for the son), Lewis speaks of a man's love for a woman and of God's jealousy that his bride be without spot or blemish (Ephesians 5:27). "For the truth which this analogy serves to emphasize is that Love, in its own nature, demands the perfecting of the beloved; that the mere 'kindness' which tolerates anything except suffering in its objects is, in that respect, at the opposite pole from Love."[60] This love, Lewis avers, "Is the consuming fire Himself, the Love that made the worlds, persistent as the artists' love for his work and despotic as a man's love for a dog, provident and venerable as a father's love for a child, jealous, inexorable, exactly as love between the sexes." Such a relentless and resourceful love may employ pain to get the attention of sluggish creatures inured in self-reference. Pain cannot be denied; it must be heeded. "God whispers to us in our pleasures, speaks in our conscience, but shouts in our pain; it is His megaphone to rouse a deaf world."[61]

Of course, the same kinds of evils that can occasion virtues not otherwise realizable can also occasion more misery. Those afflicted by pain may curse God and never repent. After the worst tsunami in history devastated the Indonesian coast in December 2004, the world heard reports of both heroic help being offered and villainous harm being perpetrated, such as looting and raping. It is difficult to fathom how much of human (and animal) suffering might be used to accomplish a good end not otherwise achievable. But, of course, the greater-good defense does not rest on calculating or surmising how a particular evil or set of evil would in fact lead to a justifiable greater good. That task is usually beyond our ken (apart from biblical examples such as Joseph).

---

[59]Lewis, *Problem of Pain*, p. 31.
[60]Ibid., p. 38.
[61]Ibid., p. 91.

Nevertheless, those who oppose theism argue that it is more reasonable to believe in gratuitous evils—evils that serve no greater goods—than to believe in a God who somehow employs evil wisely in his divine economy. The argument looks like this:

1. If God exists, there are no gratuitous evils.

2. There are gratuitous evils.

3. Therefore, God does not exist (by *modus tollens*).

There are two basic ways to respond to this challenge. First, we can reverse the argument:

1. If God exists, there are no gratuitous evils.

2. God exists.

3. Therefore, there are no gratuitous evils.

It comes down to which proposition enjoys the most rational support:

1. God exists

2. There are gratuitous evils.[62]

If the several arguments for an omnibenevolent and omnipotent and omniscient God are strong (as I have argued), then statement 1 is rationally stronger than statement 2. The problem of evil should not be tackled in an intellectual vacuum. Evil in the world *is* a possible defeater to theism and Christian theism; it is a prima facie problem. But given the wide array of reasons to believe in Christian theism—the varied arguments for God, the reliability of the Bible, the person and achievements of Jesus Christ, and so on—the claim that God does not exist loses much of its sting philosophically (however painful experienced evil may be).

Second, the Christian theist may argue that even though no evil is wasted in God's world, Christian theism itself gives us reasons why we would not be able to determine what the particular reason for any given evil might be (apart from what is revealed in the Bible). The first reason is that human beings are finite and limited in their understanding. As such, they may be puzzled by the actual nature of things, especially in a

---

[62]Nash, *Faith and Reason*, pp. 211-12.

fallen world. C. S. Lewis reflected on this fact:

> I suspect that there is something in our very mode of thought which makes it inevitable that we should always be baffled by actual existence, whatever character actual existence may have. Perhaps a finite and contingent creature—a creature that might not have existed—will always find it hard to acquiesce in the brute fact that it is, here and now, attached to an actual order of things.[63]

As God thundered to the questioning Job, "Where were you when I laid the foundations of the earth?" The series of questions posed by God in Job 38–42 all emphasize God's supremacy of power and knowledge in relation to Job. To oversimplify a profound book, the answer from God to Job seems to be, "You are in no position to know why I put you through this. But you can trust me."[64]

The second reason is that the doctrine of the Fall tells us why God's providence will remain opaque to us in some ways. Our cognitive and moral equipment, while God-created, is damaged by the effects of sin. Self-centeredness can blind us to the good of being humbled. Pride may refuse to recognize our own need to be humbled in various ways by suffering.

There is also room for some ignorance in what we know about God and his plan for the universe. While Jesus exhibited a well-integrated worldview and did not recoil from intellectual debate with the best minds of this age,[65] in several cases he did not supply explanations for specific evils. When Jesus was told of "the Galileans whose blood Pilate had mixed with their sacrifices," he simply remarked, "Do you think that these Galileans were worse sinners than all the other Galileans because they suffered this way? I tell you, no! But unless you repent, you too will all perish" (Luke 13:2-3). This appears almost rude. Perhaps those addressing Jesus wanted an explanation or a sense that those slaughtered must have deserved it. Jesus would have nothing of it. Instead of providing an explanation, he offered an exhortation to those yet living. They desperately needed to know that they too would perish unless they repented (see Matthew 4:17).

---

[63]C. S. Lewis, *God in the Dock* (Grand Rapids: Eerdmans, 1970), p. 40.

[64]See D. A. Carson "Job: Mystery and Faith," in *How Long, O Lord?* See also Eleonore Stump, "The Mirror of Evil," in *God and the Philosophers*, ed. Thomas V. Morris (New York: Oxford University Press, 1995).

[65]I defend these claims in depth in *On Jesus* (Belmont, Calif.: Wadsworth, 2003), particularly chaps. 1, 3.

Jesus continued: "Or those eighteen who died when the tower in Siloam fell on them—do you think they were more guilty than all the others living in Jerusalem? I tell you, no! But unless you repent, you too will all perish" (Luke 13:4-5). Nor did Jesus himself fully understand his own redemptive sufferings while he agonized on the cross. Otherwise, he would not have cried out in dereliction, "My God, my God, why have you forsaken me?" (Matthew 27:46). This was his outcry—even though he had predicted his death and resurrection on several occasions.

In light of these reflections it is reasonable to suppose that the ways of an all-powerful and all-knowing God will sometimes—or even often—be mysterious to us. Christian apologist and ethicist Joseph Butler (1692-1752) explains this brilliantly in his essay "Upon the Ignorance of Man":

> And as the works of God, and his scheme of government, are above our capacities thoroughly to comprehend: so there possibly may be reasons which originally made it fitting that many things should be concealed from us, which we have perhaps natural capacities of understanding; many things concerning the designs, methods, and end of Divine Providence in the government of the world. There is no matter of absurdity in supposing a veil is on purpose drawn over some scenes of infinite power, wisdom, and goodness, the sight of which might some way or other strike us too strongly; or that better ends are designed and served by their being concealed, than could be by their being exposed to our knowledge. The Almighty may cast clouds and darkness round about him, for reasons and purposes which we have not the least glimpse or conception.[66]

In Paul's doxology in Romans he exclaims,

> Oh, the depth of the riches of the wisdom and knowledge of God!
>> How unsearchable his judgments,
>> and his paths beyond tracing out. (Romans 11:33)

These unsearchable paths of God—the thick, dark, heavy mysteries of Providence—are not absurdities; they are not meaningless. Their meaning is, however, largely opaque to us now. The morally sufficient reasons for these evils may be *inscrutable*, but they are not *gratuitous*. Nevertheless,

---

[66]Joseph Butler, "Upon the Ignorance of Man (Ecclesiastes 8:16-17)," in *Fifteen Sermons Preached at the Rolls Chapel* (Boston: Hilliard, Gray, Little, and Wilkins, 1827), <http://anglicanhistory .org/butler/rolls/15.html>.

God promises his redeemed children that "in all things God works for the good of those who love him, who have been called according to his purpose" (Romans 8:28).

THE CROSS AND RESURRECTION OF CHRIST

The single greatest example of good triumphing over evil is the death of Jesus Christ on a cross outside of ancient Jerusalem. The apex of sacrificial love was displayed through the physical, mental and spiritual suffering of Jesus Christ on behalf of his enemies. No greater act of love has ever been so demonstrated, nor ever will be so. I have made the case for the reliability of the texts that report this event and for the matchless character of Christ. Yet without human rebellion against God, God's own unparalleled work of reconciliation in Christ could never have occurred. Scripture intimates that the final plan was set from the beginning when it refers to Christ as "the Lamb who was slain from the creation of the world" (Revelation 13:8).

No other worldview teaches that God Almighty humbled himself in order to redeem his sinful creatures through his own suffering and death. No other worldview endorses the idea that the supreme reality was impaled by human hands for the sake of lost souls. No founder of any other religion cried out in his sacrificial death, "My God, my God, why have you forsaken me?" (Matthew 27:46; see Psalm 22:1).

God in Christ was no stranger to agony and death. Many impugn God's allowance of evil by claiming that God is far removed from our earthly distress. But he is not. No other God bears the scars of rejection, betrayal, humiliation and crucifixion. Jesus Christ knows our pain from the inside out, because he has suffered more intensely than anyone. He is our high priest only because he sank so low as to submit to death on a cruel Roman cross for crimes he did not commit (Philippians 2:5-11). The gospel declares that God not only sympathizes with us, God empathizes with us through Christ.

E. Stanley Jones described the capacity for suffering in caring people— and in God himself.

> The higher in the scale of culture and character one goes, the more sensitiveness one manifests, the wider one's range of affection, and hence the greater capacity for suffering. When one comes to the highest life of all,

namely, God, we would expect that this sensitiveness would be manifested in its perfection. The cross says that it is. The cross is God sensitive to human sin and sorrow, so sensitive that it becomes his very own.[67]

Jesus Christ bore our sins and shared our sorrows. While many evils in this world of pain are opaque and unanswerable, the greatest evil of all time has been explained to us.

But the death of Christ was not the end. From the earliest sermons in the book of Acts to the Epistles and through Revelation and on to the proclamation of the gospel today around the world, the cross of Christ is inescapably linked to the resurrection of Christ (see chap. 22). No other religion is based on the death, burial and resurrection of its divine founder. It is in this supernatural reality that the problem of evil is best understood. If the misunderstanding of his own people could not thwart him, if the powers of darkness could not outsmart him or seduce him, if death itself could not hold him, then we have every reason to trust him as "the Beginning and the End" (Revelation 21:6). The resurrection of the crucified Christ opens up a hopeful future for every believer in Christ. This is why Paul proclaims, "What I received I passed on to you as of first importance; that Christ died for our sins according to the Scriptures, that he was buried, that he was raised on the third day according to the Scriptures (1 Corinthians 15:3-4).

The world deserves tears and anger, as we cry out with the psalmist, "My soul is in deep anguish. / How long, LORD, how long?" (Psalm 6:3). But the present world is not the fully redeemed cosmos spoken of in the book of Revelation—a world in which there is no more curse and no more tears, a world where God dwells with his redeemed creatures in perfect harmony (Revelation 21–22). Because of the reality of the resurrection of Christ from the dead, Paul looks ahead with rational hope.

> The trumpet will sound, the dead will be raised imperishable, and we will be changed. For the perishable must clothe itself with the imperishable and the mortal with immortality. When the perishable has been clothed with the imperishable, and the mortal with immortality, then the saying that is

---

[67]E. Stanley Jones, *Christ and Human Suffering* (New York: Abingdon Press, 1933). See also Kazoh Kitamori, *Theology of the Pain of God*, 5th ed. (1958; reprint, Eugene, Ore.: Wipf & Stock, 2005).

written will come true: "Death has been swallowed up in victory:

"Where, O death, is your victory?

Where, O death, is your sting?

The sting of death is sin, and the power of sin is the law. But thanks be to God! He gives us victory through our Lord Jesus Christ. (1 Corinthians 15:52-57)

Life in this world, fallen though it is, is meaningful because of the trajectory set in motion through the achievement of Christ, who is even now the supreme authority over the universe (Matthew 28:18; Colossians 1–2). Therefore, Paul exhorts Christ followers: "Therefore, my dear brothers and sisters, stand firm. Let nothing move you. Always give yourselves fully to the work of the Lord, because you know that your labor in the Lord is not in vain" (1 Corinthians 15:58). Fighting against injustice, unbelief, prejudice, poverty, violence and stupidity is not done in vain if it is done "in the Lord." Nor is it fighting God himself, because God is in the process of redeeming a fallen and groaning cosmos through the righteous work of Jesus Christ (Romans 8:18-26). This is the strongest response to the problem of evil that is available to erring and aching mortals east of Eden.

Conclusion

Take It to the Streets

Therefore, I urge you, brothers and sisters, in view of God's mercy, to offer your bodies as a living sacrifice, holy and pleasing to God—this is true and proper worship. Do not conform to the pattern of this world, but be transformed by the renewing of your mind. Then you will be able to test and approve what God's will is—his good, pleasing and perfect will.

(ROMANS 12:1-2)

A LONG BOOK DESERVES A SHORT conclusion. In a fairly comprehensive way, I have defended Christianity as objectively true, rational and significant for life. I have also critiqued its leading rivals, namely, naturalism, pantheism and Islam. Let me here sum up the work and give a parting exhortation.

To turn a phrase by John Stott made in reference to missions, God is an apologetical God, the Bible is an apologetical book, and Christ is an apologetical Christ. Therefore, it is imperative for Christians to defend and commend Christianity ardently, knowledgeably and wisely. The best method for this holy endeavor is to present Christianity as a hypothesis that passes rational testing better than rival worldviews. In using this method, Christians must offer a genuinely Christian worldview so that unbelievers can discern just what is being defended and how it differs from their own worldviews. But before the Christian worldview is advocated, various distortions must be unmasked so that a genuinely biblical perspective may shine through. Given certain philosophies afoot in recent decades, Christians need to defend a view of truth that comports with biblical revelation and reason. Further, they must persuade unbelievers that the pursuit of truth is neither quixotic nor histrionic, but virtuous. And given the tremendous prudential possibilities offered by Christianity—eternal felicity or eternal ruin—an individual should be motivated to investigate Christian truth claims seriously.

Concerning apologetics proper, natural theology commands a central place. The theological arguments leveled against natural theology fail. The ontological, cosmological, design, moral and religious-experience arguments make it rationally compelling to believe in God: a necessary being who created the world ex nihilo, who left his stamp of design on that creation at both the macroscopic and microscopic level, who is the source of objective moral truth and obligation, and who has revealed himself to various individuals through religious experience. Our consciousness and reasoning abilities are best explained by theism. Moving from the defense of monotheism to Christianity in particular, the biblical account of human nature uniquely explains both human greatness and misery.

Having laid these apologetic foundations, we argue for the historical reliability of the New Testament and the uniqueness and supremacy of Jesus based on his matchless claims and matchless credentials. The best explanation for Jesus' activities and affirmations about himself, God and the world is that he was in fact God incarnate. Critics to the contrary, there are coherent ways of understanding the incarnation that do justice to Scripture, creeds and logic. The resurrection of Christ is the lynchpin of Christian conviction and singles out Christianity from all other worldviews. A compelling case can be made for the resurrection of Christ in space-time history, given the background of belief in theism and the well-established nature of certain facts pertaining to Jesus' death and the beliefs and practices of the early church.

Several salient challenges to Christian theism require separate and extended treatment. Since so many think that all religions have equal spiritual standing, and that Christianity cannot claim supremacy, I argue that religions make incompatible truth claims that cannot be reconciled. Moreover, the biblical evidence favors the need for all people to hear and accept the gospel of Jesus Christ. Globally, Islam poses the most significant challenge to Christianity among the world's religions. Therefore, I assess its claim to have replaced Christianity and find that claim badly wanting. The problem of evil is a vexation not only for Christianity but for every worldview. While mysteries partially cloud our understanding of God's governance of a corrupted self and cosmos, the Christian worldview better explains the meaning and end of evil than does any alternative perspective. It not only explains evil but gives rational hope for meaning amid suffering and hope for a better world to come. Two final problems are taken up in appendices: the question of hell in relation to God's goodness and some challenges to the moral standing of the Hebrew Bible.

At times I despaired of ever finishing this book. What kept me going was the hope that my study, writing, teaching, preaching, debating and witnessing of more than thirty years may find fruitful expression in these pages—expression that may, by the grace of God, help many other people. But beyond that, these endeavors have led me deeper into the conviction ("fire in my bones") that Christianity is true and supremely important. While I have been a Christian since the summer of 1976, I have never stopped thinking critically about Christian truth claims. I have found the Christian message not only existentially meaningful (through all the ups and downs) but intellectually satisfying.

My hope and prayer for this book is that readers will take what is useful from this work—and from other sources—and bring apologetics to bear in all manner of endeavor. Apologetics needs to be applied to the whole of life under the lordship of Jesus Christ. We should hear apologetics ringing out from the pulpit and being discussed in every level of Christian education. Apologetics should be part of the core curriculum at Christian seminaries, colleges and high schools. Campus ministries should train their workers to defend Christianity and understand the weaknesses of other worldviews. Every level of publishing—Christian and secular—should feel the force of Christian persuasion, both at the academic and more popular levels. Christian academics, whether at Christian or secular institutions, should strive to develop a Christian perspective on their disciplines, being unashamed of the gospel, yet wise as serpents and innocent as doves (Matthew 10:16).

I could go on listing areas of apologetic influence and opportunity,[1] but

---

[1]See Douglas Groothuis, "A Manifesto for Christian Apologetics: Nineteen Theses to Shake the World with the Truth," in *Reasons for Faith: Making a Case for Christian Faith*, ed. Norman L.

the central question is whether or not Christians are willing to heed the divine call to defend what they believe before the unbelieving world, *come what may*. Heeding this call requires sustained study, moral courage and ceaseless prayer. It demands a desperate desire to see people come to the crucified, resurrected and ascended Jesus Christ, who now sits at the right hand of God. None of this can be accomplished in ways pleasing to the Lord apart from the in-filling and direction of the Holy Spirit, who is the Spirit of truth. While the Spirit may instruct us in good arguments that require long periods of study, the Spirit may also lead us in quiet ways to strike up conversations with strangers or to take other risks of outreach. We need to depend on Christ moment by moment, seeking the discernment and power of the Holy Spirit.[2]

Christians need a confident, courageous, contagious, compelling conviction that Christianity is the flaming truth the world needs to hear, that it can withstand rational testing and that the God of truth sponsors our humble apologetic efforts. Christians also need tenacity in the face of the spiritual warfare that always accompanies Christian outreach (see Acts 13:1-12). We need to put on the full armor of God and go into the battle for hearts and minds (Ephesians 6:10-18) because everything is at stake.[3]

While I have not emphasized it in this book, the supernatural manifestations of God's kingdom—signs and wonders such as healings, prophecy, visions and other miracles—provide powerful apologetic evidence that God is alive and powerful today. Affirming these demonstrations of God's character is in no sense irrational, since they indicate God's actions in the world and have been exhibited in the Scripture and throughout history. Nor should an expectancy and desire for signs and wonders replace the need for apologetic study at every level, since God's truth is communicated in both ways.[4]

So, in the end, what matters most? The triune God matters most: the

---

Geisler and Chad V. Meister (Wheaton, Ill.: Crossway, 2007), pp. 401-8.

[2]This was the secret of Francis and Edith Schaeffer's powerful ministry. See Francis Schaeffer, *True Spirituality* (Carol Stream, Ill.: Tyndale House, 1972); Edith Schaeffer, *The Tapestry: The Life and Times of Francis and Edith Schaeffer* (Waco, Tex.: Word, 1981); Colin Duriez, *Francis Schaeffer: An Authentic Life* (Wheaton, Ill.: Crossway, 2008).

[3]See Gary Kinnaman, *Winning Your Spiritual Battles* (Ventura, Calif.: Vine Books, 2003).

[4]J. P. Moreland, a highly skilled, prolific and well-respected philosopher, makes this point in his important book *Kingdom Triangle* (Grand Rapids: Zondervan, 2007).

One who has graciously revealed himself for our salvation and his greater glory through Jesus Christ, God incarnate. Therefore, it is only fitting that we embrace God's grace, seek first his kingdom, deny ourselves, take up our cross and follow Jesus Christ into kingdom engagements. Part of that high calling is to take apologetics to the streets for the glory of God.

Appendix 1

Hell on Trial

One of the ways in which the damned will be condemned is that they will see themselves condemned by their own reason, by which they claimed to condemn the Christian religion.

BLAISE PASCAL[1]

CHRISTIANITY IS THE HIGHEST-STAKES proposition imaginable (see chap. 8). There is eternal life to gain or lose, depending on our answer to God. But the loss, biblically understood, is far more than a mere forfeiture of gain; there is instead an inheritance of pain, both mental and physical, perpetually and without respite. The magnitude of the malady meted out by God against the unrepentant is monumental: hell. Herein, the unredeemed are thrown back on their own fallen resources, which fail to win either favor with God or escape from their moral guilt, since they have failed to respond rightly to what God has made known to them through general or special revelation (see chap. 25).

Hell is an apologetic problem for Christianity because it demands that we square the love of God with the eternal punishment of some of God's creatures.[2] But this problem should not be wrestled with in isolation from the cumulative case for Christian theism made in these pages (and else-

---

[1]Blaise Pascal, *Pensées*, ed. and trans. A. Krailsheimer (New York: Penguin, 1966), 175/563, p. 84.
[2]I argued in chap. 23 that a case can be made that, in the end, more people will be redeemed than will be lost.

where). A philosophical problem, even a vexing problem, need not sink an entire worldview. This does not mean that Christians should shy away from believing in or teaching this doctrine; it does mean that we should approach it with humility and not apart from the evidence for Christianity as a whole system.

This short chapter cannot possibly raise and answer all the issues related to the biblical doctrine of hell. Rather, it will address a well-known charge against Jesus' belief in hell and then lay out an account of hell that makes sense in light of crucial Christian truth claims.[3]

JESUS AND HELL[4]

Jesus speaks of a postmortem existence either with God in blessing or outside of God's blessing in a state of regret, loss and forfeiture. Jesus announces to the repentant criminal crucified next to him that he would be with Jesus in paradise that very day (Luke 23:43). To the crucified unrepentant criminal on his other side, Jesus offers no such promise. In the parable of Lazarus and the rich man, Jesus contrasts the beggar Lazarus, who "died and the angels carried him to Abraham's side," with the oppressive rich man who died and found himself in "Hades, where he was in torment" (Luke 16:19-23). Jesus also warns of a day when he will separate the "sheep" from the "goats" eternally on the basis of how people lived in response to him and to their neighbors (Matthew 25:31-46). Jesus implicitly builds on certain passages in the Hebrew Scriptures to this effect (e.g., Daniel 12:2), but he makes himself the key agent of eternal liberation and blessing, or eternal judgment and condemnation.

Jesus teaches that at death a person passes into a disembodied intermediate state—either into God's presence or away from it—and that at some future time this will be followed by Jesus' own return to earth in final

---

[3]I hold the traditional view that the biblical understanding of hell is eternal punishment. Some with a high view of Scripture have defended universalism (all are saved) or annihilationism (the wicked are destroyed, not punished eternally). Rather than respond to these minority views, I commend the work of Robert A. Peterson on this, *Hell on Trial: The Case for Eternal Punishment* (Phillipsburg, N.J.: P & R Publishing, 1995). His arguments against universalism and annihilationism are found in chaps. 8-9 respectively. See also the excellent overview of this doctrine by T. L. Tiessen, "Hell," in *Global Dictionary of Theology*, ed. William A. Dyrness and Veli-Matti Kärkkäinen (Downers Grove, Ill.: InterVarsity Press, 2008), pp. 372-76.

[4]Some of the material in this section is adapted from Douglas Groothuis, "Jesus' Metaphysics," in *On Jesus* (Bemont, Calif.: Wadsworth, 2003).

judgment. After this the permanent resurrection of the body will occur. "A time is coming when all who are in their graves will hear his [the Son of God's] voice and come out—those who have done good will rise to live, and those who have done evil will rise to be condemned" (John 5:28-29).

Jesus claims to have the authority to render final judgment.

> Not everyone who says to me, "Lord, Lord," will enter the kingdom of heaven, but only those who do the will of my Father who is in heaven. Many will say to me on that day, "Lord, Lord, did we not prophesy in your name and in your name drive out demons and perform many miracles?" Then I will tell them plainly, "I never knew you. Away from me, you evil-doers." (Matthew 7:21-23)

Such statements by Jesus have led some to reject Jesus as a sound thinker or a moral teacher. Bertrand Russell, in his famous essay "Why I Am Not a Christian," is illustrative: "There is one very serious defect to my mind in Christ's moral character, and that is that He believed in hell. I do not myself feel that any person who is really profoundly humane can believe in everlasting punishment."[5]

Russell claims that Jesus demonstrated "vindictive fury against those people who would not listen to His preaching." Moreover, Jesus' teaching that it is possible to sin against the Holy Spirit such that one is never forgiven "has caused an unspeakable amount of misery in the world." A kind person would never have unleashed such worries upon the world.[6] Furthermore, Jesus took "a certain pleasure in contemplating wailing and gnashing of teeth, or else it would not occur so often."[7] Last, Russell claims that the doctrine of hell "put cruelty into the world and gave the world generations of cruel torture; and the Christ of the Gospels, if you could take Him as his chroniclers represent Him, would certainly have to be considered partially responsible for that."[8] If Russell's charges stand, Jesus fails morally and philosophically and as such is not worthy of respect or emulation, let alone worship. Russell's judgment, however, is faulty.

First, Jesus did not engage in "vindictive fury" when predicting divine

---

[5]Bertrand Russell, *Why I Am Not a Christian and Other Essays on Religion and Related Subjects*, ed. Paul Edwards (New York: Simon & Schuster, 1957), p. 17.
[6]Ibid., pp. 12-13.
[7]Ibid., p. 18.
[8]Ibid.

judgment. He issues strong warnings at times but shows no "pleasure in contemplating wailing and gnashing of teeth." Moreover, after pronouncing seven charges (or "woes") against "teachers of the law and Pharisees" (Matthew 23:15-32), Jesus *laments* over Jerusalem for not accepting his offer of redemption. "Jerusalem, Jerusalem, you who kill the prophets and stone those sent to you, how often I have longed to gather your children together, as a hen gathers her chicks under her wings, and you were not willing" (Matthew 23:37).

While voluntarily dying on the cross, Jesus prays concerning those responsible for his crucifixion, "Father, forgive them, for they do not know what they are doing" (Luke 23:34). This is hardly vindictive, but forgiving and compassionate. Rather than being spiteful, Jesus issues *warnings* precisely because he believes in both heaven and hell. That he warns of eternal loss repeatedly does not entail that he takes any enjoyment in the idea, any more than a physician enjoys repeatedly warning an asthmatic patient that she will die if she doesn't stop smoking. If Jesus did in fact believe that an eternal sin against the Holy Spirit were possible, it would only behoove him to warn others against committing it (Mark 3:20-30). The fact that some have worried unnecessarily about committing this sin should not be credited to Jesus any more than pathologists should be blamed when hypochondriacs think they have contracted diseases they do not have.

Further, we should not isolate Jesus' teaching on hell from the claims and credentials we addressed in chapters twenty to twenty-two. Jesus was not just any person spouting opinions about divine retribution. He did not speak of such in a moral or spiritual vacuum. His statements were delivered as a man who claimed and demonstrated unique and unsurpassable authority based on moral teachings, compassionate life, multiple miracles, saving death and death-defeating resurrection from the dead. Even if his teachings on hell bother us (as, in fact, they do bother many Christians to some extent), his words should be heeded as well grounded, if he is, indeed, who the Bible claims he was.

Second, Russell's claim that the very idea of hell induced generations to cruelly torture others is terribly overstated. We can cite a few Inquisitors who tortured heretics in hopes that earthly torment might spare them eternal punishment, but this is but a small and deeply aberrational percentage of Christians throughout the ages. There is no biblical warrant for the idea that earthly torture can save one from eternal condemnation. The majority of those who purport to follow Jesus have adopted the attitude of warning and invitation with respect to Jesus' message of redemption, not the practice of torture or other forms of coercion. Torture is nowhere commended by the Jewish or Christian Scriptures (or any Christian creed) as a method of conversion, purgation or retaliation.

Third, while some regard the very idea of hell as utterly repugnant, philosophical arguments have been marshaled in support of the doctrine of hell. If one can rationally support the idea of God's perfect and infinite holiness and justice in relation to human sin and moral responsibility, the idea of the perpetual punishment of one who rejects God's offer of redemption is not without warrant.[9] As Milton's Lucifer put it in *Paradise Lost:*

> So farewell Hope, and with Hope farewell Fear,
> Farewell Remorse; all Good to me is lost;
> Evil be thou my Good. . . .
> Better to reign in Hell, than serve in Heav'n.[10]

C. S. Lewis spoke of the turning away of the creature from the Creator in these terms: "There are only two kinds of people in the end: Those who say to God, 'Thy will be done,' and those to whom God says in the end, 'Thy will be done.' All that are in hell chose it. Without that self-choice, there would be no hell."[11]

Moreover, there are biblically tenable and philosophically defensible models of hell that are not vindictive at all.[12] While the Bible does speak of God's wrath and punishment against unrepentant sin (both in time and eternity), it also affirms that God does not enjoy this in any sadistic kind of way. As Lamentations reveals: "For he does not willingly bring affliction / or grief to anyone" (Lamentations 3:33). This concern is also seen in God's cry through Ezekiel for his rebellious people: "Say to them, 'As

---

[9]In chaps. 10 (the ontological argument) and 15 (the moral argument), I defended the moral perfection of God. Chapter 23 discussed the biblical understanding of human agency in relation to God's providence.

[10]While Milton's Lucifer captures the essence of unmitigated rebellion against divine authority, the concept of "reigning in hell" is incoherent, since the biblical concept of hell allows for no such relationship between persons. Hell has no rewards.

[11]C. S. Lewis, *The Great Divorce* (New York: Harper, 2001), p. 75.

[12]See Michael J. Murray, "Heaven and Hell," in *Reason for the Hope Within*, ed. Michael J. Murray (Grand Rapids: Eerdmans, 1999), pp. 287-317; and C. S. Lewis, "Hell," in *The Problem of Pain* (1962; reprint, New York: Simon & Schuster, 1996), pp. 105-14.

surely as I live, declares the Sovereign LORD, I take no pleasure in the death of the wicked, but rather that they turn from their ways and live. Turn! Turn from your evil ways! Why will you die, people of Israel?" (Ezekiel 33:11).

THE LOGIC OF HELL

Many evangelicals are ashamed of this biblical doctrine, viewing it as a blemish to be covered up by the cosmetic of divine love. But this dishonors God's Word. Jesus warned his hearers of the eternal punishment awaiting those who reject him (Matthew 13:40-42; 25:46). If we clearly and compassionately expound the truth about hell, we may be surprised to find people responding to it in faith.

The doctrine of hell does not stand alone as a kind of ancient Christian chamber of horrors. Rather, hell is inseparable from three other interrelated biblical truths: human sin, God's holiness and the cross of Christ.

In a relativistic culture the very concept of sin must be elucidated and defended vigorously. If morality is relative to each person, then there is no moral standard that one must meet or break. But as I argued in chapter fifteen, the idea of an objective moral law is inescapable. When we are snubbed or exploited, we call out for justice. When we encounter people of grit and grace, we praise them as moral examples. Our conscience is more than mere instinct or social conditioning. Yet because there is often a great gap between our ideals and our actions, we suffer guilt and regret. Despite our denials and excuses, our consciences dog us throughout our days.

Christianity explains the global stain of human guilt by placing it in a theological framework that both sharpens its sting and makes relief possible. Sin is a moral condition that offends a holy God and removes us from his approval.

While much modern psychology assures us that guilt can be gutted through humanistic methods, the gospel faces the problem head-on. Guilt is real because we have violated the standards of goodness. Left to ourselves, we can do nothing to undo our wrongs. Forgiving ourselves is never sufficient because we are in no position to exonerate the guilty party—much like a murderer cannot grant himself or herself a stay of execution.

Lawbreakers deserve punishment. But is hell too extreme? The great American theologian Jonathan Edwards took this question up in his essay

"The Justice of God in the Damnation of Sinners."[13] Edwards argued that because God is "a being of infinite greatness, majesty, and glory," he is therefore "infinitely honorable" and worthy of absolute obedience. "Sin against God, being a violation of infinite obligations, must be a crime infinitely heinous, and deserving of infinite punishment." This helps deflect the commonly heard objection that since we are finite and only commit a finite number of sins, our punishment should be of limited duration.

Further, since we have sinned against God, this offense remains, no matter how much we suffer. Our suffering cannot atone for our own sin. The only suffering that atones for sin is that of Jesus Christ, "the Lamb of God who takes away the sins of the world" (John 1:29). Yet if a person has not rightly responded to God's overtures in special and general revelation, he or she is left outside of God's redemptive plan. Moreover, those in hell, having set themselves against God, continue to sin against him and so continue to bear the penalty for their perpetual and incorrigible sin.

Jonathan Edwards's much maligned but solidly biblical sermon "Sinners in the Hands of an Angry God" presses home the point that without Christ we have no grounds for confidence and every reason to fear hell. God, who is angry with sin, could justifiably send the unrepentant sinner to hell at any moment. Jesus himself warned, "Do not be afraid of those who kill the body but cannot kill the soul. Rather, be afraid of the One who can destroy both soul and body in hell" (Matthew 10:28).

To fathom the horror of sin and the holiness of God we must kneel before the cross of Christ. While the Scriptures command us to be like Christ, this is never presented as the basis of our salvation. Christ's sinless perfection is impossible for us to attain, "for all have sinned and fall short of the glory of God" (Romans 3:23). Because Jesus flawlessly obeyed God's moral law in our place, he is uniquely qualified to be our Savior. On the cross, Christ offered himself to the Father as a spotless sacrifice for our sin.

Sin against God is so severe that only the death of the sinless Son of God could atone for it. We see the reality of hell when the crucified Christ calls out, "My God, my God, why have you forsaken me?" (Mark 15:34).

---

[13]Jonathan Edwards, "The Justice of God in the Damnation of Sinners," in *Puritan Sage: Collected Writings of Jonathan Edwards*, ed. Vergilius Ferm (New York: Liberty Publishers, 1953).

Paul explained, "God made him who had no sin to be sin for us, so that in him we might become the righteousness of God" (2 Corinthians 5:21).

In the cross of Christ the sinfulness of sin, the holiness of God and the reality of hell are all writ large with the blood of the Lamb. Only through Christ taking on our hell through his death could sinners be reconciled to a holy God. Once this is understood, hell takes on a clarity not otherwise perceived. Apart from the cross there is no hope for forgiveness or reconciliation. Hell is the only alternative.

Only by understanding hell can we grasp the immensity of God's love. God's love took his Son to the hell of the cross for our sake. This is a costly love, a bloody love that has no parallel in any of the world's religions. Although other religions (particularly Islam) threaten hell, none offer the sure deliverance from it that Christianity offers through the sacrificial love of God himself. In this sense Jesus Christ suffered hell for his people.

In this rich theological context, we can courageously incorporate the doctrine of hell at the heart of our evangelistic and apologetic enterprise. Jesus asked what a person's life would be worth if he or she were to gain the whole world but forfeit his or her very soul (Matthew 16:26). Hell is the loss of the soul, a reality so terrible that Scripture uses a variety of ways to describe it. The graphic reports of hell in Scripture—such as the Abyss (Revelation 9:1-11), the lake of fire (Revelation 20:14), the blackest darkness (Jude 13), the weeping and gnashing of teeth (Matthew 25:30)—disclose the stark reality of eternal separation from God.

We can apply these truths in several ways. First, we should encourage biblical preaching and teaching on hell set in its proper theological setting and presented with prayer and compassion. As Francis Schaeffer said, the doctrine of hell must be taught "with tears." When I gave a campus lecture several years ago on the New Age view of Christ, I emphasized that the biblical Christ came to save people from hell. This did not repulse people, even though it was a secular campus. Students pondered what I said and many stayed to ask questions after the lecture.

Second, our everyday witness must involve a warning as well as a welcome. We welcome people to find eternal life in Christ, but we must also warn them of the eternal death awaiting those who reject God. Pascal said, "Between heaven and hell is only this life, which is the most fragile thing in the world."[14] Given the biblical warnings about hell, unbelievers end up betting their lives that Christianity is a lie. We should challenge people to investigate intently the claims of Christianity, considering all there is to gain and all there is to lose (see chap. 8).

Third, we must beseech God to alert both our non-Christian friends and the church at large to the reality of hell. Without this doctrine firmly in place, Christians will lose their evangelistic edge. And without a proper fear of God's holiness, no one should be expected to come to Christ for his gift of forgiveness and eternal life.

An apologetic that denies or shies away from the doctrine of hell is not truly a Christian apologetic. Yet this teaching must be done with compassion and tears. Such was exemplified by Francis Schaeffer, a man who believed in eternal punishment and who gave his life to rescue people from it and to lead them into the abundant life that only Jesus Christ delivers (John 10:10). When asked why he continued to defend and proclaim the gospel, even while afflicted with what would become terminal cancer, he replied that it was "sorrow for all the lost" that drove him to be a faithful witness, "regardless of the cost." To believe in "the eternal lostness of the lost without tears would be a cold and dead orthodoxy, indeed." Since each lost person is one of our kind, it would be "totally ugly and opposed to the biblical message" if we did not give our all to this task of evangelizing them.[15]

---

[14]Pascal, *Pensées* 152/213, p. 81. I have altered the wording slightly to make the point clearer.
[15]Francis Schaeffer, letter to the Rev. David H. Bryson, January 14, 1983, quoted in Peterson, *Hell on Trial*, p. 55.

Appendix 2

Apologetic Issues in the Old Testament

Richard S. Hess

AN APOLOGETICS ADDENDUM ON MATTERS relating to the Old Testament can include a great variety of items. Guided by the author of this volume and my own thoughts as to what may be of most value, I have chosen to focus on three items that might assist us in appreciating some of the major apologetics issues for this era. I will begin with a consideration of some of the chief issues addressed more popularly in recent pro-atheist books. I will then consider the so-called minimalists and criticisms of the historical witness of the Bible. Finally, I will look at perhaps the most important apologetic issue in the Old Testament, that of Deuteronomy, Joshua and divinely ordained genocide.[1]

NEW ATHEISTS AND THE OLD TESTAMENT

First, I would like to deal with a few of the specific charges made by the "new atheists." Space does not permit me to examine the details of every issue that is discussed. So I will attempt to focus on some of the main charges in three well-known books by authors also famous for taking this position: Sam Harris, *The End of Faith: Religion, Terror, and the Future of Reason;* Richard Dawkins, *The God Delusion;* and Christopher Hitchens, *God Is Not Great: How Religion Poisons Everything.*[2]

---

[1]There are, of course, other important apologetics issues; for example, the development of "monotheism" in ancient Israel. Was it early in Israel's history or something appearing only later in the seventh century B.C.? For more of this see Richard S. Hess, *Israelite Religions: An Archaeological and Biblical Survey* (Grand Rapids: Baker Academic, 2007).

[2]Sam Harris, *The End of Faith: Religion, Terror, and the Future of Reason* (New York: W. W. Norton, 2004). Richard Dawkins, *The God Delusion* (Boston: Houghton Mifflin, 2006). Chris-

Harris draws in references to the Old Testament here and there to support his opinion. A favorite text is Deuteronomy 13:6-16, partly quoted on page 18 and partly on page 82. For Harris obedience requires that you stone "your son or daughter" when they "return from yoga class advocating the worship of Krishna." It also justifies the Inquisition. The latter of course is an obvious error by Harris. It may have been used to justify the Inquisition, but that does not mean it was interpreted correctly. In fact, to apply this text to a young participant in yoga is misleading. First, the text uses a verb for "entice" (Hebrew root *swt*) that explicitly refers to those who are successful in leading others to do something (Judges 1:14), often contrary to God's will (as in Jezebel's leadership of Ahab [1 Kings 21:25]). Second, the statements attributed to those condemned to die are commands (first-person cohortatives), "We must worship other gods." Third, the issue here is not one of personal belief, but explicitly one attempting to lead the community away from its ancestral faith. Fourth, all this ignores the ancient context of this legislation. Deuteronomy is presented as an ideal set of laws and punishments in an ideal theocracy where the nation follows God. This is not unique. The legal collection of Hammurabi, hundreds of years earlier, functioned in a similar manner. It was an ideal set of laws designed to demonstrate the justice and righteousness of the king. Despite thousands of Old Babylonian texts, including court decisions, we have virtually no certain example in which this legal collection was appealed to in order to adjudicate a specific case. The same is virtually true of Deuteronomy. In fact, if we were to read the history of Israel in the Old Testament the picture is not that of a people fearfully observing this law lest they face death at the hands of their own family. The reality as presented is just the opposite. In every generation huge numbers of the people turn away from God with impunity. In fact, the era of Ahab and Jezebel is one of the few where their assassinations at the hands of Jehu are attributed in part to their sin. Yet even here the later prophet Hosea promises divine punishment on the dynasty of Jehu for the excessive brutality of Jehu's massacre of the Baal worshipers (Hosea 1:4). Mercy triumphs over judgment, as it does so often in the Old Testament. Thus the most severe of commands may be set forth at one place, but God's mercy enables Israel

---

topher Hitchens, *God Is Not Great: How Religion Poisons Everything* (New York: Twelve, 2007).

to accomplish what they could not or would not. At one point, in Deuteronomy 10:16, God commands Israel to circumcise their hearts. But later God promises that he will circumcise the hearts of the people (Deuteronomy 30:6). Yes, we can cherry pick harsh texts in the Bible. However, in the larger context the picture is different. God is characterized by mercy rather than judgment (Hosea 6:6; Matthew 9:13; 12:7).

The first problem that Richard Dawkins addresses in his chapter on the Old Testament concerns Noah's generation. The morality of Genesis 6–9 is "appalling" because God takes "a dim view of humans," so he drowns them with their children and innocent animals. A few points escape Dawkins's thirty-six-word summary at the top of page 238. First, according to the text God created all these people and thus holds an implicit right over their existence. Second, the rationale for the flood was the violence that filled the earth so that, with the exception of Noah, all the people devoted themselves to violence (Genesis 6:11-13). Unlike the comparable ancient Near Eastern flood account that Dawkins cites (Utnapishtim of the seventh-century B.C. *Epic of Gilgamesh*), the flood did not come because the gods were fed up with the noise of so many people (i.e., a means of population control). Rather, the Bible ascribes a moral cause, uncontrolled murder. This, of course, is the reason for the prohibition of murder immediately after the flood in Genesis 9:6. Third, in a text very conscious of chronology and sequence, it is important to note that Noah was five hundred years old (Genesis 5:32) at the point when the events leading up to the flood begin, and six hundred years old (Genesis 7:6) when the flood itself began. This would allow up to one hundred years during which Noah was building the ark and preparing for the flood. The story thus presents a century of mercy, during which everyone who cared to learn of the coming judgment, symbolized by the ark that was under construction, could learn of it from Noah. Unlike the Utnapishtim story, there was no command to keep this a secret. That no one, aside from Noah's family, turned from their murderous violence (cf. Genesis 4:23-24) itself testifies to the wickedness of that generation and their wanton destruction of what God had created. Finally, God could not have ended that generation and its murderous inclinations without destroying it entirely. Note that the text never states that children were killed. This is not to deny that the picture evoked would have included whole families. Rather, it stresses the terrible consequences of murder and violence in the eyes of God. Neither the murders by Cain nor Lamech ended in their own deaths. But this merciful act of God only led to greater and greater violence. Perhaps Dawkins has a better solution to end this growing cycle of bloodletting. The author of Genesis did not. That world ended and a new one was created, beginning with the righteousness of Noah.

Dawkins then turns his attention to Lot and his daughters in Genesis 19. The focus of Dawkins seems to be that of Lot offering his daughters to the angry mob who wished to rape the "men" who had come to warn Lot and his family of the impending judgment against their hometown of Sodom. This is paralleled with the terrible Judges 19 story of the gang rape of the Levite's concubine in Gibeon. Describing this as a "misogynistic ethos," Dawkins manages both to ignore the purpose of these stories and to violate the basic canons of reading Hebrew narrative. First, the purpose of these stories is not to present the ideals of how women (or men) should be treated in ancient Israel. It is to describe the ultimate lack of hospitality in both Sodom and Gibeon. Common morality throughout the ancient world (and in Israel) demanded that anyone visiting a town should be shown courtesy and hospitality. The evil men of both of these towns were not lusty homosexuals but rather those who rejected this tenet of common morality and sought to degrade and abuse visitors. In both cases their utter violation of hospitality brought terrible judgment upon them, their town and (for the incident of Judges 19) their tribe. This selfishness and lack of concern for the vulnerable lies behind Ezekiel 16:49, which identifies Sodom's sin as "they did not help the poor and needy." Its main concern was not sexuality any more than these stories were intended as models on how to treat one's daughters or other female family members. No text in the Bible presents Lot or the Levite as moral ideals. Rather, these texts describe corruption and degeneration on both sides. It is probably for this reason that those who constructed the order of the canon for the Christian Old Testament chose to put Ruth immediately after Judges. The scroll of Ruth describes a beautiful love story of faith in which a Moabitess freely takes on devotion to the God of Israel out of love for her mother-in-law and through this act comes to fall in love with Boaz of Bethlehem. The presentation here is less about the role of women or men and more about living in a world where love, peace and family can still exist as values despite the presence of cruelty and violence.

Hitchens begins his attack on the Old Testament with a critique of the Ten Commandments as found in Exodus 20.[3] His first attack lies with the warning of Exodus 20:5, where the worship of other gods invites divine punishment "to the third and fourth generation." For Hitchens this demonstrates the biblical rejection of the "reasonable assumption" that children are not guilty of their parents' offenses. The text does not make this claim. Actually, the text speaks of "visiting or bringing the sins of the fathers to the third and fourth generation of those who hate me." First, note the term *hate*. In this context of a covenant it refers to disloyalty, and the greatest disloyalty toward God is the abandonment of this deity to worship other gods. Thus, this is not a slight or insignificant offense. In treaty literature, hating someone creates an enemy and provides justification for war against them and for their death. Second, there is a reason for the third and fourth generation, rather than for the first and second or some later set of generations. It defines the length of time that people might expect to live so they could to see their grandchildren and great-grandchildren. Thus the text is suggesting that the effect of someone turning away from God will affect their family for as long as they live. The impact of a person's faith or lack thereof has a direct impact on his or her own family, and that effect remains throughout a lifetime. This is not the transference of guilt, which the Hebrew text does not claim. It is instead the inevitable impact parents and grandparents have on their families; something Hitchens does not mention. The following verse contrasts the effect of sin to those in a person's family while he or she is alive, with the effect of faithfulness and loyalty for "a thousand generations." There is no end to the positive effect that one's family can receive for one's faithfulness. This is clear from the manner in which Abraham was promised land, descendants and blessing as he remained faithful to God in test after test (Genesis 12–22).

The next complaint seems to be related to Hitchens's view that the command for everyone to keep the sabbath must be the sort of thing that "a Babylonian or Assyrian emperor might have ordered . . . to keep working and only to relax when the absolutist says so."[4] However, there are no Baby-

---

[3]Hitchens, *God Is Not Great*, pp. 98-100.
[4]Ibid., p. 99.

lonian or Assyrian legal collections (or any other known ancient Near Eastern collection of laws) that envision a time of rest for anyone, least of all slaves and work animals. The stipulation that this should take place one day in every seven is unknown outside the Bible. No Babylonian or Assyrian ever mandated a period of rest like this. It is unheard of and unique to ancient Israel. That such an amazing mercy for the most vulnerable elements in society should be interpreted as characteristic power madness by an ancient Near Eastern dictator demonstrates just how far Hitchens has wandered from a correct understanding of the culture in which the Bible was written. Because of this ignorance the contextual significance of the sabbath law is turned upside down and ascribed the opposite of the intended meaning, which would have been clear to any slave in the ancient world.

I could go on and examine each of the charges with a point-by-point refutation. However, the limitations of the space I have been given do not permit this. Instead, I have chosen three well-known books and examined the first one or two charges against the Old Testament in each. Repeatedly, misunderstandings of the language of the Old Testament and of the culture of the ancient world lead to absurd allegations that fit within a predetermined framework attacking Israel's God as he is portrayed in the Old Testament. Careful study of the text and its context consistently reveal the opposite of the intended allegations. I will now turn to two major issues of Old Testament apologetics.

MINIMALISTS AND THE OLD TESTAMENT

The issue of minimalism, or more accurately the question of the historical value of the Bible, has changed over the years in terms of the focus of ancient Israelite history. For example, in the mid-1970s the major concern was whether the patriarchs of Genesis 12–36 had any historical claim to its tradition.[5] The critics questioned the application of parallels from cuneiform archives dating to the traditional era of the patriarchs, the early second millennium B.C. They argued that such parallels could be found in

---

[5]See Thomas L. Thompson, *The Historicity of the Patriarchal Narratives: The Quest for the Historical Abraham,* Beihefte zur Zeitschrift für die alttestamentliche Wissenschaft 133 (Berlin: de Gruyter, 1974); and John Van Seters, *Abraham in History and Tradition* (London: Yale University Press, 1975). The term *minimalism* had not yet been coined or applied at this point. However, similar authors and arguments would be used in the 1990s, when the term began to be used.

cuneiform texts from a thousand years later, that the style of "history writing" in Genesis did not predate the Greeks who wrote in the fifth century B.C. and later, and that other customs and materials in Genesis could best be dated to the first millennium B.C. This was countered by a series of studies that demonstrated that the quantity and quality of many parallels in the early second millennium B.C. appear only then outside the Bible, that narrative writing of events such as found in Genesis 12–36 was known in the patriarchs' world of the second millennium B.C., and that many of the customs cited, including especially the personal names, are either exclusive to the early second millennium B.C. or match it in a statistically significant manner not found later.[6]

The late 1980s and early 1990s saw a shift that questioned whether anything in the Old Testament could be considered reliable. Behind this lay assumptions that no significant writing existed in Israel before the Hellenistic period, that there was no ethnic connection between Palestinian Jews of the third century B.C. and Palestinians before the sixth century B.C., and that a Judean state centered in Jerusalem could not be demonstrated before the late eighth century B.C. Thus all history writing in the Old Testament, including that of the postexilic period, was called into question and regarded as fairy tales.[7] In fact, much recent evidence has demonstrated that significant writing did exist in ancient Israel, that de-

---

[6]See especially the numerous studies collected in Alan R. Millard and Donald J. Wiseman, ed., *Essays on the Patriarchal Narratives* (1980; reprint, Winona Lake, Ind.: Eisenbrauns, 1983); Richard S. Hess, Philip Satterthwaite and Gordon Wenham, eds., *He Swore an Oath: Biblical Themes from Genesis 12-50*, 2nd ed. (Grand Rapids: Baker, 1994); and Alan R. Millard, James K. Hoffmeier and David W. Baker, eds., *Faith, Tradition, and History: Old Testament Historiography in Its Near Eastern Context* (Winona Lake, Ind.: Eisenbrauns, 1994). A single-authored work that represents one of the finest examples of applying ancient Near Eastern studies to the Bible is Kenneth A. Kitchen, *On the Reliability of the Old Testament* (Grand Rapids: Eerdmans, 2003), esp. pp. 313-72.

[7]See Thomas L. Thompson, *Early History of the Israelite People: From the Written and Archaeological Sources*, Studies in the History of the Ancient Near East 4 (Leiden: Brill, 1992); Thompson, *The Mythic Past: Biblical Archaeology and the Myth of Israel* (New York: Basic Books, 1999); Thompson, *The Messiah Myth: The Near Eastern Roots of Jesus and David* (New York: Basic Books, 2005); Neils Peter Lemche, *Prelude to Israel's Past: Background and Beginnings of Israelite History and Identity*, trans. E. F. Maniscalco (Peabody, Mass.: Hendrickson, 1998); Lemche, *The Old Testament Between Theology and History: A Critical Survey* (Louisville: Westminster John Knox, 2008); Philip R. Davies, *In Search of "Ancient Israel"* (Sheffield, U.K.: JSOT Press, 1992); Davies, *The Origins of Biblical Israel* (New York: T & T Clark, 2007); Davies, *Memories of Ancient Israel: An Introduction to Biblical History–Ancient and Modern* (Louisville: Westminster John Knox, 2008).

spite the deportations in and around Palestine in the first millennium B.C. an authentic memory of physical ancestors was preserved in the Old Testament that reached back to the early first millennium B.C., and that evidence exists for a Judean state before the Assyrian invasion of 701 B.C. (above all, in the attested dynasty known as "the house of David").[8] Indeed, this approach has been found problematic in so many areas that a host of monographs and collected studies have presented compelling evidence to debunk the theories.[9]

By 2000 and in the following years, the questions shifted again. This time challenges to the Bible focused on Israel's early appearance in Canaan as recorded in the book of Judges and on the period customarily identified with the united monarchy of the tenth century B.C. While each of these criticisms has its own significance and remains important up to the present, I can only consider something of the last and latest controversy. This view was popularized by the writings of the Tel Aviv University archaeologist Israel Finkelstein and the popular writer on archaeology Neil Asher Silberman.[10] This approach chose a middle way. They accepted that the

---

[8]On literacy see Richard S. Hess, "Literacy in Iron Age Israel," in *Windows into Old Testament History: Evidence, Argument, and the Crisis of "Biblical Israel,"* ed. V. Philips Long, David W. Baker and Gordon J. Wenham (Grand Rapids: Eerdmans, 2002), pp. 82-102; Hess, "Questions of Reading and Writing in Ancient Israel," *Bulletin for Biblical Research* 19 (2009): 1-9; Hess, review of *Literate Culture and Tenth-Century Canaan: The Tel Zayit Abecedary in Context,* by Ron E. Tappy and P. Kyle McCarter Jr., *Bulletin for Biblical Research* 19 (2009); William M. Schniedewind, "Orality and Literacy in Ancient Israel," *Religious Studies Review* 26, no. 4 (2000): 327-32. On the ninth-century evidence for David, see André Lemaire, "'House of David' Restored in Moabite Inscription," *Biblical Archaeology Review* 20, no. 3 (1994): 30-37; William M. Schniedewind, "Tel Dan Stela: New Light on Aramaic and Jehu's Revolt," *Bulletin of the American Schools of Oriental Research* 302 (1996): 75-90. On the general questions of authentic historical memory, see the following footnotes.

[9]Among the monographs see among others William G. Dever, *What Did the Biblical Writers Know and When Did They Know It? What Archaeology Can Tell Us about the Reality of Ancient Israel* (Grand Rapids: Eerdmans, 2001); Dever, *Who Were the Early Israelites and Where Did They Come From?* (Grand Rapids: Eerdmans, 2003); Kitchen, *Reliability of the Old Testament.* At least four conferences have produced important sets of papers challenging this critical approach. See the essays in Long, Baker and Wenham, ed., *Windows into Old Testament History;* James K. Hoffmeier and Alan Millard, ed., *The Future of Biblical Archaeology: Reassessing Methodologies and Assumptions* (Grand Rapids: Eerdmans, 2004); Richard S. Hess, Gerald A. Klingbeil and Paul J. Ray Jr., eds., *Critical Issues in Early Israelite History,* BBR Supplement 3 (Winona Lake, Ind.: Eisenbrauns, 2008); Daniel I. Block, Bryan H. Cribb and Gregory S. Smith, eds., *Israel: Ancient Kingdom or Late Invention?* (Nashville: B & H Academic, 2008). See also the important collection of John Day, ed., *In Search of Pre-Exilic Israel,* JSOT Supplement Series 406 (London: T & T Clark, 2004).

[10]Israel Finkelstein and Neil Asher Silberman, *The Bible Unearthed: Archaeology's New Vision of Ancient Israel and the Origin of Its Sacred Texts* (New York: Free Press, 2001); Finkelstein and

writings of Genesis were fiction but rejected the assumptions that the later periods of the Old Testament also lacked any historical worth. The assumption was that around 622, scribes of King Josiah of Judah collected the earlier writings and traditions of Israel to create a work that supported the "reforms" of this king. The farther back in time one went, the less historical value was present that could be ascribed to the writings. Thus the claims of Genesis and the first six or seven books of the Old Testament were almost entirely fiction, or at least legend whose kernels of truth were largely unrecoverable. There was a David and probably a Solomon who ruled in Jerusalem, but over a small kingdom rather than a great empire. Omri and Ahab provide the beginnings of historical worth in the northern kingdom of Israel, while late-eighth-century Hezekiah begins something approaching history in the southern kingdom of Judah. Although there is reason to challenge some of these findings, they have become the accepted dogma in mainstream biblical criticism.[11]

There is a cluster of issues here. However, they tend to revolve around the question of whether the written or oral traditions may have some claim to antiquity and authenticity. Insofar as historical worth is based on two or more independent witnesses, the earliest undoubted witness outside the Bible to a specific event attested in the Old Testament is the attack of Pharaoh Sheshonq (also called Shishak) against Palestine in 925 B.C. (cf. 1 Kings 14:25; 2 Chronicles 12:9). However, this does not invalidate anything purported to appear earlier in the biblical text. It simply means that we do not have an independent witness. If a text concurs with history where it can be checked, it may be reasonable to assume that the burden of proof lies with those who would argue for the absence of historicity elsewhere in the same context.

For example, the Bible claims that David and his son Solomon ruled over a kingdom that at various times comprised some or all of the modern state of Israel as well as regions beyond (see 2 Samuel 5; 8; 10). Is there any basis for this claim? Several lines of evidence bear on this question. First, it is important to note that the period that the Bible assigns to these rulers,

---

Silberman, *David and Solomon: In Search of the Bible's Sacred Kings and the Roots of the Western Tradition* (New York: Free Press, 2006).

[11]See, for example, Thomas Römer, *The So-Called Deuteronomistic History: A Sociological, Historical and Literary Introduction* (New York: T & T Clark, 2007).

the late eleventh century down to 931 B.C., was a time of weakness for the surrounding powers that might have conquered Israel and ruled in the area. This was true of Egypt and the Hittites, who had earlier impacted this region. Egypt was in decline and the Hittite empire had collapsed nearly two centuries earlier. Assyria and Babylonia were yet to rise to sufficient strength so as to influence the southern Levant.

Second, the powers that are mentioned in conflict with Israel in 2 Samuel 5, 8 and 10 include Aram, Ammon, Edom, Moab and Philistia. The Arameans are attested as early as three centuries before the eleventh century and gained strength at this time. Like Israel did, they also took control in the power vacuum left by a diminished Egypt.[12] In the region of Ammon the Amman citadel and perhaps one third of occupied sites before the eleventh century B.C. remained occupied into the tenth and ninth centuries.[13] Although it has long been assumed that there was no settlement in Edom before the eighth century, and therefore no context for a territorial state or entity, this has now been shown to be incorrect. In the lowland region of Edom south of the Dead Sea, tenth-century B.C. mining sites and forts such as Khirbet en-Nahas have been discovered.[14] The region of Moab is mentioned in Egyptian sources as early as the thirteenth century B.C. During the eleventh and tenth centuries B.C. more and more settlements were appearing in this region, suggesting an increase in statehood. The expansion and strength of the Philistines at this time is well documented.[15]

Third, twelfth-century B.C. Hazor, Megiddo and Gezer were diverse architecturally; respectively, an Israelite settlement, a Canaanite city-state and a Philistine dependency. However, in the mid-tenth century B.C. they all conformed to similar architectural forms, with casemate walls, six-chambered gateways and a palace complex (though the latter is

---

[12]K. Lawson Younger Jr., "The Late Bronze/Iron Age Transition and the Origins of the Arameans," in *Ugarit at Seventy-Five*, ed. K. Lawson Younger Jr. (Winona Lake, Ind.: Eisenbrauns, 2007), pp. 131-74.

[13]Elizabeth Bloch-Smith and Beth Alpert-Nakhai, "A Landscape Comes to Life: The Iron Age I," *Near Eastern Archaeology* 62 (1999): 108-11.

[14]Thomas E. Levy and Mohammad Najjar, "Edom and Copper: The Emergence of Ancient Israel's Rival," *Biblical Archaeology Review* 32, no. 4 (2006): 24-35, 70.

[15]Ann E. Killebrew, *Biblical Peoples and Ethnicity: An Archaeological Study of Egyptians, Canaanites, Philistines, and Early Israel 1300-1100 B.C.E.*, Society of Biblical Literature Archaeology and Biblical Studies 9 (Atlanta: Society of Biblical Literature, 2005), pp. 197-245.

not certain at Hazor). As noted in 1 Kings 9:15, these were strategic centers. Their emergent uniformity of major structures suggests the formation of a single state in this area.[16] The use of ashlar masonry resembles Phoenician styles rather than local Palestinian ones. Further, the fact that domestic architecture is not common in Solomonic Hazor or Megiddo (nor that there is any nearby population center at Megiddo) suggests that these were built and controlled by a larger territorial state, such as that described in Samuel and Kings.[17] To this evidence should now be added the large building of ashlar masonry which the excavator dates to the period of the united monarchy. Located in Jerusalem, it suggests the center of a supraregional state.[18]

Fourth, the Solomonic temple as described in 1 Kings 5–8 is paralleled both in the literary forms of the biblical text and especially in the details of comparative architectural forms found in West Semitic temples throughout Syria from the eleventh through the ninth centuries B.C.[19]

Thus the biblical picture of David and Solomon's reigns reflects the known realities of southern Canaan in the eleventh and tenth centuries B.C. More could be said, such as the already mentioned "house of David" texts coming within a century and a half of David's reign, according to the biblical text.[20] However, I leave this evidence with the reader to consider whether it provides sufficient warrant to give these texts about David and

---

[16]John S. Holladay Jr., "The Kingdoms of Israel and Judah: Political and Economic Centralization in the Iron IIA-B," in *The Archaeology of Society in the Holy Land*, ed. T. E. Levy (New York: Facts On File, 1995), pp. 368-98.

[17]Volkmar Fritz, "Monarchy and Re-Urbanization: A New Look at Solomon's Kingdom," in *The Origins of the Ancient Israelite States*, ed. V. Fritz and P. R. Davies, JSOT Supplement 228 (Sheffield, U.K.: Sheffield Academic Press, 1996), pp. 187-95; Baruch Halpern, "The Construction of the Davidic State: An Exercise in Historiography," in *The Origins of the Ancient Israelite States*, JSOT Supplement 228, ed. V. Fritz and P. R. Davies (Sheffield, U.K.: Sheffield Academic Press, 1996), pp. 44-75. Note that Finkelstein and Silberman, *David and Solomon*, would date the gates a century later. See, however, Dever, *What Did the Biblical Writers Know*, pp. 131-35, who represents a wider opinion among archaeologists and dates them to the tenth century B.C.

[18]Eilat Mazar, "Did I Find King David's Palace?" *Biblical Archaeology Review* 32, no. 1 (2006): 16-27, 70.

[19]Victor (Avigdor) Hurowitz, *I Have Built You an Exalted House: Temple Building in the Bible in Light of Mesopotamian and Northwest Semitic Writings*, JSOT Supplement 115 (Sheffield, U.K.: Sheffield Academic Press, 1992); Dever, *What Did the Biblical Writers Know?* pp. 144-57.

[20]For a tenth-century B.C. mention of David as part of a Palestinian place name mentioned by Pharaoh Sheshonq, see Kenneth A. Kitchen, "A Possible Mention of David in the Late Tenth Century BCE, and Deity *Dod as Dead as the Dodo?" *Journal for the Study of the Old Testament* 76 (1997): 29-44.

Solomon, so severely attacked in the past decade, their rightful place as authentic and ancient writings.

DEUTERONOMY, JOSHUA AND GENOCIDE

Turning in a different direction, I want to consider the question of genocide against the Canaanites as portrayed in Deuteronomy and Joshua. Perhaps more than any other issue that troubles those interested in the God of the Bible, the role played by God in warfare, and especially warfare against the Canaanites, causes concern. There are many texts to which I could refer in regard to this issue. However, Deuteronomy 20 and Joshua 1–11 are among the most frequently cited.

Deuteronomy 20:16-18 commands the complete destruction of every "city" in the land that God has given to Israel. This complete destruction, or devotion to the ban (Hebrew *herem*), is known in neighboring nations as well. However, in Deuteronomy this destruction is confined to the cities in Canaan. The term translated "city" is *ʿîr*. This term does not necessarily refer to a major urban center, as we tend to think of a city today. In the Bible this term can describe a village (Bethlehem [1 Samuel 20:6]), tent encampments (Judges 10:4) and a citadel (2 Samuel 12:26) or a fortress such as Zion in Jerusalem (2 Samuel 5:7, 9).[21] In fact, it seems often to identify a military context. Archaeologically, this conforms to many sites in the Late Bronze Age (e.g., Tell Balatah or Shechem) and in the Iron Age (e.g., Arad), where these walled fortresses were not habitations for the average persons to live. The masses lived in hamlets and other places nearby these forts. The forts themselves contained the palace, royal storehouses for the taxes "in kind," temples, some homes for the leadership and perhaps barracks for the troops. These "cities" were not the home of non-elites or of noncombatants. Rather, they represented the leadership, the military and those most involved with the oppression and rulership of the land. Thus the command in Deuteronomy 20 concerns complete destruction of those armies and forts that represent a religious faith and ideology that directly opposes that of Israel and God. In this sense it is indeed true to assert that God and Israel are holy and that they are called to destroy those who would oppose this God and his covenant people by lead-

---

[21]See Richard S. Hess, "The Jericho and Ai of the Book of Joshua," in *Critical Issues in Early Israelite History,* ed. Hess, Klingbeil and Ray, pp. 35-36.

ing them astray through their military might and ideology of force.

It is essential to understand that Deuteronomy 20 is an ideal, as already noted concerning Israelite (and much ancient Near Eastern) law. It is not a description of something that ever occurred or is purported to have occurred. For this we need to examine the first half of the book of Joshua. These texts are often understood as prima facie evidence of divinely willed genocide. Usually Joshua 6:21 and Joshua 8:25 are cited. Joshua 6:21 describes the capture of Jericho and mentions how Israel "devoted the city to the LORD and destroyed with the sword every living thing in it—men and women, young and old, cattle, sheep and donkeys." Joshua 8:25 says something similar about Ai: "Twelve thousand men and women fell that day." In both cases, the phrase *men and women* is literally "from man (and) unto woman." It is found elsewhere (1 Samuel 15:3; 22:19; 2 Samuel 6:19 [= 1 Chronicles 16:3]; Nehemiah 8:2; 2 Chronicles 15:13) always (except for 1 Samuel 22:19, where children are specifically mentioned) in parallelism with the Hebrew *kol* ("all, everyone").[22] Thus this phrase is synonymous with everyone and is stereotypical in the sense that it does not prejudice who might be in that group. It could include men or women, but not necessarily. In fact, a careful reading of Joshua 1–12 indicates that no specific noncombatants are ever named among the Canaanites; except for Rahab and her family, who are spared. This is because the Israelites did not target nor did they kill noncombatants.

In particular, Jericho and Ai should be understood as forts rather than as what we might think of towns with civilians. As already mentioned the biblical text names no specific noncombatants, except for Rahab and her family. This may in part explain the absence of archaeological evidence at these sites in the Late Bronze Age (the period of Israel's attack on Jericho and Ai, in light of the biblical chronology). If they were forts, and perhaps makeshift ones that used earlier defenses, there would be no evidence such as might be found in a conventional "city" where wealthy citizens would preserve higher quality (and therefore diagnostic) pottery and possessions. The term for "king" at both of these forts is Hebrew *melek*. This root appears in a number of examples throughout the West Semitic world with the meaning of someone in charge of a place or region, but under the

---

[22]Ibid., pp. 38-39.

power of a higher authority. See, for example, the fourteenth-century B.C. letter from the leader of Byblos who uses this root to describe Piwuri, a commissioner of the pharaoh over a region that includes Byblos.[23] Thus the "kings" of Jericho and Ai might be military administrators in charge of their forts but under authority to leaders of cities such as Jerusalem (one of the major east-west roads from Jericho connects with Jerusalem) and Bethel (cf. Joshua 8:9, 12, 17). Unlike Gibeon (Joshua 10:2) and Hazor (Joshua 11:10), neither Jericho nor Ai are mentioned as large or at the head of all those kingdoms. Therefore, views that Jericho or Ai were large cities are not based on the biblical witness. The name Ai means "ruin" and could appropriately identify a fort that was built out of existing Early Bronze Age walls.

Joshua 10–11 describe in detail the other major battles against the northern and southern coalitions. Both begin as defensive wars with an attack on their ally (Gibeon [Joshua 10:35]) and on Israel itself (Joshua 11:1-5). Thus these battles were defensive, not offensive, exercises. Either Israel had to fight or it faced extinction. Again, noncombatants are not specifically mentioned anywhere. The detailed description of Joshua 10:28-42, where "city" after "city" is destroyed, should be understood in the context of the "city" as primarily a fort for the king, the temple and the army. Understood in this way there is no reason to assume that noncombatant innocents were slaughtered in these forts. Even if the common people of Canaan chose not to join Israel as did Rahab and her family, they probably did not station themselves in these forts, as they had been emptied of their armies who went to fight Israel (and faced defeat). Knowing that the Israelites were on their way to attack these forts, the average Canaanite most likely fled to the hills where they hid until the Israelite army had passed. The biblical evidence for this is that the book of Judges knows of no Canaanite extermination. It knows only that there were plenty of Canaanites around in the next generation to lead Israel astray (e.g., Judges 2:10-13).

Neither the biblical text of Joshua nor that of Judges supports any genocide. The attacks on Jericho and Ai were assaults on military targets. The major wars that Israel fought were defensive. Canaanites remained in all regions (Judges 1) and intermarried with Israelites in the following gen-

---

[23]Ibid., pp. 39-41. The Amarna text referred to here is EA 131, lines 21-24.

erations. This is the biblical understanding of these battles. The archaeo-logical and extrabiblical textual evidence do not contradict it.

Although space does not permit further examples, it is my desire that the answers to these specific charges demonstrate that there are answers available to address these issues. They require an understanding of the grammatical and literary nature of the Hebrew text of the Old Testament, as well as the culture, archaeology and extrabiblical textual witness. It is hoped that the examples discussed here will inspire confidence and inter-est in the serious study of the Old Testament and its witness to God's mighty acts in history.

Glossary

abduction. An argument form that trades on giving the best explanation for a state of affairs, given the appropriate criteria. This is sometimes called "the inference to the best explanation." (Some view abduction as a form of induction; others put it in a unique category of inference.) In one sense, Christian apologetics is abductive in its overall method; it attempts to give the best explanation for reality on the basis of Christian theism.

actual infinite. The theoretical concept of a completed totality of items without limit. Used as part of the kalam cosmological argument.

agnosticism. Pertaining to theism, the belief that one cannot be sure as to the existence of God.

apologetics. The intellectual discipline of presenting the Christian worldview as objectively true, rationally compelling and existentially pertinent to all of life.

compatibilism. Regarding human agency, the claim that human responsibility is compatible with divine determination of the acts of human agents.

cumulative case argument. A strategy of using various lines of evidence to support a conclusion. In apologetics, this method encompasses arguments from natural theology as well as historical and anthropological evidence.

deduction. An argument form whereby the truth of the premises renders the conclusion true. See *modus ponens* and *modus tollens*.

epistemology. The philosophical discipline of examining the sources, scope and meaning of knowledge. Sometimes called "the theory of knowledge."

ethical relativism. The claim that moral truth is relative to the culture or individual.

evidentialism. In apologetics, the method of arguing inductively from the facts of history (particularly those of the life of Christ and his resurrection) directly to the truth of the Christian worldview.

ex nihilo. Latin phrase. Out of nothing, as in "creation out of nothing."

fideism. The idea that religious truth claims cannot be supported by reason and evidence, but that the believer need not provide any rational support for these religious truths.

inclusivism. The claim that while Christ is the only agent of salvation, people may be redeemed apart from a specific faith in Jesus Christ.

induction. An argument form whereby the truth of the premises makes the conclusion likely, but not certain.

ineffability. The state of not being describable by concepts or propositions. If X is ineffable (such as the Hindu concept of Nirguna Brahman), nothing intelligible can be affirmed about X.

intelligent design (ID). The scientific research program that argues that certain aspects of nature are better explained on the basis of a designing intelligence than by some non-intelligent causation.

libertarianism. Concerning human agency, the claim that for human will to be free, it must be self-determining and not determined by God (or any other outside factor).

materialism. The philosophical claim that only physical properties and entities exist. Sometimes used synonymously with *naturalism.*

metaphysics. The philosophical discipline of examining the existence and nature of things, whether God, humans, matter, etc.

modus ponens. Latin phrase. To affirm the antecedent of a deductive argument: If P, then Q; P; therefore Q.

modus tollens. Latin phrase. To deny the consequent of a deductive argument: If P, then Q; not-Q; therefore not-P.

natural theology. The rational project of arguing from some aspect of nature to existence of God as the best explanation for that aspect of nature; roughly synonymous with theistic arguments or theistic proofs.

necessary being. A being whose existence is logically necessary, that is, God.

nihilism. The perspective that reality is meaningless and absurd, lacking in any objective value or purpose.

nondualism. The belief that reality is one and indivisible; synonymous with monism.

nonrealism. The claim that there is no objective reality; all is interpretation.

numinous experience. A religious experience of a personal, holy and frightening being.

ontology. The study of being; roughly synonymous with metaphysics.

pantheism. Worldview claiming that everything that exists is divine, but the pantheistic concept of deity is nonpersonal rather than personal, as is the case with Christian theism.

particularism. A position on salvation that argues that, all things being equal, one must have faith in Jesus Christ in order to be redeemed.

perennialism. The claim that all religions teach essentially the same thing at their esoteric core. This is usually taken to be nondualism.

polytheism. The worldview that affirms a plurality of finite deities.

possible world. A description of a set of facts that would make up a hypothetical world; a maximally consistent set of propositions. The actual world is also a possible world.

postmodernism. In relation to philosophy, a cluster of philosophies claiming that truth is relative to cultures or individuals; truth thus dissolves into language games, forms of life and power plays.

potential infinite. A series of entities (events, numbers, etc.) which ever increases but never reaches an upper limit.

principle of sufficient reason. Coined by Leibniz, roughly the idea that for any positive state of affairs there is an adequate explanation for why that state of affairs exists.

qualia. Irreducibly subjective experiences of seeing colors, hearing sounds, tasting things, and so on; first-person events in minds not reducible to third-person descriptions.

realism. The claim that objective reality is at least partially knowable.

reductio ad absurdum. Latin phrase. To reduce an argument or proposition to absurdity, thus showing the original argument or proposition itself to be absurd and thus false.

Reformed epistemology. A broad philosophical movement led by Alvin Plantinga that claims that natural theology and other forms of apologetics are not necessary for one to have a warranted belief in the Christian worldview, since one can hold such beliefs in a "properly basic manner"—that is, apart from evidence.

religious pluralism. Either the merely *descriptive* claim that there are several religions functioning in any given society at one time or the *normative* claim that all the major world religions are equally salvific. John Hick is a principal spokesperson for this view.

specified complexity. A concept used in intelligent design arguments to indicate a state of affairs that is both improbable and specified. If something is an example of specified complexity, it is the product of a designing intelligence and cannot be accounted for by any naturalistic or otherwise impersonal causation.

Bibliography

Chapter 1: Introduction

Berger, Peter L., ed. *The Desecularization of the World*. Grand Rapids: Eerdmans, 1999.

Frankl, Victor. *The Doctor and the Soul*. 1955; reprint, New York: Vintage Books, 1986.

————. *Man's Search for Meaning: An Introduction to Logotherapy*. New York: Pocket Books, 1959.

Fukuyama, Francis. *The End of History and the Last Man*. New York: Avon Books, 1992.

Huntington, Samuel. *A Clash of Civilizations*. New York: Simon & Schuster, 1996.

Jenkins, Philip. *The Next Christendom*. New York: Oxford University Press, 2002.

Lewis, C. S. *The Screwtape Letters*. 1942; reprint, San Francisco: HarperSanFrancisco, 2001.

Schaeffer, Francis. "How I Have Come to Write My Books." In *Introduction to Francis Schaeffer*. Downers Grove, Ill.: InterVarsity Press, 1974.

Steiner, George. *Real Presences*. Chicago: University of Chicago Press, 1991.

Chapter 2: The Biblical Basis for Apologetics

Bell, Rob. *Velvet Elvis*. Grand Rapids: Zondervan, 2006.

Blomberg, Craig L., William Klein and Robert Hubbard Jr. *Introduction to Biblical Interpretation*. Rev. ed. Nashville: Thomas Nelson, 2004.

Boa, Kenneth, and Robert Bowman. *Faith Has Its Reasons: An Integrative Approach to Defending Christianity*. 2nd ed. Colorado Springs: NavPress, 2005.

Bruce, F. F. *The Defense of the Gospel in the New Testament*. Grand Rapids: Eerdmans, 1977.

Carson, D. A. "Athens Revisited." In *Telling the Truth*, edited by D. A. Carson. Grand Rapids: Zondervan, 2000.

Clark, David. *Dialogical Apologetics*. Grand Rapids: Baker, 1994.

Clark, Kelly James, ed. *Philosophers Who Believe*. Downers Grove, Ill.: InterVarsity Press, 1994.

Clarke, Adam. *Commentary on the Holy Bible: One-Volume Edition.* Abridged by Ralph Earle. Grand Rapids: Baker, 1967.

Downing, David C. *The Most Reluctant Convert: C. S. Lewis's Journey to Faith.* Downers Grove, Ill.: InterVarsity Press, 2002.

Fernando, Ajith. *Acts.* The NIV Application Commentary. Grand Rapids: Zondervan, 1998.

Groothuis, Douglas. "Event Specific Evangelism." In *Confronting the New Age.* Downers Grove, Ill.: InterVarsity Press, 1998.

—————. "Humility: The Heart of Righteousness." In *Christianity That Counts.* Grand Rapids: Baker, 1994.

—————. *On Jesus.* Belmont, Calif.: Wadsworth, 2003.

—————. *On Pascal.* Belmont, Calif.: Wadsworth, 2003.

—————. "Television: Agent of Truth Decay." In *Truth Decay.* Downers Grove, Ill.: InterVarsity Press, 2000.

Guinness, Os. *God in the Dark.* Wheaton, Ill: Crossway, 2006.

Hasel, Gerhart. "The Polemical Nature of the Genesis Account." *Evangelical Quarterly* 46 (1974): 81-102.

Koukl, Greg. *Tactics: A Game Plan for Discussing Your Christian Convictions.* Grand Rapids: Zondervan, 2009.

Lewis, C. S. *Surprised by Joy: The Shape of My Early Life.* New York: Harcourt, Brace & World, 1955.

MacArthur, John. *The Gospel According to Jesus.* Grand Rapids: Zondervan, 1988.

Machen, J. Gresham. "Christianity and Culture." In *Christianity, Education, and the State,* edited by John W. Robbins. Jefferson, Md.: Trinity Foundation, 1987.

Martin, Michael. *The Case Against Christianity.* Philadelphia: Temple University Press. 1993.

Montgomery, John Warwick. "Apologetics in the 21st Century." In *Reasons for Faith: Making a Case for Christian Faith,* edited by Norman L. Geisler and Chad V. Meister. Wheaton, Ill.: Crossway, 2007.

Moreland, J. P. *Love Your God with All Your Mind.* Colorado Springs: NavPress, 1997.

Moreland, J. P., and William Lane Craig. *Philosophical Foundations for a Christian Worldview.* Downers Grove, Ill.: InterVarsity Press, 2003.

Morris, Thomas, ed. *God and the Philosophers.* New York: Oxford University Press, 1995.

Murray, Andrew. *Humility.* Minneapolis: Bethany House, 2001.

Pascal, Blaise. *Pensées,* edited and translated by Alban Krailsheimer. New York: Penguin, 1966.

Plantinga, Alvin. *Warranted Christian Belief.* New York: Oxford University Press, 2000.

Schaeffer, Edith. *L'Abri.* 2nd ed. Wheaton, Ill.: Crossway, 1992

—————. *The Tapestry: The Life and Times of Francis and Edith Schaeffer.* Waco, Tex.: Word, 1981.

Schaeffer, Francis A. *The Finished Work of Christ.* Wheaton, Ill.: Crossway, 1998.
————. *The God Who Is There.* 30th anniv. ed. Downers Grove: Ill: InterVarsity Press, 1998.
Sire, James. *A Little Primer for Humble Apologetics.* Downers Grove, Ill: InterVarsity Press, 2006.
Whitlock, L. G., Jr. "Apologetics." In *Evangelical Dictionary of Theology,* edited by Walter Elwell. Grand Rapids: Baker, 1984.
Yandell, Keith. "Christianity and a Conceptual Orientation." In *Professors Who Believe,* edited by Paul M. Anderson. Downers Grove, Ill.: InterVarsity Press, 1998.

Chapter 3: Apologetic Method

Aristotle. *Metaphysics.*
Bahnsen, Greg L. *Presuppositional Apologetics: Stated and Defined,* edited by Joel McDurmon. Powder Springs, Ga.: American Vision, 2010.
————. *Van Til's Apologetic Readings and Analysis.* Phillipsburg, N.J.: Presbyterian & Reformed, 1998.
Berger, Peter. *A Rumor of Angels.* Garden City, N.Y.: Anchor Books, 1970.
Boa, Kenneth, and Robert Bowman. *Faith Has Its Reasons.* 2nd ed. Colorado Springs: NavPress, 2005.
Burson, Scott R., and Jerry L. Walls. *C. S. Lewis and Francis Schaeffer: Lessons for a New Century from the Most Influential Apologists of Our Time.* Downers Grove, Ill.: InterVarsity Press, 1998.
Carnell, Edward John. *An Introduction to Christian Apologetics.* Grand Rapids: Eerdmans, 1948.
Clark, Gordon. *Reason, Religion, and Revelation.* Philadelphia: Presbyterian & Reformed, 1961.
Clark, Kelly James. *Reason and Belief in God.* Grand Rapids: Eerdmans, 1990.
Cowan, Steve, ed. *Five Views of Apologetics.* Grand Rapids: Zondervan, 2000.
Edwards, Paul. *Reincarnation: A Critical Examination.* Amherst, N.Y.: Prometheus, 1996.
Evans, C. Stephen. *Faith Above Reason: A Kierkegaardian Account.* Grand Rapids: Eerdmans, 1998.
Feyman, Richard P. *QED: The Strange Theories of Light and Matter.* Princeton, N.J.: Princeton University Press, 1985.
Frame, John. *Apologetics for the Glory of God.* Phillipsburg, N.J.: P & R Publishing, 1994.
————. *Cornelius Van Til: An Analysis of His Thought.* Phillipsburg, N.J.: Presbyterian & Reformed, 1995.
Geivett, Douglas R. "Is God a Story? Postmodernity and the Talk of Theology." In *Christianity and the Postmodern Turn: Six Views,* edited by Myron B. Penner. Grand Rapids: Brazos Press, 2005.
Gerstner, John, R. C. Sproul and Art Lindsley. *Classical Apologetics.* Grand Rapids: Zondervan, 1984.

Griffiths, Paul. *An Apologetic for Apologetics.* Maryknoll, N.Y.: Orbis, 1991.

———. "Philosophizing Across Cultures: Or, How to Argue with a Buddhist." *Criterion* 26, no. 1 (1987): 10-14.

Groothuis, Douglas. *On Pascal.* Belmont, Calif.: Wadsworth, 2003.

———. *Truth Decay: Defending Christianity Against the Challenges of Postmodernism.* Downers Grove, Ill.: InterVarsity Press, 2000.

Habermas, Gary. *The Historical Jesus.* Joplin, Mo.: College Press, 1996.

Henry, Carl F. H. *God, Revelation, and Authority.* 6 vols. Waco, Tex.: Word, 1976-1982.

James, William. *The Will to Believe and Other Essays on Popular Philosophy.* New York: Dover, 1956.

Jubien, Michael. "Is There Truth in Fiction?" In *Contemporary Metaphysics.* New York: Blackwell, 1999.

Lapide, Pinchas. *The Resurrection of Jesus.* Minneapolis: Fortress, 1985.

Lewis, Gordon. *Testing Christianity's Truth Claims.* Chicago: Moody Press, 1976.

Mascord, Keith A. *Alvin Plantinga and Christian Apologetics.* Eugene, Ore.: Wipf & Stock, 2006.

McGrew, Timothy. "A Defense of Classical Foundationalism." In *The Theory of Knowledge: Classical and Contemporary Readings.* 2nd ed. Edited by Louis Pojman. Belmont, Calif.: Wadsworth, 1998.

Miller, Ed L., and Jon Jensen. *Questions That Matter.* 5th ed. Boston: McGraw-Hill, 2004.

Montgomery, John Warwick. *Faith Based on Fact.* Nashville: Thomas Nelson, 1978.

Moreland, J. P. *Love Your God With All Your Mind.* Colorado Springs: NavPress, 1997.

———. *Scaling the Secular City.* Grand Rapids: Baker, 1987.

Moreland, J. P., and William Lane Craig. "The Structure of Justification." In *Philosophical Foundations for a Christian Worldview.* Downers Grove, Ill.: InterVarsity Press, 2003.

Nash, Ronald. "The Evidential Challenge to Religious Belief" and "Foundationalism and the Rationality of Religious Belief." In *Faith and Reason.* Grand Rapids: Zondervan, 1988.

———. *Life's Ultimate Questions.* Grand Rapids: Zondervan, 1999.

Pascal, Blaise. *Pensées,* edited and translated by Alban Krailsheimer. New York: Penguin, 1966.

Piper, John, Justin Taylor and Paul Kjoss Helseth. *Beyond the Bounds: Open Theism and the Undermining of Biblical Christianity.* Wheaton, Ill.: Crossway, 2003.

Plantinga, Alvin. *Warrant and Proper Function.* New York: Oxford University Press, 1993.

———. *Warrant: The Contemporary Debate.* New York: Oxford University Press, 1993.

———. *Warranted Christian Belief.* New York: Oxford University Press, 2000.

Plantinga, Alvin, and Nicholas Wolterstorff, eds. *Faith and Rationality.* Notre

Dame, Ind.: University of Notre Dame Press, 1983.

Ramm, Bernard. *Varieties of Christian Apologetics.* 2nd ed. Grand Rapids: Baker, 1962.

Sanders, John, *The God Who Risks.* 2nd ed. Downers Grove, Ill.: InterVarsity Press, 2007.

Schaeffer, Francis A. *Escape from Reason.* 1968; reprint, Downers Grove, Ill.: Inter-Varsity Press, 2007.

————. "The Weakness of God's Servants." In *No Little People, No Little Places.* Downers Grove, Ill.: InterVarsity Press, 1974.

Schmidt, Alvin. *The Great Divide: The Failure of Islam and the Triumph of the West.* Boston: Regina Orthodox Press, 2004.

Sennet, James, and Douglas Groothuis, eds. *In Defense of Natural Theology.* Downers Grove, Ill.: InterVarsity Press, 2005.

Sire, James. *Naming the Elephant: Worldview as a Concept.* Downers Grove, Ill.: InterVarsity Press, 2004.

Spencer, Robert. *Religion of Peace? Why Christianity Is and Islam Isn't.* Washington, D.C.: Regnery, 2007.

Sproul, R. C. *Not a Chance: The Myth of Chance in Modern Science and Cosmology.* Grand Rapids: Baker, 1994.

Swinburne, Richard. *Is There a God?* New York: Oxford University Press, 1996.

Van Til, Cornelius. *The Defense of the Faith.* 4th ed. 1955; reprint, Phillipsburg, N.J.: P & R Publishing, 2008.

Wright, N. T. *Jesus and the Victory of God.* Minneapolis: Fortress, 1997.

————. *The New Testament and the People of God.* Minneapolis: Fortress, 1992.

————. *The Resurrection of the Son of God.* Minneapolis: Fortress, 2003.

Chapter 4: The Christian Worldview

Blamires, Harry. *The Christian Mind: How Should a Christian Think?* 1963; reprint, Ann Arbor, Mich.: Servant Books, 1978.

Bruce, F. F. *New Testament History.* Garden City, N.Y.: Doubleday, 1972.

Byrne, Peter. *God and Realism.* Burlington, Vt.: Ashgate, 2003.

Carson, D. A. *Becoming Conversant with the Emerging Church.* Grand Rapids: Zondervan, 2005.

Chesterton, G. K. *Orthodoxy.* 1908; reprint, New York: Image Books, 1959.

Corduan, Winfried. *Neighboring Faiths.* Downers Grove, Ill.: InterVarsity Press, 1998.

Dooyeweerd, Herman. *A New Critique of Theoretical Thought,* translated by David H. Freeman and William S. Young. Phillipsburg, N.J.: Presbyterian & Reformed, 1969.

Erickson, Millard. *God in Three Persons: A Contemporary Interpretation of the Trinity.* Grand Rapids: Baker, 1995.

Groothuis, Douglas. *On Jesus.* Belmont, Calif.: Wadsworth, 2003.

Guinness, Os. *The Call.* Nashville: Thomas Nelson, 1998.

—————. *Fit Bodies, Fat Minds.* Grand Rapids: Baker, 1994.

Halverson, William H. *A Concise Introduction to Philosophy.* 3rd ed. New York: Random House, 1976.

Heschel, Abraham. *God in Search of Man: A Philosophy of Judaism.* New York: Farrar, Straus & Giroux, 1976.

Kuyper, Abraham. *Lectures on Calvinism.* Grand Rapids: Eerdmans, 1931.

Kwan, Kai-Man. "A Critical Appraisal of Non-Realist Philosophy of Religion: An Asian Perspective." *Philosophia Christi,* series 2, 3, no. 1 (2001): 225-35.

Lewis, C. S. *The Great Divorce.* 1946; reprint, New York: Macmillan, 1976.

Mackie, J. L. *The Miracle of Theism.* New York: Oxford University Press, 1981.

Martin, Walter. *Kingdom of the Cults.* Minneapolis: Bethany House. 1974.

Moreland, J. P., and Scott R. Rae. *Body and Soul.* Downers Grove, Ill.: InterVarsity Press, 2000.

Moreland, J. P., and William Lane Craig. *Philosophical Foundations for a Christian Worldview.* Downers Grove, Ill.: InterVarsity Press, 2003.

Moreland, J. P. *Love Your God with All Your Mind.* Colorado Springs: NavPress, 1997.

Nash, Ronald. *Faith and Reason.* Grand Rapids: Zondervan, 1988.

—————. *The World of God and the Mind of Man.* Phillipsburg, N.J.: P & R Publishing, 1992.

Naugle, David. *Worldview: The History of a Concept.* Grand Rapids: Eerdmans, 2002.

Nietzsche, Friedrich. *The Twilight of the Idols.* In *The Portable Nietzsche,* edited and translated by Walter Kaufmann. New York: Viking Press, 1975.

Pearcey, Nancy. *Total Truth: Liberating Christianity from Its Cultural Captivity.* Wheaton, Ill.: Crossway, 2004.

Piper, John. *Don't Waste Your Life.* Wheaton, Ill.: Crossway, 2003.

—————. *God Is the Gospel.* Wheaton, Ill.: Crossway, 2005.

—————. *When I Don't Desire God.* Wheaton, Ill.: Crossway, 2004.

Poe, Harry Lee. *See No Evil: The Existence of Sin in an Age of Relativism.* Grand Rapids: Kregel, 2004.

Ramm, Bernard. *Offense to Reason: The Theology of Sin.* San Francisco: Harper & Row, 1985.

Russell, Bertrand. "A Free Man's Worship." In *Why I Am Not a Christian,* edited by Paul Edwards. New York: Simon & Schuster, 1957.

Sayers, Dorothy L. *The Letters of Dorothy L. Sayers: 1937-1943, From Novelist to Playwright.* Vol. 2, *The Letters of Dorothy L. Sayers,* edited by Barbara Reynolds. New York: St. Martin's Press, 1988.

Schaeffer, Francis A. *The Church Before the Watching World: A Practical Ecclesiology.* Downers Grove, Ill.: InterVarsity Press, 1971.

—————. *Genesis in Time and Space.* Downers Grove, Ill.: InterVarsity Press, 1972.

—————. *The God Who Is There.* 30th anniv. ed. Downers Grove: Ill: InterVarsity Press, 1998.

————. *He Is There and He Is Not Silent.* 30th anniv. ed. Wheaton, Ill.: Tyndale House, 2001.

Senor, Thomas. "The Incarnation and the Trinity." In *Reason for the Hope Within,* edited by Michael J. Murray. Grand Rapids: Eerdmans, 1999.

Sire, James W. *The Universe Next Door: A Basic Worldview Catalog.* 5th ed. Downers Grove, Ill.: InterVarsity Press, 2009.

Smart, Ninian. *Worldviews.* 3rd. ed. New York: Prentice-Hall, 1999.

Smith, R. Scott. *Truth and a New Kind of Christian.* Wheaton, Ill.: Crossway, 2005.

Swinburne, Richard. *The Christian God.* New York: Oxford University Press, 1994.

Wilberforce, William. *Real Christianity,* edited by James Houston. 1829; reprint, Minneapolis: Bethany House, 1997.

Chapter 5: Distortions of the Christian Worldview—Or the God I Don't Believe In

Buswell, Oliver J., III. *Slavery, Segregation, and Scripture.* Grand Rapids: Eerdmans, 1964.

Clark, Kelly James, ed. *Philosophers Who Believe.* Downers Grove, Ill.: InterVarsity Press, 1994.

Cole, Darrell. *When God Says War Is Right.* Colorado Springs: WaterBrook, 2002.

Copan, Paul. "Is Yahweh a Moral Monster?" *Philosophia Christi* 10, no. 1 (2008): 7-37.

Cowles, C. S., Eugene Merrill, Daniel Gard and Tremper Longman III. *Show Them No Mercy: Four Views on God and Canaanite Genocide.* Grand Rapids: Zondervan, 2003.

D'Souza, Dinesh. "Rethinking the Inquisition." In *What's So Great About Christianity.* Washington, D.C.: Regnery, 2007.

Dubos, René. *The Wooing of the Earth.* New York: Charles Scribner's, 1980.

Elwell, Walter A. *Handbook of Evangelical Theologians.* Grand Rapids: Baker, 1993.

Fitzmyer, Joseph. *The Letter to Philemon.* Anchor Bible Commentary. New Haven, Conn.: Yale University Press, 2000.

George, Robert. "Nature, Morality, and Homosexuality." In *In Defense of Natural Law.* New York: Oxford University Press, 1999.

Groothuis, Douglas. "Bacon and Pascal on Mystery Over Nature." *Research in Philosophy and Technology* 14 (1994): 191-203.

————. *On Jesus.* Belmont, Calif.: Wadsworth, 2003.

————. "Scientist and Philosopher of Science." In *On Pascal.* Belmont, Calif.: Wadsworth, 2003.

Guinness, Os. *Fit Bodies, Fat Minds.* Grand Rapids: Baker, 1994.

Hofstadter, Richard. *Anti-Intellectualism in American Life.* New York: Vintage, 1963.

Hutchinson, Robert. "You Were Called to Freedom." In *The Politically Incorrect Guide to the Bible*. Washington, D.C.: Regnery, 2007.

Irenaeus. *Against Heresies*.

Jaki, Stanley. *The Savior of Science*. Grand Rapids: Eerdmans, 2000.

Jenkins, Philip. *The Next Christendom*. New York: Oxford University Press, 2002.

Kaiser, Walter J. *Toward an Old Testament Ethics*. Grand Rapids: Baker, 1983.

Lee, Francis Nigel. "The Roots of Culture." In *The Central Significance of Culture*. Phillipsburg, N.J.: Presbyterian & Reformed, 1976.

Lewis, C. S. "Hope." In *Mere Christianity*. 1952; reprint, San Francisco: Harper-SanFrancisco, 2001.

Malik, Charles. *The Two Tasks*. Wheaton, Ill.: Billy Graham Center, 2000.

McGrath, Alister. *The Reenchantment of Nature: The Denial of Religion and the Ecological Crisis*. New York: Doubleday, 2002.

Moreland, J. P. *Love Your God with All Your Mind*. Colorado Springs: NavPress, 1997.

—————. *Scaling the Secular City*. Grand Rapids: Baker, 1987.

Morris, Thomas, ed. *God and the Philosophers*. New York: Oxford University Press, 1995.

Mouw, Richard. *When the Kings Come Marching In: Isaiah and the New Jerusalem*. Rev. ed. Grand Rapids: Eerdmans, 2004.

Noll, Mark. *The Scandal of the Evangelical Mind*. Grand Rapids: Eerdmans, 1994.

Rae, Scott. *Moral Choices*. 3rd ed. Grand Rapids: Zondervan, 2010.

Rushdoony, Rousas John. *Institutes of Biblical Law*. Nutley, N.J.: Craig Press, 1973.

Samples, Kenneth. *Without a Doubt*. Grand Rapids: Baker, 2004.

Schaeffer, Francis A. *The God Who Is There*. 30th anniv. ed. Downers Grove, Ill.: InterVarsity Press, 1998.

Schaeffer, Francis, and Udo Middleman. *Pollution and the Death of Man*. 1970; reprint, Wheaton, Ill.: Crossway, 1992.

Siegel, Bob. "Why Did God Command the Israelites to Wipe Out the Other Nations?" In *I'd Like to Believe in Jesus But . . .* Wheaton, Ill.: Campus Ambassadors Press, 1999.

Sire, James. "Jesus the Reasoner." In *Habits of the Mind*. Downers Grove, Ill.: InterVarsity Press, 2000.

Smith, Quentin. "The Meta-Philosophy of Naturalism." *Philo* 4, no. 2 (2001): 195-215.

Spencer, Robert. *The Politically Incorrect Guide to Islam and the Crusades*. Washington, D.C.: Regnery, 2007.

Stark, Rodney. *For the Glory of God: How Monotheism Led to Reformations, Science, Witch-Hunts, and the End of Slavery*. Princeton, N.J.: Princeton University Press, 2003.

————. *The Victory of Reason: How Christianity Led to Freedom, Capitalism, and Western Success.* New York: Random House, 2005.

Walls, Jerry L. "Heaven and Hell." In *The Routledge Companion to Philosophy of Religion,* edited by Chad Meister and Paul Copan. New York: Routledge, 2007.

White, Andrew D. *The Warfare of Science and Religion.* 1895; reprint, New York: George Braziller, 1955.

Whitehead, Alfred North. *Science in the Modern World.* New York: Macmillan, 1925.

Winnell, Marlene. *Leaving the Fold: A Guide for Former Fundamentalists and Others Leaving Their Religion.* Oakland, Calif.: New Harbinger, 1993.

Wittmer, Michael. *Heaven Is a Place on Earth: Why Everything You Do Matters to God.* Grand Rapids: Zondervan, 2004.

Wright, Christopher J. H. *An Eye for an Eye: The Place for Old Testament Ethics Today.* Downers Grove, Ill.: InterVarsity Press, 1983.

Chapter 6: Truth Defined and Defended

Aristotle, *Metaphysics.*

Berger, Peter. *Facing Up to Modernity: Excursions in Society, Politics, and Religion.* New York: Basic Books, 1977.

————. "The Perspective of Sociology: Relativizing the Relativizers." In *A Rumor of Angels: Modern Society and the Rediscovery of the Supernatural.* Garden City, N.Y.: Anchor Books, 1970.

Buber, Martin. *The Eclipse of God.* New York: Harper & Row, 1952.

Chesterton, G. K. *Orthodoxy.* 1908; reprint, New York: Image Books, 1959.

Corduan, Winfried. *No Doubt About It.* Nashville: Broadman & Holman, 1997.

Erickson, Millard. *Postmodernizing the Faith: Evangelical Responses to the Challenge of Postmodernism.* Grand Rapids: Baker, 1998.

————. *Truth or Consequences.* Downers Grove, Ill.: InterVarsity Press, 2001.

Ezorsky, Gertrude. "Pragmatic Theories of Truth." In *The Encyclopedia of Philosophy,* edited by Paul Edwards. New York: Macmillan, 1967.

Goldman, Alvin. *Knowledge in a Social World.* New York: Oxford University Press, 1999.

Grenz, Stanley, and John Franke. *Beyond Foundationalism.* Grand Rapids: Eerdmans, 2000.

Groothuis, Douglas. *Confronting the New Age.* Downers Grove, Ill.: InterVarsity Press, 1998.

————. "Meaning." In *Encyclopedia of Empiricism,* edited by Don Garrett and Edward Barbanell. Westport, Conn.: Greenwood Press, 1997.

————. *Truth Decay: Defending Christianity from the Challenges of Postmodernism.* Downers Grove, Ill.: InterVarsity Press, 2000.

Henry, Carl F. H. *God, Revelation, and Authority.* 6 vols. Waco, Tex.: Word, 1976-1983.

James, William. *Essays on Pragmatism*. New York: Havner, 1955.

————. *The Moral Philosophy of William James*, edited by John K. Roth. New York: Thomas Crowell, 1969.

Kenneson, Philip. "There Is No Such Thing as Objective Truth and It's a Good Thing, Too." In *Christian Apologetics in a Postmodern World*, edited by Timothy Phillips and Dennis Ockholm. Downers Grove, Ill.: InterVarsity Press, 1995.

Lovejoy, Arthur. "The Thirteen Pragmatisms, II." *Journal of Philosophy* 5, no. 2 (1908): 29-39.

Machen, J. Gresham. *Christianity and Liberalism*. 1923; reprint, Grand Rapids: Eerdmans, 2009.

McLaren, Brian. *A New Kind of Christian*. San Francisco: Jossey-Bass, 2001.

Moreland, J. P., and William Lane Craig, *Philosophical Foundations for a Christian Worldview*. Downers Grove, Ill.: InterVarsity Press, 2003.

Nash, Ronald. *Life's Ultimate Questions*. Grand Rapids: Zondervan, 1999.

Plantinga, Alvin. "The Twin Pillars of Christian Scholarship." In *Seeking Understanding: The Stobb Lectures, 1986-1998*. Grand Rapids: Eerdmans, 1998.

Russell, Bertrand. *A History of Western Philosophy*. New York: Touchstone, 1967.

————. *Philosophical Essays*. London: Longmans, Green, 1910.

Sampson, Philip J. *Six Modern Myths About Christianity and Western Civilization*. Downers Grove, Ill.: InterVarsity Press, 2001.

Schaeffer, Francis A. *The God Who Is There*. 30th anniv. ed. Downers Grove, Ill.: InterVarsity Press, 1998.

Taylor, Richard. *Metaphysics*. 4th ed. New York: Prentice Hall, 1990.

Webber, Robert. *The Younger Evangelicals*. Grand Rapids: Baker, 2002.

Wuthnow, Robert. *After Heaven: Spirituality in America Since the 1950s*. Berkeley: University of California Press, 1998.

Chapter 7: Why Truth Matters Most

Chesterton, G. K. *Orthodoxy*. 1908; reprint, New York: Image Books, 1959.

Eliot, T. S. *Murder in the Cathedral*. New York: Harcourt, Brace & World, 1963.

Feynman, Richard. *Surely You're Joking, Mr. Feynman: Adventures of a Curious Character*. New York: Bantam, 1989.

Geach, Peter. *Truth and Hope*. Notre Dame, Ind.: University of Notre Dame Press, 2001.

Groothuis, Douglas. "Jesus' Use of Argument." In *On Jesus*. Belmont, Calif.: Wadsworth, 2003.

————. *The Soul in Cyberspace*. Grand Rapids: Baker, 1997.

————. "Thomas Nagel's 'Last Word' on the Metaphysics of Rationality and Morality." *Philosophia Christi* series 2, 1, no. 1 (1999): 115-22.

————. *Truth Decay: Defending Christianity Against the Challenges of Postmodernism*. Downers Grove, Ill.: InterVarsity Press, 2000.

Hexham, Irving. "Evangelical Illusions: Postmodern Christianity and the Growth of Muslim Communities in Europe and North America." In *No Other Gods Be-*

CHRISTIAN APOLOGETICS

fore Me? edited by John Stackhouse. Grand Rapids: Baker Academic, 2001.

Huxley, Aldous. *Ends and Means.* 3rd ed. New York: Harper & Brothers, 1937.

James, William. "The Will to Believe." In *The Will to Believe.* New York: Dover, 1956.

Johnson, Phillip. *Defeating Darwinism by Opening Minds.* Downers Grove, Ill.: InterVarsity Press, 1997.

Kierkegaard, Søren. *Provocations: Spiritual Writings of Kierkegaard,* edited by Charles Moore. Farmington, Penn.: Plough, 1999.

Morris, Tom. *Making Sense of It All: Pascal and the Meaning of Life.* Grand Rapids: Eerdmans, 1992.

Nagel, Thomas. *The Last Word.* New York: Oxford University Press, 1997.

Nietzsche, Friedrich. *The AntiChrist,* section 50. In *The Portable Nietzsche,* edited by Walter Kaufmann. New York: Viking Press, 1975.

————. *Thus Spoke Zarathustra.* In *The Portable Nietzsche,* edited by Walter Kaufmann. New York: Viking Press, 1975.

Pascal, Blaise. *Pensées,* edited and translated by Alban Krailsheimer. New York: Penguin, 1966.

Peterson, Eugene. *Subversive Spirituality.* Grand Rapids: Eerdmans, 1997.

Russell, Bertrand. *Why I Am Not a Christian and Other Essays on Religion and Related Subjects,* edited by Paul Edwards. New York: Simon & Schuster, 1957.

Sayers, Dorothy. *Christian Letters to a Post-Christian World.* Grand Rapids: Eerdmans, 1969.

Stackhouse, John. *Humble Apologetics.* New York: Oxford University Press, 2002.

Westphal, Merold. *Suspicion and Faith.* Grand Rapids: Eerdmans, 1993.

Williams, Bernard. *Truth and Truthfulness.* Princeton, N.J.: Princeton University Press, 2002.

Chapter 8: Faith, Risk and Rationality

Corduan, Winfried. *Neighboring Faiths.* Downers Grove, Ill.: InterVarsity Press, 1998.

Davis, Caroline F. *The Evidential Force of Religious Experience.* New York: Oxford University Press. 1989.

Flew, Antony. *God and Philosophy.* Amherst, N.Y.: Prometheus, 2005.

Groothuis, Douglas, "Obstinacy in Religious Belief." *Sophia* 32, no. 2 (1993): 25-35.

————. "Wagering a Life on God." In *On Pascal.* Belmont, Calif.: Wadsworth, 2003.

————. "Wagering Belief: Examining Two Objections to Pascal's Wager." *Religious Studies* 30 (1994): 479-86.

James, William. *The Will to Believe.* New York: Dover, 1956.

Kreeft, Peter. *Christianity for Modern Pagans.* San Francisco: Ignatius Press, 1993.

Nash, Ronald. *Faith and Reason.* Grand Rapids: Zondervan, 1988.

Pascal, Blaise. *Pensées,* edited and translated by Alban Krailsheimer. New York: Penguin, 1966.

Rescher, Nicholas. *Pascal's Wager: A Study of Practical Reasoning in Philosophical Theology.* Notre Dame, Ind.: University of Notre Dame Press, 1985.

Rowe, William. *Philosophy of Religion.* Belmont, Calif.: Wadsworth, 1978.

Smart, Ninian. *The Philosophy of Religion.* New York: Random House, 1970.

Chapter 9: In Defense of Theistic Arguments

Bahnsen, Greg L. *Van Til's Apologetic: Readings and Analysis.* Phillipsburg, N.J.: P & R, 1998.

Barth, Karl. *Church Dogmatics: A Selection.* New York: Harper, 1961.

———. *The Epistle to the Romans.* New York: Oxford University Press, 1977.

Bavinck, Herman. *Doctrine of God,* translated by William Hendrickson. Grand Rapids: Eerdmans, 1951.

Calvin, John. *Institutes of the Christian Religion.*

Clarke, Adam. *Commentary on the Holy Bible.* Grand Rapids: Baker, 1967.

Craig, William Lane. "A Classical Apologist's Response." In *Five Views of Apologetics,* edited by Steve Cowan. Grand Rapids: Zondervan, 2000.

———. "Classical Apologetics." In *Five Views of Apologetics,* edited by Steve Cowan. Grand Rapids: Zondervan, 2000.

DeWeese, Garrett. "Toward a Robust Natural Theology: Reply to Paul Moser." *Philosophia Christi* 3, no. 1 (2001): 113-18.

Gilson, Etienne. *God and Philosophy.* New Haven, Conn.: Yale University Press, 1941.

Groothuis, Douglas. "Are Theistic Arguments Religiously Useless? A Pascalian Objection Examined." *Trinity Journal* 15 (1994): 147-61.

———. "Do Theistic Proofs Prove the Wrong God?" *Christian Scholar's Review* 29, no. 2 (1999): 247-60.

———. "Pascal's Biblical Omission Argument Against Natural Theology." *Asbury Theological Journal* 52, no. 2 (1997): 17-26.

———. "Proofs, Pride, and Incarnation: Is Natural Theology Theologically Taboo?" *Journal of the Evangelical Theological Society* 38, no. 1 (1955): 67-77.

———. "Skepticism and the Hidden God." In *On Pascal.* Belmont, Calif.: Wadsworth, 2003.

Harris, Murray J. *Jesus as God: The New Testament Use of Theos in Reference to Jesus.* Grand Rapids: Baker, 1992.

Henry, Carl F. H. *God, Revelation, and Authority.* Vol. 3, *God Who Speaks and Shows.* 6 vols. Waco, Tex.: Word, 1979.

Holder, Rodney. "Karl Barth and the Legitimacy of Natural Theology." *Themelios* 26, no. 3 (2001): 22-37.

Kierkegaard, Søren. *The Point of View of My Work as an Author,* translated by Walter Lowrie. New York: Harper & Brothers, 1962.

Lewis, Gordon R. "Schaeffer's Apologetic Method." In *Reflections on Francis Schaeffer,* edited by Ronald W. Ruegsegger. Grand Rapids: Zondervan Academie Books, 1986.

Moser, Paul. "Cognitive Inspiration and the Knowledge of God." In *The Rationality of Theism,* edited by Paul Copan and Paul K. Moser. New York: Routledge, 2003.

Pascal, Blaise. *Pensées,* edited and translated by Alban Krailsheimer. New York: Penguin, 1966.

Plantinga, Alvin. "Reason and Belief in God." In *Faith and Rationality,* edited by Alvin Plantinga and Nicholas Wolterstorff. Notre Dame, Ind.: University of Notre Dame Press, 1984.

———. *Warranted Christian Belief.* New York: Oxford University Press, 2000.

Schaeffer, Francis. *Escape from Reason.* 1968; reprint, Downers Grove, Ill.: InterVarsity Press, 2006.

Spiegel, James. *The Making of an Atheist: How Immorality Leads to Unbelief.* Chicago: Moody Press, 2010.

Stott, John. *The Message of Romans: God's Good News for the World.* The Bible Speaks Today. Downers Grove, Ill.: InterVarsity Press, 1994.

Sudduth, Michael. "The Dogmatic Model of Natural Theology." In *The Reformed Objection to Natural Theology.* Burlington, Vt.: Ashgate, 2009.

Chapter 10: The Ontological Argument

Anselm. *Proslogium.*

Craig, William Lane. "The Ontological Argument." In *To Everyone an Answer: A Case for the Christian Worldview,* edited by Francis Beckwith. Downers Grove, Ill.: InterVarsity Press, 2004.

Davis, Stephen T. *God, Reason, and Theistic Proofs.* Grand Rapids: Eerdmans, 1997.

———. *Logic and the Nature of God.* New York: Palgrave Macmillan, 1983.

———. "The Ontological Argument." In *The Rationality of Theism,* edited by Paul Copan and Paul K. Moser. New York: Routledge, 2003.

Dawkins, Richard. *The God Delusion.* Boston: Houghton Mifflin, 2006.

Ebersole, Frank. *Things We Know.* Eugene: University of Oregon Press, 1967.

Green, Michael. *I Believe in Satan's Downfall.* Grand Rapids: Eerdmans, 1981.

Grim, Patrick. "Impossibility Arguments." In *The Cambridge Companion to Atheism,* edited by Michael Martin. New York: Cambridge University Press, 2007.

Groothuis, Douglas. *Confronting the New Age.* Downers Grove, Ill.: InterVarsity Press, 1988.

Guanilo, "In Behalf of the Fool." In *St. Anselm: Basic Writings,* translated by S. N. Deane. Chicago: Open Court, 1962.

Hartshorne, Charles. *Anselm's Discovery: A Re-examination of the Ontological Argument for God's Existence.* Chicago: Open Court, 1965.

Hoffman, Joshua, and Gary Rosenkrantz. "Omnipotence." In *Routledge Companion to Philosophy of Religion,* edited by Chad Meister and Paul Copan. New York: Routledge, 2008.

Kant, Immanuel. "The Impossibility of an Ontological Proof of the Existence of God." In *The Critique of Pure Reason,* translated by Norman Kemp Smith. New York: St. Martin's Press, 1929.

Keller, Timothy. *The Reason for God: Belief in an Age of Skepticism.* New York: Dutton, 2008.

Lowe, E. J. "The Ontological Argument." In *The Routledge Companion to Philosophy of Religion,* edited by Chad Meister and Paul Copan. New York: Routledge, 2007.

Malcom, Norman. *Knowledge and Certainty: Essays and Lectures.* Englewood Cliffs, N.J.: Prentice-Hall, 1963.

Martin, Michael. *Atheism: A Philosophical Justification.* Philadelphia: Temple University Press, 1990.

Martin, Michael, and Ricki Monnier, eds. *The Impossibility of God.* New York: Prometheus, 2003.

Maydole, Robert E. "The Ontological Argument." In *The Blackwell Companion to Natural Theology,* edited by William Craig and J. P. Moreland. Malden, Mass.: Wiley-Blackwell, 2009.

Meister, Chad, and Paul Copan, eds. *The Routledge Companion to Philosophy of Religion.* Part 4. New York: Routledge, 2007.

Miller, Ed L., and Jon Jensen. *Questions That Matter.* 5th ed. Boston: McGraw-Hill, 2004.

Morris, Thomas V. *Our Idea of God: An Introduction to Philosophical Theology.* Downers Grove, Ill.: InterVarsity Press, 1991.

Nash, Ronald. *The Concept of God.* Grand Rapids: Baker, 1983.

—————. "Possible Worlds." In *Ultimate Questions.* Grand Rapids: Zondervan, 1999.

Nietzsche, Friedrich. "The Gay Science." In *The Portable Nietzsche,* translated by Walter Kaufmann. New York: Viking, 1968.

Plantinga, Alvin. *God and Other Minds.* New York: Cornell University Press, 1967.

—————. "Self-Profile." *Profiles 5,* edited by James E. Tomberlin and Peter Van Inwagen. Dordrecht: D. Reidel, 1985.

Rowe, William. "Modal Versions of the Ontological Argument." In *Philosophy of Religion: An Anthology,* edited by Louis Pojman. Belmont, Calif.: Wadsworth, 1987.

—————. *Philosophy of Religion: An Introduction.* Belmont, Calif.: Wadsworth, 1978.

Schaeffer, Francis A. *The God Who Is There.* 30th anniv. ed. Downers Grove, Ill.: InterVarsity Press, 1998.

Swinburne, Richard. *The Christian God.* New York: Oxford University Press, 1994.

—————. *The Coherence of Theism.* New York: Oxford University Press, 1977.

Wainwright, William. *Philosophy of Religion.* 2nd ed. Belmont, Calif.: Wadsworth, 1999.

Zagzebski, Linda. "Omniscience." In *Routledge Companion to Philosophy of Religion*, edited by Chad Meister and Paul Copan. New York: Routledge, 2008.

Chapter 11: Cosmological Arguments

Anscombe, Elizabeth. "'Whatever Has a Beginning of Existence Must Have a Cause': Hume's Argument Exposed." *Analysis* 3, no. 4 (1974): 150.

Barrow, John, and Frank Tipler. *The Anthropic Cosmological Principle.* Oxford: Oxford University Press, 1986.

Berlinski, David. *The Devil's Delusion: Atheism and Its Scientific Pretenses.* New York: Crown Forum, 2008.

Copan, Paul, and William Lane Craig. *Creation Out of Nothing: A Biblical, Philosophical, and Scientific Exploration.* Grand Rapids: Baker Academic, 2005.

Copleston, F. C. "A Debate on the Existence of God: Bertrand Russell and F. C. Copleston." In *The Existence of God,* edited by John Hick. New York: Macmillan, 1964.

Craig, William Lane. "Historical Statements of the Kalam Cosmological Argument." In *The Kalam Cosmological Argument.* 1979; reprint, Eugene, Ore.: Wipf & Stock, 2000.

———. *Reasonable Faith: Christian Truth and Apologetics.* 3rd ed. Wheaton, Ill.: Crossway, 2009.

———. "'What Place, Then, for a Creator?' Hawking on God and Creation." In *Theism, Atheism, and Big Bang Cosmology,* edited by William Lane Craig and Quentin Smith. Oxford: Clarendon, 1993.

Craig, William Lane, and James D. Sinclair. "The Kalam Cosmological Argument." In *The Blackwell Companion to Natural Theology,* edited by William Lane Craig and J. P. Moreland. Malden, Mass.: Wiley-Blackwell, 2009.

Craig, William Lane, and Walter Sinnott-Armstrong. *God? A Debate Between a Christian and an Atheist.* New York: Oxford University Press, 2003.

Davies, Paul. *God and the New Physics.* New York: Simon & Schuster, 1984.

Davis, John Jefferson. *Frontiers of Science and Faith: Examining Questions from the Big Bang to the End of the Universe.* Downers Grove, Ill.: InterVarsity Press, 2002.

———. "Genesis 1:1 and Big Bang Cosmology." In *Frontiers of Science and Faith: Examining Questions from the Big Bang to the End of the Universe.* Downers Grove, Ill.: InterVarsity Press, 2002.

Davis, Stephen T. "The Cosmological Argument and the Epistemic Status of Belief in God." *Philosophia Christi,* series 2, 1, no. 1 (1999): 8-10.

———. *God, Reason, and Theistic Proofs.* Grand Rapids: Eerdmans, 1997.

Davis, William C. "Theistic Arguments." In *Reason for the Hope Within,* edited by Michael Murray. Grand Rapids: Eerdmans, 1998.

Dembski, William. *No Free Lunch.* Lanham, Md.: Rowman & Littlefield, 2002.

Evans, C. Stephen, and R. Zachary Manis. *Philosophy of Religion.* 2nd ed. Downers Grove, Ill.: InterVarsity Press, 1999.

Ganssle, Greg, ed. *God and Time: Four Views.* Downers Grove, Ill.: InterVarsity Press, 2001.

Geisler, Norman, and William D. Watkins. *Worlds Apart.* Grand Rapids: Baker, 1989.

Groothuis, Douglas. "Metaphysical Implications of Cosmological Arguments." In *In Defense of Natural Theology,* edited by James Sennett and Douglas Groothuis. Downers Grove, Ill.: InterVarsity Press, 2005.

Hackett, Stuart. "The Cosmological Argument: The Argument from the Fact of Particular Existence." In *The Resurrection of Theism: Prolegomena to Christian Apology.* 1957; reprint, Eugene, Ore.: Wipf & Stock, 2009.

Hawking, Stephen. *The Theory of Everything.* Beverly Hills, Calif.: New Millennium, 2002.

Hawking, Stephen, and Roger Penrose. *The Nature of Space and Time.* The Isaac Newton Institute Series of Lectures. Princeton, N.J.: Princeton University Press, 1996.

Heidegger, Martin. *An Introduction to Metaphysics.* New York: Anchor Books, 1961.

Hilbert, David. "On the Infinite." In *Philosophy of Mathematics,* edited by Paul Benacerraf and Hillary Putnam. Englewood Cliffs, N.J.: Prentice-Hall, 1964.

Hume, David. "To John Stewart," Letter 91. In *The Letters of David Hume,* edited by J. Y. T. Greig. Oxford: Clarendon, 1932.

Jastrow, Robert. *God and the Astronomers.* 2nd ed. New York: W. W. Norton, 1992.

Johnson, David L. *A Reasoned Approach to Eastern Religions.* Minneapolis: Bethany Press, 1985.

Kenny, Anthony. *The Five Ways: St. Thomas Aquinas' Proofs of God's Existence.* New York: Schocken Books, 1969.

Leibniz, G. W. F. von. "Principles of Nature and Grace" (1714). In *Leibniz Selections,* edited by Philip P. Wiener. New York: Charles Scribner's, 1951.

Locke, John. *Essay on Human Understanding,* bk. 4. New York: J. M. Dent & Sons, 1961.

McDonnell, Craig Sean. "Twentieth Century Cosmologies." In *The History of Science and Religion in the Western Tradition: An Encyclopedia,* edited by Gary Ferngren. New York: Garland, 2000.

McInerny, Ralph. *Characters in Search of Their Author.* Notre Dame, Ind.: University of Notre Dame Press, 2001.

Miller, Ed L. *God and Reason: A Historical Approach to Philosophical Theology.* New York: Macmillan, 1972.

Moreland, J. P. *Scaling the Secular City: A Defense of Christianity.* Grand Rapids: Baker, 1987.

———. "Yes: A Defense of Christianity." In *Does God Exist? The Debate Between Theists and Atheists,* edited by J. P. Moreland and Kai Nielsen. 1990; reprint, Amherst, N.Y.: Prometheus, 1993.

Nash, Ronald. "Two Concepts of God." In *The Concept of God*. Grand Rapids: Zondervan, 1983.

Nerlich, G. C. "Popular Arguments for the Existence of God." In *Encyclopedia of Philosophy*, edited by Paul Edwards. New York: Macmillan, 1967.

Overton, John Henry. *The English Church in the Eighteenth Century*. New York: Longmans, Green, 1906.

Pascal, Blaise. *Pensées*, edited and translated by Alban Krailsheimer. New York: Penguin, 1966.

Peterson, Michael, William Hasker, Bruce Reichenbach and David Basinger. *Reason and Religious Belief*. 3rd ed. New York: Oxford University Press, 2003.

Pruss, Alexander. "The Leibnizian Cosmological Argument." In *The Blackwell Companion to Natural Theology*, edited by William Lane Craig and J. P. Moreland. Malden, Mass.: Wiley-Blackwell, 2009.

————. *The Principle of Sufficient Reason*. Cambridge, Mass.: Cambridge University Press, 2006.

Ross, Hugh. *Creation and Time*. Colorado Springs: NavPress, 1994.

Russell, Bertrand. *Our Knowledge of the External World*. 2nd ed. New York: W. W. Norton, 1929.

————. *Why I Am Not a Christian and Other Essays on Religion and Related Subjects*, edited by Paul Edwards. New York: Simon & Schuster, 1957.

Sagan, Carl. *Cosmos*. New York: Random House, 1980.

Schaeffer, Francis. *He Is There and He Is Not Silent*. 30th anniv. ed. Wheaton, Ill.: Tyndale House, 2001.

Senor, Thomas D. "The Incarnation and the Trinity." In *Reason for the Hope Within*, edited by Michael J. Murray. Grand Rapids: Eerdmans, 1999.

Sire, James W. "The Clockwork Universe: Deism." In *The Universe Next Door*. 5th ed. Downers Grove, Ill.: InterVarsity Press, 2009.

Smith, Quentin. "The Uncaused Beginning of the Universe." In *Theism, Atheism, and Big Bang Cosmology*, edited by William Lane Craig and Quentin Smith. Oxford: Clarendon, 1993.

Stannard, Russell. "Science and Religion." In *What Philosophers Think*, edited by Julian Baggini and Jeremy Stangroom. New York: Barnes & Noble, 2003.

Swinburne, Richard. *The Existence of God*. Rev. ed. New York: Oxford University Press, 1991.

Taliaferro, Charles. *Contemporary Philosophy of Religion*. Malden, Mass.: Blackwell, 1998.

Taylor, Richard. *Metaphysics*. 4th ed. New York: Prentice Hall, 1992.

Trueblood, D. Elton. *Philosophy of Religion*. Grand Rapids: Baker, 1957.

Van Til, Cornelius. *The Defense of the Faith*. Philadelphia: Presbyterian & Reformed, 1972.

Weldon, Stephen P. "Deism." In *The History of Science and Religion in the Western Tradition: An Encyclopedia*, edited by Gary Ferngren. New York: Garland, 2000.

Whitnow, G. J. "Entropy." In *Encyclopedia of Philosophy*, edited by Paul Edwards. New York: Macmillan, 1967.

Willard, Dallas. "The Three-Stage Argument for the Existence of God." In *Contemporary Perspectives in Religious Epistemology*, edited by R. Douglas Geivett and Brendan Sweetman. New York: Oxford University Press, 1992.

Wise, Kurt, *Faith, Form, and Time: What the Bible Teaches and What Science Confirms About the Age of the Universe*. Nashville: Broadman & Holman, 2002.

Yandell, Keith, and Harold Netland. *Buddhism: A Christian Exploration and Appraisal*. Downers Grove, Ill.: InterVarsity Press, 2009.

Chapter 12: The Design Argument

Barr, Stephen. *Modern Physics and Ancient Faith*. Notre Dame, Ind.: University of Notre Dame Press, 2004.

Carter, Brendon. "Large Number Coincidences and the Anthropic Principle in Cosmology." In *IAU Symposium 63: Confrontation of Cosmological Theories with Observational Data*. Dordrecht: Reidel, 1974.

Collins, Robin. "The Teleological Argument: Fine-Tuning." In *Blackwell Companion to Natural Theology*, edited by William Lane Craig and J. P. Moreland. Malden, Mass.: Wiley-Blackwell, 2009.

Craig, William Lane. *Reasonable Faith: Christian Truth and Apologetics*. 3rd ed. Wheaton, Ill.: Crossway, 2009.

Craig, William Lane, and Walter Sinnott-Armstrong. *God? A Debate Between a Christian and an Atheist*. New York: Oxford University Press, 2004.

Davis, Jimmy D., and Harry Lee Poe. *Designer Universe*. Nashville: Broadman & Holman, 2002.

Dawkins, Richard. *The God Delusion*. Boston: Houghton Mifflin, 2006.

Dembski, William. "Argument from Ignorance." In *The Design Revolution*. Downers Grove, Ill.: InterVarsity Press, 2004.

————. *The Design Inference: Eliminating Chance Through Small Probabilities*. New York: Cambridge University Press, 1998.

————. *Intelligent Design*. Downers Grove, Ill.: InterVarsity Press, 1999.

————. *No Free Lunch*. Lanham, Md.: Rowman & Littlefield, 2002.

Denton, Michael. *Nature's Destiny: How the Laws of Biology Reveal Purpose in the Universe*. New York: Free Press, 1998.

Flew, Antony, with Ray Abraham Varghese. *There Is a God*. San Francisco: HarperOne, 2007.

Glynn, Patrick. *God: The Evidence: The Reconciliation of Faith and Reason in a Postsecular World*. Rockland, Calif.: Prima, 1997.

Gonzalez, Guillermo, and Jay Wesley Richards. *The Privileged Planet*. New York: Free Press, 2004.

Groothuis, Douglas. "Proofs, Pride, and Incarnation: Is Natural Theology Theologically Taboo?" *Journal of the Evangelical Theological Society* 38, no. 1 (1995): 67-76.

Hawking, Stephen. *The Theory of Everything.* Beverly Hills, Calif.: New Millennium Press, 2002.

Hoyle, Fred. "The Universe: Some Past and Present Reflections." *Engineering and Science* (1981): 12.

Lennox, John. *God's Undertaker: Has Science Buried God?* Oxford: Lion, 2007.

Leslie, John. "How to Draw Conclusions from a Fine-Tuned Universe." In *Physics, Philosophy and Theology: A Common Quest for Understanding,* edited by R. J. Russell, W. R. Stoeger and G. V. Coyne. Vatican City: Vatican Observatory Press, 1988.

Monton, Bradley. *Seeking God in Science.* Boulder, Colo.: Broadview, 2009.

Moreland, J. P. *Scaling the Secular City.* Grand Rapids: Baker, 1987.

Moreland, J. P., and William Lane Craig. *Philosophical Foundations for a Christian Worldview.* Downers Grove, Ill.: InterVarsity Press, 2003.

Nunley, Troy. "On Elliott Sober's Challenge for Biological Design Arguments." *Philosophia Christi* 9, no. 2 (2007): 443-58.

—————. "Fish Nets, Firing Squads and Fine-Tuning (Again): How Likelihood Arguments Undermine Elliott Sober's Weak Anthropic Principles." *Philosophia Christi* 11, no. 2 (2010): 33-55.

Parsons, Keith. "Naturalistic Rejoinders to Theistic Arguments." In *The Routledge Companion to Philosophy of Religion,* edited by Chad Meister and Paul Copan. New York: Routledge, 2007.

Penrose, Roger. *The Emperor's New Mind.* New York: Oxford University Press, 1989.

—————. "Time-Asymmetry and Quantum Gravity." In *Quantum Gravity 2,* edited by C. J. Isham, R. Penrose and D. W. Sciama. Oxford: Clarendon, 1981.

Peterson, Michael, William Hasker, Bruce Reichenbach and David Basinger. *Reason and Religious Belief: An Introduction to the Philosophy of Religion.* 3rd ed. New York: Oxford University Press, 2003.

Rees, Martin. "Exploring Our Universe and Others." *Scientific American Special Issue: The Once and Future Cosmos* (2002): 87.

Ross, Hugh. "Why Such a Vast Universe?" In *Why the Universe Is the Way It Is.* Grand Rapids: Baker, 2008.

Russell, Bertrand. *Religion and Science.* 1935; reprint, London: Oxford University Press, 1961.

Sober, Elliott. "Absence of Evidence and Evidence of Absence: Evidential Transitivity in Connection with Fossils, Fishing, Fine-tuning, and Firing Squads." *Philosophical Studies* 143 (2009): 63-90.

Stenger, Victor J. *God: The Failed Hypothesis.* New York: Prometheus, 2007.

Strobel, Lee. "The Evidence of Physics." *The Case for a Creator.* Grand Rapids: Zondervan, 2004.

Swinburne, Richard. "How the Existence of God Explains the World and Its Order." In *Is There a God?* New York: Oxford University Press, 1996.

―――. "Teleological Arguments." In *The Existence of God.* 2nd ed. Oxford: Oxford University Press, 2004.

Wallace, Stan, ed. *Does God Exist? The Craig-Flew Debate.* Burlington, Vt.: Ashgate, 2003.

Wilber, Ken. *The Integral Vision.* Boston: Shambhala, 2007.

Chapter 13: Origins, Design and Darwinism

Adler, Mortimer. *The Difference of Man and the Difference It Makes.* New York: Holt, Rinehart & Winston, 1967.

Bacon, Francis. *The Advancement of Learning.* 1605; reprint, New York: Random House, 2001.

Beckwith, Francis. *Law, Darwinism, and Public Education.* Lanham, Md.: Rowman & Littlefield, 2003.

Bergman, Jerry. *Slaughter of the Dissidents: The Shocking Truth About Killing the Careers of Darwin Doubters.* Southworth, Wash.: Leafcutter Press, 2008.

Bergman, Jerry, and George Howe. *Vestigial Organs Are Fully Functional: A History and Evaluation of the Vestigial Organ Origins Concept.* Terre Haute, Ind.: Creation Research Society, 1990.

Bradley, Walter. "Why I Believe the Bible Is Scientifically Reliable." In *Why I Am a Christian,* edited by Norman Geisler and Paul Hoffman. Grand Rapids: Baker, 2001.

Broom, Neil. *How Blind the Watchmaker?* Downers Grove, Ill.: InterVarsity Press, 2002.

Burbank, Luther. *Partner of Nature,* edited by Wilbur Hall. New York: D. Appleton-Century, 1939.

Chesterton, G. K. *Orthodoxy.* 1908; reprint, New York: Image Books, 1959.

Collins, C. John. *Genesis 1–4: A Linguistic, Literary, and Theological Commentary.* Phillipsburg, N.J.: P & R, 2006.

Collins, Francis. *The Language of God.* New York: Free Press, 2006.

Darwin, Charles. *Life and Letters of Charles Darwin, Including an Autobiographical Chapter,* edited by Francis Darwin. New York: Appleton, 1898.

―――. *Origin of Species.* London: John Murray, 1859.

Dawkins, Richard. *The Blind Watchmaker.* New York: W. W. Norton, 1986.

―――. "The 'Information Challenge.'" In *Intelligent Design Creationism,* edited by Robert T. Pennock. Boston: MIT Press, 2001.

Dembski, William. *The Design Inference.* New York: Cambridge University Press, 1998.

―――. *The Design Revolution.* Downers Grove, Ill.: InterVarsity Press, 2004.

―――. *The End of Christianity: Finding a Good God in an Evil World.* Nashville: Broadman & Holman, 2009.

Denton, Michael. *Evolution: A Theory in Crisis.* Chevy Chase, Md.: Adler & Adler, 1985.

Dobzhansky, T. "Nothing in Biology Makes Sense Except in Light of Evolution." *American Biology Teacher* 35 (1973): 125-29.

Fichman, Martin. *An Elusive Victorian: The Evolution of Alfred Russel Wallace.* Chicago: University of Chicago Press, 2004.

Flannery, Michael A. *Alfred Russel Wallace's Theory of Intelligent Evolution: How Wallace's* World of Life *Challenged Darwinism.* Riesel, Tex.: Erasmus Press, 2008.

Fuller, Steve. *Science vs. Religion? Intelligent Design and the Problem of Evolution.* Malden, Mass.: Polity Press, 2007.

Geisler, Norman. "Genealogies, Open or Closed." In *Baker Encyclopedia of Apologetics.* Grand Rapids: Baker, 1999.

Gish, Duane. *Evolution: The Fossils Still Say No!* Green Forest, Ark.: Master Books, 1995.

Gould, Stephen Jay. "Evolution's Erratic Pace." *Natural History* 86 (1977): 12-16.

Grassé, Pierre-Paul. *Evolution of Living Organisms.* New York: Academic Press, 1977.

Harbin, Michael A. "Theistic Evolution: Deism Revisited?" *Journal of the Evangelical Theological Society* 40, no. 4 (1997): 639-52.

Hardin, Garret. *Nature and Man's Fate.* New York: Mentor, 1961.

Henry, Carl F. H. *God, Revelation, and Authority.* Vol. 6, *God Who Stands and Stays.* Waco, Tex.: Word, 1983.

Hitchens, Christopher. *God Is Not Great.* New York: Twelve Books, 2007.

Hitching, Francis. *The Neck of the Giraffe: Why Scientists Now Are Attacking Darwin's Theory of Evolution.* New York: New American Library, 1982.

Hunter, Cornelius. *Darwin's God.* Grand Rapids: Brazos, 2002.

———. *Darwin's Proof.* Grand Rapids: Brazos, 2003.

Johnson, Phillip. *Darwin on Trial.* 2nd ed. Downers Grove, Ill.: InterVarsity Press, 1993.

———. *Defeating Darwinism.* Downers Grove, Ill.: InterVarsity Press, 1997.

———. *Reason in the Balance.* Downers Grove, Ill.: InterVarsity Press, 1995.

———. "Theistic Naturalism and Theistic Realism." In *Reason in the Balance.* Downers Grove, Ill.: InterVarsity Press, 1995.

———. *The Wedge of Truth.* Downers Grove, Ill.: InterVarsity Press, 2000.

Koestler, Arthur. *Janus: A Summing Up.* New York: Vintage Books, 1978.

Kuhn, Thomas. *The Structure of Scientific Revolutions.* 3rd ed. Chicago: University of Chicago Press, 1996.

Lewis, C. S. "The Fall of Man," In *The Problem of Pain.* 1962; reprint, New York: Touchstone, 1996.

Lewis, Gordon R., and Bruce A. Demarest. *Integrative Theology.* Grand Rapids: Zondervan, 1990.

Lubenow, Marvin L. *Bones of Contention: A Creationist Assessment of Human Fossils.* Rev. ed. Grand Rapids: Baker, 2004.

Macbeth, Norman. *Darwin Retried.* New York: Dell, 1971.

─────. *Darwinism: A Time for Funerals: An Interview with Norman Macbeth.* San Francisco: Robert Briggs, 1985.

Machen, J. Gresham. *Christianity and Liberalism.* 1923; reprint, Grand Rapids: Eerdmans, 2009.

Mayr, Ernst. *What Makes Biology Unique? Considerations on the Autonomy of a Scientific Discipline.* New York: Cambridge University Press, 2004.

McGrath, Alister. *A Fine-Tuned Universe.* Louisville: Westminster John Knox, 2009.

Meyer, Stephen C. "The Cambrian Information Explosion: Evidence for Intelligent Design." In *Debating Design: From Darwin to DNA,* edited by William A. Dembski and Michael Ruse. New York: Cambridge University Press, 2006.

─────. *Signature in the Cell.* San Francisco: HarperOne, 2009.

Meyer, Stephen, Marcus Ross, Paul Nelson and Paul Chien. "The Cambrian Explosion: Biology's Big Bang." In *Darwinism, Design and Public Education,* edited by Angus Campbell and Stephen C. Meyer. East Lansing: Michigan State University Press, 2003.

Miller, Donald E. *The Case for Liberal Christianity.* New York: Harper & Row, 1981.

Milton, Richard. *Scattering the Myths of Darwinism.* Rochester, Vt.: Park Street Press, 1997.

Monton, Bradley. *Seeking God in Science.* Boulder, Colo.: Broadview Press, 2009.

Moreland, J. P. *Christianity and the Nature of Science.* Grand Rapids: Baker, 1989.

─────. *Love Your God with All Your Mind.* Colorado Springs: NavPress, 1997.

Moreland, J. P., and John Mark Reynolds, eds. *Three Views on Creation and Evolution.* Grand Rapids: Zondervan, 1999.

Nagel, Thomas. "Public Education and Intelligent Design." *Philosophy and Public Affairs* 36, no. 2 (2008).

Newman, Robert C., and Herman J. Eckelman Jr. *Genesis One and the Origin of the Earth.* Hatfield, Penn.: Interdisciplinary Biblical Research Institute, 1989.

Plantinga, Alvin, "Methodological Naturalism?" *Origins and Design* 18, no. 1 (1996): 18-27.

─────. "Methodological Naturalism? Part 2: Philosophical Analysis." *Origins and Design* 18, no. 2 (1997).

Ramm, Bernard. *The Christian Approach to Science and Scripture.* Grand Rapids: Eerdmans, 1954.

Raup, David. "Conflicts Between Darwin and Paleontology." *Field Museum of Natural History Bulletin* 30, no. 1 (1979): 22-29.

Reynolds, John Mark. "Getting God a Pass: Science, Theology, and the Consideration of Intelligent Design." In *Signs of Intelligence: Understanding Intelligent Design,* edited by William A. Dembski and James M. Kushiner. Grand Rapids: Brazos, 2001.

Rifkin, Jeremy, and Ted Howard. *Entropy: A New World View.* New York: Viking Press, 1980.

Ross, Hugh. *Creation and Time.* Colorado Springs: NavPress, 1994.

Schaeffer, Francis. *Genesis in Space and Time.* Downers Grove, Ill.: InterVarsity Press, 1972.

————. *No Final Conflict.* Downers Grove, Ill.: InterVarsity Press, 1975.

Schützenberger, Marcel-Paul. "The Miracles of Darwinism." In *Uncommon Dissent: Intellectuals Who Find Darwinism Unconvincing.* Edited by William Dembski. Wilmington, Del.: ISI Books, 2004.

Sermonti, Giuseppe. *Why Is a Fly Not a Horse?* Seattle: Center for Science and Culture, 2005.

Shapiro, James A., and Richard Sternberg. "Why Repetitive DNA Is Essential to Genome Function." *Biological Review* 80 (2005): 227-50.

Smith, A. E. Wilder. *The Creation of Life: A Cybernetic Approach to Evolution.* Wheaton, Ill.: Harold Shaw, 1970.

Spiegel, James. "The Philosophical Theology of Theistic Evolutionism." *Philosophia Christi* 4, no. 1 (2002): 89-99.

Sternberg, Richard. "On the Roles of Repetitive DNA Elements in the Context of a Unified Genomic-Epigenetic System." *Annals of the New York Academy of Sciences* 981 (2002): 154-88.

Strobel, Lee. *The Case for a Creator.* Grand Rapids: Zondervan, 2004.

Taylor, Gordon Ratray. *The Great Evolution Mystery.* New York: Harper & Row, 1983.

Thurman, L. Duane. *How to Think About Evolution and Other Bible-Science Controversies.* Downers Grove, Ill.; InterVarsity Press, 1978.

Tipler, Frank. "Refereed Journals: Do They Insure Quality or Enforce Orthodoxy?" In *Uncommon Dissent: Intellectuals Who Find Darwinism Unconvincing,* edited by William Dembski. Wilmington, Del.: ISI Books, 2004.

Vries, Hugo de. *Species and Varieties: Their Origin by Mutation.* 1904; reprint, New York: Garland, 1988.

Weaver, Richard. *Visions of Order: The Cultural Crisis of Our Time.* 1964; reprint, Bryn Mawr, Penn.: Intercollegiate Studies Institute, 1995.

Weikart, Richard. *From Darwin to Hitler: Evolutionary Ethics, Eugenics, and Racism in Germany.* New York: Palgrave Macmillan, 2004.

Wells, Jonathan. *Icons of Evolution.* Washington, D.C.: Regnery, 2000.

————. *The Politically Incorrect Guide to Darwinism and Intelligent Design.* Washington, D.C.: Regnery, 2006.

Wells, Jonathan, and William Dembski. "The Origin of Species." In *The Design of Life: Discovering Signs of Intelligence in Biological Systems.* Dallas: Foundation for Thought and Ethics, 2008.

West, John G. *Darwin Day in America.* Wilmington, Del.: ISI Books, 2008.

Wiker, Benjamin. *The Darwin Myth.* Washington, D.C.: Regnery, 2009.

————. "One Long Argument, Two Long Books." In *The Darwin Myth.* Washington, D.C.: Regnery, 2009.

————. "What to Make of It All?" In *The Darwin Myth.* Washington, D.C.: Regnery, 2009.

Woodward, Thomas. *Doubts About Darwin: A History of Intelligent Design.* Grand Rapids: Baker, 2003.

Chapter 14: Evidence for Intelligent Design

Alberts, Bruce. "The Cell as a Collection of Protein Machines: Preparing the Next Generation of Molecular Biologists." *Cell* 92, no. 291 (1998): 291-94.

Ankerberg, John, and John Weldon. *Darwin's Leap of Faith.* Eugene, Ore.: Harvest House, 1998.

Behe, Michael. "Answering the Scientific Criticism of Intelligent Design." In *Science and Evidence for Design in the Universe: The Proceedings of the Wethersfield Institute,* edited by Michael J. Behe, William A. Dembski and Stephen C. Meyer. San Francisco: Ignatius Press, 1999.

————. *Darwin's Black Box.* New York: Free Press, 1996.

————. "Design in the Details: The Origins of Biomolecular Machines." In *Darwinism, Design, and Public Education,* edited by John Angus Campbell and Stephen C. Meyer. East Lansing: Michigan State University Press, 2003.

————. *The Edge of Evolution.* New York: Free Press, 2007.

————. "Reply to My Critics: A Response to Reviews of Darwin's Black Box: The Biochemical Challenge to Evolution." *Biology and Philosophy* 16 (2001): 685-709.

Berger, Peter. *A Rumor of Angels.* New York: Anchor Books, 1970.

Berlinski, David. *The Devil's Delusion: Atheism and its Scientific Pretensions.* New York: Crown Forum, 2008.

Bhushan, Bharat. "Biomimetics: Lessons from Nature—An Overview." *Philosophical Transactions of the Royal Society of London* 367 (2009): 1445-86.

Bradley, Walter L., and Charles Thaxton. "Information and the Origin of Life." In *The Creation Hypothesis,* edited by J. P. Moreland. Downers Grove, Ill.: InterVarsity Press, 1994.

Bradley, Walter L., Roger L. Olsen and Charles B. Thaxton. *The Mystery of Life's Origin: Reassessing Current Theories.* New York: Philosophical Library, 1984.

Cooper, John. *Panentheism: The Other God of the Philosophers—From Plato to the Present.* Grand Rapids: Baker Academic, 2006.

Crick, Francis. *Life Itself: Its Origin and Nature.* New York: Simon & Schuster, 1981.

————. *What Mad Pursuit.* New York: Basic Books, 1990.

Darwin, Charles. *The Origin of the Species.* London: Langham, 1859.

Dawkins, Richard. *River Out of Eden: A Darwinian View of Life.* New York: Basic Books, 1995.

De Duve, Christian. *Vital Dust: Life as a Cosmic Imperative.* New York: Basic Books, 1995.

Dembski, William. "The Design Inference." In *The Design Inference.* New York: Cambridge University Press, 1998.

————. *Intelligent Design: The Bridge Between Science and Theology.* Downers Grove, Ill.: InterVarsity Press, 1999.

————. *No Free Lunch.* Lanham, Md.: Rowman & Littlefield, 2002.

Dennett, Daniel. "Universal Acid." In *Darwin's Dangerous Idea: Evolution and the Meanings of Life.* New York: Simon & Schuster, 1996.

Eden, Murray. "Inadequacies of Neo-Darwinian Evolution as a Scientific Theory." In *Mathematical Challenge to the Neo-Darwinian Interpretation of Evolution,* edited by Paul S. Moorhead. Philadelphia: Wistar Institute, 1967.

Eldredge, Niles. *The Monkey Business.* New York: Washington Square Books, 1982.

Gates, Bill. *The Road Ahead.* Rev. ed. New York: Basic Books, 1995.

Geisler, Norman, and Kerby Anderson. *Origin Science.* Grand Rapids: Baker, 1987.

Gould, Stephen Jay. "The Panda's Thumb." In *Intelligent Design Creationism,* edited by Robert T. Pennock. Boston: MIT Press, 2001.

————. *Rocks of Ages: Science and Religion in the Fullness of Life.* New York: Ballantine, 2002.

Gritt, Werner. *In the Beginning Was Information.* Bielefeld, Germany: Christliche Literature, 2000.

Harold, Franklin. *The Way of the Cell: Molecules, Organisms, and the Order of Life.* New York: Oxford University Press, 2002.

Hoyle, Fred. *The Intelligent Universe.* New York: Holt, Rinehart & Winston, 1984.

Johnson, Phillip. *Darwin on Trial.* 2nd ed. Downers Grove, Ill.: InterVarsity Press, 1991.

————. *The Wedge of Truth.* Downers Grove, Ill.: InterVarsity Press, 2000.

Koestler, Arthur. *Janus: A Summing Up.* New York: Vintage Books, 1978.

Meyer, Stephen. "The Explanatory Power of Design." In *Mere Creation: Science, Faith and Intelligent Design,* edited by William Dembski. Downers Grove, Ill.: InterVarsity Press, 2000.

————. "The Origin of Biological Information and the Higher Taxonomic Categories." *Proceedings of the Biological Society of Washington* 117, no. 2 (2004): 213-39.

————. *The Signature in the Cell.* San Francisco: HarperOne, 2009.

Milton, Richard. *Shattering the Myths of Darwinism.* Rochester, Vt.: Park Street Press, 1997.

Moreland, J. P. *Christianity and the Nature of Science.* Grand Rapids: Baker, 1989.

————. *Scaling the Secular City.* Grand Rapids: Baker, 1987.

Nagle, Thomas. "Public Education and Intelligent Design." *Philosophy and Public Affairs* 36, no. 2 (2008).

————. *The View from Nowhere.* New York: Oxford University Press, 1986.

Nelson, Paul. "The Role of Theology in Current Evolutionary Reasoning." In *Intelligent Design Creationism,* edited by Robert T. Pennock. Cambridge, Mass.: MIT Press, 2001.

Pearcey, Nancy. "You Guys Lost!" In *Mere Creation: Science, Faith and Intelligent Design*, edited by William Dembski. Downers Grove, Ill.: InterVarsity Press, 1998.

Pigluicci, Massimo. "Where Do We Come From?" In *Darwinism, Design, and Public Education*, edited by John Angus Campbell and Stephen C. Meyer. East Lansing: Michigan State University Press, 2003.

Polanyi, Michael. "Life's Irreducible Structure." *Science* 160 (1968): 1309.

Ross, Hugh. *Creation as Science*. Colorado Springs: NavPress, 2006.

Sire, James. *Naming the Elephant: Worldview as a Concept*. Downers Grove, Ill.: InterVarsity Press, 2004.

Thaxton, Charles, and Nancy Pearcey. *The Soul of Science*. Wheaton, Ill.: Crossway, 1994.

Thornhill, Richard. "The Panda's Thumb." *Perspectives on Science and Christian Faith* 55, no. 1 (2003): 30-35.

Ward, Peter, and Donald Brownlee. *Rare Earth: Why Complex Life Is Uncommon in the Universe*. New York: Springer, 2003.

Wells, Jonathan. *Icons of Evolution*. Washington, D.C.: Regnery, 2000.

Wilber, Ken. *A Brief History of Everything*. 2nd ed. Boston: Shambhala, 2001.

Wilder-Smith, A. E. *The Scientific Alternative to Neo-Darwinian Evolutionary Theory: Information Sources and Structures*. Costa Mesa, Calif.: TWFT Publishers, 1987.

Williams, George C. "A Package of Information." In *The Third Culture*, edited by John Brockman. New York: Touchstone, 1995.

Yockey, Hubert. *Information Theory, Evolution, and the Origin of Life*. New York: Cambridge University Press, 2005.

————. "Origin of Life on Earth and Shannon's Theory of Communication." *Computers and Chemistry* 24 (2000): 105-23.

Chapter 15: The Moral Argument for God

Alston, William. "What Euthyphro Should Have Said." *Philosophy of Religion: A Reader and Guide*, edited by William Lane Craig. New Brunswick, N.J.: Rutgers University Press, 2002.

Anscombe, Elizabeth. "Modern Moral Philosophy." *Philosophy* 33, no. 124 (1958): 1-19.

Benedict, Ruth. "A Defense of Ethical Relativism." In *Moral Philosophy: A Reader*, edited by Louis P. Pojman. 2nd ed. Indianapolis: Hackett, 1998.

Berger, Peter. *A Rumor of Angels*. New York: Anchor Books, 1970.

Carr, Karen L. *The Banality of Nihilism: Twentieth Century Responses to Meaninglessness*. New York: State University of New York Press, 1992.

Chesterton, G. K. *Orthodoxy*. 1908; reprint, New York: Image Books, 1959.

Clark, David, and Norman Geisler. *Apologetics in the New Age: A Christian Critique of Pantheism*. 1990; reprint, Eugene, Ore.: Wipf & Stock, 2004.

Conti, Joseph G. *The Truth About Tolerance: Pluralism, Diversity and the Culture Wars*. Downers Grove, Ill.: InterVarsity Press, 2005.

Coutois, Stephane, Nicholas Werth, Jean-Louis Panné, Andrzej Paczkowski, Karel Bartošek and Jean-Louis Margolin. "The Great Famine." In *The Black Book of Communism: Crimes, Terror, Repression.* Cambridge, Mass.: Harvard University Press, 1999.

Craig, William Lane. "Five Reasons Why God Exists." In *God: A Debate Between a Christian and an Atheist.* New York: Oxford University Press, 2004.

Frankena, William. *Ethics.* 2nd ed. New York: Prentice-Hall, 1988.

Frege, Gottlob. *Zeitscheift für Philosophie and philosophische Kritik* 100 (1892): 25-50.

Ganssle, Greg. "Necessary Moral Truths and the Need for Explanation." *Philosophia Christi* 2, no. 1 (2000): 105-12.

Groothuis, Douglas. "Ethics Without Reality, Postmodern Style." In *Truth Decay.* Downers Grove, Ill.: InterVarsity Press, 2000.

————. "Thomas Nagel's 'Last Word' on the Metaphysics and Rationality of Morality." *Philosophia Christi,* series 2, 1, no. 1 (1999): 115 20.

————. "The Truth About Truth." In *Truth Decay.* Downers Grove, Ill.: InterVarsity Press, 2000.

Guinness, Os. *The Case for Civility.* San Francisco: HarperOne, 2008.

Hallie, Philip. "From Cruelty to Goodness." In *Virtue and Vice in Everyday Life,* edited by Christina Hoff Summers and Fred Summers. 7th ed. Belmont, Calif.: Wadsworth, 2006.

————. *Lest Innocent Blood Be Shed.* New York: Harper, 1979.

————. *Surprised by Goodness.* McClean, Va.: Trinity Forum, 2002.

Hanink, James, and Gary R. Marr. "What Euthyphro Couldn't Have Said." *Faith and Philosophy* 4, no. 3 (1987): 241-61.

King, Martin Luther, Jr. "Letter from a Birmingham Jail." In *The Book of Virtues,* edited by William Bennett. New York: Simon & Schuster. 1993.

Kluckholn, Clyde. "Ethical Relativity: 'Sic et Non.'" *Journal of Philosophy* 52 (1955): 672.

Kurtz, Paul. "Opening Statement." In *Is Goodness Without God Good Enough? A Debate on Faith, Secularism, and Ethics,* edited by Robert K. Garcia and Nathan L. King. Lanham, Md.: Rowman & Littlefield, 2009.

Leff, Arthur Allen. "Unspeakable Ethics, Unnatural Law." *Duke Law Journal* 1979, no. 6 (1979): 1229.

Lewis, C. S. *Abolition of Man.* 1944; reprint, San Francisco: HarperSanFrancisco, 1974.

————. *Christian Reflections.* 1967; reprint, Grand Rapids: Eerdmans, 1978.

————. *Mere Christianity.* 1943; reprint, New York: Simon & Schuster, 1996.

Mackie, J. L. *Ethics: Inventing Right and Wrong.* New York: Penguin, 1977.

Mavrodes, George. "Religion and the Queerness of Morality." In *Philosophy of Religion: An Anthology.* 5th ed. Edited by Louis Pojman and Michael Rea. Belmont, Calif.: Thomson, Wadsworth, 2008.

Moreland, J. P. *Scaling the Secular City.* Grand Rapids: Baker, 1987.

Murdoch, Iris. *The Sovereignty of the Good.* 2nd ed. 1970; reprint, New York: Routledge, 2001.

Nagel, Thomas. *The Last Word.* New York: Oxford University Press, 1997.

Nash, Ronald. *Faith and Reason.* Grand Rapids: Zondervan, 1988.

———. *The Light of the Mind: St. Augustine's Theory of Knowledge.* Lexington: University Press of Kentucky, 1969.

———. "Possible Worlds." In *Life's Ultimate Questions.* Grand Rapids: Zondervan, 1999.

Nietzsche, Friedrich. "The Gay Science." In *The Portable Nietzsche,* translated by Walter Kaufmann. New York: Viking, 1968.

Pirsig, Robert. *Zen and the Art of Motorcycle Maintenance.* New York: William & Morrow, 1999.

Pojman, Louis. "A Defense of Ethical Objectivism." In *Moral Philosophy.* 3rd ed. Indianapolis, Hackett, 2003.

———. *How Should We Live?* Belmont, Calif.: Thomson, Wadsworth, 2005.

Rachels, James. *The Elements of Moral Philosophy.* 3rd ed. New York: McGraw-Hill, 1999.

Randall, Hastings. *The Theory of Good and Evil.* Oxford: Clarendon, 1903.

Reppert, Victor. *C. S. Lewis's Dangerous Idea: In Defense of the Argument from Reason.* Downers Grove, Ill.: InterVarsity Press, 2003.

Rose, Eugene. *Nihilism: The Root of the Revolution of the Modern Age.* Forestville, Calif.: Fr. Seraphim Rose Foundation, 1994.

Ruse, Michael. "Evolutionary Theory and Christian Ethics" In *The Darwinian Paradigm.* London: Routledge, 1989.

Russell, Bertrand. "A Free Man's Worship." In *Why I Am Not a Christian and Other Essays on Religion and Related Subjects,* edited by Paul Edwards. New York: Simon & Schuster, 1955.

Thielicke, Helmut. *Nihilism, Its Origin and Nature—with a Christian Answer.* New York: Harper & Row, 1961.

Sartre, Jean-Paul. *Existentialism and Human Emotions.* New York: Philosophical Library, 1957.

Schaeffer, Francis. *Art and the Bible.* Downers Grove, Ill.: InterVarsity Press, 2000.

Singer, Peter. *Rethinking Life and Death.* New York: St. Martin's Press, 1995.

Sire, James. "Beyond Nihilism: Existentialism." In *The Universe Next Door: A Basic Worldview Catalog.* 5th ed. Downers Grove, Ill.: InterVarsity Press, 2009.

Stirner, Max. *The Ego and Its Own.* New York: Libertarian Book Club, 1963.

Swinburne, Richard. *The Existence of God.* 2nd ed. New York: Oxford University Press, 2004.

Van Inwagen, Peter. *Metaphysics.* Boulder, Colo.: Westview Press, 1993.

Wilbur, Ken. *A Brief History of Everything.* 2nd ed. Boston: Shambhala, 2000.

Wright, N. T. *Surprised by Hope: Rethinking Heaven, the Resurrection, and the Mission of the Church*. San Francisco: HarperOne, 2008.

Yandell, Keith. "Theism, Atheism, and Cosmology." In *Does God Exist? The Craig-Flew Debate*, edited by Dan Wallace. Burlington, Vt.: Ashgate, 2003.

Zagzebski, Linda. "Does Ethics Need God?" *Faith and Philosophy* 4, no. 3 (1987): 282-93.

Chapter 16: The Argument from Religious Experience

Alper, M. *The God Part of the Brain: A Scientific Interpretation of Human Spirituality and God*. New York: Rogue Press, 2000.

Barrett, Justin. *Why Would Anyone Believe in God?* Lanham, Md.: Rowman & Littlefield, 2004.

Barrs, Jerome, and Ranald Macaulay. *Being Human*. Downers Grove, Ill.: InterVarsity Press, 1978.

Beckwith, Francis, Carl Mosser and Paul Owen, eds. *The New Mormon Challenge*. Grand Rapids: Zondervan, 2002.

Campbell, Joseph. *The Power of Myth*. New York: Doubleday, 1988.

Copan, Paul. "Does Religion Originate in the Brain?" *The Christian Research Journal* 31, no. 2 (2008).

Dyrness, William. *Christian Apologetics in a World Community*. Downers Grove, Ill.: InterVarsity Press, 1983.

Feuerbach, Ludwig. *The Essence of Christianity*, translated by George Eliot. New York: Harper & Row, 1957.

Freud, Sigmund. *The Future of an Illusion*. 1927; reprint, Garden City, N.Y.: Anchor Books, 1961.

Geisler, Norman, and Winfried Corduan. *Philosophy of Religion*. 2nd ed. Eugene, Ore.: Wipf & Stock, 2003.

Groothuis, Douglas. *Confronting the New Age*. Downers Grove, Ill.: InterVarsity Press, 1988.

————. "Was Moses Rational After All?" *The Bulletin of the Evangelical Philosophical Society* 17 (1994): 21-44.

Gruzalski, Bart. *On the Buddha*. Belmont, Calif.: Wadsworth, 2000.

Guinness, Os. "The Counterfeit Infinity." In *The Dust of Death*. 1973; reprint, Wheaton, Ill.: Crossway, 1994.

————. *God in the Dark: The Assurance of Faith Beyond a Shadow of Doubt*. Wheaton, Ill.: Crossway, 1997.

Habermas, Gary. *The Thomas Factor: Using Your Doubts to Draw Closer to God*. Nashville: Broadman & Holman, 1999.

Hart, David Bentley. *Atheist Delusions: The Christian Revolution and Its Fashionable Enemies*. New Haven, Conn.: Yale University Press, 2009.

Hick, John. *Philosophy of Religion*. 4th ed. Englewood Cliffs, N.J.: Prentice-Hall, 1990.

James, William. *The Varieties of Religious Experience.* New York: Longmans, Green, 1902.

Küng, Hans. *Does God Exist?* New York: Doubleday, 1980.

Lewis, C. S. *Mere Christianity.* 1943; reprint, New York: Simon & Schuster, 1996.

—————. *Surprised by Joy: The Shape of My Early Life.* New York: Harcourt Brace Jovanovich, 1955.

—————. *The Weight of Glory and Other Essays.* 1949; reprint, San Francisco: HarperSanFrancisco, 1980.

Martin, Walter. "Mormonism." In *The Kingdom of the Cults.* Rev. ed. Edited by Hank Hanegraff. 1967; reprint, Minneapolis: Bethany House, 1997.

—————. "The Unanswerable Argument." In *Essential Christianity.* Ventura, Calif.: Regal, 1980.

Mavrodes, George. *Belief in God: A Study in the Epistemology of Religion.* New York: Random House, 1970.

Moreland, J. P. *Kingdom Triangle.* Grand Rapids: Zondervan, 2007.

—————. *Scaling the Secular City.* Grand Rapids: Baker, 1987.

Murray, Andrew. *With Christ in the School of Prayer.* New Kensington, Penn.: Whitaker House, 1981.

Nagel, Thomas. *The Last Word.* New York: Oxford University Press, 1998.

Nicholi, Armand. *The Question of God: C. S. Lewis and Sigmund Freud Debate God, Love, Sex, and the Meaning of Life.* New York: Free Press, 2002.

Otto, Rudolf. *The Idea of the Holy.* 2nd ed. New York: Oxford University Press, 1958.

Pascal, Blaise. *Pensées,* edited and translated by Alban Krailsheimer. New York: Penguin, 1966.

Reisser, Paul C., Dale Mabe and Robert Velarde. "Is God a Dependent Variable?" In *Examining Alternative Medicine: An Inside Look at the Benefits and Risks.* Downers Grove, Ill.: InterVarsity Press, 2001.

Richards, Larry. *Every Covenant and Promise in the Bible.* Nashville: Thomas Nelson, 1998.

Rushdoony, Rousas John. *Freud.* Nutley, N.J.: Presbyterian & Reformed, 1965.

Schaeffer, Francis. *True Spirituality.* Wheaton, Ill.: Tyndale House, 1972.

Schmidt, Alvin. *The Great Divide: The Failure of Islam and the Triumph of the West.* Boston: Regina Orthodox Press, 2004.

—————. *How Christianity Changed the World.* Grand Rapids: Zondervan, 2004.

Sproul, R. C. *The Holiness of God.* Wheaton, Ill.: Tyndale House, 1985.

—————. *If There Is a God, Why Are There Atheists?* Wheaton, Ill.: Tyndale House, 1988.

Stace, W. T. *Mysticism and Philosophy.* New York: Jeremy Tarcher, 1960.

Stott, John. "God's People United in Christ." *In The Message of Romans: God's Good News for the World.* The Bible Speaks Today. Downers Grove, Ill.: InterVarsity Press, 1994.

————. *Men Made New.* Downers Grove, Ill.: InterVarsity Press, 1966.

————. *Why I Am a Christian.* Downers Grove, Ill.: InterVarsity Press, 2004.

Swinburne, Richard. *The Existence of God.* 2nd ed. New York: Oxford University Press, 2004.

Vitz, Paul. *Faith of the Fatherless: The Psychology of Atheism.* Dallas: Spence, 1999.

————. *Sigmund Freud's Christian Unconscious.* Grand Rapids: Eerdmans, 1993.

Wainwright, William. *Philosophy of Religion.* 2nd ed. Belmont, Calif.: Wadsworth, 1999.

Wiebe, Phillip H. *God and Other Spirits.* New York: Oxford University Press, 2004.

————. *Visions of Jesus.* New York: Oxford University Press, 1997.

Wilber, Ken. *A Brief History of Everything.* 2nd ed. Boston: Shambhala, 2000.

Yandell, Keith E. "Does Numinous Experience Provide Evidence That God Exists?" In *Christianity and Philosophy.* Grand Rapids: Eerdmans, 1984.

————. *The Epistemology of Religious Experience.* New York: Cambridge University Press, 1994.

————. *Philosophy of Religion.* New York: Routledge, 1999.

Zaehner, R. C. *Mysticism: Sacred and Profane.* New York: Oxford University Press, 1957.

————. *Zen, Drugs, and Mysticism.* New York: Pantheon, 1972.

Chapter 17: The Uniqueness of Humanity

Adams, Robert. "Flavors, Colors, and God." In *The Virtue of Faith.* New York: Oxford University Press, 1987.

Adler, Mortimer. *The Difference of Man and the Difference It Makes.* New York: Holt, Rinehart & Winston, 1967.

Anderson, Stephen R. *Dr. Doolittle's Delusion: Animals and the Uniqueness of Human Language.* New Haven, Conn.: Yale University Press, 2004.

Augustine. *The City of God.*

————. *The Trinity.*

Beilby, James, ed. *Naturalism Defeated? Essay on Plantinga's Evolutionary Argument Against Naturalism.* Ithaca, N.Y.: Cornell University Press, 2002.

Benson, Ophelia, and Jeremy Stangroom. *Why Truth Matters.* New York: Continuum, 2006.

Beuregard, Mario, and Denise O'Leary. *The Spiritual Brain: A Neuroscientist's Case for the Existence of the Soul.* San Francisco: HarperOne, 2007.

Chalmers, David. *The Conscious Mind.* New York: Oxford University Press, 1997.

Chesterton, G. K. *Generally Speaking.* New York: Dodd, Mead, 1929.

————. *Orthodoxy.* 1908; reprint, New York: Image Books, 1959.

Churchland, Patricia. "Epistemology in an Age of Neuroscience." *Journal of Philosophy* 84 (1987): 548-49.

Churchland, Paul. *Matter and Consciousness.* Cambridge, Mass.: MIT Press, 1984.

Clark, Gordon H. *A Christian View of Men and Things*. Grand Rapids: Eerdmans, 1952.

Cooper, John. *Body, Soul, and the Life Everlasting: Biblical Anthropology and the Monism-Dualism Debate*. Rev. ed. Grand Rapids: Eerdmans, 2000.

Corduan, Winfried. *Reasonable Faith: Basic Christian Apologetics*. Nashville: Broadman & Holman, 1994.

Darwin, Charles, to W. Graham. July 3, 1881. In *The Life and Letters of Charles Darwin*, edited by Francis Darwin. 1897; reprint, Boston: Elibron, 2005.

Descartes, René. *Meditations on First Philosophy*.

Flew, Antony. *Evolutionary Ethics*. New York: St. Martin's Press, 1967.

Green, Joel, and Stuart L. Palmer, eds. *In Search of the Soul: Four Views of the Mind-Body Problem*. Downers Grove, Ill.: InterVarsity Press, 2005.

Groothuis, Douglas. *On Jesus*. Belmont, Calif.: Wadsworth, 2003.

———. *Truth Decay*. Downers Grove, Ill.: InterVarsity Press, 2000.

Guinness, Os. *The Dust of Death*. Rev. ed. 1973; reprint, Wheaton, Ill.: Crossway, 1994.

Hasker, William. *Metaphysics*. Downers Grove, Ill.: InterVarsity Press, 1982.

Leibniz, Gottfried. *Monadology and Other Philosophical Essays*, translated and edited by Paul Schrecker and Anne Martin Schrecker. New York: Bobbs-Merrill, 1965.

Lewis, C. S. "Animal Pain." In *The Problem of Pain*. 1962; reprint, New York: Touchstone, 1996.

———. *Christian Reflections*. Grand Rapids: Eerdmans, 1987.

———. *Miracles*. 1947; reprint, San Francisco: HarperSanFrancisco, 1996.

MacKay, Donald M. *Human Science and Human Dignity*. Downers Grove, Ill.: InterVarsity Press, 1977.

Marlin, George J., Richard P. Rabatin and John L. Swan, eds. *The Quotable Chesterton*. Garden City, N.Y.: Image Books, 1987.

McGinn, Colin. *The Mysterious Flame*. New York: Basic Books, 2000.

Moreland, J. P. *Consciousness and the Existence of God*. New York: Routledge, 2008.

———. *Scaling the Secular City*. Grand Rapids: Baker, 1987.

Moreland, J. P., and Scott Rae. *Body and Soul*. Downers Grove, Ill.: InterVarsity Press, 2000.

Moreland, J. P., and William Lane Craig. *Philosophical Foundations for a Christian Worldview*. Downers Grove, Ill.: InterVarsity Press, 2004.

Mumma, Howard. *Camus and the Minister*. Brewster, Mass.: Paraclete Press, 2000.

Nietzsche, Friedrich. *Daybreak: Thoughts on the Prejudices of Morality*, translated by R. J. Hollingdale. New York: Cambridge University Press, 1985.

Oller, John W., and John L. Omdahl. "Origin of the Human Language Capacity: In Whose Image?" In *The Creation Hypothesis*, edited by J. P. Moreland. Downers Grove, Ill.: InterVarsity Press, 1994.

Pascal, Blaise. *Pensées,* edited and translated by A. J. Krailsheimer. New York: Penguin, 1985.

Penfield, Wilder. *The Mystery of the Mind.* Princeton, N.J.: Princeton University Press, 1975.

Pinker, Steven. *How the Mind Works.* New York: W. W. Norton, 1997.

Plantinga, Alvin. *Warranted Christian Belief.* New York: Oxford University Press, 2000.

Polkinghorne, John. *Quantum Theory: A Very Short Introduction.* New York: Oxford University Press, 2002.

Popper, Karl R., and John C. Eccles. *The Self and Its Brain.* London: Routledge & Kegan Paul, 1977.

Purtill, Richard. *Reason to Believe.* Grand Rapids: Eerdmans, 1974.

Reppert, Victor. "The Argument from Reason." In *Blackwell Companion to Natural Theology,* edited by William Lane Craig and J. P. Moreland. Malden, Mass.: Wiley-Blackwell, 2009.

———. *C. S. Lewis's Dangerous Idea: In Defense of the Argument from Reason.* Downers Grove, Ill.: InterVarsity Press, 2002.

Robinson, Howard. *Matter and Science.* Cambridge: Cambridge University Press, 1982.

Sartre, Jean Paul. *Being and Nothingness: An Essay on Phenomenological Ontology.* 1943; reprint, New York: Routledge, 1994.

Schwartz, Jeffrey, and Sharon Begley. *The Mind and the Brain: Neuroplasticity and the Power of Mental Force.* New York: Harper Perennial, 2003.

Searle, John. *Minds, Brains, and Science.* Cambridge, Mass.: Harvard University Press, 1984.

Shaffer, Jerome. "The Mind-Body Problem." In *The Encyclopedia of Philosophy,* edited by Paul Edwards. New York: Macmillan, 1967.

Sire, James W. *The Universe Next Door: A Basic Worldview Catalog.* 5th ed. Downers Grove, Ill.: InterVarsity Press, 2009.

Smart, J. J. C. "Materialism." *Journal of Philosophy* 22 (1963): 660.

Swinburne, Richard. *The Existence of God.* 2nd ed. New York: Oxford University Press, 2004.

Taliaferro, Charles. *Consciousness and the Mind of God.* New York: Cambridge University Press, 1994.

———. "The Project of Natural Theology." In *Blackwell Companion to Natural Theology,* edited by William Lane Craig and J. P. Moreland. Malden, Mass.: Wiley-Blackwell, 2009.

Tallis, Raymond. "The Unnatural Selection of Consciousness." *The Philosopher's Magazine.* 3rd quarter (2009): 28-35.

Taylor, Richard. *Metaphysics.* 4th ed. Englewood Cliffs, N.J.: Prentice-Hall, 1990.

Wilson, Clifford, and Donald McKeon. *The Language Gap.* Grand Rapids: Zondervan, 1984.

Wright, N. T. *The Resurrection of the Son of God*. Minneapolis: Fortress, 2003.

Yandell, Keith E. *Philosophy of Religion*. New York: Routledge, 1999.

Chapter 18: Deposed Royalty

Chesterton, G. K. *Orthodoxy*. 1908; reprint, New York: Image Books 1959.

Cuneo, Terence D. "Combating the Noetic Effects of Sin: Pascal's Strategy for Natural Theology." *Faith and Philosophy* 11, no. 4 (1994): 645-47.

Erickson, Millard. *Christian Theology*. 3 vols. Grand Rapids: Baker, 1983-1985.

Groothuis, Douglas. "Are Theistic Arguments Religiously Useless? A Pascalian Objection Examined." *Trinity Journal*, n.s., 15, no. 2 (1994).

—————. "Bacon and Pascal on Mastery Over Nature." *Research in Philosophy and Technology* 14 (1994): 191-203.

—————. "Pascal's Biblical Omission Argument Against Natural Theology." *Asbury Theological Journal* 52, no. 2 (1997): 17-26.

—————. "Proofs, Pride, and Incarnation: Is Natural Theology Theologically Taboo?" *Journal of the Evangelical Theological Society* (March 1995): 67-76.

Johnson, Paul. *Intellectuals*. New York: Harper & Row, 1988.

Lewis, Gordon R. *Testing Christianity's Truth Claims*. Chicago: Moody Press, 1976.

Lewis, Gordon R., and Bruce A. Demarest. *Integrative Theology*. Grand Rapids: Zondervan, 1990.

MacGregor, Geddes. *Introduction to Religious Philosophy*. Boston: Houghton Mifflin, 1959.

Pascal, Blaise. *Pensées,* edited and translated by Alban Krailsheimer. New York: Penguin, 1966.

Peirce, Charles. *Collected Papers of Charles Sanders Peirce,* edited by C. Hartshorne and P. Weiss. 6 vols. Cambridge, Mass.: Harvard University Press, 1931-1935.

Plato. *Phaedrus*.

Ramm, Bernard. *The Christian View of Science and Scripture*. Grand Rapids: Eerdmans, 1954.

Ross, Hugh. *Creation and Time*. Colorado Springs: NavPress, 1994.

Trueblood, D. Elton. *Philosophy of Religion*. Grand Rapids: Baker, 1957.

Schaeffer, Francis A. *The God Who Is There*. 30th anniv. ed. Downers Grove, Ill.: InterVarsity Press, 1998.

Shakespeare, William. *King Lear*.

Steiner, George. *In Bluebeard's Castle: Some Notes Towards the Redefinition of Culture*. New Haven, Conn.: Yale, University Press, 1971.

Warner, Martin. *Philosophical Finesse*. Oxford: Clarendon, 1989.

Chapter 19: Jesus of Nazareth (by Craig Blomberg)

In addition to the sources mentioned throughout the notes, see especially:

Blomberg, Craig L. *The Historical Reliability of John's Gospel: Issues and Commentary*. Downers Grove, Ill.: InterVarsity Press, 2001.

————. *The Historical Reliability of the Gospels*. 2nd ed. Downers Grove, Ill.: InterVarsity Press, 2007.

Bock, Darrell L. *The Missing Gospels: Unearthing the Truth Behind Alternative Christianities*. Nashville: Nelson, 2006. An excellent introduction to the beliefs of Gnosticism and other ancient mutations of Christianity deemed heretical, showing just how different and inferior they really are to historic Christianity when considered as entire worldviews.

Bowman, Robert M., Jr., and J. Ed Komoszewski. *Putting Jesus in His Place: The Case for the Deity of Christ*. Grand Rapids: Kregel, 2007. Debunks in detail the myth that first-century Christians did not almost uniformly believe in the deity of Christ, from the earliest stages of the New Testament onward. Makes a strong case for believing that Jesus *was* indeed divine.

Boyd, Gregory A., and Paul R. Eddy. *Lord or Legend? Wrestling with the Jesus Dilemma*. Grand Rapids: Baker, 2007. An abbreviated and more popular-level form of their larger work, *The Jesus Legend: A Case for the Historical Reliability of the Synoptic Jesus Tradition* (2007). Covers all the most important issues succinctly while fully abreast of the whole range of recent scholarship.

Evans, Craig A. *Fabricating Jesus: How Modern Scholars Distort the Gospels*. Downers Grove, Ill.: InterVarsity Press, 2006. A careful sifting of all of the sources outside the New Testament alleged by some to enable us to view the historical Jesus in radically different terms than the four canonical Gospels present. In short, the conclusion is that they fail in this endeavor.

Jones, Timothy P. *Misquoting Truth: A Guide to the Fallacies of Bart Ehrman's* Misquoting Jesus. Downers Grove, Ill.: InterVarsity Press, 2007. A point-by-point refutation of the misleading claims of Ehrman's book, *plus* an equally helpful critique of his books on the so-called lost Gospels and lost Christianities. Surveys a huge amount of scholarship and presents it in a remarkably readable, bite-size fashion.

Roberts, Mark D. *Can We Trust the Gospels? Investigating the Reliability of Matthew, Mark, Luke, and John*. Wheaton, Ill.: Crossway, 2007. In many ways, without obviously intending to do so, a simplified and very popularized form of almost the identical array of issues I treat in my book *The Historical Reliability of the Gospels*, for those who find even my semipopularization of the issues too daunting.

Chapter 20: The Claims, Credentials and Achievements of Jesus Christ

Anderson, Norman. *Jesus Christ: The Witness of History*. Downers Grove, Ill.: InterVarsity Press, 1985.

Bauckham, Richard. *Jesus and the God of Israel: God Crucified and Other Studies on the New Testament's Christology of Divine Identity*. Grand Rapids: Eerdmans, 2008.

Beckwith, Francis. "Baha'i Faith." In *New Religious Movements*, edited by Ronald Enroth. Downers Grove, Ill.: InterVarsity Press, 2005.

Blomberg, Craig L. "Further Reflections on Jesus' View of the Old Testament." In *The Scripture Project: The Bible and Biblical Authority in the New Millennium*, edited by D. A. Carson. Vol. 1. Grand Rapids: Eerdmans, forthcoming.

—————. *The Historical Reliability of John's Gospel*. Downers Grove, Ill.: InterVarsity Press, 2002.

—————. *The Historical Reliability of the Gospels*. 20th anniv. ed. Downers Grove, Ill.: InterVarsity Press, 2007.

—————. *Interpreting the Parables of Jesus*. Downers Grove, Ill.: InterVarsity Press, 1990.

Bonhoeffer, Dietrich. *The Cost of Discipleship*. New York: Touchstone, 1995.

Bowman, Robert M., Jr., and J. Ed. Komoszewski. *Putting Jesus in His Place: The Case for the Deity of Christ*. Grand Rapids: Kregel, 2007.

Brown, Michael L. *Answering Jewish Objections to Jesus*. Grand Rapids: Baker, 2003.

Bruce, F. F. *New Testament History*. Garden City, N.Y.: Doubleday, 1972.

Corduan, Winfried. *Neighboring Faiths*. Downers Grove, Ill.: InterVarsity Press, 1998.

Craig, William Lane. *Reasonable Faith*. 3rd ed. Wheaton, Ill.: Crossway, 2008.

Erickson, Millard. *God in Three Persons*. Grand Rapids: Baker, 1995.

—————. *The Word Became Flesh: An Incarnational Christology*. Grand Rapids: Baker, 1991.

Evans, Craig. "Life-of-Jesus Research and the Eclipse of Mythology." *Theological Studies* 54 (1993): 3-36.

Feinberg, Charles Lee. *Is the Virgin Birth in the Old Testament?* Whittier, Calif.: Emeth, 1967.

Frame, John. "The Apostles' View of the Old Testament." In *The Doctrine of the Word of God*. Phillipsburg, N.J.: P & R Publishing, 2010.

—————. "Jesus' View of the Old Testament." In *The Doctrine of the Word of God*. Phillipsburg, N.J.: P & R Publishing, 2010.

—————. "The Virgin Birth." In *Evangelical Dictionary of Theology*, edited by Walter A. Elwell. Grand Rapids: Baker, 1984.

Gabriel, Mark. *Jesus and Muhammad*. Lake Mary, Fla.: Charisma House, 2004.

Geisler, Norman. *Systematic Theology*. Minneapolis: Bethany House, 2002.

—————. "The Virgin Birth." In *Baker Encyclopedia of Christian Apologetics*. Grand Rapids: Baker, 1999.

Groothuis, Douglas. "The Ethics of Jesus." In *On Jesus*. Belmont, Calif.: Wadsworth, 2003.

—————. *On Jesus*. Belmont, Calif.: Wadsworth, 2003.

—————. *Jesus in an Age of Controversy*. 1996; reprint, Eugene, Ore.: Wipf & Stock, 2002.

Gruber, Elmar R., and Holger Kersten. *The Original Jesus: The Buddhist Sources of Christianity*. Rockport, Mass.: Element Books, 1995.

Gruenler, Royce. *New Approaches to Jesus and the Gospels*. Grand Rapids: Baker, 1982.

Habermas, Gary. *The Risen Jesus and Future Hope.* Lanham, Md.: Rowman & Littlefield, 2003.

Halverson, Dean, ed. *The Compact Guide to Religion.* Colorado Springs: NavPress, 1996.

Harris, Murray. *Three Crucial Questions About Jesus.* Eugene, Ore.: Wipf & Stock, 2008.

Hawthorne, G. F. "Amen." In *Dictionary of Jesus and the Gospels,* edited by Joel B. Green, Scot McKnight and I. Howard Marshall. Downers Grove, Ill.: Inter-Varsity Press, 1992.

Johnson, Paul. *Jesus: A Biography From a Believer.* New York: Viking, 2010.

Jones, E. Stanley. *The Christ of the Indian Road.* New York: Grosset & Dunlap, 1925.

Kaiser, Walter. *The Messiah in the Old Testament.* Grand Rapids: Zondervan, 1995.

Leung, Thomas I. S. "Confucianism." In *The Compact Guide to World Religions,* edited by Dean Halverson. Minneapolis: Bethany House, 1996.

Lewis, C. S. *Miracles.* New York: Macmillan, 1960.

—————. "What Are We to Make of Jesus Christ?" In *God in the Dock.* Grand Rapids: Eerdmans, 1970.

Machen, J. Gresham. *The Virgin Birth of Christ.* New York: Harper, 1930.

Marshall, I. Howard. "Son of Man." In *Dictionary of Jesus and the Gospels,* edited by Joel B. Green, Scot McKnight and I. Howard Marshall. Downers Grove, Ill.: InterVarsity Press, 1992.

Masani, Sir Rustom. *Zoroastrianism: The Religion of the Good Life.* New York: Macmillan, 1968.

McNutt, Francis. *The Nearly Perfect Crime: How the Church Almost Killed the Ministry of Healing.* Grand Rapids: Chosen Books, 2005.

Moreland, J. P. *Kingdom Triangle.* Grand Rapids: Zondervan, 2007.

Newman, Robert C. *The Evidence of Prophecy.* Hatfield, Penn.: Interdisciplinary Biblical Research Institute, 2001.

Parrinder, Geoffrey. *Avatar and Incarnation.* New York: Barnes & Noble, 1970.

Payne, Philip B. "Jesus' Implicit Claim to Deity in His Parables." *Trinity Journal,* n.s., 2, no. 1 (1981): 3-23.

Phillips, J. B. *Your God Is Too Small.* New York: Macmillan, 1979.

Prothero, Stephen. *American Jesus.* New York: Farrar, Straus, & Giroux, 2004.

Ramm, Bernard. *An Evangelical Christology: Ecumenic and Historic.* Nashville: Thomas Nelson, 1985.

Raymond, Robert L. *Systematic Theology.* 2nd ed. Nashville: Thomas Nelson, 1998.

Sayers, Dorothy L. *Are Women Human?* Grand Rapids: Eerdmans, 1971.

Schaeffer, Francis. *True Spirituality.* 30th anniv. ed. Wheaton, Ill.: Tyndale House, 2001.

Stauffer, Ethelbert. *Jesus and His Story.* New York: Alfred A. Knopf, 1974.

Stott, John. *The Authority of the Bible.* Downers Grove, Ill.: InterVarsity Press, 1974.

————. *Basic Christianity.* 2nd ed. Downers Grove, Ill.: InterVarsity Press, 1971.

————. "The Hound of Heaven." In *Why I Am a Christian.* Downers Grove, Ill.: InterVarsity Press, 2002.

Twelftree, Graham. *Jesus the Exorcist: A Contribution to the Study of the Historical Jesus.* Peabody, Mass.: Hendrickson, 1994.

————. *In the Name of Jesus: Exorcism Among Early Christians.* Grand Rapids: Baker Academic, 2007.

Warfield, B. B. "'It Says:' 'Scripture Says:' 'God Says.'" In *The Inspiration and Authority of the Bible.* 1948; reprint, Philadelphia: Presbyterian & Reformed, 1970.

————. *The Person and Work of Christ.* Phillipsburg, N.J.: Presbyterian & Reformed. 1950.

————. "The Terms 'Scripture' and 'Scriptures' as Employed in the New Testament." In *The Inspiration and Authority of the Bible.* 1948; reprint, Philadelphia: Presbyterian & Reformed, 1970.

Wells, David. *The Person of Christ.* Westchester, Ill.: Crossway, 1984.

Wenham, John. *Christ and the Bible.* 2nd ed. 1972; reprint, Grand Rapids: Baker, 1984.

Witherington, Ben, III. "Birth of Jesus." In *Dictionary of Jesus and the Gospels,* edited by Joel Green, Scot McKnight and I. Howard Marshall. Downers Grove, Ill.: InterVarsity Press, 1992.

Yamauchi, Edwin. *Jesus, Zoroaster, Buddha, Socrates, Muhammad.* Rev. ed. Downers Grove, Ill.: InterVarsity Press, 1972.

Chapter 21: Defending the Incarnation

Beversluis, John. *C. S. Lewis and the Search for Rational Religion.* 2nd ed. Amherst, N.Y.: Prometheus, 2007.

Brown, Dan. *The Da Vinci Code.* New York: Doubleday, 2003.

Buel, Jon A., and O. Quentin Hyder. *Jesus: God, Ghost, or Guru?* Grand Rapids: Zondervan, 1978.

Chesterton, G. K. *The Everlasting Man.* New York: Image Books, 1925.

Chopra, Deepak. *The Third Jesus.* New York: Harmony Books, 2008.

Collins, Gary. "The Psychological Evidence." In Lee Strobel, *The Case for Christ.* Grand Rapids: Zondervan, 1998.

Davis, Stephen T. "Jesus: Mad, Bad, or God?" In *Christian Philosophical Theology.* New York: Oxford University Press, 2006.

————. "The Mad/Bad/God Trilemma: A Reply to Daniel Howard-Snyder." *Faith and Philosophy* 21 (2004): 480-92.

Devan, Benjamin B., and Thomas W. Smythe. "The Character of Jesus Defended." *Christian Apologetics Journal* 5, no. 2 (2006): 109-40.

Durant, Will. *Caesar and Christ.* Vol. 2, *The Story of Civilization.* New York: Simon & Schuster, 1944.

Erickson, Millard. "The Development of Incarnational Christology. (1) To the

Council of Chalcedon." In *The Word Became Flesh: An Incarnational Christology*. Grand Rapids: Baker, 1991.

Groothuis, Douglas. *Confronting the New Age*. Downers Grove, Ill.: InterVarsity Press, 1988.

————. *On Jesus*. Belmont, Calif.: Wadsworth, 2003.

————. *Jesus in an Age of Controversy*. 1996; reprint, Eugene, Ore.: Wipf & Stock, 2002.

————. *Unmasking the New Age*. Downers Grove, Ill.: InterVarsity Press, 1986.

Hick, John. *The Metaphor of God Incarnate: Christology in a Pluralistic Age*. Louisville: Westminster John Knox, 1994.

Hitchens, Christopher. *God Is Not Great: How Religion Poisons Everything*. New York: Twelve Books, 2007.

Horner, David. "*Aut Deus Aut Malus Homo:* A Defense of C. S. Lewis's 'Shocking Alternative.'" In *C. S. Lewis as Philosopher*, edited by David Baggett, Gary R. Habermas and Jerry L. Walls. Downers Grove, Ill.: InterVarsity Press, 2007.

Howard-Snyder, Daniel. "Was Jesus Mad, Bad, or God . . . or Only Mistaken?" *Faith and Philosophy* 21 (2004): 456-79.

Hurtado, Larry. *Lord Jesus Christ*. Grand Rapids: Eerdmans, 2005.

Kierkegaard, Søren. *Philosophical Fragments*, translated by Edna Hong and Walter Hong. Princeton, N.J.: Princeton University Press, 1985.

Kreeft, Peter, and Ronald K. Tacelli. *Handbook of Christian Apologetics*. Downers Grove, Ill.: InterVarsity Press, 1994.

LaTourette, Kenneth Scott. *The Unquenchable Light*. New York: Harper & Brothers, 1941.

Lewis, C. S. *Mere Christianity*. 1943; reprint, New York: Touchstone, 1996.

————. "What Are We to Make of Jesus Christ?" In *God in the Dock*, edited by Walter Hooper. Grand Rapids: Eerdmans, 1970.

Lewis, Gordon R., and Bruce A. Demarest. *Integrative Theology*. Grand Rapids: Zondervan, 1990.

Machen, J. Gresham. *Christianity and Liberalism*. 1923; reprint, Grand Rapids: Eerdmans, 2009.

Montgomery, John Warwick. *History and Christianity*. Downers Grove, Ill.: InterVarsity Press, 1965.

Morris, Thomas V. *The Logic of God Incarnate*. New York: Cornell University Press, 1986.

————. *Our Idea of God: An Introduction to Philosophical Theology*. Downers Grove, Ill.: InterVarsity Press, 1991.

————. "Rationality and the Christian Revelation." In *Christian Faith and Practice in the Modern World*, edited by Mark A. Noll and David F. Wells. Grand Rapids: Eerdmans, 1988.

Pelikan, Jarslav. *Jesus Through the Centuries: His Place in the History of Culture*. New Haven, Conn.: Yale University Press, 1985.

Rhodes, Ron. *The Counterfeit Christ of the New Age Movement.* Grand Rapids: Baker, 1991.

Rushdoony, Rousas John. *The Foundations of Social Order: Studies in the Creed and Councils of the Early Church.* Vallecito, Calif.: Chalcedon, 2003.

Samples, Kenneth. *Without a Doubt.* Grand Rapids: Baker, 2004.

Schaeffer, Francis A. *The God Who Is There.* 30th anniv. ed. Downers Grove, Ill.: InterVarsity Press, 1998.

Swinburne, Richard. *Was Jesus God?* New York: Oxford University Press, 2008.

Witherington, Ben, III. *The Gospel Code: Novel Claims About Jesus, Mary Magdalene and Da Vinci.* Downers Grove, Ill.: InterVarsity Press, 2004.

Chapter 22: The Resurrection of Jesus

Anderson, J. N. D. *Christianity and Comparative Religion.* Downers Grove, Ill.: InterVarsity Press, 1971.

Anderson, Norman. *Jesus Christ: The Witness of History.* Downers Grove, Ill.: InterVarsity Press, 1985.

—————. *A Lawyer Among the Theologians.* Grand Rapids: Eerdmans, 1974.

Archer, Gleason. *Encyclopedia of Biblical Difficulties.* Grand Rapids: Zondervan, 1982.

Blomberg, Craig L. *Jesus and the Gospels: An Introduction and Survey.* 2nd ed. Nashville: B & H Academic, 2009.

Carson, D. A., and Douglas Moo. *Introduction to the New Testament.* 2nd ed. Grand Rapids: Zondervan, 2002.

Carson, D. A., ed. *From Sabbath to Lord's Day: A Biblical, Historical, and Theological Investigation.* Eugene, Ore.: Wipf & Stock, 2000.

Cetzer, C. "Excellent Women: Female Witnesses to the Resurrection." *Journal of Biblical Literature* 116 (1997): 259-72.

Charlesworth, James. *James Within Judaism.* New York: Doubleday, 1988.

Clark, David K. "Miracles in the World Religions." In *In Defense of Miracles: A Comprehensive Case for God's Action in History,* edited by R. Douglas Geivett and Gary Habermas. Downers Grove, Ill.: InterVarsity Press, 1996.

Collins, C. John. *The God of Miracles: An Evangelical Examination of God's Action in the World.* Wheaton, Ill.: Crossway, 2000.

Colson, Charles. *Loving God.* Grand Rapids: Zondervan, 1983.

Craig, William Lane. "Evidence for the Empty Tomb." In *In Defense of Miracles: A Comprehensive Case for God's Action in History,* edited by Gary Habermas and R. Douglas Geivett. Downers Grove, Ill.: InterVarsity Press, 1997.

—————. *Knowing the Truth About the Resurrection.* Ann Arbor, Mich.: Servant Books, 1988.

—————. "Opening Statements." In *Jesus' Resurrection: Fact or Figment?* edited by Paul Copan and Ronald Tacelli. Downers Grove, Ill.: InterVarsity Press, 2000.

—————. *Reasonable Faith.* 3rd ed. Wheaton, Ill.: Crossway, 2008.

Davis, Stephen T. *Risen Indeed: Making Sense of the Resurrection.* Grand Rapids: Eerdmans, 1993.

Dembski, William. *The Design Revolution.* Downers Grove, Ill.: InterVarsity Press, 2004.

Downing, David. *The Most Reluctant Convert: C. S. Lewis's Journey to Faith.* Downers Grove, Ill.: InterVarsity Press, 2002.

Earman, John. *Hume's Abject Failure.* New York: Oxford University Press, 2000.

Eddy, Paul Rhodes, and Gregory Boyd. *The Jesus Legend.* Grand Rapids: Baker, 2007.

Edwards, James R. *Is Jesus the Only Savior?* Grand Rapids: Eerdmans, 2005.

Edwards, William D., Wesley J. Gabel and Floyd E. Hosmer. "On the Physical Death of Jesus Christ." *Journal of the American Medical Association* 255, no. 11 (1986): 1455-63.

Flew, Antony. "Miracles." In *The Encyclopedia of Philosophy,* edited by Paul Edwards. New York: Macmillan, 1967.

Flew, Antony, and Gary Habermas. "My Pilgrimage from Atheism to Theism: A Discussion Between Antony Flew and Gary Habermas." *Philosophia Christi* 6, no. 2 (2004): 197-211.

Flew, Antony, and Roy Abraham Varghese. *There Is a God.* San Francisco: HarperOne, 2007.

Fuller, Reginald. *The Formation of the Resurrection Narratives.* New York: Macmillan, 1971.

Geisler, Norman. *Baker Encyclopedia of Christian Apologetics.* Grand Rapids: Baker, 1999.

Geisler, Norman, and Abdul Saleeb. "An Evaluation of the Qur'an." In *Answering Islam.* Rev. ed. Grand Rapids: Baker, 2002.

Geivett, Douglas R. "The Epistemology of Resurrection Belief." In *The Resurrection of Jesus: John Dominic Crossan and N. T. Wright in Dialogue,* edited by John Dominic Crossan, N. T. Wright and Robert B. Stewart. Minneapolis: Fortress, 2006.

Green, Michael. *The Empty Cross of Jesus.* Downers Grove, Ill.: InterVarsity Press, 1984.

Groothuis, Douglas. *Jesus in an Age of Controversy.* 1996; reprint, Eugene, Ore.: Wipf & Stock, 2002.

Habermas, Gary R. "Explaining Away Jesus' Resurrection: The Recent Revival of Hallucination Theories." *The Christian Research Journal* 23 (2001): 26-31.

————. "Resurrection Claims in Non-Christian Religions." *Religious Studies* 25 (1989): 167-77.

————. "The Resurrection of Jesus and Recent Agnosticism." In *Reasons for Faith: Making a Case for the Christian Faith,* edited by Norman L. Geisler and Chad V. Meister. Wheaton, Ill.: Crossway, 2007.

————. "Resurrection Research 1975 to the Present: What Are Critical Scholars Saying?" *Journal for the Study of the Historical Jesus* 3, no. 2 (2005): 135-53.

——. *The Risen Jesus and Future Hope.* Lanham, Md.: Rowman & Littlefield, 2003.

——. "A Summary Critique: Questioning the Existence of Jesus." *The Christian Research Journal* 22, no. 3 (2000): 54-56.

Habermas, Gary, and Antony Flew. *Did Jesus Rise from the Dead?* edited by Terry L. Miethe. San Francisco: Harper & Row, 1987.

——. *Resurrected? An Atheist and Theist Dialogue,* edited by John Ankerberg. Lanham, Md.: Rowman & Littlefield, 2005.

Habermas, Gary, and Michael Licona. *The Case for the Resurrection of Jesus.* Grand Rapids: Kregel, 2004.

Harris, Murray. *From Grace to Glory: Resurrection in the New Testament.* Grand Rapids: Zondervan, 1990.

Hume, David. *An Enquiry Concerning Human Understanding,* edited by T. Beauchamp. Oxford: Oxford University Press, 2001.

Hume, David. "Of Miracles." In *Writings on Religion,* edited by Antony Flew. Chicago: Open Court, 1992.

Hurtado, Larry. *How on Earth Did Jesus Become a God?* Grand Rapids: Eerdmans, 2006.

——. *Lord Jesus Christ.* Grand Rapids: Eerdmans, 2005.

Josephus. *Antiquities of the Jews.*

Justin Martyr. *Dialogue with Trypho.*

Keener, Craig. *Gift and Giver: The Holy Spirit for Today.* Grand Rapids: Baker Academic, 2001.

Kreeft, Peter, and Ronald Tacelli. *Handbook of Christian Apologetics.* Downers Grove, Ill.: InterVarsity Press, 1994.

Ladd, George Eldon. *I Believe in the Resurrection of Jesus.* Grand Rapids: Eerdmans, 1975.

Lapide, Pinchas. *The Resurrection of Jesus.* Minneapolis: Augsburg, 1983.

Lewis, C. S. *Miracles: A Preliminary Study.* 1947; reprint, HarperSanFrancisco, 1996.

——. "Myth Became Fact." In *Christian Reflections.* Grand Rapids: Eerdmans, 1970.

Martin, Michael. *The Case Against Christianity.* Philadelphia: Temple University Press, 1993.

McCann, Frank. "Divine Conservation." In *Guide to the Philosophy of Religion,* edited by Phillip L. Quinn and Charles Taliaferro. New York: Blackwell, 1997.

Metzger, Bruce. *Historical and Literary Studies: Pagan, Jewish, and Christian.* Grand Rapids: Eerdmans, 1968.

Miethe, Terry L, ed. *Did Jesus Rise from the Dead? The Resurrection Debate.* New York: Harper & Row, 1987.

Montgomery, John Warwick. *Human Rights and Human Dignity.* Grand Rapids: Zondervan, 1986.

————. *Tractatus Logio-Theologicus.* Bonn: Verlag für Kultur und Wissenschaft, 2002.

————. *Where Is History Going? A Christian Response to Secular Philosophies of History.* Minneapolis: Bethany Fellowship, 1969.

Moule, C. F. D. *The Phenomenon of the New Testament.* Naperville, Ill.: Alec R. Allenson, 1967.

Paley, William. *A View of the Evidences of Christianity* 1.1.1. London: John W. Parker, 1859.

Pascal, Blaise. *Pensées,* edited and translated by Alban Krailsheimer. New York: Penguin, 1966.

Pliny. *Letters.*

Porter, W. J. "Creeds and Hymns." In *Dictionary of New Testament Background,* edited by Craig Evans and Stanley E. Porter. Downers Grove, Ill.: InterVarsity Press, 2000.

Ramm, Bernard. *Protestant Christian Evidences.* Chicago: Moody Press, 1967.

Robinson, John A. T. *The Human Face of God.* Philadelphia: Westminster Press, 1973.

Rordorf, Willy. *Sunday: The History of the Day of Rest and Worship in the Earliest Centuries of the Christian Church.* Philadelphia: Westminster Press, 1968.

Samples, Kenneth. *Without a Doubt.* Grand Rapids: Baker, 2004.

Schaeffer, Francis A. *The God Who Is There.* 30th anniv. ed. Downers Grove, Ill.: InterVarsity Press, 1998.

Schonfield, Hugh. *The Passover Plot.* New York: Bantam Books, 1966.

Sire, James W. *The Universe Next Door: A Basic Worldview Catalog.* 5th ed. Downers Grove, Ill.: InterVarsity Press, 2009.

————. *Why Should Anyone Believe Anything at All?* Downers Grove, Ill.: InterVarsity Press, 1994.

Starkie, Thomas. *A Practical Treatise of the Law of Evidence.* London: n.p., 1833.

Strobel, Lee. *The Case for Christ.* Grand Rapids: Zondervan, 1998.

Swinburne, Richard. *The Resurrection of God Incarnate.* New York: Oxford University Press, 2003.

————. "The Vocation of a Natural Theologian." In *Philosophers Who Believe,* edited by Kelly James Clark. Downers Grove, Ill.: InterVarsity Press, 1994.

————. "The Significance of the Resurrection." In *The Resurrection of God Incarnate.* New York: Oxford University Press, 2003.

Taliaferro, Charles, and Anders Hendrickson. "Hume's Racism and His Case Against the Miraculous." *Philosophia Christi* 4, no. 2 (2003): 427-42.

Tertullian. *On Spectacles.*

Thayer, Thomas Baldwin. *Christianity Against Infidelity.* Cincinnati: John A. Gurley, 1849.

Wenham, John. *Easter Enigma.* 1984; reprint, Eugene, Ore.: Wipf & Stock, 2005.

Wright, N. T. *The Challenge of Jesus*. Downers Grove, Ill.: InterVarsity Press, 1999.

————. "Christian Origins and the Resurrection of Jesus: The Resurrection of Jesus as a Historical Problem." *Sewanee Theological Review* 41, no. 2 (1998): 107-23.

————. "Jesus' Resurrection and Christian Origins." *Gregorianum* 83, no. 4 (2002): 615-35.

————. *The Resurrection of the Son of God*. Minneapolis: Fortress, 2003.

————. *Surprised by Hope: Rethinking Heaven, the Resurrection, and the Mission of the Church*. San Francisco: HarperOne, 2008.

Yamauchi, Edwin. *Jesus, Zoroaster, Buddha, Socrates, Muhammad*. Rev. ed. Downers Grove, Ill.: InterVarsity Press, 1972.

Chapter 23: Religious Pluralism

Adler, Mortimer. *Truth in Religion: The Plurality of Religions and the Unity of Truth*. New York: Macmillan, 1990.

Aldwinkle, Russell. *More Than a Man: A Study in Christology*. Grand Rapids: Eerdmans, 1976.

Barrett, David B., George Thomas Kurian and Todd M. Johnson, eds. *World Christian Encyclopedia: A Comparative Survey of Churches and Religions in the Modern World*. Vol. 1, *The World by Countries: Religionists, Churches, Ministries*. 2nd ed. New York: Oxford University Press, 2001.

Blomberg, Craig. *Jesus and the Gospels*. 2nd ed. Nashville: Broadman & Holman, 2009.

Campbell, Joseph. *The Power of Myth*. New York: Anchor Books, 1988.

Chesterton, G. K. *Orthodoxy*. 1908; reprint, New York: Image Books, 1959.

Clark, David. *To Know and Love God*. Wheaton, Ill.: Crossway, 2003.

Corduan, Winfried. "Religion: Study and Practice." In *Neighboring Faiths*. Downers Grove, Ill.: InterVarsity Press, 1998.

————. *A Tapestry of Faiths*. Downers Grove, Ill.: InterVarsity Press, 2002.

Erickson, Millard. "The Salvation of Those Incapable of Faith." In *How Shall They Be Saved?* Grand Rapids: Baker, 1996.

Fernando, Ajith. *Sharing the Truth in Love*. Grand Rapids: Discovery House Publishers, 2001.

Geivett, Douglas, and W. Gary Phillips. "A Particularist View." In *Four Views of Salvation in a Pluralistic World*, edited by Dennis L. Okholm and Timothy R. Phillips. Grand Rapids: Eerdmans, 1996.

Groothuis, Douglas. *Confronting the New Age*. Downers Grove, Ill.: InterVarsity Press, 1988.

————. "Myth and the Power of Joseph Campbell." In *Christianity That Counts*. Grand Rapids: Baker, 1994.

————. "Nondualism on Trial." *Journal of the International Society of Christian Apologetics* 1, no. 1 (2008): 105-12.

————. *Unmasking the New Age*. Downers Grove, Ill.: InterVarsity Press, 1986.

Guinness, Os. "The East No Exit." In *The Dust of Death*. Wheaton, Ill.: Crossway, 1994.

Hackett, Stuart. *Oriental Philosophy: A Westerner's Guide to Eastern Thought*. Madison: University of Wisconsin Press, 1979.

Halverson, Dean. *The Compact Guide to Religion*. Colorado Springs: NavPress, 1996.

Hanh, Thich Nhat. *Living Buddha, Living Christ*. New York: Riverhead Books, 1995.

Hick, John. *A Christian Theology of Religions*. Louisville: Westminster John Knox, 1995.

————. *An Interpretation of Religion*. New Haven, Conn.: Yale University Press, 1989.

————. "Jesus and the World Religions." In *The Myth of God Incarnate*, edited by John Hick. London: SCM, 1977.

Hodge, Charles. *Justification by Faith Alone*. Hobbes, N.M.: Trinity Foundation, 1995.

Huxley, Aldous. *The Perennial Philosophy*. 1944; reprint, New York: Meridian Books, 1969.

James, William. *The Varieties of Religious Experience: The Works of William James*, edited by Frederick Burkhardt. Cambridge, Mass.: Harvard University Press, 1985.

Kärkkäinen, Veli-Matti. *An Introduction to the Theology of Religions: Biblical, Historical, and Contemporary Perspectives*. Downers Grove, Ill.: InterVarsity Press, 2003.

King, Richard. *Indian Philosophy: An Introduction to Hindu and Buddhist Thought*. Washington, D.C.: Georgetown University Press, 2007.

Maharaj, Rabi. *Death of a Guru*. Eugene, Ore.: Harvest House, 1984.

Markham, Ian. "Truth and Religion." In *Routledge Companion to Philosophy of Religion*, edited by Chad Meister and Paul Copan. New York: Routledge, 2008.

————. *A World Religions Reader*. 2nd ed. Oxford: Blackwell, 2000.

Moreland, J. P, and Tim Muelhoff. *The God Conversation*. Downers Grove, Ill.: InterVarsity Press, 2007.

Nash, Ronald H. *Faith and Reason: Searching for a Rational Faith*. Grand Rapids: Zondervan, 1988.

————. *Is Jesus the Only Savior?* Grand Rapids: Zondervan, 1995.

————. *When a Baby Dies*. Grand Rapids: Zondervan, 1999.

Netland, Harold. *Dissonant Voices: Religious Pluralism and the Quest for Truth*. Grand Rapids: Eerdmans, 1991.

————. *Encountering Religious Pluralism*. Downers Grove, Ill.: InterVarsity Press, 2001.

Newbigin, Lesslie. *The Gospel in a Pluralist Society.* Grand Rapids: Eerdmans, 1989.

Parrinder, Geoffrey. *Avatar and Incarnation.* New York: Barnes & Noble, 1970.

Pinnock, Clark. *A Wideness in God's Mercy: The Finality of Christ in a World of Religions.* Grand Rapids: Zondervan, 1992.

Prabhavanada, Swami, and Frederick Manchester. *The Upanishads: Breath of the Eternal.* New York: Mentor, 1957.

Radhakrishnan, S. *The Hindu Way of Life.* New York: Macmillan, 1964.

Radhakrishnan, Sarvepalli, and Charles A. Moore, eds. *A Sourcebook in Indian Philosophy.* Princeton, N.J.: Princeton University Press, 1957.

Rosenberg, Joel C. *Inside the Revolution: How the Followers of Jihad, Jefferson, and Jesus Are Battling to Dominate the Middle East and Transform the World.* Carol Stream, Ill.: Tyndale House, 2009.

Sheikh, Bilquis, and Richard H. Schneider. *I Dared to Call Him Father: The Miraculous Story of a Muslim Woman's Encounter with God.* Lincoln, Va.: Chosen Books, 2003.

Sire, James W. "Journey to the East: Eastern Pantheistic Monism." In *The Universe Next Door: A Basic Worldview Catalog.* 5th ed. Downers Grove, Ill.: InterVarsity Press, 2009.

Smith, Huston. *The Soul of Christianity.* San Francisco: HarperSanFrancisco, 2005.

Sproul, R. C. *Faith Alone: The Evangelical Doctrine of Justification.* Grand Rapids: Baker, 1995.

Warfield, B. B. "Are There Few That Be Saved?" *Biblical and Theological Studies,* edited by Samuel Craig. Phillipsburg, N.J.: Presbyterian & Reformed, 1968.

Weibe, Phillip. *Visions of Jesus: Divine Encounters from the New Testament to Today.* New York: Oxford University Press, 1997.

Wilber, Ken. *Sex, Ecology, Spirituality: The Spirit of Evolution.* 2nd ed. Boston: Shambhala, 2000.

Wright, Christopher J. H. *The Mission of God.* Downers Grove, Ill.: IVP Academic, 2006.

Yandell, Keith E. "On the Alleged Unity of All Religions." *Christian Scholar's Review* 6 (1976): 140-55.

Yun, Brother, and Paul Hattaway. *The Heavenly Man.* Grand Rapids: Monarch, 2002.

Chapter 24: Apologetics and the Challenge of Islam

Abdul-Haqq, Abdiyah. *Sharing Your Faith with a Muslim.* Minneapolis: Bethany House, 1980.

Caner, Ergun Mehmet, and Emir Fethi Caner. *Unveiling Islam: An Insider's Look at the Muslim Life and Beliefs.* Grand Rapids: Kregel, 2002.

Cooper, Anne, and Elise Maxwell. *Ishmael My Brother: A Christian Introduction to Islam.* London: Monarch, 2004.

Darwish, Nonie. *Cruel and Usual Punishment: The Terrifying Implications of Islamic Law.* Nashville: Thomas Nelson, 2008.

Fallaci, Oriana. *The Force of Reason.* New York: Rizzoli, 2006.

————. *The Rage and the Pride.* New York: Rizzoli, 2002.

Gabriel, Mark. "Leaving the University." In *Jesus and Muhammad.* Lake Mary, Fla.: Charisma House, 2004.

Geisler, Norman, and Abdul Saleeb. "An Evaluation of the Qur'an." In *Answering Islam.* Rev. ed. Grand Rapids: Baker, 2002.

Hexham, Irving. "Evangelical Illusions: Postmodern Christianity and the Growth of Muslim Communities in Europe and North America." In *No Other Gods Before Me?* edited by John Stackhouse. Grand Rapids: Baker Academic, 2001.

Kitchen, Kenneth. *On the Reliability of the Old Testament.* Grand Rapids: Eerdmans, 2003.

Moucarry, Chawkat. *The Prophet and the Messiah: An Arab Christian's Perspective on Islam and Christianity.* Downers Grove, Ill.: InterVarsity Press, 2001.

Parshall, Phil. *Muslim Evangelism: Contemporary Approaches to Contextualization.* Waynesboro, Ga.: Gabriel Publishing, 2003.

Phillips, Melanie. *Londonistan.* New York: Encounter Books, 2007.

Rassamini, Jerry. *From Jihad to Jesus: An Ex-Muslim's Journey of Faith.* Chattanooga, Tenn.: Living Ink, 2006.

Saleeb, Abdul. "Islam." In *To Everyone an Answer,* edited by Francis Beckwith, William Lane Craig and J. P. Moreland. Downers Grove, Ill.: InterVarsity Press, 2004.

Spencer, Robert. *Religion of Peace? Why Christianity Is and Islam Isn't.* Washington, D.C.: Regnery, 2007.

————. *Stealth Jihad.* Washington, D.C.: Regnery, 2008.

Tov, E. *Textual Criticism of the Hebrew Bible.* 2nd ed. Minneapolis: Fortress, 2001.

Weigel, George. *The Cube and the Cathedral: Europe, America, and Politics Without God.* New York: Basic Books, 2005.

Ye'orr, Bat. *Eurabia.* Madison, N.J.: Farleigh Dickinson University Press, 2005.

Chapter 25: The Problem of Evil

Augustine. *Confessions.*

————. *Enchiridion on Faith, Hope, and Love,* translated by J. F. Shaw. Chicago: Henry Regnery, 1961.

Bales, Kevin. *Ending Slavery: How We Free Today's Slaves.* Berkeley: University of California Press, 2007.

Batstone, David. *Not for Sale.* San Francisco: HarperOne, 2007.

Bettenson, Henry, ed. *The Early Christian Fathers.* London: Oxford University Press, 1956.

Bonhoeffer, Dietrich. *The Cost of Discipleship.* New York: Touchstone, 1995.

Boyd, Greg. *Satan and the Problem of Evil.* Downers Grove, Ill.: InterVarsity Press, 2001.

Boyd, Jeffrey. *Being Sick Well.* Grand Rapids: Baker, 2005.

Butler, Joseph. "Upon the Ignorance of Man (Ecclesiastes 8:16-17)." In *Fifteen Sermons Preached at the Rolls Chapel.* Boston: Hilliard, Gray, Little, and Wilkins, 1827.

Carson, D. A. *How Long, O Lord?* Grand Rapids: Baker, 1991.

Carter, Alan. "On Pascal's Wager: Or All Bets Are Off?" *Philosophia Christi,* series 2, 3, no. 2 (2001): 511-16.

Clark, Gordon. *Religion, Reason, and Revelation.* Philadelphia: Presbyterian & Reformed, 1961.

Corduan, Winfried. *No Doubt About It.* Nashville: Broadman & Holman, 1994.

Dyrness, William. *Christian Apologetics in a World Community.* Downers Grove, Ill.: InterVarsity Press, 1983.

Edwards, Paul. *Reincarnation: An Examination.* New York: Prometheus, 1996.

Frame, John. *Apologetics to the Glory of God.* Phillipsburg, N.J.: Presbyterian & Reformed, 1994.

———. "Human Responsibility and Freedom." *The Doctrine of God.* Phillipsburg, N.J.: P & R Publishing, 2002.

Feinberg, John. *No One Like Him.* Wheaton, Ill.: Crossway, 2001.

Geisler, Norman. "Harold Kushner." In *Baker Encyclopedia of Christian Apologetics.* Grand Rapids: Baker, 1999.

Griffiths, Paul. "Apologetics in Action: Buddhists and Christians on Selves." In *An Apologetic for Apologetics.* Maryknoll, N.Y.: Orbis, 1991.

Groothuis, Douglas. "Are All Bets Off? A Defense of Pascal's Wager." *Philosophia Christi,* series 2, 3, no. 2 (2001): 517-24.

———. *On Jesus.* Belmont, Calif.: Wadsworth, 2003.

Helm, Paul. *The Providence of God.* Downers Grove, Ill.: InterVarsity Press, 1994.

Henry, Carl F. H. "The Resurgence of Process Philosophy." In *God, Revelation, and Authority.* Vol. 6, *God Who Stands and Stays.* Waco, Tex.: Word, 1983.

Hick, John. *Evil and the God of Love.* Rev. ed. New York: Palgrave Macmillan, 2007.

Hobart, R. E. "Free Will as Involving Determinism and Inconceivable Without It." In *Metaphysics: The Big Questions,* edited by Peter Van Inwagen and Dean W. Zimmerman. Malden, Mass.: Blackwell, 1998.

Jones, E. Stanley. *Christ and Human Suffering.* New York: Abingdon, 1933.

Kushner, Harold. *When Bad Things Happen to Good People.* New York: Schocken, 1981.

Lewis, C. S. *The Abolition of Man.* 1944; reprint, San Francisco: HarperSanFrancisco, 1974.

———. "Divine Omnipotence." In *The Problem of Pain.* New York: Touchstone, 1966.

————. *Mere Christianity*. 1952; reprint, New York: HarperCollins, 2001.

Mill, John Stuart. *Three Essays on Religion*. 1874.

Murray, Michael. *Nature Red in Tooth and Claw*. New York: Oxford University Press, 2008.

Nash, Ronald. *Faith and Reason*. Grand Rapids: Zondervan, 1988.

Nash, Ronald, ed. *Process Theology*. Grand Rapids: Baker, 1987.

Nelson, Mark T. "Naturalistic Ethics and the Argument from Evil." *Faith and Philosophy* 8, no. 3 (1991): 368-79.

Netland, Harold. *Dissonant Voices*. Grand Rapids: Eerdmans, 1991.

Piper, John, Justin Taylor and Paul Kjoss Helseth, eds. *Beyond the Bounds: Open Theism and the Undermining of Christianity*. Wheaton, Ill.: Crossway, 2003.

Plantinga, Alvin. *God, Freedom, and Evil*. Grand Rapids: Eerdmans, 1974.

Roth, John K. "A Theodicy of Protest." In *Encountering Evil*, edited by Stephen T. Davis. Louisville: Westminster John Knox, 2001.

Rotholz, James. *Chronic Fatigue Syndrome, Christianity, and Culture*. Binghamton, N.Y.: Hayworth Medical Press, 2002.

Rushdoony, Rousas John. *Revolt Against Maturity: A Biblical Psychology of Man*. Fairfax, Va.: Thoburn Press, 1977.

Russell, Bertrand. *History of Western Philosophy*. 1945; reprint, New York: Simon & Schuster, 1972.

Schaeffer, Francis. *He Is There and He Is Not Silent*. 30th anniv. ed. Wheaton, Ill.: Tyndale House, 2001.

Spiegel, James. *The Benefits of Providence: A New Look at Divine Sovereignty*. Wheaton, Ill.: Crossway, 2005.

Stump, Eleonore. "The Mirror of Evil." In *God and the Philosophers*, edited by Thomas V. Morris. New York: Oxford University Press, 1995.

Swinburne, Richard. *Providence and the Problem of Evil*. New York: Oxford University Press, 1998.

Talbot, Mark R. "True Freedom: The Liberty That Scripture Portrays as Worth Having." In *Beyond the Bounds: Open Theism and the Undermining of Christianity*, edited by John Piper, Justin Taylor and Paul Kjoss Helseth. Wheaton, Ill.: Crossway, 2003.

Wainwright, William. *Philosophy of Religion*. 2nd ed. Belmont, Calif.: Wadsworth, 1999.

Warfield, B. B. "On the Emotional Life of Our Lord." *Biblical and Theological Studies*. New York: Scribners, 1912.

Watts, Alan. *The Way of Zen*. New York: Vintage Books, 1957.

Weisel, Elie. *Night*. New York: Avon Books, 1969.

Whitehead, Alfred North. *Process and Reality*. 1929; reprint, New York: Free Press, 1982.

Wright, R. K. McGreggor. "The Incoherence of the Free Will Theory." In *No Place for Sovereignty*. Downers Grove, Ill.: InterVarsity Press, 1996.

Zaehner, R. C. *Hinduism*. New York: Oxford University Press, 1983.

Chapter 26: Conclusion

Duriez, Colin. *Francis Schaeffer: An Authentic Life*. Wheaton, Ill.: Crossway, 2008.

Groothuis, Douglas. "A Manifesto for Christian Apologetics: Nineteen Theses to Shake the World with the Truth." In *Reasons for Faith: Making a Case for Christian Faith*, edited by Norman L. Geisler and Chad V. Meister. Wheaton, Ill.: Crossway, 2007.

Moreland, J. P. *Kingdom Triangle*. Grand Rapids: Zondervan, 2007.

Schaeffer, Edith. *The Tapestry: The Life and Times of Francis and Edith Schaeffer*. Waco, Tex.: Word, 1981.

Schaeffer, Francis. *True Spirituality*. Carol Stream, Ill.: Tyndale House, 1972.

Appendix 1: Hell on Trial

Edwards, Jonathan. "The Justice of God in the Damnation of Sinners." In *Puritan Sage: Collected Writings of Jonathan Edwards*, edited by Vergilius Ferm. New York: Liberty Publishers. 1953.

Lewis, C. S. *The Great Divorce*. New York: Harper, 2001.

———. "Hell." In *The Problem of Pain*. 1962; reprint, New York: Simon & Schuster, 1996.

Murray, Michael J. "Heaven and Hell." In *Reason for the Hope Within*, edited by Michael J. Murray. Grand Rapids: Eerdmans, 1999.

Pascal, Blaise. *Pensées*, edited and translated by Alban Krailsheimer. New York: Penguin, 1966.

Peterson, Robert A. *Hell on Trial: The Case for Eternal Punishment*. Phillipsburg, N.J.: P & R Publishing, 1995.

Russell, Bertrand. *Why I Am Not a Christian and Other Essays on Religion and Related Subjects,* edited by Paul Edwards. New York: Simon & Schuster, 1957.

Tiessen, T. L. "Hell." In *Global Dictionary of Theology*, edited by William A. Dyrness and Veli-Matti Kärkkäinen. Downers Grove, Ill.: InterVarsity Press, 2008.

Appendix 2: Apologetic Issues in the Old Testament

Bloch-Smith, Elizabeth, and Beth Alpert-Nakhai. "A Landscape Comes to Life: The Iron Age I." *Near Eastern Archaeology* 62 (1999): 108-11.

Block, Daniel I., Bryan H. Cribb and Gregory S. Smith, eds. *Israel: Ancient Kingdom or Late Invention?* Nashville: B & H Academic, 2008.

Davies, Philip R. *Memories of Ancient Israel: An Introduction to Biblical History—Ancient and Modern*. Louisville: Westminster John Knox, 2008.

———. *The Origins of Biblical Israel*. New York: T & T Clark, 2007.

———. *In Search of 'Ancient Israel.'* Sheffield, U.K.: JSOT Press, 1992.

Dawkins, Richard. *The God Delusion*. Boston: Houghton Mifflin, 2006.

Day, John, ed. *In Search of Pre-Exilic Israel*. JSOT Supplement Series 406. London: T & T Clark, 2004.

Dever, William G. *What Did the Biblical Writers Know and When Did They Know It? What Archaeology Can Tell Us About the Reality of Ancient Israel.* Grand Rapids: Eerdmans, 2001.

―――――. *Who Were the Early Israelites and Where Did They Come From?* Grand Rapids: Eerdmans, 2003.

Finkelstein, Israel, and Neil Asher Silberman. *The Bible Unearthed: Archaeology's New Vision of Ancient Israel and the Origin of Its Sacred Texts.* New York: Free Press, 2001.

―――――. *David and Solomon: In Search of the Bible's Sacred Kings and the Roots of the Western Tradition.* New York: Free Press, 2006.

Fritz, Volkmar. "Monarchy and Re-Urbanization: A New Look at Solomon's Kingdom." In *The Origins of the Ancient Israelite States.* JSOT Supplement 228. Edited by V. Fritz and P. R. Davies. Sheffield, U.K.: Sheffield Academic Press, 1996.

Halpern, Baruch. "The Construction of the Davidic State: An Exercise in Historiography." In *The Origins of the Ancient Israelite States.* JSOT Supplement 228. Edited by V. Fritz and P. R. Davies. Sheffield, U.K.: Sheffield Academic Press, 1996.

Harris, Sam. *The End of Faith: Religion, Terror, and the Future of Reason.* New York: W. W. Norton, 2004.

Hess, Richard S. *Israelite Religions: An Archaeological and Biblical Survey.* Grand Rapids: Baker Academic, 2007.

―――――. "The Jericho and Ai of the Book of Joshua." In *Critical Issues in Early Israelite History.Critical Issues in Early Israelite History,* edited by Richard S. Hess, Gerald A. Klingbeil and Paul J. Ray Jr. BBR Supplement 3. Winona Lake, Ind.: Eisenbrauns, 2008.

―――――. "Literacy in Iron Age Israel." In *Windows into Old Testament History: Evidence, Argument, and the Crisis of "Biblical Israel,"* edited by V. Philips Long, David W. Baker and Gordon J. Wenham. Grand Rapids: Eerdmans, 2002.

―――――. "Questions of Reading and Writing in Ancient Israel." *Bulletin for Biblical Research* 19 (2009): 1-9.

Hess, Richard S., Philip Satterthwaite and Gordon Wenham, eds. *He Swore an Oath: Biblical Themes from Genesis 12-50.* 2nd ed. Grand Rapids: Baker, 1994.

Hitchens, Christopher. *God Is Not Great: How Religion Poisons Everything.* New York: Twelve, 2007.

Hoffmeier, James K., and Alan Millard, eds. *The Future of Biblical Archaeology: Reassessing Methodologies and Assumptions.* Grand Rapids: Eerdmans, 2004.

Holladay, John S. Jr. "The Kingdoms of Israel and Judah: Political and Economic Centralization in the Iron IIA-B." In *The Archaeology of Society in the Holy Land,* edited by T. E. Levy. New York: Facts on File, 1995.

Hurowitz, Victor (Avigdor). *I Have Built You an Exalted House: Temple Building in the Bible in Light of Mesopotamian and Northwest Semitic Writings.* JOST Supplement 115. Sheffield, U.K.: Sheffield Academic Press, 1992.

Killebrew, Ann E. *Biblical Peoples and Ethnicity: An Archaeological Study of Egyp-*

tians, Canaanites, Philistines, and Early Israel 1300-1100 B.C.E. Society of Biblical Literature Archaeology and Biblical Studies 9. Atlanta: Society of Biblical Literature, 2005.

Kitchen, Kenneth A. "A Possible Mention of David in the Late Tenth Century BCE, and Deity *Dod as Dead as the Dodo?" *Journal for the Study of the Old Testament* 76 (1997): 29-44.

————. *On the Reliability of the Old Testament.* Grand Rapids: Eerdmans, 2003.

Lemaire, André. "'House of David' Restored in Moabite Inscription." *Biblical Archaeology Review* 20, no. 3 (1994): 30-37.

Lemche, Neils Peter. *The Old Testament between Theology and History: A Critical Survey.* Louisville: Westminster John Knox, 2008.

————. *Prelude to Israel's Past: Background and Beginnings of Israelite History and Identity,* translated by E. F. Maniscalo. Peabody, Mass.: Hendrickson, 1998.

Levy, Thomas E., and Muhammad Najjar. "Edom and Copper: The Emergence of Ancient Israel's Rival." *Biblical Archaeology Review* 32, no. 4 (2006): 24-35, 70.

Mazar, Eilat. "Did I Find King David's Palace?" *Biblical Archaeology Review* 32, no. 1 (2006): 16-27, 70.

Millard, Alan R., and Donald J. Wiseman, eds. *Essays on the Patriarchal Narratives.* 1980; reprint, Winona Lake, Ind.: Eisenbrauns, 1983.

Millard, Alan R., James K. Hoffmeier and David W. Baker, eds. *Faith, Tradition, and History: Old Testament Historiography in Its Near Eastern Context.* Winona Lake, Ind.: Eisenbrauns, 1994.

Römer, Thomas. *The So-Called Deuteronomistic History: A Sociological, Historical, and Literary Introduction.* New York: T & T Clark, 2007.

Schniedewind, William M. "Orality and Literacy in Ancient Israel." *Religious Studies Review* 26, no. 4 (2000): 327-32.

————. "Tel Dan Stela: New Light on Aramaic and Jehu's Revolt." *Bulletin of the American Schools of Oriental Research* 302 (1996): 75-90.

Thompson, Thomas L. *Early History of the Israelite People: From the Written and Archaeological Sources.* Studies in the History of the Ancient Near East 4. Leiden: Brill, 1992.

————. *The Historicity of the Patriarchal Narratives: The Quest for the Historical Abraham.* Beihefte zur Zeitschrift für die alttestamentliche Wissenschaft 133. Berlin: de Gruyter, 1974.

————. *The Messiah Myth: The Near Eastern Roots of Jesus and David.* New York: Basic Books, 2005.

Van Seters, John. *Abraham in History and Tradition.* New Haven, Conn.: Yale University Press, 1975.

Younger, K. Lawson, Jr. "The Late Bronze/Iron Age Transition and the Origins of the Arameans." In *Ugarit at Seventy-Five,* edited by K. Lawson Younger Jr. Winona Lake, Ind.: Eisenbrauns, 2007.

Name Index

Subject Index

Scripture Index